Teaching Composition at the Two-Year College

Background Readings

EDITED BY

Patrick Sullivan

English Department
Manchester Community College

Christie Toth

Department of Writing & Rhetoric Studies
University of Utah

TYCA Advisory Panel

Holly Hassel, Jeffrey Klausman, Carolyn Calhoon-Dillahunt,
Leslie Roberts, Joanne Giordano, Jeff Andelora, Jeff Sommers,
Jan Lombardi

bedford/st.martin's
Macmillan Learning
Boston | New York

For Bedford / St. Martin's

Vice President, Editorial, Macmillan Learning Humanities: Edwin Hill
Editorial Director, English: Karen S. Henry
Senior Publisher for Composition, Business and Technical Writing,
    Developmental Writing: Leasa Burton
Executive Editor: Karita France dos Santos
Production Editor: Lidia MacDonald-Carr
Media Producer: Melissa Skepko-Masi
Production Coordinator: Carolyn Quimby
Executive Marketing Manager: Joy Fisher Williams
Project Management: Linda DeMasi, DeMasi Design and Publishing Service
Director of Rights and Permissions: Hilary Newman
Permissions Manager: Kalina Ingham
Senior Art Director: Anna Palchik
Cover Design: William Boardman
Composition: Achorn International, Inc.
Printing and Binding: RR Donnelley and Sons

For information, write: Bedford/St. Martin's, 75 Arlington Street, Boston, MA 02116
    (617-399-4000)

ISBN 978-1-319-02257-0

Acknowledgments
Text acknowledgments and copyrights appear at the back of the book on pages 681–83, which constitute an extension of the copyright page. Art acknowledgments and copyrights appear on the same page as the art selections they cover.

Preface

We welcome you to this scholarly collection for writing teachers at two-year colleges. With 1,108 two-year colleges nationwide, the need for this kind of book is urgent. Millions of degree-seeking students in the United States enroll at two-year colleges every year, and virtually all of them will be required to take at least one writing course. Indeed, roughly half of all U.S. college students now take their introductory composition courses at two-year colleges. To date, however, there has been no critical sourcebook assembled specifically for writing teachers at the two-year college. This book seeks to fill that gap by focusing on the distinctive challenges and opportunities that writing instructors encounter in two-year college classrooms.

As readers will see, we have included a number of landmark essays that will be of interest to anyone who teaches composition, but what makes this collection unique is the wide selection of essays devoted specifically to teaching at the two-year college. In fact, many of the essays included here were written for our major professional journal, *Teaching English in the Two-Year College*. Others were written by and for community college teacher-scholars. We have selected these essays because we believe that they will be of great value to teachers—whether they are new to the profession or more seasoned veterans—who seek fresh and innovative ways to engage the work they do as teachers of writing.

Writing instructors at two-year colleges have many demands on their time. They typically manage a heavy teaching load, and many are adjunct/contingent faculty working at more than one institution. They are busy with the everyday work of teaching writing: designing courses and curricula, responding to and evaluating student writing, and meeting with students to discuss drafts of essays. Given these responsibilities, it is often difficult for faculty to find time to keep up with scholarly developments. This collection of essays is designed to meet these instructors' needs by providing an up-to-date, practice-oriented, and comprehensive overview of the field that teachers can use as a resource for ongoing professional development. We have kept the chapters short so that instructors will be encouraged to explore issues that interest them, knowing they can do so over the course of a few days by reading a small set of carefully selected essays.

A Focus on the Practical

Our collection of essays emphasizes practical scholarship, with particular attention to the key question teachers face every day: "Theory is all well and good, but how can I use it in the classroom on Monday?" Most of the essays in this collection address pragmatic issues, focusing on the essential task of applying scholarship to local classroom practice in thoughtful and effective ways. We hope this collection will help writing teachers at two-year colleges navigate the ongoing process of translating theory into practice—and practice into theory—in their classrooms.

This approach is reflected in the way many of the chapters in this book are organized. A large number of chapters open with key theoretical essays in our field about the nature of language, literacy, and learning. These selections are followed by essays from two-year college teacher-scholars that illustrate how theory can be applied to the two-year college setting. The "Responding to Student Writing" chapter, for example, begins with a canonical essay by Nancy Sommers, which is paired with an award-winning essay by Carolyn Calhoon-Dillahunt and Dodie Forrest, "Conversing in Marginal Spaces: Developmental Writers' Responses to Teacher Comments," that translates Sommers's work into pragmatic, locally grounded practices for the two-year college classroom. We believe readers will find this organizational approach—which showcases two-year college English instructors' expertise in what Ernest Boyer calls "the scholarship of application" (23)—engaging, relevant, and gratifying.

Fresh Ways to Think about Teaching Writing

The field of writing studies is always evolving, and so is the higher education policy landscape, particularly when it comes to two-year colleges. This volume is designed to help two-year college English faculty respond to these changes and develop new ways of engaging the work of teaching writing. We seek to accomplish this in two ways: (1) by highlighting scholarship written by two-year college teacher-scholars themselves; and (2) by featuring work that engages the unique challenges and conditions of the two-year college in innovative ways. Much of the scholarship in this volume is recent, and it therefore provides even veteran two-year college teacher-scholars with some of the best new thinking about effective writing pedagogy.

We have organized the book to facilitate learning about, discussing, and implementing this important work. The book is divided into six sections, each of which addresses key areas of concern for teachers of writing at the two-year college:

1. An Introduction to the Two-Year College

2. Preparing to Teach

3. Translating Theory into Practice

4. Rethinking "Business as Usual"

5. Diverse Student Populations

6. The Profession of English at the Two-Year College

Each of these parts opens with a short editorial essay that identifies major themes and contextualizes the selected readings within a wider scholarly conversation. The sections of the book are organized into topical chapters, each of which can focus discussion at department meetings, inform professional development activities, and guide departmental policies and classroom practices.

After a brief overview of the mission and history of the modern two-year college, the remainder of the book is devoted to practical applications of scholarship that will be of immediate value to teachers in their classrooms. The subjects we address include preparing to teach, designing writing courses and assignments, teaching for transfer of learning, fostering critical and creative thinking, integrating reading and writing, responding to student writing, teaching academic literacies, thinking carefully about the five-paragraph essay and the teaching of "grammar," reforming developmental education, and teaching diverse student populations. The final unit of the collection examines issues of professional identity and the role of contingent faculty.

Our goal is to make it easy and convenient for two-year college writing faculty to discuss and implement these fresh ideas.

A Research-Based Resource for Researchers, Graduate Students, and Teachers

This volume has benefited from close ties to our major national professional organization, the Two-Year College English Association (TYCA). First of all, to prepare for our work on this book, we designed and distributed a national survey to TYCA members, asking our colleagues what research and scholarship was important to them as teachers of writing at the two-year college. To our knowledge, this is the first survey of its kind about the use of academic scholarship among this cohort of English teachers—an important group of educators who teach roughly half of all composition classes nationwide. The survey was conducted in 2013 and was supported by the TYCA Executive Committee. We received 174 responses from across the nation. These survey responses were crucial in helping us gather material for this collection: it confirmed many of our initial ideas about what work to include and drew our attention to additional resources that have been important to two-year college writing faculty across the nation. In very real ways, this book reflects the accumulated experience and wisdom of those 174 two-year college teacher-scholars who responded to our survey. (For more on the findings of this survey, see Toth and Sullivan.) Furthermore, the 2013–2014 TYCA Research Committee, a group with deep working knowledge of current scholarship, also consulted on key topics and readings for this volume. This book in its final form is the result of extensive consultation, collaboration, and teamwork.

While two-year college writing instructors are the primary audience for this collection, we have also designed this book to serve as a resource for researchers, graduate students, and aspiring community college faculty who seek an introduction to writing instruction at the two-year college. This book can be used for faculty professional development workshops at two-year colleges, as a textbook in graduate-level courses, and as a reference guide for individual scholars, programs, and departments at both two- and four-year institutions.

This volume attempts to engage and honor the diverse scope of two-year college writing teachers' professional roles, which extend beyond the classroom to include hiring, training, and mentoring adjunct faculty; developing assessment and placement procedures; addressing issues related to diversity, access, and opportunity; engaging in ongoing professional development with colleagues; and keeping abreast of new academic and policy developments that are changing the way we think about two-year college writing instruction. This book is designed to help our colleagues at the two-year college do this important work thoughtfully and skillfully, informed by current theory and research in the field of writing studies, as well as other disciplines relevant to teaching at open admissions institutions.

Humility and Respect

We present this book with humility about the limits of our own experience and with great respect for the important work our readers do, day in and day out, with their students and colleagues. Although we (Patrick and Christie) come to this work from different institutional positions, we share a deep commitment to two-year colleges and their students and faculty. Different editors might well have assembled a very different book from the one readers now hold in their hands. We have endeavored to select scholarship that we regard as important and innovative based on our own academic and professional trajectories, and, whenever possible, we have selected work that could be put to immediate, practical use in the classroom. We understand that this collection is far from the final word on the complex and ever-evolving discipline of composition studies.

This volume has been an extraordinarily gratifying project to work on, one that has deepened our appreciation for the intellectual work and important societal contributions of two-year college teachers-scholars-activists. We hope that readers will find the resources we have assembled here useful to the everyday joys and challenges of teaching writing at "democracy's colleges" (Boggs).

Acknowledgments

Because we personally know so many of the contributors in this volume, this book feels like a grand gathering of old friends. It is a great honor, indeed, to acknowledge the community of teacher-scholar-activists represented in this book and also the larger group of colleagues who do the important work of teaching writing every day in classrooms at two-year colleges across America. We dedicate this book to you.

We would especially like to thank the editors of our major scholarly journal, *Teaching English in the Two-Year College*, for giving a voice to two-year college English teachers.

We are deeply indebted to our superb team of editors at Bedford/ St. Martin's, especially Karita France dos Santos, Rachel Childs, Evelyn Denham, Dmitriy Rapoport, Elise Kaiser, Lidia MacDonald-Carr, and Linda DeMasi of DeMasi Design and Publishing Service.

Patrick would like to thank his colleagues at Manchester Community College, and his family—Susan, Bonnie Rose and Richard, and Nicholas—for their ongoing enthusiasm and support for his work.

Christie thanks her many TYCA friends and mentors, as well as her two-year college students, past and present, who are the reason for the work. There are never enough thanks for Ben.

Works Cited

Boggs, George. "Democracy's Colleges: The Evolution of the Community College in America." Prepared for the White House Summit on Community Colleges. Washington: American Association of Community Colleges, 19 Aug. 2010. PDF file.

Boyer, Ernest L. *Scholarship Reconsidered: Priorities of the Professoriate.* Jossey-Bass, 1990.

Toth, Christie, and Patrick Sullivan. "Toward Local Teacher-Scholar Communities of Practice: Findings from a National TYCA Survey." *Teaching English in the Two Year College*, vol. 43, no. 3, 2016, pp. 247-73.

How They Got Here

Steve Straight

—for my students

> Rich carried his high school diploma to the local
> bank in 1975 and learned job after job, treated
> everyone he met with respect and humility and
> rose to the corner office with the desk, two chairs,
> and tall ficus plant, his two sons in college. After
> the bank was swallowed, and swallowed again,
> the new boss took the train straight from Yale,
> spent the year convincing him that bad spelling
> and plain words would number his days, and all
> his confidence slid through a trap door down
> a long, dark shaft.
>
> Michelle emerged from the fog of neglect and doubt
> that her family had pumped into her room for years.
> Thirty, with a small child, unemployed and still
> chained to her father's house, she walked three
> miles here each day, swapping shoulders with
> her load of books every few steps and dreaming
> of the day when one of the directions would not
> be uphill.
>
> Masako sat quietly in the back of the room, sitting
> up straight to peer over the tall grass of Japanese
> that surrounded her. Weeded out of the college
> track back in Japan, she became housewife for an
> engineer whose company sent him abroad. Now
> in the new world everyone spoke so fast, and even
> her quick fingers riffling through the two-way
> dictionary could find no trace of the idioms and
> clipped words that peppered her professor's
> sentences.
>
> Hank was a runner. Each day his Indian legs
> pushed up the Wickham Park hills or his feet
> slapped the cinder track as he tried to keep a step
> ahead of the neighbor's dog, his brothers' fists,
> his mother's tears. About the time his knees
> gave out and everything caught him at once,
> the local trade school coughed him out with
> the other misfits and outlaws, more than a
> few with talent collecting under their fingernails.

From *The Water Carrier*, reprinted edition. Curbstone, 2004, pp. 19–21.

Butch walks the jungle path every day, a morning
mist rising as he fingers the trigger of his M-16,
the metal like part of his arm. He's on point, has
circled around to where the enemy should be, and
with each short breath the hairs in his nose work
like antennas. Suddenly a figure jumps out from
the brush a short way off, and before he can
recognize the voice or face, it's the boy he practically
adopted from the village, who taught him trust
when he had none, dead at his feet, the gun
hot in his hand. Now, his brain has decided it's
time to get it all down.

Kate lay on the hard cot of chronic fatigue
for the last two years of high school, the thin
mattress absorbing her tears and sweat, hour
after hour watching her breath and imagining
her hands and feet heavy and warm until they
were. As a last resort, her father found a magician
in New Jersey with spells of peroxide drip, new
medicines, and pink vials of vitamin shots
she could taste within minutes, until one day,
from the nightmare no one understood, she awoke.

Kendall, pegged in third grade as "mischievous,"
by ninth grade "dangerous," whose father thought
the Army would help him pay attention, who
washed out of basic and washed up here, drums
all his fingers on the desk as the papers are handed
back, frowns at the comments littering the margins,
then looks up surprised when his professor
tells him he has a lot to say.

Contents

PART SIX: THE PROFESSION OF ENGLISH AT THE TWO-YEAR COLLEGE 573

An Introduction to the Two-Year College

In 1946, President Truman appointed a special commission to chart a new course for higher education in America. The document produced by this commission, commonly referred to as the Truman Commission Report, reimagined the role of colleges and universities in America in profound and enduring ways. It is one of the most significant documents ever produced in the United States on the subject of higher education.

This document is clearly the product of a unique historic moment—the years immediately following the cataclysm of World War II. The suffering and trauma of the war informed the thinking of the commission in powerful ways, and this report reflects a moment of historic clarity about human dignity and worth. No longer willing to accept higher education's long association with wealth and privilege, the commission envisioned a broader, more inclusive function for colleges in postwar America. Instead of serving as a bastion of privilege, the commission imagined a "much larger role for higher education in the national life." Informing this vision is an inspiring belief in individual potential and agency:

> Education that liberates and ennobles must be made equally available to all. Justice to the individual demands this; the safety and progress of the Nation depend upon it. America cannot afford to let any of its potential human resources go undiscovered and undeveloped. (p. 8 in this volume)

To achieve this end, the commission called for "the establishment of a network of public community colleges that would charge little or no tuition, serve as cultural centers, be comprehensive in their program offerings with emphasis on civic responsibilities, and would serve the area in which they were located" (33–34). This is the moment when the modern two-year college—with its mandate to democratize the nation's postsecondary system—was born. Today's two-year colleges are the living legacy of this inspiring vision for American higher education.

We begin Part One of this collection with a brief excerpt from the Truman Commission Report, followed by recent national statistics about demographics and enrollment at two-year colleges from the American Association of Community Colleges. As readers may know, the term "two-year college" is often used interchangeably with "community college," and also includes two-year branch campuses of universities as well as many technical and tribal colleges. There are currently 1,108 two-year colleges nationwide. These institutions have become a foundational part of America's system of higher education, serving a large and diverse student population. Many students at two-year colleges come from groups that have historically been marginalized and underrepresented in postsecondary education.

At the core of the modern two-year college's mission and institutional identity is its open admissions policy, providing opportunity and access to any student with a high school diploma or GED. This commitment to access has generated its share of triumphs and successes, of course, but it has also created challenges, particularly in terms of meeting the needs of students who are unprepared for the challenges of college-level work. Nonetheless, as Mike Rose has suggested, "One of the defining characteristics of the United States is its promise of a second chance; this promise is central to our vision of ourselves and to our economic and civic dynamism. When we are at our best as a society, our citizens are not trapped by their histories" (xiii). The two-year college has become a place where individuals from all walks of life can reinvent themselves and work toward building better futures for themselves and their families. In this spirit, we conclude the first chapter with Nell Ann Pickett's landmark essay, which famously describes two-year colleges as "democracy in action."

The second chapter examines important issues related to race, class, and definitions of "success" at two-year colleges. Here we highlight enduring questions that two-year college writing teachers continue to engage. Richard Rothstein examines the many factors that can affect student lives *outside* the classroom, often influencing their educational experiences in ways that are invisible, unacknowledged, or misunderstood by both instructors and policymakers. The excerpt we include from Jenny Stuber's book *Inside the College Gates* reports on the relationship between social class and postsecondary education. Stuber's work suggests that socioeconomic background can shape a student's experience at college in powerful and often negative ways. Finally, Patrick examines how we might think more productively about the notion of success at open admissions institutions. Are simple graduation rates, like those used by selective institutions, an appropriate way to measure student success in these settings? Patrick suggests that the distinctive mission and student populations at open admissions colleges require more nuanced thinking about this important question.

Finally, our third chapter highlights two important essays that historicize the work of two-year college English faculty. As the saying goes, you can't know where you're going until you know where you've been. "Professing at the Fault Lines: Composition at Open Admissions Institutions" was published in 1999, and Cynthia Lewiecki-Wilson and Jeff Sommers were among the first two-year college teacher-scholars to publicly champion open admissions composition teaching as "an intellectually productive and transformative site of disciplinary practice" (p. 78). Readers may note a somewhat combative tone in this essay, as Lewiecki-Wilson and Sommers seek to challenge common misconceptions, "negative assumptions" (p. 60), and "elitist attacks" (p. 79) about the work of two-year college English teachers. They suggest that the teaching of writing in these contexts has been "central to the historical formation and continuing practice of composition studies" (p. 60) and conclude with a powerful and still-resonant challenge to our discipline: "Can composition studies survive if open admissions education does not?" (p. 79).

Holly Hassel and Joanne Giordano's more recent essay, "Occupy Writing Studies" (2013), responds to this important question, providing emphatic validation for the work done by two-year college composition faculty. Hassel and Giordano call on the discipline to begin "rethinking" scholarly practices to focus more attention on the teaching of writing at the two-year college and the needs of two-year college English faculty: "These often ignored postsecondary writing teachers need a more effective and extensive body of scholarship that offers research-based best practices that are relevant to the daily work that they do" (p. 84). Hassel and Giordano also examine the various means by which "academic hierarchies are maintained and reproduced in professional discourses and processes" and how these "hierarchies are largely tied to student preparation and institutional resources" (p. 83). The two essays in this chapter highlight the sustained efforts of two-year college teacher-scholars to forge a discipline that embraces the distinctive demands of writing instruction at open admissions institutions.

Taken together, the selections in Part One document a significant social and cultural transformation in postsecondary education in America, tracing the development of the modern two-year college from its birth in 1947 to its current position as an essential, integral part of our system of higher education in America. This work suggests that we have arrived at a moment when the study of writing instruction at two-year colleges may be moving from the margins to the mainstream of our discipline. As the many essays by two-year college faculty in this volume suggest, this transformation has been accomplished through the dedication and activism of two-year college teacher-scholars themselves. Their important work has helped to make a living reality of the Truman Commission's bold, idealistic vision for the two-year college in America.

Works Cited

Rose, Mike. *Back to School: Why Everyone Deserves a Second Chance at Education*. New Press, 2012.

History and Mission of the Two-Year College

Higher Education for Democracy

President's Commission on Higher Education

The Truman Commission Report, from which this excerpt is taken, was published in 1947 and is one of the most important documents ever written about higher education in America. This report was published under the title Higher Education for American Democracy. *The report was revolutionary in the comprehensive changes it proposed for higher education in America. It recommended that the United States turn away from European forms of education and instead develop its own education system and curriculum, tailored to a democracy. The report included specific recommendations, such as trying to double college attendance by 1960, integrating vocational and liberal arts education, and extending free public education through the first two years of college. It also called for eradicating religious and racial discrimination, increasing federal funding for scholarships and fellowships, and closing the educational quality gap between wealthier and poorer states. The brief section excerpted here captures the ambitious scope of the report in its intent to open up access to higher education.*

From *Higher Education for American Democracy: A Report of the President's Commission on Higher Education.* Vol. 1. *Establishing the Goals.* Harper & Brothers, 1947, p. 101.

A merican colleges and universities must envision a much larger role for higher education in the national life. They can no longer consider themselves merely the instrument for producing an intellectual elite; they must become the means by which every citizen, youth, and adult is enabled and encouraged to carry his education, formal and informal, as far as his native capacities permit.

This conception is the inevitable consequence of the democratic faith; universal education is indispensable to the full and living realization of the democratic ideal. No society can long remain free unless its members are freemen, and men are not free where ignorance prevails. . . . Education that liberates and ennobles must be made equally available to all. Justice to the individual demands this; the safety and progress of the Nation depend upon it. America cannot afford to let any of its potential human resources go undiscovered and undeveloped.

2016 Community College Fast Facts

American Association of Community Colleges

The American Association of Community Colleges (AACC) is the primary advocacy organization for the nation's community colleges. The association represents 1,108 two-year, associate degree–granting institutions and 12 million students. The AACC's "Fast Facts" provides convenient access to reliable national data about community colleges and their students, including enrollment trends and demographic information about students attending community colleges. This AACC fact sheet is updated annually.

continued

Figure1.

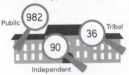

Fast Facts

February 2016

Number and Type of Colleges[1]

Public **982**

Tribal **36**

90 Independent

1,108 Total number of community colleges

26%
Public community colleges with on campus housing[10]

Headcount Enrollment (Fall 2014)[2]

Program Type	#	%	Attendance	#	%
Credit	7.3M	60%	Part-time	4.5M	62%
Noncredit[3]	5.0M	40%	Full-time	2.8M	38%
TOTAL	**12.3M**	**100%**	**TOTAL**	**7.3M**	**100%**

Estimated change from Fall 2014–Fall 2015: -2.4%.[4]

Demographics of Students Enrolled for Credit

Ethnicity[2]	%	Age[5]	%	Gender[2]
White	49%	Average	28	
Hispanic	22%	Median	24	
Black	14%	≤21	37%	
Asian/Pacific Islander	6%	22-39	49%	
Native American	1%	40+	14%	
Two or more races	3%			
Other/Unknown	4%			
Nonresident Alien	1%			

57% Women
43% Men

Other Student Demographics[5]

First generation to attend college – 36%
Single parents – 17%
Non-U.S. citizens – 7%
Veterans – 4%
Students with disabilities – 12%

Representation of Community College Students Among Undergraduates (Fall 2014)[2]

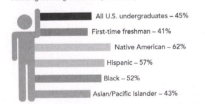

All U.S. undergraduates – 45%

First-time freshman – 41%

Native American – 62%

Hispanic – 57%

Black – 52%

Asian/Pacific Islander – 43%

Employment Status (2011–2012)[5]

Full-time students employed full time – 22%
Full-time students employed part time – 40%
Part-time students employed full time – 41%
Part-time students employed part time – 32%

Student Financial Aid (2011–2012)[5]

% of students applying

62% Federal aid
72% Any aid

% of students receiving

Any aid – 58%
Federal grants – 38%
Federal loans – 19%
State aid – 12%
Institutional aid – 13%

% of Federal Aid Received by Community Colleges (2013–2014)[6]

Pell Grants – 36%
Federal Work Study – 18%
Federal Supplemental Educational Opportunity Grants – 23%

Average Annual Tuition and Fees (2015–2016)[7]

Community Colleges (public, in district) – $3,430
4-year colleges (public, in state) – $9,410

Degrees and Certificates Awarded (2013–2014)[8]

795,235 Associate degrees

494,995 Certificates

Bachelor's degrees awarded by 88 public and 58 independent colleges [1,8]

Community College Revenues by Source (2013–14)[9]

Sources	Revenue	%
Tuition	$17,242,025,437	29.5%
Federal	$8,264,032,954	14.1%
State	$17,442,989,183	29.8%
Local	$10,568,296,830	18.1%
Other	$4,929,830,599	8.4%
TOTAL	**$58,447,175,003**	**100.0%**

Source

[1] AACC membership database, January 2016.
[2] NCES. (2015). IPEDS Fall 2014 Enrollment Survey [AACC analysis].
[3] AACC membership database, 2016 [AACC analysis].
[4] National Student Clearinghouse. (2015). Term Enrollment Estimates Fall 2015.
[5] NCES. (2015). 2011–12 National Postsecondary Student Aid Study (NPSAS:12) [AACC analysis].
[6] College Board. (2015). Trends in Student Aid: 2015.
[7] College Board. (2015). Trends in College Pricing: 2015.
[8] NCES. (2015). IPEDS 2013-2014 Completion Survey [AACC analysis].
[9] NCES. (2015). IPEDS 2013–14 Finance Survey Files [AACC analysis].
[10] NCES. (2015). IPEDS 2014 Institutional Characteristics Survey File [AACC analysis].

Courtesy American Association of Community Colleges (AACC).

The Two-Year College as Democracy in Action

Nell Ann Pickett

In her 1997 Chair's Address to the Conference on College Composition and Communication (CCCC), Pickett describes community colleges as "democracy in action." This speech signaled an important moment of recognition for two-year colleges as institutions and for the national Two-Year College English Association (TYCA) as an organization. The 1997 CCCC convention celebrated national TYCA's establishment after years of activism by two-year college faculty within the National Council of Teachers of English. TYCA continues to honor Pickett's record of leadership through the Nell Ann Pickett Service Award, which is given annually to a teacher-scholar who has made important contributions to two-year college professionalism.

I am a graduate of a two-year college, and I am proud of it. It is an honor to stand here today as your colleague—and as a two-year college teacher. The two-year college is the bringer of dreams to hundreds of thousands of persons across this country, and that I can take part in that dream remains for me the highest honor.

A student wrote on the first day of class:

> My grandpa used to say, "Only in America does a poor man have a chance." Well, I'm here to tell you that if my Grandpa was here today, I'd tell him that only at a college like this does a poor guy who messed up his life get another chance.

This student, in his mid-twenties, was enrolled at Hinds Community College the month after his release from the county penal farm for dealing drugs. (Propitiously, the penal farm is just across the highway from the college.)

He was afraid. He was ashamed. And he had grave doubts about his future. But he came to a college that would take him in, and he was embraced by a faculty who did not care where he came from, just that he had. He had come to better his opportunities and as he said, "to get a clean start." And so the work began. And so did a dream. At the end of almost two years at Hinds, no longer afraid for his future, James is to graduate this summer with an Associate in Applied Science degree in drafting and design technology; he plans to transfer in the fall to a state university. His story is a common one, for the community college is in the business of serving the community. And the best way to serve is to put back into the community.

From *College Composition and Communication*, 1998, vol. 49, no. 1, pp. 90-98.

"Only at a college like this," James wrote.

It is because of the Jameses and the Pecks, the Barbaras, the Mary Jeans, the Eileens—and yes, the Nell Anns—that I entitle this address, "The Two-Year College as Democracy in Action."

In the fall of 1966, I was hired at what was then Hinds Junior College on a one-year appointment replacing a teacher on leave. The one-year appointment suited [me]. I had been teaching at the university level for four years, preceded by three years in high school. Before settling into a career of teaching and before completing a PhD, I wanted to be sure that the level of institution and its expectations complemented my interest in classroom teaching.

At Hinds, I was returning to the two-year college from which I had graduated ten years earlier with an Associate in Arts degree and a major in English. To this day, I have the 3×5 cards on which I had written the valedictory address I gave at graduation. As support on that occasion, my mentor English teacher Jim El Byrd Harris held a copy of those cards so that if I got so nervous I couldn't talk, the speech would be delivered. This morning, a friend and predecessor in this office—Lynn Troyka—holds a copy of the text I'm reading from. So no matter how my knees shake or my voice quivers, this address—now that it's written—will be given.

What I would like to center my remarks around is how an assignment to teach technical writing at a community college has shaped much of my professional life—and continues to shape it. Like many two-year college English teachers who have been around for a while, I've taught everything in the curriculum—including developmental courses, honors courses, writing courses, literature courses. The courses I most often teach, however, form a two-semester sequence of technical writing.

These technical writing courses are service courses for students majoring in such areas as child development, commercial art, criminal justice, dental assisting, drafting and design, electronics, hospitality and tourism management, landscape management, nursing, paralegal studies, veterinary technology. Most of the students are working toward an Associate in Applied Science degree and plan to enter the workforce full-time upon completion of the program at Hinds. Most of them work at one or more jobs, and most will be in school two and a half to five or more years off and on to meet the requirements for the so-called two-year program.

While most are full-time students (12 or more hours per semester), an increasing number are part-time—particularly those in the 30-to-50 age bracket, the baby-boomer generation. The community college often serves these persons through courses at nontraditional times and locations. Taking education to the people—democratizing education—enables individuals to realize the dream of bettering their lives.

Two years ago, Peck Sullivan, 32, a full-time supervisor at a container corporation, decided to do something to get his life out of a rut and to make life better, reports Andy Kanengiser. He has a high school equivalency certificate. He wants to become a nurse. "It would be great to help people," he explains. "I want to make more money and better the lifestyle for our family" (1). Sullivan enrolled at a convenient community college site and is taking two classes a semester. He's making As and Bs. His wife, Brenda, 31, an insurance company employee, is proud of his decision to enter college. She states, "I've been begging him to do it. This is a man who has the brain to do more with his life. I just wish he had done it sooner." Peck Sullivan comments about his leap to college: "I was nervous and didn't know what to expect. The kids are so much younger, but they made me feel pretty welcome" (1).

Mentioning that 27.2 is the average age for Hinds students in associate degree programs gets a "So what?" response from traditional students—those 17, 18, or 19 years of age. Nontraditional students, such as Peck Sullivan, listen with a different ear, a comforting ear, when they begin to understand what that means: of the 13,000 students at Hinds, more than half are 27 or older. At 32 years of age, wanting something better in life, Sullivan is thus in the mainstream of students in two-year colleges across the nation.

Currently, approximately ten million people across the nation are enrolled in both credit and noncredit courses in two-year colleges, according to a telephone interview with the American Association of Community Colleges. This estimate is not surprising. Consider the implications of this statement from AACC: "There are approximately 1300 community colleges strategically located within 25 miles of 95 percent of the nation's population base." Further, AACC reports that "the majority of the nation's first-time in college freshmen, minority students, and women are enrolled" in two-year colleges (*Responding to the Challenge* 5).

But let's narrow the spectrum for the moment and consider the numbers of persons enrolled in credit courses in one state, the state of Mississippi. According to the Mississippi State Board of Community and Junior Colleges, in the 1995–96 academic year:

- 69% of first-year college students were enrolled in community colleges;

- 54% of all college students were enrolled in community colleges.

Let me interject a bit of background. Two-year colleges have been a part of Mississippi higher education since the 1920s. In fact, the state of Mississippi has the oldest state-wide system of two-year colleges in the nation. Further, community colleges in Mississippi emerged from agricultural high schools that provided education and training, work assignments, and dormitories. My institution, founded in 1917, first offered college courses in 1924.

In Mississippi, as in other states, a community college is the most cost-effective choice in higher education. For FY 1996, the Mississippi State Board of Community and Junior Colleges lists the average yearly tuition and required fees in Mississippi:

- Private colleges and universities $6,190
- Public universities $2,446
- Public community colleges $936

Stated another way, for the same amount of money a student can attend a private college or university for one semester, or attend a community college for four semesters and still have $1200 left over. Or for the same amount of money, a student can attend a public university for one semester, or a community college for three semesters.

Additional statistics concerning Mississippi are particularly significant because of concerted efforts to enroll underrepresented population groups. Last year

- 28% of all community college students were minority (Mississippi State Board); 36% of the state's population was minority (*Mississippi Almanac* 68).

- 67% of all associate degrees were awarded to women (Mississippi State Board); 52% of the state's population was female (*Mississippi Almanac* 68).

Historically, these two groups—minorities and women—have been underrepresented in higher education not only in Mississippi but across the nation.

Mary Jean Evans is in my Technical Writing II class this semester. In two months, Mary Jean, 38 years of age, will realize a dream come true. She will graduate in May with an Associate in Applied Science degree and a major in paralegal technology. Married at 16, she is the mother of three children. A full-time student since she began college two years ago, she is also the accountant for her husband's business. She serves as president of the Paralegal Club, and she works 20 hours a week in a legal firm as a paralegal intern. She writes, "My goal is to excel to my fullest potential; I value my family first but I expect a lot from myself. I think a real important accomplishment for me is to attend school, maintain good grades, and still be the mother and wife I want to be."

For Mary Jean, the only good grade is an A. One year ago at midsemester, she had a B in civil litigation; she talked with the teacher about dropping the course. Astounded to learn that hers was the highest average in the class, Mary Jean responded, "I want to learn everything that a course has to offer."

Peck Sullivan and Mary Jean Evans continue to juggle the realities of the demands of school, work, and family. And the realities of our students are the realities that we as teachers in two-year colleges deal with each day. Syllabi, assignment sheets, paper-due dates, student conferences, portfolio reviews—these are always fluid. Or we lose the student. And the student loses contact with formal education and training—at least for the time being. Encouraging students, making every class meeting relevant to students' goals, using teaching/learning materials that students can identify with: these realities are the continuous challenge for us as teachers. And the challenges can be very frustrating.

Let me share one such frustration. When I was hired in the fall of 1967 as "permanent" faculty at Hinds, I was asked to teach the two sections of technical writing. I said "Sure," and was handed the textbook used since the college first offered technical writing in 1962. This textbook was a revision and extension of *The Engineer's Manual of English*, first published in 1933. The first weeks of class, students and I both realized that this textbook did not meet our needs. It was written for engineering majors in their junior or senior year of college who had completed their general education requirements and many of their engineering requirements.

In desperation, I began producing multipage handouts to get us through the term. Then for the next term, my colleague Ann Laster was also assigned to teach technical writing. All the while, my department chair and I were contacting publishers and publishing representatives pleading for them to send us examination copies of their technical writing books suitable for first- and second-year students. There was no such book.

We visited businesses and industries, we talked with technicians in the workplace, we gathered examples of writing they did on the job. And we read and read and read. We worked closely with technical instructors, audited technical classes, attended craft committee meetings, and made lots of assignments that required students to research what would be expected of them in the workplace. The college supported us and encouraged us.

The following summer, the college gave us a stipend to refine and expand the units on explaining procedures, describing mechanisms, giving various kinds of reports, and writing business letters. The vocational offset printing department at the college printed our materials as a spiral-bound book. That fall, several publishing representatives asked for a copy of our "homemade" book. Shortly, we had offers of contracts from four major publishing houses. We signed a contract, and soon the book was in production.

What happened next was to be the biggest shock of my life. We began to get urgent phone calls from the editor in New York:

First call: We have arranged for a published professor at a well-known Eastern university to write an introduction and to be listed as the senior author.

Our response: We don't know this man. He has had no part in writing this book. Forget it.

Second call: Our editorial staff has decided that using your initials plus last names is sufficient on the title page.

Our response: We like our full names—Nell Ann Pickett, Ann A. Laster. Use those full names or just tear up the contract.

Third call: Identification of your institution is not necessary on the title page.

Our response: We are from Hinds Junior College, in Raymond, Mississippi, and that's the way we want to be known.

Naive as we were, those phone calls within a week just didn't set right with us; there was something innately unfair. Our gut reply was: "Forget this book publishing notion." After all, we had not sought a publisher. Our sole reason for writing and assembling *Effective Communication for the Technical Student* in the summer of 1968 was to offer appropriate classroom materials for our students.

Those telephone calls from the senior editor were our first experience in being treated as inferior because (1) we were women and (2) we taught in a two-year college. As we mulled over those phone calls, we realized that the publisher had made certain judgments:

- A technical writing textbook aimed at the two-year college market was indeed needed and would sell.

- This publishing house wanted to go on record as producing the first technical writing textbook designed specifically for freshman and sophomore level courses.

Further,

- A technical writing textbook authored by two women would not be creditable. (Sada A. Harbarger in her 1923 technical writing textbook was referred to only as S. A. Harbarger, Robert J. Connors points out, "perhaps because the publisher felt that many readers might resent a woman claiming to be able to teach technical writing" [335].)

- A technical writing textbook by two-year college teachers, particularly teachers from a rural, deep South state, would not sell.

- The only voice to be trusted in making publishing decisions is the voice of the publisher.

Well, the book came out several months later than scheduled. Through the grapevine, we learned that two cantankerous Mississippi women were blamed for costing the publisher a bundle of money because they would not listen to reason about something as inconsequential as names and college identification on a title page and an introduction written by a guest author. We also learned that when the publisher telephoned us with those urgent messages, the front matter—the last folio to be printed—was already in press.

Those bits of information were being fed to us with the expectation that two neophyte authors, who happened to be female and who taught in a two-year college, at press time would not question the judgment of an editor at a 175-year-old publishing company. But we felt great pride in being female and in choosing to teach in a two-year college. In that first publishing venture, our focus was sharing with others the classroom materials that we had developed for our students. Although at that point in our lives we did not have the vocabulary to articulate the unfairness we felt in the senior editor's insistences, there was never any doubt about our stance. Accept our work and us for what we are.

Now working on the eighth edition of this textbook (for release in fall 1998), we continue to experience the full support of our college and of our colleagues—and, yes, of senior editors.

I'd like to share another major influence early in my Hinds teaching career that bonded me with the two-year college. The English department chair, Jim El Byrd Harris, said to me, "Nell Ann, there's a new professional organization for two-year college faculty, and I want you to go to the next meeting. I think you and it can grow together." That meeting was the February 1968 annual convention of the Southeastern Conference on English in the Two-Year College, now known as TYCA-Southeast. The site of that third annual meeting of the new organization was Biloxi, Mississippi. Several hundred people were expected—the lure of the beautiful Mississippi Gulf Coast in winter—who could resist? History was made that weekend, but not in the way we had anticipated. In Biloxi, there was a four-inch snowfall, part of a band of sleet and snow that paralyzed the deep South. Rather than the three hundred we had expected, the three dozen of us who had arrived a day early were the only ones at the conference.

One of the early arrivers was Elisabeth McPherson, featured speaker. Liz, harbinger and champion, whom we specifically honor and commemorate on this day, was chair of CCCC in 1972—the first two-year college person elected to the office. Throughout her life, Liz was a leading voice in the democracy of the two-year college, of the development of the two-year regional organizations, of students' rights to their own language, and of students' rights to educational opportunity.

Since my first attendance at the Regional in Biloxi, I have returned each year. The two-year Regionals have come to mean informative sessions, learning, sharing, belonging, a professional home. It is no wonder that there is such excitement about the inauguration of the Two-Year College English Association-National this week at this conference in Phoenix, for it was CCCC that 32 years ago, in 1965, inaugurated the seven two-year college Regionals.

In closing, I want to comment on an expanding emphasis in the two-year college—workforce improvement—and how it is undergirded by the openness, the acceptance, the flexibility in programming in the two-year college. Let me share one example of how workforce initiatives are making a difference in persons' lives, as reported by Marcy Lamm.

Eileen Rubin, an insurance executive, lost her job, her livelihood, and her self-esteem. Through the local community college, she established an even more rewarding career.

Rubin, through new management of the company where she had worked for years, found herself in a no-win situation. She says, "All of a sudden everything I did was wrong. I could see it [a pink slip] coming, and there wasn't a darn thing I could do about it" (Lamm 11). She quit before she was squeezed out.

At 43 years of age, her world began to crumble. In spite of her strong qualifications and job leads, she could not find employment. Her husband's income was supporting her and their 10-year-old son. But her executive salary had supplied the major income for the family. "I was depressed. I was scared for my family that I was letting them down. I thought nobody's going to want to hire me. I thought I was too old" (11).

Then she attended a career seminar at the community college sponsored by its Women in Trades and Technology program. The series of aptitude tests that she took highlighted her interest in health care and nursing, manifested years earlier as a premed major at Rutgers University. Rubin enrolled in the community college nursing program and graduated with an associate degree in nursing in May 1995. Within a week, she was employed in her new profession, and she continues to receive promotions. Rubin reports that in her new life as a registered nurse she is happier and spends more time with her family, and "my priorities are very different" (12).

Eileen Rubin, in her early 40s, states to the world: "I will never again put work first." Rubin, through a community college, learned new skills that helped her cope with the challenge of workplace competition. She experienced firsthand the concepts enumerated in the AACC's *Developing the World's Best Workforce*. Community colleges

- are accessible to virtually all Americans;

- provide diverse programs and services; and

- receive high ratings from employers for the quality of programs and for program responsiveness to employer needs.

Community colleges have emerged as vanguard institutions in preparing an efficient, skilled, and adaptable workforce.

I salute all the Eileens and the Jameses, the Pecks, and the Mary Jeans across this country. And I salute the 1300 two-year colleges—colleges that bring hope, opportunity, fulfillment of dreams to a large segment of our population for whom otherwise higher education would be very difficult, if not impossible.

Community colleges are open door, they are accessible, they are affordable, they are cost efficient, they offer a broad array of programs and services, and they open the way for transferring to four-year institutions or entering/reentering the workforce.

Familiar words from the Declaration of Independence remind us of the basis of our democracy: "We hold these truths to be self-evident . . ."— you know the rest of the sentence. The abstractions "created equal," "certain unalienable rights," "life, liberty, and the pursuit of happiness" become realities for many because of their community college experiences.

Community colleges are indeed democracy in action.

Works Cited

American Association of Community Colleges, Commission on Workforce and Community Development. *Responding to the Challenge of Workforce and Economic Development: The Role of America's Community Colleges*. Washington, DC: AACC. May 1996.

American Association of Community Colleges. *Developing the World's Best Workforce: An Agenda for America's Community Colleges*. Annapolis Junction, MD: Community College P, 1996.

Connors, Robert J. "Technical Writing Instruction in America." *Journal of Technical Writing and Communication* (1982):329–52.

Kanengiser, Andy. "Lifelong Learning Boom Crowds Campuses." *The Clarion-Ledger* [Jackson, MS.] 8 Jan. 1997:A1, 5.

Lamm, Marcy. "Women's Mid-Life Crises Often Inspire New Careers, Upgraded Self-Esteems." *The Clarion-Ledger* [Jackson, MS.] 3 Nov. 1996:B11–12.

Mississippi Almanac 1997–1998. Yazoo City: Computer Search and Research, 1997.

Mississippi State Board of Community and Junior Colleges. "Mississippi Community and Junior Colleges." Fact Sheet. Jackson, MS: n.d.

2

Access and Opportunity

Social Class, Student Achievement, and the Black–White Achievement Gap

Richard Rothstein

In the preface to Class and Schools, *the source of the following selection, Lawrence Mishel writes, "Richard Rothstein asks us to view the black-white and low- to middle-income achievement gaps with a wider lens. His revealing and persuasive analysis of how social class shapes learning outcomes forces us to look at the differences in learning styles and readiness across students as they enter school for the first time. Further, he prods us to consider the influence of income, health, safety, and other gaps affecting students as they proceed through school. Even the racial and income gaps facing adults play a role, particularly as students look to their elders for signs of a payoff to education and sometimes find the evidence lacking. Consequently, according to Rothstein, addressing the achievement gap requires no less than a significant transformation of social and labor policy along with extensive school reform." The excerpt that follows is from the first chapter of Rothstein's book.*

From *Class and Schools: Using Social, Economic, and Educational Reform to Close the Black–White Achievement Gap.* Economic Policy Institute, 2004, pp. 13-17 and 19-24.

The Legacy of the Coleman Report

The 50th anniversary of the Supreme Court's desegregation decision in *Brown vs. Board of Education* has directed renewed attention to the persistent achievement gap between black and white students. The court's ruling was an early hint that American public education should be judged on whether schools produce racially equal outcomes. When it relied on sociological reasoning, particularly that of Kenneth Clark, to show that segregation inevitably led black students to achieve less, the court spurred a debate in which Americans continue to engage.[1] If equal resources do not produce equal achievement, what will?

By 1964, 10 years after the court decision, the achievement gap remained huge. Many districts resisted integration. Advocates of equality were convinced that a gap persisted simply because, whether segregated or integrated, black children continued to attend more poorly financed schools.

So Congress then ordered a study to prove, once and for all, that blacks attended inferior schools and that this caused their relatively low achievement. Most people thought the proposed study was somewhat silly; after all, why prove once again that blacks attended inferior schools? But James S. Coleman, a sociologist then at Johns Hopkins University, accepted the charge and concluded, to his own consternation, that variation in school resources had very little—almost nothing—to do with what we now term the test score gap between black and white children. Instead, the family backgrounds of black and white students, their widely different social and economic conditions, accounted for most of the difference.[2]

Since the Coleman report, refuting this conclusion has been an obsession of education research. Surely, there were flaws in Coleman's analysis. He found, for example, more variation in achievement within schools than between them, but left mostly unexplored whether relative teacher effectiveness might explain this variation more than student background. Nonetheless, scholarly efforts over four decades have consistently confirmed Coleman's core finding; no analyst has been able to attribute less than two-thirds of the variation in achievement among schools to the family characteristics of their students.

Yet no matter how often confirmed, the claim remains counterintuitive. Why should poverty mean a child can't learn to read, write, and compute? Surely, a good teacher can guide any child, regardless of skin color or family income, to do these things. Surely, throughout our history, poor children have used education to rise in the United States, and poverty was no fatal impediment. If today there is an achievement gap, common sense says that schools must not be doing for blacks what they did for immigrants and other poor youngsters since the nation's founding.

This [selection] endeavors to show why socioeconomic differences *must* produce an achievement gap between students from different social classes, why these differences have always produced such a gap (myths about a golden age of immigrant achievement notwithstanding), and why this unpleasant reality actually makes the most compelling common sense. Children from lower social classes and from many racial and ethnic minorities, even in the best schools, will achieve less, on average, than middle-class children.

Some Common Misunderstandings about the Achievement Gap

Three misunderstandings about the achievement gap cloud public discussion about the pathways by which social class influences learning.

First, the Coleman report's finding that families are a much bigger influence than school quality on achievement is too easily misinterpreted as the notion that "schools don't make a difference." Since it is apparent that schools make a big difference—as the late Senator Daniel Patrick Moynihan (and a co-author, Frederick Mosteller) quipped, "children don't think up algebra on their own"[3]—we are tempted simply to dismiss Coleman's claim. But what the Coleman report argued is not that schools don't influence achievement but rather that the quality of schools attended by black and white children has little influence on *the difference* in average achievement between black and white students. If we describe *average* achievement, schools clearly have the biggest influence of all. This is common sense, and it is not wrong. Whether children learn math is schools' responsibility, but you will be better at predicting *which* children do better in math, and which do worse, if you know their social class backgrounds.

Think of Coleman's finding this way: all students learn in school, but schools have demonstrated limited ability to affect differences in the rate at which children from different social classes progress. Children from higher social classes come to school with more skills and are more prepared to learn than children from lower classes. All children learn in school, but those from lower classes, on average, do not learn so much faster that they can close the achievement gap.

A second misunderstanding stems from the loose way that the "achievement gap" is described in public discourse. Scholars and educators used to portray the gap in relative, or "norm-referenced" terms. A description of this type leads to the conclusion that average black achievement is from one-half to a full standard deviation below average white achievement. In other words, if average white students are at about the 50th percentile of a national test score distribution, then average black students would be somewhere between about the 16th and the 31st percentile in that distribution.[4]

In contrast, policy makers now typically report achievement in "criterion-referenced terms"—they ask not how students rank in comparison to national averages (or norms), but whether they passed a specific point on a scoring scale. This point is usually termed "proficiency." So instead of asking how black students achieve, on average, relative to whites, policy makers ask what percentage of blacks passed the cut point, and how this compares to the percentage of whites who did so.

This shift in measurement causes great mischief because the gap now depends on how difficult the cut point is. If very simple skill levels are judged proficient, most students of both races can pass the test. If more skill is required, fewer will pass. The simpler the level, the smaller the gap.[5] Effective schools can ensure that close to 100% of students, regardless of race or social class, pass simple tests. These schools can then claim to have closed the gap because both blacks and whites pass the proficiency point equally. But if the same students took somewhat more difficult tests, achievement gaps would re-appear.

. . . [M]any claims by those who now brag that their particular approaches can close the gap have been based on this statistical sleight of hand—if you set a cut score low enough, you can eliminate the gap without in any way changing average achievement of students from different social classes. (And . . . this is a strategy that federal law now invites states to adopt.)

So to be clear: when the following pages describe why differences in social class *must* produce a big achievement gap, they refer to a gap in *average* achievement in the wide range of skills that schools should produce—not only basic math and literacy, but also the ability to reason and create; an appreciation of history, science, art, and music; and good citizenship, self-discipline, and communication skills.

The third misunderstanding is to equate group averages and the performance of all individuals within the group. We all know highly successful students from lower-class backgrounds, and it is tempting to conclude that their success proves that social class cannot be what impedes most disadvantaged students. But there is a distribution of achievement in every social group, and these distributions overlap. While average achievement of lower-class students is below average achievement of middle-class students, there are always some middle-class students who achieve below typical lower-class levels. And there will always be some lower-class students who achieve above typical middle-class levels.[6] Demography is not destiny, but students' social and economic family characteristics are a powerful influence on their relative *average* achievement.

These three clarifications should be kept in mind in any discussion of causes of the achievement gap between white and black students or between middle-class and low-income students. First, schools do make a big difference in the level, if not in the variation, of achievement. Second, socioeconomic differences are less of a bar to closing the achievement gap if the gap is measured only as the difference between groups in low-level proficiency. And, third, the power of social class to predict average performance is not inconsistent with high achievement of some students from lower classes. Any average includes relatively higher and relatively lower performance of some in the group.

If these three misunderstandings are not permitted to cloud our thinking, then the Coleman report's conclusion seems not at all counter-intuitive; indeed, it makes perfect sense that the economic, educational, and cultural characteristics of families have powerful effects on learning, effects that even great schools cannot obliterate, on average. . . .

Social Class Differences in Childrearing

To take full advantage of school, children should enter ready to learn, and their after-school, weekend, and summer activities should reinforce their learning. But children differ in how ready they are to learn when they enter school, and these differences are strongly influenced by their social class backgrounds.

Parents of different social classes tend to raise children somewhat differently. More educated parents read to their young children more consistently and encourage their children to read more to themselves when they are older.[7] Most parents with college degrees read to their children daily before the children begin kindergarten; few children whose parents have only a high school diploma or less benefit from daily reading. White children are more likely than blacks to be read to or told stories in pre-kindergarten years.[8] Young children of college-educated parents are surrounded by more books at home while children of less-educated parents see fewer books.[9]

A five-year-old who enters school recognizing some words and who has turned pages of many stories will be easier to teach than one who has rarely held a book. The second child can be taught, but, with equally high expectations and effective teaching, the first will more likely pass a reading test than the second. So the achievement gap begins.

As discussed earlier, this is not a determinist description. Some low-income children are naturally quick learners, take to school well, and respond so well to high expectations that after a few years of school they read better than typical middle-class children. Some middle-class children get no support for learning from troubled families, and some low-income parents organize life around a dream of college. But *on average*, a typical middle-class child who began to read at home will have higher lifetime achievement than a typical low-income child who was taught only in school, even if each benefits from good curriculum, effective teaching, and high expectations. If a society with such social class differences wants children, irrespective of social class, to have the same chance to achieve academic goals, it should find ways to help lower-class children enter school having the same familiarity with books as middle-class children have.

By kindergarten, almost all upper-class children, about half of middle-class children, and fewer than one in five lower-class children have used computers.[10] This difference is not due solely to expense — lower-class families have televisions, and they could obtain computers if they were valued — but rather to differences in how parents from different social classes use computers themselves. If parents routinely sit at computers, toddlers will sit on their parents' laps and play with the mouse and keyboard. If computers are rarely used by parents, their children will be less proficient, even with computers at home. Some school reform proposals include distributing computers to children's families, expecting that this will help close the achievement gap. But while it may help a little, such a distribution will not do much. If schools filled kindergartens with computers, or even distributed them to families, the advantages of children who also learned at home would persist, because differences in computer literacy practices that parents model will not have been affected.

Some people acknowledge the impact of such differences on student achievement but find it hard to accept that good schools should have so difficult a time overcoming them. This challenge would be easier to understand if Americans had a broader international perspective on education. Although many countries' students do better on academic tests, on average, than Americans, class backgrounds influence *relative* achievement everywhere. The inability of schools to overcome the disadvantage of less literate home backgrounds is not a peculiar American failure but a universal reality. The number of books in students' homes, for example, consistently predicts scores within almost every country.[11] Turkish immigrant students suffer from an achievement gap in Germany, as do Algerians in France, as do Caribbean, African, Pakistani, and Bangladeshi pupils in Great Britain, and as do Okinawans and low-caste Buraku in Japan.[12]

An international reading survey of 15-year-olds, conducted in 2000, found a strong relationship in almost every nation between parental occupation and student literacy. The gap between literacy of children of the highest-status workers (like doctors, professors, lawyers) and the lowest-status workers (like waiters and waitresses, taxi drivers, mechanics) was even greater in Germany and the United Kingdom than it was in the United States. In France the gap was about the same as in the United States, while in the Scandinavian countries and Korea it was smaller. There were similar disparities between other social classes. The gap between the literacy of children of middle-class workers (like teachers, accountants, engineers) and of children of lower-status workers was about the same in the United States and the United Kingdom, greater in Germany than in the United States, and slightly smaller in France than in the United States.[13] After reviewing these results, a U.S. Department of Education summary concluded that "most participating countries do not differ significantly from the United States in terms of the strength of the relationship between socioeconomic status and literacy in any subject."[14] Remarkably, the department published this conclusion at the same time that it was guiding a bill through Congress that demanded every school in the nation abolish social class differences in achievement within 12 years. It was enacted as the "No Child Left Behind" law.

Just as giving away computers won't overcome these gaps, so urging less-educated parents to read to children can't fully compensate for differences in school readiness. If children see parents read to solve their own problems or for entertainment, children are more likely to want to read themselves.[15] Parents who bring reading material home from work demonstrate by example to their children that reading is not a segmented burden but a seamless activity that bridges work and leisure.[16] Parents who read to children but don't read for themselves send a different message.

How parents read to children is as important as whether they do; more educated parents read aloud differently. When working-class parents read aloud, they are more likely to tell children to pay attention without interruptions or to sound out words or name letters. When they ask children about a story, questions are more likely to be factual, asking for names of objects or memories of events.[17] Parents who are more literate are more likely to ask questions that are creative, interpretive, or connective, like "what do you think will happen next?" "why do you think this happened?" "does that remind you of what we did yesterday?"[18] Middle-class parents are more likely to read aloud to have fun, to start conversations, to provide an entree to the world outside. Their children learn that reading is enjoyable and are more motivated to read in school.[19]

Stark social class differences arise not only in how parents read but in how they converse. Explaining events in the broader world to children, in dinner talk, for example, may have as much of an influence on test scores as early reading itself.[20] Through such conversations, children develop vocabularies and become familiar with contexts for reading in school.[21] Educated parents are more likely to engage in such talk and to begin it with infants and toddlers, conducting pretend conversations long before infants can understand the language. Typically, middle-class parents "ask" infants about their needs, then provide answers for the children ("Are you ready for a nap, now? Yes, you are, aren't you?"). Instructions are more likely to be given indirectly: "You don't want to make so much noise, do you?"[22] This kind of instruction is really more an invitation for a child to work through the reasoning behind an order and to internalize it. Middle-class parents may not think of themselves as conducting academic instruction for infants, but that is what they are doing with this indirect guidance.

Yet such instruction is quite different from what policy makers nowadays consider "academic" for young children: explicit training in letter and number recognition, letter-sound correspondence, and so on. Such drill in basic skills is unlikely to close the social class gap in learning.

Beginning in 1998, the federal government surveyed a national sample of kindergartners and their parents. The government intends to continue monitoring this sample of children as they move through school. Results so far illustrate how complex are the social class differences in children's academic preparation.

The survey includes data on family income, mother's education, father's education, mother's occupational status, and father's occupational status. Families, mothers, and fathers were ranked on these measures and then the five measures were averaged to create a composite called socioeconomic status, or SES. All children can then be divided into five SES quintiles, with those from the highest 20% of families by SES in the top quintile, and those from the lowest 20% of families by SES in the bottom quintile.[23]

As you would expect, entering kindergartners from higher social classes have more books in their homes and are read to more frequently by their parents. Yet surprisingly, smaller proportions of parents from higher SES quintiles than from lower SES quintiles believed that their children should know how to count when they first entered kindergarten. Smaller proportions of parents from higher SES quintiles believed that their children should know the alphabet letters before kindergarten.

Similarly in this government survey, black parents were more likely than white parents to believe that their children should count and know the alphabet when they entered kindergarten.[24]

In a few years, the government will report survey results on this group of kindergartners when they have third grade test scores. It is probably safe to predict that the average math and reading scores of higher-SES children, fewer of whose parents believe that their children should know the alphabet and count before kindergarten, will, in third grade, be higher than the average scores of children whose parents expected them to master the mechanics of reading and math before kindergarten. These parents from higher social classes were confident that raising children in an environment where literacy was valued and modeled would be a more important determinant of children's own literacy than drilling these children in the basics.

This relative lack of concern among higher-SES and white parents about very young children's mastery of the mechanics of reading and arithmetic does not mean that middle-class parents do not expect their children to absorb a familiarity with letters and numbers more naturally. "Touch and feel" books are among middle-class children's first toys. Later, alphabet blocks, magnetic letters on refrigerator doors, and labels taped on walls or objects are commonplace. Adult conversations vary by social class and become part of infants' and toddlers' background environments. When educated parents speak to each other in children's presence, even if the children are not being addressed directly, these parents use larger vocabularies and more complex sentences than less-educated parents do. Although middle-class preschoolers don't use advanced vocabulary words or sentence constructions themselves, they have an advantage when they hear their college-educated teachers speak or when these words and constructions are first encountered in books.

Soon after middle-class children become verbal, parents typically draw them into adult conversations so children can practice expressing their own opinions. Inclusion this early in adult conversations develops a sense of entitlement in children; they feel comfortable addressing adults as equals and without deference. Children who want reasons rather than simply submitting to direction on adult authority develop intellectual skills upon which later academic success in school will rely. Certainly, some lower-class children have such skills and some middle-class children lack them. But, on average, a sense of entitlement is social class-based.[25]

Working-class parents typically maintain firmer boundaries between adult and child worlds and are less likely to conduct conversations with pre-verbal children. Except when it is necessary to give a warning or issue other instructions, these parents less often address language directly to infants or toddlers. Unlike middle-class parents, working-class parents are less likely to simplify their language (using "baby talk") to show pre-verbal children how to converse, before the children are naturally ready to do so. If children need instruction, the orders are more likely to be direct, undisguised in question form.[26]

Working-class adults are more likely to engage in conversation with each other as though their infants, even older children, were not present. These parents make less of a deliberate effort to name objects and develop children's vocabularies. Such parents assume that children will learn to talk naturally. The children do, but not with the same sophistication as middle-class children. One study of black and white working-class families in the rural South in the 1970s found that black parents made a deliberate effort to teach pre-verbal children to name objects and to speak, but then were more likely than white working-class parents to abandon this activity once the children began talking; the black parents were more likely to view the job of teaching children to speak as having now been accomplished.[27]

The point here is not that there are childrearing practices, specific to the social classes, that are identical over time and geography. Rather, it is that such patterns do exist, and that they are bound to have an influence on how children learn, at what rate they learn, and what instructional approaches will be most effective in schools.

Today, these social class differences may help to explain why schools have more success in narrowing the achievement gap at lower grades, only to see it widen later on. In the upper grades, when posing more open-ended questions increasingly becomes a way to learn, middle-class children do what comes naturally to them. Lower-class children may succeed with direct instruction when learning basic skills, but are less prepared for the inquiry learning that is more important to academic success in upper grades. Tests in primary years have more questions of fact, identification, or simple recall, questions like those that children of lower-class families are used to answering when stories are read to them. But tests in the later grades contain more questions requiring abstract reasoning or conceptualization, the kinds of questions about stories that lower-class children are unused to answering but with which middle-class children have more experience.[28]

Notes

1. Clark argued that segregation created a feeling of inferiority, and that it was difficult for the achievement of black children to overcome this stigma.
2. For discussions of the historical context of the Coleman report, see Moynihan 1968; Mosteller and Moynihan 1972; and Grant 1973.
3. Mosteller and Moynihan 1972.
4. Henceforth, for simplicity, I will say that, compared to white students who are on average at the 50th percentile, black students are on average at about the 23rd percentile.
5. To be more precise, the achievement gap will disappear if the proficiency point is either excessively simple, or excessively difficult. If you ask fourth graders to take a test with questions like the addition of 2+2, almost all from every socioeconomic group will get it right, and so there will be no test score gap. If you ask fourth graders to take a test that requires solving differential equations, almost none will do so, and there also will be no test score gap. The biggest test score gap between students from two socioeconomic groups will appear if proficiency is defined as the midpoint between the average scores of students from those groups.
6. If the average black student scores at about the 23rd percentile in a national normal distribution in which the average white student scores at the 50th percentile, about one-quarter of the black students are statistically likely to score higher than the average-scoring white student.
7. Bianchi and Robinson 1997; Hoffereth and Sandberg 2001.
8. Denton and Germino-Hauskens 2000, Table 20, p. 52. Of children whose mothers have at least a bachelor's degree, 59% are read to daily. Of children whose mothers have no more than a high school diploma or equivalent, 39% are read to daily. Of children whose mothers have less than a high school diploma, 36% are read to daily. Of white children, 49% are read to daily. Of black children, 35% are read to daily.

   Of children whose mothers have at least a bachelor's degree, 93% are read to at least three times a week. Of children whose mothers have no more than a high school diploma or equivalent, 75% are read to at least three times a week. Of children whose mothers have less than a high school diploma, 63% are read to at least three times a week. Of white children, 86% are read to at least three times a week. Of black children, 68% are read to at least three times a week.
9. Denton and Germino-Hauskens 2000, Table 19, p. 51. Of children whose mothers have at least a bachelor's degree, 71% have more than 50 books in their homes; of children whose mothers have only a high school diploma,

37% have this many books; of children whose mothers did not graduate from high school, only 14% have this many.

10. Rathburn and West 2003, Table 4.
11. Torney-Purta et al. 2001, p. 65.
12. Other countries do not track their achievement gaps with as much precision as we do in the United States. In some countries, there is resistance to collecting data by income or ethnicity because of a feeling that this somehow legitimizes a non-assimilationist ideology (Rothstein 2000a). For descriptions of gaps in other nations, see Begag 1990; Castles et al. 1984; Garner 2004; Neuman and Peer 2002; OFSTED 1999; Ogbu 1992b; and Sciolino 2004. For a discussion of poor educational attainment of low-income children of all ethnicities in Great Britain, see Ermisch 2001.
13. OECD 2001.
14. Lemke 2002, p. 37; Figure 17, p. 44.
15. Snow and Tabors 1996.
16. Lareau 1989.
17. Mikulecky 1996.
18. See also Britto and Brooks-Gunn 2001, who report on a survey that included only poorly educated single African American mothers. Within this group, more expressive language use during book reading predicted children's achievement, but the survey does not lead to any reliable conclusions regarding whether the use of expressive language is related to social class.
19. Mikulecky 1996.
20. Mikulecky 1996.
21. Snow and Tabors 1996.
22. See Lareau 2003 for a general discussion of these childrearing pattern differences.
23. Tourangeau et al. 2002, Section 7.4.2, pp. 7–18.
24. Portas 2004. Additional data analysis provided to the author by Carole A. Portas. In the lowest 20% of families by socioeconomic status, 79% of parents believed that their children should know the alphabet letters when they entered kindergarten. But only 55% of families from the highest 20% of families by socioeconomic status shared this belief. For believing that children should know how to count at kindergarten entry, the shares were 71% and 50%, respectively.
25. Lareau 2002, 2003.
26. Heath 1983.
27. Heath 1983.
28. Heath 1983.

Bibliography

Begag, Azouz. 1990. "The 'Beurs,' Children of North-African Immigrants in France: The Issue of Integration." *Journal of Ethnic Studies* 18(1): 1–14.

Bianchi, Suzanne M., and John Robinson. 1997. "What Did You Do Today? Children's Use of Time, Family Composition, and the Acquisition of Social Capital." *Journal of Marriage and the Family* 59(May): 332–344.

Castles, Stephen, with Heather Booth and Tina Wallace. 1984. *Here for Good. Western Europe's New Ethnic Minorities*. London: Pluto Press.

Denton, Kristen, and Elvira Germino-Hauskens. 2000. *America's Kindergartner's. Findings from the Early Childhood Longitudinal Study, Kindergarten Class of 1998–99, Fall 1998*. NCES 2000-070. Washington, D.C.: U.S. Department of Education, National Center for Education Statistics.

Garner, Richard. 2004. "Chinese Perform Better in English Than White Children." *Independent Education*, February 25.

Grant, Gerald. 1973. "Shaping Social Policy: The Politics of the Coleman Report." *Teachers College Record* 75(1): 17–54.

Heath, Shirley Brice. 1983. *Ways With Words*. Cambridge, England: Cambridge University Press.

Hoffereth, Sandra L., and John F. Sandberg. 2001. "How American Children Spend Their Time." *Journal of Marriage and the Family* 63(May): 295–308.

Lareau, Annette. 1989. *Home Advantage: Social Class and Parental Intervention in Elementary Education: Theory, Research, Practice*. Thousand Oaks, Calif.: Sage.

Lareau, Annette. 2002. "Invisible Inequality: Social Class and Childrearing in Black Families and White Families." *American Sociological Review* 67(October): 747–776.

Lareau, Annette. 2003. *Unequal Childhoods*. Berkeley: University of California Press.

Lemke, Mariann, et al. 2002. *Outcomes of Learning. Results from the 2000 Program for International Student Assessment of 15-Year-Olds in Reading, Mathematics, and Science Literacy*. NCES 2002-115. Washington, D.C.: U.S. Department of Education, Office of Educational Research and Improvement.

Mikulecky, Larry. 1996. *Family Literacy: Parent and Child Interactions*. Washington, D.C.: U.S. Department of Education. <http://www.ed.gov/pubs/FamLit/parent.html>

Mosteller, Frederick, and Daniel P. Moynihan. 1972. "A Pathbreaking Report." In Frederick Mosteller and Daniel P. Moynihan, eds., *On Equality of Educational Opportunity*. New York, N.Y.: Random House.

Moynihan, Daniel P. 1968. "Sources of Resistance to the Coleman Report." *Harvard Educational Review* 38(1): 23–36.

Neuman, Michelle J., and Shanny Peer. 2002. *Equal from the Start: Promoting Educational Opportunity for All Preschool Children—Learning from the French Experience*. New York, N.Y.: The French-American Foundation.

OFSTED (Office for Standards in Education). 1999. *Raising the Attainment of Minority Ethnic Pupils*. HMI 170. London, England: OFSTED Publications Centre. Author.

Ogbu, John. 1992b. "Understanding Cultural Diversity and Learning." *Educational Researcher* 21(8): 5–14, 24.

OECD (Organization for Economic Cooperation and Development). 2001. *Knowledge and Skills for Life: First Results from the OECD Programme for International Student Assessment PISA 2000*. Paris, France: OECD.

Portas, Carole A. 2004. "Early Childhood Care and Education and Its Relationship to Reading Achievement at the Start of Kindergarten." Paper prepared for the annual meeting of the American Education Finance Association, Salt Lake City, Utah, March 12.

Rathburn, Amy, and Jerry West. 2003. *Young Children's Access to Computers in the Home and at School in 1999 and 2000*. NCES 2003-036. Washington, D.C.: U.S. Department of Education, Office of Educational Research and Improvement.

Rothstein, Richard. 2000a. "When Culture Affects How We Learn." *New York Times*, October 11.

Sciolino, Elaine. 2004. "France Seems to Try Acting Affirmatively on Muslims." *New York Times*, January 15.

Snow, Catherine, and Patton Tabors. 1996. "Intergenerational Transfer of Literacy." Washington, D.C.: U.S. Department of Education. <http://www.ed.gov/pubs/FamLit/transfer.html>

Torney-Purta, Judith, Rainer Lehman, Hans Oswald, and Wolfram Schulz. 2001. *Citizenship and Education in Twenty-Eight Countries: Civic Knowledge and Engagement at Age Fourteen*. Amsterdam, the Netherlands: International Association for the Evaluation of Educational Achievement.

Tourangeau, Karen, et al. 2002. *User's Manual for the ELCS-K First Grade Public-Use Data Files and Electronic Code Book*. NCES 2002-135. Washington, D.C: U. S. Department of Education, Office of Educational Research and Improvement.

Inside the College Gates: Education as a Social and Cultural Process

Jenny Stuber

In her book Inside the College Gates, *sociologist Jenny Stuber explores how students from different social class backgrounds navigate the college environment. She finds that social class plays an important role in structuring students' college experiences, providing social and cultural resources for navigating life both inside and outside the classroom; it also shapes students' class consciousness and how they make sense of their own and others' social class positions. The excerpt that follows, from the first chapter of Stuber's book, situates her research within existing educational research and makes a convincing case that we should view education as both a possession and a process. While many researchers have focused on higher education as a variable or a quantity to be attained (a "possession"), Stuber explores higher education as a process—as an extended period of socialization and identity development, where students gain not just human capital, but social and cultural capital as well. Ultimately, she shows that the "experiential core" of higher education—the places outside of the classroom, heavily influenced by peer norms and interactions—plays a critical role in structuring students' experiences in college and reproducing social class inequality.*

From *Inside the College Gates: How Class and Culture Matter in Higher Education*. Lexington, 2011, pp. 1-15.

Education and Class Inequality

Schools within the United States have long been hailed as the "great equalizers." Regarded as institutions that function according to merito-cratic principles, our nation's schools are envisioned as the setting in which the American Dream can be realized; a place where students are given the opportunity to overcome the circumstances of their birth through individual effort and competition. Time and again, school re-forms have been enacted in order to more perfectly realize this goal by enhancing access and equity for students regardless of their race, class, and gender identities (Ravitch 2001; Tyack and Cuban 1995). Scholars credit, moreover, the expansion of higher education—first through the Morrill Act of 1862 and later following World War II through the G.I. Bill—as the force that gave birth to a strong American middle class (Kerbo 2009). Classic and contemporary sociological research confirms these perceptions, showing that schooling does, indeed, function as a cor-rective to racial inequalities (Condron 2009; Downey et al. 2004) and that social mobility is strongly predicted by how much education a per-son completes (Blau and Duncan 1967; Sewell and Hauser 1975).

A more critical strain of scholarship challenges this optimistic view. Scholars within this tradition assert that educational institutions play a "sifting and sorting" role (Collins 1971, 1979; Spring 1976), whereby they contribute to—rather than ameliorate—social inequalities. With respect to higher education, one source of stratification is the initial de-cision to attend college. Researchers find a decades-long pattern whereby high school students from the highest SES quartile are nearly twice as likely to enroll in some type of post-secondary education compared to students in the lowest quartile (Roksa et al. 2007). A second source of stratification is the decision of where to enroll. This research shows that students from the first and second SES quartiles are greatly over-represented at highly selective colleges and universities (Bowen and Bok 2000; Carnevale and Rose 2004). The fact that lower-income students are more likely to enroll in community colleges and less-selective insti-tutions has powerful consequences for social stratification, given their association with lower graduation rates and lower earnings over time (Brint and Karabel 1989; Carnevale and Rose 2004; Gerber and Cheung 2008). Finally, researchers have focused on retention as a third source of class-based stratification in higher education. While 88 percent of second-generation students return for a second year, only 73 percent of first-generation students do so (Warburton, Burgarin, and Nunez 2001). In general, first-generation students—a common proxy for class status—are "less likely to stay enrolled or attain a bachelor's degree after five years" (Pascarella et al. 2004: 250) compared to their second-generation peers.

Carried to its logical conclusion, this research leads to the asser-tion that if lower-income students were given greater access to higher education and more tools to complete their degrees, our nation's colleges and universities would become the "great equalizers" many imagine them to be. While such inequalities are serious and deserving of attention, my contention is that the dramatic increase in college enrollments, coupled with the diversification of the higher education landscape, has fundamentally altered the relationship between higher education and class inequality. With nearly 70 percent of high school students going on to some form of higher education (National Center for Education Statistics 2009), the relevant questions are no longer simply whether students go to college, where they go, or even whether they complete their degree. Given the ongoing expansion of higher education, it is increasingly important that researchers examine the stratifying processes that take place on college campuses.

In their 2008 review of sociological research on higher education, Mitchell Stevens, Elizabeth A. Armstrong, and Richard Arum called for greater attention to the ways in which stratification occurs outside of the classroom. Although students gain important skills and human capital within the classroom, they acquire other valuable social and cultural resources within their friendship networks and through their extracurricular involvements. While all students acquire social and cultural capital while in college, some students gain more than others. Consequently, students' social and extracurricular experiences offer different—and unequal—opportunities for gaining valuable social and cultural capital and, in doing so, operate as a site for social stratification within higher education.

The foregoing sociological debate over the source of inequality within higher education is rooted in two distinct theoretical approaches to education. Moreover, these theoretical approaches are grounded in two distinct perspectives on the meaning of social class and the dynamics of class reproduction. As I elaborate below, one of these perspectives conceives of education as a possession; this perspective leads to questions about who attends and who graduates. The other perspective conceives of education as a process; this perspective leads to questions about what happens to students while they are enrolled. . . . [T]hese theoretical orientations—to the extent that they are supported empirically— provide different recommendations for how to make institutions of higher education more egalitarian in terms of social class.

Education as a Possession

When theorizing the relationship between education and social inequality, some scholars approach education as a possession, as a discrete, measurable trait that defines a person. Frequently operationalized as "years of schooling completed" or "highest degree attained," these studies treat education as a variable that predicts and is predicted by other sociologically relevant characteristics (occupational status, earnings, parental education, mate selection, life expectancy, and more). According to Mitchell Stevens and his coauthors (2008), this research portrays higher education as a "sieve," where educational institutions are conceptualized as gradually filtering out students from lower social class backgrounds (Sorokin ([1927] 1959).

This framework has been used profitably to understand processes of social mobility. These researchers find that those who attain the highest degrees from the most prestigious institutions originate from the most privileged social classes; yet they also show that "educational attainment" is the primary basis upon which privileged occupational positions are allocated. Researchers working within this tradition have developed increasingly complex statistical models whose goal is to predict the extent to which family background, cognitive ability, peer influence, and educational attainments predict subsequent occupational attainments and earnings (Blau and Duncan 1967; Featherman and Hauser 1978; Roksa et al. 2007; Sewell et al. 1969). Since the late 1960s—assisted by emerging computer technologies—this research tradition has been incredibly fertile. Indeed, a recent edited volume showcases efforts to apply these models to educational access and attainment across nations (Shavit et al. 2007).

Yet as higher education has expanded and diversified, this research tradition has encountered new challenges. Because the U.S. higher education landscape now contains approximately 4200 degree-granting institutions, there is incredible variability in the quality and reputation associated with the degrees they grant. This diversification makes it more difficult to conceive of education as a possession that has a uniform, quantifiable meaning. While quantitative models may treat a bachelor's degree from a highly selective university and one from a nonselective university as equivalents, the consequences of these two degrees may be quite different when measured as occupational outcomes or other life experiences. The expansion of higher education, in essence, has reduced "vertical" differentiation in educational attainment; meaning, there is less variability among adults in terms of the amount of education they have received. Because of this, there is greater need to explore "horizontal" differentiation in higher education; that is, to examine differences among people with the same level of education (Gerber and Cheung 2008) For example, researchers could examine how occupational and economic outcomes are impacted by differences among graduates in terms of the selectivity of institution attended, major course of study, and academic performance.

Although the expansion of higher education has prompted scholars to ask more nuanced questions about the meaning of a college degree, there are still limitations to this perspective. In focusing on educational attainment as a possession, many of these studies end up treating education as a "black box." Rather than looking at what happens to an individual who is in the process of attaining a particular level of education, these studies treat educational attainment as an input or output; a window into some other relevant phenomena—occupational attainment or earnings, for example—but rarely worthy of attention in its own right. As such, the underlying mechanisms that produce particular outcomes remain unexplored. There are exceptions, of course. Developers of the Wisconsin Model of Educational Attainment made a major contribution by incorporating "social psychological" variables into their models, namely in terms of identifying aspirations and peer networks (Sewell and Hauser 1975) as mechanisms underlying educational attainment. Similarly, other scholars theorize that educational attainment plays a "signaling" function, whereby it acts as a proxy for valued social and cultural attributes, such as perseverance and knowledge of high culture (Collins 1979).

Critical of this tradition, Mitchell Stevens (2007: 102) argues that "sociologists' enduring penchant for quantification"—wherein measures of educational attainment have been treated as not only necessary, but sufficient, representations of the educational process—"have tended to obscure the essentially cultural character" of the educational experience. By conceptualizing education as "a static quantity akin to money," research that treats education as a possession offers only partial insight into the ways in which education is linked to social class inequality.

Education as a Process

In theorizing the relationship between education and social inequality, a more recent strand of research conceptualizes education as a process. Where the seminal tradition uses quantitative models to predict discrete educational and economic outcomes, the newer tradition uses quantitative and qualitative methods to explore social processes, peer cultures, and symbolic "outcomes." Those working within this tradition argue that researchers must examine what happens to students while they are in school—rather than summarizing their time spent there as a discrete number—to better understand the connection between education and social inequality.

To examine education as a process is to conceptualize schools as incubators (Stevens et al. 2008). Those who view schools as incubators seek to open the "black box" that characterizes much of the variable-based, outcome-oriented research; the image of the incubator, after all, calls to mind a transparent environment in which the growth of a living creature can be monitored. Applied to educational research, colleges and universities are conceptualized as sites for "incubating" valued social and cultural competencies. Indeed, it is this notion that I intend to invoke in the title to this book. The image of the college gates—a common symbol emblazoned upon college websites and postcards—suggests a significant entry point into a sheltered, developmentally unique world. The social and cultural competencies that are honed while in college are partially cultivated in the classroom, but because students spend only about fifteen hours each week within formal academic environments, most of this cultivation takes place outside of the classroom. By focusing on the social and extracurricular domain of higher education, researchers seek to extend the rich tradition within the sociology of education that has produced insight into the social worlds of primary and secondary students (Adler and Adler 1998; Bettis 2003; Eckert 1989; Eder 1987, 1995; Pascoe 2007; Thorne 1993; Willis 1977). Together, these works make the essential point that schools are intensely social places, second only to the family of origin as a setting in which socialization and identity formation takes place.

Research that views education as a process mirrors a broader shift in sociological studies of stratification. During the 1970s, feminist scholars argued that studies that define social class location as synonymous with occupational position—the prevailing sociological approaches at the time—provide limited insight into class inequality and social reproduction. These researchers drew attention to women's roles in the class structure, showing that privileged women's participation in cultural institutions and philanthropic organizations allows them to wield power and reproduce their class interests by establishing social and cultural standards (Beisel 1996; Domhoff 1970; McCarthy 1991; Ostrander 1984; Ostrower 2002). Other scholars contributed to this tradition by examining women's roles in class reproduction as part of their parenting roles (Brantlinger 2003; Lareau 1989, 2003; Reay 1998). As privileged women socialize their children in class-specific ways and actively promote their children's interests and protect advantages within schools (and other institutional settings), they simultaneously engage in social reproduction. On the domestic front, women construct class identities and engage in social class projects by maintaining homes that are meticulously clean (Collins 1992) and yards that are attractively landscaped (Kefalas 2003)—efforts that help them gain class respectability when their husbands' occupational efforts do not. Together, this research made an important contribution by showing that social class is not derived solely from a person's occupational identity and experiences, and that social class processes and the reproduction of class inequality take place in multiple social locations.

In addition to feminist scholars, cultural scholars of the 1970s made similarly important contributions to the study of class inequality. The "cultural turn" in sociology refers to an intellectual movement in which scholars brought renewed attention to the role of meaning and symbols in structuring our lived experiences. In studies of social stratification, the cultural turn resulted in understandings of "social class" that moved beyond measures of income, wealth, or occupation. Instead, they conceived stratification as a complex process that generates and is generated by multiple, conceptually distinct hierarchies. That is, social stratification reflects not simply the fact that some people have greater access to economic resources than others, but also the fact that some people have greater access to valued cultural/symbolic resources than others.

As a major proponent of this perspective, French sociologist Pierre Bourdieu wrote: "It is . . . impossible to account for the structure and functioning of the social world unless one reintroduces capital in all its forms and not solely in the one form recognized by economic theory" (1986: 97). Two forms of "capital" that Bourdieu emphasized were social and cultural capital. Researchers define social capital as a resource for social action that inheres in social relations (Bourdieu 1986; Coleman 1988; Portes 1998). In processes of social stratification it is valuable because it provides access to information about and meaningful pathways into desired social experiences and positions. Cultural capital—which exists in embodied, objectified, and institutionalized forms (Bourdieu 1986)—includes a person's educational qualifications, knowhow, comportment, and tastes. Within social interaction, it operates as a system of symbolic cues that social actors use to regulate access to places and positions; a yardstick for determining who is "one of us" (Lamont 1992). These forms of capital play a role in class reproduction—the perpetuation of class inequality and the class structure—because they are typically acquired through socialization within the family of origin (Bourdieu and Passeron [1977] 1990).

In terms of how these forms of capital matter within educational settings, an important assumption is that educational settings and other dominant social institutions are not neutral settings; rather, these scholars argue, they operate according to the cultural rules, norms, and expectations of the dominant classes (Lareau 1989; Bourdieu and Passeron [1977] 1990). Students who enter school already equipped with these cultural resources have a "leg up" on those who are only just becoming familiar with the culture of schools and the dominant classes. Cultural capital, then, in the form of cultural attitudes, preferences, and behaviors functions as an invisible, interactional resource that selects and conditions some students for success while identifying others as unworthy of academic or social distinction (Bourdieu and Passeron [1977] 1990).

Despite the fact that social stratification reflects multiple, conceptually distinct hierarchies, the material hierarchies and the symbolic/cultural hierarchies that structure class inequalities are ultimately inseparable. Thus, in order to understand the relationship between class inequalities and higher education, researchers must pay attention to the social and cultural processes that play out on college and university campuses. Through their peer cultures, college students sort themselves into friendship groups and social networks that are stratified and segregated; further, these peer groups often overlap with or provide entrée into extracurricular involvements. Both of these settings, moreover, provide different and unequal opportunities for acquiring social and cultural capital. Thus, as college students move through the social and extracurricular domains of their campuses, they hone their social and cultural competencies, while acquiring additional social and cultural resources. Beyond the campus walls, these resources again come into play as individuals use them to navigate social, marital, and job markets (Armstrong 2007; DiPrete and Buchmann 2006; Schwartz and Mare 2005; Stevens 2007). While college students' degrees surely represent different and unequal attainments of human capital, education is also the process that incubates within students different and unequal attainments of social and cultural capital.

References

Adler, Patricia A. and Peter Adler. 1998. *Peer Power: Preadolescent Culture and Identity*. New Brunswick, NJ: Rutgers University Press.

Armstrong, Elizabeth A. 2007. "College Culture and Social Inequality." Working paper. Sociology Department, Indiana University.

Beisel, Nicola. 1996. *Imperiled Innocents: Anthony Comstock and Family Reproduction in Victorian America*. Princeton, NJ: Princeton University Press.

Bettis, Pamela J. and Natalie G. Adams. 2003. "The Power of the Preps and a Cheerleading Equity Policy." *Sociology of Education* 76: 128–42.

Blau, Peter M. and Otis Dudley Duncan. 1967. *The American Occupational Structure*. New York: Wiley.

Bourdieu, Pierre. 1986. "The Forms of Capital." Pp. 241–58 in *Handbook of Theory and Research for the Sociology of Education*, edited by John G. Richardson. New York: Greenwood.

Bourdieu, Pierre and Jean-Claude Passeron. [1977] 1990. *Reproduction in Education, Society, and Culture*. Translated by Richard Nice. Newbury Park, CA: Sage.

Bowen, William G. and Derek Bok. 2000. *The Shape of the River: Long-Term Consequences of Considering Race in College and University Admissions*. Princeton, NJ: Princeton University Press.

Brantlinger, Ellen A. 2003. *Dividing Classes: How the Middle Class Negotiates and Rationalizes School Advantage*. New York: Routledge-Falmer.

Carnevale, Anthony P. and Stephen J. Rose. 2004. "Socioeconomic Status, Race/Ethnicity, and Selective College Admissions." Pp. 101–56 in *America's Untapped Resource: Low-Income Students in Higher Education*, edited by Richard D. Kahlenberg. New York: Century Foundation Press.

Coleman, James S. 1988. "Social Capital in the Creation of Human Capital." *American Journal of Sociology* 94: S95–S120.

Collins, Randall. 1971. "Functional and Conflict Theories of Educational Stratification." *American Sociological Review* 36: 1002–19.

———. 1979. *Credential Society: An Historical Sociology of Education and Stratification*. New York: Academic Press.

———. 1992. "Women and the Production of Status Cultures." Pp. 213–31 in *Cultivating Differences: Symbolic Boundaries and the Making of Inequality*, edited by Michèle Lamont and Marcel Fournier. Chicago: University of Chicago Press.

Condron, Dennis J. 2009. "Social Class, School, and Non-School Environments, and Black/White Inequalities in Student Learning." *American Sociological Review* 74: 683–706.

DiPrete, Thomas and Claudia Buchmann. 2006. "Gender-Specific Trends in the Value of Education and the Emerging Gender Gap in College Completion." *Demography* 43:1–24.

Domhoff, G. William. 1970. *The Higher Circles: The Governing Class in America*. New York: Random House.

Downey, Douglas B., Paul von Hipple, and Beckett Broh. 2004. "Are Schools the Great Equalizer?: Cognitive Inequality During the Summer Months and School Year." *American Sociological Review* 69: 613–35.

Eckert, Penelope. 1989. *Jocks and Burnouts: Social Categories and Identity in the High School*. New York: Teachers' College Press.

Eder, Donna (with Catherine C. Evans and Stephen Parker). 1995. *School Talk: Gender and Adolescent School Culture*. New Brunswick, NJ; Rutgers University Press.

Eder, Donna and Stephen Parker. 1987. "The Cultural Production and Reproduction of Gender: The Effect of Extra-Curricular Activities on Peer-Group Culture." *Sociology of Education* 60: 200–13.

Featherman, David L. and Robert M. Hauser. 1978. *Opportunity and Change*. New York: Academic.

Gerber, Theodore P. and Sin Yi Cheung. 2008. "Horizontal Stratification in Post-secondary Education: Forms, Explanations, and Implications." *Annual Review of Sociology* 34: 299–318.

Kefalas, Maria. 2003. *Working-Class Heroes: Protecting Home, Community, and Nation in a Chicago Neighborhood*. Berkeley, CA: University of California Press.

Kerbo, Harold. 2009. *Stratification and Inequality*. Boston: McGraw-Hill.

Lamont, Michèle. 1992. *Money, Morals, and Manners*. Chicago: University of Chicago Press.

Lareau, Annette. 1989. *Home Advantage: Social Class and Parental Intervention in Elementary School*. London: The Falmer Press.

———. 2003. *Unequal Childhoods: Class, Race, and Family Life*. Berkeley: University of California Press.

McCarthy, Kathleen D. 1991. *Women's Culture: American Philanthropy and Art, 1830–1930*. Chicago: University of Chicago Press.

National Center for Education Statistics (NCES). 2009. *The Condition of Education 2009*. Washington, DC: National Center for Education Statistics, U.S. Government Printing Office.

Ostrander, Susan A. 1984. *Women of the Upper Class*. Philadelphia: Temple University Press.

Ostrower, Francie. 2002. *Trustees of Culture: Power, Wealth, and Status on Elite Arts Boards*. Chicago: University of Chicago Press.

Pascarella, Ernest T., Christopher T. Pierson, Gregory C. Wolniak, and Patrick T. Terenzini. 1994. "First-Generation College Students: Additional Evidence on College Experiences and Outcomes." *Journal of Higher Education* 75: 249–84.

Pascarella, Ernest T., Patrick T. Terenzini, and Gregory S. Blimling. 1994. "The Impact of Residential Life on Students." Pp. 22–52 in *Realizing the Educational Potential of Residence Halls*, edited by Charles C. Schroeder and Phyllis Mable. San Francisco: Jossey Bass.

Pascarella, Ernest T. and Patrick T. Terenzini. 2005. *How College Affects Students: Volume 2, A Third Decade of Research*. San Francisco, CA: Jossey Bass.

Pascoe, C. J. 2007. *Dude, You're a Fag: Masculinity and Sexuality in High School*. Berkeley: University of California Press.

Portes, Alejandro. 1998. "Social Capital: Its Origins and Applications in Modern Sociology." *Annual Review of Sociology* 24: 1–24.

Ravitch, Diane. 2001. *Left Back: A Century of Failed School Reforms*. New York: Simon and Schuster.

Reay, Diane. 1998. *Class Work: Mothers' Involvement in their Children's Primary Schooling*. UCL Press: London.

Roksa, Josipa, Eric Grodsky, Richard Arum, and Adam Gamoran. 2007. "United States: Changes in Higher Education and Social Stratification." Pp. 165–91 in *Stratification in Higher Education: A Comparative Study*, edited by Yossi Shavit, Richard Arum, and Adam Gamoran. Palo Alto, CA: Stanford University Press.

Schwartz, Christine R. and Robert Mare. 2005. "Trends in Educational Assortative Marriage from 1940–2003." *Demography* 42: 621–46.

Sewell, William and Robert Hauser. 1975. *Education, Occupation, and Earnings*. New York: Academic Press.

Shavit, Yossi, Richard Arum, and Adam Gamoran. 2007. *Stratification in Higher Education: A Comparative Study*. Palo Alto, CA: Stanford University Press.

Sorokin, Pitirim A. [1927] 1959. *Social and Cultural Mobility*. New York: Free Press.

Stevens, Mitchell L. 2007. *Creating a Class: College Admissions and the Education of Elites*. Cambridge, MA: Harvard University Press.

Stevens, Mitchell L., Elizabeth A. Armstrong, and Richard Arum. 2008. "Sieve, Incubator, Temple, Hub: Empirical and Theoretical Advances in the Sociology of Higher Education." *Annual Review of Sociology* 34: 127–51.

Thorne, Barrie. 1993. *Gender Play: Boys and Girls in School*. Brunswick, NJ: Rutgers University Press.

Tyack, David and Larry Cuban. 1995. *Tinkering Towards Utopia: A Century of Public School Reform*. Cambridge, MA: Harvard University Press.

Warburton, Edward C., Rosio Bugarin, and Anne-Marie Nuñez. 2001. *Bridging the Gap: Academic Preparation and Postsecondary Success of First Generation Students* (NCES 2001-153). Washington, DC: National Center for Education Statistics, U.S. Government Printing Office.

Willis, Paul. 1977. *Learning to Labour: How Working-Class Kids Get Working-Class Jobs*. New York: Columbia University Press.

Measuring "Success" at Open Admissions Institutions: Thinking Carefully about This Complex Question

Patrick Sullivan

Can we measure "success" at open admissions institutions the same way that we measure success at traditional, selective admissions institutions—that is, by composite graduation rates? In this article, Patrick suggests that we can't. Even when community college students indicate—either informally in class, or formally on surveys such as the Community College Survey of Student Engagement—that they want to graduate and transfer to a four-year institution, they often have only a vague notion of what this means. Many are first-generation college students who have no firsthand or family experience with college, and many have only an emerging sense of what it takes to earn a degree. Patrick suggests that when the typical community college student says that he or she wants to "obtain a bachelor's degree"—a key marker in the body of research devoted to this question—this student often means something very different from the typical student at a selective admissions institution who says exactly the same thing.

Graduation rates continue to be used as the standard benchmark for success at most institutions of higher learning, including community colleges (Wilt), even by those who should know that the use of such a marker of success at open admissions institutions is highly problematic. Using this benchmark for community colleges becomes particularly troublesome when it is used in comparison with graduation rates at selective admissions institutions. This practice is problematic because these two kinds of institutions are very different in terms of mission and student body and because this practice avoids or simplifies complexities that are unique to the learning communities at open admissions institutions.[1] There are many ways to measure success at our nation's colleges and universities, of course, and some of these do not dispose themselves conveniently to data collection or simple means of quantifiable measurement.

Nonetheless, there appears to be a dark and troubling mystery at the heart of the community college enterprise that was famously discussed by Burton Clark in 1960 ("The 'Cooling-Out' Function in Higher Education") and has since been taken up again in more recent work by Ira Shor and others (see Brint and Karabel; Carter; Monk-Turner; Rouse; Shor, "Our" and *When*; Sternglass; Traub, *City* and "What"). To state this as plainly, fairly, and unequivocally as I can, I cite a passage

From *College English*, 2008, vol. 70, no. 6, pp. 618-32.

from a recent report by the United States Department of Education (National Center for Education Statistics) entitled *Profiles of Undergraduates in U.S. Post-secondary Education Institutions: 2003–04, With an Analysis of Community College Students* (2006):

> Student persistence is of concern to educators and policymakers because large numbers of students who begin their college education in community colleges never complete it. For example, among a cohort of first-time freshmen who enrolled in community colleges in 1995–96, some 48 percent had either completed a credential (36 percent) or transferred to a 4-year institution (12 percent) 6 years after first enrolling (Hoachlander, Sikora, and Horn 2003). In contrast, among students who first enrolled in 4-year colleges or universities, 63 percent had completed a bachelor's degree, and another 18 percent were still enrolled or had completed an associate's degree or certificate (Berkner, He, and Cataldi 2003). (iii; see also Tinto)

This is a question, of course, that is never far removed from most discussions about student "success" at community colleges. It also frequently comes into play in more theoretical discussions about the value of open admissions institutions nationwide (see Dougherty; Brint and Karabel). It is an issue, furthermore, that has come to play a vital role in the daily lives of English teachers at open admissions institutions—as we engage the work of designing and teaching basic writing and college-level curriculum and as we discuss policy and practice related to workload, class size, assessment, and other matters. It is an issue, moreover, that continues to cause divisiveness and misunderstanding between colleagues at four-year institutions and those at public two-year institutions, especially in English departments, where common purpose and common challenges should be fostering a spirit of cooperation and collegiality.

This is a matter of special urgency for our profession because community colleges have never been more central to the enterprise of higher education in this country than they are today. Approximately 46 percent of all U.S. undergraduates now attend community colleges (American Association; see also Millward, Powers, and Crump; "Percent"). Teachers of English at our nation's community colleges are now routinely called on by college committees, statewide and systemwide task forces, and, increasingly, interventionist legislatures to address issues related to "student success." English teachers are regarded as essential contributors to these conversations because they teach English—and, thus, the foundational college-level skills of reading, writing, and thinking—and because they have, like English teachers at all levels of instruction, historically provided leadership at their schools on issues related to assessment, retention, developmental education, and other endeavors related to student success. Invariably, competing notions about how to use research data related to "student success" find their way to the center of these conversations. In recent years, these discussions have become increasingly politicized, and they are increasingly conducted as high-stakes endeavors. For better or worse, discussions about "success" at open admissions institutions also very often turn out to be discussions about the work that English teachers do as providers of both basic literacy and college-level reading and writing instruction. For all of these reasons, it is vitally important that members of our profession think carefully about how we measure student success at open admissions institutions.

Access and Opportunity

Community colleges offer all kinds of students—and especially nontraditional students and students from the most marginalized and financially disadvantaged sectors of our society—what no other college or university has ever offered them before: opportunity, hope, and the chance to build more prosperous and satisfying futures for themselves. This is an unprecedented development in the long history of higher education, and it is to our enduring credit that we have helped shape the substance and character of this system (see Baker; Cohen and Brawer; Cook and King, *Improving* and *Low*; Dougherty; Fox; Griffith and Conner; Lavin and Hyllegard; Pickett, p. 11 in this volume). How can we ever expect to measure or quantify this gift of hope?

Of course, open admissions policies generate challenges as well, and perhaps the most longstanding and troublesome of these are students who come to community colleges unprepared to do college-level work. As John and Suanne Roueche note in *High Stakes, High Performance* (1999),

> On average, almost 50 percent of all first-time community college students test as underprepared for the academic demands of college-level courses and programs and are advised to enroll in at least one remedial class. This percentage of underprepared students has not changed significantly across the United States in the last two decades, and there is no evidence that it will be reduced in the near future, although in individual states percentages have fluctuated. (5)

Selective admissions institutions also enroll underprepared students, but, as the editors of a recent report from the United States Department of Education (National Center for Education Statistics) note, public two-year institutions are "more likely than other types of institutions" to offer "remedial" reading or writing courses, and they offer "a greater number of different remedial courses, on average" (*Remedial*). This is as we might expect, given the very different admissions policies and missions of these institutions.

Measuring success for students at open admissions institutions is complicated by a variety of factors, and such measurements must therefore be conducted with great care and thoughtfulness. Is, say, a 50 percent overall graduation rate acceptable? Should it be more? What would be reasonable to expect? And how should we define "success" for our underprepared students? Would it be graduation with an associate's degree? Completion of a certificate program or a vocational track curriculum that would provide them with employable skills? Successful completion of one full year of study? Successful completion of at least one college-level course? Finishing at least one basic writing class? Counseling underprepared students to enter the workplace? Helping these students discover that, fortunately or unfortunately, college may not be for them? Would, say, an overall 30 percent graduation for our most underprepared students be acceptable?

Graduation Rates at Selective Institutions

The major point of this essay is that we cannot measure success at open admissions institutions the same way that we measure success at traditional, selective admissions institutions — typically, by composite graduation rates. Yale, for example, has a graduation rate of over 90 percent (Yale). Obviously, for such schools, as well as for state colleges and universities with selective admissions, it makes sense to use composite graduation rates, at least as one marker of institutional success. Even in this regard, however, different demographic populations often have very different graduation rates, and the composite scores reported by universities often mask such differences. To cite one important example noted in a recent issue of *The Journal of Blacks in Higher Education* (2006),

> According to the most recent statistics, the nationwide college graduation rate for black students stands at an appallingly low rate of 42 percent. This figure is 20 percentage points below the 62 percent rate for white students. Here, the only positive news we have to report is that over the past two years the black student graduation rate has improved by three percentage points. ("Black" 88)

At Yale, the graduation rate for black students is 89 percent. But at other institutions, the discrepancy is much larger. At the University of Michigan, for example, the graduation rate for white students is 88 percent, but for black students it is 67 percent. At Bates, the graduation rate for white students is 88 percent, but for black students it is 64 percent. There are significant gaps at many other highly selective institutions as well ("Black" 91). So, even if we seek to measure "success" in this way — by graduation rates — we must be careful to disaggregate these data and to look carefully at what such data tell us (see Karabel; United States *Profiles*). We must also look at the formidable variety of personal and academic skills and attitudes that students bring with them when they are granted admission to selective and highly selective institutions. Should open admissions institutions be asked to compare themselves with these kinds of institutions when it comes to using graduation rates to measure success? I don't think so.

"Success" at Open Admissions Institutions

Using composite graduation rates to measure success for students at open admissions institutions is a bad idea for a number of reasons. First of all, many students who enroll at open admissions institutions specifically indicate that they are *not* attending college in order to earn an associate's degree or to transfer to a four-year institution. For example, the 2005 Community College Survey of Student Engagement (CCSSE) report, "Engaging Students, Challenging the Odds," shows how various student goals are at our nation's community colleges. The data regarding "goals" cited in this report were gathered from over 130,000 community college students nationwide:

> Students' Primary Goals [Note: Students could select more than one "primary goal."]
>
> Complete a certificate program: 29%
>
> Obtain an associate degree: 57%
>
> Transfer to a four-year college or university: 48%
>
> Obtain or update job-related skills: 41%
>
> Self-improvement/personal enjoyment: 40%
>
> Change careers: 30% (4)

Furthermore, even when community college students indicate—either informally, in class, or formally, on surveys such as the CCSSE—that they want to graduate and "transfer" to a four-year institution, they often have only a vague notion of what this means. Many are first-generation college students who have no firsthand or family experience with college, and many have just a limited sense of what it takes to earn a degree. I would like to suggest that when the typical community college student says that he or she wants to "obtain a bachelor's degree"—a key marker in the body of research devoted to this question, as we will see—this student is saying something very different than when the typical student at a selective admissions institution says exactly the same thing.

This became clear to me recently as I talked with some of my daughter's high school friends about their plans for college. When I spoke with these young men and women about their plans, almost all of them talked about college without the least trace of doubt or equivocation. Most of them had college-educated parents, and they all had an absolute sense of clarity and certainty that they were going on to earn bachelor's degrees. It was just a matter of deciding what college they would attend. Most of them had a variety of appealing options.

Although each of these students would answer yes to a survey question that asked if they planned to attend college after high school and pursue a bachelor's degree, there is no way to account in such a survey for the absolute sense of sureness with which they would answer the question. I might even be tempted to use a word such as "entitlement" here to characterize this disposition toward college and the earning of a bachelor's degree (issues related to class are certainly at work here; see Fox; Griffith and Connor; Lareau; Rothstein; Tough). Of course, as educators who believe in the transformative power of education, most of us would like to see this attitude more widely held.

There is considerably less sureness, however, among most of the students that I work with at my community college, especially among my basic writing students. Many basic writers, as we know, are first-generation college students, many come from the most socially marginalized and financially disadvantaged groups in our culture, and many bring a long history of academic frustration and failure to our classrooms (see Fox; Karabel; Shor "Our"; Sternglass; Sullivan; Traub, *City* and "What"; see also Mutnick). But this sense of "unsureness" is something that many students who attend my open admissions college share, whether they are basic writers or not. As research suggests, the same appears to be true of many who attend community colleges nationwide. This is something that English teachers are likely to notice because our pedagogy often brings us in close contact with individual students, as we meet with them individually in and out of class to discuss assigned readings and drafts of essays. Although many community college students answer yes to survey questions about planning to get some kind of degree, many often have no idea what this means, how they might go about earning such a degree, or even what an associate's or bachelor's degree is, for that matter.

Educational Attainment and Persistence

This is why studies conducted by McCormick (1997), Pascarella et al. (1998), Carter (2001), and others, suggesting that enrollment at a community college "reduces" students' "degree aspirations" (Pascarella and Terenzini 380), seem to me to be misleading and misguided—and the result of an unfortunate unfamiliarity with community colleges and community college students (even though some of these researchers clearly value the work that community colleges do). Especially when such researchers talk about "educational attainment and persistence," for example, as Pascarella and Terenzini do in *How College Affects Students:*

A Third Decade of Research (2005), they can seem almost dismissive of community colleges:

> Pascarella and his colleagues found that community college students who entered with plans to complete a bachelor's degree were, after two years of college, 20 to 30 percent more likely than their four-year counterparts to have reduced their degree aspirations below a bachelor's degree. The same net trend, although not statistically significant, was apparent after the first year of college. Other students report findings consistent with those of Pascarella and his colleagues. (380)

For the record, reducing anyone's aspirations—about college, about life, or about anything else—is the last thing most community college teachers, counselors, administrators, staff members, or presidents want to do. The phrasing here, and the incomplete understanding of students who attend open admission institutions that this formulation suggests, is quite unfortunate. Scholars continue to be puzzled by these data, and many have attempted to find some way to explain them (see Pascarella "New"; Pascarella and Terenzini 429–33). None of them, to my mind, has offered us anything satisfactory. Unfortunately, this pernicious idea related to community colleges continues to have wide social currency and considerable political influence in state legislatures.

Pascarella, Edison, Nora, Hagedorn, and Terenzini (1998), for example, discuss why "beginning postsecondary education at a two-year college tends to inhibit degree attainment" (180). They note a number of possible explanations, including the difficulties related to transferring and the problems that students encounter adjusting to a new academic culture at transfer institutions. They also note that community colleges themselves might be in the business of "cooling out" student aspirations (drawing on Burton Clark's still powerfully present notion), especially those students from nonwhite, working-class, and lower- and lower middle-class demographics (180). Researchers have continued to wonder why students who enroll at four-year colleges with selective admissions persist and complete work for bachelor's degrees at a statistically higher rate than those who begin their academic careers at community colleges with what appear to be roughly comparable qualifications and family backgrounds. What is particularly puzzling about these data is that students who appear to have identical educational aspirations (as well as other similarities in terms of academic skills, family income, and parental educational achievement) obtain bachelor's degrees at very different rates.

As I have reviewed this research and reflected on the many students that I have encountered in twenty years of teaching at a community college, I believe that this difference can be explained in a number of ways that contest these claims. Perhaps the most important difference is that students who enroll at these different institutions *appear* to have expressed to researchers and survey takers that their goals are identical—i.e., that they plan to "obtain a bachelor of arts degree," the key benchmark in this research (see, for example, Pascarella, Edison, Nora, Hagedorn, and Terenzini 181). In fact, however, in all sorts of subtle and not so subtle ways, *their goals are not by any means identical.*

The very act of applying to a selective admissions institution suggests—and, in fact, *requires*—a much more significant level of commitment to one's educational future. It is, in itself, an important marker for predicting persistence toward "obtaining a bachelor of arts degree." Students who pursue this educational option often have very different attitudes about college—even though both students might answer a survey question related to their academic goals in exactly the same way.

First of all, we need to understand that applying to a selective admissions institution requires careful, long-term planning, virtually throughout a student's entire high school career. To apply to such an institution, one must prepare for and take standardized tests, arrange to have letters of recommendation submitted, and complete an application and essay. To be admitted, one must also have earned strong grades in high school. When students apply to such schools, they also know that they will be involved in a competitive process and that admission is not guaranteed.

These schools are also significantly more expensive than community colleges, and they require from admitted students a significant financial commitment. Most students must be ready to assume some level of debt in order to attend such schools. Students must also embrace considerable challenges in terms of lifestyle. The vast majority of students attending selective admissions institutions move away from home for the first time, happily or reluctantly (often it's a little of both, of course), and they must forsake the comforts of familiar homes, neighborhoods, and communities. At these institutions, students typically live in dorms, where they encounter many new people and experience a new local culture, new daily rhythms, and new challenges related to food, friendships, social interaction, and workload. Attending a selective four-year institution requires a very significant level of commitment from students—financially, emotionally, and psychologically—as the parents of these students know only too well.

Attending a community college, on the other hand, requires a much less significant personal commitment. Applying to an open admissions institution is much easier—and this is by design, of course. Standardized test scores and letters of recommendation are usually not required, and one's grades in high school are also not a factor. When students apply to such schools, they also know that, if they meet the basic general admissions requirements (usually a high school degree or a GED), their admission is guaranteed. Long-term planning in high school is not necessary. Students can decide even two or three days before a fall semester begins, for example, to attend a community college and be admitted, regardless of poor high school grades. Community colleges are also significantly less expensive than selective admissions institutions, and they do not require of admitted students a radical change in lifestyle. The vast majority of students attending community colleges live either at home with their parents or in their own apartments or homes. They can continue to live in their hometown, and they can continue to maintain current friendships, jobs, and a network of community ties.

Attending a community college requires a much different level of commitment from students in almost every area of their lives. This profile difference helps explain the graduation data that continues to puzzle researchers. It seems clear that, even among those who self-identify in similar ways to data collectors about their degree aspirations, there is a very real qualitative difference between the level of commitment that students bring to the enterprise of completing a bachelor's degree, indicated simply by where they choose to attend college. This difference explains a great deal in terms of commitment and persistence differences between these two cohorts of students.

To put this idea in its simplest form, I pose this question: If all things are equal in terms of a student's economic status, academic preparation, level of family educational attainment, etc. (to the best of our ability to measure these variables), which of the following students has demonstrated the greater commitment to "obtaining a bachelor's degree"?

- Student #1, who applies to, is accepted at, and then chooses to attend an institution that *offers* a bachelor's degree.

  or

- Student #2, who attends an institution that *does not offer* a bachelor's degree [i.e., a community college].

I think the answer is obvious. Is it any wonder that community college students persist at a significantly lower rate in "obtaining a bachelor of arts degree" than those who attend selective admissions institutions? I do not mean to suggest that every student who attends a community college with the goal of "obtaining a bachelor's degree" fits this profile, but a considerable number of students do. This may well account for some of the differences in graduation rates. In fact, many students who attend a community college and indicate a desire to eventually earn a bachelor's degree have a "cooler" commitment to that goal than those who attend selective admissions institutions that offer bachelor's degrees. We just don't have the mechanism yet to measure that difference accurately. Our institutions aren't "cooling them out." These students come to us with "cooler" expectations and commitment to begin with, even though both types of students may answer simple questions on surveys about their goals in exactly the same way.

"Six Distinct Populations"

Recent research has begun, in fact, to make more careful and finely nuanced distinctions among the many different types of students who attend community colleges, and this work provides us with a better picture of what community colleges actually do and how we might better measure "success" for students who attend them. We also now appear to be able to measure "motivation" more accurately.

For example, in a recent report from the United States Department of Education (National Center for Education Statistics), entitled *Profiles of Undergraduates in U.S. Post-secondary Education Institutions: 2003–04, With an Analysis of Community College Students* (2006), the editors offer us a much more sophisticated profile of community college students than many I have previously encountered. They identify "six distinct populations" of students attending these institutions:

> In a recent report, Adelman (2005) used data from the postsecondary transcripts of 1992 high school graduates to develop "portraits" of six distinct populations who attend community colleges. These portraits were based on the credits earned by traditional college-age students (23 or younger) in various degree programs. The first two portraits described students likely to persist and included students in (1) traditional academic paths leading to a transfer and bachelor's degree, and (2) occupational credential paths leading to vocational credentials or associate's degrees awarded by community colleges. The remaining four groups of students were much less successful in earning credits and completing credentials. These groups included (3) students with relatively weak high school academic preparation who struggled to acquire community college credits and then stopped; (4) students who withdrew almost immediately after enrollment with few if any credits earned; (5) those who were based in other institutions (i.e., taking most courses in another institution, primarily in 4-year colleges); and (6) a small population of "reverse transfers" with "declining momentum toward credentials at any level." (19)

For those of us who teach at community colleges, this probably sounds about right. Furthermore, when disaggregated like this, the numbers related to graduation and "success" look very different, as the editors make clear. The "cooling out" function disappears:

> The results of this study suggest that students who enroll in community colleges with a strong commitment toward completing a program of study, whether to transfer to a 4-year college or obtain a degree or certificate, maintain their enrollment for 1 year at relatively high rates. Yet such students made up just 49 percent of those enrolled in community colleges in 2003–04 [. . .].
>
> The findings from this study help explain why community college students complete associate's degrees or certificates at relatively low rates. That is, graduation rates are typically based on all students enrolled in

> degree programs, yet findings from this study indicate that a substantial proportion of students enrolled in formal degree programs do not necessarily intend to complete a degree. (37)

As welcome as this news is, it probably doesn't surprise anyone who works at a community college. We certainly attract our share of "highly motivated" and well-prepared students who are capable of distinguishing themselves at any college in the nation. Many of them, in fact, transfer and do just that, earning bachelor's degrees, master's degrees, and Ph.D.'s, as a number of my former students have done. Highly motivated students choose to begin their academic careers at a community college for a host of reasons. Sometimes it's just simple economics. For example, some students come from middle-class families and, as a recent report of the American Council on Education notes, "have become less likely to choose certain types of institutions [selective admissions institutions] because their families make too much money to qualify for financial aid, but too little for the students to attend without assistance" (4). Sometimes it's convenience and ease of access or even a question of an important relationship that they are unwilling to leave (a parent or family member, typically).

But we also attract other kinds of students as well. Some, for example, attend community colleges as "experimenters," as Manski (1989) and Grubb (1991) have noted: these students attend low-cost, low-risk open admissions institutions to give college "a try." Success for such students might well be measured in terms of finding an answer to the question, "Is college for me?" Helping students find an answer to this question probably should be considered "success" as well. Students typically turn to community colleges, rather than to four-year institutions, to seek an answer to that question. There are other types of students as well. The research is emphatic on this point: students attend open admissions institutions for all kinds of reasons.

Different Kinds of Material Conditions, Different Kinds of Lives

Finally, students who attend open admissions institutions typically live very different lives than those who attend traditional selective admission institutions, even if they all might answer questions related to long-term academic goals in similar ways (i.e., indicating the desire to "earn a bachelor's degree"). Some research acknowledges this variable, and some does not.

When we talk about persistence and "success" at open admissions institutions, it is important to remember that many students who attend such institutions typically live very complex lives. Many are handling adult challenges that traditional undergraduates simply do not have to concern themselves with (work and family being primary), and this, of course, puts them more at risk relative to long-term ventures such as earning a college degree (see Duncan and Brooks-Gunn; Ellwood and Kane; Grissmer, Kirby, Berends, and Williamson; Lee and Burkam; Masset and Denton; Mayer; Pickett, p. 11). We know, for example, that 60 percent of students at two-year colleges work more than 20 hours per week; 34 percent spend 11 or more hours caring for dependents; and 20 percent spend "significant time" (6 to 20 hours per week) commuting to and from classes (Community College Survey "Engagement" 4; see also Community College Survey "Engaging"). In contrast, students who attend selective admissions institutions typically have fewer responsibilities outside of the classroom. It seems clear that these two cohorts of students are very different populations of students meeting different kinds of challenges.

Furthermore, for students who attend college part-time, a large segment of the student body at most open admissions institutions and an increasing demographic nationwide (see United States, *Condition*), the long-term goal of earning a college degree can pose almost impossible challenges. Students routinely speak to me about this problem (and in the most heartbreaking of terms). One such student, who did excellent work all semester in one of my composition classes, recently spoke to me quite tearfully about her long-term prospects for a degree: "At this rate, I'm never going to finish. I'll be 40 years old before I complete my associate's degree, and I just can't bear that." Working toward a degree by taking one or two courses per semester requires extraordinary determination, resourcefulness, and perseverance. This is another risk factor that complicates chances for "success" for students at community colleges.

Conclusion

This essay began with "a dark and troubling mystery":

> Student persistence is of concern to educators and policymakers because large numbers of students who begin their college education in community colleges never complete it.

I hope this essay will help alleviate some of this concern and help colleagues who are unfamiliar with open admissions institutions understand why this lack of completion might naturally be the case. We may finally be able to put to rest Burton Clark's ideas about the "cooling-out function." (Clark's essay continues to be among the most widely cited works in the scholarly literature devoted to community colleges.)

It seems clear that we must begin to think more carefully about how we measure "success" at open admissions institutions, especially in terms of how we compare the work done at these institutions with that done at selective admissions institutions. We must begin to build a definition of "success" at community colleges that takes into account open admissions policies, as well as the community college's unique mission within the system of higher education in this country. Most important, we must develop a definition of "success" that acknowledges the unique complexities, challenges, and material conditions that typically come into play for students who attend open admissions institutions.

As we seek to understand what "success" means for students on our different campuses, we must also help ensure that administrators and policymakers attend carefully to the way that we use research data to define and measure student success at open admissions institutions. Conflicting notions about how to use research data invariably find their way to the center of such discussions, often hindering productive dialogue and action. There is a great deal at stake here, and it is my hope that this essay will help us do this important work more effectively.

We face many common challenges as teachers of college English, and it is time to forge the kind of collegial, collaborative relationships that will help us meet these challenges together. It is time for all of us—those who teach at open admissions institutions and those who teach at selective admissions institutions—to move beyond the misunderstanding and mistrust that has plagued our profession for years. It is my hope that this essay will contribute in some small way to moving that important work forward and help those unfamiliar with open admissions institutions to better understand the good work being done at America's community colleges.

Notes

1. Just a note here about terminology: The vast majority of public two-year colleges are open admissions institutions. In 2002–2003, for example, "95.4% of public two-year colleges had an open admissions policy, compared to 12.5% of public four-year colleges" (Millward, Powers, Crump 1). Most of these public two-year institutions refer to themselves as "community colleges." "Open admissions institution" and "community college" have therefore come to be used interchangeably.

Works Cited

Adelman, C. *Moving Into Town—and Moving On: The Community College in the Lives of Traditional-Age Students*. U.S. Department of Education. Washington, DC: Office of Vocational and Adult Education, 2005.

American Association of Community Colleges. "Fast Facts" January 2006. 8 May 2007 http://www.aacc.nche.edu/Content/NavigationMenu/AboutCommunity Colleges/Fast_Facts1/Fast_Facts.htm.

American Council on Education. *Choice of Institution: Changing Student Attendance Patterns in the 1990s*. ACE Issue Brief. June 2004. 3 September 2006. 8 May 2007 http://www.acenet.edu/programs/policy.

Baker, George A., III, ed. *A Handbook on the Community College in America: Its History, Mission, and Management*. Westport, CT: Greenwood, 1994.

Berkner, L., He, S., and Cataldi, E. *Descriptive Summary of 1995–96 Beginning Postsecondary Students: Six Years Later (NCES 2003-151)*. U.S. Department of Education. Washington, DC: National Center for Education Statistics, 2003.

"Black Student College Graduation Rates Remain Low, But Modest Progress Begins to Show." *The Journal of Blacks in Higher Education*. Winter 2005/ 2006: 88–96. Also available online at: http://www.jbhe.com/features/50_black student_gradrates.html.

Brint, Steven, and Jerome Karabel. *The Diverted Dream: Community Colleges and the Promise of Educational Opportunity in America: 1900–1985*. New York: Oxford UP, 1989.

Carter, Deborah. *A Dream Deferred? Examining the Degree Aspirations of African American and White College Students*. New York: Routledge Falmer, 2001.

Clark, Burton. "The 'Cooling-Out' Function in Higher Education." *American Journal of Sociology* 1960 (65): 569–76.

Cohen, Arthur, and Florence Brawer. *The American Community College*. 4th ed. San Francisco: Jossey-Bass, 2002.

Community College Survey of Student Engagement. "Engagement By Design: 2004 Findings." The University of Texas at Austin, Community College Leadership Program. 2004. 8 May 2007 www.ccsse.org.

———. "Engaging Students, Challenging the Odds." The University of Texas at Austin, Community College Leadership Program. 2005. 8 May 2007 www .ccsse.org.

Cook, Bryan, and Jacqueline E. King. *Improving Lives Through Higher Education: Campus Programs and Policies for Low-Income Adults*. ACE Issue Brief. Washington, DC: ACE, 2005.

———. *Low-Income Adults in Profile: Improving Lives Through Higher Education*. Washington, DC: ACE, 2004.

Dougherty, Kevin. *The Contradictory College: The Conflicting Origins, Impacts, and Futures of the Community College*. Albany: SUNY P, 2001.

Duncan, Greg, and Jeanne Brooks-Gunn, eds. *Consequences of Growing Up Poor*. New York: Russell Sage Foundation, 1997.

Ellwood, David T., and Thomas J. Kane. "Who Is Getting a College Education? Family Background and the Growing Gaps in Enrollment." *Securing the Future: Investing in Children from Birth to College*. Ed. Sheldon Danziger and Jane Waldfogel. New York: Russell Sage Foundation, 2000. 283–324.

Fox, Tom. *Defending Access: A Critique of Standards in Higher Education*. Portsmouth, NH: Boynton/Cook, 1999.

Griffith, Marlene, and Ann Connor. *Democracy's Open Door: The Community College in America's Future*. Portsmouth, NH: Boynton/Cook, 1994.

Grissmer, David W., Sheila Nataraj Kirby, Mark Berends, and Stephanie Williamson. *Student Achievement and the Changing American Family*. Santa Monica, CA: RAND, 1994.

Grubb, N. "The Decline of Community College Transfer Rates: Evidence from National Longitudinal Surveys." *Journal of Higher Education* 62 (1991): 184–217.

Hoachlander, G., A. Sikora, and L. Horn. *Community College Students: Goals, Academic Preparation, and Outcomes (NCES 2003-164)*. U.S. Department of Education. Washington, DC: National Center for Education Statistics, 2003.

Karabel, Jerome. *The Chosen: The Hidden History of Admission and Exclusion at Harvard, Yale, and Princeton.* Boston: Houghton Mifflin, 2005.

Lareau, Annette. *Unequal Childhoods: Class, Race, and Family Life.* Berkeley: U of California P, 2003.

Lavin, David E., and David Hyllegard. *Changing the Odds: Open Admissions and the Life Chances of the Disadvantaged.* New Haven, CT: Yale UP, 1996.

Lee, Valerie E., and David T. Burkam. *Inequality at the Starting Gate: Social Background Differences in Achievement as Children Begin School.* Washington, DC: Economic Policy Institute, 2002.

Manski, Charles F. "Schooling as Experimentation: A Reappraisal of the College Dropout Phenomenon." *Economics of Education Review* 8 (1989): 305–12.

Masset, Douglas, and Nancy Denton. *American Apartheid: Segregation and the Making of the Underclass.* Cambridge, MA: Harvard UP, 1993.

Mayer, Susan. *What Money Can't Buy: Family Income and Children's Life Chances.* Cambridge, MA: Harvard UP, 1997.

McCormick, Alexander. *Transfer Behavior Among Beginning Postsecondary Students: 1989–94* (Statistical Analysis Report no. NCES 97-226). Washington, DC: U.S. Department of Education, Office of Educational Research and Improvement, National Center for Education Statistics, 1997.

Millward, Jody, Lois Powers, and Rebecca Crump. *TYCA Two-Year College Facts and Data Report: 2005.* Sept. 2005. 26 Aug. 2007 http://www.ncte.org/groups/tyca/featuredinfo/122335.htm.

Monk-Turner, Elizabeth. *Community College Education and Its Impact on Socioeconomic Status Attainment.* Mellen Studies in Education. Vol. 41. Lewiston, NY: Edwin Mellen, 1998.

Mutnick, Deborah. "On the Academic Margins: Basic Writing Pedagogy." *A Guide to Composition Pedagogies.* Ed. Gary Tate, Amy Rupiper, and Kurt Schick. New York: Oxford UP, 2001. 183–202.

Pascarella, Ernest. "New Studies Track Community College Effects on Students." *Community College Journal* 69 (1999): 8–14.

Pascarella, E., M. Edison, A. Nora, L. Hagedorn, and P. Terenzini. "Does Community College Versus Four-Year College Attendance Influence Students' Educational Plans?" *Journal of College Student Development* 39 (1998): 179–93.

Pascarella, Ernest T., and Patrick T. Terenzini. *How College Affects Students. Volume 2: A Third Decade of Research.* San Francisco: Jossey-Bass, 2005.

"Percent of Degree-Granting Institutions with First-Year Undergraduates Using Various Selection Criteria for Admission, by Type and Control of Institution: 2000–01, and 2002–03." Table 311. Digest of Education Statistics, 2003. June 2005. National Center for Education Statistics. 2004. 8 May 2007 http://nces.ed.gov/programs/digest/d03/tables/dt311.asp.

Rothstein, Richard. *Class and Schools: Using Social, Economic, and Educational Reform to Close the Black-White Achievement Gap.* Washington, DC: Economic Policy Institute, 2004.

Roueche, John E., and Suanne D. Roueche. *High Stakes, High Performance: Making Remedial Education Work.* Washington, DC: Community College Press, 1999.

Rouse, Cecilia Elena. "Democratization or Diversion? The Effect of Community Colleges on Educational Attainment." *Journal of Business Economics and Statistics* 13.2 (1995): 217–24.

Shor, Ira. "Our Apartheid: Writing Instruction and Inequality." *Journal of Basic Writing* 16.1 (1997): 91–104.

———. *When Students Have Power: Negotiating Authority in a Critical Pedagogy.* Chicago: U of Chicago P, 1996.

Sternglass, Marilyn. *Time to Know Them: A Longitudinal Study of Writing and Learning at the College Level.* Mahwah, NJ: Lawrence Erlbaum Associates, 1997.

Sullivan, Patrick. "Cultural Narratives about Success and the Material Conditions of Class at the Community College." *Teaching English in the Two-Year College* 33 (2005): 142–60.

Tinto, Vincent. *Leaving College: Rethinking the Causes and Cures of Student Attrition.* 2nd ed. Chicago: U of Chicago P, 1993.

Tough, Paul. "What It Takes to Make a Student." *New York Times Magazine* 26 Nov. 2006: 44–51+.

Traub, James. *City on a Hill: Testing the American Dream at City College.* New York: Addison, 1994.

———. "What No School Can Do." *New York Times Magazine* 16 Jan. 2000: 52+.

United States. Department of Education, National Center for Education Statistics. *The Condition of Education 2002.* "Nontraditional Undergraduates." 2002. 21 June 2007 http://nces.ed.gov/programs/coe/2002/analyses/nontraditional/index.asp.

———. *Profiles of Undergraduates in U.S. Post-secondary Education Institutions: 2003–04, With an Analysis of Community College Students.* 2006. 10 Oct. 2007 http://nces.ed.gov/pubs2006/2006184.pdf.

———. *Remedial Education at Degree-Granting Postsecondary Institutions in Fall 2000.* Nov. 2003. 19 Oct. 2007 http://nces.ed.gov/surveys/peqis/publications/2004010/index.asp.

Wilt, Richard. "Community College Graduation Rates Matter." *Community College Times* 4 July 2006: 6.

Yale University, Office of the Registrar. "Yale University 6-Year Graduation Rates for Yale College Students." 20 Apr. 2006. 21 June 2006 http://www.yale.edu/oir/open/pdf_public/W041_YC_Grad_Rates.pdf.

3

Composition Studies and the Two-Year College

Professing at the Fault Lines: Composition at Open Admissions Institutions

Cynthia Lewiecki-Wilson and Jeff Sommers

According to authors Cynthia Lewiecki-Wilson and Jeff Sommers, "At the time we set out to write this piece, community and two-year colleges were experiencing a wave of public and political bashing (combined in some states with legislation) about remedial classes, time to completion, and so on—attacks that have since spread to all of higher education. We wanted to point out that open-admissions students and their teachers actually resided in all kinds of institutional spaces, and that particular approaches to teaching writing benefited open-admissions students—a rich, process-focused curriculum that encourages them to acknowledge and explore their own life experiences, for example. We wanted to give their teachers a voice and respect for the work they do, and we argued that teachers didn't just impart rules, but that they and their students in such writing classrooms are engaged in knowledge-making."

From *College Composition and Communication*, 1999, vol. 50, no. 3, pp. 97-121.

Consider these views:

- A 1993 history of the emerging composition/rhetoric discipline concludes that it is not yet fully a field, that it has no research method it can call its own, and warns that the "costs" of professionalizing might be borne by students "in the margin," affect relationships with colleagues, and "come at the expense of practitioners."[1]

- A recent assessment of graduate Rhetoric and Composition programs locates the discipline in the (re)production of graduate teachers of rhetoric and composition, not in undergraduate writing courses, and argues for greater attention to professional development in graduate programs as a way to improve the discipline.[2]

- A theorist of the history of composition studies argues that we should both resist and affirm composition's disciplinary status. The "both/and" approach marks comp as "post disciplinary." Although maintaining the importance of undergraduate classroom practices, this stance reads such practices as "predisciplinary" aspects of comp, whereas "credentialing activities" like grad programs and institutional spaces like writing program administration provide the necessary "cultural capital" to expand composition's space in the university.[3]

- New York City mayor Rudolph W. Giuliani wages a public "war" on the city's six community colleges, declaring that their students are unprepared for college work, that courses created to meet the needs of students are "remedial" (many of these are first-year writing courses), and that the teaching of these courses should be shifted "to other institutions." The mayor brags that this policy will "reduce the number of students in the system by at least 75 percent." News analysts recognize the mayor's move as an easy, popular way to win support and further his political ambitions. In May 1998, the mayor and the governor successfully "push" the board of trustees to ban all "remedial" courses at the city's 11 senior colleges, apparently shifting these courses to the six community colleges, which "are already filled to overflowing." Incoming students who do not pass gateway placement exams in reading, writing, and math will be barred entrance, ending the open admissions policy established in 1970. During this public campaign of ridicule, confusion and duplicity abound as the mayor first attacks the community colleges, then the senior colleges. No one is quite sure what will happen at the city's community colleges, and in several of the institutions the two co-exist at the same site.[4]

In these mostly paraphrased accounts we have purposely omitted the names of authors to shift attention from disputing with individuals, which is not our aim. Instead, we want to emphasize what these different narratives have in common, which is that they structure perceptions so that it is very difficult to see, let alone seriously consider, any possibility of satisfying intellectual work occurring between composition teachers and their students in open admissions programs. Whether the current state of composition studies is seen as "predisciplinary," as a "professional discipline," as "postdisciplinary," or, as in the case of Giuliani's campaign against City College, in need of the disciplinarian's rod of punishment, each view overlooks the teaching-practice/knowledge-production relationship, and so disregards the teaching of writing in two- and four-year open admissions programs—except as a site for the discipline of punishment, applied to both students and teachers, and legitimated through metaphors of deficit.

We, the authors, profess our discipline at a professional faultline, a site where contradictions meet. We teach at a two-year open access branch of a state university; we are also members of a department with a composition and rhetoric graduate program. We routinely encounter negative assumptions about open admissions students, teachers, and programs from our own students, faculty, and administrators, from their counterparts on the main campus, and from the public. In both the public's and the profession's stories about open admissions education, composition figures poorly: ignored or erased from histories of the discipline; consigned to a "skills" or "remediation" category; or worse, publicly made the scapegoat by ambitious politicians who have no real interest in writing education.

Why should compositionists care about two- and four-year open admissions education? In the following pages, we describe the social materiality of teaching in such locations. We want you to see that the "discipline" of composition takes place in the interactions of teachers and students in open admissions composition classes. For this brief space we thus ask that you reverse the usual thinking about open admissions education. Rather than regarding it as at the "margin" of our profession, we want you to consider the teaching of writing in open admissions sites as central to the historical formation and continuing practice of composition studies. We ask you to reflect on how such a shift in thinking might change views of the profession and redirect attention to work compositionists need to do for the future—questions we will return to at the end of this essay.

To reverse your normal patterns of thought, we are consciously trying to provoke "a crisis of representation." Susan Carlton argues that such a crisis can be a powerful rupture. In her view one occurred when rhet/comp doctoral programs were created and thereby "shift[ed] the material conditions of the field" (81). She claims that "institutional placement" can act "as a 'lever' to displace disciplinary practices and to institute postdisciplinary ones" (81). But how far does the doctoral program lever extend? We doubt that it can be expected to stretch itself all the way down the hill or across town, from research universities to open admissions institutions—which do employ doctoral graduates, but often do not have professional programs, budgets, departmental spaces, etc., with which "composition" can wield institutional leverage. And institutional forces are certainly not the only, or even the most powerful ones, being felt in classrooms today. Again, we ask you to reverse thinking for a moment, and consider a different lever, pulled by other forces. What if the "lever" that will be moving the discipline extends from the other direction, from the current "extracurricular" attack on open admissions education?

Double Consciousness: Seeing Ourselves/ As Others See Us

Our first step in provoking a crisis of representation is to describe us, the Others of composition. For this project, we interviewed nine compositionists who have taught or currently teach at two- or four-year open admissions institutions.[5] Some have previously taught at such sites; some teach in colleges, divisions, or programs that formerly served open admissions students. Not only are we a disparate group, but describing our institutional sites is complicated as well. These are varied, not easy to categorize: a two-year community college in the mountain west; a city university classroom in which most students speak first languages other than English; a suburban commuter branch college of working-class, multi-aged students; or a southern four-year college where many entering students speak non-standard dialects, to name just a few varied sites. The institutional map is made even harder to draw when we include subfield boundaries, such as basic writing, developmental writing, or ESL. These courses may be offered within large research universities or colleges, further obscuring the picture of where open admissions composition teaching occurs. Because it occurs at many different institutional sites, this teaching can often remain invisible when academic maps and disciplinary boundaries are usually drawn.

Presenting a picture of our students is equally complicated. Who are the students in open admissions composition classrooms? From our experience and those of our informants, we would say they can be extremely diverse, even when institutions offer a range of first writing courses. Mary Soliday, at City College of New York, told us: "The primary challenge for me as a teacher is that classes are so diverse. One may have several truly excellent writers sitting alongside writers who have trouble composing more than a paragraph." Not all students are "basic writers," a term whose definition is not intrinsic, but which depends on the particular array of placement tests and course options that create hierarchies among entering college writers. Whether or not basic writers are mainstreamed or separated into special courses varies with institutions. *The Journal of Basic Writing* has published a vigorous and ongoing debate about the benefits or drawbacks of separate courses.[6] Soliday has reported her success mainstreaming basic writers into a year-long writing course, and efforts like hers and Barbara Gleason's now take on bigger stakes in light of the banning of "remedial" courses in the City College system. While City College has a large minority enrollment,[7] many open admissions composition classes are predominantly white, as are many basic writers. Jacqueline Jones Royster and Rebecca Taylor caution that we should be careful in forming generalizations about the identities of these students. In contrast to the stereotype of the urban minority student, Royster and Taylor point out that the basic writer at Ohio State might more likely be a white, rural male who has grown up on a farm and is not conversant with popular culture (because he has no access to cable TV, for example). "'Location' becomes exacerbated by the pressures of multiply defined experiences of marginality, based not only on personal identity but also on social and institutional identity—or non-identity" (29). They note that research has focused mostly on "*student* identity" and that "explorations of *teacher* identity seem almost absent" (31). Instead of objectifying students as somehow "basic" (31), they call for inquiry about teachers. "Questions concerning the professionalization, scholarly commitment, and even work ethics of our basic writing teachers seem to arise frequently. How do such institutionally driven doubts affect basic writing scholarship and pedagogy?" (33–34).

In the following descriptions of our identities as composition teachers of open admissions students, we both invoke the idea of an identity as well as complicate notions of an open-admissions-teacher identity. We want to affirm the warning against stereotyping and objectifying open admissions writers as well as their teachers. Our survey did, however, yield some answers to Royster and Taylor's question. Respondents described again and again how public pressures work against good teaching practices. When headlines trumpet the deficiencies of students entering college, states react by eliminating funding and credit for basic writing courses, or by mandating a single curriculum, entrance testing, or gateway exams. In such a climate, compositionists at open access institutions often feel a sense of schizophrenia, torn between their knowledge that teaching writing is important and challenging and the harsh public voices attacking their enterprise.

These contradictions can produce frustration, but they can also more positively generate a "double consciousness," like that described by W. E. B. Du Bois: "a peculiar sensation. . . . One ever feels his [and her] twoness" (16–17). While we purposely employ this racial homology to represent our awareness of our own otherness, we do not do so to objectify our difference but as a strategy to explore the particular kind of knowledge produced in the complex and contradictory site of an open admissions writing class. It remains important to keep in mind that most open admissions teachers are white and middle-class. "What is likely," Royster and Taylor state, "is that the teacher will probably not share particular identities with the students . . . including factors such as histories of academic success, institutional status, and 'cultural' sense of being" (29). To this likely scenario, though, we would add the possibility that the open admissions teacher *may* (though not always will) share with students an experience of being seen as the Other. The open admissions teacher who has developed a double consciousness may be able to help students understand how they are located within institutions and written (off) by them, and help guide students to re-write themselves as agents rather than objects of learning.

While teaching composition to open admissions students may sometimes feel as though it is waged on a battlefield, our interviewees asserted repeatedly that it is intellectually satisfying, although that aspect of our work remains invisible to the public and the profession. Respondents expressed a deep commitment to the ideals of democracy, to "developing critical literacy and democratic habits" through writing, as Ira Shor now at CUNY Graduate School told us, and to the "open door," which many noted is now being slammed shut. Howard Tinberg of Bristol Community College (MA) wrote to us: "I consider the teaching of composition to be pound for pound the most important task that any college teacher can undertake. I believe so because I think we comp teachers are in the business of training decent and ethical citizens. Other courses may pay lip service to such ends; we act on them."

What may mark the greatest difference between teaching composition in research university programs and at two- and four-year open access institutions, programs, or divisions is the impact of local histories and conditions. The pendulum swings of public enthusiasm or ridicule for open access education affect teaching at these sites, particularly in the way that public will becomes translated into local legislation. Local conditions vary widely, we found, and may come in the form of entrance and exit exams mandated by the institution or in its articulation agreements with senior colleges (as at CCNY). Some states require state-wide assessments or exit exams that drive local curricula, as in Florida, or the Regents Literacy Exam in Georgia. Many states (California, South Carolina, Georgia, and New York, just to name a few) are tightening admissions requirements and eliminating or disallowing developmental courses. Such external pressures—along with the national trend of cost cutting and reliance on more part-time faculty—also make open admissions composition teachers sometimes feel isolated and besieged. Unlike faculty at research universities, we often conduct our professional work outside of an English department buffer zone, in an interdisciplinary department perhaps, which can very often put us in the middle of the political fray—whether that be campus-wide or community-wide.

The Opening and Closing Door: A Revolving History of Populism and Purification

A short walk through the key moments in open admissions education that respondents identified, as well as those we found recorded in the official histories, quickly dispels the myth that current attacks on open admissions education are new. In identifying the key events leading to open admissions at CUNY, Ira Shor listed the student protests of the late 60s which "forced the CUNY Board of Higher Education to implement open admissions." Shor noted, though, that even in the early 70s open admissions at CUNY came "under constant attack from authorities in government, media, and private enterprise" and "required constant defense."[8]

Our own institution, an open admissions regional branch of Miami University, was conceived and built in the mid-60s, in a brief heyday of civic optimism just after some successes of the civil rights movement and before antiwar student protests and their resulting backlash. This double movement, enthusiasm for open admissions followed or even accompanied by fear and a turning against the new student populations, marks not only recent history, but in fact was also part of the community college movement from the start. As Allen A. Witt et al. point out in their history of junior and community colleges: "In an interesting relationship, populists *and* elitists in higher education were both responsible for the growth of junior and community colleges. Populists wanted to provide access to higher education for the masses, whereas elitists hoped to purify higher education by providing separate institutions for the teaching of lower-division students" (xviii).

Junior colleges started appearing sporadically over one hundred years ago, spurred in part by the social mandate after the Civil War to broaden avenues to literacy by increasing the number of schools, although as Pederson notes many were segregated institutions that remained so until the 1950s (181). The large influx of immigrants from 1900 to 1920, Ratliff points out, also exerted pressure to increase access to public higher education (12). There were (and are) wide variations in the kinds of open access programs, divisions, or institutions that developed—as many variations, in fact, as there are local histories. By the 1920s, junior colleges became a nationally accredited and standardized system of schooling, though one taking many forms. Some, associated with comprehensive and research universities, provided the first two years of education in regional, accessible locations; the University of Chicago was a pioneer of this model. Others, often located in rural areas, were former four-year colleges that had contracted to two-year programs. Large state systems developed in California, Texas, Illinois, Missouri, Kansas, Michigan, and other states, primarily in the West and Midwest. Some city universities also began as two-year open access institutions or adapted a Chicago style model of lower open access divisions and a senior college (see Witt et al., chs 1–5).

Always in a tenuous position, urban community colleges in particular faced fierce opposition. "Those who believe that the challenges now facing America's urban community colleges—from cultural diversity and conflict, to remediation and testing, to political intervention—are of recent origin might do well to look to . . . history" (Pedersen 180).

By the late 1930s, "nearly one-tenth of the students in American higher education were enrolled in junior colleges" (Witt et al., 96). By 1990 two-year and junior colleges had nearly six million students in 1200 institutions, accounting for almost 45% of all students in higher education (Witt et al., 262). Even more significant are the minority enrollment statistics. The U.S. Department of Education reported that in 1991, of all students enrolled in higher education, 56.5% of Hispanic students, 41.9% of African American students, 40% of Asian students, and 36% of Caucasian students were enrolled in two-year institutions (Padron 88).

If, as many of our respondents feel, a new battle is being waged against open access education, it seems apparent, considering these figures, that at this particular historical moment the effect will be (dare we say its goal is?) to restrict minorities' access to education. Compare the student population before and as a result of open admissions at CUNY. According to the *Washington Post*, before open admissions in 1969, CUNY's freshman class was 96% white and 4% non-white, whereas in 1997 the makeup of the first-year class was 32% white and 68% non-white (Harden).

The opening up of higher education to previously excluded populations was a key event of open admissions education cited by both Nancy Thompson and Rhonda Grego. They see the current erosion of support for open access education as part of a broader erosion of support for programs that promote racial equity such as affirmative action. Both teach in the Southeast, at the University of South Carolina and at historically black Benedict College, respectively. They pointed to the civil rights movement of the 1960s, which in their region brought a new population into the university.

However, the double movement of populism and purification was at work nearly a century before the civil rights movement and is illustrated by a story Grego drew from her research on the teaching of writing during the period of Reconstruction. At that time when the doors to education were briefly opened to African Americans, the first black undergraduate from Harvard came to the University of South Carolina and created an experimental program, what he and the faculty called a sub-freshman class. "It was truly for students who had been admitted to college," Grego explained, "but they were going to give them the space and training to adjust to the institution and more traditional classes. They did it for a year. Then the board of trustees told them you can't do that . . . it's not sanctioned. You're letting in those you know are going to take an extra year. This is a time when higher education institutions were solidifying and forming their identity, a time when English studies were trying to appear more scientific. So this attitude isn't something that came along with the sixties. It was there from the very beginning of modern higher education."

Open Access Teaching: Attending to the Literate Acts of Students, Renewal through Repetition

The next step in provoking a crisis of representation is to make visible what compositionists actually do at open admissions institutions. Their work differs from that of colleagues in research universities because open admissions compositionists *do* teach first-year writing, again and again, and because they must give lots of attention to students and their writing, or—simply put—they will lose them. Nell Ann Pickett has explained this aspect of her teaching career at a two-year college: "The realities of our students are the realities that we as teachers in two-year colleges deal with each day. Syllabi, assignment sheets, paper-due dates, student conferences, portfolio reviews—these are always fluid. Or we lose the student. . . . Encouraging students, making every class meeting relevant to students' goals, using teaching/learning materials that students can identify with: these realities are the continuous challenge for us as teachers" (p. 15 in this volume).

Our interviewees wrote of instituting changes in response to the needs of their students and of reinventing their teaching along with the emerging discipline of composition studies. Nancy Thompson recalled the innovative ways her southern university eventually responded to the challenge of the civil rights movement, in the late 60s and early 70s creating multidisciplinary courses and programs to serve the needs of a new African American population. Partly because no one else was interested in basic writing at that time, Thompson felt she had enormous freedom to experiment in her teaching. Reflecting from the vantage point of more than twenty years, she realizes now, she said, that film studies and feminism influenced her approaches to teaching writing and that she practiced an early form of cultural studies. "I don't remember when I began emphasizing the writing process, but I always was aware of and emphasized different cultures; that has always been an important part of what I like about teaching. I worked with Chicano students in Arizona, and then I came to South Carolina to work with African American students." Today Thompson teaches graduate classes and runs the writing studio,[9] but "has to fight to be able to teach a freshman class."

Stephen Ruffus, of Salt Lake Community College, echoed Thompson's memory of innovative freedom; he believes that open admissions education has led the way in "non-standard approaches to learning."[10] And it is true that just as open admissions compositionists have developed with the field, they have also influenced it. Consider Mina Shaughnessy's work on basic writing, Ira Shor's on critical pedagogy and working-class students, Mary Soliday and Barbara Gleason's on mainstreaming basic writers, Rhonda Grego and Nancy Thompson's on the writing studio. Indeed, every teacher we interviewed has published work that comes from teaching open admissions students.

Because open admissions compositionists teach first-year writing again and again, they have opportunities to grow and develop and to reflect on their evolution. How have they changed over the course of their careers? When asked to reflect on the changes in her teaching of composition over nearly thirty years, Helon Raines of Armstrong Atlantic State University (GA) recounted: "When I began teaching at the University of Southern Mississippi in 1970, I was hired one week, handed a grade book, a textbook, given a room assignment and sent into the classroom the next week. I had no training. Today, fortunately, I have no memory of what I taught or how I taught it." Between the early 70s and 80s composition was becoming a field and process pedagogies took root. Raines identified several key events of that formative period that have transformed her teaching of writing including: the shift from current-traditional rhetoric to process writing; new approaches in grading, evaluating, and assessing writing; the emergence of comp as a professional discipline with conferences, journals, and graduate training; writing center and writing across the curriculum advances; expanded notions of literacy; the development of national and regional Writing Projects; and the validation of multiple kinds of research and scholarship in writing.

Rhonda Grego recalled that when she first started teaching composition as a graduate student in a Rhetoric and Comp PhD program in the early 80s, "process" didn't really get much respect. She and others in the program paid lip-service to process approaches; they used student workshopping of papers, for instance. But the grad students nevertheless felt "there was a kind of message about people who did process work that it was a little soft, that there wasn't as much academic valuing of the process approach as there was the more intellectual history of rhetoric or argumentation." Looking back now, Grego sees her current teaching grew from the dissatisfactions that she first sensed then. "We would model" for students a close rhetorical reading of a text, and "somehow, magically, they were to take the topic" and connect it to their own papers. "I see now, I guess I always felt, that there was a lot going on in that gap. There was a kind of silence there, and then it would be peer draft workshop day." Over the years and in response to her students' needs, Grego has developed new approaches to fill that gap. She now does more responding to early stage writing, helping to articulate implicit pathways of development and alternative strategies.

Jeff Sommers' first teaching experience, as an adjunct, resembled Helon Raines': handed a book one day, in front of the class the next, with no preparation to teach composition. A year later, he was a full-time instructor at a community college, teaching five sections of composition in a program that addressed basic writing students as deficient writers. The program emphasized a self-paced program of grammar instruction with little writing required. As he learned about classroom management and student needs, he also discovered that he was slipping extra writing work into the class schedule. As time went on, Jeff convinced his chair to allow him to experiment with teaching a process pedagogy, even receiving funding to attend a summer seminar on composition teaching. By that time, he had begun to see that teaching composition to the varied and fascinating students he was encountering at the community college could be very stimulating. When the opportunity arose later in his career, Jeff sought a position at an open admissions institution, leaving a teaching job at a four-year university to come to Miami Middletown.

Those early experiences at an open admissions campus have influenced his work ever since. At Miami, he has had the opportunity not only to teach at a two-year open admissions campus, but has also been involved in graduate education, working with new teaching assistants and returning public school teachers attending Miami's site of the National Writing Project. As he teaches those courses on pedagogy, he is aware that his experiences at open admissions campuses are now influencing the graduate students he teaches.[11] He is thus passing along, however indirectly, the lessons of the two-year composition classroom.

Cindy Lewiecki-Wilson became interested in composition while she was writing her dissertation and teaching as an adjunct instructor. Like Rhonda Grego, she used the term "process" in graduate school as a TA, but did not actually teach much process then; program constraints such as mass exit exams kept her teaching current-traditional. She realizes now that no matter how process-centered a teacher wishes to be, if students must pass (or fail) the course by means of a timed prompt, producing a single piece of writing with no chance for revisions, then a pedagogy emphasizing a few narrow forms of argumentation and surface correctness prevails. In the mid-80s she taught composition as an adjunct in a strong composition program, one that trained its grad students and adjuncts in pedagogy; however, an exit exam there also drove the curriculum. As her teaching evolved, she added conferences, peer workshopping, and allowed limited revising, but only when she moved to her present position at a two-year regional campus did she really develop a pedagogy emphasizing multiple and creative revising and portfolio assessment.[12] She also started applying theory to the writing classroom, asking students to analyze the social forces that shape writing and writers. In part, her teaching evolved out of necessity. The students she now teaches have such differing levels of preparation that they need creative process and revision strategies. Their economic and social precariousness constantly threatens to overwhelm them and calls for critical analysis. In part, local conditions (no exit exams) freed her to develop. She has also become more personal in the classroom, asking students to speak out about their lives in their writing, to connect their experiences to cultural and social critique, to undertake community-based writing projects.

Institutional structure has affected Cindy's teaching in other ways. Because two-year campuses are more interdisciplinary, and faculty in English often teach the same courses and have the same students, there are opportunities for collaboration. At her campus, English faculty regularly present at conferences, do research, and write together. They are currently working together to create a new option for a first-semester composition class that provides extra workshop support for students who need it. Cindy also works with non-English faculty and administrators on campus-wide writing issues. Though two-year campus faculty have the opportunity to shape the way the larger institution considers writing issues, this opportunity is also a responsibility. There is no graduate writing administration to authorize attitudes or do institutional program building. If those faculty committed to composition as a discipline do not do hands-on institutional and community alliance building, they risk losing the freedom to teach composition in the ways they know are best. Faculty at Miami Middletown, for example, have been resisting pressure to institute a computerized skills test instead of actual student writing to place students in writing courses. Not only do they reject such a test as a legitimate way to assess writing, but they are also fearful that a skills-centered curriculum might be imposed at some future time. As Ira Shor has warned, "Top-down testing has little to do with bottom-up learning and a lot to do with institutional control" ("Our Apartheid" 98). On a two-year campus, resistance cannot take place only in individual classrooms; compositionists cannot afford to be remote, individual scholars and experts. They have to step across the boundaries of their classrooms and teach and speak to others—for example, explaining to administrators and faculty in other departments, why editing skills are only a sub-set of the knowledges a writer needs to practice and learn, and why open admissions students, in particular, need time to practice the processes of writing, of rethinking and rewriting, of critical thinking, cultural analysis, self-expression.

Cindy also works with high school English teachers and occasionally with graduate students on the main campus. This location, straddling the usual division lines of high school, college, and research university practices of English, requires a compositionist to be a writer and translator all the time—to think of audience, purpose, and situation—to write and rewrite disciplinary knowledge again and again. Cindy sees her interests in gender, race, class, and disability issues in writing, literature, and women's studies, not as separate fields, but as a single subject, concerning issues of "writing and difference," and one that is anchored in her teaching and the learning in an open admissions institution.

Howard Tinberg also noted how student differences have influenced the evolution of his teaching. "Looking back at one of my old syllabuses plainly shocked me," he wrote. "I had used it prior to coming to the community college. It was bold, innovative, organizing an *entire* semester's work in composition around ethnographic research. I was shocked because of its boldness and because it reminded me of the adjustments that I had made when coming to my current position: I quickly learned when moving to an open access college that I needed to be attuned to the needs of a wide range of student abilities and to the busy, often harried lives of those students." Although Tinberg laments that his current syllabus is "safer" and there is a "circularity of the path" he has taken—he now teaches a research paper again—he also acknowledges how his thinking has changed: "I am more convinced than I have been in a long time that a required writing course demands plenty of opportunity for reading and evaluation and synthesis of that reading." He explains that he still assigns journals, but "I now try to situate my journal assignment within the content of the course."[13] Tinberg's story is one of gradual change and evolution in teaching, influenced, in a positive way, by the repeated teaching of first-year writing courses.

Evolution and renewal were themes that recurred in the commentaries of our respondents and one Jeff pointed to as well. Jeff recalled his "Kafka class," a nightmarish, surreal experience for him to teach. A number of years ago, while teaching three sections of the same first-year composition course, he realized one of the classes was inert. Activities that would encourage active interest and participation later in the day in his other two classes would elicit no response at all from this group. The students never laughed, never joked, never asked questions, and they never even seemed irritated at what they must have perceived as Jeff's terminal lack of any interesting qualities as an instructor. The situation was so demoralizing that Jeff pleaded with the three students in the class who had some sparks of energy to transfer to one of his other two classes where they would be taking the same course but would get much more out of it. His motivation was mostly on their behalf because he could see at times that they were suffering when their classmates remained so passive, but he was also thinking of himself: He wanted them to know that he was a better teacher than they had been experiencing.

Five years later, a familiar name appeared on Jeff's class list in English 112, the second-semester composition course. Lisa had been one of the students in the "Kafka class," but this Lisa was nothing like that earlier version from years before. She was always prepared for class, always willing to participate in class discussion. She was lively, animated, bright, insightful. She actually became something of a class leader. This time, Jeff was delighted to have Lisa in class. Lisa's explanation for the change was "Oh, I just grew up, that's all." But she also commented that she had seen that first course as valuable, even though she had not taken it seriously enough, and given a second chance, she came back to the same instructor.

The experience was significant for Jeff. While the change in Lisa was the most striking one he has ever experienced in a student, connecting with former students again is common for him. He recently had a student in the second-semester composition course who was completing the sequence he had begun in Jeff's first-semester course 14 years earlier. He also had another student who was repeating the course five years later because, she said, the first time around she had not applied herself enough to earn a grade she could live with. Jeff frequently teaches the siblings, parents, children, and friends of former students as well, all of whom arrive in his classes with a preconceived notion of who he is as an instructor because of their own prior experiences with him, either firsthand or through the conversations they have had with someone close to them who has been in one of his classes.

Where English faculty teach the same courses over and over again, often teaching multiple sections of writing courses at the same time, opportunities for development are always available. Professors as well as students have second chances to reinvent themselves, as Howard Tinberg described. Lisa had changed as she matured. She came back and excelled in a setting similar to the one in which she had been less-than-successful before. But Jeff saw himself as also having had a second chance. He strives to teach his best every term, but he acknowledges that he had something to prove to Lisa (and himself) as much as she had something to prove to herself and to him. Every time Jeff walks into a class and discovers students who are taking his course because they have done so once before or because big sister recommended it, he feels that same need to work harder to prove that the recommendation was deserved. Jeff's teaching has evolved through repeated opportunities to teach the same course. Once he realized how poorly things were going in the "Kafka class," he began to see repetition as his chance to try out new strategies, to rehearse them almost. He would critique his plans and then make revisions and use those strategies in his more responsive classes. It was while teaching the "Kafka class," for example, that he changed the classroom seating arrangement from rows of desks to a circle, a change that became permanent. By the time Lisa came back to Jeff's composition class, he had incorporated a number of strategies into his teaching as regular features that had been born out of the desperation he felt in the earlier class. She benefited from Jeff's being a more accomplished teacher in part *because of* not *in spite of* the unfortunate first experience.

For Mary Soliday, teaching at CCNY has provided her with the opportunity to reflect and reinvent her own teaching. She noted that in many of her classes she had problems with attendance and lateness that interfered with her efforts to "create a community of writers." "These are pervasive ills at CCNY, since most of our students have such full and complex lives. But rather than blame the students, I began to think that their behaviors reflected resistance to my teaching, and so I started reconsidering my approach." She explained how her experience with colleague Barbara Gleason in implementing a FIPSE grant allowed them to "mainstream basic writers into one year-long course." When the grant concluded, she discovered that she could not simply carry its activity over into one-semester courses, so she began a process of adaptation. She now uses her syllabus to teach students about the writing process, "a process which I believe is particularly powerful for students whose lives are so complex that, unlike myself at their age, they can't stay up all night to write a paper even if they wanted to. My syllabus contains all the assignments written out on it, plus the basic information about the course, and I constantly refer the students to it, emphasizing that writing a little bit at a time will fit in better with lives cut up by commuting, child care, work, and study."

Soliday concluded that "many of these changes in my teaching are developmental—I simply have gained more experience both as a teacher of writing and as a teacher at CCNY." But she also noted that "other changes have resulted from institutional pressures that a responsible teacher cannot ignore and that theory never fully accounts for. In some cases, institutional reaction and harsh penalties against students have probably pushed me towards a deeper concern about students' errors." She noted that she discusses rhetorical form continuously throughout the course and even incorporates a good deal of explicit grammar instruction into the course from the first day of the term. "I've begun spending more time analyzing the major patterns of error in students' writing and dealing explicitly with these in class and conference." Her path is reminiscent of Howard Tinberg's in its circularity as she has gradually seen the need to move back to Mina Shaughnessy's work in error analysis while teaching at the very same place where the approach was developed.

This theme of teaching evolution, renewal, and reflection is apparent in a number of the stories we were told. Melissa Sue Kort of Santa Rosa Junior College (CA) related an anecdote from one of her current writing courses. "Last week, a student brought a paper to me that began with a description of being assaulted and raped in a locker room on campus. The incident had been widely publicized, but the victim's name withheld. The student wrote that as she was being attacked 'I found myself thinking of Joan Didion and a point she made in her essay "Sentimental Journeys"'" (an essay we had been discussing in class). She went on to argue in favor of protecting the anonymity of rape victims." Reading the student's paper in class, Kort described herself as "frozen," trying to figure out "how to maintain the student's privacy, give her the tutorial she obviously desired, and offer sympathy, support, and encouragement." She managed the challenge and noted that the student had only one absence that term and earned the best grade in the class.

As Kort's teaching day continued, she encountered a student who apologized for having missed the past two classes because of brain surgery to remove a tumor. She had managed to keep up with the assigned work and expressed concern that her absences might affect her grade. But Kort also reported on a tutorial with a student who "had put so little effort into his paper that he hadn't even managed to press the 'spell check' key on the computer." And a number of other students in that same class "complained that I had made them study the material on their own, rather than 'giving' it to them." She concluded, "Perhaps these tales of the best of times, the worst of times, in some way hint at the challenges and frustrations of teaching English in the two-year college. One minute a student will infuriate me; the next, a student will astound me with her commitment in the face of a 'real life' that would probably have flattened me. I respect them tremendously, the ones who earn my respect; that respect tempers my attitude towards their less dedicated, less prepared, less focused peers, and renews my energy for the task."

Kort also reflected on her earliest days as a teacher twenty years ago, noting that her evolution began almost immediately. "Most of my students were coming off the graveyard shift. I knew this because they were freshly showered, barely awake. I did this sort of how-to-make-sentences approach." She learned, however, that the model of teaching she was using was a real problem. Her students were "grownups," yet she was instructing them at the level of composing basic sentences and paragraphs. "They were planning on college class papers, not single paragraph entries," but "they were being taught as if they were children rather than being given experiences that were appropriate to their adulthood." She even remembers that her first job interview took place in a "remedial classroom" where the tables and chairs were child-size. "That epitomized the attitudes that somehow if you were remedial you were a child, whether or not you were thirty or forty or even twenty-five." Over the years Kort has changed. "I start my freshman comp class now with a selection from *The Pedagogy of the Oppressed*," and although some are resistant, students usually "acknowledge that they have been trained to be passive in class."

Helon Raines provides a story of her own evolution as a teacher of composition. At the start of her career as a graduate student in 1970 her approach was "the product, one-draft, research-paper-emphasis, lecture mode." In 1976 she was "still using prose models" and recalls presenting a seminar for other graduate students on the "efficacy of the method." Her composition teaching began to evolve in the mid-80s when she regularly attended the Wyoming Conference on Teaching Freshman and Sophomore English. "From that time on, I was experimenting with many different methods, moving away from the strict prose models approach with the typical assignment of writing a description, then a narrative, then a process analysis, then a definition."

Over the past 13 years, Raines' teaching has "moved," to use her word, "from teaching courses which did not include much informal writing to using journals, double-entry notebooks, reading logs, in class responses to questions, and other forms of writing to learn. I moved from having a mid-term and a final exam to what I have come to call 'meditations' (informal writings that I do not grade but just check) so that in my classes today, by the end of the term, students do nothing but workshopping while I conference individually with students. Since about 1990, the final exam time is a performance and celebration with five or six students reading their essays selected by their response groups and everyone writing peer response notes to the essays which I distribute to the author after I read them." She also described changes in her grading procedures and responses to student writing. "My assessment has changed from evaluating the first draft of a paper with a letter grade and, if the paper was revised, averaging the two grades together, to reading multiple drafts, and only giving a 'pencil grade' if the student asks for one." Implicit in this history is Raines' notion of "movement." Her teaching story is one of evolution, and that evolution was influenced, for the better, by her teaching situation at a two-year campus where she taught lots of students in lots of writing courses.

Teachers at open access institutions have not given up process approaches. In fact, they still struggle to get their colleagues to see the benefits of teaching process, including peer workshopping, revisions, and portfolios. However, they have incorporated process into courses that focus on critical thinking, cultural studies, ethnography, and/or literacy. Several stated that they have stopped using journals; others use them but for more content-based writing and metacognitive reflection. If these teachers are "post-process," as Ruffus describes himself, they are likewise and at the same time struggling to maintain process pedagogy and convince their current-traditional colleagues of its benefits. Helon Raines wrote, "I do not care so much that everyone adopt newer methods, and in fact I have often made the case why it would *not* be an ideal world" if everyone taught the same way. "However, I do think every composition teacher should be able and willing to know what the issues are." Raines, who taught at a community college for many years and is now at a four-year state university, notes that at both institutions about half the teachers "are committed to a process methodology with revision, peer response, and collaborative learning." On the other hand, she writes, "all faculty at the community college consider themselves composition experts," see "teaching composition as difficult, as something that not everyone can do well simply by virtue of having degrees in English," and "usually feel their work is challenging and rewarding, even if under-valued by others."

In "Composing English Studies," Richard Miller argues for "the importance of seeing composition as the institutional site reserved for investigating acts of reading and writing as evidenced in and by student texts. . . . as the field whose very expertise lies in initiating students into an exploration of how meaning gets made—the institutional location, in short, where student work rather than the literary text serves as the principal subject of study" (169). As those we interviewed attest to, open admissions compositionists put student acts of reading and writing at the center of their disciplinary practice, regarding the teaching of first-year writing as both the practice of their discipline and the site of knowledge production.

Looking Ahead from the Point of View of Open Admissions Teaching

While Rhonda Grego commented that she thinks composition will "survive backlash. I'm of the hopeful variety of person. I prefer to be an optimist," her research colleague and writing partner, Nancy Thompson, voiced concerns that were less optimistic: "I wonder if Freshman English might not be dying out at my institution. We have a university 101 that is an introduction to university experience. With Freshman English being so caught up in preparing students to be English majors, I'm not sure if the university is going to continue to tolerate that for all students." The picture our respondents presented of the future proved to be a mix of hopes and fears, optimism and pessimism.

Mary Soliday, who generally considers her evolution as a teacher positively, also commented on the negative pressures that have driven some of the changes she has made. She now sees "that remediation and its bedfellow, mass assessment, are wicked responses to open admissions students in the context of the late 1990s. Most of the students I have had don't need remediation: They just need more sustained practice to develop as writers; they need intellectually stimulating college courses taught by committed teachers." Soliday's observations were echoed by other respondents who also look ahead to a future where continued evolution as teachers may be restricted or even made impossible by the elimination of courses and reliance on adjuncts.

To Sylvia Holladay, those external pressures led her to retire after nearly forty years of teaching, deciding that she could contribute more effectively outside the classroom and outside a formal position in an institution. "For one who has dedicated her life to open admissions humanitarian higher education, it is definitely but sadly time to make the transition to doing something else." The factors that led Holladay to this conclusion sound very much like Soliday's "wicked responses." Holladay explained that the Florida State Legislature and Department of Education have implemented new regulations in the late 90s that "had the effect of closing the open door, of eliminating open admissions." She listed a number of these regulations:

> All students entering the community colleges must take a statewide multiple-choice computerized test for placement. All students who take basic courses must take a statewide multiple-choice exit test to pass the course. The

> Legislature in the name of uniformity and equality passed a law that the General Education core at all universities and community colleges cannot exceed 36 credit hours. We had to trim 6 hours. We lost college-level reading and a laboratory science courses as well as college survival skills — courses that most of our AA students need.

Holladay also discussed how these regulations affected her campus and her teaching. Her college was compelled to abandon its own writing placement assessment in favor of a multiple choice test and had to modify its curriculum in ways that were not pedagogically sound, simply to conform to uniform course numbering throughout the state system. "All of these changes," she concluded, "go against what I as a compositionist know to be effective pedagogical practice. These changes have caused widespread frustration, low morale, and burnout among comp instructors."

Ira Shor also spoke of similar external pressures and their deleterious effect. He described his college as

> underfunded and understaffed; classes too large; individual attention hard to get; counseling and advising services too thin; required courses offered too infrequently to help students make progress towards a degree; and growing reliance on adjunct faculty making student academic experience uneven and unpredictable. The constant conservative political attacks on this besieged public university system demoralize students and teachers in an atmosphere of constant cutbacks.

When asked what is the most difficult task he faces as a teacher, Shor identified the challenge of getting students to "take responsibility for their education by negotiating the curriculum in a critical-democratic pedagogy. Students have no prior experience with democratic participation in curriculum because school and colleges have presented only authoritarian power relations, with unilateral decision-making from the top down." Shor warned that "unless current trends are halted, writing instruction will become more and more a part-time teacher enterprise, with more outside testing and tracking of students who will be charged higher-tuition for a lower-quality education."

For Howard Tinberg and Helon Raines the look ahead is not as bleak, but their expectations are, at best, mixed. Tinberg said, "Five years from now, I fear one of two things happening: that the only people teaching freshman writing will be part-time instructors, or, and this is equally problematic, that the full-time people teaching that course will have neither the energy nor commitment to discipline their teaching. I worry about the professionalism of English instruction at the two-year college even as I celebrate the possibilities for change." Helon Raines told us that she expected that "departments will continue to teach writing classes that are different from those taught in the 50s and 60s in name only." She added, however, "I do expect to see more writing in all courses or a requirement of sophomore level writing courses for many. . . . Writing should take a much more central role in the curriculum than it ever has in the past or at present."

The future appears to be bringing both the promise and threat of more emphasis on technology. At Miami University Middletown, we have already seen a number of technology initiatives at our campus—ranging from reductionist writing placement by computerized editing tests, instead of the writing sample we had formerly used, to a push for faculty to create their own web sites for their courses. While the English department, at least for the moment, successfully replaced the computerized placement test with a writing sample, our concerns remain. With the increased investment in technology, we will continue to feel pressures from the administration to use that investment. Already teaching one class that incorporates its own web site, Jeff envisions composition courses using the Internet more regularly and welcomes the change—with a cautionary note. When we teach on the Internet and provide students with easy access to the same links we use in our research and class preparation, we diffuse our own authority somewhat in the classroom, a move that can be exciting and productive. However, Jeff fears that administrators will rush to embrace "distance learning" via the Internet, neglecting the very strength of the campus, the personal contact between faculty and students.

As Cindy looks to the future, she thinks it will be increasingly necessary for compositionists to explain their discipline to the public. We have to translate the discipline of our work to those outside our classrooms, not only in terms of how students learn to write and make meaning, but by also describing the ways compositionists have learned to read and respond to student writing. We need to give reasons for our more complex readings of student literacies and advocate for the importance of critical literacy. Without a counter-discourse about writing, the public slips back into the simplified language of grammar skills, deficits, and remediation and uses it against the most disempowered.

The Fate of Open Admissions and the Future of Composition Studies

The sites we have described, two- and four-year colleges that serve open admissions students, grew rapidly 20 to 30 years ago, but there are many signs that the broad-based social commitment to educating open admissions students is ending. During this same period, composition as a discipline came into being. All the respondents who have been teaching since the 1970s identified the formation of the discipline as one of the most important factors in advancing their teaching and scholarship. And as composition programs and teachers dedicated to teaching writing developed to meet the needs of open admissions students, they and their students in part helped shape this field and create new sub-fields. Just as research universities provide the necessary conditions for their faculty to teach and research in narrowly defined fields, two- and four-year open admissions institutions and programs provide the opportunity for compositionists to hone their discipline. Yet our respondents also report their very real struggles to maintain the best disciplinary practices at their institutions amid state-mandated testing, requirements that negatively impact on curriculum, and cutbacks that lead to loss of courses and full-time faculty. These conditions exert pressure to move backward, as Helon Raines said, to pre-process models, even as many of those we surveyed wish to move ahead to extend their teaching to include post-process social critiques.

In "Disciplining Students; Whom Should Composition Teach and What Should They Know?" James Slevin traces the roots of the word *discipline* to restore its older meaning of the learner learning and teacher teaching. Presently, the word is "conceptualized as a spatial object . . . defined by . . . boundaries . . . in an agonistic relationship to others" (155). Teaching is seen as outside the boundary, as the application of disciplinary knowledge. Slevin asks his readers to instead understand *discipline* as having to do with the acts of "transmission and transformation . . . includ[ing] all the agents, students as well as teachers, who engage in this activity" (156). "The prevailing view of disciplinary work," he points out, "underpins the idea not only of research as the defining disciplinary activity but also of the research university as our 'idea of the university'" (159). When the discipline of composition studies is redefined as the teacher teaching and the student learning, it is possible to see that disciplinary knowledge about writing is transformed in students' acts of composing and revising and teachers' of assigning and responding to writing; then it is also possible to see the open admissions institution not at the margin but at the center of such disciplinary activity. Such a reversal, we would argue, should change the way we think about the future of composition studies. Royster and Taylor end their essay on "Constructing Teacher Identity in the Basic Writing Classroom" by asking these questions: "Should we be moving as a profession to draw more colleagues to basic writing as an area to which one is professionally devoted and not just generally interested? . . . Who are we thinking of when we think of 'basic writing teachers' for the twenty-first century? What are the pedagogical implications of our answers? What are the implications for teacher training?" (43)

We have been arguing that the profession should see open admissions composition teaching not as a low-level site merely for the application of knowledge, but as an intellectually productive and transformative site of disciplinary practice. Coming to such an understanding is only a first step, but one that may lead compositionists to undertake and value different kinds of work in the future. When open admissions composition teaching is seen as central, it becomes clear that working to preserve open admissions programs is as crucial to the future of the discipline as preserving and enlarging graduate programs, and that translating the practices and theories of the undergraduate writing classroom to academic colleagues in other departments and to the public is as important as conducting research and writing to one another in scholarly journals.

Time is running short for open admissions students, however. Decisions about testing, course offerings, and bilingual education are being leveraged by ambitious political figures who use simplified arguments waged against the most vulnerable students in public education to shape opinion and garner support for their careers. California votes down bilingual education. The mayor and governor of New York pressure the trustees of City University to end open admissions. These actions come from outside the university. While composition and rhetoric has been busy institutionalizing itself within the university, outside its walls, rhetoric has been used against itself to shape a new policy of closing off access and limiting opportunities.

In a listserv discussion of the debacle at CUNY, Karen Greenberg wrote, "This is a nightmare that I still cannot believe is happening." How do we awake from the nightmare? What will happen to the teaching of writing as the commitment to open admissions students is withdrawn, as is currently happening around the country? Will composition, as a discipline, retract solely to the preserves of large research universities and their graduate programs, and can it survive there? How can composition, as a disciplined source of pride, growth, and renewal, resist and counter elitist attacks? We would put our final challenge even more boldly: Can composition studies survive if open admissions education does not?

Notes

1. "The meaning of *composition* has been shifting from a course title to a conceptual paradigm for an emerging discipline . . . as yet, composition studies is not universally accepted as a field of study, and it has no research methodology of its own, relying instead on (sometimes ill-fitting) borrowings from other disciplines. . . . But what is the cost of emphasis on professionalism? . . . How would disciplinary legitimacy affect our relationship with students in the margin? With our colleagues? Would disciplinary status come at the expense of practitioners?" (Phillips et al. 461).

2. Miller et al., "Present Perfect and Future Imperfect," surveyed grad students in composition and rhetoric and argue for "(re)-conceiving professionalization within departments," that "programs need to learn how to be accountable to and for the student-scholars writing within and being written by those programs" (394). The authors are sensitive to the danger of "clone" thinking (406)—what James Slevin warns is the circularity of disciplinary reasoning—but they do mean grad students in rhet/comp when they mention student writers; "programs" refer to grad programs, not the core writing courses for undergraduates; jobs are defined by rhetoric and

composition positions advertised in the MLA job list (400), not all jobs teaching composition; in regard to "accountability," they ask, "How can the field of rhetoric and composition become more accountable to its graduate students?" rather than, say, being accountable as teachers of first-year writers (401).

3. In "Composition as a Postdisciplinary Formation," Susan Carlton acknowledges that disciplinary formations can stifle creativity and serve merely to reproduce social hierarchies, but nevertheless she hopes composition will use its disciplinary status to "invent possibilities for change within the university space" (86). From our perspective, this entire discussion of disciplinarity assumes a single common, institutional space—the research university—which, we would remind readers, is only *one kind* of higher education space.

4. See Levy for a report of Giuliani's demands. For an analysis of the mayor's ambitions, see Barry. Patricia Williams, writing in *The Nation*, comments, "some awfully powerful people have lapsed into an astonishing degree of cavalier anti-intellectualism, their thoughtlessness abetted by logo-like catch phrases whose chief attributes are minimalist condescension, succinct class bias and sleekly coded racism" (10). For accounts of the trustees' decision, see Arenson's two articles.

5. A note on method: Interviews were conducted in October and November, 1997, by email, written correspondence, and in taped personal and telephone interviews. See below for a complete list of interviews.

6. See *JBW*, Vols. 1, 2, 3 (1997).

7. According to Arenson, minorities make up 67% of senior college enrollment. "CUNY estimates that 38 percent of white students would have trouble meeting the new standard, compared with 46 percent of black students, 51 percent of Asian students and 55 percent of Hispanic students" ("Weakest Students" A 19).

8. See Shor's *Culture Wars* for his history of attacks on higher education.

9. See Grego and Thompson for a description of their Studio program.

10. See Holladay, pp. 31ff, for an extended discussion of the impact of two-year campuses on composition instruction.

11. See Powers-Stubbs and Sommers' comparison of two- and four-year discourse communities.

12. See Lewiecki-Wilson for a description of teaching comp in the two-year college classroom.

13. See Tinberg's "Theory as Healing" for a description of the evolution of theory in Tinberg's teaching.

Interviews

Grego, Rhonda. Personal Interview, tape-recorded and transcribed. Nov. 1997.

Holladay, Sylvia A. Written Interview. Nov. 1997.

Kort, Melissa Sue. Telephone Interview, tape-recorded and transcribed. Nov. 1997.

Raines, Helon. Written Interview. Oct. 1997.

Ruffus, Stephen. Email Interview. Nov. 1997.

Shor, Ira. Email Interview. Nov. 1997.

Soliday, Mary. Written Interview. Oct. 1997.

Thompson, Nancy. Personal Interview, tape-recorded and transcribed. Nov. 1997.

Tinberg, Howard. Email Interview. Nov. 1997.

Works Cited

Arenson. Karen. "New York City's College System Enters Unknown in Policy Shift." *New York Times*, 28 May 1998: A 1, B 6.

———. "CUNY to Tighten Admissions Policy at 4-Year Schools." *New York Times*, 27 May 1998: A 1, A 19.

Barry, Dan. "Giuliani's War on City Colleges: Wider Audience?" *New York Times* 30 Jan. 1998: A 17.

Carlton, Susan Brown. "Composition as a Postdisciplinary Formation." *Rhetoric Review* 14 (1995): 78–87.

Du Bois, W. E. B. *The Souls of Black Folks.* Chicago: A. C. McClurg, 1903. Rpt. Fawcett 1961.

Greenberg, Karen. Open letter sent to recipients of CBW-L (Conference on Basic Writing List) <CBW-L@TC.UMN.EDU> 27 May 1998.

Grego, Rhonda, and Nancy Thompson. "Repositioning Remediation: Renegotiating Composition's Work in the Academy." *CCC* 47 (1996): 62–84.

Harden, Blaine. "Reading, Writing and Ruckus: City University of New York's Tougher Standards Anger Many." *Washington Post*, 2 June 1998: A 3.

Holladay, Sylvia A. "Order Out of Chaos: Voices from the Community College." *Composition in the Twenty-First Century: Crisis and Change.* Eds. Lynn Z. Bloom, Donald A. Daiker, and Edward White. Carbondale: Southern Illinois UP, 1996. 29–38.

Levy, Clifford J. "Giuliani Demands Community Colleges Drop Remedial Courses." *New York Times* 30 Jan. 1998: A 17.

Lewiecki-Wilson, Cynthia. "Teaching in the 'Contact Zone' of the Two-Year College Classroom: Multiple Literacies/Deep Portfolio." *Teaching English in the Two-Year College* 21 (1994): 267–76.

Miller, Scott L., Brenda Jo Brueggemann, Bennis Blue, and Deneen M. Shepherd. "Present Perfect and Future Imperfect: Results of a National Survey of Graduate Students in Rhetoric and Composition Programs." *CCC* 48 (1997): 392–409.

Miller, Richard E. "Composing English Studies." *CCC* 45 (1994): 164–79.

Padron, Eduardo J. "Hispanics and Community Colleges." *A Handbook on the Community College in American: Its History, Mission, and Management.* Ed. George A Baker, III. Westport: Greenwood, 1994. 82–93.

Pedersen, Robert. "Challenges Facing the Urban Community College: A Literature Review." *A Handbook on the Community College in American: Its History, Mission, and Management.* Ed. George A. Baker, III. Westport: Greenwood, 1994. 176–89.

Phillips, Donna Burns, Ruth Greenberg, and Sharon Gibson. "*College Composition and Communication:* Chronicling a Discipline's Genesis." *CCC* 44 (1993): 443–65.

Powers-Stubbs, Karen, and Jeff Sommers. "'Where We Are Is Who We Are, But It Doesn't Have to Be That Way': Two- and Four-Year Faculty Discourse

Communities." *Politics and Writing at the Two-Year Campus.* Eds. Keith Kroll and Barry Alford. Portsmouth: Boynton, 2001.

Ratliff, James L. "Seven Streams in the Historical Development of the Modern American Community College." *A Handbook on the Community College in American: Its History, Mission, and Management.* Ed. George A. Baker, III. Westport: Greenwood, 1994. 3–16.

Royster, Jacqueline Jones, and Rebecca Greenberg Taylor. "Constructing Teacher Identity in the Basic Writing Classroom." *Journal of Basic Writing* 16 (1997): 27–50.

Shaughnessy, Mina. *Errors and Expectations.* New York: Oxford UP, 1977.

Shor, Ira. *Culture Wars: School and Society in the Conservative Restoration 1969–1984.* Chicago: U of Chicago P, 1986.

———. "Our Apartheid: Writing Instruction & Inequality." *Journal of Basic Writing* 16 (1997): 91–104.

Slevin, James F. "Disciplining Students: Whom Should Composition Teach and What Should They Know?" *Composition in the Twenty-First Century: Crisis and Change.* Ed. Lynn Z. Bloom, Donald A. Daiker, Edward M. White. Carbondale: Southern Illinois UP, 1996. 153–65.

Soliday, Mary. "From the Margins to the Mainstream: Reconceiving Remediation." *CCC* 47 (1996): 85–100.

Soliday, Mary, and Barbara Gleason. "From Remediation to Enrichment: Evaluating a Mainstreaming Project." *Journal of Basic Writing* 16 (1997): 64–78.

Tinberg, Howard. "Theory as Healing." *Teaching English in the Two-Year College* 24 (1997): 282–90.

Williams, Patricia. "Honey, I Shrunk the Classroom." *Nation* 20 April 1998: 10.

Witt, Allen A., James L. Wattenbarger, James F. Gollattscheck, and Joseph E. Suppiger. *America's Community Colleges: The First Century.* Washington, DC: American Association of Community Colleges, 1994.

Occupy Writing Studies: Rethinking College Composition for the Needs of the Teaching Majority

Holly Hassel and Joanne Baird Giordano

According to authors Holly Hassel and Joanne Baird Giordano, the selection that follows resulted from their "increasingly urgent sense that professional development opportunities, graduate training, and access to professional resources are misaligned with the actual work that most English instructors do at two-year colleges and less selective universities. The erosion of tenure lines and the growth of student enrollment at open-admissions institutions signal that writing studies is in a new era requiring rigorous assessment of the professional needs of practitioners and a realistic revision of the training experiences provided by graduate programs in

From *College Composition and Communication*, vol. 65, no. 1, 2013, pp. 117-39.

English." This article draws from the coauthors' research and teaching at a two-year college and argues for a shift in thinking that places access institutions at the center, not the margins, of the profession.

In 2002, *College Composition and Communication* published John Lovas's "All Good Writing Develops at the Edge of Risk," which emerged from the previous year's Conference on College Composition and Communication Chairs address. In it, Lovas critiques the omission of two-year college students and faculty from the professional knowledge base of first-year writing, arguing, "You cannot represent a field if you ignore half of it. You cannot generalize about composition if you don't know half of the work being done. . . . much of the theorizing in our profession about basic writing, assessment, grading practices, teaching methods, and text production by students has a thin empirical base" (276). A decade later, we take up this claim and call once again for greater professional attention to the work happening in two-year colleges. Like Lovas, we believe that not enough has been said in scholarly conversations about marginalization of open-admissions and two-year campuses from professional dialogues even though such campuses are sites of engaging and essential work where almost half of all college students start their postsecondary educations.

In this essay, we address misconceptions about teaching writing in the two-year college and question the professional discourse that marginalizes teaching at open-admissions and two-year campuses from writing studies.[1] We first place our argument in the context of demographics about teaching college writing, including student populations, institutional types, and employment statuses. We provide details about the wide range of students and student learning needs that two-year college educators confront (and enjoy) in their work. We examine how academic hierarchies are maintained and reproduced in professional discourses and processes and explain how those hierarchies are largely tied to student preparation and institutional resources. We press college composition instructors to embrace an open-access mission of higher education. Ultimately, we call for a scholarly reimagination that repositions two-year college teaching at the center of our disciplinary discourse about college composition and argue for the greater participation of two-year college faculty and contingent instructors in writing studies knowledge making to create a broader and more accurate knowledge base from which to make curricular and instructional decisions and, ultimately, to reshape the profession.

Status, Exclusion, and Writing Studies

For the purposes of our essay, we distinguish between two kinds of institutions. There are institutions like ours that admit all students who meet the minimal criterion of having a high school diploma or its equivalent, or who can demonstrate through a standardized test that they have the "ability to benefit" from higher education (see Sullivan and Nielson). These we contrast with institutions that have any additional admission criteria and that reject applicants. With comparatively heavy teaching loads, open admission policies, and spare budgets, open-admissions and two-year campuses do not enjoy the same cultural status as selective institutions.[2] Unfortunately, this low status obscures 1) the important cultural and educational function of two-year campuses, 2) the engaging work at such institutions, and 3) the relationship of teaching and learning that happens at two-year colleges from our collective knowledge about the teaching of college composition (see Lewiecki-Wilson and Sommers, p. 58 in this volume).

Given the large role that teaching remedial or introductory college writing at less-selective institutions plays in higher education, published research in writing studies should include and account more fully for such teaching. A majority of postsecondary writing instructors will not spend their careers teaching upper-division courses, training graduate students, or researching narrowly focused issues in rhetoric and composition. David Laurence reports on behalf of the Modern Language Association, for example, that of 82,400 faculty members whose principal field is English, *almost half* (47.9 percent) teach at Carnegie Associate's institutions. As Laurence writes, "Despite the extraordinarily high percentage of faculty members teaching off the tenure track in two-year colleges, the 8,704 English faculty members holding tenured and tenure-track positions in two-year colleges outnumber the tenured and tenure-track English faculty in every other sector." In other words, the most common faculty experience in teaching English is at a two-year college.

Further, teaching off the tenure-track is increasingly the norm for college faculty. Figures vary, but an account is provided by the *Chronicle of Higher Education*: "full- and part-time adjuncts, graduate students, and postdoctoral fellows account for well over three fourths of all faculty appointments" (Schmidt). A more nuanced accounting from the American Association of University Professors points to 41.1 percent of faculty as part-time, 15.1 percent as full-time, non-tenure track, and 19.4 percent as graduate student employees. In four-year institutions, the MLA report observes, 60 percent of faculty in English departments work off the tenure track. In two-year colleges, the figure rises to approach 80 percent of English instructors.[3]

These often ignored postsecondary writing teachers need a more effective and extensive body of scholarship that offers research-based best practices that are relevant to the daily work that they do; moreover, our disciplinary knowledge base is incomplete if not informed by this work. Unless intellectual engagement in the form of inquiry, reading, research, and writing becomes part of the professionalization of all postsecondary writing teachers—including those working in teaching-intensive institutions and off the tenure track—writing studies has a very incomplete picture of the teaching and learning of college composition.

This underrepresentation is revealed through a brief analysis of the review practices that shape scholarly publication by the inclusion or exclusion of two-year college perspectives in professional exchanges of knowledge. For example, the 2012 Conference on College Composition and Communication program included 478 concurrent sessions. Just 12 of those sessions were identified in the program as "Sessions Presented by Two-Year College Faculty" (27). Though certainly two-year college faculty presented in other sessions not specifically identified as two-year sessions, these numbers reveal the mismatch between the number of instructors who teach at two-year institutions (almost half) and their representation on the CCCC program, 2.5 percent. Similarly, an examination of the *CCC Reviewers for 2011–2012* in the June 2012 issue of *CCC* demonstrates how underrepresented two-year college scholars are in the gatekeeping function that shapes how the field of writing studies is represented in our flagship journal. Of the 184 reviewers named and thanked in that feature, 4 are from two-year campuses, or around 2 percent. The editorial introduction to that issue, "Tracing Intersections," notes that peer review is "at the heart of epistemological and scholarly practice" (554) and is a critical part of the method by which we shape knowledge in the field. We agree with Kathleen Blake Yancey that peer review is the signature methodology by which disciplinary knowledge is established, and the name itself suggests collegiality among disciplinary peers. If two-year college teacher-scholars are not adequately represented among the corps of those who both produce and review what becomes the baseline knowledge for members of our profession, then we are not benefiting from the experiences of two-year faculty.[4]

Teaching and Learning in the Two-Year College

According to the American Association of Community Colleges, 44 percent of all US undergraduates are enrolled at community colleges. Like many two-year college learners, a majority of students in our own statewide, two-year institution of access arrive at college with the potential to *become* proficient college-level readers and writers, but they aren't yet ready for postsecondary academic reading and writing in their first semester. Many take a full year of composition before they have enough experience with source-based writing and critical reading to enroll in a transfer-level research course, which is the starting point for most writers at more-selective universities that admit primarily well-prepared students.[5] A few students even require two years of writing instruction to become eligible to take a second-semester writing course; in other words, they are still "first-year" writers in their third college year. For most instructors, working with underprepared college students is the daily reality of teaching college composition.

Writing instructors at two-year institutions face a class of students with an extremely varied pathway to a transfer-level composition course. After implementing changes to our process for placing students into first-year writing courses and to our placement test cut scores, for example, we faced many questions from administrators regarding the effectiveness of those changes. Data we collected to assess our new placement process reveal what a writing classroom in an open-admission institution often looks like and how it might differ from one at an institution with more specific admission criteria than our own institution's. We examined institutional data and collected information about the curricular path of all students who began their college education in a non-degree credit writing course (either basic composition or a workshop course for multilingual writers) on our campus in fall 2010. Data sources for these ninety-three students included their academic profiles (high school grades and English curriculum, test scores, and recommended placement) as well as their grades in all courses they took in the first two years of college. Their average score on the English portion of the ACT standardized test was 12.9, and the average ACT reading score was 15.25. Since the benchmark set by ACT for likely success in degree-credit composition is 18, these students were, at least on this measure, extremely unprepared for college reading and writing. Tracking these students' academic outcomes, we learned that the overall average college GPA for this group of students was 1.95, below the cutoff for good standing; indeed, 46 percent of the students were on final probation, probation, or suspension within two years. However, over half were in good standing after four semesters of college. Of the thirty-nine students (41 percent) who successfully made their way through the first-year writing sequence (consisting of a non-degree credit course, first-semester credit-bearing composition, and a transfer-level, research-based writing course), students averaged 3.33 semesters to complete the sequence. Most students who had to repeat a course en route to Composition II needed to take Composition I twice, while three multilingual students purposefully repeated a developmental course to develop more fully as writers before moving to credit-bearing composition. These data illustrate the challenges of teaching at an open-admission campus where instructors struggle to create effective programs, instruction, and interventions that will move students to even a basic level of college literacy readiness.

However, academic outcomes for the students who successfully completed the writing program sequence demonstrate that learners who are excluded from most institutions can become proficient postsecondary writers at two-year colleges. Further, the teaching experience of instructors at open-admission campuses is likely to include a broad range of students with a great deal of variation in their precollege experiences and an enormous variety of academic needs as they prepare to achieve the learning outcomes for college writing courses. For instance, at our own institution, we keep records of students' placement profiles as part of our multiple measures approach.[6] In fall 2012, our campus had first-year students with ACT scores in English as low as 8 and as high as 36, and ACT reading scores ranging from 10 to 35. Though these students will likely not find themselves in the same first-semester writing course during the same semester, many of them will *eventually* find themselves in a writing course with writers whose initial assessments varied widely, as underprepared students move through the developmental curriculum and into the core, transfer-level writing course. Some instructors will be working with students initially unprepared to do college-level work who will ultimately take a research-based and transfer-level writing course in a classroom with students who direct-tested into that course, perhaps through standardized test scores, Advanced Placement credit, or a high school dual enrollment program. As a result, many—perhaps most—college writing instructors at open-access campuses must continually develop an expansive, flexible, and constantly revised sense of the answers to these two questions: What is college-level writing? How do we know when a student is ready to do it? One of the most interesting aspects of working at an open-admission, two-year campus is that these two framing questions have multiple answers and require continual reflection and adaptation.

The Maintenance of Academic Hierarchies

An important question, then, is why has writing studies so narrowly centered its work on college composition at four-year institutions? Lovas's essay provides a partial explanation—the publication expectations of the tenure process at such campuses. However, we cannot ignore that academia's hierarchical structure contributes in important ways to the shaping of our disciplinary knowledge—a hierarchy that is, in our judgment, imagined in some ways and true in others. In terms of the work that faculty, instructors, and administrators do at varying types of institutions, the status difference lies primarily in the selectivity of the institution and the resources each institution has, not in the relative value of the kinds of work that professionals do. Teaching-intensive work, including teaching in the lower division, is as equally valuable to the higher education enterprise as teaching in the upper division, mentoring graduate students, or conducting the scholarship of discovery (per Boyer's *Scholarship Reconsidered*) most characteristic of Research I institutions.[7] To understand why the lack of knowledge about writing instruction at two-year colleges persists, it's important to acknowledge how academic hierarchies are maintained.

Where hierarchies most stand out in higher education institutions is in the nature of the students who enroll in them. As the July 2012 *Chronicle of Higher Education* symposium, "Has Higher Education Become an Engine of Inequality?" explains, the biggest difference between our types of institutions is in the resources allocated to the students who attend them, and the social mechanisms that "sort" students into colleges and universities are the primary sources of hierarchies. For example, Richard Kahlenberg observes in "Magnifying Social Inequality" that students who have the most resources typically go to colleges with the most resources and vice versa: "Low-income and minority students are concentrated in community colleges, which spent an average of $12,957 per full-time-equivalent student in 2009, while higher-income and white students are disproportionately educated at private four-year research institutions, which spent an average of $66,744 per student." Social class also predicts a student's likelihood of earning a degree, with 50 percent of children whose families earn more than $90,000 earning a BA by age twenty-four, while one in seventeen children whose family income is less than $35,000 will have that same educational outcome (Wolin). Community colleges also serve minority students at a rate that is larger than proportional to the overall population. The American Association of Community Colleges asserts that "Community colleges have historically enrolled approximately half of all undergraduate students of color" (Mullin 7–8). The Community College Research Center reports that 51 percent of all Hispanic undergraduates enrolled at a two-year college, as did 31 percent of African American students, with African American students making up 20 percent of the overall student population at two-year colleges (Bailey, Jenkins, and Leinbach 13; "Community College FAQs").

Many of the arguments (see Wilson; Goldrick-Rab; Bailey) in the *Chronicle* forum suggest that the solution to such social and institutional inequality is to attract more low-income students to high-status institutions, which will produce increases in graduation rates. However, this solution fails to recognize that first-generation or working-class students face more challenges (cultural, academic, and financial) that often make a four-year institution a poor match for their learning needs. What these numbers do demonstrate is the function of social class in predetermining students' likelihood of earning a college degree, the way that students' baccalaureate ambitions evolve during their work at the two-year college, and the critical importance of research and inquiry needed at open-door institutions if we as a profession are truly interested in expanding access to higher education for greater numbers of Americans.

At the same time, we fully acknowledge — and are troubled by — the low retention and persistence rates at two-year campuses, that is, the number of students who continue from their first semester to their second, and then to the subsequent academic year. Sociologists and education theorists since 1960 have built on Burton Clark's essay "The 'Cooling Out' Function in Higher Education" as an analytical lens for forming arguments about the social function of open-admissions institutions, arguments that are not very flattering to two-year colleges.

Specifically, Clark advanced the thesis that community colleges serve as a sort of holding pen for students with low academic ability, and that "while some students of low promise are successful, for large numbers failure is inevitable and *structured*," and that ultimately such a student has "been allowed to become involved but [his or her] destiny is to fail" (571). Clark's provocative thesis has been explored more fully and has been complicated since his article's publication (Brint and Karabel; Beach), but Clark's claims seem still to hold a great deal of explanatory power for policymakers who are increasingly hostile to open-admissions campuses (see, for example, Fain ["How to"] for current attempts to eliminate open-admissions policies).

Another explanation for the dismal cultural perception of two-year college campuses is their greater reliance on contingent faculty, whose labor conditions often exclude them from full participation in the profession. Recent research has linked the use of contingent faculty to decreased student retention and reductions in transfer rates, such as Kevin M. Eagan and Audrey Jaeger's study that found "a significant and negative association between students' transfer likelihood and their exposure to part-time faculty instruction" (180). They observe that "for every 10% increase in students' exposure to part-time faculty instruction, students tended to become almost 2% less likely to transfer" (180). We agree with those who attribute this decline in student success to the inequitable working conditions in which many contingent faculty teach, including a lack of basic material resources that are preconditions to effective teaching (office space, technology access, library privileges, etc.). We would add to this explanation that contingent status often also equals exclusion from an institution's professional resources that help instructors develop as teachers (for example, involvement in workshops, support for professional memberships, funding to attend conferences, and financial support for disciplinary scholarship or research on student learning). . . . A lack of equal access to resources essentially results in instructors with the least professional support working with the most at-risk and underprepared students. Inequitable working conditions create a recipe for a disciplinary crisis that has a profound effect on the students who attend two-year colleges and their ability to get the education that open-admissions institutions aspire to provide.

In some ways, then, the low status of the open-admission institution has partly been reinforced by the notion that the function of the community college is to create the illusion of democratic access to education. Though not all community college students intend to transfer, the Community College Survey of Student Engagement results from 249,548 students show that the vast majority of students at two-year colleges nationally identify transfer (71 percent) or obtaining an associate degree (79 percent) as a primary or secondary educational goal; however, just one in five actually do transfer (Fain, "Graduate"). The average, six-year baccalaureate-achievement rate nationally for students who begin their studies at community colleges, which data from the National Student Clearinghouse show is, on average, 12 percent (National Center). In contrast, according to the 2011 Community College Survey of Student Engagement in our own statewide two-year institution, 94 percent of students identify transfer to a four-year college or university as a primary or secondary educational goal. Nevertheless, just 44 percent of our students each year ultimately transfer to a baccalaureate-granting institution, with numbers at some of our thirteen campuses as high as 50 percent (University of Wisconsin Colleges). With a 70 percent graduation rate (for students who ultimately transfer) over six years, the overall graduation rate of new freshman students beginning in our two-year institution hovers around 23 percent or 29 percent over eight years (Nettesheim).[8] It's also notable that approximately 19 percent of students who attend our state's flagship university (with its 83 percent six-year graduation rate for new freshmen) can be categorized as first-generation college students, while the numbers for our open-admission institution are 66 percent (Office of Academic Planning and Research; Nettesheim).

We have two thoughts on these data. First, though we are reluctant to agree that this structured failure is indeed part of the role of the open-access college, we recognize that the promulgation of this view is one way that academic hierarchies are maintained—in other words, that "low-promise" students at institutions of access either aren't college material, or that the school they attend is not a real college. Second, if postsecondary institutions have any social aspirations to achieve the college completion agenda that aims to increase the number of US residents with higher education credentials, then "structured failure" at the two-year college is unacceptable.

Writing studies professionals are perhaps in the best position to stage an intervention to increase the academic success and retention of students whose only pathway to a college degree is through an open-access institution.[9] Writing studies is a "high-contact" discipline because college composition is a near-universal requirement for a college degree and because two of the defining characteristics of writing classes are individual conferencing and ongoing feedback on student texts. As a result, writing instructors reach nearly every student enrolled in a post-secondary writing class. They may interact with students through multiple semesters of non-degree credit writing or as they repeat a credit-bearing academic writing course. The ubiquitous and engaged nature of teaching college writing means that we are well-positioned to develop increasingly better ways of preparing students to meet the rigorous expectations of college-level reading, writing, and thinking.

As reenvisioned, a more inclusive writing studies profession should account for the complex and diverse needs of students who enroll at institutions of access and should better meet the professional needs of the instructors who teach those students. Without such a research base, most instructors cannot find their teaching realities reflected in the published literature. Certainly, faculty (including those with contingent status) who teach in two-year colleges and other open-admissions institutions need to advocate for greater representation in scholarly publications and the national conversations that shape the profession of teaching college writing. We also need to do a much better job of helping members of the profession who work outside of two-year institutions understand the importance of the work that takes place at open-admissions colleges. However, two-year college faculty don't have the primary responsibility for being more included (or arguing more forcefully for inclusion) in the professional organizations and activities that shape writing studies, especially given the hierarchical way that higher education usually privileges the voices of professionals at research universities over the majority who teach at other institutions. Our professional organizations and the most privileged groups in writing studies (i.e., those who work at high-status, high-resource institutions) have an intellectual, scholarly, and moral obligation to work toward creating an inclusive profession that fully accounts for the diverse range of teaching and learning experiences in postsecondary writing.

The Disciplinary Benefits of Recentering

Though some readers might take issue with our characterization of two-year college teaching as substantially different from teaching at other kinds of institutions, there are meaningful differences between working at an open-admission institution and working at a campus with admissions criteria beyond a high school diploma or its equivalent. To fully comprehend the experience of writing students in the United States, we need a better picture of the paths they take to college writing classes. Because teaching and learning in the two-year college is distinct from other settings, additional data, research, and systematically collected evidence are essential for helping instructors more effectively do what they are employed to do.

Certainly in some ways, CCCC has recognized one part of that work, basic writing. For example, the 2013 CCCC Convention included a special thread on basic writing, and publications such as *The Journal of Basic Writing* focus on the needs of students in non-degree credit composition. However, basic writing does not define or capture two-year college teaching. While most basic writing is taught in the two-year college, it is not taught only in two-year colleges, and two-year college faculty teach many other courses including intermediate composition, technical and business writing, and a wide range of other first- and second-year courses in English. To identify basic writing as a defining feature of the work of two-year college teaching is to misunderstand the teaching and learning that happens in such institutions.

The broad range of college preparation levels for writers who enroll at open-admissions institutions not only provides new and challenging teaching and learning experiences for instructors teaching in two-year colleges, but also has important scholarly benefits for the profession. As part of the previously discussed project to assess changes to our placement process and curriculum, a group of sixty-seven students consented to share writing from their first-year courses, including developmental composition, academic reading courses, first-year writing, and, for more advanced students, sophomore writing in other disciplines. The purpose of this study was to document in a richer and more specific way how our students were developing as writers across the composition curriculum; we also needed to identify the barriers students faced in completing the core writing requirement. We knew from institutional data that low percentages of students at our statewide campuses moving from non-degree credit writing through the composition sequence earned high grades that marked proficiency in academic writing. For example, institutional reports showed that students who began their college career in the core, degree-fulfilling writing courses were 2.5 times as likely to earn As compared to students who began in non-degree credit writing—and fewer than a third of basic writing students eventually complete the core writing course at all.

In 2010, we invited the approximately 1,400 students on our campus to participate in our study of students' transition to college writing, using an electronic survey and distributing consent forms in first-year writing courses. Sixty-seven students consented to participate (though we were only able to draw meaningful conclusions about fifty-four students because the other thirteen did not complete the first semester or did not complete any writing courses). Over the course of two years, we collected student writing through student self-submission and the assistance of campus composition instructors sharing participating students' drafts. Students began at all levels of the first-year writing program—developmental writing, first-semester credit-bearing composition, or direct placement into a core transfer research course. This permitted us to examine the entire range of students at our open-access campus. We collected an average of 6.2 papers per student, for a total of 359 pieces of formal writing, primarily from composition classes, though some students shared work they had produced for courses in other disciplines. After identifying participants, we returned to our initial placement data (collected for all students during the placement assessment process) and examined how those students progressed as writers over their first two college years. At the end of the first academic year, we analyzed the collected writing in relation to our writing program's learning outcomes and the students' initial placement profiles. We conducted the same process again in the second year for students who took three or four semesters to complete the core writing requirement.

Nineteen of the fifty-four participants took a first-semester, non-degree credit composition course. Our analysis of the writing that they produced during their first college year revealed four key findings that illustrate the benefits of conducting research at an institution that admits the full range of students who enroll in higher education.

First, about half of these students had difficulty with the conventions of standard written English (which their low standardized test scores reflected), but the others had sentence-level skills that were indistinguishable from research participants who received a degree-credit composition placement. However, the needs of these writers were different from most participants who began college in a more advanced course because the basic writers lacked experience with writing in formal academic ways. We learned a great deal about participating students' educational backgrounds through self-assessment essays produced at the point of placement; the self-assessment and reflection writing they completed for their basic writing course; and the many writing assignments of varying purposes and genres that they completed over the first and second years. For example, one student, Violet, acknowledged in a piece of self-assessment writing: "In high school I didn't really prepare for college. None of my friends help me at all on preparing for college, I would have to say my family members were mainly the only ones that did a little bit on preparing me for college." Another participating student, June, wrote in a self-assessment essay: "My academic learning was very limited at my high school. The reason I say that is because, a small town like [her hometown] just teaches you the basic, to pass a student through high school"; in a separate essay she wrote: "I remember we always wrote essays on our self, family, or place that we cared about. We didn't do any research papers, or papers we had to write after we read a book." Another student, Kevin, confessed in a reflective letter: "Coming into my senior year, I had to decide if I wanted an easy class or a hard college based class. I decided to take the easy class because it was my final year of high school. I wanted to enjoy it more instead of wanting to work harder. I deeply missed a crucial opportunity to get better knowledge in writing." This theme repeated itself throughout the student writing, helping us to draw conclusions that can inform curricular change and make decisions about, for example, appropriate textbooks or pedagogical approaches that will both reflect best practice based on disciplinary knowledge and reflect systematically collected evidence about the students we serve in our own classrooms and their learning needs.

Second, all of the students who were placed into a non-degree composition course had difficulty with critical and analytical reading. Most of them completed writing assignments at some point in their first two college years that asked student writers to analyze, respond to, or in some other way write about a reading they had done for class. Students either could not write effectively about difficult college-level texts or could not reflect their understanding and subsequent analysis of such texts in their writing. Illustrative of this gap is a journal comment by a participating student, Suav: "As a reader, I think that I am only at like a freshmen level because I haven't really read an entire book since my freshman year [of high school]. Reason why is because I don't really have anyone but my friends to talk to and ask questions about school readings." Suav, like many of our participating students who began in developmental writing, either chose not to enroll in or did not have access to a literacy-rich high school curriculum, and as a first-generation college student, he did not have family support for his academic learning.

Third, the other, most challenging areas of college writing for these students were a lack of familiarity with academic conventions and rhetorical knowledge. We identified fifteen students of fifty-four (about a quarter) who did not demonstrate an understanding of basic academic conventions such as using signal phrases to introduce sources, using formal academic tone, or referring to authors by their last names. An example of this is from a student, Wayne, whose use of informal language permeated his formal writing in the first semester: "In the beginning of the course I was always like I don't need this class, I don't know why Im in here." For many of the students who began in non-degree credit writing courses, then, academic conventions, more than sentence-level correctness, presented the biggest barrier to their readiness for degree-credit coursework (not just in writing courses).

Fourth, another fifteen students of our fifty-four (not entirely the same group as those developing their knowledge of academic conventions) did not demonstrate a command of rhetorical knowledge, primarily in their ability to make appropriate choices for a particular audience or rhetorical purpose. For example, one participating student, Tammy, struggled into her third semester with making choices that fit a specific rhetorical purpose. A good example of this is in her first-semester writing course, when she was asked to write an analysis of an advertisement. Tammy frequently conflated the genre conventions of analysis she was supposed to be doing with the advertising rhetoric she was critiquing, as when she writes about several ads for cosmetics: "Every girl wants to be pretty so this can make some women want to go out and make their eyes dazzle." In her third-semester course, English 102, Tammy continued to have difficulty meeting the needs of academic readers; she had still not quite mastered the use of signal phrases to orient readers to sources, or she presented obvious and factual information in lieu of analysis (for example, noting in a paragraph on organ donation that organs require life support to stay alive).

In identifying these skills and readiness gaps faced by students with particular placement profiles and who started at different points in our composition sequence, we created knowledge useful in confirming the appropriateness of our placement test cut scores, in advocating for expanding a "multiple measures" placement process on all thirteen of our campuses, and in producing suggested revisions to our three-course writing sequence to place greater emphasis on critical reading, writing from sources, and a wider variety of academic genres and rhetorical purposes. For practically all the students across our composition sequence, our research demonstrates that standardized test scores can sometimes be a proxy for select proficiencies, but they almost never demonstrate a student's ability in the most important skill sets, including knowledge of academic conventions, rhetorical knowledge, and processes. Further, all ten of the students in our study who started in the transfer-level research course struggled with critical and analytical reading of texts. Our research provides us with evidence to show that 1) the students our institution serves benefit from substantial experience with critical reading and writing about reading before completing the transfer research course, and 2) textbooks and assignments that focus on sentence-level exercises or paragraph writing aren't a good fit for the needs of students in our developmental program.

As we draw additional conclusions from this research study, several lessons stand out to us for the purposes of our present argument. First, this kind of research—studying the needs of students who are served by open-admissions institutions and who hope to access the opportunity that higher education presents—can only be done at two-year institutions. Students with poor academic preparation, low test scores, or poor grades are overrepresented—potentially only represented in open-admissions and two-year campuses during their first year. For example, the study described above has led us to examine the relationship between students' standardized test scores and the quality of writing they produced in the first year of college. Our analysis includes a wide variety of writers—students who by any measure would be excluded from higher education except at institutions of access, as well as students whose test scores and academic records could admit them to most colleges in the country—all of whom might be in the same classroom at a two-year college. What the results of such research can do is 1) specifically and in a systematic way document the learning needs and gaps of students who hope to pursue a college education but who have academic and language deficiencies that prevent them from entering into a degree-credit college curriculum, 2) help inform our own curriculum and instruction within our institution to better match the learning needs of this array of students if we hope to move more students from remedial writing to transfer-level coursework, 3) provide research-based recommendations that can help build a body of knowledge to inform the work of developmental and degree-credit writing instruction nationally, and 4) inform national position statements on best practices in writing instruction to bring evidence-based instructional practices and shared disciplinary values to the field. With increasing numbers of students in the United States enrolling in college each decade, many of whom have not necessarily taken an academically rigorous high school curriculum or who are returning to school after some years away, it's more imperative than ever that the research produced on writing and reading in college reflect the complete spectrum of college writers.[10]

Further, there is a benefit to the institution to have such inquiry take place on teaching-intensive campuses whose mission is focused on serving the needs of students versus producing scholarship of discovery. Teaching-focused research produces new knowledge that can be funneled back into the work of the students and instructors in that institution. One advantage of using instruction at an open-access institution as a starting point for developing a research question is that the intersections between research and teaching can translate a problem or professional frustration into an engaging line of scholarly inquiry. As teacher-scholars, we have received significant professional benefits from researching and teaching students whose educational pathways and life experiences bring them to our two-year campus. One key value of our research comes from using what we learn from systematically analyzing the writing that students produced over their first college year to enhance our own teaching to help students transition more successfully through the first-year writing program. When two-year college faculty conduct scholarship, they can subsequently use the findings from this systematic inquiry to lead their institution in adapting policies, practices, and pedagogies that respond to the specific needs of the students (as documented in another article in this issue). More important, this kind of work then becomes part of the departmental conversation that informs policy and practice within the institution.

Additionally, there is a benefit to the profession of writing studies when research into first- and second-year writing reflects the material and academic realities of the students in postsecondary writing classrooms because such scholarship grants our profession a fuller understanding of what writing instruction in college looks like. Some key and unexplored questions about what it means to be a college writer can be answered only through research at institutions that admit many different kinds of college writers. For example, we used the findings from our study to write a peer-reviewed article (see Hassel and Giordano, p. 219) that ultimately, we hope, contributed to the body of knowledge on the teaching of writing.

There is certainly *some* work by two-year college instructors and about two-year college writing already taking place, but it has limitations. For example, a number of two-year college scholars have documented through case studies and anecdotes the particular challenges of the students who are served by two-year institutions and faculty who teach there (see Holladay; Tinberg; Valentino). The *What Is College-Level Writing?* series of volumes published by NCTE and coedited by two-year college scholars are other prominent examples (Sullivan, Tinberg, and Blau). Howard Tinberg and Jean-Paul Nadeau's *The Community College Writer: Exceeding Expectations* also showcases the intellectual work of both instructors and students that is happening in two-year colleges. Recent issues of *WPA: Writing Program Administration* have featured articles about WPA work in the two-year college (Calhoon-Dillahunt) and programs for student veterans (authored by two-year college scholar Marilyn Valentino, "Serving"). *College English*'s first issue of 2013 tackles questions about policy and underprepared students (Sullivan and Nielson). Our professional resources are making an effort to include voices from two-year college faculty and students.

However, we note two limitations to the current range of scholarship on the teaching of writing at the two-year college. First, these voices should be at the center of our national conversations about teaching college writing if we hope to accurately represent the sheer number of faculty and students who are teaching and learning in such settings and to provide professional resources that meet the needs of instructors and students at two-year colleges. Second, the profession can benefit from more systematic inquiry into student learning in the writing classroom that takes place at two-year colleges. For example, in *Teaching English in the Two-Year College*, the major journal for two-year college English professionals, the primary publication emphasis has historically been on teacher reflection and classroom narratives rather than articles emerging from systematic inquiry or from a formal research design (see Hassel, for an assessment of research gaps for two-year college teaching). All of the professional resources in our field must work together to fill in these gaps and better meet the needs of the members of our profession.

Recommendations and Conclusions

To bring about this rethinking of college composition, our profession must support more research conducted at two-year colleges, research that can then inform the graduate training of instructors who will likely spend their teaching careers at such institutions. Both coauthors serve in administrative capacities that involve evaluating, mentoring, and training new instructors in our statewide program, and we continually hear common refrains: "it was a major adjustment to teach this student population"; "I was unprepared to work with these students"; "I was trained to teach [creative writing, literature, rhetoric], and now I primarily teach developmental composition"; "these students struggle to read college-level texts, and I didn't take coursework in reading pedagogy." More scholarship emerging from open-enrollment institutions would provide a stronger knowledge base for the training of future professionals in the teaching of college writing. Writing studies work at institutions of access is teaching-intensive, and it almost always requires instructors to adapt their pedagogical approaches to meet the needs of students who aren't prepared for college reading and writing. The efforts of this sometimes ignored majority are essential to higher education, and their work is both engaging and rewarding. An increased emphasis on teaching and learning at two-year colleges and other institutions of access is vitally important if we are to meet the needs both of college writers and of the members of our profession.

To close, we turn to the work of one of our students who discusses her experiences with academic writing by balancing the realities of her prior learning with optimism for the future (with an attitude mirrored by many of the nearly 140 college writers we have studied over the past five years): "In high school, I only had the basic writing courses which did not prepare me for college writing. Also, as a second English learner, writing is always a challenge for me. As a second semester college student, I hope to find out more about the relationship between writing and learning." We echo the thinking of this college writer. We, too, hope to find out more about the relationship between writing and postsecondary learning at two-year colleges and other institutions of access to higher education, and we hope that many others will join us in exploring that issue and related questions that will provide our profession with a clear picture of what it means both to be a college writer and to teach college writing.

Notes

1. We should note that in most two-year institutions, teaching English and teaching writing are nearly synonymous; though many campuses teach sophomore-level literature, creative writing, film studies, or writing courses, most instructors at two-year campuses can expect to teach primarily first-year writing, basic writing, or other developmental and learning support courses as the majority of their teaching load.
2. We acknowledge that the spectrum of institutional types in American higher education is much broader than what we refer to here; the Carnegie Classification of Institutions of Higher Education offers a nuanced range of categories across undergraduate and graduate instructional programs, enrollment profile, undergraduate profile, size, and setting (see Carnegie Foundation).
3. Space limitations prevent us from discussing in depth here the specific concerns of contingent faculty. Please see Arnold et al. and our forthcoming chapter for other arguments we have made about contingent faculty in writing studies.
4. Certainly the teaching-intensive nature of the work at two-year and open-admissions institutions limits the ability of faculty who work in those settings to contribute to writing studies in the form of professional service activities at the same level as faculty teaching at research institutions. However, these differing professional responsibilities cannot entirely explain the virtual omission of two-year faculty from the peer-review process and conference program.
5. For example, in our own University of Wisconsin system, students at the three most selective campuses start in the "second-semester" or transfer-level, research-focused writing course, while at most other campuses in our system, students will take two semesters of degree credit writing.

6. See Holly Hassel and Joanne Giordano ("FYC Placement") for a discussion of this placement work.

7. For example, Ernest L. Boyer outlines his vision of multiple types of scholarship: scholarship of discovery, the traditional type of inquiry that "contributes not only to the stock of human knowledge but also to the intellectual climate of a college or university"; scholarship that integrates knowledge across disciplines and specialties; scholarship of application, which may include service activities emerging from the professional knowledge of the faculty member; and the scholarship of teaching, which applies the rigorous methodology of disciplinary research to the classroom and to the learning needs of students.

8. See Patrick Sullivan's essay "Measuring 'Success' at Open Admissions Institutions" (p. 42) for a discussion of the contrast between students who begin their educations at four-year campuses and those who start at two-year campuses.

9. See Pegeen Reichert Powell's essay "Retention and Writing Instruction" for a more thorough treatment of this relationship between retention and writing studies.

10. The current public discourse around the "college completion agenda," accompanied by the increasing investment in educational reform of philanthropic foundations like Lumina and the Gates Foundation, provides a more urgent incentive than ever before for educators and professional organizations to find systematic, evidence-based, discipline-specific ways of improving our work in the classroom. See Linda Adler-Kassner and Kristine Hansen for discussions (and critiques) of related and varying educational reform efforts.

Works Cited

ACT, Inc. "What Are ACT's College Readiness Benchmarks?" *College Readiness: Issues in College Readiness.* ACT. 2010. Web. 16 Aug. 2012.

Adler-Kassner, Linda. "The Companies We Keep or The Companies We Would Like to Try to Keep: Strategies and Tactics in Challenging Times." *WPA: Writing Program Administration* 36.1 (2012): 119–40. Print.

American Association of Community Colleges. "Fast Facts." Web. 26 June 2012.

American Association of University Professors. "Resources on Contingent Appointments: Trends in Faculty Status, 1975–2009." Web. 28 Feb. 2013.

Arnold, Lisa, Laura Brady, Maggie Christensen, Joanne Giordano, Holly Hassel, Ed Nagelhout, Nathalie Singh-Corcoran, and Julie Staggers. "Forum on the Profession." Ed. Mike Palmquist and Sue Doe. *College English* 73.4 (2011): 409–27. Print.

Bailey, Thomas R. "Equity and Community Colleges." *Chronicle of Higher Education* 2 July 2012. Web. 28 Feb. 2013.

Bailey, Thomas, Davis Jenkins, and Timothy Leinbach. "What We Know about Community College Low-Income and Minority Student Outcomes: Descriptive Statistics from National Surveys." *Community College Research Center.* Teachers College, Columbia University. Jan. 2005. Web. 21 Feb. 2013.

Beach, Josh. *Gateway to Opportunity?: A History of the Community College in the United States.* Sterling, VA: Stylus, 2012. Print.

Boyer, Ernest L. *Scholarship Reconsidered: Priorities of the Professoriate.* Princeton: Carnegie Foundation for the Advancement of Teaching, 1990. Print.

Brint, Steve, and Jerome Karabel. *The Diverted Dream: Community Colleges and the Promise of Educational Opportunity in America, 1900–1985.* New York: Oxford UP, 1989. Print.

Calhoon-Dillahunt, Carolyn. "Writing Programs without Administrators: Frameworks for Successful Writing Programs in the Two-Year College." *WPA: Writing Program Administration* 35.1 (2011): 118–35. Print.

Carnegie Foundation for the Advancement of Teaching. "Standard Listings." *Carnegie Foundation.* Web. 20 Mar. 2013.

Clark, Burton. "The 'Cooling Out' Function in Higher Education." *American Journal of Sociology* 65.6 (1960): 569–76. Print.

Community College Research Center. "Community College FAQs." *Community College Research Center.* Teachers College, Columbia University. Web. 21 Feb. 2013.

Conference on College Composition and Communication. *Writing Gateways.* Conference Program for the Sixty-Third Annual Convention. St. Louis. 2012. Print.

Eagan, Kevin M., and Audrey Jaeger. "Effects of Exposure to Part-Time Faculty on Community College Transfer." *Research in Higher Education* 50.2 (2009): 168–88. *Academic Search Complete.* Web. 25 Feb. 2013.

Fain, Paul. "Graduate, Transfer, Graduate." *Inside Higher Ed* 8 Nov. 2012. Web. 27 Mar. 2013.

———. "How to End Remediation." *Inside Higher Ed* 4 Apr. 2012. Web. 20 Mar. 2013.

Goldrick-Rab, Sara. "Renewing the Commitment." *Chronicle of Higher Education* 2 July 2012. Web. 28 Feb. 2013.

Hansen, Kristine. "The Composition Marketplace: Shopping for Credit versus Learning to Write." *College Credit for Writing in High School: The "Taking Care of" Business.* Ed. Kristine Hansen and Christine Farris. Urbana: NCTE, 2010. 1–39. Print.

Hassel, Holly. "Research Gaps in *Teaching English in the Two-Year College.*" *Teaching English in the Two-Year College* 40.4 (2013): 343–63. Web.

Hassel, Holly, and Joanne Giordano. "Contingency, Access, and the Material Conditions of Teaching and Learning in the 'Statement of Principles.'" *A Statement in Recension: The Principles and Standards for the Postsecondary Teaching of Writing for the 21st Century University.* Ed. Randall McClure, Michael Pemberton, and Dayna Goldstein. Parlor Press (forthcoming).

———. "FYC Placement at Open-Admission, Two-Year Campuses: Changing Campus Culture, Institutional Practice, and Student Success." *Open Words: Access and English Studies* 5.2 (2011): 29–59. Web.

Holladay, Sylvia. "Order out of Chaos: Voices from the Community College." *Composition in the Twenty-First Century: Crisis and Change.* Ed. Lynn Z. Bloom, Donald A. Daiker, and Edward M. White. Carbondale: Southern Illinois UP, 1996. 29–38. Print.

Kahlenberg, Richard. "Magnifying Social Inequality." *Chronicle of Higher Education* 2 July 2012. Web. 22 Feb. 2013.

Laurence, David. "Demography of the Faculty: A Statistical Portrait of English and Foreign Languages." Modern Language Association and the Association of Departments of English. 2008. Web. 27 June 2012.

Lovas, John. "All Good Writing Develops at the Edge of Risk." *College Composition and Communication* 54.2 (2002): 264–88. Print.

Mullin, Christopher. *Why Access Matters: The Community College Student Body.* (Policy Brief 2012-01PBL). Washington: American Association of Community Colleges, 2012. Web. 22 Feb. 2013.

National Center for Public Policy and Higher Education. "Affordability and Transfer: Critical to Increasing Baccalaureate Degree Completion." National Center for Public Policy and Higher Education. June 2011. Web. 29 Aug. 2012.

Nettesheim, Gregg. "First Generation Students in the UW–Colleges." *Academic Matters: A Publication of the University of Wisconsin–Colleges Office of Academic Affairs* 9.1 (2009): 4–6. Web. 22 Feb. 2013.

———. "Re: New retention reports available." Message to Holly Hassel. 13 Apr. 2012. Email.

Office of Academic Planning and Research. "Retention and Graduation Rates for Undergraduates." University of Wisconsin–Madison. 10 July 2012. Web. 16 Aug. 2012.

Powell, Pegeen Reichert. "Retention and Writing Instruction: Implications for Access and Pedagogy." *College Composition and Communication* 60.4 (2009): 664–82. Print.

Schmidt, Peter. "AAUP Proposes Giving Contingent Faculty a Much Bigger Role in College Governance." *Chronicle of Higher Education* 28 June 2012. Web. 28 Feb. 2013.

Sullivan, Patrick, and David Nielson. "'Ability to Benefit': Making Forward-Looking Decisions about Our Most Underprepared Students." *College English* 75.3 (2013): 319–43. Web.

Sullivan, Patrick, and Howard Tinberg, eds. *What Is "College-Level" Writing?* Urbana: NCTE, 2006. Print.

Sullivan, Patrick, Howard Tinberg, and Sheridan Blau, eds. *What Is 'College-Level' Writing? Vol. 2: Assignments, Readings, and Student Writing Samples.* Urbana: NCTE, 2010. Print.

Tinberg, Howard. *Border Talk: Writing and Knowing in the Two-Year College.* Urbana: NCTE, 1997. Print.

Tinberg, Howard, and Jean-Paul Nadeau. *The Community College Writer: Exceeding Expectations.* Urbana: NCTE, 2010. Print.

University of Wisconsin Colleges. "Institutional Accreditation Self-Study Report." 2012. Web. 28 Feb. 2013.

Valentino, Marilyn. "2010 Chair's Address: Rethinking the Fourth C: Call to Action." *College Composition and Communication* 62.2 (2010): 364–78. Print.

———. "Serving Those Who Have Served: Preparing for Student Veterans in Our Writing Programs, Classes, and Writing Centers." *WPA: Writing Program Administration* 36.1 (2012): 164–78. Print.

Wilson, William Julius. "The Role of Elite Institutions." *Chronicle of Higher Education* 2 July 2012. Web. 28 Feb. 2013.

Wolin, Richard. "Fading Glory Days." *Chronicle of Higher Education* 2 July 2012. Web.

Yancey, Kathleen Blake. "From the Editor: Tracing Intersections." *College Composition and Communication* 63.4 (2012): 552–77. Print.

PART TWO

Preparing to Teach

As we know, "preparing to teach" involves much more than simply drafting a day's lesson plan or copying a handout. It is a complex, ongoing process of research, planning, experimentation, and reflection that continues each semester *and* throughout a teacher's professional career. Although the selections in this part of our book might at first glance appear to be geared toward *new* writing instructors, we believe that even seasoned veterans will find much that is valuable in these readings. Anyone wishing to refresh, deepen, or rejuvenate their teaching practice will find inspiration and direction here. In fact, much of this material is quite recent and offers important new perspectives on some of the most essential aspects of our work. The readings in this chapter provide pragmatic approaches to pedagogy and curriculum for two-year college writing faculty at any stage of their career.

We begin Chapter 4 with a landmark essay by Richard Fulkerson, who provides a historical overview of the major theoretical approaches to teaching composition that emerged in our discipline over the second half of the twentieth century. This is one of the most influential surveys of writing pedagogy ever published, and it is essential reading for anyone in our profession. We pair Fulkerson's overview with a well-known essay by Mark Reynolds, who celebrates two-year college writing teachers as "knowledge makers" and calls on two-year college writing teachers to be active participants in the our discipline's scholarly conversations. This essay and the edited collection it introduced—*The Profession of English in the Two-Year College*—helped establish the expectation that two-year college English faculty would be active teacher-scholars.

The Two-Year College English Association (TYCA) affirms this professional expectation in two important documents: "Research and Scholarship in the Two-Year College" (2003; rev. 2010) and "Characteristics of the Highly Effective Two-Year College Instructor of English" (2012). Both documents are available online at the national TYCA Web site (http://www.ncte.org/tyca). The "Research and Scholarship" statement offers a compelling rationale for the value of scholarship to two-year college English faculty:

> At two-year colleges, good teaching matters most, but this committee views scholarship as a prerequisite and a corequisite for good teaching—because teachers' scholarship legitimizes their expertise, informs their classroom practice, and provides their students with models for intellectual inquiry. (3–4)

Writing faculty at two-year colleges are always busy. Nonetheless, our profession regards engagement with research and scholarship as an essential and ongoing component of good teaching. In fact, professional development might be understood as a continuous process of engagement with emerging theory and research with the goal of improving practice. Thus, in some very important ways, we are always "preparing to teach."

Chapters 5, 6, and 7 foster this kind of engagement by focusing on key issues related to writing course preparation. Chapter 5 presents recent interdisciplinary scholarship on course design. We begin with Sheridan Blau's essay about how we conceptualize the role of reading as we prepare to teach writing—a key concern for compositionists and a vitally important aspect of writing course design. Among the dispositions that Blau identifies as essential for 21st century literacy are a "willingness to suspend closure—to entertain problems rather than avoid them" (p. 155 in this volume), a "tolerance for ambiguity, paradox, and uncertainty" (p. 157), and "intellectual generosity and fallibility: willingness to change one's mind, to appreciate alternative visions, and to engage in methodological believing as well as doubting" (p. 157). We conclude this chapter with Patrick's essay on student motivation in the writing classroom. Surveying a wide variety of research on motivation, much of which has been produced outside of our discipline, Patrick recommends that teachers designing writing courses attend carefully to student motivation, as it is an essential prerequisite for any kind of real learning and engagement. Patrick offers a number of pragmatic classroom strategies for nurturing students' intrinsic motivation for writing drawn from his own experiences teaching at a two-year college.

Another resource we highly recommend for teachers designing writing courses is Ken Bain's book *What the Best College Teachers Do*, based on a fifteen-year study of some of the best teachers in the United States across a wide range of disciplines and institutions. In his chapter entitled "How Do They Prepare to Teach?" Bain notes that the planning that excellent teachers do *before* they teach is just as important as anything else they do in or out of the classroom. He finds, for example, that the best teachers seek to create a "natural critical learning environment" by presenting students with "intriguing, beautiful, or important problems, authentic tasks that will challenge them to grapple with ideas, rethink assumptions, and examine their mental models of reality" (18). Although we were not able to include selections from Bain's book in this collection, his book was mentioned by a number of respondents to our survey of TYCA members (see Preface p. v) and is recommended for anyone wishing to design—or redesign—a writing course.

Chapter 6 focuses on a central but often overlooked and undertheorized aspect of teaching: designing writing assignments. We open this chapter with an excerpt from John Bean's *Engaging Ideas: The Professor's Guide to Integrating Writing, Critical Thinking, and Active Learning in the Classroom*. In this selection, "Using Writing to Promote Thinking," Bean discusses the importance of "awakening students to the existence of problems all around them" (p. 187). He theorizes writing as "both a process of doing critical thinking and a product that communicates the results of critical thinking" (p. 188). Bean offers a variety of pragmatic suggestions for designing writing assignments that foster such thinking. This book was also praised by a number of respondents to our national TYCA survey.

In the excerpt we feature from their recent book, *The Community College Writer*, Howard Tinberg and Jean-Paul Nadeau also provide very pragmatic advice about assignment design. Both Tinberg and Nadeau are two-year college writing teachers, and the guidelines they provide are drawn directly from their own research and practice. Tinberg and Nadeau recommend that teachers "show students what success looks like," "spell out criteria for success," "suggest processes for succeeding," "develop incremental stages for complex writing tasks," "allow for formative and substantive feedback" and "provide ample opportunities for drafting" and revision (pp. 199–200). These recommendations align with decades of composition research on genre knowledge, writing processes, and assessment practices. For those interested in learning more about assignment design, we recommend Muriel Harris's essay "Assignments from Hell." Harris distills over twenty-five years of work in writing centers and offers writing teachers practical suggestions for designing effective assignments. We also recommend Lynda Holmes's article "What Do Students Mean When They Say, 'I Hate Writing'?" which examines why students sometimes struggle to respond to writing assignments and what we can do to help them more productively approach this work.

Finally, Chapter 7 examines the nature of writing expertise and the transfer of learning—two of the most important and debated issues in our profession at the moment. Anne Beaufort is an important voice in this discussion, and the excerpt we include here from her widely referenced book, *College Writing and Beyond*, provides a convenient overview of her thinking on this subject. Beaufort suggests that strong writers draw on five knowledge domains whenever they write:

1. Discourse community knowledge

2. Writing process knowledge

3. Subject matter knowledge

4. Genre knowledge

5. Rhetorical knowledge

According to Beaufort, foregrounding these five domains helps students frame their work in productive ways that encourage knowledge transfer beyond the writing classroom.

In their award-winning article, "Transfer Institutions, Transfer of Knowledge," Holly Hassel and Joanne Giordano bring the conversation about learning transfer to the two-year college setting. Hassel and Giordano study the development of rhetorical adaptability among an often overlooked group of underprepared writers: those who "occupy a misty nether land where they are neither basic writers nor proficient college-level writers" (p. 221). Hassel and Giordano find that such writers often revert to precollege strategies when confronted with new writing challenges. To address this tendency, Hassel and Giordano "emphasize the importance of cultivating students' metacognition as part of the writing curriculum, highlight the benefits of process pedagogy at all stages of precollege and first-year composition, and argue for text-based writing assignments in introductory writing courses" (p. 222). These findings have important implications for anyone teaching writing in two-year colleges, and also demonstrate why staying current with developments in our discipline is so important.

As TYCA's 2004 "Guidelines for the Academic Preparation of English Faculty at Two-Year Colleges" suggest, effective writing teachers are "reflective practitioners and flexible teacher-scholars" who "ground their teaching in theory and research" (4). Regardless of where an instructor is in his or her career, "preparing to teach" means staying current with research and scholarship and bringing the best of that work into one's pedagogy. We believe the material in this collection facilitates such engaged and reflective teaching practice.

Works Cited

Bain, Ken. *What the Best College Teachers Do*. Harvard University Press, 2011.

Harris, Muriel. "Assignments from Hell." *What Is "College-Level" Writing? Vol. 2: Assignments, Readings, and Student Writing Samples*. Edited by Patrick Sullivan, Howard Tinberg, and Sheridan Blau. NCTE, 2010, pp. 233-53.

Holmes, Lynda A. "What Do Students Mean When They Say, 'I Hate Writing'?" *Teaching English in the Two-Year College*, vol. 29, no. 2, 2001, pp. 172-78.

Two-Year College English Association. "Guidelines for the Academic Preparation of English Faculty at Two-Year Colleges." *Two-Year College English Association*, 20 Nov. 2004. Web. Accessed 5 Apr. 2016.

- - -. "Research and Scholarship in the Two-Year College." *Teaching English in the Two-Year College*, vol. 39, no. 1, 2010, pp. 7-28.

Theory, Scholarship, and Practice

Composition at the Turn of the Twenty-First Century

Richard Fulkerson

In reference to the following selection, author Richard Fulkerson explains, "I argue that examining two collections of essays designed for the preparation of new writing teachers and published twenty years apart provides some important clues to what has occurred to composition studies in the interval. Building on the framework I established in two previous CCC articles, I argue that composition studies has become a less unified and more contentious discipline early in the twenty-first century than it had appeared to be around 1990. The present article specifically addresses the rise of what I call critical/cultural studies, the quiet expansion of expressive approaches to teaching writing, and the split of rhetorical approaches into three: argumentation, genre analysis, and preparation for 'the' academic discourse community."

About every ten years, frustration drives me to try to make personal sense of composition studies, a discipline for which I was not trained but into which I have been inexorably drawn.[1] As I revise this manuscript, I direct a doctoral program that prepares about half of the students to become writing professors, and for the first time in over

---

From *College Composition and Communication*, 2005, vol. 56, no. 4, pp. 654-87.

a decade, I am (Acting) Director of First-Year Composition. Selecting texts and devising a syllabus for our teaching assistants to use in multiple sections raised again those large questions of who we are, what we wish to achieve with students, and how we ought to go about it.

In 1990, when I attempted to survey the composition landscape ("Composition in the Eighties"), I wrote with some optimism and sense of progress that as a field we had achieved a consensus about our goals: we agreed that we were to help students improve their writing and that "good writing" meant writing that was rhetorically effective for audience and situation. But we still disagreed over what sort of pedagogy would best reach the goal—over whether to assign topics, how to assign topics, and what type of topics to assign; over the role of readings and textbooks; over peer-response groups; over how teachers should grade and/or respond to writing. I called this situation "axiological" consensus and "pedagogical diversity." Invoking the Cheshire Cat's advice to Alice, I said we agreed, in other words, on where we were trying to go but not on the best route to it: on ends but not means.

Forecast

In what follows, I intend to revisit the metatheory I suggested in "Composition in the Eighties," using it to interpret and critique what I see as the terrain of composition around the turn of the twenty-first century. My central claim is that we have diverged again. Within the scholarship, we currently have three alternative axiologies (theories of value): the newest one, "the social" or "social-construction" view, which values critical cultural analysis; an expressive one; and a multifaceted rhetorical one. I maintain that the three axiologies drive the three major approaches to the teaching of composition. I will treat them with the following designations and in this order: (1) critical/cultural studies [CCS], (2) expressivism, and (3) procedural rhetoric.[2]

Specifically I shall argue that the "social turn" in composition, the importation of cultural studies from the social sciences and literary theory, has made a writing teacher's role deeply problematic. I will argue that expressivism, despite numerous poundings by the cannons of postmodernism and resulting eulogies, is, in fact, quietly expanding its region of command. Finally, I'll argue that the rhetorical approach has now divided itself in three.[3]

Mapping Comp-landia: Now and Then

We can get a suggestive picture of large-scale changes in the discipline by looking at two volumes published twenty years apart, each designed to introduce novices to alternate ways to teach college writing. In 1980 the National Council of Teachers of English published *Eight Approaches to Teaching Composition*, edited by Tim Donovan and Ben McClelland. To it we can compare the recent (2001) collection of bibliographical es-

Table 1. Two Views of the Composition Landscape

Timothy Donovan and Ben McClelland, eds. *Eight Approaches to Teaching Composition.* Urbana, IL: NCTE, 1980.	Gary Tate, Amy Rupiper, and Kurt Schick, eds. *A Guide to Composition Pedagogies.* New York: Oxford, 2001.
1. "Writing as Process," Don Murray	1. "Process Pedagogy," Lad Tobin
2. "The Prose Models Approach," Paul Eschholz	2. "Expressive Pedagogy," Christopher Burnham
3. "The Experiential Approach," Stephen Judy	3. "Rhetorical Pedagogy," William Covino
4. "The Rhetorical Approach," Janice Lauer	4. "Collaborative Pedagogy," Rebecca Moore Howard
5. "The Epistemic Approach," Kenneth Dowst	5. "Cultural Studies and Composition," Diana George and John Trimbur
6. "Basic Writing," Harvey Wiener	6. "Critical Pedagogy," Ann George
7. "The Writing Conference," Thomas Carnicelli	7. "Feminist Pedagogy," Susan Jarratt
8. "Writing in the Total Curriculum," Robert Weiss	8. "Community-Service Pedagogy," Laura Julier
	9. "The Pedagogy of Writing Across the Curriculum," Susan McLeod
	10. "Writing Center Pedagogy," Eric Hobson
	11. "On the Academic Margins: Basic Writing Pedagogy," Deborah Mutnick
	12. "Technology and the Teaching of Writing," Charles Moran

says *A Guide to Composition Pedagogies*, edited by Gary Tate, Amy Rupiper, and Kurt Schick. As composition has become more diverse, the eight "approaches" from 1980 have increased to twelve "pedagogies" in the 2001 collection. Table 1 gives a chapter outline, with authors, for each collection.

In their introduction, Donovan and McClelland stress the shift from product to process, still a relatively new idea in 1980. Citing both Richard Young and Janet Emig, they endorse the metaphor that a Kuhnian "paradigm shift" has occurred in composition. Significantly, they point out that approaches 2 to 5 (that is, the models approach, the experiential, the rhetorical, and the epistemic) all "accommodate the process approach" (xiii), one version of which Don Murray presents as the volume's first and context-setting chapter.

Although both collections open with a chapter on writing as process (about which more later), the "prose models" approach, taken seriously in 1980, is missing from the new volume. Stephen Judy's experiential approach more or less matches up with expressive pedagogy as Chris Burnham defines it. Both volumes have a chapter on the rhetorical approach.

The major difference shows up in chapters 5 to 8 of the new volume. They have no parallels in the older one. These four chapters represent variations of the major new area of scholarly interest in composition as we begin the twenty-first century, critical/cultural studies (CCS), showing the impact of postmodernism, feminism, and British cultural studies.[4]

In addition, the rhetorical aims and techniques of the contributors have changed, representing a growing "scholarizing" of the field. In *Eight Approaches*, practitioner-experts explain how to use the approach each favors. The editors describe the chapters as "case studies which record the authors' attempts to put it all together — at least for themselves and their students" (xiii). Murray includes charts to help the aspiring process teacher; Paul Eschholz lists thirty authors who have interested his students as models. Janice Lauer traces a single student paper through its growth and reprints the final copy. Citations to related works are minimal (ranging from seven for Murray and for Wiener up to twenty-six for Lauer, with an average of sixteen). In contrast, the chapters in the newer collection are heavy, scholarly bibliographical surveys. Susan Jarratt's article on feminism cites well over a hundred sources, as does William Covino's on rhetoric, with an average of seventy citations per essay for the whole. Despite the editors' claims to have produced the volume for students just coming into the field (vi), it frequently makes daunting reading even for old hands.

Analytical Scheme

In "Composition in the Eighties" I postulated that in order to have a philosophy of composition upon which you can explicitly erect a course, you must answer four questions:

1. The axiological question: in general, what makes writing "good"?

2. The process question: in general, how do written texts come into existence?

3. The pedagogical question: in general, how does one teach college students effectively, especially where procedural rather than propositional knowledge is the goal? And

4. The epistemological question: "How do you know that?" which underlies answers to all the others.

I will employ these four questions (and others) in order to examine critically the variant contemporary approaches to teaching college writing.

By the time I finish, then, I hope to have filled in the boxes in the following grid:

Perspective on Composition	Evaluative Theory	View of Process	View of Pedagogy	Epistemology Assumed
Current/ Traditional Rhetoric [C/T]				
Expressivism				
Critical/Cultural Studies [CCS]				
Procedural Rhetoric				

Note that, in contrast to the two collections above, I include no "process perspective." Instead, one heading for each perspective is "view of process." All composition perspectives assume some view of the writing process; that is, any concept of composing and/or teaching composition must presuppose an answer to "How are texts produced?" It is widely acknowledged that C/T composition truncates "process" as much as possible (outline, write, edit, receive grade, do exercises). Each of the other approaches is capable of and likely to encourage students to learn and employ more extensive "processing."[5]

Here is an important demurrer about that chart, however. As a tidy four-by-four grid, it seems to imply that there are separate and systematic sets of characteristics for each "perspective"—our perspectives, four pedagogies, four views of process, and four epistemologies. But it isn't that simple. Since I name the "perspective" for evaluation theory (axiology), those two will necessarily match. But although the perspective influences the pedagogical and process views and reflects epistemological assumptions, there is no neat one-to-one pattern. Different scholars who primarily value "expressiveness" in writing may not share either epistemology or pedagogy or view of process. And a dyed-in-the-wool CCS advocate might share pedagogical and epistemological assumptions with someone professing essentially rhetorical values.

Social Theories, Critical/Cultural Studies Approaches

Judging from the published scholarship of the last thirteen years, cultural studies has been the major movement in composition studies, no surprise to readers of our leading journals. A sort of foundational publication was *Cultural Studies in the English Classroom*, edited by Jim Berlin and Michael Vivion in 1992. It included articles about entire English programs that had shifted to cultural studies (such as Carnegie Mellon, Pitt, and the SUNY–Albany doctoral program) as well as accounts of individual courses at other schools. In 1995 came *Left Margins: Cultural Studies and Composition Pedagogy*, by Karen Fitts and Alan France. In addition to hundreds of theoretical articles, there are a good many ethnographic accounts of courses using cultural studies, including Russel Durst's *Collision Course* and Douglas Hunt's *Misunderstanding the Assignment*, as well as Mark Hurlbert and Michael Blitz's collection *Composition and Resistance*.

More to the point are the extensive bibliographical essays in the Tate, Rupiper, and Schick volume. The one explicitly on topic is "Cultural Studies and Composition," by John Trimbur and Diana George, which cites 111 sources, and says, "cultural studies has insinuated itself into the mainstream of composition" (71). Whether cultural studies is as widespread in composition classrooms as in our journals is actually an open question. Answering it would require survey data we simply do not have. Closely related is "Critical Pedagogy," by Ann George. For my purposes, feminist composition (treated by Jarratt) is similar to these two. All three focus on having students read about systemic cultural injustices inflicted by dominant societal groups and dominant discourses on those with less power, and upon the empowering possibilities of rhetoric if students are educated to "read" carefully and "resist" the social texts that help keep some groups subordinated. Andrea Greenbaum has recently argued that cultural studies approaches, critical approaches, many feminist approaches, and even postcolonial approaches can all be seen as similar "emancipatory movements in composition."

I acknowledge that treating the three pedagogies as bibliographically separate makes sense. Trimbur and George note that the originating trinity of cultural studies are Richard Hoggart (*The Uses of Literacy*, 1957), Raymond Williams (*Culture and Society*, 1958, and *The Long Revolution*, 1961), and E. P. Thompson (*The Making of the English Working Class*, 1963) (73), but the "big three" of critical pedagogy, according to Ann George, are Paulo Freire, Henry Giroux, and Ira Shor (93). Feminist theory cannot be so cleanly anchored, but no one would nominate any of the six just-named authors.

It's important to emphasize that in CCS the course aim is not "improved writing" but "liberation" from dominant discourse. Here is how Ann George puts it: "[C]ritical pedagogy engages students in analyses of the unequal power relations that produce and are produced by cultural practices and institutions [. . .], and it aims to help students develop the tools that will enable them to challenge this inequality" (92). And here are some satiric but revealing thoughts of a new graduate teaching assistant, prior to entering her first-year CCS classroom: "[Students] will be astonished as I, layer by layer, unveil their ideology. They will gawk when I expose the simulacra. They will not be able to stop their pens when questioning their role in the university, the cultural formation of gender roles and expectations, racial stereotypes, and the ethical practices of the titans of industry" (Heimer 17). James Berlin, surely the most famous CCS advocate, defined the goal of the social composition course saying, "Our larger purpose is to encourage our students to resist and to negotiate [. . .] hegemonic discourses—in order to bring about more personally humane and socially equitable economic and political arrangements" ("Composition" 50).

Certainly it's misleading to talk of a single "cultural studies" or "critical" or "feminist" pedagogy. A tremendous variety of courses fit the CCS rubric. But here, as I understand it, are the essential features that would justify categorizing a writing course, including feminist courses, under the CCS heading.

1. The central activity of the course is interpretation. The interpretation may be of readings, either about cultural theory or the experiences of a cultural group or individual (Richard Rodriguez, Victor Villanueva, Paulo Freire, Gloria Anzaldúa, and other authors are popular). Alternatively, students may interpret cultural artifacts—ads, TV shows, minority language use, popular songs, etc. Most often, both sorts of "texts" are used.

2. Frequently, multiple texts reflect one theme: the course or a major chunk of it might be about family, the Vietnam War, education, the sixties. (For real examples, see George and Trimbur's anthology *Reading Culture*.)

3. The interpretive moves assume the artifact/text reveals certain deep structural truths about power in American society, specifically ways in which the dominant culture dominates, in terms of race, class, gender, sexual orientation, etc.

4. Students write papers interpreting social artifacts, usually selected in connection with the course theme(s). Some courses involve a fairly elaborate enactment of writing as an extended, recursive, complex process.

5. The course goal, as framed by Berlin and others, is to empower or liberate students by giving them new insights into the injustices of American and transnational capitalism, politics, and complicit mass media.

In fact, some writers remark that their courses would not necessarily need to be in English departments. Patricia Bizzell and Bruce Herzberg's CCS textbook, *Negotiating Difference*, features documents focusing on six moments of cultural conflict in U.S. history. It would be a superb foundation for a course in history. Other courses could equally well exist in a sociology department or an anthropology department, or even in an environmental science department.

What can be learned by interrogating critical/cultural studies courses using my four features of a philosophy of composition? First, although the pedagogy as outlined above is pretty flexible, one principle is clear. It would be inappropriate in a course about cultural hegemony for the teacher to be an oppressor, so most discussions of such courses invoke a democratic, often Freirean, classroom, based on reading assigned texts and then having problem-posing discussions. Second, there is no agreed-on view of writing as a process. There may be heuristic questions about the artifacts; teachers may respond to multiple drafts, and often drafts are shared in peer-response groups to encourage revision. A portfolio with a reflective entry may well be used. But neither extended processing nor the portfolio is inherently related to the approach. And descriptions of other courses suggest that the complex process is often cut short, perhaps by restricting prewriting/invention to "reading" and to class or small-group discussion. Just what one might expect in a course in a different department.

The epistemological assumptions always include a claim that knowledge is socially constructed through dialectic exchanges. After all, such courses are part of the "social turn" in composition. And since cultural artifacts, including texts and codes of behavior, are taken as proof about the nature of a culture, ethnographic research receives high credibility as a knowledge source. Epistemological assumptions are crucial to such courses on two levels: (1) they determine what sort of scholarly research is acceptable as grounding for the approach itself (as is true for any approach), and (2) they also control what students are taught regarding "proof" in their own reading and writing. The idea that one can accurately infer features of cultural hegemony from readings and other artifacts within one's own culture is itself a crucial epistemological assumption. The pedagogical claims, although sometimes based on ethnographic case studies, are never said to be generalizable but always local. Their epistemic status is that of sophisticated lore. "I saw this happen," or "I did this and it helped my students."

In point of fact, virtually no one in contemporary composition theory assumes any epistemology other than a vaguely interactionist constructivism. We have rejected quantification and any attempts to reach Truth about our business by scientific means, just as we long ago rejected "truth" as derivable by deduction from unquestioned first principles. For us, all "truth" is rhetorical, dialectally constructed, and provisional. Even our most empirical journal, *Research in the Teaching of English*, now publishes primarily ethnographic studies.

Finally, what of axiology? What counts as good writing in a cultural studies course? (CCS scholars are not much help on this since even in describing their classes and assignments they rarely include samples of student writing.) What we come down to is that the writing in such a course will be judged by how sophisticated or insightful the teacher finds the interpretation of the relevant artifacts to be. In other words, papers are judged in the same way they would be in any department with a "content" to teach. This is just the way a history professor would judge a paper, or a chemistry prof, or a business prof. Thus the standard of evaluation used is, I assert, actually a mimetic one—how close has the student come to giving a "defensible" (read "correct") analysis of the materials.

Axiologically, CCS courses resemble the popular and durable literature-based composition courses. In both types, students read texts judged important by the teacher. They write about those texts, and their work is evaluated based on how well it shows that they understand and can perform the interpretive approach. The difference is that the lit/comp courses use belletristic texts, which students must interpret to the teacher's satisfaction, while the CCS course uses any text or other artifact thought to reveal cultural principles. In both courses, the writing is essentially a display of valued intellectual interactions with the relevant texts and is judged accordingly. Ungenerously, one could argue that this does not produce a writing course at all—any more than a sociology course in race relations that uses extensive writing is a writing course. Certainly it provides students with extensive practice in writing and with getting feedback—although it isn't clear whether the feedback is mainly about writing or mainly about culture and how to "read" it.

Both the lit-based course and the cultural studies course reflect, I suspect, content envy on the part of writing teachers. Most of us (still) have been trained in textual analysis: we like classes built around texts to analyze. (And I am certainly not immune to that envy. I *enjoy* leading discussions of complex nonfiction that challenges students to think hard about basic beliefs.)

Let me attempt to further concretize this portrait of CCS as contemporary mimeticism by examining Russel Durst's *Collision Course: Conflict, Negotiation, and Learning in College Composition*, one of the most thoughtful and realistic CCS ethnographies. At Durst's university, students take a two-quarter sequence of writing courses, which follow a standardized syllabus and use the same texts. Durst spent the first two quarters of successive years observing two teachers in the program, occasionally participating in the classroom, reading student papers, and interviewing selected students. In other words, pretty much the full panoply of classroom ethnography by an outside observer. In the first and relatively traditional course, students write in various genres, based on personal experience. The second-quarter course uses a cultural studies approach, which Durst asserts to be typical of current approaches to teaching writing. He invokes Freire, Bizzell, Giroux, Shor, and Trimbur for its underlying philosophy (3). In this second course, using Gary Colombo, Robert Cullen, and Bonnie Lisle's *Rereading America* (1992 edition), the students write four major assignments on separate cultural themes: "[T]he standard syllabus asked students to read and write about the nature of family structures, the issue of money and success as reflected in the American dream, and aspects of prejudice, discrimination, and group membership" (17). Each student picked a fourth topic from the book as the basis of a research project, which counted double.

Durst is careful to say, "Though I believe in and teach a critical literacy approach that locates students in a larger cultural and historical context, my goal as a teacher and program director is not to turn first-year students into critical intellectuals and political activists" (6). Durst began his ethnographic study with the hypothesis that what students wanted and expected from a composition course in college conflicted with what teachers using a critical pedagogy were mostly interested in: "first-year students typically enter composition with an idea of writing and an understanding of what they need to learn about writing that are dramatically at odds with the views and approaches of the teacher" (2). The students are "career-oriented pragmatists who view writing as a difficult but potentially useful technology" (2). Durst wanted to investigate the connection between the "social turn" in composition and the "more traditional concern in the field with the teaching of writing, as in strategies, approaches, and techniques. [. . .] I see unresolved, even unacknowledged tensions between these areas of concern" (4). Since the program had a first course in this more traditional format and a second course emphasizing cultural studies, Durst was in an ideal position to compare student reactions to the two approaches.

Most of the book deals with the second course as taught by Sherry Stanforth, a "doctoral student interested in critical theory, feminism, composition studies, and creative writing" (19). She is already a published author and has been identified as an outstanding teacher who gets "consistently strong evaluations" (19). She has some of the same students for both courses, and Durst met regularly with several of them throughout both quarters. He also observed and took field notes on half of Stanforth's class meetings (30). In the later chapters, he narrates a plethora of classroom events that frustrated him and many of the teachers. "As course subject matter began to focus more on political issues, the conflict between many students' views and those of the textbook became more pronounced" (142). Teachers "lamented the horrific ignorance of individual [student] writers who misapplied citations or misinterpreted the central idea of an argument" (161). The students didn't listen to NPR or read the *Atlantic Monthly* or the *New Yorker*, and thus were unaware that what they were studying was actually a hot public topic (161); "helping them evolve as socially just citizens seemed overwhelming, especially for first-year teaching assistants. In between conferences and classes, they sat around the office together, pondering the ongoing confusion of their work. Was the goal to teach them better values or better writing or both?" (161). And the students, as Durst sees them, engage in "twin resistance" (128). They resist politically, claiming "they are being force-fed a liberal ideology'" (128). And they resist intellectually "the work they are being asked to do in reading what seem to them unnecessarily abstruse essays and taking on the difficult task of forming and supporting interpretations of what they are finding out are surprisingly complex issues" (128).

In addition to paralleling literature-based "composition" courses and displaying our content envy, most CCS courses seem inappropriate to me for two reasons. First, reading, analyzing, and discussing the texts upon which the course rests are unlikely to leave room for any actual teaching of writing. So we get a "writing" course in which writing is required and evaluated, but not taught. I agree with Gary Tate, who remarked, "if we are serious about teaching *writing* rather than literature or politics or religion, we can—should—make the writing of our students the focus (content) of the course" ("Empty" 270).

The second problem is the likelihood of indoctrination. Teachers dedicated to exposing the social injustice of racism, classism, homophobia, misogyny, or capitalism cannot perforce accept student viewpoints that deny such views or fail to register their contemporary relevance. Maxine Hairston's notorious "Diversity, Ideology, and Teaching Writing," accusing CCS teachers of indoctrinating their students with leftist views, was widely denounced, provoking more written responses than any other article during Richard Gebhardt's six-year tenure as editor of *College Composition and Communication*. Hairston claimed that cultural studies composition teachers "show open contempt for their students' values" (119), and engage in "facile non-logical leap[s]" (121), all the while perverting the purpose of writing classes and turning them into leftist political indoctrination.

The standard response accused Hairston of ideological naivete, arguing that she assumed her own pedagogy to be ideology-free but that since all pedagogies are always already political, she must be incorrect (and thus also unenlightened). Therefore, her critique of CCS courses could be denounced as well as ignored.

Logically that argument means no pedagogy can be accused of indoctrination, because the accuser's hands would necessarily also be unclean. In other words, there could be no grounds for distinguishing between a teacher who overtly forces students to echo his or her politics in their writing and one who tolerates alternative positions. All education becomes equally indoctrinating; I take such a position to be an obvious absurdity.

It was unfortunate that Hairston expressed her views so intemperately, liberally engaging in ad hominem argument and provoking the same from many respondents, and even more unfortunate that she later had to acknowledge seriously misquoting Cy Knoblauch, after identifying him as one CCS ideologue. Both features substantially reduce her ethos. She also described her own classroom approach in a vague way that made her seem an extreme expressivist, who would accept whatever her students said on primarily personal topics. That was not an accurate view of her teaching (see Jolliffe et al.).

Most scholars who examine a CCS course ethnographically or narrate such a course of their own go out of their way to say the teachers are careful not to indoctrinate students. Students are "free" to write their papers from any perspective they choose. They have only to make a thoughtful case for their position. The problem is that a socially committed teacher will rarely find contrary views presented by an undergraduate to be sufficiently "thoughtful," any more than a literature scholar will find an undergraduate reinterpretation of "Hills Like White Elephants" convincing. In addition, a student who knows his or her instructor's own political views will probably not choose to oppose them with a grade at stake.

Contemporary Expressivist Composition

At least one approach to feminist pedagogy does not fall under critical/cultural studies, even though it is still designed to help free students from patriarchy and even though it does include readings. It is essentially a consciousness-raising and coming-to-voice class, in which female students are provided a safe place to share and explore experiences and viewpoints. Many traditional features of academic writing, such as having a clear argumentative thesis and backing it up to convince a reader, are put on a back burner (see especially Annas). Contemporary feminists might regard such a course as retrograde (see Greenbaum's discussion of "bitch pedagogy" and her critique of the self-effacement and self-sacrifice implied by the commonly held view that, for women, an "ethic of care" is most appropriate).

Such courses are one variety of the enduring category of the expressivist composition class, a category which seems to be going strong, despite the groundswell of cultural/critical pedagogies. In the Tate, Rupiper, and Schick volume, Chris Burnham writes the bibliographical chapter on expressive pedagogy, and it's worth quoting his definition at length (starting with the presumption of the rhetorical triangle):

> Expressivism places the writer in the center, articulates its theory, and develops its pedagogical system by assigning highest value to the writer and her imaginative, psychological, social, and spiritual development and how that development influences individual consciousness and social behavior. Expressivist pedagogy employs freewriting, journal keeping, reflective writing, and small group dialogic collaborative response to foster a writer's aesthetic, cognitive, and moral development. Expressivist pedagogy encourages, even insists upon, a sense of writer presence even in research-based writing. This presence—"voice" or ethos—whether explicit, implicit, or absent, functions as a key evaluation criterion when expressivists examine writing. (19)

Notice that the overriding goal is to "foster [. . .] aesthetic, cognitive, and moral development," not to improve written communication or encourage critical thinking. Writing is a means of fostering personal development, in the great Socratean tradition of "knowing thyself." Burnham invokes both Thomas Merton and bell hooks as sponsoring voices for the viewpoint (20). One crucial axiological goal is to have students write with "voice"—although Burnham doesn't commit the 1960s mistake of referring to the student's "authentic" voice.

The current hotbed of expressivism seems to be the NCTE affiliate the Assembly for Expanded Perspectives on Learning (AEPL), which publishes yearly the *Journal of the Assembly for Expanded Perspectives on Learning* (founded by Alice Brand in 1995). The assembly began as a special-interest group, "Beyond the Cognitive Domain," started by Robert Graves and Brand, which met at the 1991, 1992, and 1993 CCCC Conventions. When the interest group became the AEPL, James Moffett was the first member. The group continues to hold well-attended daylong preconvention workshops at CCCC, and several edited collections of articles by members have appeared. (See Brand and Graves; Foehr and Schiller.) Other recent presentations of complex expressive views include books by Marshall Alcorn; Jeffrey Berman; and Charles Anderson and Marian MacCurdy.

Of course, there is no single "expressive" way to teach composition, any more than there is a single CCS way. Some expressive teachers are interested in helping students mature and become more self-aware, more reflective. Others are interested in writing as healing or therapy. Some are most interested in creative self-expression. Some have students choose their own topics; others have concerns they want students to address. And another sort of expressivism involves asking students to write the classic personal *essai*. (See Paul Heilker and Kurt Spellmeyer for arguments about the value to our students of essayist literacy.)

Recently Karen Surman Paley criticized the easy and common denigration of expressivist teaching, in *I-Writing: The Politics and Practice of Teaching First-Person Writing*. For her dissertation, she did ethnographic case studies of two female teachers at Boston College, including audiotaped student interviews. She says the results "deconstruct the social construction of 'expressivism' as a naïve pedagogy" (x) and "demonstrate that 'expressivist' programs are much more complicated than they have been made out to be" (xiii). To the extent that she argues for allowing first-person narrative to be a part of composition (both first-year and advanced), Paley does an excellent job, both in critiquing the work of Berlin and Lester Faigley that rejects autobiographical narrative out of hand, and in demonstrating that in the classrooms she observed, even autobiographical narrative often raises issues related to the holy political trinity of class, race, and gender.

But Paley seems to defend the wrong victim in the wrong way because the courses she observed do not look expressivist in the first place. The first-year course required four papers: an autobiographical narrative, an "analysis," a persuasive argument, and a research paper. In the advanced course, no topics or genres were assigned; students were to choose their own topics and write once a week. Paley, however, identifies the Boston College program as "expressivist" (56). The only reason I can determine is that it is directed by Lad Tobin, who received his doctorate from the University of New Hampshire under Don Murray et al. and who has often written about expressivism and its relationship to "process pedagogy." The inclusion of a single autobiographical narrative in the first course is a perfectly standard practice and doesn't warrant labeling the course "expressive."

In addition, one would not "defend" a truly "expressive" course by saying that it actually does address issues of social consciousness—class, race, gender, ethnicity, etc. It would be defended by showing that it led to greater self-awareness, greater insight, increased creativity, or therapeutic clarification of some sort. To say that such a course "actually" does involve cultural studies issues is to give the game away by accepting the values of a quite different composition philosophy.

Just as no one actually knows how widespread CCS composition courses are, the same is true for expressive courses grounded in the views and experiences of the student authors. We have lots of indirect evidence for both.

A Digression on Process and Post-Process

It's simply inaccurate to equate "process" teaching with an expressive axiology, although the two were entwined in the influential early work of Don Murray. Tobin, writing in the Tate, Rupiper, and Schick volume, remarks that "it was not unusual to hear 'process' and 'expressivism' used almost interchangeably" (9). I think his chapter on "Process Pedagogy" encourages the confusion, even though he points out that "a teacher could emphasize the organic nature of the composing process but not assign or even allow personal writing" (9). Those who are committed to an expressive axiology nowadays do generally teach an extended writing process, a process of invention and discovery. So do many of those committed to what I have called the mimetic axiology of cultural studies. And so do those who are primarily committed to teaching students from the perspective of a rhetorical axiology ("good" writing is writing that works effectively for the readers in the rhetorical context). Jim Berlin said it well: "Everyone teaches the process of writing, but everyone does not teach the *same* process. The test of one's competence as a composition instructor [. . .] resides in being able to recognize and justify the version of the process being taught" ("Contemporary" 777). There are complicated historical reasons that the "process revolution" of the 1970s also became identified with the advocacy of unique expressive voice. But probably most process teaching today derives more from the cognitive and problem-solving research of Linda Flower and John Hayes plus pioneering work by Janet Emig, Nancy Sommers, and Sondra Perl, not to mention the rhetoric revival—led by figures like Edward P. J. Corbett—than it does from the individualistic advocacy of Don Murray and Ken

Macrorie. At any rate, to equate one's view of process with the overall aim of an approach is a category error. All approaches necessarily include views of process. (For a related discussion that attempts to identify separate theories of process that correspond to three major "views" of composition, see Faigley's "Competing Theories of Process: A Critique and a Proposal.")

As for our being "post-process," I tend to share Lynn Bloom's view (expressed at the Miami Conference on Composition in the Twenty-First Century in 2001) that the term is an oxymoron. But there is no agreed-upon meaning for it; it may just be the latest way of showing yourself to be *au courant*. One meaning is that as a field we no longer do research into writing processes. That is certainly accurate (although not necessarily progress), but it isn't what the term seems to refer to most of the time. Thomas Kent argues that "process" implies a set of regular, sequential procedures that writers do or should go through, in short, a production formula. And since writing isn't formulaic but "hermeneutic guess-work" (3), process research and theory were essentially mistaken from the start. It's true that "process" in some classrooms and textbooks did (and no doubt still does) become reduced to formulaic steps. Tobin even tells of overhearing a colleague tell a student, "You have not done any freewriting here. You can't just jump from brainstorming straight to composing. You can't skip steps" (11). But such linear rigidity was never faithful to what the process researchers learned. So Kent attacks a straw character. A third definition takes "process" to mean the romanticized view of the isolated writer seeking inspiration and striving to make personal meaning alone in a garret, together with the resulting personal texts. Since we have rejected that view of process and emphasize all writing as social, we are, therefore, "post-process." This viewpoint too makes a category error by equating expressivism as an axiology with a process based on genius and inspiration. It further presumes a reductive notion of what a genuinely expressive writing course involves. Thus it commits the straw-character fallacy twice. (See my "Of Pre- and Post-Process: Reviews and Ruminations.")

Rhetorical Approaches to Composition

When the Council of Writing Program Administrators (WPA) approved in 1999 a statement of minimal standards for what a first-year writing course should accomplish, neither critical cultural studies approaches nor expressive ones were much reflected in the document, officially approved by the organization of people who actually direct programs ("WPA Outcomes"). That statement lists broad desired outcomes under four headings: Rhetorical Knowledge, Critical Thinking, Processes, and Knowledge of Conventions. Under each heading is a bulleted list of six to ten outcomes—the bulk of which are pretty traditional. They emphasize writing effectively for different audiences, seeing writing as an extended process of multiple tasks and drafts, and learning to control surface features and formatting. The only gestures I see toward a cultural studies agenda are the fourth and seventh entries under "Critical Thinking, Reading, and Writing." The fourth says students should "understand the relationships among language, knowledge, and power," and the seventh suggests that faculty in all disciplines should help students learn "the relationships among language, knowledge, and power in their fields."

As I see this document, it is fully in the dominant tradition of composition in the 1970s and 1980s. Let's call that tradition procedural rhetoric. Using my four dimensions of a philosophy of composition, we can say that this constellation of approaches shares an axiological commitment to judging writing by suitability to the context ("situation and audience"), including concern for classical issues of *pathos*, *ethos*, and *logos*. Its theory of the writing process says that writing is a complex extended set of (teachable) activities in which a wide variety of invention procedures may be valuable, and an equal variety of drafting and revision activities. Its pedagogical assumptions are flexible, although lecture is eschewed. One standard metaphor for the teacher in a rhetorically grounded classroom is that of a coach helping students master a variety of activities (procedural knowledge). Another is that of an experienced guild member, a master craftsperson, to the student as apprentice. Teacher modeling, followed by student performance, followed by critique, followed by further practice would be an appropriate learning sequence. This may be a collaborative or democratic classroom; very likely part of the extended writing process will include peer-revision groups. And teacher commentary, either written or oral, will be given on drafts of papers. Readings may be used but are not the center of the class activity.

Epistemologically, adherents of this view believe that values and decisions are reached through dialectic, but they do not take a radical antifoundational view. Rhetorical teachers would generally not be comfortable with the claim that "all truth [reality] is a social construct"; they grant that evidentiary statements can be true or false (i.e., that "facts" do exist), and that some claims are better founded than others.

In contemporary composition practice, I see rhetorical philosophies taking three different emphases: composition as argumentation, genre-based composition, and composition as introduction to an academic discourse community.

Ironically, these topics are not now discussed much in our leading journals. Maybe this material is just too "traditional" to warrant much space. To find major articles on argument theory and argument teaching, one does better by looking to related fields. *Informal Logic* carries many directly relevant articles, as does *Argumentation and Advocacy* from the field of speech and rhetoric. The bulk of genre theory is found in collections rather than journals, although a good deal of it was also published in speech communication in the eighties (see Campbell and Jamieson; Miller).

Although the Tate, Rupiper, and Schick bibliographical collection is strong on various dimensions of cultural studies and on expressivism, it is unfortunately weak on rhetorical approaches. The extensive essay entitled "Rhetorical Pedagogy," by William Covino, is misnamed and ill-fitted to the volume. Although Covino cites over one hundred sources about rhetoric, ranging from Plato and Aristotle through Thomas Sprat to Walter Ong and Chaim Perelman, he focuses on history and theory. A graduate student who read all the cited material would be well prepared to write a comprehensive exam over both classical and modern rhetoric, but the student would know little about contemporary rhetorical pedagogy. Ironically, in the predecessor volume to Tate, Rupiper, and Schick, *Eight Approaches to Teaching Composition*, Janice Lauer did a far better job of explaining how to enact a rhetorical approach in the classroom. What the Tate, Rupiper, and Schick collection needs are three further bibliographical essays: one on "Argumentation and Composition," a second on "Genre Theory and Composition," and a third on "Discursive Communities and the Teaching of Composition."

Despite the shortage of composition scholarship on argumentation, evidence indicates that treating writing as argument for a reader is widespread. There are two relevant edited volumes on argumentation (see Emmel, Resch, and Tenney; and Barnett). And the growth and success of argument-based textbooks in the last twenty years has been phenomenal (see Rottenberg; Ramage, Bean, and Johnson; Clark; Lunsford and Ruszkiewicz; Williams and Colomb; Faigley and Selzer; Fahnestock and Secor; Crusius and Channell). The WPA statement, with its call for making students aware of the need to have a thesis and to write for an audience, supports this outlook. (See also Gerald Graff's *Clueless in Academe*, in which he argues that all academic discourse is argument characterized by certain preferred intellectual "moves" that should be shared explicitly with students.) In fact, even CCS teachers actually want argument from their students: claims about oppression, race, or the American Dream are to be grounded in close readings of various social "texts"; assertions of cultural patterns are to be backed up with artifactual data.

Durst's case study of Sherry Stanforth demonstrates how composition teachers may expect students to produce arguments but fail to share that expectation with students. One assignment in Stanforth's first-quarter course is to "explain a concept"—"not only by presenting factual information but by doing so in an interesting, critical, and creative manner that would appeal to an audience" (96). After some class discussion, student groups of four are given concepts on which to generate ideas for writing. After an oral report from one of the groups, Stanforth praises their work: "These people didn't just define. They discussed their topic as a problem and also proposed some solutions. They went way beyond just a boring, pointless listing of information" (97–98). Now, in this course, the assignments are supposed to progress by mode or genre. This assignment to "explain a concept" will be followed by a "problem/solution" paper and then by an "argument." But, of course, when Stanforth praises this group's work on their concept explanation by saying that they perceived the concept as a problem and also offered solutions, she indicates both that the sequence is problematic and that what she would in fact find "interesting" and thus reward would be a concept paper that also takes a stand, makes an argument.

And indeed, this turns out to be the case on the actual assignment. The whole class seems confused by how to go about the task, and Stanforth asks Cris, one of the case-study students, what the main point of her paper is to be. Cris says she wants "to show people that tattooing is an art, it's not what other people think" (Durst 101). The teacher's question and the student's answer both reveal that this task is actually to make an argument for a reader. The entire situation would be much clearer if everyone involved recognized this was the case and could discuss the task in the language of argumentation: claim, evidence, assumption, counterviews, refutation. Later in the lesson, Stanforth stresses the need to narrow the topic and decides to model the process. She asks for a sample topic from the students. Someone proposes Halloween, and she spends several minutes demonstrating ways to limit that topic. Durst remarks, "she emphasized that the essay should be focused around a thesis and main point that the writer wanted to make about Halloween" (101). The students remain "puzzled" (101), which doesn't seem too surprising. What Stanforth wants is for them to take a topic they are familiar with, locate an arguable issue within it that would be interesting to an (unspecified) audience, and then develop an argument with a thesis, necessarily including sufficient explanation of the concepts involved. Matters would go more smoothly if that expectation were shared with the students, perhaps even built into the class.

I would not want to argue that there is an "argumentation approach" to teaching composition. For many, probably most, of the "approaches" discussed in these two central collections twenty years apart could fit under such a broad rubric. And "argumentation" certainly can't be called a full "philosophy" of composition because the relevant features of argumentation imply only an axiology (rhetorical), not a particular pedagogy or view of writing as a process, nor even a coherent epistemology. In fact, the specialists in teaching students to argue and critique arguments, members of the informal logic and speech debate communities, disagree dramatically about how argumentation should be taught (not to mention how it should be analyzed and assessed). Many of us know that we want arguments from students, but we differ on what topics they should argue about, on how explicitly to "teach" argument, over how to assess it, and over the role of "logic," either formal or informal, in such a course. (See my "Technical Logic, Comp-Logic, and the Teaching of Writing.")

The second dominantly rhetorical approach at the turn of the twenty-first century, and a major concern in composition scholarship, involves the direct study of "genre." "Genre" is the contemporary heir to what Paul Eschholz called "The Prose Models Approach: Using Products in the Process" in the Donovan and McClelland volume. "Genre" is also the contemporary incarnation of what we (properly) disparage as a "modes of discourse" approach (see Robert Connors, "The Rise and Fall of the Modes of Discourse").

The scholarship on teaching "composition as genre" would require a full-length chapter of the sort in the Tate, Rupiper, and Schick collection. (For a start, see the collections by Berkenkotter and Huckin; Bishop and Ostrom; and Freedman and Medway.) Most discussions of genre in the last decade have paid homage to the contextual/situational definition offered by Carolyn Miller, in contrast to the older idea of a genre as a form/formula (such as the genre "Elizabethan sonnet"). Miller developed her definition specifically to describe oral genres; as has often been the case, rhetorical scholars in speech communication have beaten those of us in composition studies to the punch (see Foss as well as Campbell and Jamieson). As I have written elsewhere in connection with *Newsweek* "My Turn" columns, the consensus in speech-rhetoric is that a rhetorical genre exists when common subject matter plus a common provocative exigence (see Miller) leads to discourses manifesting "a constellation of forms that recurs in each of its members. These forms, *in isolation*, appear in other discourses. What is distinctive about the acts in a genre is the recurrence of the forms *together* in constellation" (Campbell and Jamieson 20).

In "Genre-Based Pedagogies: A Social Response to Process," Ken Hyland provides an excellent overview of the current situation, even though his study focuses on English as a Second Language. The grounding for a genre-based approach is the identification of a number of those "relatively stable [. . .] types of utterances" (Bakhtin 64) that scholars have thought valuable enough for students to justify explicit teaching of the generic features and the genre's social contexts. As Hyland puts it, "from a genre perspective [. . .] people don't just write, they write to accomplish different purposes in different contexts and this involves variation in the ways they use language" (19). Because "the features of a similar group of texts depend on the social context of their creation and use" and because "those features can be described in a way that relates a text to others like it and to the choices and constraints acting on text producers [. . .] every successful text will display the writer's awareness of its context and the readers who form part of that context" (21). Thus the genre approach has a relatively clear (rhetorical) axiology, and Hyland also describes the implied pedagogy: "Genre pedagogies assume that writing instruction will be more successful if students are aware of what target discourses look like" (26). Thus teachers explain both required and optional features of the genre in question, as well as any constraints on order of elements. Students and teachers are likely to examine several samples of the target genre plus their rhetorical contexts prior to students' launching their own projects.

Genre-based courses and CCS courses thus share an extensive focus on close reading of texts and on culturally determined patterns, but the goals of the reading differ. In the CCS course, the students are to read critically and cite the texts read in their own papers on related topics. In the genre course, the readings serve as discourse models from which students can generalize. Both approaches presume that texts are socially constructed and intertextual. Genre researchers often study multiple instances of a target discourse in order to discern its features; they also do classroom research that quantifies in order to determine how successfully a genre has been taught. Thus, implicitly, genre approaches to composition rest on a quasi-scientific epistemology. The only feature of a full philosophy of composition they lack is an overt perspective on process. Most discussions of actual genre-based classes, as well as current genre textbooks, indicate that writing processes are assumed to be extensive, multiple-draft activities, frequently with peer-group feedback. Invention practices, however, seem to be restricted to imitating required features of the target genre.

In a recent and elaborate analysis Anis Bawarshi, after arguing that repeated social situations give rise to genres (including the first-year writing syllabus) and that generic features guide the "invention of the writer" in both senses of that phrase, surprisingly concludes that, therefore, we should have students actually investigate and write about genres as the essence of the class. He forms "semester-long groups, each adopting a specific academic discipline," which "study the discipline through its genres" (163). "Students still write arguments, but these arguments are about writing, about the rhetorical choices writers make and how their genred positions of articulation organize and elicit these choices" (163). Bawarshi's vision of the first-year writing class is of a group of students who become discourse analysts in search of field-specific academic genres.

As a practical matter, for composition outside of ESL contexts, genre-based composition is now likely to be found either in courses devoted to argument genres or in technical writing, where the idea of learning quite specific, even discipline-specific, writing genres has been entrenched and is largely without controversy.

For first-year courses, although a number of major textbooks use a genre approach, Rise Axelrod and Charles Cooper's *St. Martin's Guide to Writing* has become the modern classic of the type. It shows a sort of transitional link between the old modes pedagogy and a contemporary genre pedagogy, as well as the shift from the C/T product orientation to extended process. Older modes texts either classified full discourses into some variety of the EDNA modes (exposition, description, narration, argument), or they were snippet anthologies in which fragments of discourses were reproduced to illustrate a given method of elaborating a single point. (The archetype here is *Prose Models*, by Harry Levin, which originally included a paragraph from *The Grapes of Wrath* to illustrate "description" and a couple of paragraphs from Orwell about military parade marching to demonstrate comparison and contrast.)

Axelrod and Cooper classify full-length discourses rather than snippets, devoting a chapter to each genre chosen; the chapters include extensive directives for students to use suggested processes of invention, arrangement, revision, and group response. Some chapters are just EDNA modes in process dress (such as a narrative writing assignment and later an argument). Others, however, come closer to being actual writing genres, such as a profile or a policy recommendation.

The more fully evolved first-year argumentation texts that coherently use a genre approach tend to accept some modern version of classical Greek and Roman stasis theory. (See Fulkerson, *Teaching the Argument in Writing*; Fahnestock and Secor, "Teaching Argument: A Theory of Types" and *A Rhetoric of Argument*.)

Stasis theory asserts that only a limited number of claim types can be "at issue" in dialectal discourse. If one can identify the type of claim, that knowledge has immediate generic implications concerning what features must, may, or must not be included, and even some traditionally expected orders of presentation. Joining this quasilogical analysis of claim plus elaboration with a specific exigency of situation and thus a specific set of intended readers further assists in defining both the requisite and the disallowed moves. So a text arguing for a claim of a specific stasis (such as evaluation), especially within a context including exigency and audience, gives rise to what can be called an argument genre.

This is reasonably well-settled ground, so there is little contemporary scholarship discussing it. But the central textbook, John Ramage, John Bean, and June Johnson's *Writing Arguments* (now into its sixth edition), continues to lead the sales of argument textbooks, and newer argument textbooks nearly all demonstrate some variation on the stasis-based genre approach. (See Faigley and Selzer; Williams and Colomb; Crusius and Channell.)

The major modern stasis types, common in the scholarship but even more evident in textbooks, include definition, generalization or interpretation, causation, evaluation, and policy recommendation. Typically, a textbook chapter presenting a stasis-based argument genre for students will include background discussion of the types of situations the genre is likely to arise in, discussion of the features—obligatory or optional—the genre involves, some invention guidelines or prompts, some revision questions, and several model texts (perhaps including unsuccessful attempts), both student-authored and professional. The pedagogy is essentially the classical one of imitation.[6]

The third variety of "procedural rhetorical" is the "discourse community" view implied by David Bartholomae in his famous article "Inventing the University," and elaborated in *Facts, Artifacts, and Counterfacts: Theory and Method for a Reading and Writing Course*, coauthored with Anthony Petrosky. Beginning students (especially those identified as "basic" writers) are presumed to be neither cognitively deficient nor linguistically impoverished. As outsiders, they simply lack experience with the "academic discourse community" and its conventions. In order to introduce them to that community, they are asked to read a sequence of difficult texts, often on a single theme, and write regularly, also about that theme. The goal is to allow students to read, write, and reason as they will be expected to do in other college courses, and thus to absorb the sorts of rhetorical moves that will help them survive in college. The discourse community approach assumes that most college writing responds to other texts, that it relies on close reading, that the student text will present an interpretive argument, that the preferred method of reasoning is citing textual evidence for one's position, while also indicating awareness of alternative positions, and that students must learn to take on vocabulary and some syntactic and organizational features of academic discourse.

Bartholomae's approach resembles CCS in being based on "reading" and using extensive materials relating to a single theme, and in giving little direct advice about either genre or process. (The student is the one who must "invent the university.") But the approach is still essentially rhetorical in that the student text will be judged on the basis of how well it meets the demands of the expected academic audience, of how well it suits the logos, pathos, and ethos accepted in the academy.

The concept of introducing students into a new discourse community has produced a good deal of controversy. At first it seemed like a good way to conceive of weak writers without challenging their literacy—they were just not "members" of the discourse community they needed to enter, and such membership was just a matter of learning a new set of literacy conventions. But then a whole series of complicated issues arose. Is there such a thing as "academic discourse"? Or would students need really to learn the conventions of the major field they intended to work within, or indeed of all the fields they had to take courses in? Doesn't the idea of "academic" discourse, with its concern for critical thinking, definition of terms, citation of evidence, and preferred reasoning patterns, give an unfair advantage to students from middle and upper classes (especially whites), who are likely to have a greater familiarity with such texts prior to college? Is it in fact an act of hegemonic imperialism to insist that students not use their own languages but master that of their professors? (Don't students, in the famous NCTE document's phrase, "have a right to their own language"?) Composition teachers who object to the entire idea of having students learn to conform their writing to the demands of the academic discourse community are thus unlikely to adopt this version of procedural rhetoric.

Conclusions and Implications

Although it's always nice to map a large and complicated region of study so that novices, at the least, can more easily navigate it, what does any of this matter? In other words, as we sometimes ask of students, "So what?" What does this look, at approximately the last fourteen years of college composition theory, show? I confess that frequently during the project I felt I was saying nothing that would not already be obvious to any scholar who has been paying attention. Nevertheless, here are my suggestions about where the discussion leaves us.

1. Composition has become much more complex with the significant growth of cultural studies, postmodernism in comp, genre theory, and discourse community theory (not to mention issues of assessment, placement, service, teacher preparation, etc.).

2. At the turn of the twenty-first century, there is a genuine controversy—*within* the field, not in the eyes of the public, the administration, or the legislature—over the goal of teaching writing in college. Are we teaching students to write in order that they should become successful insiders? Or are we teaching them to write so that they are more articulate critical outsiders? (Or even so that they "know themselves"?) The major divide is no longer expressive personal writing versus writing for readers (or whatever oppositional phrase you prefer: "academic discourse," "formal writing," "persuasion"). The major divide is instead between a postmodern, cultural studies, reading-based program, and a broadly conceived rhetoric of genres and discourse forums (Jim Porter's term [137]).

3. While a composition philosophy can be examined by asking about axiology, epistemology, pedagogy, and process, the options are neither interdetermined nor independent. Planning a composition course isn't quite like ordering from a menu, in which the main course you want is largely unconnected to what you choose for an appetizer, soup, and dessert. On the other hand, you probably would not want egg rolls as an appetizer followed by pizza and refried beans. Axiology (what you want to achieve) has implications for, but doesn't determine, processes (what moves you think students need to learn), and both are involved with pedagogy (how you will conduct class to enable the process to achieve the goal). And how you answer any of those questions will depend in part on your epistemology. It's easy to create a course that is self-contradictory and thus baffling to students. We may teach one thing, assign another, and actually expect yet a third.

4. Even though we disagree among ourselves, those outside of English—including the public who pay tuition and taxes, the

deans, presidents, and politicians who demand accountability, and the students themselves—in general hold a still different view of what we should be up to than we do.

5. There is no ultimate ground, no empirical, dialectical, or Platonic basis, for proving that one approach is proper. I do not intend this remark to ally me with postmodern antifoundationalism. I simply accept the old epistemological axiom that you cannot derive an "ought" from an "is."

6. Yet if a university or a department is serious about seeing writing courses as constituting a "program" or some portion of a larger scheme of "general education," some degree of commonality is likely to be required.

7. Preparing our graduate students in composition for the discourse community they must enter to succeed as composition professors is becoming increasingly difficult. It is natural to imitate our literary colleagues and produce PhD-holders created in our own image(s). "If you got your degree at South Florida, then you are post-everything. University of Pittsburgh grads are into cultural studies. Purdue and Arizona State products know rhetorical traditions." But limiting students to understanding one dominant perspective disadvantages them. Programs will have to make serious choices and perhaps prepare students as utility players able to fit into several positions, rather than teach them the field's "best practices." A new tenure-track PhD may have been well prepared in teaching composition for her alma mater using Approach A, yet be required to shift smoothly to Approach X in her new home.

If you accept my analysis, then no matter which of my four questions you pose, composition studies is a less unified field than it was a decade ago. We differ about what our courses are supposed to achieve, about how effective writing is best produced, about what an effective classroom looks like, and about what it means to make knowledge. If the Tate, Rupiper, and Schick volume reflects our current standing as a field, the various "sociocultural pedagogies" have become the center. Process has been deemphasized, although each axiology accommodates some version of it. Classroom practices are in dispute, but tending toward an emphasis on reading. If, however, the WPA Statement accurately reflects the views of program directors, then perhaps procedural rhetoric is dominant in reality though not in publications. But the actual question of what is good writing is more problematic than ever. Bob Broad, in *What We Really Value*, says that every department should spend at least a semester using a complex ethnographic procedure that leads to Dynamic Criteria Mapping in order to discover the multitude of "real" textual features it values, which can then be shared with students.

In *The Making of Knowledge in Composition*, Steve North asserted that "composition faces a peculiar methodological paradox: its communities cannot get along well enough to live with one another, and yet they seem unlikely to survive [. . .] without one another" (369). If you think that is a dangerous situation, as North and I do, then early in the twentieth-first century, composition studies is in for a bumpy ride. Maybe Gary Olson was not just engaging in hyperbole when he told *Chronicle of Higher Education* writer Scott McLemee that "the field of composition studies is on the verge of 'what undoubtedly will come to be known as "the new theory wars"'" (A17).

Notes

1. The research leading to this paper was pursued with the help of a grant from the Texas A&M–Commerce Organized Research Committee during the spring of 2003. I thank the committee for its support.

2. There are also still plenty of current-traditionalist teachers. Their views don't appear in publications, but signs of their existence show up in anecdotes about papers being failed for comma errors, and in the continued sales of handbooks and workbooks. My best proof rests on studies of commenting practices carried out by several doctoral students in our program, using Richard Straub and Ron Lunsford's analytical model. They have collected marked papers from teachers in Texas, Oklahoma, and Arkansas, and used the teacher responses to infer teachers' current-traditional values. In his most recent book, Straub in fact found the same thing. But this is probably no surprise. Current-traditional formalists you shall have always with you.

3. My argument will necessarily be based on indirect evidence: published scholarship, textbooks, a few organizational documents, and personal discussions. There is no available and current synthetic account of what goes on in college writing classrooms in the United States: the syllabi, writing assignments, readings, classroom procedures. Most observers presume that a disjunct exists between published theory and daily practice, with the practice being much less philosophically consistent than the scholarship. Although we have many ethnographic accounts of separate classrooms, we desperately need a comprehensive empirical study of what actually goes on nationwide.

4. As in the earlier volume, the final chapters are not so much "pedagogies" as considerations of important related issues: WAC and basic writing are in both; writing center pedagogy now replaces "tutorials"; and technology has become important enough to get a chapter of its own now, as does service-learning, whose philosophical basis is quite unclear.

5. I have deliberately chosen to omit from the list of perspectives several topics treated in both the Tate, Rupiper, and Schick and the Donovan and McClellan volumes: writing across the curriculum and basic writing, as well as service-learning and computers and composition. By leaving these topics out of my heuristic grid, I do not mean to imply they are unimportant. But I do not see them as constituting "approaches" to composition.

6. A vivid contrast between a CCS approach and a rhetorical (genre) approach results from looking at the work of John Trimbur. Diana George and he edited what is probably the first anthology for cultural studies, *Reading Culture*, now in its fifth edition (2004). The book has an introductory procedural chapter, "Reading the News," followed by thematic chapters pulling together materials on topics such as "Generations," "Schooling," and "Work." So it is no surprise that Tate, Rupiper, and Schick tapped the same two authors to write on cultural studies. In addition, Trimbur gets credit for the earliest use of the term "post-process" in print for his multiple review "Taking the Social Turn: Teaching Writing Post-Process." Trimbur also coedited *The Politics of Writing Instruction: Postsecondary* (1991) with Richard Bullock, and wrote "Cultural Studies and the Teaching of Writing" (1988). He also wrote one of the critical responses to Hairston, in fact. Based on such publications, one would presume Trimbur belongs to the "camp" of scholars who consistently support postmodern and post-process CCS approaches to composition. His scholarly credentials for such a role are impeccable.

Yet Trimbur has also questioned some CCS tenets: "I worry that post-modernism has based its authority on a kind of intellectual blackmail that makes it difficult to argue against the current climate of radical disbelief without sounding hopelessly naïve, unfashionable, and incipiently totalitarian" ("Composition Studies: Postmodern or Popular" 131). He further pushed to separate cultural studies from postmodernism, saying, "the notion of the popular revises the severe textualism of postmodernism." And he criticized postmodernists for commonly assuming that "the effective meanings of social texts can be deciphered from the constitutive surfaces of popular entertainment and mass-mediated culture by acts of critical reading" (127). He favorably cited Dave Morley saying, "[T]he meaning produced by the encounter of text and subject cannot be read off straight from its 'textual characteristics' or discursive strategies" (128).

In ironic contrast, Trimbur also wrote a more recent successful textbook, *The Call to Write* (1999 and 2002), which joins extensive treatments of writing as process with a series of chapters presenting argument genres, including chapters on the evaluative review, the recommendation proposal, and the report, plus the traditional library research project. He says the book treats "eight of the most familiar genres" (1st ed. 115), and sums up his rationale as follows: "Studying and experimenting with the eight genres can help you expand your repertoire of writing strategies so that you can respond flexibly and creatively to a range of situations that call on you to write" (115). The book was advertised as the first rhetoric written to conform to the composition outcomes from the WPA guidelines. The second edition actually reprints the guidelines in a chapter on "public documents" (203–05).

The chapters contain elaborate discussions of the "call" (exigency) that might produce a given genre, plus suggestions for audience analysis, process materials, and both student and professional example texts. There are, in addition, chapters on critical reading, on collaboration, and on writing essay tests. This book could scarcely be a greater contrast to *Reading Culture*, which gives students writing tasks such as the following:

> Read Barbara Kantrowitz and Keith Naughton's entire article in the November 12, 2001 *Newsweek*. Jot down your own account of what

happened in your school or community immediately following 9/11. But don't stop there. Step back and ask, from your own perspective several years later, what the meaning of those events is. Write an essay that both describes what happened around 9/11 and what you now see as its meaning. (5th edition 81)

Note that neither genre nor audience is indicated, and no process advice given (here or anywhere in the book), other than "read" and "write."

Works Cited

Alcorn, Marshall W., Jr. *Changing the Subject: Discourse and the Constructions of Desire*. Carbondale: Southern Illinois UP, 2002.

Anderson, Charles M., and Marian M. MacCurdy, eds. *Writing and Healing: Toward an Informed Practice*. Urbana, IL: NCTE, 2000.

Annas, Pam. "Style as Politics: A Feminist Approach to the Teaching of Writing." *College English* 47 (1985): 360–71.

Axelrod, Rise B., and Charles R. Cooper. *The St. Martin's Guide to Writing*. 4th ed. New York: St. Martin's, 1994.

Bakhtin, M. M. "The Problem of Speech Genres." *Speech Genres and Other Late Essays*. Ed. Caryl Emerson and Michael Holquist. Trans. Vern W. McGee. Austin: U of Texas P, 1986. 60–102.

Barnett, Timothy. *Teaching Argument in the Composition Course: Background Readings*. Boston: Bedford, 2002.

Bartholomae, Donald. "Inventing the University." *When a Writer Can't Write: Studies in Writer's Block and Other Composing Process Problems*. Ed. Mike Rose. New York: Guilford, 1985.

Bartholomae, Donald, and Anthony Petrosky. *Facts, Artifacts, and Counterfacts: Theory and Method for a Reading and Writing Course*. Upper Montclair, NJ: Boynton, 1986.

Bawarshi, Anis. *Genre and the Invention of the Writer: Reconsidering the Place of Invention in Composition*. Logan: Utah State UP, 2003.

Berkenkotter, Carol, and Thomas N. Huckin, eds. *Genre Knowledge in Disciplinary Communication: Cognition/Culture/Power*. Hillsdale, NJ: Erlbaum, 1995.

Berlin, James. "Composition and Cultural Studies." *Composition and Resistance*. Ed. C. Mark Hurlbert and Michael Blitz. Portsmouth, NH: Boynton, 1991. 47–55.

———. "Contemporary Composition: The Major Pedagogical Theories." *College English* 44 (Dec. 1982): 765–77.

Berlin, James, and Michael Vivion, eds. *Cultural Studies in the English Classroom*. Portsmouth, NH: Boynton, 1992.

Berman, Jeffrey. *Risky Writing: Self-Disclosure and Self-Transformation in the Classroom*. Amherst: U of Massachusetts P, 2002.

Bishop, Wendy, and Hans Ostrom, eds. *Genre and Writing: Issues, Arguments, Alternatives*. Portsmouth, NH: Heinemann, 1997.

Bizzell, Patricia, and Bruce Herzberg. *Negotiating Difference: Cultural Case Studies for Composition*. Boston: Bedford, 1996.

Brand, Alice Glarden, and Richard L. Graves, eds. *Presence of Mind: Writing and the Domain beyond the Cognitive*. Portsmouth, NH: Boynton, 1994.

Broad, Bob. *What We Really Value: Beyond Rubrics in Teaching and Assessing Writing*. Logan: Utah State UP, 2003.

Bullock, Richard, and John Trimbur, eds. *The Politics of Writing Instruction: Postsecondary*. Portsmouth, NH: Boynton, 1991.

Burnham, Christopher. "Expressive Pedagogy: Practice/Theory. Theory/Practice." Tate, Rupiper, and Schick 19–35.

Campbell, Karlyn Kohrs, and Kathleen Hall Jamieson. "Form and Genre in Rhetorical Criticism: An Introduction." *Form and Genre: Shaping Rhetorical Action*. Ed. Karlyn Kohrs Campbell and Kathleen Hall Jamieson. Falls Church, VA: Speech Communication Assn., 1977. 9–32.

Clark, Irene. *The Genre of Argument*. Fort Worth: Harcourt, 1998.

Colombo, Gary, Robert Cullen, and Bonnie Lisle, eds. *Rereading America: Cultural Contexts for Critical Thinking and Writing*. 2nd ed. New York: Bedford, 1992.

Connors, Robert. "The Rise and Fall of the Modes of Discourse." *CCC* 32 (Dec. 1981): 444–63.

Crusius, Timothy W., and Carolyn Channell. *The Aims of Argument*. 4th ed. Boston: McGraw, 2003.

Donovan, Timothy R., and Ben W. McClelland, eds. *Eight Approaches to Teaching Composition*. Urbana, IL: NCTE, 1980.

Durst, Russel K. *Collision Course: Conflict, Negotiation, and Learning in College Composition*. Urbana, IL: NCTE, 1999.

Emig, Janet. *The Composing Processes of Twelfth Graders*. Urbana, IL: NCTE, 1971.

Emmel, Barbara, Paula C. Resch, and Deborah S. Tenney, eds. *Argument Revisited, Argument Redefined: Negotiating Meaning in the Composition Classroom*. Thousand Oaks, CA: Sage, 1996.

Fahnestock, Jeanne, and Marie Secor. *A Rhetoric of Argument*. 2nd ed. New York: McGraw, 1990.

———. "Teaching Argument: A Theory of Types." *CCC* 34 (Feb. 1983): 20–30.

Faigley, Lester. "Competing Theories of Process: A Critique and a Proposal." *College English* 48 (Oct. 1986): 527–42.

Faigley, Lester, and Jack Selzer. *Good Reasons*. 2nd ed. New York: Addison, 2003.

Fitts, Karen, and Alan W. France, eds. *Left Margins: Cultural Studies and Composition Pedagogy*. Albany: SUNY P, 1995.

Flower, Linda, and John R. Hayes. "A Cognitive Process Theory of Writing." *CCC* 32 (Dec. 1981): 365–87.

Foehr, Regina Paxton, and Susan A. Schiller, eds. *The Spiritual Side of Writing: Releasing the Learner's Whole Potential*. Portsmouth, NH: Boynton, 1997.

Foss, Sonya. *Rhetorical Criticism: Exploration and Practice*. Prospect Heights, IL: Waveland, 1989.

Freedman, Aviva, and Peter Medway, eds. *Learning and Teaching Genre*. Portsmouth, NH: Boynton, 1994.

Fulkerson, Richard. "Composition in the Eighties." *CCC* 41.4 (Dec. 1990): 409–29.

———. "*Newsweek* 'My Turn' Columns and the Concept of Rhetorical Genre: A Preliminary Study." *Defining the New Rhetorics*. Ed. Theresa Enos and Stuart Brown. Sage Series in Written Communication 7. Newbury Park, CA: Sage, 1993. 227–43.

———. "Of Pre- and Post-Process: Reviews and Ruminations." *Composition Studies* 29.2 (Fall 2001): 93–119.

———. *Teaching the Argument in Writing.* Urbana, IL: NCTE, 1996.

———. "Technical Logic, Comp-Logic, and the Teaching of Writing." *CCC* 39 (Dec. 1988): 436–52.

George, Ann. "Critical Pedagogy: Dreaming of Democracy." Tate, Rupiper, and Schick 92–112.

George, Diana, and John Trimbur. *Reading Culture.* 5th ed. New York: Pearson, 2004.

Graff, Gerald. *Clueless in Academe: How Schooling Obscures the Life of the Mind.* New Haven: Yale UP, 2003.

Greenbaum, Andrea. *Emancipatory Movements in Composition: The Rhetoric of Possibility.* Albany: SUNY P, 2002.

Hairston, Maxine. "Diversity, Ideology, and Teaching Writing." *CCC* 43 (May 1992): 179–93.

Heilker, Paul. *The Essay: Theory and Pedagogy for an Active Form.* Urbana, IL: NCTE, 1996.

Heimer, Carrie. "Forty-Eight Eyeballs." *What to Expect When You're Expected to Teach.* Ed. Anne Bramblett and Alison Knoblauch. Portsmouth, NH: Boynton, 2002. 11–14.

Hunt, Douglas. *Misunderstanding the Assignment: Teenage Students, College Writing, and the Pains of Growth.* Portsmouth, NH: Boynton, 2002.

Hurlbert, C. Mark, and Michael Blitz. *Composition and Resistance.* Portsmouth, NH: Boynton, 1991.

Hyland, Ken. "Genre-Based Pedagogies: A Social Response to Process." *Journal of Second Language Writing* 12 (2003): 17–29.

Jolliffe, David, Michael Keene, Mary Trachsel, and Ralph Voss, eds. *Against the Grain: A Volume in Honor of Maxine Hairston.* Cresskill, NJ: Hampton, 2002.

Kent, Thomas. "Introduction." *Post-Process Theory: Beyond the Writing Process Paradigm.* Ed. Thomas Kent. Carbondale: Southern Illinois UP, 1999.

Levin, Harry. *Prose Models: An Inductive Approach to Writing.* New York: Harcourt, 1964.

Lunsford, Andrea A., and John Ruszkiewicz. *Everything's an Argument.* Boston: Bedford, 1999.

McLemee, Scott. "Deconstructing Composition: The 'New Theory Wars' Break Out in an Unlikely Discipline." *Chronicle of Higher Education* 21 Mar. 2003. A16–A17.

Miller, Carolyn R. "Genre as Social Action." *Quarterly Journal of Speech* 70 (May 1984): 151–67.

Murray, Don. "Writing as Process: How Writing Finds Its Own Meaning." Donovan and McClelland 3–20.

North, Stephen M. *The Making of Knowledge in Composition: Portrait of an Emerging Field.* Upper Montclair, NJ: Boynton, 1987.

Paley, Karen Surman. *I-Writing: The Politics and Practice of Teaching First-Person Writing.* Carbondale: Southern Illinois UP, 2001.

Perl, Sondra. "Writing Process: A Shining Moment." *Landmark Essays on Writing Process.* Ed. Sondra Perl. Davis, CA: Hermagoras, 1994. xi–xx.

Porter, Jim. *Audience and Rhetoric.* Englewood Cliffs, NJ: Prentice, 1992.

Ramage, John, John Bean, and June Johnson. *Writing Arguments.* 6th ed. New York: Pearson, 2004.

Rottenberg, Annette T. *Elements of Argument.* 6th ed. Boston: Bedford, 2000.

Shor, Ira. *Empowering Education: Critical Teaching for Social Change.* Chicago: U of Chicago P, 1987.

Sommers, Nancy. "Revision Strategies of Student Writers and Experienced Adult Writers." *CCC* 31 (Dec. 1980): 378–88.

Spellmeyer, Kurt. *Common Ground: Dialogue, Understanding and the Teaching of Composition.* Englewood Cliffs, NJ: Prentice, 1993.

Straub, Richard. *The Practice of Response: Strategies for Commenting on Student Writing.* Cresskill, NJ: Hampton, 2000.

Straub, Richard, and Ronald Lunsford. *Twelve Readers Reading: Responding to College Student Writing.* Cresskill, NJ: Hampton, 1995.

"Students' Right to Their Own Language." Spec. issue of *CCC* 25 (Fall 1974).

Tate, Gary. "Empty Pedagogical Spaces and Silent Students." Fitts and France 269–73.

Tate, Gary, Amy Rupiper, and Kurt Schick, eds. *A Guide to Composition Pedagogies.* New York: Oxford, 2001.

Tobin, Lad. "Process Pedagogy." Tate, Rupiper, and Schick 1–18.

Trimbur, John. *The Call to Write.* 1st and 2nd eds. New York: Longman, 1999, 2002.

———. "Composition Studies: Postmodern or Popular." *Into the Field: Sites of Composition Studies.* Ed. Anne Ruggles Gere. New York: MLA, 1993. 117–32.

———. "Taking the Social Turn: Teaching Writing Post-Process." *CCC* 45.1 (1994): 108–18.

Trimbur, John, and Diana George. "Cultural Studies and Composition." Tate, Rupiper, and Schick 71–92.

Trimbur, John, et al. "Reply to Maxine Hairston: Diversity, Ideology, and Teaching Writing." *CCC* 44.2 (1993): 248–55.

Williams, Joseph M., and Gregory G. Colomb. *The Craft of Argument* 2nd ed. New York: Addison, 2003.

"WPA Outcomes Statement for First-Year Composition." *WPA: Writing Program Administration* 23.1/2 (Fall/Winter 1999): 59–66.

Young, Richard. "Paradigms and Problems: Needed Research in Rhetorical Invention." *Research on Composing: Points of Departure.* Ed. Charles R. Cooper and Lee Odell. Urbana, IL: NCTE, 1978. 29–47.

Two-Year College Teachers as Knowledge Makers

Mark Reynolds

After providing a brief history of two-year colleges and a discussion of faculty roles, Mark Reynolds's essay examines the many ways two-year faculty members have found to carry on research and scholarly activities despite considerable obstacles. In addition to traditional scholarship and research through accepted avenues, two-year college teacher-scholars have authored a number of the profession's most widely used and popular textbooks. Reynolds concludes his essay with suggestions for many areas where two-year college professionals can contribute valuable knowledge to the discipline and to the academy at large. The Two-Year College English Association continues to honor Reynolds's long record of promoting teacher-scholarship through the annual Mark Reynolds Award for Best Article in Teaching English in the Two-Year College.

Introduction

Because of the nature and history of two-year institutions, their faculty did not routinely envision themselves as knowledge makers within the discipline of English studies. Two-year colleges have always concentrated on only the first two years of undergraduate education. In English, those years focus on developing the fundamentals of academic writing and reading, work usually relegated to graduate students in universities and often deemed by the academy as of lesser importance. In addition, two-year-college teachers have not seen themselves as specialists, researchers, or scholars in the classic sense. Because they teach nonspecialized courses at the introductory level of the discipline, their expertise is most often judged elementary or surface level, suitable for the nonspecialist, the generalist, or the less highly degreed. Many in the academy have also considered the two-year teacher's work as rudimentary rather than dealing with theory, abstract ideas, or formal research. Two-year-college teachers historically have been most concerned with pedagogy and praxis, with translating the complex into the simple for students, instead of discovering knowledge, defining new territory, or communicating complex ideas to peers.

Faculty members in the vast majority of two-year colleges have not had to conduct research or publish to get or keep a job. One exception has been faculty on two-year branch campuses of major state universities in states such as Ohio and Pennsylvania, where faculty have been held to the same tenure and promotion requirements as those on the

---

From *The Profession of English in the Two-Year College*, edited by Mark Reynolds and Sylvia Holladay-Hicks. Boynton/Cook, 2005, pp. 1-15.

universities' main campuses. The majority of two-year faculty members, however, unlike their university colleagues, were hired to teach, not to publish or create disciplinary scholarship. Two-year-college faculty members also work in institutions that admit any and all with a high school diploma or its equivalent. Thus, these open-door institutions have often been viewed erroneously as having no standards. They are different, too, from much of higher education because comprehensive community colleges and two-year technical colleges place great emphasis on preparing students for the world of work after only a year or two of attendance. Most of the academy has not been able to relate to such utilitarian purposes, to training in skills such as automotive mechanics, computer drafting, nursing, cosmetology, air conditioning and refrigeration, welding, masonry, home health aid, postal management, and many other fields of employment.

In these institutions, some designated "junior," where the majority has had no system of professional or academic rank, faculty members have been commonly labeled "instructors." A concentrated effort throughout their history to avoid rank has resulted both from the strong emphasis placed on teaching and from the democratic spirit implicit throughout the two-year college's history and purpose for existing. As a result, those outside the institutions, especially those in universities, have tended to view two-year-college faculty merely as teachers, seldom as scholars or researchers. However, as Elizabeth Nist and Helon Raines have pointed out,

> Reasons exist for the predominance of two-year colleges naming all faculty "instructor," none of which has to do with value, ability, or education. Yet, "instructor" in university language designates the bottom of the academic hierarchy and connotes fewer degrees, less experience and/or ability, and minimal, if any scholarship or publication. (65)

For all of these reasons, then, the academy has seldom judged the two-year-college faculty member capable of making significant contributions to knowledge. Nor has it paid much attention to their efforts, judging them unworthy or insignificant. In fact, a national survey of faculty, conducted by The Carnegie Foundation for the Advancement of Teaching in 1997, dispels several stereotypes about community college faculty, including the one that they do not engage in or appreciate scholarly research. According to that report,

> The average difference in the amount of time that community college faculty and those of baccalaureate institutions spend each week performing research or comparable scholarly activities is only 2.3 hours. In addition, almost 80 percent of community college faculty engage in consulting or professional service. ("Casting" 45)

History and Purposes

As indicated, much of the faculty role within two-year colleges has resulted from these institutions' historical origins and specialized functions. The most significant factor in their founding came from the efforts of some prominent university presidents to separate the first two years of college education from the last two. As early as the 1850s, several university presidents were calling for new institutions to take on the role of general education. Henry Tappan, president of the University of Michigan, William Rainey Harper, president of the University of Chicago, David Starr Jordan, president of Stanford University, and Alexis Lange, dean of the School of Education at the University of California, are usually given credit for encouraging such a split in the first decade of the twentieth century. Jordan, in particular, wanted to split the first two college years from the rest of the university in order to create a university more akin to its European ancestors, an elite institution focused on research and scholarship. He is credited with initiating the terms "junior" and "senior" colleges to refer to the two divisions. In 1901, two additional years were added to the high school in Joliet, Illinois, creating what has traditionally been labeled as the nation's first junior college (Cohen and Brawer 6–13).

Paralleling the division of universities into upper and lower strata, initiatives began in many separate localities in the country to create educational institutions of higher learning that responded to particular local needs and provided educational opportunities beyond high school to the less affluent. This response to the local communities in which they are located has been a hallmark of two-year colleges from their beginnings. Often, this response has been in the form of workforce preparation, preparing the local population as workers for a particular business or industry in the community. At other times, this function has meant addressing a significant area population with unique needs, especially by offering English as a Second Language programs to large immigrant populations. Community colleges in New York City, Chicago, Miami, and in parts of Texas and California offer examples of the latter. Responding to their local communities has always meant, as well, providing a variety of enrichment and leisure-time activities to area citizens (see Griffith and Connor for other descriptions of local response).

Since their founding in the early 1900s, two-year colleges have always sought to fill specific needs in American higher education beyond the traditional high school years. As a result, two-year institutions occupy an unusual position, lodged between the high school and the university, often seeming to belong to neither, and yet often integrally tied to both even though distinctly unlike either. As a result, these institutions have had to forge their own identity within their local environments, and they consider responses to local needs an important function.

Faculty have always been encouraged and, in some cases expected, to be involved in their communities. Colleges have traditionally tailored activities specifically to meet the needs of local constituencies, whether in the form of particular courses, workforce training, or cultural and enrichment programs. In English departments, such activities may have taken the form of computerized writing courses designed for a local industry, courses in technical or business writing, creative writing workshops at a community center, life writing courses at a retirement center, a discussion by a faculty member of Ebonics at a local civic club, or a topic such as "religion and literature" for a local religious group.

As a result of their open admissions policies, a major purpose of two-year colleges has been to provide training in basic skills to the large number of area students who enroll with deficiencies in language and mathematical skills. English departments have, therefore, created extensive programs of basic skills training—courses in remedial or developmental or basic writing and reading. In many colleges, these programs have several levels and include courses in study skills, orientation to college, library use, and either the incorporation of ESL courses within a basic skills program or the development of a separate ESL program, depending on local needs. In such programs, English teachers might work closely with counselors, learning skills specialists, librarians, speech teachers, specialists in learning disabilities, or occupational therapists.

According to Glen Gabert, it is the open admissions policy that "has been one of the most misunderstood characteristics of community colleges and has led to charges that they are second-rate institutions with low standards. It is more accurate to say that community colleges admit anyone who demonstrates reasonable potential for success in the program to which they seek admission" (15). Moreover, many separate programs, such as nursing, within institutions do have set admission requirements.

It has mainly been this basic skills function, often located within English departments on two-year campuses, with its heavy remedial emphasis, that has caused the academy to view two-year colleges as something less than collegiate, as more allied to the high school than the university, attending to a population that is not and never will be "college material." The remedial and vocational functions together cause some to consider two-year colleges both inappropriate and unworthy of being included within the higher education spectrum.

History shows, however, that the two-year college is the single most important element in what has been called the democratization of American higher education. That fact is self-evident when one observes the dramatic increase in the numbers of these institutions from the 1960s into the 1990s. At least one two-year college is located in every congressional district. Currently, over 1,400 public and private two-year colleges enroll over two million students full-time and an additional 3.6 million students part-time (*The ERIC Review* 25). Such numbers are impressive, considering the ever-increasing costs of higher education. Low costs alone have continued to attract students who, in the past, would only have attended a four-year college or university. According to statistics, approximately fifty percent of all students begin their higher education in two-year colleges (Doucette and Roueche 1). However, only about one-fifth of those continue their education by enrolling in the upper levels of colleges or universities.

Those who do, nevertheless, constitute a significant number, a number that will continue to increase with the rising costs of higher education. These are the students who fulfill the transfer mission of two-year colleges, completing the first two years of a four-year undergraduate education, equivalent to the first two years at most four-year colleges and universities. Significantly, studies consistently show that those transferring from two-year colleges to four-year colleges perform as well as or better than students who begin their work at the senior institution (see Gaskins, Holt, and Roeger).

It is also in fulfilling the transfer function that two-year colleges have been most like four-year colleges and universities. Two-year institutions offer both regular and advanced college composition, creative writing, and technical writing, a great variety of literature courses from traditional introductory courses to surveys of British and American literature, world literature, multicultural literature, and more specialized courses in women's literature, mystery, science fiction, and Native American and African American literature. In increasing numbers since their inception, two-year colleges have developed honors programs, and offer special honors courses to excellent students capable of high levels of performance in any educational setting.

Faculty as Knowledge Makers

Because their primary concern has been teaching, two-year-college faculty members belong to that large body of practitioners who have contributed to what Stephen North has called lore, the knowledge that emanates from classrooms across the country and from teacher practice, much of which never gets written down but which circulates widely through practice and talk and, consequently, becomes knowledge.

Two-year-college faculty members traditionally have heavy teaching loads, three to six classes each term, and large numbers of students. Most of their teaching centers on composition and requires time-consuming paper reading. Such heavy workloads in and of themselves are major reasons so few two-year-college teachers have been active knowledge makers who have produced published accounts of their knowledge either through journal articles or book-length studies. Because of such workloads, many teachers have not felt connected to their discipline in formal ways. They cannot relate to the faculty who have the time, institutional support, and financial support for research, publication, or conference attendance and presentations. For years, many felt that what got published in the discipline's journals had little relevance to their daily work in the classroom.

However, with the establishment of the journals *Teaching English in the Two-Year College* (1974) and the *Journal of Basic Writing* (1978), two-year-college practitioners had places that welcomed their academic writing and knowledge making. These journals, in particular, have allowed two-year-college teachers to give reports of their work and have encouraged them to provide accounts of classroom practice. Indeed, with the establishment of a journal particularly for them, two-year-college English teachers have been much more prolific in their publishing efforts. Major journals in the discipline such as *College English* and *College Composition and Communication* have routinely published the work of two-year-college teachers and have kept one or more on their editorial boards and a number among their manuscript reviewers. These actions have encouraged and recognized the work of two-year-college English teachers and also provided incentives for their participation in the discipline's conversations.

Many two-year teachers have also produced textbooks that are repositories of their knowledge, many of them pioneering works and among the most widely used college texts. Pickett, Laster, and Staples' technical writing textbook, which was the first on this subject at the introductory college level, is one of them. The first technical writing textbook by two-year-college teachers for two-year-college students, it is now in its eighth edition. (See Pickett, "A Quarter Century," for an account of the early travails two-year-college teachers faced getting textbooks published.) Audrey Roth's research manual, also in its eighth edition, grew from the author's experiences at Miami-Dade Community College and has been one of the most widely used guides at both two- and four-year institutions for introducing research methodology to beginning college students. The textbook by Elizabeth and Gregory Cowan, *Writing* (Wiley 1980), was one of the first and, perhaps, the most successful to incorporate the pedagogy of the process approach to writing. Both authors' experiences grew from their long years of teaching in two-year colleges. John Langan has had great success with his composition textbooks, especially those for basic writing and developmental reading. The composition texts and handbooks of Lynn Troyka and Diana Hacker have been among the most widely used in the nation's two- and four-year institutions. Hundreds of other two-year-college teachers have also written successful textbooks that convey their expertise on a variety of subjects. All of these texts are full of practitioner's lore, of knowledge useful to teachers. They represent the foundation of what is being taught throughout the first two years of college writing and reading in all institutions.

Another outlet for two-year teacher knowledge has been professional conferences. In 1965, the Conference on College Composition and Communication of the National Council of Teachers of English established seven regional conferences on English in the two-year college. Since that time, most of these regional conferences have conducted major professional meetings where two-year-college faculty have gathered to hear presentations about their teaching and professional concerns. The meetings have attracted nationally known scholars and such literary figures as Eudora Welty and James Dickey. The large numbers of attendees over the years and the longstanding success of these annual meetings attest to their value to two-year-college teachers and others. . . . These meetings have been major sites for teachers to pass on their knowledge. However, because the proceedings have not routinely been published, such knowledge too often has taken the form of North's lore.

Two-year-college teachers have also been active in all the major national professional organizations, giving papers at their meetings, serving on their committees, and often publishing in their journals. Their numbers have not been great, and their efforts most often have been individual ones; nonetheless, two-year-college participation has been long, regular, and constant, if not widespread, in NCTE, CCCC, MLA, ADE, CEA, the regional MLAs, and numerous regional and state professional organizations. This participation is even more remarkable when one remembers that many of these instructors work in institutions where research, scholarship, publishing, indeed knowledge making itself, is not valued. Two-year-college instructors have often engaged in these activities at their own expense and without institutional rewards. They do so for their personal intellectual stimulation and satisfaction, because they are serious scholars and researchers, and because they are motivated to contribute to the discipline's knowledge from their unique perspective. With the establishment of the Two-Year College English Association (TYCA) within the National Council of Teachers of English in 1996, and the Committee on Community Colleges within the Modern Language Association in 1997, opportunity for professional growth and development for two-year-college English faculty has expanded significantly.

Kinds of Knowledge Two-Year-College Teachers Make

Two-year-college teachers are required in most institutions to have only a master's degree, although many do have Ph.D.s, D.A.s, and Ed.D.s. While most faculty members do not view themselves as specialists in a narrow field within the discipline, they do consider themselves experts in the teaching of the first two college years of their discipline and in the craft of teaching itself. They more often consider themselves generalists, adaptable to students and settings and able to take complex materials and discover ways to communicate them effectively to varied audiences. It is in this teaching expertise that the academy might well learn most from two-year-college teachers. The majority long ago eschewed the lecture as the primary means of conveying material. They have long been knowledgeable about collaborative learning and the social construction of meaning. They long ago embraced the use of media in teaching, and they have been pioneers in the use of technology in the classroom (see Reynolds "Twenty-Five Years"; and *Teaching English in the Two-Year College* Special Issue).

They have also been pioneers in the development of writing centers, locales where they have addressed the needs not just of underprepared students, but also of students in all disciplines across their institutions. Howard Tinberg has published a monograph on the serious work that goes on in two-year-college writing centers. He makes a strong case that two-year-college faculty are experts in the dissemination of knowledge, more than in knowledge itself. His study demonstrates the strong commitment of a group of cross-disciplinary faculty to the teaching of writing to diverse students. Tinberg's work is an excellent example of the kinds of knowledge making two-year-college faculty have contributed and are capable of contributing to the discipline. Other examples of significant scholarly endeavors over the years by two-year English faculty include Paul Oehler's discography of American literature set to music, Jane Maher's biography of Mina Shaughnessy, Randy Cross' rescuing of T. S. Stribling's editions of long out-of-print Southern novels, and Karen Castelluci Cox's development of story cycle theory.

Because most two-year-college English departments are quite small, there has always been a good deal of cross-disciplinary interaction among the disciplines on two-year campuses, much more so than one usually finds at a university. It is not at all uncommon for faculty in English to combine for interdisciplinary work with faculty from mathematics, psychology, history, nursing, even automotive mechanics. Such work may take the form of team-teaching, of creating special courses for local businesses or industries, of collaboration for work with honors students, of campus committee work, writing center tutorials, or study skills labs. It is not uncommon for such faculty to meet and work together daily in environments that are integrated institutionally, providing a much more holistic and cohesive faculty than found on most four-year campuses. At some colleges, Santa Fe Community College in Gainesville, Florida, for example, faculty offices have not been organized by departments, but are interspersed campus-wide so that an English faculty member's office may be next door to a computer instructor's or a cosmetology instructor's. Such an arrangement makes for a more cohesive and integrated faculty community, one that encourages interdisciplinary solutions to campus problems and especially student learning.

It is probably in the teaching of nontraditional students that two-year-college teachers have produced the most valuable knowledge. Faculty members confront students who are first-generation college students for the most part—commuters, holders of part- and full-time jobs, with an average age of twenty-nine, and who view education often as a stop-in and stop-out event to be managed when their lives can accommodate a course or two: ". . . their lives zig and zag. They leave school to take a job or have a baby or reorganize their lives; they come back, perhaps with a different goal, a different attitude, once, twice, three times" (Griffith and Connor 20). Working with such students takes special teachers, special means, dedication, and determination. And yet, as Griffith and Connor demonstrate, many such students succeed only because of two-year colleges. Anne Ruggles Gere, Mike Rose, Smokey Wilson, and others have attested to the importance of community colleges in the lives of such students. Without them, millions of students would never succeed, and it is the two-year-college system within higher education that Kurt Spellmeyer has praised for proving "so successful that it now even seems prosaic" (39).

In addition to dealing with nontraditional students, two-year-college teachers have been pioneers in the teaching of writing and reading to the underprepared student. Smokey Wilson, Peter Dow Adams, John Langan, Lynn Troyka, Audrey Roth, Jane Peterson, and others are among the two-year-college teachers who have devoted their lives to finding the most effective methods of teaching basic language skills to academically unprepared students. Their knowledge exists in numerous professional articles and in textbooks they have prepared and class tested with thousands of students. Wilson has been particularly active in interrogating the nontraditional student and those needing special help with basic skills. Her scholarship, discussed in a number of published sources, is a model for others who would like to learn how to teach these students.

Most two-year-college teachers knew about diversity and multicultural students long before it became fashionable to discuss them. It may well be in the teaching of diverse students that two-year-college knowledge making will prove most valuable to future educators. ESL programs have been established in community colleges in large urban areas for many years. The teaching of reading, writing, and language skills to non-native speakers has been a priority in many two-year colleges. The two-year college has been a major factor in the assimilation of thousands of immigrants into the American mainstream. Peter Dow Adams, Mike Anzaldúa, Alan Meyers, and Loretta Kasper have been among those involved with knowledge making in ESL in two-year colleges. It is two-year-college teachers who most often help students navigate the border crossings necessary to move not just across poverty or social class or cultural boundaries, but also across language barriers of all kinds.

Another area in which two-year-college teachers have been knowledge makers is in the preparation of students for the world of work. This area of education is the one most alien to the academy. Many on the two-year campus have long been comfortable talking about job application letters, resume preparation, on-the-job writing, technical writing, lab reports, and other areas of applied writing because their students have been greatly concerned with such writing. Because many students en-roll in one- or two-year technical programs that lead to employment after their course work, they need specialized writing courses related to their job training. This is true of nursing students, computer drafting students, office administration students, and others. English faculty often teach specialized writing courses for these students or at least assist the students with course assignments in writing centers.

Not only has the concern been with what current students might need, but two-year colleges have also often been called on to meet the needs of local businesses or industries that have a specific and immedi-ate need for employee training. That training might be in the form of routine business letters or reports, or it might be more specialized in the form of a specific kind of technical writing. Few in university En-glish departments routinely respond to such community needs. Yet the flexibility of most two-year-college teachers allows them to take on such teaching assignments, on campus or off.

The most hopeful areas for two-year knowledge making lie in the recent calls for new definitions of scholarship and for valuing teaching and the scholarship of teaching and learning. The plea to extend the definitions of what constitutes scholarship to include systematic in-quiry through either the synthesis, interpretation, or application of knowledge as called for by the Commission on the Future of Community Colleges and the Carnegie Foundation for the Advancement of Teach-ing (Boyer) offers expanded opportunities to two-year-college faculty. George Vaughan has advocated valuing intellectual work other than original research, such as instructional materials, bibliographies, op-ed pieces, computer software, and technical innovations. Those represent activities with which most two-year-college teachers have had wide ex-perience. Spellmeyer, recognizing the power of the community college, has urged a view of knowledge and knowledge making that seems com-patible with the democratic spirit of two-year colleges when he sug-gests that "non-specialists" can be considered as knowledge makers (44).

Sidney Dobrin also has recognized the need, particularly in compo-sition studies, to expand knowledge resources. Essential to the field's development are, he says,

> ... multiple modes of inquiry, multiple types of knowledge. Current thinking in composition recognizes that theory and practice are not self-contained. They not only rely on each other in transformative flux but also are dependent upon continued multimodal inquiry from various locations within the field in order to continually inform rhetoric and composition. (24–25)

No one is more knowledgeable about what is needed to expand knowl-edge in English studies than two-year-college faculty members. They have been at the forefront of teaching writing at all levels to diverse populations. Their knowledge about literacy production and transmission is especially valuable. Their expertise in dealing with nontraditional students, with multicultural audiences, with all the attendant issues of gender, race, class, and ethnicity can be the source of valuable and useful information to all of higher education as student populations in all settings only grow more diverse and more nontraditional.

What is needed now is for local knowledge to become global and be translated into theory whenever possible. The theory must be discussed and debated. Those within two-year colleges must come to see themselves as having knowledge worth sharing with the academy as a whole. Additionally, the academy must demonstrate a willingness to consider the knowledge generated by its two-year-college counterparts. Dobrin's comments about those teaching writing are appropriate for everyone throughout higher education:

> . . . whether engaged in theoretical pursuit or consumed by teaching six sections of basic writing [compositionists] need to explore the ways in which theory from various ideological and epistemological backgrounds influences both the theoretical inquiries and the diurnal practice that makes up the field's bread and butter. (155)

Conclusion

By virtue of their unique location, sitting as they always have *between* the university and the secondary school, two-year-college faculty are in an important position to offer knowledge about those who move on to the university and those who will move from two-year settings to the world of work. Two-year faculty themselves, occupying this interborder position are, as Howard Tinberg says, "quintessentially postmodern," possessing "no single identity, but rather have shifting and blurred identities. Like the subject of postmodern anthropology, we move in a variety of worlds. We are the educational 'mestizas,' the translatable teachers" (x–xi). Characterizing himself, he offers a profile of many two-year faculty:

> A Ph.D. steeped in literary theory and trained in the traditional canon, I strain here and in my classroom to find a language that has currency for theorists as well as for practitioners. I publish, I give papers at professional conferences, and I teach. I work to connect to all these activities; I try to translate them across borders. In my professional writing, I try to strike a balance between the public and the private, the academic and the expressive, the abstract and the classroom-based. In my teaching, I seek to use theory as guide to my practice and look to practice to engender theory. (xi)

It is this unique position that has created problems for the two-year teacher in the past, but it may well be that this position will be one of strength, a place from which the new knowledge needed by the discipline for the future can be most productively engendered.

Nellie McKay, a Modern Language Association representative to the 1987 English Coalition Conference, indicated the importance of listening to multiple professional sources of knowledge, particularly two-year-college teachers:

> I was impressed by the makeup of the group and learned a great deal from listening to those who are more in the trenches than I am—not only elementary and secondary school teachers but especially from those who teach in community colleges. (1)

She goes on to suggest that those in the universities, because of the pressures for research, neglect attention to "'the teaching of reading, writing, speaking, and listening' or to the prime issues in the way students learn." It is in these essential areas that two-year-college teachers can be most helpful to their university colleagues. If two-year-college teachers will share the knowledge they have acquired from their serious attention to teaching, knowledge about transmitting ideas to varied audiences, their work with technology in varied settings, and their expertise at workforce training, they can make valuable contributions to the discipline's knowledge. They can participate in the most productive ways with their colleagues throughout the academy to educate citizens in the twenty-first century.

It is essential that higher education encourage two-year-college faculty to become more active participants in the national discussion. Two-year faculty have much to teach the discipline of English and much to contribute to the direction higher education will take in the new century. Recent trends toward valuing teaching, toward more acceptance of classroom-based research, toward more emphasis on literacy education, and toward the use of technology in classrooms highlight areas where two-year teachers possess expertise. With the recent national initiatives to assure all citizens the equivalent of the first two years of a college education, major attention is shifting to the nation's two-year colleges. As higher education becomes more expensive, society will be more inclined to support the work of two-year colleges than it will those engaged in canon debates and theory wars. If university English departments do go the way of departments of classics, as Harold Bloom has suggested (17), or dissolve into departments of cultural studies, as Michael Berube has indicated, two-year colleges will be in place and ready to assume teaching the skills of reading and writing to all of tomorrow's students.

Works Cited

Berube, M. 1996. Address. National Council of Teachers of English Convention. Chicago Hilton, Chicago. (Nov 21.).

Bloom, H. 1994. *The Western Canon: The Books and School of the Ages.* New York: Harcourt.

Boyer, E. L. 1990. *Scholarship Reconsidered.* Princeton: Carnegie Foundation for the Advancement of Teaching.

"Casting New Light on Old Notions: A Changing Understanding of Community College Faculty." 1998. *Change* (Nov./Dec.): 43–47.

Cohen, Arthur M., and Florence B. Brawer. 2003. *The American Community College.* 4th ed. San Francisco: Jossey.

Commission on the Future of Community Colleges. 1988. *Building Communities: A Vision for a New Century.* Washington, DC: American Association of Community and Junior Colleges.

Cross, R. K. 1985. "Introduction." In *The Forge*, by T. S. Stribling. Tuscaloosa: U of Alabama P.

———. 1985. Introduction. In *The Store*, by T. S. Stribling. Tuscaloosa: U of Alabama P.

———. 1986. "Introduction." *Unfinished Cathedral*, by T. S. Stribling. Tuscaloosa: U of Alabama P.

Cross, R. K., and J. T. McMillan, eds. 1982. *Laughing Stock: The Autobiography of T. S. Stribling.* Memphis: St. Luke's.

Cowan, G., and E. Cowan. 1980. *Writing.* New York: Wiley.

Cox, K. Castellucci. 1998. "Magic and Memory in the Contemporary Story Cycle: Gloria Naylor and Louise Erdrich." *College English* 60: 150–2.

Dobrin, S. I. 1997. *Constructing Knowledges: The Politics of Theory-Building and Pedagogy in Composition.* Albany: State U of New York P.

Doucette, D., and J. E. Roueche. 1991. "Arguments with Which to Combat Elitism and Ignorance about Community Colleges." *Leadership Abstracts* 4.13. Austin: League for Innovation in the Community College.

The ERIC Review. 1996. 5.1/2.

Gabert, G. 1991. *Community Colleges in the 1990s.* Bloomington: Phi Delta Kappa.

Gaskins, J., D. Holt, and E. Roeger. 1998. "Do Two-Year College Students Write as Well as Four-Year College Students? Classroom and Institutional Perspectives." *Teaching English in the Two-Year College* 25: 6–15.

Gere, A. R. 1996. "Stories Out of School." *Teaching English in the Two-Year College* 23: 9–18.

Griffith, M., and A. Connor. 1994. *Democracy's Open Door: The Community College in America's Future.* Portsmouth: Heinemann.

Maher, J. 1997. *Mina P. Shaughnessy: Her Life and Work.* Urbana: NCTE.

McKay, Nellie. "From a Letter to Wayne Booth." What Is English? Peter Elbow. New York and Urbana: MLA and NCTE, 1990. 1–2.

Nist, E. A., and H. H. Raines. 1995. "Two-Year Colleges: Explaining and Claiming Our Majority." In *Resituating Writing: Constructing and Administering Writing Programs*, edited by J. Janangelo and K. Hansen, 59–70. Portsmouth: Heinemann.

North, S. M. 1987. *The Making of Knowledge in Composition: Portrait of an Emerging Field.* Portsmouth: Heinemann.

Oehler, P. 1998. "A Discography of American Literature Set to Music—Part II." *Teaching English in the Two-Year College* 26: 25–28.

———. 1994. "I Sing the Body Electric: A Selected Discography of American Literature Set to Music." *Teaching English in the Two-Year College* 21: 309–16.

Pickett, N. A. 1994. "A Quarter Century and Beyond: My Story of Teaching Technical Communication." In *Two-Year College English*, edited by M. Reynolds, 134–43. Urbana: NCTE.

Pickett, N. A., A. A. Laster, and K. E. Staples. 2000. *Technical English: Writing, Reading, and Speaking.* 8th ed. New York: Addison.

Reynolds, M. 1990. "Twenty-Five Years of Two-Year College English." *Teaching English in the Two-Year College* 17: 230–35.

Reynolds, M., ed. 1994. *Two-Year College English: Essays for a New Century.* Urbana: NCTE.

Rose, M. 1989. *Lives on the Boundary: The Struggles and Achievements of America's Underprepared.* New York: Free.

Roth, A. J. 1999. *The Research Paper: Process, Form, and Content.* 8th ed. Belmont: Wadsworth.

Spellmeyer, K. 1996. "Inventing the University Student." In *Composition in the Twenty-First Century: Crisis and Change*, edited by L. Z. Bloom, D. A. Daiker, and E. M. White, 39–44. Carbondale: Southern Illinois U P.

Teaching English in the Two-Year College. 1996. Special Issue on Technology (October).

Tinberg, H. B. 1997. *Border Talk: Writing and Knowing in the Two-Year College.* Urbana: NCTE.

Vaughan, G. 1994. "Scholarship and Teaching: Crafting the Art." In *Two-Year College English,* edited by M. Reynolds, 212–21. Urbana: NCTE.

Wilson, S. 1997. "Acts of Defiance (and Other Mixed Messages): Taking Up Space in a Sub-Collegiate Course." *Teaching English in the Two-Year College* 24: 291–303.

———. 1994. "What Happened to Darleen? Reconstructing the Life and Schooling of an Underprepared Learner." In *Two-Year College English*, edited by M. Reynolds, 37–53. Urbana: NCTE.

Designing Writing Courses

Performative Literacy: The Habits of Mind of Highly Literate Readers

Sheridan Blau

In this essay, Sheridan Blau discusses the knowledge required for what he calls "disciplined literacy"—that is, a student's ability to interpret and respond to texts critically—which he views as necessary for "full participation in civic and economic life" (p. 154). Blau suggests that exercising disciplined literacy requires three foundational literacies: textual literacy, intertextual literacy, and performative literacy, the latter of which is what enables the activation and use of other forms of knowledge. Blau outlines seven habits of mind that make up performative literacy and offers concrete strategies for fostering these habits of mind in the classroom.

Definitions of literacy change in changing historical and educational contexts, and may even change from one administration to another in federal and state governments. Miles Myers (1996) identified five conceptions of literacy that have dominated American educational thought in different periods from colonial times to the present.

"Signature literacy," knowing how to sign one's name, was the conventional standard for literacy in the American Colonies until the Revolutionary War. From the Revolutionary War to the Civil War, the prevailing

From *Voices from the Middle*, 2003, vol. 10, no. 3, pp. 18–22.

standard was that of "recording literacy," which was generally defined by legible penmanship in copying short documents and the ability to read and spell simple words. From the Civil War to the time of the First World War, the standard was "recitational literacy," demonstrated by memorizing and reciting patriotic speeches and pieces of canonical literature.

In the period from about 1916 to 1985, schooling became directed at producing students who had achieved "analytic literacy," a standard that entailed a shift from oral reading to silent reading and from memorization to comprehension and analysis. This typically required readers in junior and senior high schools to study a common body of texts and engage in such activities as identifying main ideas and themes, recognizing technical features like point of view and figures of speech, and describing literary elements like plot, character, and setting.

The fifth and latest form of literacy, which has been called "critical literacy," or what I call "disciplined literacy," requires students to become more active, responsible, and responsive readers than ever before—readers who may be trusted to select many of the texts they will read in school, who are invited to produce their own interpretations of texts (rather than merely accept the interpretations of their teachers), and who are frequently expected to recognize, criticize, and even resist the values and vision of the world advanced by or inscribed in literary and nonliterary texts. Such a disciplined literacy, the principal features of which are now reflected in most national and state standards documents in the English language arts (Woodward and Halbrook, 1999), represents a new ambition for public schooling, but it is the kind of literacy that has always been possessed by the intellectual and literary elite of every culture. To aspire to such a literacy for all students is to aspire to full participation in civic and economic life for all citizens in a democratic republic (Blau, 2001).

What Skills or Knowledge Does Disciplined Literacy Require?

If students are actually to exercise such a complex and thoughtful form of contemporary literacy, they will have to simultaneously acquire what amounts to three different kinds of foundational literacy beyond those that may have traditionally and explicitly been taught in school under the heading of literacy. I define these as *textual literacy*, *intertextual literacy*, and *performative literacy* (Blau, 2003).

Textual literacy refers to the procedural knowledge that allows a reader to move from summarizing or retelling the plot of a story, to constructing a plausible interpretation, to reflecting critically on a text. This set of moves is governed largely by the rules of evidentiary reasoning and entails a process of thinking that is parallel to what we usually mean by critical thinking.

Intertextual literacy is akin to what E. D. Hirsch (1987) calls cultural literacy. Reading specialists have frequently described this as prior conceptual and informational knowledge that readers need to make sense of what they read, beyond what they would understand merely by pronouncing and decoding the words of a text. A reader reading a phrase that refers to Joseph's coat of many colors may know all the individual words and understand the possessive and descriptive signifiers and still not have any idea what the phrase refers to. What that reader may be missing is a familiarity with the biblical story of Joseph and his brothers in the book of Genesis.

Performative literacy can be identified as an enabling knowledge—knowledge that enables readers to activate and use all the other forms of knowledge that are required for the exercise of anything like a critical or disciplined literacy. It also represents a set of literate practices without which readers cannot continue to grow in knowledge and literary competence through their reading experience. This enabling form of knowledge—performative literacy—is essential to functioning as a fully enfranchised reader in 21st-century schools.

Performative Literacy in Action

I have identified seven traits as constitutive of performative literacy, each one associated with actions and dispositions that distinguish more competent from less competent readers.

1. A capacity for sustained focused attention. This attribute may seem so obviously required for the reading of difficult texts that it hardly needs to be mentioned. However, when students fail to give close, sustained attention to texts, their complaint of not understanding the text is often interpreted as an inability to comprehend. When simple lack of appropriate effort is treated—as it often is—as a symptom of insufficient mastery of some sub-skill of reading, students are likely to be offered forms of instructional assistance that support inattention and confirm the students' own mistaken notion that they lack some specialized body of knowledge or reading skills that distinguish them from their teachers.

2. Willingness to suspend closure—to entertain problems rather than avoid them. Again, the difference between expert and less than expert readers seems to reside in the operation of the will rather than in the wit. It's not that expert readers immediately apprehend meaning in a text and do so with a sharper vision than less skilled readers, but that they are more willing to endure and even to embrace the disorientation of not seeing clearly, of being temporarily lost. The most productive readers will even sacrifice whatever comfort they may find in a coherent and apparently complete reading to notice discontinuities or possible contradictions in their understanding of a text. Instead of ignoring or rushing in to plug up such gaps with weak evidence or rationalizations, they will probe them, opening up the possibility that their own formerly comfortable reading will collapse or require reconstruction.

3. Willingness to take risks—to offer interpretive hypotheses, to respond honestly, to challenge texts, to challenge normative readings. This characteristic is closely related to a willingness to entertain problems, and both of them are functions of what we might more globally identify as intellectual courage. First, we want to note that any time a reader offers an independent interpretation of a text in a classroom or community of other readers, a risk and a responsibility are both concomitantly undertaken. The responsibility is to make the case (Rex and McEachen, 1999) in support of the proffered interpretation through a process of evidentiary reasoning. The risk is that the case won't stand up to interrogation by other readers or even to the reasoning process necessary to demonstrate its plausibility.

Intellectual courage may also be required when readers feel called upon by their own experience and knowledge to offer readings that might be socially stigmatized or deemed unacceptable by particular communities of readers. Such readings and such courage may be particularly appropriate, however, in the most traditional English classrooms where literature is sometimes offered up by teachers in what they may see as their obligatory role as the high priests of the canonical culture—a role that many parents and school boards continue to think appropriate for teachers—and where all texts taught seem to demand reverence as the only acceptable response, a reverence that often requires the deadening of perceptiveness and critical inquisitiveness rather than their quickening.

If we want our students to be engaged readers, likely to notice what they notice in the course of their reading and to record it for later reflection, we will probably value their literary irreverence as much as their sense of literary awe. Students need at least enough lack of reverence—or, more positively, a sufficient sense of the value of their responses and their right to talk back to texts—to be willing to recognize when a text speaks against them as well as for them, when it represents an ideology that they might prefer to resist rather than admire.

4. Tolerance for failure—a willingness to re-read and re-read again. This attribute is probably related to intellectual courage and is surely related to a capacity for sustained attention, but it refers more specifically to a reader's possession of a kind of faith in the process of reading and faith in one's self as a reader that allows a reader to read a text a second time after feeling bewildered or blank in a first reading, and then to re-read again when the second reading is hardly more satisfying than the first.

How much re-reading and frustration can a competent reader tolerate? More than an incompetent reader can. In fact, one of the principal differences between expert readers and those who appear less skilled is that the more accomplished have a greater capacity for failure. They are at least willing to experience failure more often, framing their failure not so much as failure but as a part of the difficulty that comes with the territory of reading difficult texts.

5. Tolerance for ambiguity, paradox, and uncertainty. Closely related to an ability to suspend closure, this tolerance is less a matter of patience and faith in one's capacity to solve problems than one of accepting the limitations and developmental nature of our understanding and the paradoxical, ambiguous, and provisional condition of most human knowledge at any moment. The least competent readers tend to confuse intellectual sufficiency with certainty and completed knowledge, and are inclined to equate uncertainty with ignorance, and ambiguity or paradox with confusion. Readers who read texts looking for secure and certain answers to their questions may also read the world with a similar passion for certainty and with a similar intolerance for the moral complexity and ambiguity that resist simplistic formulations.

6. Intellectual generosity and fallibility: willingness to change one's mind, to appreciate alternative visions, and to engage in methodological believing as well as doubting (Elbow, 1986). This characteristic refers to a constellation of related traits that allow readers to learn from and be influenced by texts and discourse about texts. The strongest readers will generally argue persuasively for their own readings of texts and be able to demonstrate the deficiencies of arguments for alternative readings. But they also show a capacity to experiment with—to try on and, as it were, to believe—alternative perspectives and to recognize the possibilities of alternative or multiple constructions of meaning. In this process, they also show themselves to be fallibilists—persons capable of changing their minds, capable of learning from their encounter with other readings to look in a new way, and therefore to adopt a perspective that is more comprehensive than their own former vision.

7. A capacity to monitor and direct one's own reading process: metacognitive awareness. As any attentive teacher knows, and as a growing body of formal research studies have shown us (see summaries of research in Schoenbach et al., 1999; Beers, 2002; Olson, 2002), a major difference between strong and weak readers has to do with the way strong readers monitor the progress of their understanding as they move through a text, self-correcting as necessary and recognizing when they need to re-read or re-focus their attention or take some other step to assist themselves in understanding what they are reading. Readers who are used to monitoring their reading are less likely to feel defeated by difficult texts because they are aware of the difference between understanding and not understanding and recognize their own resources for focusing or re-directing their attention in precisely the ways I have been describing under the other dimensions of performative literacy.

Fostering Performative Literacy in Classrooms

Performative literacy can be developed in students when literature is taught in a way that recognizes that reading, like writing, is a process of text construction—a process through which meaning is made in the head of the reader (and later reconstructed and made more visible, perhaps, through writing) through the reader's encounter or transactions with words on a page and in the course of conversations with other readers. To recognize that reading is a process of meaning making or text construction is to recognize that it is a process very much like writing, involving the same false starts; the same vision and re-vision, drafting and redrafting; and all the same perils, opportunities (including opportunities for collaboration and consultation), and recursiveness of writing.

To see reading as such a process of composition will not only link the teaching of reading with the teaching of writing, it will also foster in students the kind of respect and capacity for tentativeness, for confusion, for sustained attention, for failure, for metacognitive awareness, particularly if what is foregrounded and honored in the course of instruction is the efficacy of the reading process rather than any predetermined product or content knowledge that a teacher feels obligated to transmit. In short, instruction directed toward fostering performative literacy must focus on the processes of reading and re-reading, placing an equal or greater emphasis (yet not an exclusive emphasis) on what student readers learn about their own capacity as readers in their transactions with difficult texts as on any established body of knowledge about those texts. A number of instructional approaches meet this criterion, including the following:

- Assignments that make reading processes visible. These might include double-entry journals where students record lines with responses and reflections on them from each reading and re-reading of a text; or simpler reading logs that ask students to keep track of their questions and other responses with each reading and re-reading.

- Assignments that not only honor but encourage students to identify what they don't understand. The point is to move away from assignments that identify comprehension as a product and instead help students see comprehension as a process (Beers, 2002). Examples include having students use sticky notes to flag what they didn't understand as they are reading; having students underline specific words or phrases that caused confusion; having students write about how they came to understand a particular text.

- Cold reading (what my colleagues in the South Coast Writing Project and Literature Institute for Teachers call "pants-down reading") that involves working with students on a poem or short story that the teacher has never read before and with which the teacher is likely to experience difficulties in understanding—difficulties that will enable the teacher to collaborate authentically with students in the construction of meaning and to exemplify the traits and actions that constitute performative literacy.

Finally, just as the teaching of writing as a process has been found to thrive most successfully in a culture of instruction that supports collaboration, tentativeness, risk taking, collegiality, and opportunities to publish written work for an identifiable community of readers, so will classrooms seeking to enable students as fully functioning readers need to become communities of practice in which performative literacy is culturally valued and honored in both theory and practice. When we accomplish that, then we'll be nurturing a literacy that really matters in the 21st century.

References

Beers, K. (2002). *When kids can't read: What teachers can do*. Portsmouth, NH: Heinemann.

Blau, S. (2001). Politics and the English language arts. In C. Dudley-Marling & C. Edelsky (Eds.), *The fate of progressive language policies and practices* (pp. 183–208). Urbana, IL: NCTE.

Blau, S. (2003). *The literature workshop: Teaching texts and their readers*. Portsmouth, NH: Heinemann.

Elbow, P. (1986). Methodological doubting and believing: Contraries in inquiry. In P. Elbow, *Embracing contraries: Explorations in learning and teaching*. New York: Oxford University Press.

Hirsch, E. D. (1987). *Cultural literacy: What every American needs to know*. Boston: Houghton Mifflin.

Myers, M. (1996). *Changing our minds: Negotiating English and literacy*. Urbana, IL: NCTE.

Olson, C. B. (2002). *The reading/writing connection: Strategies for teaching and learning*. New York: Allyn & Bacon.

Rex, L., & McEachen, D. (1999). If anything is odd, inappropriate, confusing, or boring, it's probably important: The emergence of inclusive academic literacy through English classroom discussion practices. *Research in the Teaching of English*, 34, 65–131.

Schoenbach, R., Greenleaf, C., Cziko, C., & Hurwitz, L. (1999). *Reading for understanding: A guide to improving reading in middle and high school classrooms*. San Francisco: Jossey-Bass.

Woodward, K., & Halbrook, A. (1999). National initiatives in English language arts. In K. Woodward (Ed.), *Alignment of national and state standards: A report by the GED testing service* (pp. 65–93). Washington, DC: American Council on Education.

"A Lifelong Aversion to Writing": What If Writing Courses Emphasized Motivation?

Patrick Sullivan

This essay begins with a disturbing claim made by Linda Brodkey about the state of writing instruction in America:

> *While it appears to take longer in some cases than in others, composition instruction appears to have succeeded best at establishing a lifelong aversion to writing in most people, who have learned to associate a desire to write with a set of punishing exercises called writing in school: printing, penmanship, spelling, punctuation, and vocabulary in nearly all cases; grammar lessons, thesis sentences, paragraphs, themes, book reports, and library research papers in college preparatory or advanced placement courses.*

Patrick suggests that there may be some validity to this claim, and proposes that teachers of writing address this lifelong aversion problem by carefully attending to student motivation. The key variable, for Patrick, is a student's "intrinsic motivation" for writing, which can be nurtured in writing classes. The author provides examples from his own teaching practice at a two-year college to demonstrate how this might be accomplished. As Patrick says, "unless students are engaged, interested, and intrinsically motivated, the best curriculum in the world will not make much difference in terms of learning" (p. 182).

With all due respect to the many excellent scholars working in the field of composition, I would suggest that the single most important sentence in the last twenty-five years of composition scholarship occurs in Linda Brodkey's essay "Writing Permitted in Designated Areas Only":

> While it appears to take longer in some cases than in others, composition instruction appears to have succeeded best at establishing a lifelong aversion to writing in most people, who have learned to associate a desire to write with a set of punishing exercises called writing in school: printing, penmanship, spelling, punctuation, and vocabulary in nearly all cases; grammar lessons, thesis sentences, paragraphs, themes, book reports, and library research papers in college preparatory or advanced placement courses. (220)

From *Teaching English in the Two-Year College*, 2011, vol. 39, no. 2, pp. 118-40.

These are disturbing words, indeed—but important ones, too, it seems to me. In this essay, I engage the issue of "aversion" that Brodkey raises and address it in relation to the growing body of scholarship related to intrinsic motivation and my own experience in the composition classroom.

Before turning to intrinsic motivation, I want to consider the validity of Brodkey's claim: Is it true that we encounter significant levels of "aversion" to reading and writing in our typical high school English classes, in our basic writing classrooms, in our first-year composition courses? Let us answer this question with as much candor and courage as we dare. Personally, I have taught composition at an open admissions institution now for over twenty years, and I have encountered my fair share of aversion to writing, especially in my basic writing classes. I have also worked with a number of area high school English teachers over the last several years, and I have heard plenty about student aversion to writing from them as well. Is it possible that the most lasting and significant learning outcome many students take away from English classes is a lifelong aversion to writing? Alas, I think it may be.

Another way to begin understanding the scope and significance of this problem is to ask a corollary question: How many students do we routinely encounter in high school and college English classes who are curious about ideas, who enjoy reading and have done a lot of it, and who are enthusiastically committed to becoming better writers? Not nearly as many as there should be, it seems to me, given how much time students spend in English classes, K–12.

Furthermore, I believe that at least part of our current national "college readiness" crisis stems directly from this "aversion" problem. In *The Condition of College and Career Readiness*, for example, the American College Testing Association (ACT) reports that only 66 percent of all ACT-tested high school graduates met the English College Readiness Benchmark for writing in 2010, which tests usage, mechanics, and rhetorical skills (8). An even smaller number (52 percent) met this benchmark for reading (8). In broad terms, these numbers indicate that roughly half of all high school graduates who took the ACT are not ready to be successful college-level readers, writers, or thinkers. These data are drawn from tests taken by 1.57 million students, approximately 47 percent of all 2010 high school graduates in the nation. The National Center for Education Statistics reports, moreover, that 37.6 percent of all students "took a remedial course" in college in the 2007–08 academic year, the most recent year for which data is available (United States, *Profile*). The number for students attending public two-year public institutions, the vast majority of which are open admissions institutions, was 44.5 percent (*Profile*).

There is justifiable concern, of course, about this poor performance. It is expensive and, in the long run, dangerous in terms of the nation's economic vitality, global competitiveness, and national security—for all the obvious reasons. In 1998, for example, Breneman and Haarlow estimated that "remedial education costs the nation's public colleges and universities about $1 billion annually" (2; see also Saxon and Boylan). The Strong American Schools organization notes in its 2008 report with the chilling title, *Diploma to Nowhere*, that the number of "remedial" students in American colleges now exceeds 1 million (1,305,480), incurring an estimated cost to taxpayers of over two billion dollars (3). A number of recent high-profile reports have attempted to engage and address this problem, including the U.S. Department of Education's *A Test of Leadership*, the American Association of Colleges and University's *College Learning for the New Global Century*, Achieve's *Closing the Expectations Gap 2007*, and Stanford University's Bridge Project report, *Betraying the College Dream: How Disconnected K–12 and Postsecondary Education Systems Undermine Student Aspirations* (Venezia, Kirst, and Antonio). I do not want to put too fine a point on this, other than to note that there is a great deal at stake here.

I believe that our national "remediation problem" is directly related to our "aversion" problem. After all, two of the three most important gateway college readiness skills are taught primarily by English teachers—reading and writing (the other gateway skill, of course, is math). My argument here is a simple one: we must attend carefully and systematically to issues related to motivation because students who are motivated typically do not underachieve. Recent research has provided a compelling theoretical argument for this focus on motivation. This work suggests that intrinsic motivation is a prerequisite for any kind of significant learning or achievement. I think it is essential that English teachers begin to engage this research carefully and begin developing curriculum designed specifically to promote and nurture motivation.

"Intrinsic" versus "Extrinsic" Motivation

The first step I believe we need to take as we begin engaging our "lifelong aversion" problem is to think carefully about student motivation and how we attempt to nurture and promote student engagement in English classes. There are many different ways that we might theorize even the general purpose of education, for example, that will make important differences in how we develop writing assignments, classroom activities, and curriculum for our students. For me, no one gets it better than Yeats: "Education is not the filling of a bucket, but the lighting of a fire." The presence or absence of this "fire," of course, affects everything students experience in our classrooms, usually in profound ways. As we know, students who are engaged and motivated learn almost effortlessly. Those who are not almost always struggle, resist, and often fail. Unmotivated students also often become disruptive and troublesome influences in our classrooms.

What Yeats is talking about here is "intrinsic" motivation, the kind of passion for a subject that leads to deep and significant student learning. As Alfie Kohn notes,

> Psychologists typically distinguish between "intrinsic" and "extrinsic" motivation, depending upon whether one sees a task as valuable in its own right or merely a means to an end. . . . Adults who consistently do excellent work, and students whose learning is most impressive, are usually those who love what they do, not those who see what they do as a way to escape a punishment. (*Case* 22)

I think as a profession we need to do a much better job creating activities, learning environments, and writing projects for students that target this kind of intrinsic motivation. In fact, I would like this to become one of our primary goals as English teachers, across institutional boundaries and at all grade levels. If we can inspire sincere student interest in reading, writing, and thinking, everything else, it seems to me, will take care of itself, without us having to lecture, harangue, prod, threaten, test, quiz, or plead. We all try to do this to some extent, of course. I am proposing that we make it one of the *primary guiding principles of our profession*, in an attempt to reverse the production of lifelong aversion to writing in students. To do this, of course, will require creativity, patience, and perhaps even courage.

Recent Research on Motivation

There has been a great deal of groundbreaking work done on motivation during the last twenty-five years or so, and all of it points to the importance of intrinsic motivation. This research has very significant ramifications for teachers of English. As Daniel Pink notes, however, in his book *Drive: The Surprising Truth about What Motivates Us*, there is currently a "mismatch between what science knows" about motivation and what organizations, educators, and parents do in terms of motivation (145). Anderman and Anderman make exactly the same point in their recent book, *Classroom Motivation* (v).

Edward Deci is perhaps the most important scholar in this field of study, and his published work on intrinsic motivation (much of which he co-authored with Richard M. Ryan) has become foundational. What he has to say about motivation, for example, in his book *Why We Do What We Do* (which he wrote for a popular audience with the help of *New York Times* science writer Richard Flaste), is something that I think all teachers (as well as principals, superintendents, legislators, advocates for national and statewide testing programs, and citizens concerned about education) should hear:

> [A]ll the work [Richard M.] Ryan and I have done indicates that *self-motivation*, rather than external motivation, is at the heart of creativity, responsibility, healthy behavior, and lasting change. . . . Because neither compliance nor defiance exemplifies autonomy and authenticity, we have continuously had to confront an extremely important—seemingly paradoxical—question: How can people in one-up positions [i.e., in positions of authority], such as health care providers or teachers, motivate others,

such as their patients or students, who are in one-down positions, if the most powerful motivation, leading to the most responsible behavior, must come from within—if it must be internal to the self of the people in the one-down positions? . . . In fact, the answer to this important question can be provided only when the question is reformulated. The proper question is not, "how can people motivate others?" but rather *"how can people create the conditions within which others will motivate themselves?"* (9–10; see also Deci and Ryan, *Handbook*; Deci and Ryan, *Intrinsic*).

Deci also laments the loss of motivation that seems to accompany attendance at school:

For young children, learning is a primary occupation; it is what they do naturally and with considerable intensity when they are not preoccupied with satisfying their hunger or dealing with their parents' demands. But one of the most troubling problems we face in this culture is that as children grow older they suffer a profound loss. In schools, for example, they seem to display so little of the natural curiosity and excitement about learning that was patently evident in those very same children when they were three or four years old. What has happened? (19)

Deci also poses a very important question for teachers, one that I think is vital for all English teachers at all levels of instruction and across institutional boundaries: "Why is it that so many of today's students are unmotivated, when it could not be more clear that they were born with a natural desire to learn?" (19). The problem Deci and Flaste are describing here, of course, is exactly the problem I am addressing in this essay.

As Ryan and Powelson suggest, it seems imperative that we not "conceive of the central goal of 12 years of mandatory schooling as merely a cognitive outcome" (62). Instead, the goal should be to create learners who are "willing and even enthusiastic about achieving something in school, curious and excited by learning to the point of seeking out opportunities to follow their interests beyond the boundaries of school" (62). This motivation needs to come from our students' own natural curiosity, interests, and passions. It should be characterized, as Ryan, Koestner, and Deci note, by "genuine interest, enjoyment and excitement" (189).

Boiled down to its most essential, this body of work suggests that educators need to pay careful attention to motivational factors in the classroom—in terms of course design, general course outcomes, assignment design, and a whole host of "smaller," less obvious aspects of classroom environment and classroom management strategies.

Motivation and Composition Scholarship

Situating my argument here within the long history of composition scholarship is not difficult, since there has not been a great deal of attention paid to intrinsic motivation in our literature. Part of the reason for this is that much of this research has been conducted outside of our discipline, and, as we know, it sometimes takes many years for work conducted in other disciplines to make its way into our scholarly conversations. This appears to be changing, however. A recent special issue of *English Journal*, for example, was devoted entirely to motivation (Lindblom). There has also been some significant discussion of intrinsic motivation in the scholarship related to reading instruction (in Atwell's *The Reading Zone* and *In the Middle* and in Smith and Wilhelm's *Reading Don't Fix No Chevys*). Again, however, many writing teachers are not familiar with research related to reading development.

Alfie Kohn has also been doing important work on this subject for many years, but he is a bit of an absolutist in terms of classroom applications of intrinsic motivation, and this appears to have contributed to keeping intrinsic motivation on the periphery of our scholarly conversation. His theoretical discussions of intrinsic motivation have obviously been groundbreaking. But his practical classroom suggestions can sometimes strike readers as impractical. Unfortunately, this may be part of the reason why intrinsic motivation is not more widely discussed and implemented in classrooms. Kohn suggests, for example, that we "reduce the number of possible grades to two: A and Incomplete. The theory here is that any work that does not merit an A isn't finished yet" (*Punished* 208). I personally find this idea very appealing, but it is not an easy idea to operationalize in the classroom. Like Kohn, I believe that any student work that has not earned an A or a B is simply unfinished — and I tell my students this. Nonetheless, like most teachers, I still find myself at the end of the semester reporting final grades other than A and Incomplete.

Kohn also argues against most kinds of "praise" (*Punished* 96–116), and much of what he says about this subject is important. Obviously, certain kinds of praise can damage intrinsic motivation, especially if such praise is perceived as empty, unearned, or used to manipulate or control. But praise doesn't always have to be damaging as Kohn acknowledges (106–110). Deci, Koestner, and Ryan, for example, have shown in an important study published a few years after Kohn's famous book, *Punished by Rewards*, that "verbal rewards" (i.e., positive feedback) do not have much of an effect on children but *do* have a consistently "significant positive impact" on the intrinsic motivation of college students: "verbal rewards — or what is usually labeled positive feedback in the motivation literature — had a significant positive impact on intrinsic motivation, although the effect on free-choice behavior was found for college students but not children" (653). Part of the reason for this, as we will see, is "age effects" and the cognitive sophistication of older students that enables them to distinguish between different kinds of praise.

The subject of motivation is clearly a very complex area of human psychology, as Deci, Koestner, and Ryan demonstrate, for example, in their exhaustive meta-analytic review of 128 research studies examining the effects of extrinsic reward on intrinsic motivation. In this essay I attempt to chart a pragmatic "middle way" for teachers of English—offering our profession a practical, replicable way to begin applying the wisdom of Kohn, Deci, and Ryan in the classroom. My argument here is that we can begin doing this by focusing on three key teaching strategies: *variety*, *choice*, and *disguised repetition*. To show how these three key strategies can be used in a classroom, I share examples from my own teaching practice, using a basic writing course that I teach at my open admissions institution, where issues of motivation come into play every day. I would like to see our profession situate intrinsic motivation at the very heart of what we do in our classrooms.

What Do Students Say about English Classes?

One way to begin exploring this subject is to ask students themselves what they have enjoyed, valued, and learned in their English classes. I have been doing this recently in my classes, and the results have been fascinating. Here is the simple survey I have been using:

1. Taking into account all of your experiences in English classes throughout your years in school, what kinds of assignments and activities in English classes have inspired you to enjoy reading and writing?

2. What kinds of assignments and activities in English classes have led you to dislike reading and writing?

3. If you could design curriculum to promote enjoyment of reading and writing in, say, a junior high school or senior high school English class, what kinds of activities and assignments would you include and why?

Here is one typical response:

1. Throughout my experiences in English classes I have typically only had very traditional assignments which have included reading either a book, play, or some other reading and then writing a paper on it. I feel these are beneficial to an extent but they tend to become somewhat repetitive rather quickly. One activity that I particularly liked was one involving a movie. We watched *Blood Diamond* in class. We did this after reading a book dealing with child soldiers. We were then asked to pick an aspect of the movie (i.e., the symbolism of diamonds, what they represent) and write a paper on it. Although this assignment did involve a paper, it was more enjoyable to me because of watching a film that so closely

paralleled the book we were reading. It made it much more interesting.

2. Like I said above, reading and then writing a paper is beneficial to an extent, but doing the same thing over and over again doesn't, in my opinion, instill a love of reading and writing. I think assignments that tend to involve creativity and different mediums are far more interesting.

3. Creative assignments. Reading more recent literature as it may be easier to relate to. Activities involving more mediums. Perhaps things like, film, music, and theatre.

I think there is important wisdom here that confirms what the research on intrinsic motivation is telling us about student engagement and learning.

I have also recently completed work as one of the editors of the second volume of *What Is "College-Level" Writing?: Assignments, Readings, and Sample Student Writing,* and my work on this book has greatly deepened my appreciation for intrinsic motivation. We included three student-authored essays in this book, inviting these college students to talk about their writing histories and to discuss landmark experiences in their precollege writing careers. To my great surprise, all three of our student contributors singled out creative assignments as crucial to nurturing their interest in English as a subject. These creative assignments appear to have one thing in common—they introduce variety, choice, and disguised repetition into the curriculum. That is, they are assignments that involve reading, writing, and thinking, but they do not present themselves to students as typical English assignments.

Casey Maliszewski is one of our student contributors, and she was home-schooled from kindergarten through twelfth grade. She attended a community college after getting her GED, and she served from 2007–08 as the international president of Phi Theta Kappa, the international honor society for junior, community, and technical colleges. She recently received her Bachelor of Arts degree from Mount Holyoke College (majoring in sociology) and is currently in her second year at Columbia Law School. Creative assignments were crucial to her development as a writer:

My parents' creative approach to English was no formal writing—none. My writing assignments consisted of fiction stories, poems, fables, and journals, just enough to get a handle on basic grammar. I remember marveling when my friends told me of their latest book report due. Asking my mother why I never had to do any book reports, she responded with a shriveled face as if she had just tasted bad milk. "Book reports made me hate reading when I was kid. I do not want to do the same thing to you." I suppose my parents' approach worked because I always was and still am an obsessive reader.

One story assignment comes to mind during my earlier years of high school work. My assignment was to write a fable about why robins are red breasted. First, I had to do research on the computer on what a fable was and what components it consisted of (a brief story that features animals, inanimate objects, and forces of nature to illustrate a moral lesson). Then, I had to find a fable already written to get an example. Last, I had to let my imagination do the rest. Such an assignment might seem odd, but by this time I was used to these creative assignments from my parents. (257–58)

Casey notes in her essay that completing these creative assignments throughout her high school years kindled in her "a great interest in writing." Casey is now an active and joyful learner, and despite never having written a formal essay until she was preparing for her GED, she has had a very successful college career.

Lindsay Larsen, one of our other student contributors, reports a similar experience:

One of the best assignments I had in high school was to create a newspaper about Romeo and Juliet, and my friend and I wrote articles about the tragic events in the play, including police reports about the deaths of Romeo, Juliet, Mercutio, and other characters, and an investigative article on apothecaries. In middle school, I had a teacher who had us write creative works for every book or poem we were reading—we created a poem version of Poe's "The Pit and the Pendulum," or wrote a creative piece on the Holocaust after reading about Anne Frank. Creative assignments helped open my imagination and helped me grow as a thinker. With creative writing assignments, you are not restricted to a certain form and your ideas are not stifled. The real world is filled with different problems and issues, and dealing with them in creative ways will help you immensely in life. Creative assignments allow for more freedom and less boredom for students. It is important to master all forms of writing, and this in turn will improve a student's essays. (282–83)

It seems to me there is important wisdom here.

A "Captive Audience"

Obviously, some students we meet in English classes are, indeed, enthusiastic and motivated learners. I think it is also probably fair to say, however, that a large number of students that we meet in English classes (especially K–12 and in basic writing classes) are not. They do not *necessarily* bring a compelling interest in reading, writing, or thinking with them into our classrooms, and they often simply try to "get through" and "survive" English classes.

Think about it for a second: There are millions of students in English classes across the country at this very moment—in primary and secondary schools, in basic writing classes, and also in first-year composition courses—who *do not particularly want to be there*. In some very real ways, they are a "captive audience"—*captive*, of course, accurately suggesting a condition of being unhappily and "forcibly confined or restrained" and "unable to escape." It is our job to help these students *want* to be in English classes—day after day, year after year. We cannot continue to present as self-evident the value of reading and writing. We need to work every day to help students *discover, experience*, and *feel* the joys of reading and the magic of written communication. It has become very clear to me that traditional motivational chestnuts like "This class will really help you improve your SAT scores" are not working.

How "Aversion" Is Created and Nurtured

I believe that there are many factors that help promote aversion to writing in our school systems and classrooms. Some of this aversion appears simply to be the result of our profession not having systematically engaged the issue of intrinsic motivation before. Certainly, some of this aversion is also created by high-stakes local, national, and state-mandated standardized testing programs. Such programs negatively affect motivation in all sorts of ways. One obvious factor, of course, is the proportion of class time available to spend on any activities other than preparing for high-stakes tests, taking such tests, and reviewing the results of these tests. The relief and joy that the students at Tyler Heights Elementary School express in Linda Perlstein's book, *Tested*, for example, when their state-mandated testing cycle ends and the school is free to move on to different kinds of learning activities suggests what is at stake here in terms of motivation and student success. The change is so significant, in fact, that one young student remarks, "It feels like a different school" (246). A qualitatively different kind of engagement and student learning also begins to take place.

Some of this aversion is also probably our own fault. We have relied perhaps too much on traditional kinds of assignments, traditional classroom strategies, and readings drawn from what Lynn Bloom calls the "essentially conservative" essay canon (417), which results in a few "classic" essays and readings getting assigned over and over again. Most high school reading lists focus on a very narrow list of traditional titles which dominate reading assignments year after year. Furthermore, as Smith and Wilhelm note, teachers canonize (and have students write about) certain kinds of texts—especially those that allow readers to provide nuanced interpretations (195)—at the expense of others. Smith and Wilhelm's interviews with male students in middle school and high school provide compelling evidence for broadening the variety of readings we assign, teach, and invite students to write about. One of the students Smith and Wilhelm interview, in fact, addresses this issue—and speaks to our aversion problem—with devastating effect: "I will read books that other people tell me I should read—except for my English teachers" (143).

Aversion is also created in structural and systematic ways by national and statewide curriculum requirements and by less than helpful or sympathetic superintendents, principals, deans, department chairs, and parents. There is much working against us here.

Balance

I am not arguing here that we should abandon "rigor" and "high standards." We obviously need to continue to design curriculum that provides traditional kinds of challenges for students as readers, writers, and thinkers. That being said, however, I believe that the typical K–12, basic writing, and first-year composition (FYC) English class clearly needs to achieve a richer, more diverse blend of reading and writing activities.

Proportionately, it seems to me that we should probably devote approximately 20 percent of our class time to this important endeavor, with the remainder dedicated to traditional kinds of assignments and activities. This is the approximate percentage of time that I devote to this kind of work in my classes, and the results have been encouraging. (I provide specific examples from my own teaching practice below.) Practically speaking, I do not think we necessarily even need to see immediate positive results from this work with all students in every class. I think we need to think longitudinally across the entire span of students' academic experience in English classes. Somewhere along the line, and hopefully before they come to college, we want that "fire" to be lit. And we will no doubt need to be patient. It may take years and many positive experiences in English classrooms for some students to finally enjoy reading, writing, and thinking.

I think it makes sense to look at this kind of curriculum development as a long-term, low-risk, high-yield investment strategy, one that has the potential to pay extraordinary dividends over the course of a student's academic career. It also has the potential to generate great value for students after they leave school, potentially producing adults in great numbers who will become thoughtful, passionate, lifelong learners. There is also no more important gift that we can hope to give to our nation and to our democracy than this: citizens who like to read, write, and think.

Not All Students Are Resistant Learners

Before moving forward with a discussion of practical classroom strategies, I would like to state for the record that I do not believe that all students are resistant writers and learners. In my twenty-five years of teaching English, I have certainly had the pleasure of working with many enthusiastic, fully engaged students. But I must also say, in terms of full disclosure, that I have also worked with many students who have not been particularly engaged.

I also do not wish to diminish or dismiss the literacies that students possess or to suggest that what I define here as reading, writing, and thinking is the only type of reading, writing, and thinking that is worth doing. That being said, I do seek to situate my argument here in the important and ongoing national conversation about "college readiness" and preparing students to be successful college-level readers, writers, and thinkers. I believe attention to intrinsic motivation has the potential to dramatically improve students' ability to be successful in college.

Practical Classroom Applications

There are probably a million different ways to nurture intrinsic motivation in the English classroom, and this in itself should make this enterprise fascinating and enjoyable for teachers. In the remainder of this essay, I describe how I have targeted intrinsic motivation and blended this element of my teaching practice with more traditional kinds of assignments and activities in one of the classes that I teach, English 93, the final course in the three-course basic writing sequence that we offer at my open admissions institution. For purposes of illustrating a general pedagogical strategy, I believe this course is a good choice to discuss here because it likely resembles writing courses taught at many other colleges and in many high schools as well. I also think this class is a good choice because it is a site where I routinely encounter strong "aversion to writing." Obviously, students cannot be considered "ready for college" if they do not like to read, write, or think (Sullivan, "Open" 6–9). So the stakes are high here in terms of our national conversation related to articulation, "college readiness," and alignment across institutional boundaries.

Three Major Essays with Challenging, College-Level Readings

The core of my English 93 class is built around three major essays, and these assignments are traditional and challenging. English 93 is designed to help students transition from basic writing to college-level reading, writing, and thinking, and I take this learning outcome very seriously. I seek to assign college-level readings and have students engage college-level ideas and issues. I have discussed assignments for this class elsewhere (Sullivan, "What"), but for the purposes of this essay, I would like to provide specific examples of the type of readings that I ask students to respond to so that readers can get a sense of the broader pedagogical ecology of this classroom. Here are the readings from the three major assignments that I used in the fall 2010 semester:

1. Listening: James Baldwin, "Sonny's Blues"

2. Cultural Critique

   a. Ruth Benedict, from *Patterns of Culture* (chapter 1: "The Science of Custom")

   b. Kathryn Edin and Maria Kefalas, from *Promises I Can Keep: Why Poor Women Put Motherhood before Marriage* (introduction, chapters 1, 2, 6, and conclusion)

3. Intelligence

   a. Alfred W. Munzert, Kim Munzert, and Alfred Munzert, *Test Your IQ* (a timed self-scoring IQ test)

   b. Howard Gardner, from *Frames of Mind* (excerpts) and *Multiple Intelligences,* chapter 1 (pages 3–24) and chapter 4 (pages 53–62)

   c. Daniel Goleman, from *Emotional Intelligence* (chapters 3, 4, 5, 6, and 12; pages 33–90 and pages 189–99)

As we work on these units as a class, I do most things English teachers typically do: I assign journal writing for each of these readings; I discuss the readings in class with my students; I have students develop rough drafts of their essays in response to these readings; and I meet with each student individually to talk about and assess the progress of their drafts. I also require students to meet with a tutor at our Writing Center. So this is serious, focused work.

These three major writing projects, along with other traditional kinds of activities that I have designed for this class take up roughly 80 percent of my class time (this includes introducing students to important research and theory related to reading, writing, and thinking as well as work related to motivation).

Variety, Choice, and Disguised Repetitions

I devote the remainder of my available time to activities designed to promote and nurture intrinsic motivation. My focus here is on adding variety, choice, and disguised repetitions to my curriculum. By design, this turns out to be about 20 percent of my total class time. Some of the days I use for these activities I consider "gimmees." I have found, for example, that students are usually incapable of doing much new work on days when major essays are due, so I can use these days however I wish without feeling like I might be "wasting" class time. For the remainder, I use what I think of as "good work days," valuable teaching days when students are likely to be mentally fresh and willing to work hard. I could, of course, be using this class time to do more traditional kinds of work or having students engage in more repetitions of traditional work (which until recently I have always done), but I have come to believe that the time I spend in class on activities designed to nurture intrinsic motivation is very worthwhile. These activities, regardless of when they are scheduled, really do make a significant positive difference in the way students think about my class and about "English." They also nurture a positive long-term attitude toward reading and writing. For the remainder of this essay, I would like to share with readers how I attempt to realize this in my classroom.

Variety

Writing about Art on Campus

In calling for introducing more variety into our curriculum, I am following the work of composition scholars like Curtis and Herrington and their important research on writing development in the college years. In their 2003 essay in *College Composition and Communication*, Curtis and Herrington call for broadening the types of writing students are required to do (86–88). (As Lunsford and Lunsford have shown, there does not appear to be much variety in the English curriculum. Most of the writing assigned in FYC, for example, is either argument or close analysis [793].) I am also following the advice of Alfredo Lujan, who suggests that students should have to "write and write often in multigenres: stories, personal essays, critical essays, parodies, poems, freewrites, letters to teachers, journals, jingles, reader responses, lists" (56). I am also following Kohn, who likewise supports bringing more variety into our classrooms (*Punished* 220). I am also responding here to the testimony of Casey Malszewski and Lindsay Larsen, the two student contributors to *What Is "College-Level Writing" (Vol. 2)* that I cited earlier, both of whom argue persuasively, it seems to me, for bringing more variety into our curriculum. I believe variety is one very important way we can nurture intrinsic motivation. Variety can serve to deepen students' understanding and appreciation of writing, and it can make the classroom experience more diverse and interesting. It also allows different kinds of learners to encounter different kinds of challenges, provides pacing and rhythm over the course of the semester, and disguises repetitions.

One example of how I introduce variety into my English 93 class is writing about art on campus. Here I am following the work of Elliot Eisner, who argues persuasively in *The Arts and the Creation of Mind*, in favor of curricular diversity as well as for the value of incorporating art and aesthetics into our curriculum. As he suggests, "Meaning is not limited to what words can express" (280). We are blessed to have a campus extraordinarily rich in artwork (we have student and professional art on many walls and public places on campus, and we have a gallery). The assignment I describe here is designed to diversify our class's writing activities and to have students engage art and aesthetics. This assignment also helps students work on their concentration and observational skills. Good writers, I tell them, are good observers, and they are able to sustain focus and concentration. This activity also provides me with an excellent opportunity to talk about audience and to highlight the difference between reader-based and writer-based prose (Flower). This assignment requires students to imagine an audience that is unfamiliar with their work of art and then write for it. This helps my basic writing students begin to make the crucial cognitive transition from writing for themselves (writer-based) to writing for others (reader-based), a key transition point for developing writers. Finally, I also like to do some things with my classes during the semester that get my students up and moving in order to show them that writers do more than just sit in front of computers all day and write.

For this assignment, we tour the campus looking at art. I ask students to select a work they like and then return to it and study it carefully. Students then write about the work they select. Here is the assignment:

Writing about Art on Campus

Today, we will tour the campus looking at the art on display. Your job will be to find a piece of art that you really like. Once you have found a work you like, I would like you to write a response to the piece you've selected. I will be collecting these at our next class meeting, and you will be presenting the work you chose to the class in a short speech. Word count: 350 word minimum!

Here's how our day will go:

- We will spend 30 minutes touring campus and taking notes.
- I would like you to select a work that you want to write about and then return to it to sit in front of it. Please spend some time looking at it carefully. I'd like you to take notes and begin a preliminary draft of your response (at least 15 minutes).
- Take a picture of the work you've chosen so you can show it to the class. Convert it to a .jpeg at home and bring it to class on your flash drive.
- We will all return to class during the final 10 minutes of class to finish up this activity and begin writing our responses.

Here's what I would like you to do in each paragraph:

Paragraph 1: Please describe the piece of art that you have selected as carefully and fully as you can. Please assume that the audience you are writing for has not seen the work you have selected. Readers will only be able to "see" your work of art from your written description, so make it full and strong!

What is it? (A painting? A sculpture? Pottery?)

What is it made of? (Paint? Wood? Steel? Something else?)

What colors or textures or patterns does it feature that you find interesting or appealing?

Paragraph 2: Think carefully about the piece you've selected.

What does it make you feel?

What does it make you think?

Does it recall or remind you of anything?

Why do you like this piece of art?

Why did you select it?

This kind of assignment adds a very welcome element of variety to the semester, and most students find the assignment fascinating and enjoyable, regardless of how much exposure they have had to art before. Many students develop a proprietary sense of ownership toward the work they have chosen, and for this reason they usually look forward to writing and speaking about it. All of this helps nurture intrinsic motivation for writing, and students are still required to "read" their piece of art carefully, think about why the piece moves them, and then write an effective description and response. I feel we have much to gain from making variety a hallmark of our curriculum development.

Choice

Reading for Pleasure

Choice is something that everyone interested in motivation and teaching agrees is important. It is one of Kohn's three major curricular recommendations for teachers, along with richer, more meaningful content and more opportunities for students to collaborate (*Punished* 213–26). It is foundational to Atwell's approach to teaching reading (*Middle* 37–39; *Reading* 26–35). It is supported by many other reading scholars as well, including DeBenedictus, Manning and Manning, and Worthy, Turner, and Moorman. Deci and Flaste also consider it essential in the classroom because it helps promote intrinsic motivation and autonomy (34–36, 144–49). My own journey toward providing students with choice has been a long one. I highlight one assignment here that resulted from this important journey.

I have always wanted my English 93 students to love reading, but I was never willing to devote any class time to this important learning outcome. I also believed until recently that this was something students should really be able to get to on their own. For many years, I would simply tell students that they should love reading, and I thought that they would. Like most teachers, I felt as if I already had enough material to cover, and I would always think, "I just can't spare the time."

I have recently changed my mind about this, though, and as a result I have developed an assignment that targets this learning outcome specifically—getting students to enjoy reading. My thinking now is this: "If I really believe this is an important outcome for my courses—if I really want students to read on their own for pleasure—I ought to have an assignment that specifically targets that outcome." So learning how to "read for pleasure" and seeing reading as enjoyable are the two major things I am after here. I also want students to begin to see the library for the miraculous and amazing place it is. So in response to this thinking, I developed the following book review activity, with the goal of designing a "book report" assignment that even Casey's Mom could love:

Essay #3: Book Review!

For this assignment, I am asking you to select a book from the library about a subject that interests you. It can be fiction, poetry, biography, a graphic novel, a book about art or food or national parks—anything that you are interested in. Once you have done this, I would like you to write a review of the book that will include the following:

1. An interesting and creative introduction that will get readers interested in reading your review.
2. Author, title, publication date, and subject.
3. Why you selected this book.
4. What you found interesting in this book.
5. What you enjoyed in this book.
6. What you learned from this book.
7. Please include at least two quotes from your book and discuss why you found these quotations important or interesting.
8. Your overall assessment of the book.

The guidelines are as follows:

1. The book cannot be one you are reading for another class.
2. The book cannot be one that you've read before.
3. I would like this book to be one you've always wanted to read or about a subject you've always wanted to know more about.
4. You may also purchase a book at a bookstore or borrow it from your home library or a friend.

Your focus here should be on enjoyment! Have some fun! You can organize your review however you want—but I want you to think creatively and remember that you are writing for an audience, as we will be posting these reviews on our class website. Reviews should be approximately 750 words in length.

Each student will also be presenting a 2-minute speech on the book they have chosen to read.

To prepare for this assignment, about a week before we begin this activity I survey my students about their reading practices and what subjects interest them. I then personalize my feedback to them as we look around the library. Here are some comments my students made last semester about the subjects they wanted to read about:

- Society, psychological issues, urban life, political issues, other cultures, their beliefs and way of life.

- I would like to read about a true story, nothing fiction.

- I would like to read about something exciting or a bio on someone.

- I want to read more, but not sure what I want to read about.

- I like to read about the military.

- I do not like books, books make me tired and bored. I hate books so I do not want to read any book.

Once we are in the library, I meet with students individually and help them find a book they are happy with. Some students choose urban fiction, some choose books about sports, some choose popular novels, and some surprise me with what they pick. I let students choose anything they want. If I can see a spark of interest and enthusiasm, then I know they have the right book.

This activity is also designed to address our national "aversion to reading" problem, a problem linked in many important ways to our "aversion to writing" problem. As Worthy, Turner, and Moorman suggest, research related to student reading is not encouraging:

> While most children begin their school careers with positive attitudes toward reading, many show a steady decline in reading attitudes and voluntary reading as they progress through school (Allington, 1975; McKenna, Ellsworth, & Kerr, 1995; Shapiro & White, 1991). Negative attitudes become especially prevalent beginning in middle and high school years (Anderson, Tollefson, & Gilbert, 1985; Cline & Kretke, 1980). In fact, according to a report from the California Department of Education (cited in Morrow, 1991), 70% of the over 200,000 sixth graders surveyed almost never read for pleasure. Other researchers paint similarly bleak pictures of students' leisure reading. (296)

I think it is imperative that we design and implement curriculum to reverse this unfortunate trend.

I am also attempting with this assignment simply to plant seeds that may flower later in students' lives or careers, even if they do not bear the immediate fruit of turning students instantly into voracious readers.

Following this activity, I do a satisfaction survey to see what students like about this assignment and what they learned from it. Most really enjoy it. Here is a representative sampling of this feedback:

- I enjoyed reading what I wanted.

- I learned books are different than movies.

- I enjoyed the assignment because it was a nice break from all the hardcore college books. It was fun.

- I learned that everyone has a different preference in what they like to read for fun. Each was unique in its own way.

- Yes, I liked my book.

- Yes, I liked it because we got to pick whatever we wanted to read. It was nice to have a little freedom.

- Yes, I enjoyed the opportunity to read what I chose.

- I learned that there are lots of books in the library that I would like to read.

In terms of course design and the overall rhythm and trajectory of this class, I place this assignment immediately after the most challenging assignment of the semester, as a kind of palate cleanser and enjoyable interlude before we begin the intense final weeks of the semester. As one of the comments above suggests, students are very aware of pacing and rhythm issues in classes ("I enjoyed the assignment because it was a nice break from all the hardcore college books. It was fun."). I find that this break allows students to concentrate more fully and with more engagement on the final writing projects to come.

Disguising Repetitions

The Bonnie Awards

I believe the testimony from our student contributors to volume 2 of *What Is "College-Level" Writing?* tells us a great deal about the value of disguising repetitions. They have shown us how powerfully these kinds of creative assignments can affect student engagement, motivation, and learning. I think there is a great deal we have to gain from thinking creatively and designing activities that "disguise repetitions" in our classrooms—that is, developing assignments that require students to read, write, and think, but that do so in ways that are creative and nontraditional. I would like to see us make this a central part of curriculum development at all levels of English instruction.

One of the ways that I disguise repetitions in my English 93 class is a playful awards ceremony I have developed called the Bonnie Awards (named after my daughter). I have found this activity does a great deal to nurture intrinsic motivation.

Before I describe this activity, it would be useful to first discuss what we know about "rewards," a subject which Kohn has written about extensively. I think it is important for teachers interested in nurturing intrinsic motivation to have a clear understanding of what the current research says about rewards, as this is a subject that routinely comes into play in all sorts of ways in our classrooms and schools (the honor roll, the National Honor Society, Phi Theta Kappa, the dean's list, the president's list). As the title of his best-known book suggests, Kohn has argued famously that students are "punished by rewards" because "rewards undermine interest" (140). Again, I believe that Kohn makes a very important point here. Reward systems that seek to "bribe" students into controlling or improving behavior and performance will be effective only in the short term—and they will often actually do more damage than good to long-term motivation and learning. And this kind of incentivization can never be as powerful or as transformative as intrinsic motivation in terms of a student's long-term success. But as with the issue of "praise," more recent research related to rewards has complicated our understanding of how students respond to rewards. Research has shown, for example, that certain kinds of rewards can be worthwhile and can nurture intrinsic motivation. There are a number of variables that come into play here, as Deci, Koestner, and Ryan suggest, including the age of the student and how a student perceives the intention of a reward:

> For more than 25 years, we have argued that predictions about the effects of rewards necessitate a differentiated analysis of how the rewards are likely to be interpreted by the recipients based on a consideration on the type of rewards (Deci, 1971, 1975), the type of contingency [i.e., what kind of performance or behavior is required to earn the reward] (Ryan et al., 1983), the type of participants (Deci et al., 1975), and the type of interpersonal climate within which the rewards are administered (Deci, Nexlek, et al., 1981; Ryan et al., 1983). (658)

Rewards can function in different ways, and this is particularly dependent on how students perceive the intention of these rewards—their "functional significance" (Deci, Koestner, and Ryan 628). Rewards that are perceived to control or influence behavior and self-determination will have a negative effect on intrinsic motivation. Rewards that are "positively informational"—that is, rewards that are used as "indicators of competence" (628)—can be positive motivators: "where rewards are positively informational, they are predicted to provide satisfaction of the need for competence and thus to enhance motivation" (628; see also Ryan, Mims, and Koestner).

The Bonnie Awards were designed with these kinds of variables in mind, and this activity has been designed in a way that is consistent with what research tells us about nurturing intrinsic motivation. After students submit their work for one of my major assignments (usually my second major assignment, around midterm), essays that have earned a B+ or better are presented to the class as our Bonnie Award nominees. I copy these essays and distribute them to students along with a Bonnie Award ballot. Everyone in class is asked to submit votes in five categories:

1. Best Overall Performance by a Writer in an English 93 Class

2. Best Engagement of the Big Ideas in the Readings

3. Best Use of Readings

4. Best Introduction

5. Most Fun to Read

I continue to be impressed each semester by how well this activity works. Intrinsic motivation for reading, writing, and thinking surges once students realize that someone other than me will read their work and that their work on this essay will have some meaning beyond "learning how to write." Students also are usually eager to read the work of their peers. I am always surprised how much I am able to gain simply by framing a rather standard peer writing activity in this way.

In terms of the variables Deci, Koestner, and Ryan discuss related to rewards, this assignment has been designed to maximize impact on intrinsic motivation:

The type of rewards: These awards are symbolic and playful, and students clearly recognize this (and enjoy it).

The type of contingency: Students receive a letter grade for their essay independent of the Bonnie Awards. These awards are, in some important ways, simply extensions of grades they have already earned. Winners are selected by their classmates (not by me).

The type of participants: These are college students, and as Deci, Koestner, and Ryan note about "age effects," "college students have greater cognitive capacity for separating the informational and controlling aspects of rewards" (656). My students clearly understand that this activity has been designed to motivate them to do their best writing, to reward excellent work, and to help them learn from other writers in the class.

The interpersonal climate: Again, the climate is playful, friendly, and supportive, and students understand and appreciate this.

This activity works in many positive ways. It provides me with an opportunity to publicly recognize excellent work in my class. It also provides students with an opportunity to read strong writing produced by their classmates. And it has proved to be an especially powerful learning activity for my less accomplished writers because they get to see how other students—some sitting right next to them—have responded successfully to the same assignment they struggled with. For many students, these essays often speak more eloquently and powerfully about good writing than anything I can say in class about it. It has proved to be a very powerful learning and teaching tool.

After students have read each of the essays and submitted their ballots, we discuss the essays together as a class. I ask students to identify the qualities that they liked about the essays they chose as winners, and we develop a rubric for "good writing" that comes out of this student work. Here is one such rubric that we developed from one of these discussions:

Qualities You Liked about the Bonnie Award Essays

1. Depth. Personal engagement.
2. Engaged readings effectively.
3. Used personal experience well (related to the readings; used experience to explore and discuss ideas in readings).
4. Used quotes from the readings. Then explained the quotes. Then discussed the quote and the meaning.
5. Good intro! Got my attention!
6. Flow! Stayed on topic. Good transitions. I got involved with reading it!
7. Juicy details! ("el encondido"/"Merengue and Bachata/palm trees, sunny beaches, colorful cement houses").
8. Engaged me as a reader.
9. The writing is alive.
10. Good paragraphs and good grammar.
11. Rhythm.
12. Interesting to read.
13. The writer appears to care that the writing is interesting!

This is a pretty impressive rubric coming from basic writing students.

I complete this project with an Academy Award–style ceremony that I conduct to announce the winners in each category. I present Bonnie Awards that I make myself to the winners. I've had students tell me with a smile long after a particular semester has ended that they still keep their Bonnie Awards proudly displayed in their homes. This activity orients student writers in a very positive way toward their work and toward each other. It is also simply a creative way to disguise repetitions—a way that invites students to read student writing and then talk about the components of good writing in ways that engage their attention and interest.

Conclusion

Speaking about American high schools and the discouraging news coming from ACT about college readiness, Jack Jennings, president of the Center on Education Policy in Washington, D.C., recently touched on precisely this issue of intrinsic motivation: "We haven't figured out how to improve them [high schools] on a broad scope and if our kids aren't dropping out physically, they are dropping out mentally" (Banchero). That's very well said, it seems to me. The key phrase here, it seems to me, is "dropping out mentally." As I argue in this essay, and as current research suggests, unless students are engaged, interested, and intrinsically motivated, the best curriculum in the world will not make much difference in terms of learning. Furthermore, if our goal is to create active and engaged lifelong learners and to build a strong democracy full of thoughtful, curious, intellectually vibrant, and well-read adults, a great deal is at stake here in terms of what goes on in English classes. After all, this is the primary place where Americans learn to read, write, and think.

Since I have begun targeting intrinsic motivation in this way, I have noticed improved student engagement and performance. The pacing of my classes is different, and many students appear to be able to make it to the end of the class and still stay engaged. Students are also very perceptive and recognize the efforts I am making on their behalf in this regard. They have communicated to me in all sorts of ways how much they appreciate the nontraditional, "creative" curricular elements I have built into my classes, even as they recognize the value and importance of the more traditional work we do together.

I think there is probably less urgency to concern ourselves with intrinsic motivation in upper-level and advanced placement classes, as the students who have made it to these curricular levels have already demonstrated some degree of motivation and can be assumed to be ready to focus on serious business—although I personally think it is important to target intrinsic motivation at all curricular levels. (I do so in all my courses, including the upper-level college courses I teach.) But for students in basic writing classes in college, for students in high school English classes, and for all those students in K–8 English classes, I think it is very clear that there is much we need to do in terms of nurturing intrinsic motivation.

As English teachers, we have in our care the most potent of all human creations—written language. We need to provide opportunities for students to experience for themselves the joy of reading and the power of language to move, transform, and inspire. It is a privilege to be given this task. Let us begin finding ways to light this "fire"—so that reading and writing become an essential and beloved part of our students' lives.

Works Cited

Achieve, Inc. *Closing the Expectations Gap 2007: An Annual 50-State Progress Report on the Alignment of High School Policies with the Demands of College and Work.* 2007. Web. 8 May 2009.

American Association of Colleges and Universities. *College Learning for the New Global Century.* Washington: AACU, 2007. Print.

American College Testing Program [ACT]. *The Condition of College and Career Readiness 2010*. 2010. Web. 27 Nov. 2010.

Anderman, Eric M., and Lynley Hicks Anderman. *Classroom Motivation*. Upper Saddle River: Prentice Hall, 2009. Print.

Atwell, Nancie. *In the Middle*. 2nd ed. Portsmouth: Boynton/Cook, 1998. Print.

———. *The Reading Zone*. New York: Scholastic, 2007. Print.

Banchero, Stephanie. "Scores Stagnate at High Schools." *Wall Street Journal* 16 Aug. 2010. Web. 26 Nov. 2010.

Bloom, Lynn Z. "The Essay Canon." *College English* 61.4 (1999): 401–30. Print.

Breneman, D. W., and W. N. Haarlow. "Remediation in Higher Education: A Symposium Featuring Remedial Education: Costs and Consequences." *Fordham Report* 2.9 (1998): 1–22. Print.

Brodkey, Linda. "Writing Permitted in Designated Areas Only." *Higher Education under Fire*. Ed. Michael Berube and Cary Nelson. New York: Routledge, 1995. 214–37. Print.

Curtis, Marcia, and Anne Herrington. "Writing Development in the College Years: By Whose Definition?" *College Composition and Communication* 55.1 (2003): 69–90. Print.

DeBenedictus, Deb. "Sustained Silent Reading: Making Adaptations." *Voices from the Middle* 14.3 (2007): 29–37. Print.

Deci, Edward L., and Richard Flaste. *Why We Do What We Do: Understanding Self-Motivation*. New York: Penguin, 1996. Print.

Deci, Edward L., Richard Koestner, and Richard M. Ryan. "A Meta-Analytic Review of Experiments Examining the Effects of Extrinsic Rewards on Intrinsic Motivation." *Psychological Bulletin* 125.6 (1999): 627–68.

Deci, Edward L., and Richard M Ryan, eds. *Handbook of Self-Determination Research*. Rochester: U of Rochester P, 2002. Print.

———. *Intrinsic Motivation and Self-Determination in Human Behavior*. New York: Plenum, 1985. Print.

Eisner, Elliot W. *The Arts and the Creation of Mind*. New Haven: Yale UP, 2004. Print.

Flower, Linda. "Writer-Based Prose: A Cognitive Basis for Problems in Writing." *College English* 41.1 (1979): 19–37. Print.

Kohn, Alfie. *The Case against Standardized Testing: Raising the Scores, Ruining the Schools*. Portsmouth: Heinemann, 2000. Print.

———. *Punished by Rewards: The Trouble with Gold Stars, Incentive Plans, A's, Praise, and Other Bribes*. Boston: Houghton Mifflin, 1993. Print.

Larsen, Lindsay. "Disappearing into the World of Books." Sullivan, Tinberg, and Blau 280–92. Print.

Lindblom, Ken, ed. *Motivating Students*. Spec. issue of *English Journal* 100.1 (2010). Print.

Lujan, Alfredo. "The Salem Witch Trials: Voice(s)." Sullivan, Tinberg, and Blau 41–57. Print.

Lunsford, Andrea, and Karen Lunsford. "'Mistakes Are a Fact of Life': A National Comparative Study." *College Composition and Communication* 59.4 (2008): 781–806. Print.

Maliszewski, Casey. "Home Schooled." Sullivan, Tinberg, and Blau 257–66. Print.

Manning, G. L., and M. Manning. "What Models of Recreational Reading Make a Difference?" *Reading World* 23.4 (1984): 375–80. Print.

Perlstein, Linda. *Tested: One American School Struggles to Make the Grade*. New York: Holt, 2007. Print.

Pink, Daniel. *Drive: The Surprising Truth about What Motivates Us*. New York: Riverhead, 2009. Print.

Ryan, Richard M., Richard Koestner, and Edward Deci. "Ego-Involved Persistence: When Free-Choice Behavior Is Not Intrinsically Motivated." *Motivation and Emotion* 15 (1991): 185–205. Print.

Ryan, Richard M., Valerie Mims, and Richard Koestner. "Relation of Reward Contingency and Interpersonal Context to Intrinsic Motivation: A Review and Test Using Cognitive Evaluation Theory." *Journal of Personality and Social Psychology* 45.4 (1983): 736–50. Print.

Ryan, Richard M., and Cynthia L. Powelson. "Autonomy and Relatedness as Fundamental to Motivation and Education." *Journal of Experimental Education* 60 (1991): 49–66. Print.

Saxon, D. Patrick, and Hunter R. Boylan. "The Cost of Remedial Education in Higher Education." *Journal of Developmental Education* 25.2 (2001): 2–8. Print.

Smith, Michael W., and Jeffery D. Wilhelm. *Reading Don't Fix No Chevys: Literacy in the Lives of Young Men*. Portsmouth: Heinemann, 2002. Print.

Strong American Schools. *Diploma to Nowhere*. Washington: Strong American Schools, 2008. Print.

Sullivan, Patrick. "An Open Letter to Ninth Graders." *Academe* January/February 2009: 6–10. Print.

———. "What Can We Learn about 'College-Level' Writing from Basic Writing Students? The Importance of Reading." Sullivan, Tinberg, and Blau 233–53. Print.

Sullivan, Patrick, Howard Tinberg, and Sheridan Blau, eds. *What Is "College-Level" Writing?* Vol. 2: *Assignments, Readings, and Sample Student Writing*. Urbana: NCTE, 2010. Print.

United States. Department of Education, National Center for Education Statistics. *Profile of Undergraduate Students: 2007–08*. Table 6.2: Percentage of first- and second-year undergraduates who reported ever taking a remedial course after high school graduation. 2010. Web. 27 Nov. 2010.

———. *A Test of Leadership: Charting the Future of U.S. Higher Education*. Washington: U.S. Department of Education, 2006. Web.

Venezia, Andrea, Michael Kirst, and Anthony Antonio. *Betraying the College Dream: How Disconnected K–12 and Postsecondary Education Systems Undermine Student Aspirations*. Final Policy Report from Stanford University's Bridge Project, 2003. Web.

Worthy, Jo, Margo Turner, and Megan Moorman. "The Precarious Place of Self-Selected Reading." *Language Arts* 75.4 (1998): 296–304. Print.

Designing Writing Assignments

Using Writing to Promote Thinking

John Bean

The book from which this selection is taken was praised by a number of respondents to our national survey of TYCA members as an essential resource for teachers of writing. This is not surprising, as John Bean synthesizes research from a variety of disciplines and then skillfully translates that research into pragmatic, up-to-date suggestions for integrating writing, critical thinking, and active learning in the classroom. The excerpt we feature here focuses on strategies for designing writing activities that promote critical thinking—a key concern for all writing instructors. Bean reviews some of the general principles linking writing to learning and critical thinking, and then offers specific classroom strategies for promoting critical thinking and strong writing.

In his now classic study of pedagogical strategies that make a difference, Richard Light (2001) examined the connection between writing and student engagement. "The results are stunning," he claims:

> The relationship between the amount of writing for a course and students' level of engagement—whether engagement is measured by time spent on

---

From *Engaging Ideas: The Professor's Guide to Integrating Writing, Critical Thinking, and Active Learning in the Classroom*, 2nd ed. Jossey-Bass, 2011, pp. 1-14.

the course, or the intellectual challenge it presents, or students' level of interest in it—is stronger than the relationship between students' engagement and any other course characteristic. . . . (55)

More recent research, conducted jointly by the National Survey of Student Engagement (NSSE) and the Council of Writing Program Administrators (WPA), has shown that for promoting engagement and deep learning the number of writing assignments in a course may not be as important as the design of the writing assignments themselves (Anderson, Anson, Gonyea, and Paine, 2009). Good assignments, this research has shown, give students opportunities to receive early feedback on their work, encourage meaning-making, and clearly explain the instructor's expectations and purpose. . . .

[My aim] is to give professors a wide range of options for bringing the benefits of engaged learning to students. My premise, supported by an increasing body of research, is that good writing assignments (as well as other active learning tasks) evoke a high level of critical thinking, help students wrestle productively with a course's big questions, and teach disciplinary ways of seeing, knowing, and doing. They can also be designed to promote self-reflection, leading to more integrated, personally meaningful learning. Moreover, the benefits do not accrue only to students. Professors who successfully integrate writing and other critical thinking activities into their courses often report a satisfying increase in their teaching pleasure: students are better prepared for class, discussions are richer, and student performance improves.

But the use of writing and critical thinking activities to promote learning does not happen through serendipity. Teachers must plan for it and foster it throughout the course. This [selection] suggests a sequence of steps that teachers can take to integrate writing and critical thinking into their courses. It then addresses four negative beliefs that often discourage teachers from taking these steps—the beliefs that integrating writing into a course will take time away from content, that writing assignments are not appropriate for some disciplines or courses, that assigning writing will bury a teacher in paper grading, and that assigning writing requires specialized expertise. Because these beliefs raise important concerns, I seek to supply reassuring responses at the outset. . . .

Steps for Integrating Writing and Critical Thinking Activities into a Course

This section surveys eight steps teachers can take to integrate writing and critical thinking activities into a course.

*Step 1: Become Familiar with Some of the General Principles
Linking Writing to Learning and Critical Thinking*

To appreciate how writing is linked to learning and critical thinking, we can begin with a brief discussion of how we might define critical thinking.

CRITICAL THINKING ROOTED IN PROBLEMS

Although definitions in the pedagogical literature vary in detail, in their broad outlines they are largely elaborations, extensions, and refinements of the progressive views of John Dewey (1916), who rooted critical thinking in the students' engagement with a problem. Problems, for Dewey, evoke students' natural curiosity and stimulate both learning and critical thought. "Only by wrestling with the conditions of the problem at first hand, seeking and finding his own way out, does [the student] think" (188).

Part of the difficulty of teaching critical thinking, therefore, is awakening students to the existence of problems all around them. Meyers (1986), who agrees with Dewey that problems are naturally motivating, argues that teachers ought to begin every class with "something that is a problem or a cause for wonder" (44). Meyers quotes philosopher and chemist Michael Polanyi, who claims that "as far down the scale of life as worms and even perhaps amoebas, we meet a general alertness of animals, not directed towards any specific satisfaction, but merely exploring what is there: an urge to achieve intellectual control over the situations confronting [them]" (41).

Presenting students with problems, then, taps into something natural and self-fulfilling in our beings. In his fifteen-year study of what the best college professors do, Ken Bain (2004) shows that highly effective teachers confront students with "intriguing, beautiful, or important problems, authentic tasks that will challenge them to grapple with ideas, rethink their assumptions, and examine their mental models of reality" (p. 18). Set at the appropriate level of difficulty, such "beautiful problems" create a "natural critical learning environment" that engages students as active and deep learners. Similarly, Brookfield (1987) claims that critical thinking is "a productive and positive" activity. "Critical thinkers are actively engaged with life" (5). This belief in the natural, healthy, and motivating pleasure of problems—and in the power of well-designed problems to awaken and stimulate the passive and unmotivated student—is one of the underlying premises of this book.

DISCIPLINARY VERSUS GENERIC DOMAINS FOR CRITICAL THINKING

Not all problems, however, are *academic* problems of the kind that we typically present to students in our classrooms or that we pose for ourselves in doing scholarly research. Academic problems are typically rooted within a disciplinary conversation: to a large extent, these problems are discipline-specific, as each discipline poses its own kinds of questions and conducts inquiries, uses data, and makes arguments in its own characteristic fashion. As Anne Beaufort (2007) has shown, to think and write like a disciplinary professional, students must draw not only on subject matter knowledge, but also on knowledge about the discipline's genre conventions, its methods of argument, its typical kinds of evidence, its ways of referencing other researchers, and its typical rhetorical contexts and audiences. . . .

But certain underlying features of critical thinking are generic across all domains. According to Brookfield (1987), two "central activities" define critical thinking: "identifying and challenging assumptions and exploring alternative ways of thinking and acting" (71). Joanne Kurfiss (1988) likewise believes that critical thinkers pose problems by questioning assumptions and aggressively seeking alternative views. For her, the prototypical academic problem is "ill-structured"; that is, it is an open-ended question that does not have a clear right answer and therefore must be responded to with a proposition justified by reasons and evidence. "In critical thinking," says Kurfiss, "all assumptions are open to question, divergent views are aggressively sought, and the inquiry is not biased in favor of a particular outcome" (2).

THE LINK BETWEEN WRITING AND CRITICAL THINKING

Given this view of critical thinking, what is its connection with writing? Quite simply, writing is both a process of doing critical thinking and a product that communicates the results of critical thinking. . . . [W]riting instruction goes sour whenever writing is conceived primarily as a "communication skill" rather than as a process and product of critical thought. If writing is merely a communication skill, then we primarily ask of it, "Is the writing clear?" But if writing is critical thinking, we ask, "Is the writing interesting? Does it show a mind actively engaged with a problem? Does it bring something new to readers? Does it make an argument?" . . . [E]xperienced writers begin by posing two kinds of problems—what we might call subject matter problems and rhetorical problems. Subject matter problems drive the writer's inquiry. The writer's thesis statement is a tentative response to a subject matter problem; it poses a contestable "answer" or "solution" that must be supported with the kinds of reasons and evidence that are valued in the discipline. But writers also think critically about rhetorical problems: Who is my audience? What genre should I employ and what are its features and conventions? How much do my readers already know about and care about my subject matter problem? How do I want to change my audience's views? What alternative views must I consider? Writers produce multiple drafts because the act of writing is itself an act of problem solving. Behind the scenes of a finished product is a messy process of exploratory writing, conversation, and discarded drafts. . . .

Step 2: Design Your Course with Critical Thinking Objectives in Mind

Once teachers are convinced of the value of critical thinking, the next step is to design a course that nurtures it. What is such a course like? In her comprehensive review of the literature on critical thinking, Kurfiss (1988) examined a wide range of successful disciplinary courses devoted to the teaching of both subject matter and critical thinking. In each case, she explains, "the professor establishes an agenda that includes learning to think about subject matter. Students are active, involved, consulting and arguing with each other, and responsible for their own learning" (88). From this review, she derives eight principles for designing a disciplinary course that supports critical thinking:

1. Critical thinking is a learnable skill; the instructor and peers are resources in developing critical thinking skills.

2. Problems, questions, or issues are the point of entry into the subject and a source of motivation for sustained inquiry.

3. Successful courses balance challenges to think critically with support tailored to students' developmental needs.

4. Courses are assignment centered rather than text and lecture centered. Goals, methods, and evaluation emphasize using content rather than simply acquiring it.

5. Students are required to formulate and justify their ideas in writing or other appropriate modes.

6. Students collaborate to learn and to stretch their thinking, for example, in pair problem solving and small group work.

7. Several courses, particularly those that teach problem-solving skills, nurture students' metacognitive abilities.

8. The developmental needs of students are acknowledged and used as information in the design of the course. Teachers in these courses make standards explicit and then help students learn how to achieve them (88–89).

[My aim is] to help teachers develop courses that follow these guidelines. Of key importance are Kurfiss's principles 2, 4, and 5: a good critical thinking course presents students with "problems, questions, [or] issues" that make a course "assignment centered rather than text [or] lecture centered" and holds students responsible for formulating and justifying their solutions orally or in writing. This [selection] particularly emphasizes writing assignments because they are perhaps the most flexible and most intensive way to integrate critical thinking tasks into a course and because the writing process itself entails complex critical thinking. But much attention is also given to class discussions, small group activities, and other teaching strategies that encourage students to work collaboratively to expand, develop, and deepen their thinking. Attention is also given throughout to the design of problems at appropriate levels of difficulty, to the developmental needs of students, and to the importance of making expectations and criteria clear (principles 1, 3, and 8).

Step 3: Design Critical Thinking Tasks for Students to Address

A crucial step in teaching critical thinking is to develop good problems for students to think about. Tasks can range from enduring disciplinary problems to narrowly specific questions about the significance of a graph or the interpretation of a key passage in a course reading. The kinds of questions you develop for students will depend on their level of expertise, their current degree of engagement with the subject matter, and the nature of question asking in your own discipline.

When I conduct workshops in writing across the curriculum, I like to emphasize a disciplinary, content-driven view of critical thinking by asking faculty to write out one or two final examination essay questions for one of their courses—questions that they think require both subject matter knowledge and critical thinking. We then discuss the kinds of critical thinking needed and the relative difficulty of each question, sometimes offering suggestions on ways to improve questions to elicit the kinds and levels of critical thinking the teacher seeks. When we have appreciated the value of these questions for promoting critical thinking, I suggest that it is a shame to waste them on a timed exam, where students spend only an hour or so on task. Such questions and dozens more like them can be integrated into the fabric of a course, where they can stimulate curiosity, drive inquiry, and promote learning. . . .

Step 4: Develop a Repertoire of Ways to Give Critical Thinking Tasks to Students

Once you have developed a stockpile of critical thinking problems based on your course's subject matter, you can choose from dozens of ways to integrate them into your course. I present numerous options for giving critical thinking problems to students. These include the following:

1. *Problems as formal writing assignments.* Formal writing assignments, which require revision and multiple drafts, keep students on task for extended periods and are among our most powerful tools for

teaching critical thinking. They can range in length from one-paragraph "microthemes" to major research projects within a disciplinary genre. . . . [E]ffective academic assignments usually require that the student formulate and support a thesis (or test a hypothesis) in response to a problem. Such problem-centered assignments, which are primarily argumentative or analytical, are more effective for developing critical thinking than topic-centered assignments, which students often interpret as asking for information ("Write a research paper on one of the following topics").

2. *Problems as thought-provokers for exploratory writing.* Although students normally write only a few formal papers for a course, they can do behind-the-scenes exploratory writing on a daily basis. . . . [T]his kind of low-stakes writing . . . is a seedbed for generating and growing ideas. Exploratory writing records the actual process of critical thinking while simultaneously driving it forward. Perhaps more than any other instructional tool, exploratory writing transforms the way students study for a course because it can make active critical thinking about course subject matter part of each day's homework. . . .

3. *Problems as small group tasks.* Disciplinary problems make powerful collaborative learning tasks. Small groups can be given a set time to brainstorm possible solutions to a problem or to seek a best solution by arriving at a consensus or a reasoned "agreement to disagree." In a plenary session, groups report their solutions and present their justifying arguments using appropriate reasons and evidence. The instructor usually critiques the groups' solutions and often explains how experts in the discipline (for whom the teacher is spokesperson) might tackle the same problem. During plenary sessions, the instructor both models and coaches disciplinary ways of making arguments, also attending to the generic critical thinking skills of looking at the available evidence and considering alternative views. . . .

4. *Problems as starters for class discussions.* Discussion classes can begin with one or two critical thinking problems written on the chalkboard or posted in advance on an electronic discussion board as "questions of the day." The teacher guides the discussion, encouraging students to appreciate and manage complexity. (If students have addressed these questions the night before in an exploratory thinking piece, they will be both eager and prepared for class discussion.) Other ways to get students actively addressing critical thinking problems include classroom debates, panel discussions, and fishbowls. . . .

5. *Problems as practice exam questions.* . . . One of the best approaches [to coax more student learning and critical thinking out of essay exams] is to give practice exams that students write for homework on a self-timed basis. Feedback is provided through in-class discussion of representative essays.

The point of all these strategies is to model for students a view of knowledge in which inquirers must develop and support provisional answers to disciplinary problems. By actively using new concepts and information, students engage course material on a deeper level.

Step 5: Develop Strategies to Include Exploratory Writing, Talking, and Reflection in Your Courses

Good writing, I like to tell my students, grows out of good talking—either talking with classmates or talking dialogically with oneself through exploratory writing. A key observation among teachers of critical thinking is that students, when given a critical thinking problem, tend to reach closure too quickly. They do not suspend judgment, question assumptions, evaluate evidence, imagine alternative answers, play with data, enter into the spirit of opposing views, and just plain linger over questions. As a result, they often write truncated and underdeveloped papers. To deepen students' thinking, teachers need to build into their courses time, space, tools, and motivation for exploratory thinking. Closely connected to exploratory tasks are reflective tasks aimed at encouraging students to think metacognitively about their own thinking processes, to connect learning in one course to other courses or to their own lives, to transfer skills from one setting to another, and to integrate their learning. . . .

Step 6: Develop Strategies for Teaching How Your Discipline Uses Evidence to Support Claims

To grow as critical thinkers, students need to learn how different disciplines use evidence to support arguments. According to Richard Light (2001), "A surprising number of undergraduates describe learning how to use evidence to resolve controversies in their field, whatever their field, as a breakthrough idea" (122). Light describes the bafflement of first-year students as they shift from discipline to discipline, encountering different ways that disciplines gather and use evidence to address problems. Some disciplines derive their evidence from observations of natural or cultural phenomena, sometimes converted to numbers, subjected to statistical analysis, and displayed in graphs and tables. Other disciplines use qualitative data from ethnographic observations, focus group transcripts, or interviews. Still others analyze aural, visual, or verbal texts housed in libraries, historical archives, art galleries, museums, popular media archives, or websites.

What new students don't see is how these different kinds of data function as evidence in support of a claim. Teachers can accelerate students' understanding of a field by designing assignments that teach disciplinary use of evidence or that help students analyze the thinking moves within an evidence-based argument. Closely related to disciplinary use of evidence is use of disciplinary genres such as experimental reports, ethnographies, design proposals, or disciplinary papers suitable for presentation at an undergraduate research conference. . . .

Step 7: Develop Effective Strategies for Coaching Students in Critical Thinking

Besides giving students good problems to think about, teachers need to critique students' performances and to model the kinds of critical thinking they want students to develop. According to Meyers (1986), teachers of critical thinking will often spend much of their class time as "referees, coaches, and mentors rather than as lecturers and purveyors of the truth . . . For most of us," he continues, "this is a worthwhile but difficult shift" (39). [There are] numerous ways that teachers can coach critical thinking, including guiding discussions, critiquing solutions developed by small groups, writing comments on student drafts, holding conferences, sharing autobiographical accounts of their own thinking and writing processes, discussing strengths and weaknesses of sample papers, breaking long assignments into stages, and stressing revision and multiple drafts. An equally important aspect of coaching is providing a supportive, open classroom that values the worth and dignity of students. . . .

Step 8: When Assigning Formal Writing, Treat Writing as a Process

In most kinds of courses, the student "product" that most clearly exhibits the results of critical thinking is a piece of formal writing addressing an open-ended problem. Too often, however, what the student submits as a finished product is in an unrevised draft, the result of an undeveloped and often truncated thinking process that doesn't adequately confront all the available evidence, consider alternative views, examine assumptions, or imagine the needs of a new reader. Much of the thinking promoted by writing occurs during the messy process of revision when the writer's ideas gradually become focused and clarified. No matter how much we exhort students to write several drafts and to collaborate with peers, most of our students will continue to write their papers on the night before they are due unless we structure our courses to promote writing as a process.

Teachers can get better final products, therefore, if they design their courses from the outset to combat last-minute writing, to promote exploratory writing and talking, and to encourage substantive revision. Promoting such exploration is one of the functions of progressive writing centers, where experienced tutors or consultants can help students understand the demands of an assignment, brainstorm ideas, and revise their papers through multiple drafts. On many campuses the director of the writing center is one of an instructor's most important resources for developing ways to incorporate writing into a course. . . .

Four Discouraging Beliefs and Some Encouraging Responses

The steps just described can help teachers integrate writing and critical thinking activities into their courses. However, many teachers who are tempted to do so may be held back by negative beliefs or misconceptions about what happens when a teacher begins developing a pedagogy using writing and critical thinking. It will be helpful, therefore, to address these beliefs at the outset. Based on discussions with faculty from across the disciplines, I find the following four misconceptions the most pervasive and potentially discouraging.

Misconception 1: Emphasizing Writing and Critical Thinking in My Courses Will Take Time Away from Content

Many faculty, understandably concerned about coverage of material, do not want to shift class time away from content. In addressing this conundrum, one must first distinguish between how much a teacher "covers" in a given course and how much students actually learn in a meaningful and usable way. Much of the literature on best pedagogical practices suggests that less is more. For example, Robert Zemsky (2009), founding director of the University of Pennsylvania's Institute for Research on Higher Education, argues that "no one has sufficient time or gray matter to master a knowledge base that is growing exponentially every decade or so." Rather than focus exhaustively on content coverage, Zemsky urges educators to prioritize content, focusing on high-priority material while simultaneously teaching the critical thinking and problem-solving skills needed to acquire and apply new knowledge:

> Discussions of the changing nature of knowledge often morph into what a successful learning outcome would be if detailed content were actually becoming less important than a well-executed learning process. The former is static; the latter is dynamic in the sense that learning processes change as the learner seeks new knowledge and tackles new problems.

In my experience, integrating writing and critical thinking components into a course can increase the amount of subject matter that students actually learn. My assertion may seem counterintuitive until one realizes that these assignments can restructure the way students study outside of class. Critical thinking tasks—which require students to *use* their expanding knowledge of subject matter to address disciplinary problems—motivate better study habits by helping students see their learning as purposeful and interesting. If tasks are designed to improve academic reading, students often learn to read textbooks more powerfully and to interact more critically with primary source readings. With more confidence that students can learn from assigned readings, teachers can, if they choose, redirect some class time away from lecturing over the readings toward critical discussions, small group problem solving, or other critical thinking activities. . . .

Misconception 2: Writing Assignments Are Unsuitable in My Course

Most teachers believe that writing applies naturally to English courses, to liberal arts courses, and to certain specialized courses in their fields. They may not, however, believe that writing is equally appropriate in their own courses. These doubts are frequently expressed by teachers of quantitative or technical courses or ones that focus on basic facts, concepts, or algorithmic procedures that, according to the teacher, must be "committed to memory" before the student can move on to problem solving and analysis. If we apply some conceptual blockbusting, however, we see that writing assignments can be used profitably in any course. (My point is exemplified by the wide range of disciplines represented—accounting, physics, chemistry, all levels of mathematics, nursing, business, education, and engineering, as well as the humanities and social sciences.) By conceptual blockbusting, I mean primarily rethinking what constitutes a *writing assignment*. . . . Whatever a teacher's goals for a course, writing assignments can be designed to help students meet them.

Misconception 3: Adding More Writing to My Course Will Bury Me in Paper Grading

Many teachers would gladly require more writing in their courses if it were not for the need to mark and grade all those papers. If teachers do not currently assign any writing in their courses, adding a writing component will admittedly require extra work, although not necessarily more total time devoted to teaching if some of the teacher's current preparation or conference time is shifted toward responding to writing. If teachers already require writing in their courses (say, a couple of essay exams and a term paper), following the[se] suggestions . . . might *reduce* the total time they spend on student writing while simultaneously making that time more rewarding for themselves and more productive for students. The NSSE/WPA research cited at the beginning of this [selection] (Anderson, Anson, Gonyea, and Paine, 2009) has shown that what matters in using writing to promote deep learning is not the amount of writing in a course but the quality of the writing assignments themselves.

There are many ways to work writing into a course while keeping the paper load manageable. Some methods require no teacher time (for example, in-class freewriting); some, minimal time (perusing a random selection of entries from a guided journal or class discussion board); and some, very modest time (assigning write-to-learn microthemes using models feedback). Even when you require several formal essays or a major research paper, you may employ any number of timesaving strategies to reduce the paper load. The key is to decide how much time you are willing to spend on student writing and then to plan your courses to include only what you can handle—always remembering that you do not have to read everything a student writes.

Misconception 4: I Am Not Knowledgeable Enough About Writing and Grammar to Help Students with Their Own Writing

Many teachers across the curriculum will admit that English was not their favorite subject. Although they produce competent professional writing in their own fields, they believe that because they struggle with their own writing and because they do not know grammatical terminology or composition theory, they lack the skills to help students. [I hope] to allay these fears. Because the best teacher commentary focuses primarily on ideas and development, no special terminology is needed. Teachers simply need to be honest readers, making comments like these:

"I got lost in this part."

"You need more evidence here."

"You seem to be overlooking Baker's research on this problem. Can you summarize and respond to Baker's views?"

"Excellent point!"

A main key to teaching writing . . . is teaching students how to revise. The more teachers struggle to revise their own writing, the more they can serve as role models for students. In short, your own experience as an academic writer and reader, combined with your expertise in how scholars in your field inquire and argue, should be all the background you need to help your students with their writing.

Conclusion: Engaging Your Students with the Ideas of Your Course

The steps suggested here for integrating writing and critical thinking assignments into a course can increase students' engagement with subject matter and improve the quality of their work. Moreover, these suggestions do not call for rapid, complete makeovers of a course. It is possible to make changes in a course gradually—trying a few new activities at a time, looking for strategies and approaches that fit your discipline and subject matter, that work for your students, and that accord with your own personality and teaching philosophy.

Some teachers make only minimal changes in their courses. I know of one teacher, a brilliant lecturer, who has changed nothing in his courses except for adding a series of nongraded "practice essay exams." He collects the exams (written out of class, self-timed by students), keeps a record of who submits them, reads randomly selected ones in search of representative problems as well as models of excellent exams, and then holds class discussions of what constitutes a good answer. He is very happy with this minimalist approach and offers persuasive anecdotal evidence that this practice has improved students' study habits as well as the quality of their actual essay exams.

But I know of other teachers who have radically transformed their classrooms, moving from a teaching-centered to a learning-centered pedagogy, from lecture-based courses to inquiry-based courses using exploratory writing, collaborative learning, lively discussions, and other strategies for engaging students in inquiry and debate.

References

Anderson, P., Anson, C., Gonyea, B., and Paine, C. Using results from the Consortium for the Study of Writing in College. Webinar handout. *National Survey of Student Engagement*, 2009. Retrieved April 26, 2010, from http://nsse .iub.edu/webinars/TuesdaysWithNSSE/2009_09_22_UsingResultsCSWC /Webinar%20Handout%20from%20WPA%202009.pdf

Bain, K. *What the Best College Teachers Do*. Cambridge: Harvard University Press, 2004.

Beaufort, A. *College Writing and Beyond: A New Framework for University Writing Instruction*. Logan, Utah: Utah State University Press, 2007.

Brookfield, S. D. *Developing Critical Thinkers: Challenging Adults to Explore Alternative Ways of Thinking and Acting*. San Francisco: Jossey-Bass, 1987.

Dewey, J. *Democracy and Education*. New York: Macmillan, 1916.

Kurfiss, J. G. *Critical Thinking: Theory, Research, Practice, and Possibilities*. ASHE-ERIC Higher Education Report No. 2. Washington, D.C.: ERIC Clearinghouse on Higher Education and the Association for the Study of Higher Education, 1988.

Light, R. J. *Making the Most of College: Students Speak Their Minds*. Cambridge: Harvard University Press, 2001.

Meyers, C. *Teaching Students to Think Critically: A Guide for Faculty in All Disciplines*. San Francisco: Jossey-Bass, 1986.

Zemsky, R. "The To Do List." *Inside Higher Ed*, Sept. 14, 2009. http://www .insidehighered.com/views/2009/09/14/zemsky

Implications for Teaching and Research

Howard Tinberg and Jean-Paul Nadeau

Discussing findings from a institutional study of two-year college student writers, Howard Tinberg and Jean-Paul Nadeau emphasize the importance of well-designed writing assignments for optimum student engagement and development. They offer six essential criteria for effective assignments, synthesized from writing assignments across a number of disciplines and informed by conversations with student writers as well as faculty from a variety of disciplines. Their criteria speak to the wide variety of courses and writing tasks assigned within the broad mission of comprehensive community colleges.

Designing Assignments

When we began this study, we hypothesized that faculty at our college were assigning writing in classes other than the first-year required English courses and that writing assignments would reflect the complex mission of the college, promoting both academic and workplace literacy. Our work in the multidisciplinary writing center provided some basis for our assumptions: while the majority of the writing that tutors see in the center comes from English courses, roughly 40 percent comes from social sciences, most conspicuously criminal justice, history, human services, and psychology. Writing comes as well from dental hygiene, biology, and art. We need to keep in mind, however, that the writing center serves students well beyond their first semester—which, of course, is our focus in this study. A study of our cohort portfolios strongly supports the perception that a preponderance of writing done in that first semester occurs in the required English courses only.

That fact has implications for our second hypothesis in that the writing done in English courses favors the essay over other forms of composition—a genre that, for all intents and purposes, lives mostly in the classroom and not in the workplace. We conclude that what David Russell calls the "myth of transience" is alive and well at Bristol: in other words, the idea that writing instruction in an English course transfers easily to writing done in any course (Russell 3). "Talking with the pen or keyboard," as it were, calls for the same set of skills whatever the discipline or course or genre. But, as with the mission of the community college itself, our assessment of these matters is complex and dialogic. Writing assignments that emerge from the college's career areas

From *The Community College Writer: Exceeding Expectations*. Southern Illinois University Press, 2010, pp. 115-18.

strongly suggest a workplace-specific set of criteria. We point, for example, to an interview assignment in occupational therapy, for which students need to "integrate relevant academic knowledge through case study" and demonstrate "skills of self awareness, listening, and therapeutic communication." While occupational therapy can hardly claim a monopoly on the importance of listening skills, this assignment has moved well beyond assessing written performance on the basis of paragraph logic or clarity of thesis—conventional markers of the academic essay. Rather, students are asked, as part of their assignment, to do what is expected at the job and to report on whether they have met expectations. The same can be said of communication students, who are asked by their instructor to compose a "feature news story" for the college newspaper. Students need not only to be able to conduct an interview effectively, they need to demonstrate a knowledge of the news story genre, which, while sharing similarities with the essay, is also distinctively different (especially in its attention to capturing an urgency and immediacy as expressed in speech and described behavior).

Students will achieve little, of course, unless the assignments provide the opportunity for engagement and growth. "Given the right conditions," asserts George Hillocks, "nearly all students can become engaged" (21). What are those conditions? Put another way, what features must an effective assignment have? Conversely, what flaws in assignment design prevent student engagement and development? Guided by our study and our years of work in the writing center, we offer these characteristics as essential to effective design of assignments for our students:

1. *Show students what success looks like.* Many of our students have never seen some of the forms of writing required in college and would benefit by seeing genres "in action." What, for example, does an annotated bibliography look like? When Andrew, a student in our cohort, was asked to write a film review, he had had little exposure to the genre. He became familiar with the genre by seeking out examples.

2. *Spell out criteria for success.* Many of our students have sufficient motive to succeed but need directions on the road. Many also lack a vocabulary and metaknowledge for talking about successful writing. What makes for an effective piece of college-level writing? Or as Kim, one of our cohort asked of her English instructor, What constitutes a "perfect paper"?

3. *Suggest processes for succeeding.* More than one of our students commented on what they saw as a key difference between high school and college—at least in regards to writing instruction in English courses. In high school, they assert, a task would be given but with little direction as to how to achieve it. In college, they claim, students are shown not only what they are to produce but how to go about doing it. Realizing that it is hardly fair to generalize on all writing instruction—at either the high

school or college level—we take the point seriously nonetheless: process matters. Students need to be shown how to go about achieving success: what steps ought to be taken?

4. *Develop incremental stages for complex writing tasks.* Imagine being asked, as Kim and her fellow students were, to write an "autobiography" in your general psychology course in which you apply the theories of Erickson and Maslow. Left to your own devices to complete the assignment, you might be tempted to begin with what you know best: your own story. And so you tell your story, compelling as it is. But you lose sight of the second half of the assignment: to theorize your account through the lens of Erickson and Maslow. You attempt to jury-rig the theory to your narrative but end up adding a new and somewhat disconnected section to your paper. How might this have been avoided? An assignment divided into several stages might have prevented this problem: the student could have been asked to engage the theories initially through a summary exercise. She might then have been asked to synthesize her sources: where are the overlaps? Where do they differ? These steps could have been followed with the beginning of an analysis, stipulating a hypothesis that could enable her to manage her own life story.

5. *Allow for formative and substantive feedback.* Student after student in our project called upon faculty to provide guidance through their written feedback, feedback that could then be employed to improve their writing. While our access to faculty commentary was limited, what we saw in cohort portfolios provided important lessons: private notes or check marks (whose meaning is known only by the faculty member) do little to promote student learning. Feedback that is not grounded in the assignment criteria does nothing but confuse the student and further reinforces perceptions of faculty bias and subjectivity. The most useful feedback was rooted in clearly and explicitly stated criteria. In addition, we noted the facilitative nature of effective commentary, affirming what Knoblauch and Brannon (over two decades ago) called the "writer's ongoing pursuit of meanings" (130).

6. *Provide ample opportunities for drafting.* Another clear difference between high school and college writing instruction, our students claimed, was the sheer amount of revision expected in college (at least in the first semester). We were impressed by our students' willingness to allow their writing to go through several drafts in response to faculty feedback. While in some cases the revision seemed nothing more than attending to localized editing matters (to move a grade from A– to A), in other situations students engaged in changing global features of their writing, such as gaps in logic or the lack of grounding detail. As a group, our students were more than willing to undertake significant changes to their work. Shall we not give them the opportunity to do so?

Works Cited

Hillocks, Jr., George. *Teaching Writing as a Reflective Practice*. New York: Teachers College, 1995.

Knoblauch, C. H., and Lil Brannon. *Rhetorical Traditions and the Teaching of Writing*. Upper Montclair, NJ: Boynton/Cook, 1984.

Russell, David. *Writing in the Academic Disciplines: A Curricular History*. 2nd ed. Carbondale: Southern Illinois University Press, 2002.

Teaching for Transfer of Learning

The Question of University Writing Instruction

Anne Beaufort

The selection that follows is excerpted from the first chapter of Anne Beaufort's College Writing and Beyond. *In it, she asks us to consider "what knowledge domains best represent the mental schema employed in expert writing performances? And what knowledge domains—or mental schema—do writers need to invoke for analyzing new writing tasks in new discourse communities? If we can articulate these knowledge domains and apply them to shaping curriculum, we can then contextualize writing instruction more fully and have a basis for teaching for transfer, that is equipping students with a mental schema for learning writing skills in new genres in new discourse communities they will encounter through life" (p. 212 in this volume).*

> *Anne:* What's your sense of yourself as a writer now, compared to four years ago?
>
> *Tim:* Uh, well, shoot. Four years ago I would have said, you know, I've got . . . I don't know . . . Four years ago, before taking classes here, I would have said, well that's not really writing . . . realizing that . . . it's not like a particular genre that qualifies as writing. Okay, now you can use style or you pay attention to this, but it's like, you

From *College Writing and Beyond: A New Framework for University Writing Instruction.* Utah State University Press, 2007, pp. 5-22.

know, whenever you scribble something down, I mean anytime you
sit down at the keyboard then that's writing. Even if it's one, two,
three, four . . .

—Tim, senior year of college

Anne: Do you think you grew as a writer?

Tim: In college? Oh yeah, yeah.

Anne: How?

Tim: Well, I grew to enjoy it and I think I enjoyed it because I was set
free, and in being set free I think I found that I had some skill at
it . . . I had occasions that were handed to me (laughs). Write! Well,
might as well make this fun.

—Tim, two years after college

This book has two stories to tell: the story of Tim's somewhat limited
growth as a writer (from this researcher's perspective) between the
time he started a freshman writing class at a major US university until
two years after he had graduated from school; and second, more argument than story, a case for a re-conceptualization of writing instruction
at the post-secondary level. In an earlier ethnography, I examined the
struggles of four writers to acclimatize themselves to the demands of
writing in college and then in the workplace. Out of that work came a
beginning articulation of the nature of writing expertises and a demonstration of why transfer of writing skills from one social context to another is a major issue as yet given too little attention in conceptions of
writing curricula. In this work — a blended genre of both ethnography
and argument — I draw on the data of a longitudinal case study of one
writer bridging from high school writing instruction to freshman writing and then to writing in his two majors, history and engineering, to
answer the fundamental question college administrators, college professors in disciplines other than composition studies, and business leaders ask: why graduates of freshman writing cannot produce acceptable
written documents in other contexts? At the same time, for those readers who are well acquainted with the scholarship that answers that question, I provide additional empirical work and pragmatic suggestions . . .
that may aid the effort to build more coherent writing instruction at the
post-secondary level. And for theorists and critics who have not focused
on these issues, I hope to provide food for thought on the nature of writing expertise. I see the issues I raise here as relevant to all venues for
college-level writing instruction: freshman writing programs, writing-in-
the-disciplines programs, programs to train teaching assistants and tutors in teaching of writing, and writing center pedagogies.

We know that writing is a complex cognitive and social activity and that the mental processes involved as well as the contextual knowledge bases that must be tapped are enormous. Writing skill is honed over a lifetime. A ten- or a fourteen-week college course in expository or argumentative writing is only a small step on the journey. But given that that step is costing universities in the US (and ultimately, taxpayers) billions of dollars in their collective budgets every year and that there are major industries (publishing, testing) associated with these programs, the question, more finely tuned is, "Could these expenditures of dollars and human capital be made more wisely?" What has recent research in literacy studies or composition studies told us about why Dick and Jane cannot write documents of use to employers or colleagues at the end of college? And how could this research be applied to re-conceptualizing writing curricula and teacher training and tutor training?

The biggest, most costly aspect of writing instruction at the post-secondary level is the compulsory writing course offered in the freshman year to most college students. Some in the field of writing instruction (Petraglia 1995) have already suggested that freshman writing as an enterprise in US institutions of higher education should just close shop: the "products" (i.e., graduates of freshman writing) are unfinished, the gains are too minute to show up in most assessment processes, and the cost–benefit ratios are too small. I have a different view based on my research, my understanding of colleagues' research, and my reading in fields that speak to the transfer of learning problem. Freshman writing, if taught with an eye toward transfer of learning and with an explicit acknowledgment of the context of freshman writing itself as a social practice, can set students on a course of lifelong learning so that they know *how to learn* to become better and better writers in a variety of social contexts.

You may ask what qualifies me to set such a bold agenda for a single book, based on a single case study. I make my argument humbly, with great respect for those many teachers (including those who taught Tim) who work arduously, with great dedication to their students' growth as writers, whose insights may render my views flawed and limited. But I base my views on my own teaching of college writers, my experience mentoring teachers of writing and directing two writing programs at two universities in the US with very different student populations, my work on state-mandated assessment of writers, and my research. In the spirit of numbering my days, I am willing to take the risk to write this now. I hope that teachers, researchers, administrators, and publishers will be willing to listen and continue working with me on the agenda I set forth in this book. . . .

Problems in University-Level Writing Instruction

In France and England, when I say I teach writing at the university level I am met with puzzled looks. A common response is: "Writing? Don't university students in the US know how to write already?" Formal writing instruction in most European countries ends in high school. In the US, if I say I teach writing, the next question is, "You teach creative writing?"

And yet, I am part of an American tradition of teaching expository and argumentative writing at the university level that was started in US higher education in the late 1800s at Harvard. This enterprise now employs thousands of teachers (many part time), supports over 60 Ph.D. programs in which historical, theoretical, and classroom-based research on the teaching of writing is carried out, and represents a healthy percentage of the college textbook industry's revenues. Academic writing is one of two courses generally required of all college students (the other, a math course). Many campuses also have an upper-division writing program or writing-in-the-disciplines program as well, and a campus writing center where students can seek individualized help on writing projects.

Periodically, journalists, or politicians, or scholars critique this compulsory college level writing course. I concern myself here with the critiques of other scholars, which have generally come from two perspectives. The first critique they make is based on social constructionism and activity theory and the related perspectives of literacy studies, genre theory, and critical theory. From these theoretical vantage points, all acts of writing—and writing instruction—are viewed as socially situated human activities. Writing literacy is a form of political and social capital. Genres perform social functions. Writers assume subject positions and political positions through the genres they employ.

This leads to a critique of freshman writing that goes something like this: because it is a compulsory course, taught in isolation from other disciplinary studies at the university as a basic skills course, this social context leads freshman writing to become a course in "writing to produce writing" (Dias 2000), or to "do school" (Russell 1995). For the majority of students, freshman writing is not a precursor to a writing major. It is an isolated course, an end in itself, a general education requirement to be gotten out of the way. If taught within an English department, or by teachers who are primarily trained in English or comparative literature, students may perceive it as an English course, and yet the course is often a poor step-child to literature courses in English or comparative literature departments and usually suffers the same isolationist lack of intellectual and social moorings.

But why does this lack of institutional grounding for freshman writing matter? Because usually there is no overt linking of the course to any intellectual discipline (even the disciplines of Rhetoric or Composition Studies are usually not invoked in freshman writing), the overriding social context for students becomes the institutional requirement of the course itself. So writing papers is perceived by students as an activity to earn a grade rather than to communicate to an audience of readers in a given discourse community and papers are commodified into grades, grades into grade reports, grade reports into transcripts, etc. This condition is a serious detriment to motivating writers and to teaching writers to be sensitive to authentic social contexts for writing. This condition also misleads students into thinking writing is a generic skill that, once learned, becomes a "one size fits all" intellectual garb. This in turn leads to misappropriation of principles taught in the course in other contexts where some of those principles are not helpful, or, as cognitive psychologists would say, negative transfer of learning occurs.

On the other hand, no course, no writing situation is without a social context. Given the backgrounds of those who typically teach writing courses and their interests in literature, creative writing, or cultural studies, students in writing courses are most often schooled in the discourse community norms and genres associated with literary studies or cultural studies or journalism (especially the sub-set of creative nonfiction). If students begin to learn some of the literacy practices of these discourse communities, there is some benefit. But what leaves students short-changed as they move into other course work and fields is that the particular discourse community (or communities) in which the teacher is situating himself or herself is not made explicit. And this leads to the second issue with a generic skills course in writing: the transfer of learning issue.

Most teachers of writing think of themselves as generalists. The particular institutional context of their classes and the future endeavors of their students are of less concern than the challenges of equipping students with basic skills. But research in composition studies and linguistic anthropology and literacy studies in the last 30 years has shown there is really no viable commodity called "general writing skills" once one gets beyond the level of vocabulary, spelling, grammar, and sentence syntax (and some would argue that even at the sentence level, writing is specific to particular discourse communities' needs). McCarthy's landmark study documented how little a student may gain from a generic writing skills course. Others have repeatedly documented over and over the context-specific expectations about what counts as "good writing" (Bazerman 1982, Berkenkotter et al. 1988, Brandt 1990, Canagarajah 1997, Fahnestock and Secor 1991, Faigley and Hansen 1985, Heath 1983). Writing standards are largely cultural and socially specific. And yet, novice writers usually get little instruction in how to study and acquire the writing practices of different discourse communities.

Russell (1995) explains the problem with the assumption that there exists a set of "general writing skills" by drawing a sports analogy: it is as if there were a course in general ball handling that were intended to teach skills applicable to playing jacks, tennis, baseball, and soccer. Given the way freshman writing is typically taught, graduates of these courses could easily think the standards for writing they have been given in freshman writing are universal. They are ill-prepared to examine, question, or understand the literacy standards of discourse communities they are encountering in other disciplines, in the work world, or in other social spheres they participate in. This can result in negative transfer of learning: what worked for a freshman writing essay is inappropriately applied to writing in history, or social sciences, or the sciences or in business. The student must learn, through failed attempts at such transfer of supposed "general" writing skills, how to adapt to the standards and purposes for writing in new discourse communities. And there is significant documentation of students' inabilities, unassisted, to grasp these discourse community differences that affect writers' roles and the texts produced.

In addition to these overriding problems—the inexplicit, or isolated social context of most generic writing courses that teach one way of writing (useful in freshman writing, and somewhat in literature, journalism, or comparative literature courses), rather than teaching a set of tools for analyzing and learning writing standards and practices in multiple contexts, i.e., to facilitate transfer of learning—there are other concrete problems with the typical curriculum in freshman writing. As part of the lack of clarity about what discourse community or communities freshman writing is within or attempting to approximate, there is the problem of a subject matter to write about within the context of a particular discourse community's values and standards. Even textual or rhetorical or literary analyses of texts—common assignments in freshman writing—are often conducted without students having solid grounding in the subject matter of the texts being analyzed and the discourse communities these texts come from. So again, the writing is being analyzed without examining how subject matter, rhetorical occasion, and discourse community context interact. It is a commonly held belief that the only subject of generic writing courses is "writing," and yet students read and write on a variety of subjects without attention to the effect of a given subject matter on written expression.

Kaufer and Young (1993) point out, writing with "no content in particular" wrongly assumes "pretty much the same skills of writing will develop no matter what content is chosen" (78). In contrast to this position, Kaufer and Young highlight what the relationship of subject matter to development of writing skills is: (a) a language act is a composite of form and meaning; (b) subject matter constrains writing, that is, it is not simply a passive environment; and (c) subject matter makes a significant difference in the particular writing skills that get learned (p. 83).

Some teachers of freshman writing offer a smorgasbord of readings on a variety of topics from week to week, which keeps the level of engagement with ideas and information more superficial (Dias 2000). Others let students choose their own subjects to research and write about across a semester. At best, if the curriculum is laid out in either of these ways, the teacher can only sit on the intellectual sidelines of the subject matter the student is exploring, asking questions a generalist would ask. And if a writing course is theme-based, with readings focused on a single intellectual topic, as is the case in the data I will present here, it is not uncommon for the subject matter to be secondary to writing process instruction; or, the subject matter is presented to writing students as an object for rhetorical study in a sealed chamber of rhetorical perspectives that are divorced from the full-range of socially embedded dynamics in a given text. Again, writing becomes writing for the sake of a writing class, rather than writing for the sake of intellectual pursuits. And the skills taught are without grounding in, or acknowledgment of, the effects of subjects and their social contexts on writing activity.

And there are problems beyond having an engaging subject matter that invites intellectual curiosity and exploration and teaches the interrelatedness of content and form in texts. Without serious intellectual engagement in the problems of a particular subject matter, standards of assessment are skewed toward writing process skills and superficial treatment of subject matter is "excused," which is a missed opportunity to hook students on intellectual pursuits and to stretch their critical thinking skills.

As Kaufer and Young mention, without a specific subject matter rooted in a specific discourse community, the genres assigned are not explicitly named as genres "belonging to" or part of the practices of particular discourse communities; they are what some have called "school genres." So students perceive what they write as either "universal" forms of writing, or forms idiosyncratic to freshman writing or school writing. Typical genres assigned in freshman writing in the US include the personal narrative (is this a genre akin to the literary essay, a subspecialty within the broader discourse community of journalism? Or does it take a particular form peculiar to freshman writing?), the academic essay (a school genre that is a variation on the op ed piece in a newspaper if mostly opinion, or a variation on various essay forms found in different disciplines within the humanities—history, philosophy, etc.), and the "research paper." As Larson (1982) points out, "research paper" defines not a genre but a method of developing subject matter. Or some assign the "textual analysis," again, a school genre, variations of which could be located in any of the humanities depending on the type of texts being analyzed. These genres are taught as if they were universal standards for communicating in all disciplines and yet hardly any discipline outside freshman writing would consider these assignments authentic to the genre requirements of their particular discourse communities.

For example, here is a writing assignment developed by a novice freshman writing teacher. It is an assignment in search of a genre and discourse community to belong to.

> Choose as your topic a place that is significant to you. It can be a neighborhood, a favorite hangout, a monument, or a childhood home. Describe the place in your own words and explain its personal import to you. Combine

your personal opinion with historical information which explains the site's significance to the greater population. I want you to use Annie Dillard as inspiration for this essay, but keep in mind the difference between memoir, which she writes, and the academic essay, which you will write.

Invoking Annie Dillard as the model for students to follow in executing the assignment suggests the journalistic discourse community Dillard writes in, and the genre of the literary essay. And yet, students are to write an academic essay. What is the relation between Dillard's work and an academic essay? And what disciplines in academe take as their subject matter neighborhoods and how would those disciplines be thinking about and writing about such subject matter? If the teacher had wanted students to follow in the journalistic tradition of Dillard, at least the target discourse community would have been clear. But the target "academic essay" is in need of a specific disciplinary anchor to be a well-grounded intellectual and communicative task for these students. And unfortunately, this assignment is not an isolated example. Look at the teaching apparatus in almost any college writing text and the writing assignments suggested will reveal the same problems.

Related Problems with Writing-in-the-Disciplines and Writing Center Approaches

At this point, readers no doubt think I am going to propose a writing-in-the-disciplines or freshman seminar approach to introductory college level writing courses. In this approach to introductory college writing instruction, teachers in a range of disciplines offer seminars on topics within their fields and work on students' writing intensively. Smit (2004) proposes such a model with a three-course sequence across the majors: a first course, "Introduction to Writing as Social Practice," would begin to acquaint students with the ways in which language is socially situated. A second and third course would introduce students to writing practices of distinct discourse communities. At many schools, courses in the major are designated as writing-intensive, and in these courses more attention is given to students' writing as the course subject matter is taught.

Writing courses in the major bypass the problem of contextualizing writing instruction in a discourse community. But while a more overt disciplinary basis to the writing instruction can solve the problem of writing that is devoid of a well-identified social context within which the writing is grounded and motivated, research in these approaches to writing instruction has uncovered other problems. Dias points out: "Writing [can be] defined . . . in the disciplinary courses primarily as a way of displaying learning" (2000). So teachers give assignments that lead students to feel they are simply demonstrating that they read the book or listened to the lectures rather than engaging in the intellectual work of the discipline through writing tasks. For example, a historian asks students to compare a novel and several primary sources, attempting to (a) get the students more interested in the subject matter and (b) prevent plagiarism. But historians rarely would take on such a task. The student knows, and the teacher knows, the writing is for purposes of gate-keeping/grade-giving.

A second problem with discipline-specific writing courses, taught by disciplinary experts, is the experts' difficulties in making overt the knowledge about writing standards they have learned from a slow acculturation process, rather than by direct instruction (Kaufer and Young 1993). As Russell (1995) says,

> A discipline uses writing as a tool for pursuing some object. Writing is not the object of its activity. Thus, writing tends to become transparent, automatic, and beneath the level of conscious activity for those who are thoroughly socialized into it. . . . As a result, experts may have great difficulty explaining these operations to neophytes. (70)

Or, as Polanyi (1966) would say, the knowledge of disciplinary writing conventions has become tacit knowledge, beneath the level of consciousness. To instruct newcomers requires making that tacit knowledge conscious.

A third problem with writing instruction in disciplinary settings is the issue of teaching students to learn how to learn the conventions of writing in new situations they will encounter. As Kaufer and Young (1993) point out, a unified theory that takes into account general and context-specific writing skills is needed for executing a solid writing curriculum. If the writing instruction is context-specific and students are not given the kinds of intellectual tools and frameworks for being able to become astute at learning to be flexible writers, they will not be able to adapt to a variety of writing situations.

In addition to the need for individuals assigning and coaching writing appropriately in their respective fields, Young and Leinhardt (1998) point out a critical need for ". . . models for the systematic instruction of disciplinary writing." In spite of the writing-across-the-curriculum movement (WAC) in higher education in the US since the early 1980s, there is little documentation of successful disciplinary writing curricula that are systematic in their approach, i.e., offering a sequence of writing assignments and instruction that explicitly move students progressively toward more complex and more expert writing performances as they pursue their major fields of study.

Writing center tutors have an even greater challenge: eliciting from writers who come for help what the context is for the writing task they want help with. Often, novice writers are not clear what the task requirements are and do not understand the discourse community expectations embedded in the writing task. Or, the writing assignment itself is vague or confusing, leaving both tutor and writer in a difficult situation.

While no theoretical framework can solve some of the problems writing tutors may face, there is room for a more robust theory of writing instruction that could serve tutors and students well.

Much of the current scholarship in writing center practice (Boquet 2002, Briggs and Woolbright 2000, Grimm 1999, Harris 1998, Hobson 1994, Pemberton and Kinkead 2003) combines expressivist views (supporting the individual writer in finding his/her voice) and social constructionist views (meaning in written texts is often created through collaborative dialogue between writer and tutor) and writing process approaches (how to help the writer develop a more robust writing process). But the move in writing center practice away from being directive or product-focused leads to very general approaches to guiding writers in revising drafts. Stephen North's dictum to "work with the writer, not the writing" is often invoked. The advice to "review the essay with the writer for development and organization" (Ryan 2002) is typical of tutoring guides. It is understandable that writing center tutor training guides treat superficially the context-specific aspects of writing and focus largely on a very general set of guidelines for academic writing. But, if tutors added to their approaches to coaching writers a framework for assisting students in understanding how to analyze the context-specific nature of writing activities, the tutors could better promote the kinds of learning-how-to-learn skills all advanced writers need. Furthermore, the oft-cited dichotomy between working to produce better writing versus producing better writers could be set aside, as both goals could be accomplished through applying a more robust theory of writing expertise to tutor practices.

These then are some of the manifestations I see of a less than fully articulated conceptual model of writing expertise and a limited, seldom-invoked conceptual model for aiding writers to transfer learning from one context to another. . . . I explain now the theoretical model for writing expertise I have worked out, based on the data in this and my earlier research, that can provide us with greater clarity about the components of a successful approach to instructing writers who have advanced beyond issues of sentence-level fluency.

A Conceptual Model of Writing Expertise

If there is no such thing as writing expertise, or "general" writing skill, but rather, individual expert writing performances, as Bazerman (1994) argues, then there is a need to conceptualize writing in a whole other way. While writing expertise does not transfer wholesale from one writing context to another, it is possible to identify the common knowledge domains within which writers must develop context-specific knowledge. The literature on expertise suggests that experts not only have very rich, deep, context-specific knowledge, but they also have mental schema, or heuristics, with which to organize knowledge and aid problem-solving and gaining new knowledge in new situations. So the question becomes, what knowledge domains best represent the mental schema employed in expert writing performances? And what knowledge domains—or mental schema—do writers need to invoke for analyzing new writing tasks in new discourse communities? If we can articulate these knowledge domains and apply them to shaping curriculum, we can then contextualize writing instruction more fully and have a basis for teaching for transfer, i.e., equipping students with a mental schema for learning writing skills in new genres in new discourse communities they will encounter throughout life.

If asked what they teach, most teachers of university-level writing would probably articulate some or all of the following: writing process knowledge (how to get writing done, from pre-drafting to final draft), rhetorical modes (narrative, exposition, persuasive writing, etc.), audience awareness, voice, style, grammar, and mechanics. Some might include genre knowledge or critical thinking or research skills. Conspicuously missing from the list is subject matter knowledge or discourse community knowledge. And also absent is a sense of a whole, a way of conceptualizing how the different aspects of writing are related and fit together. An examination of composition readers and rhetorics and writing handbooks would, for the most part, mirror our partial and fragmented views of writing instruction, with a few notable exceptions.

The same fragmentation is true in the theoretical and empirical literature in composition studies. The only overviews in composition studies of writing expertise are Carter's (1990), Bryson's (1991), and Smagorinsky and Smith's (1992). They outline in broad strokes the nature of research into expertise and general versus context-specific ways of thinking of writing skills. Others have identified single components of the domain knowledge and skills associated with expert writers' performances: writing process skills (Flower and Hayes 1981, Perl 1979, Sommers 1980), subject matter knowledge and rhetorical knowledge (Geisler 1994), and types of rhetorical strategies specific to particular fields of expertise (Fahnestock 1986, Fahnestock and Secor 1991, Herrington 1988). What is needed is a more inclusive model that can account for the multiple knowledge domains activated in expert writing performances. As an engineer must understand certain laws of physics, chemical properties of materials, etc. to create the desired product, so too, the writer must engage a considerable body of writing knowledge in acts of composing.

As a starting place to take into account the domains of knowledge writers employ, I use the model of writing expertise theorized from the data in my ethnographic study of writers' transitions from academic to professional writing (1999). Briefly, the model consists of five overlapping yet distinct domains of situated knowledge entailed in acts of writing: discourse community knowledge, subject matter knowledge, genre knowledge, rhetorical knowledge, and writing process knowledge.

Figure 1. Conceptual Model: Expert Writers Draw on Five Knowledge Domains

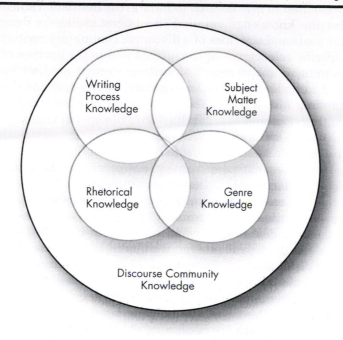

As depicted in Figure 1, these knowledge domains, all integral to writing expertise, overlap and interact with each other. Labeling a particular aspect of writing expertise as one or the other dimension is at times difficult, given their interactive functions (Prior 1994). Nonetheless, for purposes of teasing out as many of the knowledge domains that comprise writing expertise as possible in this study, the distinctions are maintained at the same time that the interactive aspects are depicted.

Here is further articulation of this conceptual model. First, the overarching concept: a theory of discourse communities. What writing expertise is ultimately concerned with is becoming engaged in a particular community of writers who dialogue across texts, argue, and build on each other's work. Discourse communities exhibit a particular network of communicative channels, oral and written, whose interplay affects the purposes and meanings of the written texts produced within the community. Based on a set of shared goals and values and certain material/physical conditions, discourse communities establish norms for genres that may be unique to the community or shared with overlapping communities and roles and tasks for writers are appropriated within this activity system (Beaufort 1997). While some critique a theory of discourse community, I find the components of discourse communities I have isolated in my research to have great heuristic value.

Besides the knowledge entailed in understanding and engaging the broader goals and activities of a discourse community, writers must engage a specific subject matter considered within the purview of a discourse community. In this aspect of writing, experts are both drawing on existing knowledge bases (i.e., background knowledge) and doing the critical thinking necessary for the creation of "new" or "transformed" knowledge (Bereiter and Scardamlia 1987, Bloom 1971) that is interactive with and is influenced by the discourse community. Such critical thinking includes knowing how to frame the inquiry, what kinds of questions to ask or analytical frameworks to use in order to "transform" or inscribe documents with new meaning(s).

Writers must also develop knowledge of genres whose boundaries and features the discourse community defines and stabilizes. Slevin's (1998) postmodern definition of genre and Bawarshi's (2003) excellent exposition of the ways genres serve writers in the process of creating texts are rich discussions of genres as a tool for writers and are a much-needed replacement to the limited theories of text types from classical rhetoric. Some (Devitt 2004) would argue that genre knowledge is all-encompassing and a theory of discourse community is superfluous, but my research suggests both are necessary. I have found that genres such as the essay or the grant proposal vary greatly from one discourse community to another, and these variations become clear and understandable as one considers variations between discourse communities.

In addition to discourse community knowledge, subject matter knowledge, and genre knowledge, writers must address the specific, immediate rhetorical situation of individual communicative acts (Ede and Lunsford 1984, Lunsford and Ede 1996). This includes considering the specific audience and purpose for a particular text and how best to communicate rhetorically in that instance. The rhetorical moment is also affected by the social context—material conditions, timing, social relationships, etc. within the discourse community. And finally, writers must have writing process knowledge, i.e., knowledge of the ways in which one proceeds through the writing task in its various phases. This procedural knowledge associated with writing process is also affected by the material, socially specific particulars of a given writing situation or "community of practice" (Flower 1994, Rogoff 1994).

An illustration of one particular writing task familiar to academics may bring these abstract conceptions of the components of writing expertise into clear focus: let us examine the writing of an abstract of a journal article or book. An abstract is a *genre* (or sub-genre—part of another genre) read by those in several different *discourse communities*—researchers in the writer's field (biology, for example), librarians who need to build library collections and those who put bibliographic information on publications into databases, and editors of publications in the writer's field. Across these diverse discourse communities, there is a common *rhetorical occasion* that prompts the need for abstracts—namely, readers' need to quickly ascertain if there is "news" of interest in the longer work the abstract announces—or just how to categorize the *subject matter* of the piece—and the writer's need to interest others in the new work. Like the first paragraph of a news or feature story in journalistic venues, or movie trailers shown in theaters before a film's release, the abstract must convey information succinctly, clearly, and with a sense of urgency, beckoning the reader to continue reading. Besides being well versed in all aspects of the subject matter being reported on, say, stem cell research, the writer of the abstract must know what the required content is for *the genre* of an abstract. Should it include a mention of research methods? The research problem? The main thesis? A sense of the subject's importance to this group of readers? Genre knowledge entails knowing what content is required, what is not; how best to sequence the content; what specific needs the readers will have, and how common or technical a vocabulary to use. And finally, the writer must find the best *writing process* for getting the abstract written: should s/he write it first, as a focusing device to guide composing the rest of the piece? Or should it be written last, after the writer has discovered, through writing, what s/he has to say? Should s/he just copy and paste from key lines in the body of the piece, or summarize the piece in a fresh way? These are the writing process decisions and know-how that complete the five domains of writing knowledge a writer draws on for this particular task.

Combined then, the five knowledge domains articulated here (including an expanded notion of subject matter knowledge that includes a critical thinking component) form the theoretical framework I will use for analyzing aspects of writing expertise Tim exhibited in freshman writing, in history, and in engineering over a six-year period. This conceptual framework will also inform the recommendations for restructuring university-level writing instruction in ways that will increase the likelihood of positive transfer of learning.

Such a position could be critiqued as positivist or foundationalist, i.e., as falsely implying that learning is a matter of "pouring in" knowledge to the blank slate of a person's mind and that the subject matter to be learned (i.e., writing knowledge) is fixed and stable. Those who would raise this critique might argue that knowing is only situational and dialogic—for the moment—and there are no fixed "categories" of knowledge. To those of this philosophical bent, I offer two comments: first, to conceptualize writing knowledge in distinct yet overlapping categories does not inherently imply either that those categories are fixed and discrete, or that learning is a rote affair, a matter of simply "banking" such knowledge. I would agree with Bereiter and Scardemalia, ". . . what counts with cooks and experts is what they do with the material in their pantries or memory stores" (1993, p. 45). Or, as they state more directly, ". . . we have to find [expertise] in the ongoing process in which knowledge is used, transformed, enhanced, and attuned to situations" (46). Gaining writing expertise only takes place, I believe, in the context of situational problem-solving, or, as others have demonstrated, through legitimate participation in apprenticeship situations (Heath 1983, Lave and Wenger 1991, Prior 1994). As Flower states, "The meaning of a literate act will not lie solely in the resources on which it draws, the conventions in which it participates, or the context to which it responds, but in the ways writers use and even transform their knowledge and resources to take action" (1994, p. 37). So a theory of writing expertise provides the schema that can guide a developmental process that empowers the individual writer, rather than place any limitations on writers.

To those who do not feel satisfied that there is enough of a critical, liberal agenda in this theory of writing expertise, I would say, yes, the theory is apolitical in the sense that no particular political agenda is being promoted and no one interest group is being catered to. But on the other hand, this view of expertise is crucial to the legitimate social causes of literacy, employment, and effective communication—to empowering all across gender, race, ethnic, and class lines to write effectively in a range of social contexts.

What I do is name the types of resources from which writers draw to create texts and a way of organizing a schematic for those resources. Again, to draw on Bereiter and Scardamalia's work on the nature of expertise, ". . . knowledge is not just one more factor . . . knowledge is a large part of what must be explained and not something that lies in the background" (1993, p. 44). Others have represented writing knowledge as a combination of content knowledge and rhetorical knowledge (Geisler 1994), or procedural knowledge and declarative knowledge (Berkenkotter et al. 1989), or knowledge of text types and the linguistic features of written discourse. What I am proposing here is a fuller accounting of the knowledge domains expert writers employ than has been given in other accounts, not to win some philosophical argument about the nature of truth, but rather, to try to get at a more fine-grained and unified sense of what is going on when we study writers' behaviors and a broader view of what we should consider in creating writing curricula.

References

Bawarshi, Anis. *Genre and the Invention of the Writer: Reconsidering the Place of Invention in Composition.* Logan, UT: Utah State University Press, 2003.
———. "The Genre Function." *College English* 62, no. 3 (2000): 335–360.
Bazerman, Charles. "Scientific Writing as a Social Act." In *New Essays in Technical and Scientific Communication*, edited by P. Anderson, 156–184. Farmingdale, NY: Baywood, 1982.
———. *Constructing Experience.* Carbondale, IL: Southern Illinois University Press, 1994.

Beaufort, Anne. *Writing in the Real World: Making the Transition from School to Work*. New York: Teachers College Press, 1999.

———. "Operationalizing the Concept of Discourse Community: A Case Study of One Institutional Site of Composing." *Research in the Teaching of English* 31, no. 4 (1997): 486–529.

Bereiter, Carl, and Marlene Scardamalia. *Surpassing Ourselves: An Inquiry into the Nature and Implications of Expertise*. Chicago: Open Court, 1993.

———. *The Psychology of Written Composition*. Hillsdale, NJ: Lawrence Erlbaum Associates, 1987.

Berkenkotter, Carol, Thomas Huckin, and John Ackerman. "Conventions, Conversations and the Writer: Case Study of a Student in a Rhetoric Ph.D. Program." *Research in the Teaching of English* 22 (1988): 9–44.

Berkenkotter, Carol, Thomas N. Huckin, and John Ackerman. "Social Context and Socially Constructed Texts: The Initiation of a Graduate Student into a Writing Research Community." Center for the Study of Writing. U.C. Berkeley, 1989.

Bloom, B.S., ed., *Taxonomy of Educational Objectives Handbook: Cognitive Domain*. New York: McGraw-Hill, 1971.

Boquet, Elizabeth H. *Noise from the Writing Center*. Logan, UT: Utah State University Press, 2002.

Brandt, Deborah. *Literacy as Involvement: The Acts of Writers, Readers, and Texts*. Carbondale IL: Southern Illinois University Press, 1990.

Briggs, Lynn C., and Meg Woolbright, eds., *Stones from the Center: Connecting Narrative and Theory in the Writing Center*. Urbana, IL: National Council of Teachers of English, 2000.

Bryson, Mary, Carl Bereiter, Marlene Scardamalia, and Elana Joram. "Going Beyond the Problem as Given: Problem Solving in Expert and Novice Writers." In *Complex Problem Solving: Principles and Mechanisms*, edited by Robert J. Steinberg and Peter A. Frensch, 61–84. Hillsdale, NJ: Lawrence Erlbaum Associates, 1991.

Canagarajah, A. Suresh. "Safe Houses in the Contact Zone: Coping Strategies of African-American Students in the Academy." *College Composition and Communication* 48, no. 2 (1997): 173–196.

Carter, Michael. "The Idea of Expertise: An Exploration of Cognitive and Social Dimensions of Writing." *College Composition and Communication* 41, no. 3 (1990): 265–286.

Devitt, Amy J. *Writing Genres*. Carbondale: Southern Illinois University Press, 2004.

Devitt, Amy J., Mary Jo Reiff, and Anis Bawarshi. *Scenes of Writing: Strategies for Composing with Genres*. New York: Pearson Longman, 2004.

Dias, Patrick. "Writing Classrooms as Activity Systems." In *Transistions: Writing in Academic and Workplace Settings*, edited by Patrick Dias and Anthony Paré, 11–29. Cresskill, NJ: Hampton Press, 2000.

——— and Anthony Paré, eds. *Transitions: Writing in Academic and Workplace Settings*. Cresskill, NJ: Hampton Press, 2000.

Ede, Lisa, and Andrea Lunsford. "Audience Addressed/Audience Invoked: The Role of Audience in Composition Theory and Pedagogy." *College Composition and Communication* 35, no. 2 (1984): 155–71.

Fahnestock, Jeanne. "Accommodating Science: The Rhetorical Life of Scientific Facts." *Written Communication* 3, no. 3 (1986): 275–296.

Fahnestock, Jeanne, and Marie Secor. "The Rhetoric of Literary Criticism." In *Textual Dynamics of the Professions: Historical and Contemporary Studies of Writing in Professional Communities*, edited by Charles Bazerman and James Paradis, 76–96. Madison: University of Wisconsin Press, 1991.

Faigley, Lester, and K. Hansen. "Learning to Write in the Social Sciences." *College Composition and Communication* 34 (1985): 140–149.

Flower, Linda. *The Construction of Negotiated Meaning: A Social Cognitive Theory of Writing*. Carbondale, IL: Southern Illinois University Press, 1994.

Flower, Linda, and John R. Hayes. "A Cognitive Process Theory of Writing." *College Composition and Communication* 32, no. 4 (1981): 365–387.

Geisler, Cheryl. *Academic Literacy and the Nature of Expertise: Reading, Writing and Knowing in Academic Philosophy*. Hillsdale. NJ: Lawrence Erlbaum Associates, 1994.

Grimm, Nancy. *Good Intentions: Writing Center Work for Postmodern Times*. Portsmouth, NH: Boynton/Cook Publishers, 1999.

Harris, Muriel. "Writing Center Theory and Scholarship." In *Theorizing Composition: A Critical Sourcebook of Theory and Scholarship in Contemporary Composition Studies*, edited by Mary Lynch Kennedy, 364–371. Westport, CT: Greenwood Press, 1998.

Heath, Shirley Brice. *Ways with Words*. Cambridge: Cambridge University Press, 1983.

Herrington, Ann. "Teaching, Writing and Learning: A Naturalistic Study of Writing in an Undergraduate Literature Course." In *Advances in Writing Research: Vol 2. Writing in Academic Disciplines*, edited by David Jolliffe, 133–166. Norwood, NJ: Ablex, 1988.

Hobson, Eric H. "Writing Center Practice Often Counters Its Theory. So What?" In *Intersections: Theory-Practice in the Writing Center*, edited by Joan A. Mullin and Ray Wallace, 1–10. Urbana, IL: National Council of Teachers of English, 1994.

Kaufer, David, and Richard Young. "Writing in the Content Areas: Some Theoretical Complexities." In *Theory and Practice in the Teaching of Writing: Rethinking the Discipline*, edited by Lee Odell, 71–104. Carbondale: Southern Illinois University Press, 1993.

Larson, Richard L. "The 'Research Paper' in the Writing Course: A Non-Form of Writing." *College English* 44, no. December (1982): 811–816.

Lave, Jean, and Etienne Wenger. *Situated Learning: Legitimate Peripheral Participation*. Cambridge: Cambridge University Press, 1991.

Lunsford, Andrea A., and Lisa Ede. "Representing Audience: 'Successful' Discourse and Disciplinary Critique." *College Composition and Communication* 47, no. 2 (May) (1996): 167–179.

McCarthy, Lucille Parkinson. "A Stranger in Strange Lands: A College Student Writing across the Curriculum." *Research in the Teaching of English* 21, no. 3 (1987): 233–265.

Pemberton, Michael A., and Joyce Kinkead, eds. *The Center Will Hold: Critical Perspectives on Writing Center Scholarship*. Logan, UT: Utah State University Press, 2003.

Perl, Sondra. "The Composing Process of Unskilled College Writers." *Research in the Teaching of English* 13, no. 4 (1979): 317–336.

Petraglia, Joseph, ed. *Reconceiving Writing, Rethinking Writing Instruction*. Mahwah, NJ: Lawrence Erlbaum Associates, 1995.

Polanyi, Michael. *The Tacit Dimension*. Garden City, NY: Doubleday & Company, 1966.

Prior, Paul. "Response, Revision, Disciplinarity: A Microhistory of a Dissertation Prospectus in Sociology." *Written Communication* 11, no. 4 (1994): 483–533.

Rogoff, Barbara. "Developing Understanding of the Idea of Communities of Learners." *Mind, Culture, and Activity* 1, no. 4 (1994): 209–229.

Russell, David. "Activity Theory and Its Implications for Writing Instruction." In *Reconceiving Writing, Rethinking Writing Instruction*, edited by Joseph Petraglia, 51–77. Mahwah, NJ: Erlbaum, 1995.

Ryan, Leigh. *The Bedford Guide for Writing Tutors, Third Edition*. New York: Bedford/St. Martins, 2002.

Slevin, James F. "Genre Theory, Academic Discourse, and Writing within Disciplines." In *Audits of Meaning*, edited by Louise Z. Smith, 3–16. Portsmouth, NH: Boynton/Cook Publishers, 1988.

Smagorinsky, Peter, and Michael W. Smith. "The Nature of Knowledge in Composition and Literary Understanding: The Question of Specificity." *Review of Educational Research* 62, no. 3 (1992): 279–305.

Smit, David W. *The End of Composition Studies*. Urbana, IL: Southern Illnios University Press, 2004.

Sommers, Nancy. "Revision Strategies of Student Writers and Experienced Adult Writers." *College Composition and Communication* 31, no. 4 (1980): 378–388.

Young, Kathleen McCarthy, and Gaea Leinhardt. "Writing from Primary Documents: A Way of Knowing in History." *Written Communication* 15, no. 1 (1998): 25–68.

Transfer Institutions, Transfer of Knowledge: The Development of Rhetorical Adaptability and Underprepared Writers

Holly Hassel and Joanne Baird Giordano

This essay earned the Mark Reynolds Award for Best Article in Teaching English in the Two-Year College *for 2009. About the research that they report on in this essay, Holly Hassel and Joanne Baird Giordano note that "in 2007, we were part of a small group of English instructors at our two-year campus who were increasingly troubled by success rates for underprepared college readers and writers in our writing program. With our campus colleague, Christina Marty, we subsequently designed a first-semester writing course that focused on critical reading and writing from sources to address gaps between students' preparation and our institution's writing courses. We focused on a cohort of students not often acknowledged in research and scholarship—students who are neither basic writers nor*

From *Teaching English in the Two-Year College*, 2009, vol. 37, no. 1, pp. 24-40.

proficient college-level writers. We conducted a research study to examine students' transition between the revised course and our second-semester core research course. The project and its findings became the starting point for substantial revisions to our writing program."

"It takes time to get a feel for the roles that readers can be expected to comfortably play in the modern academic world."

—Walter Ong, "The Writer's Audience Is Always a Fiction"

Although transferring to a baccalaureate program is not a universal goal of two-year college students, many enter open admission institutions intending to pursue a four-year degree. *Change*, a publication of the Carnegie Foundation for the Advancement of Teaching, reported in 2006 that "40 percent of all first-time freshmen begin their postsecondary careers in community colleges" and that 79% of those students planned to go on for a bachelor's degree. The same survey data showed that 15–20% of students who began at a two-year college actually went on to complete a bachelor's degree within six years (Doyle). These numbers reveal, fairly dramatically, that, despite their plans for degree completion, many students who begin their studies at two-year institutions are at risk for probation, suspension, and dropping out of higher education.[1]

How do we explain these numbers? Patrick Sullivan's opinion essay, "Measuring 'Success' at Open Admissions Institutions," in the July 2008 issue of *College English* (p. 42 in this volume) can contribute to our professional understanding, as teachers at two-year institutions, of this low level of degree attainment by students who begin their careers at our campuses. Calling for a reassessment of what constitutes success for students enrolling at these colleges, Sullivan persuasively argues that students at open admission universities have often invested less and prepared less for the goal of "obtaining a bachelor's degree," a phrase that he believes our students use in different ways than students who begin at selective and residential baccalaureate-granting universities.

Sullivan's essay provides an important context for understanding student writers at open admission institutions; they may intend to pursue upper-division coursework but are still learning what it means to achieve a college degree, as they further refine their expectations and struggle to meet the demands of higher education. We strongly concur with Sullivan's analysis of the "personal and academic skills and attitudes" that students bring with them to their work at two-year institutions and of how they are different from students at more selective institutions; at the same time, we hope to extend Sullivan's discussion with our current essay. In addition to the differing levels of financial, emotional, and psychological commitment required in advance of students' enrollment in four-year institutions (versus two-year institutions), we need to consider the sometimes significant, but not insurmountable, gap between the precollege preparation of our students and the reading and writing skills necessary for transferring to four-year institutions.

What we hope to do in this essay is make clearer the needs and abilities of a specific student population with whom many of us work at the two-year college. Kelly Ritter, in her September 2008 *College Composition and Communication* essay, "Before Mina Shaughnessy: Basic Writing at Yale, 1920–1960," calls for research into the "silent or invisible student populations that are at risk of being forgotten through the convenience of standardized histories and limiting labels" (39). We respond to Ritter's call for a "re-definition of *basic* in composition studies using local, institutional values rather than generic standards of correctness" (12) by reevaluating the skills and needs of beginning college writers at open admission, two-year institutions. These students can occupy a misty nether land where they are neither basic writers nor proficient college-level writers. Many of these students leave high school with an emerging understanding of academic writing and, thus, test out of developmental and nondegree preparatory courses. At the same time, they lack the more advanced critical reading skills and rhetorical strategies necessary for enrolling in and successfully completing most writing-intensive college courses. This often-ignored student population may be ready for degree-credit writing courses at open admission campuses while remaining unprepared for the core first-year composition course required by most four-year institutions. Thus, this group of students enters its first year of college on our campus—and at many other open admission institutions across the country—with standardized test scores that are acceptable for admission to higher education. However, these scores also suggest that those students aren't able to perform critical reading tasks, even though they may comprehend basic (generally, informational) college-level texts at the level of "literal recall," "low inference," and "high inference" (*Achieve* 16). The additional skills of analysis and interpretation that require more complex cognitive skills are still developing in this student population, which may not be immediately obvious from the students' ACT or other placement test scores. Furthermore, this student population may be able to punctuate sentences correctly and adhere to conventions for standard written English usage, even as they are still developing the higher-order analysis, thinking, and organizational skills that are required in college-level writing.

With so much attention paid to defining basic writers, the language and semantics of basic writing, and the sorts of educational experiences that may or may not benefit students who are unprepared to do college-level reading and writing, the student we address faces very particular challenges to success in his or her college career. In this essay, we describe the results of a scholarship of teaching and learning project that conducted a qualitative study of the writing development of 21 student writers during the first year of college, tracking their progress in an English 101 course[2] and following them as they moved into the core, transfer-level composition course. We use the writing of three students as case studies to illustrate the challenges that beginning college writers face as they transition from introductory to degree-requirement composition courses and attempt to meet the demands of increasingly complex reading and writing tasks.

Our classroom research reveals that students who straddle the basic/developmental writing and college-level writing borderland struggle to translate instruction into rhetorical adaptability. When faced with challenging new reading and writing tasks in the core, transfer-level composition course, students in our study reverted to rhetorical strategies typical of pre-English 101 instruction. Our findings emphasize the importance of cultivating students' metacognition as part of the writing curriculum, highlight the benefits of process pedagogy at all stages of precollege and first-year college composition, and argue for text-based writing assignments in introductory writing courses.

Although, admittedly, it is difficult to characterize "prevailing views" in any field, in composition/writing studies it would be fair to assert that influential voices within the field (Brooke, Mirtz, and Evans, 1994; Downs and Wardle, 2007) have resisted the assumption that first-year composition courses prepare students for writing in the academy, even as others have explored the necessity of this position (Knodt, 2006). For example, Downs and Wardle proposed that instructors might approach first-year and sophomore-level composition courses as "Introduction to Writing Studies," rejecting the idea that "[w]hile some general features of writing are shared across disciplines . . . these shared features are realized differently within different academic disciplines, courses, and even assignments," rightly calling it a "category mistake" to assume that first-year composition can prepare students for all of the rhetorical demands of their college educations (556). However, it is our contention that our writing program at a two-year, open admission institution, and at others like it, must necessarily bear the responsibility of preparing students for the academic writing that they can expect to do in their college career after—or concurrent with—their first-year composition course(s). It is precisely this challenge—to help students cultivate a rhetorical adaptability that will take them into their future coursework—that we take up in this essay.

Method of Study

Our project began with the development of a redesigned English 101 course focused on bridging the gap between precollege writing and the core composition course. We approached our classroom research and the design of the bridge course with recommendations by research in the field of writing and the recommendations of our disciplinary organizations in mind (Writing Study Group of the National Council of Teachers of English Executive Committee, 2004; Council of Writing Program Administrators, 2000; see also Heaney, 2006; Maloney, 2003). Recognizing, as April Heaney does, that at-risk student populations "experience higher levels of frustration with critical reading and academic writing" (29) than their academically better-prepared counterparts, we structured the course around critical reading and source-based writing, specifically on the topic of cultural identity and academic literacy.

This emphasis in form and content reflects contemporary disciplinary trends outlined in Lunsford and Lunsford's 2008 *College Composition and Communication* essay, "Mistakes Are a Fact of Life: A National Comparative Study," a replication of a 1986 study of "error" in student writing that examines the shifts in the last two decades in demands placed on students in their writing courses. The authors observe that the contemporary trend in writing instruction in the United States is academic writing that is research- or argument-focused, with the majority (473) of the 877 essays that they studied asking students to make supported or marginally supported arguments. In their quantitative study of error, two major findings are relevant to our current discussion. First, the average length of student essays analyzed had doubled during that time period, from approximately two pages to a little over four pages. Second, the sort of essay that students had been assigned changed dramatically: "Although the first study included some reports and a fair number of readings of (mostly) literary texts, the majority of the papers were personal narratives" (793). As Lunsford and Lunsford note, contemporary writing instruction has replaced personal narrative and literary analysis with argument and research, suggesting that "student writers today are tackling the kinds of issues that require inquiry and investigation as well as reflection and that students are writing more than ever before" (Lunsford and Lunsford 793). Given the heavy emphasis on research and argument that Lunsford and Lunsford document, nearly all college students can expect to do writing that takes a position and that engages with the ideas of others.

Most important, our research methodology was designed with both the recognized practices in our field and disciplinary conventions in mind, including close reading of texts (student writing), discourse analysis and rhetorical analysis, the inclusion of student assignments designed to measure metacognitive dimensions of the writing process, and a portfolio assessment that documented student growth over two semesters. Our study uses student writing as evidence for the conclusions that we draw. Perhaps most crucial for the purposes of the present discussion was our collection of the first essay from the students' English 102 class that addressed the targeted learning outcome. Of the twenty-two students who were initially enrolled in the fall English 101 course, fourteen students completed the specified assignment in the spring.[3]

Over the course of two semesters, the research team (the two authors, the English 101 instructor whose course we studied, and a tutorial writing specialist) used a rubric to evaluate the learning outcome: "Independently adapt a self-generated text's thesis, structure, and style to a particular writing task defined by audience and purpose." Each level of performance was characterized not just as "meets" or "exceeds" expectations but was judged by our assessment of the student's readiness to move into the core writing course. The research team met twice per week in the Fall 2007 semester to analyze each student's writing and document the student's growth over the course of the two English 101 assignments, according to their success in each of the five features (audience, purpose, thesis, structure, style) described on the rubric. The collective judgments about each student's fall semester writing were then used as a basis for contrasting with the student's first essay in the core writing course, in conjunction with instructor narrative assessments using our project rubric. We made holistic judgments about the students' achievement of the learning outcome as demonstrated by their English 102 essay, designated by the various instructors of those courses.

For the purposes of this essay, we discuss our findings drawn from our analysis of the first essay from the transfer-level course (English 102) that our English 101 students completed. Although we encourage readers to consider the limitations of generalizing from our small sample, we also see our analysis as part of the tradition in writing studies research that values discourse analysis, close reading, case studies, and other sorts of established, qualitative research methods that are used widely in the field of composition studies.

Audience and Purpose: Case Studies in Rhetorical Choice

The key observation of our research team's study of student writing involves the challenge that students face responding to new rhetorical situations with appropriate college-level reading and writing strategies. When moving into the more advanced writing course, students struggled to translate their English 101 learning into rhetorical flexibility—that is, the ability to make appropriate choices for (and determine the contours, shape, and demands of) new writing assignments when the purpose, audience, and, subsequently, structural and stylistic conventions had changed. Similarly, students had difficulty completing writing tasks that required accompanying college-level reading strategies. If the primary goal of our project was to measure the learning outcome that we initially posed as our research question (i.e., adapting an essay to the demands of a specific writing task), by all objective measurements, most students failed to achieve this outcome. Of the fourteen students who moved into the core-level composition course, ten received assignments that mirrored the types of source-based writing tasks that they had completed in English 101 (meaning that we were unable to measure, really, their ability to adapt to new sorts of writing tasks). Four students received an unfamiliar type of writing task that required critical analysis of sources, and they subsequently failed to meet the expectations for their English 102 assignment targeting our learning outcome.

More specifically, ten students wrote argumentative essays that required them to conduct independent research, take a position on a topic, and support that position with evidence. Students had practiced this sort of rhetorical task frequently in the English 101 course (which didn't necessarily demand that students read their source material critically, simply that they comprehend its content). Similar source-based research assignments are common in the transfer-level course, both on our campus and at most institutions (as Lunsford and Lunsford documented). Of the ten students, nine completed the new research assignment at a proficiency level that met or exceeded their performance on the less difficult final source-based essay in the bridge course—although most of them tended to report on information rather than analyze sources. The remaining student did not demonstrate proficiency at adapting to the expectations of a college audience in English 101 (which she was taking for a second time), and she did not pass the core transfer-level course.

More interesting, perhaps, were the students who were faced with an entirely different sort of task that required them to adapt to a new rhetorical situation and engage critically with an unfamiliar text. In the bridge composition section that we studied, both marginally prepared and more advanced students for this level struggled to adapt their rhetorical choices to new writing tasks, specifically those that asked them to do independent research, read sources critically, and formulate a thesis independently. We have chosen to focus in detail here on three of the students whose English 102 assignments required them to tackle writing assignments that were very rhetorically different from those that they had successfully completed in English 101. Not surprisingly, we concluded that underprepared students (if these students are representative) have difficulty adapting their reading and writing strategies to meet the needs of a college-level academic audience that they have not previously encountered.

Whitney: A Case Study in Rhetorical Regression

Whitney tested into a nondegree credit basic writing course but chose to enroll in English 101. At the beginning of the semester, she struggled to make the transition to college-level writing and thinking. In the first paper, she was asked to synthesize two sources in response to the writing prompt "What is an educated person?" Whitney's thesis statement,

"Therefore, Richard Rodriquez and William Cronon both discuss the importance of being and [sic] educated person, and also what it means as well," displayed an attempt to find commonalities between the two sources but, like the rest of her essay, tended toward shallow comparisons. Her essay explicitly failed to meet the demands of the assignment of synthesizing two sources; instead, she used precollege strategies, such as listing, summarizing, and reporting on information rather than analyzing and taking an independent position. Whitney represents many underprepared students who enter college with the understanding that academic writing means summarizing the ideas of others rather than developing a complex thesis based on evidence. Thus, in the early 101 essays, the main point of her entire essay and subsequent topic sentences for each paragraph became secondary to reporting on assigned readings.

Her metacognitive awareness of the writing process was also at a considerably novice level. When assessing her final portfolio, Whitney wrote that a strength is that "I do maint [sic] points very well and that I stick with them," even as she said later that she still needed to work on this: "sometimes I forget what my point was." Her understanding of revision was also at a very emerging level. In describing her revision process, Whitney noted, "My last paper did not have any main points in it at all, I thought it was to hard to put in main points. Then I figured out the different topics that I stuck with and put main points in." For her, they were less important parts of the essay that she could add to later drafts. Whitney's self-evaluation for the course portfolio further revealed an evolving but inadequate rhetorical knowledge of controlling ideas. She identified creating and adhering to main points as one of her strengths — although her actual essays produced throughout the study suggest otherwise.

Whitney's self-analysis of her final essay demonstrated an emerging understanding of college-level paragraphs, organized around key supporting points that advance the thesis. She clearly recognized that the paragraphs of her essay entirely lacked main points and instead focused on general informational topics. Nevertheless, she was unable to transfer that knowledge successfully to her own writing, because she tried to insert argumentative topic sentences into the essay *after* drafting it rather than developing the essay based on a thesis statement and supporting points. Thus, over the course of her first semester, Whitney began to develop a sense of what the main points of paragraphs should look like in a college essay (using assertive topic sentences), but she still struggled to adapt her writing process in a way that would allow her to structure an essay on a new topic with new demands using that knowledge.

Like many marginally prepared students on our campus, Whitney made substantial progress toward writing at a college level during the bridge course while still retaining some precollege writing strategies.

Whitney especially progressed in her use of specific evidence in support of her claims. Although the thesis of her final essay is not quite at a college level, it takes a position rather than stating a topic: "Language use is adapted differently with different people, with different language, and with different discourse communities. Realizing how language adapts to different situations and different discourse communities is shocking." Her understanding of *how* to take a position is limited, and she relies heavily on a precollege strategy, by focusing on a directional statement that presents a list of topics for each section of the essay. Furthermore, Whitney, like many developing college writers, mistakes editorial commentary or value judgments for analysis. She did attempt to deal with abstraction in her thesis, in contrast to earlier essays that were more informational and less complex, and she goes on to support this thesis more successfully than in her earlier work, using specific examples such as "That brings me into my polish [sic] speaking language. I speak it very slow and soft and I am not confident in what I am saying." She provides similar examples for her analysis of her language adapting at home with her family and with her boyfriend.

And yet, it is apparent from Whitney's final paper that managing any kind of evidence that isn't personal example is still a struggle and thus signals the difficulty that she subsequently faced with managing a complex text in the core transfer-level course. For example, in her discourse analysis paper, Whitney organized her paper in a way that is intuitive for novice writers but that more sophisticated writers eventually move past, especially in their management of sources. When conducting self-analysis, she understood paragraphs as units of meaning, but when attempting to integrate outside field research, she simply let it stand as independent paragraphing, using topic sentences that report on her methods for conducting research rather than advancing the thesis: "I had an interview with my polish [sic] speaking grandma" and "I had another interview which was my boyfriend." Even at the end of the bridge course, which was focused on critical reading and source-based writing, Whitney was struggling to manage information that she didn't generate herself.

Predictably, Whitney completely failed to meet instructor expectations in a transfer-level course assignment that asked her to analyze a scholarly article critically, take a position on a text, and find and integrate sources independently into an essay. It's important to note that Whitney met instructor expectations on the first few assignments for the second semester course, which asked her to take a position using familiar strategies used in the English 101 course. Whitney performed the least successfully on an assignment also undertaken by two of her other 101 classmates who ended up in the same 102 section (Jana and Sarah, discussed in the following section). This assignment asked students to "select a critical article [from a shared class text on the *Harry Potter* series] and develop three questions about the article that encourage analysis and discussion. As the assignment explained, "For each question, you will write a one-page (exactly one-page) response." Students were asked to incorporate examples from the article and from one credible outside source to support their response to the questions. Whitney ignored assignment instructions by beginning her paper "To start off with I will provide a brief summary of the article 'Controversial Content in Children's Literature' out of the book *Critical Perspectives on Harry Potter*." Rather than write an analysis or argument, Whitney responded with unsupported opinions and relied heavily on popular culture rather than on outside credible scholarly sources to support her claims:

- "I feel that personally this issue of Cedric's death should not be an issue."

- "For instance, I was watching a C.S.I. show and there was a scene during the show were [sic] the detectives were at a dumpster pulling out a dead prostitute."

- "I really don't feel that teenage boys are going to get lost in the fantasy of Harry Potter and start to believe in an evil force or stat [sic] to join forces with an occult or cult."

Whitney failed to adapt her writing according to the assignment instructions and regressed to informal academic tone, although her instructor reported that she successfully completed argumentative essays that did not require independent analysis of sources.

Jana: A Case Study in Rhetorical Conservatism

Surprisingly, even students who demonstrated better preparation for the transfer-level course did not demonstrate a proficiency in adapting their writing strategies to unfamiliar academic tasks, although they completed earlier assignments with a fairly advanced level of proficiency when asked to take a position using familiar strategies from the bridge course. Jana provides a fascinating example of a student who was highly successful in English 101, even at adapting to the purpose and audience of college-level writing assignments. However, her self-assessment survey reveals that she had a low level of metacognitive awareness about her own writing—that is, she could define the terms "purpose" and "audience" in a rote way but was unable to self-assess those features effectively in her own writing, a limitation that we argue prefigured the challenges that she faced in the English 102 course. For instance, when asked to "briefly describe how you made decisions about the following elements as you drafted this essay," Jana's analysis of her purpose is disconnected from the requirements of the assignment and instead focuses on her thesis: "This is a big one, I use this [sic]. I figure out what point I am trying to get a cross [sic] with this paper. I work it out from there usually." Her description of how she makes decisions about audience suggests a similarly incomplete understanding of college-level writing strategies: "I basically base it on either the students or the teacher, [sic] it helps a little but not that much." This disconnection between Jana's performance on fairly straightforward college writing tasks in English 101 and her awareness of her own rhetorical strategies is indicative of what becomes a later problem with a more difficult English 102 essay, where she failed to meet expectations for most learning outcomes because she was unable to adapt to the demands of an unfamiliar assignment that required her to find and analyze a source independently.

Interestingly, in the English 101 course, Jana successfully analyzed and synthesized two sources assigned by the instructor. She was able to offer an intermediate-level thesis that responded to the writing prompt and achieved the purpose of the assignment, which was to synthesize two assigned texts. Her thesis for essay two, "Rodriguez and Cronin [sic] both discuss the importance of being not only educated but also being a part of society," recognizes that she needs to pull out similar features of the two texts on education. She broke her thesis into subtopics that analyzed commonalities between the two texts while taking a position. For the bridge course assignment, Jana clearly understood the writers' arguments and organized her essay using a complex structure that synthesized the ideas of both writers in each paragraph rather than addressing each text in two completely separate sections of her essay, as less advanced writers in the same class tended to do. Her topic sentences organized her essay around themes that the two assigned readings shared:

- "both are stimulating [sic] quick to discuss what it means to be a truly educated person."

- "Rodriguez and Cronon discuss that you must learn everything that has been learned."

- "Being free is an important part of both the *Hunger of Memory* book by Rodriguez and *Only Connect* [sic] by Cronon. It is important because of the contrast with this issue."

- "Another very important contrast that is made by both Rodriquez [sic] and Cronon is ethnicity and heritage."

For many underprepared college students, the intellectually sensible way to organize texts is by summarizing what each writer says—even though the task of synthesis demands that they integrate the two sources at a more sophisticated level. In this sense, Jana's organizational strategy showed her to be writing at an advanced level that demonstrated readiness for English 102.

In contrast, Jana was unable to analyze sources in the transfer-level course when required to find them independently. In completing the same assignment on the critical article on the *Harry Potter* series that Whitney was asked to do, despite having succeeded at an intermediate to advanced level in the bridge course at analyzing assigned course texts, Jana reverted to pre-101 rhetorical strategies. In addition, she failed to meet instructor expectations for addressing the purpose and scope of an unfamiliar but only slightly more difficult analysis assignment in English 102. For example, Jana did not pose a critical analysis question about the scholarly essay, as the assignment directed, nor did she assert a thesis that made an argument in response to the question, failing to respond to — or perhaps accurately interpret — the assignment prompt. Surprisingly, she didn't have a thesis statement. Besides making these misjudgments about the purpose of the assignment, this student writer made inappropriate decisions about audience needs, such as including an online "Wiktionary" definition for the term "death." In short, she focused on the topic of the article (death), not on the text, and primarily discussed her feelings about death rather than engaging analytically with the independently located text.

Jana also demonstrated a disjunction between her performance on the English 101 essays and the English 102 assignment in her ability to make judgments about conventions and adhere to sentence-level expectations, diction, and style. For example, in her work for the bridge course, even in the earliest essay that we studied, she achieved a command of formal academic tone and style on a par with or beyond that of her classmates. By contrast, in her 102 essay, she frequently relied on conversational and informal language, such as "So, I guess that" and "Let's just say that." She often directly addressed the reader with phrases such as "I will give you something else to consider." Her multiple misjudgments in tone reveal a lack of rhetorical knowledge about how to address a college audience — a misjudgment demonstrated much less frequently in her work for the 101 course. She repeatedly used second person "you" and directly addressed the reader, such as imploring her audience to "imagine" particular scenarios. She also failed to find scholarly sources, as required by the assignment, and used inappropriate metarhetoric (such as "In an article I was reading").

Jana and Whitney were not the only students to cling to precollege writing approaches. Jana reverted to informational writing instead of applying the new techniques that she had learned in the bridge course; Whitney appeared to return to an informal tone, use of popular rather than academic research sources, and editorial commentary instead of analysis. Sarah, another student from our study enrolled in the same 102 course, remained attached to her own precollege rhetorical tool: a five-paragraph essay format that she had used successfully in high school. Sarah's reliance on the five-paragraph structure limited her ability to develop her ideas fully in the English 101 course. In the next course, that same strategy made it impossible for Sarah to adapt her writing to address the needs of a new audience and adhere to the requirements for the article analysis assignment.

To us, these are instructive examples because of the disconnect between the expectations of the assignment and the students' ability to achieve them, especially given their previous performance on essays that required them to use formal academic tone and meet a demanding rhetorical purpose, such as analysis and synthesis. In our notes about Jana's overall English 101 development, we commented on her improvement through the writing process and her ability to proofread and minimize sentence-level errors and indicated that she seemed ready to move on to English 102. Although she did retain the ability to cite correctly in MLA style, Jana was unable to apply much of what she had learned about academic writing conventions in the bridge course when faced with a new (but not especially complex) type of source-based assignment the following semester. It is notable that the English 102 instructor reported that Jana was able to transfer her knowledge of college-level rhetorical strategies and writing conventions to other, more familiar types of assignments.

Melanie: A Case Study in Literacy, Technology, and Metacognition

Melanie is an appropriate example of an advanced basic writer/novice proficient writer whose work reveals how students may not appear to be "at risk" in their early coursework, but, as they move into new rhetorical tasks and more demanding coursework—and, in this case, new writing environments—their risk for probation and suspension increases dramatically. As an English 101 student, Melanie earned high grades but moved into an entirely online English 102 course that required writing and reading strategies that were very different from those that she used in 101 and coupled those demands with the reading and writing intensity of online learning. She eventually dropped out of the course, but not before completing the first two assignments. Cynthia Selfe has argued that writing teachers have an obligation to pay attention to the ways that "technology is now inextricably linked to literacy and literacy education in this country" (414). Melanie's performance in the bridge and online 102 courses is a clear illustration of this relationship between literacy and technology.

In English 101, Melanie, like many of her peers, made substantial progress toward developing college-level writing strategies while still demonstrating an incomplete understanding of academic writing conventions. For example, her second essay used an inappropriately informal tone and showed a weak command of the content of the reading. Melanie was able to write a thesis that supported a claim about the two assigned texts: "In the articles 'Only Connect' and *Hunger of Memory*,

Cronon and Rodriguez describe that becoming a member of society is very important in becoming a well-educated person." Even though the wording is shaky, Melanie offers a somewhat complex idea, that education is an initiation into a society, and the bulk of her essay demonstrates some of the important cosmetic features of academic writing, such as topic sentences, transitions between ideas, and relatively error-free sentences. However, she often used summary rather than analysis and struggled to make substantive connections between the two texts. Melanie's final essay in English 101 made these same missteps — with a distracting and inappropriate use of metadiscourse and conversational tone. As a result of her ability to write a satisfactory thesis and support it with examples from a text, she passed the English 101 course with a relatively high grade, even though some of her work did not demonstrate substantial thinking about the texts under discussion. However, this inconsistency persisted into 102 and was indeed part of the explanation for her failure to complete the core course.

At the time of our initial analysis of Melanie's work, we were curious about what it was in the final English 101 assignment that led her to regress in her command of formal academic tone. A close analysis of her work reveals why Melanie can be characterized as an at-risk student writer, namely, her still-emerging command of judging audience and purpose. For example, although the final assignment on discourse communities for English 101 asked students to analyze their own language use — an assignment that should have signaled expectations for formal academic tone and analysis — Melanie mistook the assignment as an invitation to discuss both personal experience and personal feelings about language. Her self-assessment noted, "I just wrote as I would normally talk in a group of people," revealing that she had enough understanding to characterize her tone accurately but not enough rhetorical knowledge to recognize that it was inappropriate for the assignment. Consequently, when Melanie was asked to complete a difficult assignment in the transfer-level, online English 102 course, she made missteps similar to those of Sarah, Jana, and Whitney.

Two major misconceptions reveal themselves in Melanie's approach to the online 102 assignment: First, she used an informal tone for a formal essay assignment, an "Exploratory Essay" that asked her to chart her thinking process as she researched a topic during the second phase of a research process. Second, this metacognitive assignment demanded that students demonstrate a sophisticated and advanced level of self-awareness, because they needed to document their reading and writing process as they conducted research and worked toward a larger research essay. However, Melanie reverted to a precollege rhetorical strategy, reporting on information, specifically, how to care for the elderly and working in a nursing home as a nursing assistant, rather than a discussion of the multiple perspectives that her research process *should* have revealed to her as she engaged in investigation and inquiry about the topic.

Our Classrooms

Based on these findings, we advocate an expansion of the professional definition of "underprepared" or "at-risk" student writers. The current disciplinary understanding accounts only for students who place specifically into noncredit college courses; in fact, many students whose test scores, and perhaps even timed writing samples, place them into degree-credit courses may not bring with them the sorts of sophisticated reading and writing skills that instructors expect for college-level coursework (see Ritter, 2008). Our study revealed four major challenges that underprepared students face in adapting their reading and writing strategies as they move from introductory classes into core transfer-level composition courses and that are relevant to thinking about pedagogical approaches to both of these courses:

1. When faced with an assignment that was perhaps different but not necessarily more difficult, students floundered or failed to make suitable judgments about how to meet the needs of the reading audience.

2. These developing writers struggled to take a position on a *text* instead of using the text to report on information or support a claim; they reverted to the precollege strategy of commenting on the ideas or topics in the sources versus analyzing the sources.

3. Students were fairly successful at analyzing and synthesizing sources from shared class readings; however, they struggled to analyze independently located sources and seemed to have difficulty transferring college-level reading strategies to new, unfamiliar texts.

4. Particularly telling is the reversion to high school rhetorical strategies. When they encountered something new or different, these students didn't build on the strategies and techniques that they had learned in English 101; they instead reverted to precollege strategies, even though, according to the 101 and 102 instructors, these same students had performed adequately and sufficiently at a college level on more familiar assignments.

All of the students that we studied entered the English 101 course ostensibly vetted by standardized test scores as prepared to do college-level work; nine out of fourteen students in our study successfully completed the first source-based writing assignment in the core transfer course when faced with a writing task that required them to take a position and support a thesis with evidence. Similarly, three out of the four students who struggled to adapt to an unfamiliar sourced-based writing task in the core course successfully completed other argumentative writing assignments that were similar to those from the 101 course. The other student dropped out of the course before completing other assignments.

Although these numbers may be dismaying from an instructional perspective, because they suggest that students were ill-prepared for new rhetorical situations and writing tasks, we can be heartened by Lunsford and Lunsford's findings that the majority of programs in the United States are asking students to do argumentative writing with or without supporting evidence. That is, these students are prepared to do the kinds of writing that they are most likely to encounter in their college career. In this sense, our instructional design was successful. A bigger challenge is how to design learning experiences that cultivate rhetorical adaptability and the ability to analyze a text independently because so much of the work that students do in the first year of college and beyond requires a solid foundation in these skills.

From a pedagogical perspective, we argue strongly for providing under-prepared and at-risk student writers with writing courses that engage students in critical reading, writing from sources, and taking a position on complex topics, as David Bartholomae argued as long ago as 1993 and Rodby and Fox claimed again in 2000. Our study has shown, and James Gentile has noted, that a challenging college-level reading and writing assignment "calls the student to move beyond the self; to think in the context of others, and of texts, and of ideas; and then through that process, to move back to the self, informed and critical" (325). Similarly, Patrick Sullivan has claimed that, in a college-level composition course, "having a student read, consider, and respond to multiple readings grouped around a thematic question or issue would be ideal, in my judgment. The primary goal, regardless of the number of readings assigned, is to introduce students to an ongoing conversation that is multilayered and complex" ("Essential" 17). We concur with Gentile and Sullivan that adapting to academic writing tasks and developing college-level thinking depends heavily on a student's ability to use appropriate reading strategies to move beyond precollege approaches (such as reporting on information) to analysis, synthesis, and evaluation.

Source-based writing is a major focus of core transfer-level composition courses and writing-intensive classes in the disciplines, and yet many (if not most) students enter open admission two-year institutions still developing the ability to understand, critically read, and write about academic texts, or, at least, their ACT scores suggest this.[4] For example, when reading assignments are disconnected from writing tasks in introductory composition courses, students miss a key opportunity to develop the critical reading and thinking skills that are necessary for successfully enrolling in higher-level college courses. Our analysis of students' source-based writing suggests that underprepared students develop critical reading skills slowly, over the course of more than one semester. Therefore, text-based writing assignments in introductory composition courses play a crucial role in preparing students for more advanced coursework, both in English and in other disciplines. Furthermore, we argue that many underprepared students cannot successfully make the leap to source-based writing assignments in transfer-level courses without first receiving multiple opportunities to write about reading, discuss college-level texts, and think independently and critically about what they read.

Our study also reinforces the "WPA Outcomes Statement for First-Year Composition," which asserts knowledge of processes as an important learning outcome for first-year composition. Our English 101 students who moved into English 102 sections that emphasized student conferences, process pedagogy, and portfolio assessment were better able to meet instructor expectations, especially when their initial efforts were wildly off-base. Similarly, many of the students in the English 101 class who made the most progress toward developing the writing skills necessary for enrolling in the core composition course also spent the most time working on multiple revisions of each essay. Underprepared writers are still developing the ability to adapt their rhetorical strategies to college-level writing situations, and they understand how thinking, reading, and writing at a college-level are substantively different from what they did in high school. Therefore, timely instructor feedback and multiple opportunities for revision provide students with the rhetorical knowledge that is necessary for making the transition to transfer-level composition courses and other disciplines that require both the same type of skills and new and different skills (see Durst in Smagorinsky 2006). Adaptability and intellectual agility require that students can make judgments about new tasks that they haven't encountered before.

In 1975, rhetorician Walter Ong perceptively observed that "Writing calls for difficult, and often quite mysterious, skills. Except for a small corps of highly trained writers, most persons could get into written form few if any of the complicated and nuanced meanings they regularly convey orally" (57). Our current study must be framed by an awareness that we do not live in a world or work in institutions where clear communication of ideas can remain a mysterious skill for the few, and we, as English teachers in the two-year college, are explicitly charged with its de-mystification. We recognize that the cultivation of rhetorical adaptability is a lifelong process; more advanced students bring with them a greater comfort level with texts and ideas than the students that we have identified as "underprepared." This may be a frustrating acknowledgment for writing instructors who work with at-risk student populations. However, we are heartened by the recognition that instruction *does* make a difference for students in remedying a lack of preparation to make an academic argument, knowing that, when those students are prepared to take on the sorts of writing tasks common in academia, they can meet that challenge.

Notes

1. The University of Wisconsin System's Office of Professional and Instructional Development funded this project through a 2007–2008 Undergraduate Teaching and Learning Grant. Christina McCaslin, Deb Timoney, and Annette Hackbarth-Onson were also members of the research team. Special thanks to Christina McCaslin for her analysis of student writing and feedback on this essay. Additional thanks to the anonymous readers and to Jeff Sommers at *Teaching English in the Two-Year College,* whose suggestions helped shape our revisions.
2. Our three-sequence course, English 098: Basics of Composition, English 101: Composition I, and English 102: Composition II, does not easily divide the student population based on placement as developmental; that is, English 101 students are a border student population who demonstrate the ability to use standard written English (sometimes not) but who lack the more sophisticated critical reading, writing, thinking, and research skills that would prepare them for the core course.
3. Three students failed or withdrew from 101, one completed 101 successfully but did not enroll in 102, one student completed 102 but not the designated assignment, one student retook 101, one student transferred to another institution, and one student enrolled in 102 but left the course before completing the designated assignment.
4. For example, the average ACT score in reading for developmental and bridge course students on our campus is 18 (out of 36), a score that ACT's "College Readiness Standards" indicate will prepare students to "Identify a clear main idea or purpose of straightforward paragraphs in uncomplicated narratives," "Locate simple details at the sentence and paragraph level in uncomplicated passages," and "Draw simple generalizations and conclusions . . . in uncomplicated passages" (see www.act.org/research for more).

Works Cited

Achieve, Inc. *Aligned Expectations?: A Closer Look at College Admissions and Placement Tests.* Washington, DC: Achieve, 2007.

Bartholomae, David. "The Tidy House: Basic Writing in the American Curriculum." *Journal of Basic Writing* 12.1 (1993): 4–21.

Brooke, Robert, Ruth Mirtz, and Rick Evans. *Small Groups in Writing Workshops: Invitations to a Writer's Life.* Urbana, IL: NCTE, 1994.

Council of Writing Program Administrators. "WPA Outcomes Statement for First-Year Composition." Council of Writing Programs Administrators. April 2000. 21 July 2008 http://www.wpacouncil.org/positions/outcomes.html.

Downs, Douglas, and Elizabeth Wardle. "Teaching about Writing, Righting Misconceptions: (Re)Envisioning 'First-Year Composition' as 'Introduction to Writing Studies.'" *College Composition and Communication* 58.4 (2007): 552–84.

Doyle, William. "Community College Transfers and College Graduation: Whose Choices Matter Most?" *Change* (May/June 2006). 21 July 2008. http://www.carnegiefoundation.org/change/sub.asp?key=98&subkey=1711&=true.

Durst, Russel. "Writing at the Postsecondary Level." *Research on Composition: Multiple Perspectives on Two Decades of Change*. Ed. Peter Smagorinsky. New York: Teachers College P, 2006. 78–107.

Gentile, James. "College-Level Writing: A Departmental Perspective." Sullivan and Tinberg 311–29.

Heaney, April. "The Synergy Program: Reframing Critical Reading and Writing for At-Risk Students." *Journal of Basic Writing* (2006): 26–52.

Lunsford, Andrea A., and Karen J. Lunsford. "Mistakes Are a Fact of Life: A National Comparative Study." *College Composition and Communication* 59.4 (June 2008): 781–806.

Knodt, Ellen Andrews. "What Is College Writing For?" Sullivan and Tinberg 146–57.

Maloney, Wendy Hall. "Connecting the Texts of Their Lives to Academic Literacy: Creating Success for At-Risk First-Year College Students." *Journal of Adolescent and Adult Literacy* 46.8 (2003): 264–74.

Ong, Walter. "The Writer's Audience Is Always a Fiction." *Cross-Talk in Comp Theory: A Reader*. Ed. Victor Villanueva. 2nd ed. Urbana, IL: NCTE, 2003. 55–76.

Ritter, Kelly. "Before Mina Shaughnessy: Basic Writing at Yale, 1920–1960." *College Composition and Communication* 60.1 (September 2008): 12–45.

Rodby, Judith, and Tom Fox. "Basic Work and Material Acts: The Ironies, Discrepancies, and Disjunctures of Basic Writing and Mainstreaming." *Journal of Basic Writing* 19.1 (2000): 84–99.

Selfe, Cynthia. "Technology and Literacy: A Story about the Perils of Not Paying Attention." *College Composition and Communication* 50.3 (1999): 411–36.

Sullivan, Patrick. "An Essential Question: What Is 'College-Level' Writing?'" Sullivan and Tinberg 1–30.

Sullivan, Patrick, and Howard Tinberg. *What Is College-Level Writing?* Urbana, IL: NCTE, 2006.

Writing Study Group of the National Council of Teachers of English Executive Committee. "NCTE Beliefs about the Teaching of Writing." NCTE. November 2004. 21 July 2008 http://www.ncte.org/about/over/positions/category/write/118876.htm.

Translating Theory into Practice

The selection and arrangement of the readings in this section highlight pragmatic classroom applications of landmark scholarship. We seek here to celebrate the intellectual work that two-year college faculty undertake on a daily basis as they translate theory into practice—and practice into theory—as "knowledge makers" in their local pedagogical contexts (see Reynolds p. 139 in this volume). One message that came through loud and clear in our national survey of Two-Year College English Association (TYCA) members was the desire for scholarship that was both *practical* and *relevant* to two-year college working conditions, student populations, and daily teaching activities. The chapters in this section showcase the translation of theory from multiple disciplines into practice in two-year college writing classrooms.

Chapter 8 focuses on promoting critical and creative thinking. We begin with two important statements about critical thinking. First, we feature an excerpt from the highly influential Delphi Report, one of the most important documents ever written on this topic. Published in 1990, this report was developed and endorsed by a team of scholars from the American Philosophical Association. The full title of the report suggests its ambition: *Critical Thinking: A Statement of Expert Consensus for Purposes of Educational Assessment and Instruction.* (Interested readers can find the full report online.) We include the committee's succinct summary statement on the "Affective Dispositions of Critical Thinking," a short, bulleted list that summarizes much of the committee's wisdom about critical thinking. This list can be discussed with students and used to shape assignments and classroom activities.

We follow the Delphi Report with an excerpt from the "Framework for Success in Postsecondary Writing," a document developed collaboratively by the Council of Writing Program Administrators, the National Council of Teachers of English, and the National Writing Project. This statement, which draws on Arthur Costa and Bena Kallick's seminal work on "habits of mind," represents our discipline's best current thinking about the dispositions and orientations necessary for successful college writing. Both of these documents are readily adaptable for classroom use across many instructional levels. They can also help shape departmental conversations about curriculum and pedagogy.

We conclude this chapter with an essay written by Frost McLaughlin and Miriam Moore, two-year college teacher-scholars who discuss their efforts to assess critical thinking in student writing. In a research study they conducted at a cross-sector Symposium on Thinking and Writing at the College Level, McLaughlin and Moore found that evaluators often valued "correctness" and "voice" over critical thinking, which they suggest is much more difficult to assess. Echoing the language of previous readings in this chapter, they note that teaching approaches which promote critical thinking may be at odds with approaches that prioritize the development of a student's "authentic" voice:

> Without open-minded thinking as a basis of approaching the writing task—the thinking that prompts the writer to consider alternative approaches and possible outcomes—the writer may not achieve the level of reasoning we expect in freshman writing. This thoughtful, fair-minded approach with its resulting careful reasoning, often expressed in a clear but neutral tone, may well be one of the distinguishing features of "college-level" thinking and writing. (pp. 256–66)

Perhaps most importantly, McLaughlin and Moore's work highlights the importance of consciously examining the potentially conflicting values and theories that underpin our writing pedagogies.

Chapter 9 focuses on an increasingly important issue in our profession: the integration of reading and writing at all levels of writing instruction. Reading proficiency among writing students has become a key part of the discussions about developmental education reform currently sweeping the country (for more on this, see Part Four, Chapter 14). As David Jolliffe notes in "Learning to Read as Continuing Education,"

> At every college and university where I have taught in the past twenty-five years—and this list includes four state universities, a private liberal arts college, and a large Catholic university—the talk about student reading is like the weather: Everybody complains about it, but nobody does anything about it. (p. 271)

Jolliffe is a nationally recognized expert on the subject of reading, and in the excerpt we feature from this essay he reviews current approaches to integrating reading and writing instruction. In the second selection in this chapter, "A Framework for Rereading in First-Year Composition," Dan Keller extends this discussion by focusing on the importance of *re*reading. Like Jolliffe, Keller suggests that *how* we teach students to read is as important as *what* we ask them to read. He urges teachers of writing to make "curricular space for rereading" (p. 283).

We conclude this chapter with an essay by Katie Hern, a writing teacher at a two-year college in California and a national leader in developmental education reform. Hern discusses the art of selecting readings for classes, including developmental courses, and makes a compelling case for what is at stake when we make decisions about the readings we include in two-year college writing courses. Asking "What will you have your students read?" Hern notes,

> This might be the most important decision you'll make as an English teacher. A good choice means engaged students who integrate the texts in their own writing and produce stronger essays. A poor choice means suffering all semester—low energy in the classroom, frustrated students not doing the reading, essays that are heavy on generalities and light on evidence. (p. 294)

Hern's recommendations have been developed through long experience working with two-year college students and faculty. For those interested in learning more about integrating reading and writing, we recommend Cheryl Hogue Smith's "Interrogating Texts: From Deferent to Efferent and Aesthetic Reading Practices" and Patrick's "What Can We Learn about 'College-Level' Writing from Basic Writing Students?: The Importance of Reading." Both of these essays discuss pragmatic concerns related to teaching reading and writing in two-year college settings.

Chapter 10 focuses on responding to student writing. We begin with Nancy Sommers's canonical study of instructors' written responses to student writing. The conclusion Sommers draws from this research is both famous and alarming: "For the most part, teachers do not respond to student writing with the kind of thoughtful commentary which will help students to engage with the issues they are writing about or which will help them think about their purposes and goals in writing a specific text" (pp. 304–5). Sommers recommends that writing teachers embrace a much more ambitious, generative understanding of revision, one that is characterized by

> a sense of revision as discovery, as a repeated process of beginning again, as starting out new, that our students have not learned. We need to show our students how to seek, in the possibility of revision, the dissonances of discovery—to show them through our comments why new choices would positively change their texts, and thus to show them the potential for development implicit in their own writing. (p. 306)

We conclude this chapter with Carolyn Calhoon-Dillahunt and Dodie Forrest's award-winning essay, "Conversing in Marginal Spaces," which engages in direct conversation with Sommers's ongoing work on the subject of responding to student writing. After attending a session at the 2005 CCCC Convention at which Sommers shared the results of a four-year longitudinal study of Harvard student writers, Calhoon-Dillahunt and Forrest developed their own study:

> [W]e felt inspired to conduct our own empirical study of student response to teacher feedback, one that focused on community college writers, specifically developmental writers. What would *these* students, in some ways the very antithesis of Harvard students, have to say? Would *our* students at Yakima Valley Community College—many of them first-generation students, academically underprepared, ethnically diverse, and most holding down jobs or raising families or both while attending school in the most economically challenged area of Washington State—value feedback as a resource for revision and personal writing growth as Harvard student Tiffany Threadcraft did? (p. 308)

Calhoon-Dillahunt and Forrest discovered that the developmental writers they surveyed, "like the Harvard students in Sommers's study, read and appreciated teacher commentary and found 'suggestions/constructive criticism' to be the most helpful" (p. 311). However, their study also showed that students were not skilled readers of teacher comments. They suggest that two-year college instructors must actively work to *teach* their students how to read and apply feedback on their papers. Calhoon-Dillahunt and Forrest's research demonstrates the importance of consciously considering institution type when making and sharing pedagogical knowledge.

Finally, Chapter 11 takes up Patrick's and Howard Tinberg's well-known question, "What is 'college-level' writing?" (Sullivan and Tinberg; Sullivan, Tinberg, and Blau). The pair of readings presented here focus on what it means to teach "academic literacy" at institutions that include many different disciplinary communities, each with its own conventions and expectations for writing. In the first selection, David Russell examines the history of postsecondary writing instruction in the United States, pointing out the complexities inherent in the very idea of a generalized course on "college writing" when disciplinary discourses vary so widely.

In his groundbreaking book *Border Talk: Writing and Knowing in the Two-Year College*, excerpted here, Howard Tinberg famously suggests that two-year college writing faculty are "border crossers," and as such they possess unique insights into what it means to navigate the diversity of academic literacies. Tinberg suggests that "to teach at a community college is to be 'in translation'"—in translation between "disciplines and institutions, between the local and the global, the practical and the theoretical, the private and the public, the two-year college and the research university" (p. 337). He suggests that this unique location positions two-year college writing teachers in powerful ways as we seek to map "disciplinary ways of knowing" with our colleagues and our students (p. 340).

Indeed, the intellectual work of translating between theory and practice across multiple disciplines, geographies, and institution types—work that the essays in these chapters highlight—may be a distinctive professional strength of two-year college writing teachers. Christie Toth, Brett Griffiths, and Kate Thirolf refer to this professional disposition as "transdisciplinary cosmopolitanism" (p. 598), viewing it as a powerful orientation from which more narrowly disciplined university faculty might learn.

Works Cited

Costa, Arthur L., and Bena Kallick, eds. *Learning and Leading with Habits of Mind*. ASCD, 2008, pp. 16-38.

Smith, Cheryl Hogue. "Interrogating Texts: From Deferent to Efferent and Aesthetic Reading Practices." *Journal of Basic Writing*, vol. 31, no. 1, 2012, pp. 59-79.

Sullivan, Patrick. "What Can We Learn about 'College-Level' Writing from Basic Writing Students? The Importance of Reading." Sullivan, Tinberg, and Blau, pp. 233-53.

Sullivan, Patrick, and Howard Tinberg, eds. *What Is "College-Level" Writing?* NCTE, 2006.

Sullivan, Patrick, Howard Tinberg, and Sheridan Blau, eds. *What Is "College-Level" Writing?* Vol. 2: *Assignments, Readings, and Student Writing Samples.* NCTE, 2010.

CHAPTER

8

Fostering Critical and Creative Thinking

Dispositions of the Good Critical Thinker

Dr. Peter A. Facione

Regarding the following selection, author Peter Facione writes, "The landmark 1990 APA Delphi Report presents the findings of a two-year project to articulate an international expert consensus definition of 'critical thinking.' The experts found that critical thinking is best understood, taught, and modeled for students as the process of purposeful and reflective judgment. In the Delphi Report an international panel of experts identify the attributes of ideal critical thinkers as well as the specific skills that are engaged in the process of purposeful, reflective judgment. The report includes detailed pedagogically focused tables and specific recommendations relating to critical thinking instruction and assessment. Over the past 25 years this report has been adopted by educators at every level and in every discipline, as well as by business, military, healthcare, and technology professionals seeking to make the idea of 'critical thinking' practical, positive, and applicable. Today the Delphi conceptualization is used throughout the world. It grounds academic requirements, courses, textbooks, peer-reviewed research, dissertations, competitively funded grants, institutional accreditation projects, and numerous assessment tools used for educational and employment purposes when evaluating an individual's or a group's reasoning skills and

From "The Delphi Report Executive Summary," *Critical Thinking: A Statement of Expert Consensus for Purposes of Educational Assessment and Instruction.* (ERIC Document No. ED315423). 1990.

mindset attributes are important." Teachers seeking additional detail can download the complete Delphi Report online.

FINDING: To the experts, a good critical thinker, the paradigm case, is habitually disposed to engage in, and to encourage others to engage in, critical judgment. She is able to make such judgments in a wide range of contexts and for a wide variety of purposes. Although perhaps not always uppermost in mind, the rational justification for cultivating those affective dispositions which characterize the paradigm critical thinker are soundly grounded in CT's personal and civic value. CT is known to contribute to the fair-minded analysis and resolution of questions. CT is a powerful tool in the search for knowledge. CT can help people overcome the blind, sophistic, or irrational defense of intellectually defective or biased opinions. CT promotes rational autonomy, intellectual freedom and the objective, reasoned and evidence-based investigation of a very wide range of personal and social issues and concerns.

The majority (61%) regard the dispositions listed in Table 1 as part of the conceptualization of CT. The consensus (83%) is that good critical thinkers can be characterized as exhibiting these dispositions.

Table 1. Affective Dispositions of Critical Thinking

Approaches to Life and Living in General:

* inquisitiveness with regard to a wide range of issues,
* concern to become and remain generally well-informed,
* alertness to opportunities to use CT,
* trust in the processes of reasoned inquiry,
* self-confidence in one's own ability to reason,
* open-mindedness regarding divergent worldviews,
* flexibility in considering alternatives and opinions,
* understanding of the opinions of other people,
* fair-mindedness in appraising reasoning,
* honesty in facing one's own biases, prejudices, stereotypes, egocentric or sociocentric tendencies,
* prudence in suspending, making, or altering judgments,
* willingness to reconsider and revise views where honest reflection suggests that change is warranted.

Approaches to Specific Issues, Questions or Problems:

* clarity in stating the question or concern,
* orderliness in working with complexity,
* diligence in seeking relevant information,
* reasonableness in selecting and applying criteria,
* care in focusing attention on the concern at hand,
* persistence though difficulties are encountered,
* precision to the degree permitted by the subject and the circumstance.

RECOMMENDATION: Just as with the cognitive dimension of CT, when conceiving of the education or assessment of critical thinkers, it is important to consider ways of developing materials, pedagogies, and assessment tools that are effective and equitable in their focus on these affective dispositions. The cultivation of these dispositions is particularly important to insure the use of CT skills outside the narrow instructional setting. Persons who have developed these affective dispositions are much more likely to apply their CT skills appropriately in both their personal life and their civic life than are those who have mastered the skills but are not disposed to use them.

Framework for Success in Postsecondary Writing

CWPA, NCTE, and NWP

This document is the product of an unprecedented collaboration among perhaps the three most important professional organizations devoted to writing instruction in the United States—the Council of Writing Program Administrators, the National Council of Teachers of English, and the National Writing Project. It reflects our profession's best current thinking about college readiness and the skills and dispositions that students need in order to be successful college-level readers, writers, and thinkers. Of note here is the focus on dispositional characteristics and habits of mind— something quite new to discussions of college writing and college readiness. The excerpt we include here is the Executive Summary. The entire document (which is quite brief) can be shared and discussed with students in writing classes, used for creating writing rubrics, and employed by departments to guide curriculum revision and development. The full document is conveniently available online. Readers who would like to learn more about the Framework—how it arrived at its present shape and a sampling of professional responses to it—should consult the special 2012 symposium devoted to it in College English: "On the Framework for Success in Postsecondary Writing" *(74.6: 520–53).*

Executive Summary

The concept of "college readiness" is increasingly important in discussions about students' preparation for postsecondary education.

This Framework describes the rhetorical and twenty-first-century skills as well as habits of mind and experiences that are critical for college success. Based in current research in writing and writing pedagogy, the Framework was written and reviewed by two- and four-year college

From "Framework for Success in Postsecondary Writing." 2011.

and high school writing faculty nationwide and is endorsed by the Council of Writing Program Administrators, the National Council of Teachers of English, and the National Writing Project.

Habits of mind refers to ways of approaching learning that are both intellectual and practical and that will support students' success in a variety of fields and disciplines. The Framework identifies eight habits of mind essential for success in college writing:

- Curiosity—the desire to know more about the world.

- Openness—the willingness to consider new ways of being and thinking in the world.

- Engagement—a sense of investment and involvement in learning.

- Creativity—the ability to use novel approaches for generating, investigating, and representing ideas.

- Persistence—the ability to sustain interest in and attention to short- and long-term projects.

- Responsibility—the ability to take ownership of one's actions and understand the consequences of those actions for oneself and others.

- Flexibility—the ability to adapt to situations, expectations, or demands.

- Metacognition—the ability to reflect on one's own thinking as well as on the individual and cultural processes used to structure knowledge.

The Framework then explains how teachers can foster these habits of mind through **writing, reading, and critical analysis** experiences. These experiences aim to develop students'

- Rhetorical knowledge—the ability to analyze and act on understandings of audiences, purposes, and contexts in creating and comprehending texts;

- Critical thinking—the ability to analyze a situation or text and make thoughtful decisions based on that analysis, through writing, reading, and research;

- Writing processes—multiple strategies to approach and undertake writing and research;

- Knowledge of conventions—the formal and informal guidelines that define what is considered to be correct and appropriate, or incorrect and inappropriate, in a piece of writing; and

- Ability to compose in multiple environments—from traditional pen and paper to electronic technologies.

Integrating Critical Thinking into the Assessment of College Writing

Frost McLaughlin and Miriam Moore

Clear and logical thinking is central to good writing. In order to emphasize the role of thinking in writing, Professors McLaughlin and Moore integrated the assessment of thinking into a rubric that they and colleagues used across disciplines to assess student writing. This article discusses the development of this rubric and explores how instructors from three contexts (high school / college dual-enrollment, two-year colleges, and four-year colleges) interpreted and applied it to two sample papers. The authors discuss variations in instructor responses to sample student writing, focusing specifically on the disparate weights assigned to logic and voice. These differences highlight variations in what instructors value across the contexts in which writing is taught, as well as the challenges in describing and assessing critical thought in writing.

When writing teachers at any level get together to assess student essays, they often disagree in their evaluations of the writing at hand. This is no surprise as writing is a complex process, and in evaluating it, teachers go through a complex sequence of thoughts before emerging with an overall assessment. Chris Anson describes this process of reading and responding reflectively to student writing as first involving "a complicated, rich internal response, much of it never shared with the writer." According to Anson, "In most cases, the internal response is more elaborate and less strictly pedagogical than the external response. Good teaching requires a highly complex process as we read, collect impressions, formulate an internal response, [and] choose which of the many impressions and ideas the student should receive" (373).

When teachers try to translate this rich response to student writing into a grade, commentary, or rubric score, they necessarily simplify and sometimes reduce the various reactions that they experience. Rubrics afford a shortcut to this rich response by focusing teachers' attention on certain aspects of writing. In fact, the elimination of some of the complexity of responding to writing is both an advantage and a shortcoming of rubrics in that while rubrics can reduce the number of steps needed to evaluate writing by bypassing the filtering process described by Anson, in doing so they necessarily narrow the focus of the teacher's attention to certain features. The problems with such shorthand tools, noted in works like Bob Broad's *What We Really Value* and Maja Wilson's *Rethinking Rubrics in Writing Assessment*, are well known. Besides

From *Teaching English in the Two-Year College*, 2012, vol. 40, no. 2, pp. 145-62.

failing to embrace comprehensively all of the elements that comprise sophisticated writing and thinking, rubrics often present instead features that tend to stand out and allow easy assessment, often countable features, like the level of detail and correctness. Less obvious and more difficult-to-assess features like incisive analysis and the rhetorical use of tone or metaphor are rarely represented in writing rubrics, though they are clearly valued by sophisticated readers. Omitting such rhetorical features becomes, then, a matter of practicality for rubrics, especially as the more complex the rubric generally, the less intelligible to the student and the less useful to the teacher in focusing attention and saving time. Rubrics are especially useful for instructors in disciplines other than English who are often uncomfortable with the messy job of grading student writing and want "the clean, easy fix" that David Martins points out rubrics provide in his article on the relationship between the use of rubrics and the "material conditions" of teaching (124).

As a result of their simplicity, rubrics tend to look and feel somewhat elementary, rewarding basic writing features like organization and correctness more proportionally than they do nuance or precision. Likewise, critical thinking, or the complexity of thought and analysis that is expected in "college-level" writing, is often not included in writing rubrics. Sometimes added as a separate category to writing rubrics, critical thinking appears in its simplest terms as a measurement of whether the logic is clear rather than whether the thinking is complicated, open-minded, or contextually appropriate. Critical thinking can become just another "skill" like those Susan Fanetti, Kathy M. Bushrow, and David L. DeWeese describe as forming the sort of "static rubric" used to evaluate "standardized test writing" (80), which they view as inherently in opposition to those analytic and critical thinking skills required in college that are "resistant to large-scale, objective standardization" (78). Though the authors address the more general effect of standardization in high school writing instruction (and its mismatch with college instruction), they also point out the role that rubrics play in quantifying and reducing writing into simple and sometimes inappropriate but measurable skills.

Despite these shortcomings and because of the prevalent use of rubrics in writing assessment, we chose to develop a rubric designed both to measure critical thinking in writing and, at the same time, to reflect its value. We wanted to develop an uncomplicated method for college faculty across the disciplines to measure critical thinking in written assignments. In doing so, we join Martins in his expressed need for a time-saving tool and Chris Stroutholpoulos and Janet L. Peterson in their desire for a flexible tool. (Stroutholpoulos and Peterson combined a required core of traits with a set of optional ones in their rubric for assessing writing.) Our goal was to develop a streamlined rubric that is sufficiently simple and adaptable to be easily used by faculty who assign writing across disciplines. The critical thinking in writing rubric

(CTWR) combines two critical thinking elements with three writing elements (and one optional research element).

Arguably the educational buzzword of this decade, *critical thinking* is as elusive a concept as *college-level writing*. In using the term *critical thinking*, we mean the fairly complicated reasoning that we want college students to practice. Such reasoning involves "purposeful, self-regulatory judgment which results in interpretation, analysis, evaluation, and inference, as well as explanation of the evidential, conceptual, methodological, criteriological, or contextual considerations upon which that judgment is based" (Facione 2). To do this, we began by grouping the following skills under the label *Logic*: "Consistently and accurately interprets evidence, draws warranted conclusions, analyzes alternative perspectives and evaluates where appropriate" (language adapted from the Facione and Facione Holistic Scoring Rubric). This rubric category also encompasses three levels of Bloom's Revised Taxonomy of cognitive skills: understanding (which includes interpretation), analyzing, and evaluating (Anderson and Krathwohl 67–68). To incorporate the initial phase of thinking critically about a writing topic—an ordered and reflective approach to the writing task—we used the terms *thoughtful* and *organized* in the rubric element *Focus*: "Effectively addresses the writing task in a thoughtful and organized manner." This element reflects a rich array of cognitive activities—understanding the writing task (context, audience, thesis, etc.), responding in a logical and complex manner, and accomplishing the rhetorical demands of the problem. While the complexity of *Focus* posed some practical problems for group assessments, the element does communicate the proper attributes of the critical approach to an assignment. In this sense, the element *Focus* in the CTWR combines three of the seven "key areas of critical thinking" as defined by William Condon and Diane Kelly-Riley at Washington State University in their critical thinking rubric: "identification of a problem or issue," "establishment of a clear perspective on the issue," and "location of the issue within an appropriate context(s)" (59) as well as four of the sixteen "analytic scale traits" of the Cognitive Level and Quality of Writing Assessment (CLAQWA) rubric developed at the University of South Florida: "assignment requirements," "main idea," "audience," and "purpose" (*CLAQWA Online*). By loading this element with the integral attributes of problem and solution conception, we have both complicated and simplified the assessment process.

The terms embedded in *Focus* also reflect a general attitude that is evident in mature writing from its inception and clearly results in an overall coherence and organization in the written product. This *thoughtful* attitude may be the sum of Bloom's revised taxonomy—to *remember, understand, apply, analyze, evaluate,* and *create*—or it may be more the affective or dispositional traits of the critical thinker, as characterized by authors of the consensus statement known as "The Delphi Report" (Facione). Those dispositional traits include approaching problems with clarity, orderliness, diligence, reasonableness, care, persistence, and precision (13). A student's initial approach to a writing assignment has much to do with the complexity of thought and the organization of its final form.

We developed the CTWR over time, using an adapted version of the Writing Assessment Rubric used by the Virginia Community College System (VCCS) as a basis, and presented it to faculty cross-disciplinary work groups as part of our college's Quality Enhancement Plan (QEP), as well as to English faculty groups like the southeastern regional conference of the Two-Year College Association (TYCA-SE). In our largest forum, the first biennial Symposium on Thinking and Writing at the College Level (March 2011), we used the rubric with a group of eighty participants, most of whom were English instructors teaching first-year composition to students in three different contexts: high schools with dual-enrolled students, community colleges, and four-year universities. Teachers of dual-enrolled courses in first-year composition were in the majority at this event, with teachers at two- and four-year campuses comprising the minority. What we noticed immediately during the assessment session was a wider variation in response, both in the rating of rubric elements and in the ensuing discussion, than had been evident in our previous uses of the rubric. Previously, when using a pilot version of the CTWR with cross-disciplinary faculty at Lord Fairfax Community College, faculty response was generally spread between two contiguous ranks, with a fairly low number of outlying ranks. The same was true for the ranking done by English faculty attending a TYCA-SE presentation on using the CTWR to assess critical thinking in writing. However, the larger number of participants in our cross-context symposium group showed much more divergence across ranks than before.

Two changes in the conditions under which we were now using the rubric were immediately obvious: First, symposium participants came from more varied contexts than had previous users of the rubric; these earlier groups were all two-year college faculty members from both English and other disciplines. Second, the writing samples that symposium participants assessed were different from the samples we had used previously. Whereas in the earlier sessions we had used lengthy student samples from a sociology course and short samples from our freshman composition courses, this time we used two very different student essays written in freshman composition to fulfill an assignment in definition, samples that we felt illustrated the presence and absence of critical thinking in a fairly clear way. (See Appendix A for the writing assignment that generated the samples and Appendixes B and C for the sample essays.) To our surprise, symposium participants varied significantly in their ratings of the two samples, especially in their assessment of *Focus* and *Logic*, the two rubric elements designed to reflect aspects of critical thinking. What follows in this article is an analysis of the diverse symposium response to those student samples.

Before looking at specific responses to the samples, it is important to note that while we made the samples electronically available to participants before the symposium, no "norming" of participants was done prior to or during the symposium. Indeed, no discussion of what critical thinking is or looks like in college writing took place before or during the assessment. (This lack of preliminary discussion or "norming" remained constant during the development of our rubric, as one of our goals was to design an easy-to-use instrument that cross-disciplinary faculty could use without training.) Our intent in assembling a mixed group of instructors who were ostensibly teaching the same course of freshman composition, albeit in different settings, was simply to begin the conversation about what distinguishes college-level thinking in writing. In doing this we were following the lead of Patrick Sullivan and Howard Tinberg, whose two volumes entitled *What Is "College-Level" Writing?* provided part of the impetus for our parallel questioning of what "college-level" thinking is exactly. Both volumes present provocative essays on a range of perspectives on this topic. Indeed, in his opening chapter of the first volume, "An Essential Question: What Is 'College-Level' Writing?" Patrick Sullivan lists five questions to consider, the first being "What kinds of intellectual work do colleagues and students around the country associate with the concept of college-level writing?" (19). This is the absorbing question that we are attempting to answer when we assess the critical thinking in student writing using our rubric. Our exploration of this aspect of writing assessment did not need to involve—in fact, in our opinion, needed to avoid—the "scoring guidelines and rater training" used to ensure a high level of interrater reliability (Huot 557). What we were looking for was not a "reliable" set of responses to the critical thought in samples of student writing but instead the rich, differentiated range of response that is natural to faculty assessing thinking within different contexts and disciplines. That is essentially what we found in the symposium response to our student samples.

Using clicker technology, then, symposium participants rated each element from the CTWR in both sample papers. We purposely did not track responses to individuals, nor did we track them to instructional setting (high school, community college, and four-year university), our purpose being to raise the issues surrounding the features of "college-level" thinking and writing rather than to resolve them. Similarly, our aim in this article is to address the issue of critical thinking as an important component of "college-level" writing and to discuss the problems attendant in its assessment. Like our colleagues who first posed this question about "college-level" writing, we eschew a single, easy answer and try to find answers among the varied experience and perspectives of our colleagues in multiple disciplines and contexts. In developing a writing rubric that includes elements of critical thinking, however, we are clearly attempting to articulate how those elements can be identified, analyzed, and evaluated as part of the writing assessment process.

As noted previously, the CTWR, which has undergone a substantial editing process during its development, was not available to participants before using it at the symposium. From its use with other community college faculty and students, we had simplified the CTWR to six categories with four possible ratings, or ranks: Superior, Skilled, Adequate, and Inadequate. By removing the high-stakes differentiation between a passing (D) and failing (F) rank through combining them into one labeled "Inadequate," we hoped to make assessment easier. Further, at the suggestion of students, we omitted descriptions of all ranks but the highest—essentially removing descriptions of all but the best aspects of writing in the CTWR. By omitting numerical or letter grades and using only single-word descriptors, we sidestepped the conflict that such grade designations create for teachers during assessment as well as the impulse of students to revise minimally to get to the next rank. The rubric shown in Figure 1 is the result of these changes.

Results

The results that we collected in real time using clicker technology during the symposium assessment surprised us. While we did not discuss the ratings during the assessment session beyond remarking on interesting or widely disparate results and informally asking participants to volunteer reasons for their ratings, the responses in this forum were sufficiently different from our previous results, as well as different from each other, to motivate our analysis and its discussion in this paper. While neither sample paper was extremely good or bad in our opinion, we thought the essays did demonstrate the features of critical thinking by their absence and presence. The first sample, an essay defining the term *jocks* (see Appendix B), appeared to us to provide an engaging example of a distinctive style, or voice, but to lack the thoughtful analysis that we expect of college-level thinking and writing. The second essay, which defines the term *creativity* (see Appendix C), while lacking both detailed development and a distinctive voice, did appear to us to demonstrate some of the features of complex thinking. Many symposium participants, however, saw the sample essays differently. Because we were interested in assessing the thinking in the two writing samples, our analysis focuses on two elements in the rubric—*Focus* and *Logic*—and the various ranks (Superior, Skilled, Adequate, and Inadequate) our participants gave them.

A. Response to "Jocks"

The writing sample defining the term *jocks* was deemed to be "Superior" in *Focus* by 25% of participants, Skilled by 38%, Adequate by 20%, and Inadequate by 17%. If *Focus* is defined as "effectively" addressing "the

Figure 1. Critical thinking in writing rubric (CTWR) for college-level writing

Element	Superior	Skilled	Adequate	Inadequate
Focus Effectively addresses the writing task in a thoughtful and organized manner				
Logic Consistently and accurately interprets evidence, draws warranted conclusions, analyzes alternative perspectives, and evaluates where appropriate				
Content Substantially develops ideas through specific details, reasons, and examples				
Style Consistently uses language that is precise, varied, and vivid; employs diverse and appropriate sentence structure throughout				
Correctness Makes few errors in usage, grammar, punctuation, and spelling				
Research Consistently selects appropriate source material; correctly integrates outside source information; cites information accurately				

writing task in a thoughtful and organized manner," how could freshman composition teachers, albeit from different levels and contexts, evaluate that criterion with such widely disparate results? One answer may be that there are two criteria under scrutiny in *Focus*—*thoughtful* and *organized* manner—making the element more complicated to assess. The first aspect, *thoughtful*, is difficult to measure, the second less so. The paper defining *jocks* is clearly organized in the sense that it introduces the term *jock* with detailed description that renders a clear image, then describes the motivation, attire, and habitat of this type of person, and concludes by positioning jocks in reference to "others." However, in the case of a *thoughtful* focus, the paper cannot be said to approach the definition task with careful consideration or reflection. In fact, the very pace of the essay projects a fast and funny satire of the brainless and brawny athlete stereotype. Herein may lie the reason for the polar assessments of the paper's *Focus* as Superior and Inadequate: where some participants may have viewed the essay's pace and tone to be evidence of a carefully devised rhetorical strategy, others (including ourselves) may view its core content as providing a stereotype that is easy for most high school students to exploit. The humor is amusing, the voice clear and interesting, yet the thinking behind the definition is in no way nuanced, nor, we would argue, is its inception *thoughtful*.

The second element of the CTWR that embodies critical thinking is *Logic*, which consists of four parts, two of which (points 3 and 4 below) correspond to cognitive processes in Bloom's classification of educational objectives: *analysis* and *evaluation*:

> *Logic:* (1) Consistently and accurately interprets evidence, (2) draws warranted conclusions, (3) analyzes alternative perspectives, and (4) evaluates where appropriate

Only 3% of the participants rated the *Logic* of *jocks* as Superior, 17% rated it Skilled, 36% Adequate, and 43% Inadequate. This is a clear statement by participants that something is lacking in the logic of the definition of *jocks*. To us, the stereotype of the brutish jock is simplistic, both in its original conception (*Focus*) and in its lack of conclusion, interpretation, analysis, or evaluation of the topic. Indeed, the paper could be said to be overly simple in its reasoning, ending essentially where it began.

Table 1. Symposium Ratings for the Writer's Focus in Sample A

Sample A	Superior A	Skilled B	Adequate C	Inadequate D/F
Focus	25%	38%	20%	17%

Table 2. Symposium Ratings for the Writer's Logic in Sample A

Sample A	Superior A	Skilled B	Adequate C	Inadequate D/F
Logic	3%	17%	36%	43%

B. Response to "Creativity"

The second essay, which attempts to define the more abstract term *creativity*, was rated higher in *Focus* and similar in *Logic* to the ratings of the *jocks* definition. When asked whether this essay on *creativity* "effectively addresses the writing task in a thoughtful and organized manner," 21% of participants rated it as Superior, 38% as Skilled, 28% as Adequate, and 14% as Inadequate. When we compare these results to the *Focus* ratings of the radically different *jocks* paper (see Table 3), we find a rather similar pattern, though there is a substantial difference in the lowest ranking. That the student thought in a careful and organized manner about defining *creativity* seems less clear to our participants than the fact that the paper is not deficient in its *Focus*. In contrast, only 2% of participants rated *Logic* in the definition of *creativity* to be Superior, 28% Skilled, 58% Adequate, and 12% Inadequate.

If we break down *Logic* into its parts—*interprets, concludes, analyzes alternatives, and evaluates effectively*—this essay would seem to us to satisfy the first part by interpreting the conventional definition of *creativity* correctly (in paragraph 1), the second by drawing warranted conclusions about its application in other domains (paragraphs 2–4), and the third by rejecting the limits of the conventional perspective on creativity (paragraphs 1, 2, and 4). Most (86%) participants rated the paper as either Skilled or Adequate in *Logic*, while 12% ranked the *Logic* as Inadequate. Generally, then, participants agreed that the paper's *Logic* was Adequate where we would have rated it as Skilled, if not Superior.

Table 3. Symposium Ratings for the Writer's Focus and Logic in Samples A and B

	Superior A	Skilled B	Adequate C	Inadequate D/F
Sample A				
Focus	25%	38%	20%	17%
Logic	3%	17%	36%	43%
Sample B				
Focus	21%	38%	28%	14%
Logic	2%	28%	58%	12%

Discussion

As noted previously, the overall assessment of the student samples by symposium participants was not what we expected. While we were relatively sure that the humorous details of Sample A's definition of *jocks* would elicit a much higher rating in *Content* and *Style* than the sometimes thin and consistently neutral tone of Sample B, in our judgment Sample B was clearly superior to Sample A in terms of critical thinking. We were also fairly certain that a similar imbalance would exist in the element *Correctness*, as the definition of *creativity* was nearly error free while the definition of *jocks* was riddled with surface errors. Both of our hunches were correct. Nevertheless, we were not prepared for the disparity in overall ratings of the two papers, due in part to our incorrect prediction of Sample B's superior ratings in thinking (*Focus* and *Logic*).

The clicker-generated sum of the five feature ratings shows that participants were fairly evenly divided in their overall rating of Sample A, while nearly half (41%) the participants ranked Sample B as Adequate work, nearly a third as Skilled, and the others were each 15%, representing a more traditional curve (see Table 4: Overall Symposium Ratings, Samples A and B).

Our assumption is that certain elements of writing command more attention than others, dominating raters' perception of other elements. For some, perhaps even most, composition teachers at the college level, *Correctness* is a minimum requirement of "college-level" writing but not one that they would likely cite as more important than others—though its deficiency could elicit a failing rank overall. For other instructors, an attribute like voice (which is only one aspect of the element *Style* in our rubric) can be the most compelling feature of an essay, overriding the rating of other elements. When we asked symposium participants during our assessment session to explain their rankings of the two definition samples, a few mentioned the absence and presence of voice. One participant said of the *creativity* definition that there is "no reflection of humanity in this paper—no reflection of voice—no personality; it is hard to distinguish between style and content here—is it a lack of examples or lack of flair?" For some participants, there appears to be conflict over the importance of content versus the importance of flair (which we interpret to mean *voice*). One participant commented that the first writer couldn't control his flair and the second is "almost 'textbook-like' in tone," as if the second writer is striving for an academic voice. In contrast to these responses from participants, we find the neutral but precise academic voice to be satisfactory for carrying out the task of defining a highly abstract term like *creativity*, though a more interesting voice would not necessarily detract from the definition.

This brings up an intriguing possibility: for some English teachers voice appears to be paramount while for others it is not so important or, in some cases, is even a distraction. In his chapter in part 1, "High School

Table 4. Overall Symposium Ratings for Samples A and B

Sample A	Superior A	Skilled B	Adequate C	Inadequate D/F
Focus	25%	38%	20%	17%
Logic	3%	17%	36%	43%
Content	19%	37%	37%	7%
Style	53%	33%	13%	2%
Correctness	9%	29%	36%	27%
Total	**22%**	**31%**	**28%**	**19%**
Sample B				
Focus	21%	38%	28%	14%
Logic	2%	28%	58%	12%
Content	2%	9%	58%	32%
Style	7%	26%	51%	16%
Correctness	44%	46%	9%	0%
Total	**15%**	**29%**	**41%**	**15%**

Perspectives," of volume 1 of *What Is "College-Level" Writing?* Alfredo Celedon Lujan discusses his stance in support of a writing pedagogy that privileges voice:

> *Boring:* College-level writing must have a strong thesis statement. College-level writing is tightly woven and unified—buttressed by topic, transitional, and parallel sentences that flow seamlessly and thematically from paragraph to paragraph. College-level writing must have an introduction, body, and conclusion. It is demonstrated in essays, papers, stories, journals, research projects, lab reports, reader responses, articles, etc. It conforms to state and national standards and adheres to the conventions of correctness. *Boring.* (41)

This characterization of college writing echoes the comments of some of our participants regarding the definition of *creativity*. After recounting a youthful experience in writing a research paper, Lujan poses the question "What is acceptable and genuine student writing today?" to which he responds: "I'd say good writing rings true with *voice* authenticity (Ken Macrorie, Peter Elbow, Nancy Martin . . . , Donald Graves, Peter Stillman). As far as I know, the nebulous term *voice* has been kicked around for the last quarter of a century, *mas o menos.*" Lujan then asks, "What is voice in writing?" and answers, "to simplify, it is, perhaps, when the writer recognizes in her or his prose or poetry a style, tone, personality, and rhythm that work" (43). Lujan then expands this definition, saying,

"Writing without voice is breathing without rhythm—is speaking without body language, accent, dialect, or inflection. When a student writes, she or he is talking on paper" (44).

There are two striking differences between Lujan's perception of voice and our own. First, we struggle to teach first-year writers the difference between speech and writing; between the casual, limited lexicon of speech and the rich, considered lexicon of writing. Second, though placing voice at the center of writing is, as Lujan points out, certainly a familiar concept to those who are grounded in earlier literature of writing pedagogy, and clearly many of our participants regarded the second essay (on *creativity*) as hopelessly lifeless and lacking *voice,* we find that clear, neutral tone an entirely acceptable academic voice and preferable to a dramatic, emotional voice when the primary goal is to communicate complicated ideas.

We think perhaps the variety of modes practiced in high school writing, creative modes like personal narrative or fiction or poetry, make voice a more highly valued characteristic of writing in the K–12 context than does the exclusively expository writing done by the majority of students in freshman composition and other college courses. In "Voice in Writing Again: Embracing Contraries," Peter Elbow, an early and prominent voice promoting the importance of voice, recently raised the need to reconsider voice critically, arguing against the conventional "either/or" stance and for a "both/and" approach to voice, and we concur. The presence of voice in writing does not preclude the presence of critical thinking; neither does it reflect its presence. Voice has little to do with the logic of a paper; logical conclusions can be expressed in a neutral academic voice (which is, of course, itself a very specific "voice") or it can be expressed in a conspicuously dramatic voice. Neither type of expression has much to do with the internal logic or critical focus of an essay. When we attempt to assess thinking in writing, we need to analyze its representation carefully, ignoring the specific mode of expression, or "voice." This is more difficult than it sounds as we are often swayed in our assessment of reason by the rhetorical strategy with which it is communicated. Yet isn't this precisely what we aim for in the teaching of critical thinking—the ability to separate emotional appeal from compelling logic and evidence? Pedagogically we needn't abandon the cultivation of voice in writing as long as the writing is undergirded by critical thought. If a particular voice—or any aspect of style, for that matter—is appropriate for academic writing, and this varies according to discipline and even subdiscipline, then it, too, can be valued separately. We are not sure why this group assessment raised the issue of *voice* or why the rankings of the essay defining *jock* were so lacking in agreement, but we suspect it was both the blatant tone of that essay and the diverse composition of the assessing group. It occurs to us that high school teachers, including those who teach some dual enrollment courses, sometimes teach a broader range of genres, including fiction, poetry, and narrative genres in which *voice* is essential.

We are not alone in surmising that certain features like voice may override the evaluation of other features of writing. Chris Thaiss and Terry Myers Zawacki in their research on different discourses across the disciplines in four-year George Mason University faculty found to their surprise that after judging student samples as poor and good, "the 'poor' paper was judged by a plurality of cross-disciplinary participants to be the best in the sample—because they regarded it as having the 'freshest voice' and 'taking the most risk' [remarkably similar to the comments made during our symposium session] in its approach to the research—while they downgraded the 'excellent' [in Thaiss and Zawacki's view] paper as 'conventional, saying nothing new even though competently written" (1). This inconsistency is highlighted by the disagreement about the importance of logic and voice among some of our symposium participants. One participant used language similar to that of the Thaiss and Zawacki survey responses to describe what was lacking in the *creativity* definition, saying that although the paper is mechanically correct, the writer is "not taking chances" in the paper. This symposium participant continues, asking whether precision and correctness might not be inversely related to voice: "Does correctness go up when voice goes down?" Another participant pointed out that "the purpose of writing varies more in K–12 than it does in college," that Sample A represents an "emotional rant versus a logical definition," and that it thus "excels in one way but fails in another." Certainly purpose and genre vary more in K–12 English classes, where creative writing is sometimes an option in writing assignments (see the poems submitted as journal samples that Lujan presents as embodying his conception of voice), than they do in freshman composition and writing done in cross-disciplinary courses. In those courses the writing is always expository and often restricted to very specific genre requirements. And while we agree with the faculty at George Mason University in expressing the need for open-mindedness in college writing, and we assume open-minded thinking will be expressed in fairly neutral tones, the results of Thaiss and Zawacki's faculty survey also reflect a desire for more than conventional reportage or neutral analysis in college-level writing across disciplines.

Weights provide a method of controlling the values we place on a specific element of writing in any given assignment. Because our main objective was to provide a way to assess critical thinking in all student writing, including writing done in non-English disciplines, we intentionally did not assign weights to individual components of the CTWR. In fact, we wanted to sidestep the controversy of valuing any single aspect of writing and thinking more than another in our presentation, while offering the potential for individual instructors to do so. Were we to assign equal values to, say, *Style* and *Logic* in using the CTWR, *Logic* would outweigh voice as the latter is only one aspect of *Style* (diction and sentence construction being examples of other aspects of style). In this way, the reduction that rubrics impose upon the assessment of writing, which we acknowledge, makes clarity exceedingly important in the use of rubrics with students. If we determine that critical thinking is more important in freshman writing than, say, mechanics, we should weight those elements accordingly. An example of this sort of adaptation of the CTWR is the omission of the element *Style* by two members of our faculty who used the CTWR in biology and philosophy courses. Neither instructor felt that style was important for her discipline or for the specific assignment she was evaluating. For our purposes as English teachers, all of the writing elements—*Content, Style,* and *Correctness*—are important, as are the critical thinking elements, *Focus* and *Logic*.

Clearly, we should show students in our evaluation of their writing, rubric or otherwise, what elements we value and how much. For us, nuanced thinking is more valuable than voice, and that shows in the CTWR element descriptions, where we include thinking in both *Focus* and *Logic*. A few participants commented in a symposium survey that they would prefer removing the thinking from the first element, *Focus*, restricting its rating to organization; however, we prefer to keep *thoughtful manner* in that description because we value the thinking of the piece over some other elements that we do not include, like risk-taking and unconventional expression. If we do not distinguish between detailed content and complex thought, for example, or between interesting voice and interesting ideas, we may be encouraging students to short circuit their thinking in lieu of whatever qualities they observe to be prioritized in evaluation. The value we place on critical thinking in college writing is part of a larger cloth, we believe, in that most academic disciplines place a similar value on thinking, whether or not they make this priority clear to students.

This preference for nuanced, objective thinking appears to be borne out in the three attributes of good writing that Thaiss and Zawacki found George Mason faculty to value across the disciplines:

1. Clear evidence in writing that the writer(s) have been persistent, open minded, and disciplined in study.

2. The dominance of reason over emotion or sensual perception.

3. An imagined reader who is coolly rational, reading for information, and intending to formulate a reasoned response. (58–59)

College-level writing, it seems, values the well-reasoned point over its dramatic rendering. Perhaps reasoning, then, is a salient feature of college writing. Whether it is as important in high school writing is certainly worth examining in greater detail in the future.

In conclusion, the assessment of critical thinking takes time and often complicates the act of writing assessment. Sometimes the most highly detailed and interesting student writing is not the product of complicated thinking but rather of strong feeling. Yet voice is not a substitute for thinking, though it can certainly enhance the expression of thought. At the same time, when students try to think complexly, their writing sometimes reflects complication in awkward constructions, misused words, and tedious detail. The stage and purpose of the writing assignment have everything to do with the weight instructors assign different features of writing, and rubrics—when used—should certainly reflect the relative importance of these elements. In the end, Elbow's advocating a "both/and" approach to considering voice in writing is quite sound, as a clear, neutral voice can bring welcome clarity to complicated abstract ideas.

In a chapter of the second volume of *What Is "College-Level" Writing?* Ronald F. Lunsford, John Kiser, and Deborah Coxwell-Teague discuss whether high school students should be exempt from freshman composition when they pass the AP exam at a high level. Examining three essays in the article, the authors touch on the sorts of writing assignments high school students face in preparation for AP writing exams. They conclude that students should probably receive college credit for high AP scores, but that they should not be exempt from college writing courses because the high scores do not reflect the same coursework, perhaps because of the nature of the writing assignments. According to the authors, these different assignments raise "the issue of whether personal writing provides a sufficient indicator of mastery of the skills a first-year writing course should develop." Lunsford, Kiser, and Coxwell-Teague are "not convinced" that personal narrative does require the same skills that analysis and argument do (97). In a similar vein, we are not convinced that the "academic voice" we try to cultivate in writing at the college level is the same "voice" that personal narrative cultivates. And while we are well aware of the deadened voice that is sometimes imposed on student writing by the constraints of an assignment, we do not see academic voices as the "passive, dispassionate, and objective" language used by writers who are simply transferring information from one source to their own essay instead of discovering or inventing new truths as described by Gregory Shafer in "Living in the Post-Process Writing Center" (294). The goal of helping students to find their own "authentic" voices in personal narrative may well be appropriate at earlier stages of a student's writing development, yet that student's personal voice or expression is less important than the actual thinking reflected in college writing. Indeed, it may be that the open-mindedness required by critical thinking is expressed more naturally in the neutral tone of academic writing. This brings us back to the purpose of including *thoughtful* as a descriptor in the CTWR element *Focus*. Without open-minded thinking as a basis of approaching the writing task—the thinking that prompts the writer to consider alternative approaches and possible outcomes—the writer may not achieve the level of reasoning we expect in freshman writing. This thoughtful, fair-minded approach with its resulting careful reasoning, often expressed in a clear but neutral tone, may well be one of the distinguishing features of "college-level" thinking and writing.

Appendix A

Definition Essay

A. Requirements for Essay

- Outline/planning sheet

  In planning your paper, select a "real" audience; that is, write to a group of people such as readers of a publication, an assembly of people for a single purpose, etc. Then adjust your level of explanation and vocabulary accordingly. Also, plan your strategy of introduction, your way of both broaching the topic and engaging the interest of your audience. This planning sheet is required as the cover sheet to your essay.

- Peer review comments

  Turn in the peer review comments on your rough draft with the following: cover sheet, essay outline, at least 2 drafts.

- Final paper

Be sure to double space and use a 12-point font to complete the 500+ word essay.

B. Organization

There is no rigid paragraph-by-paragraph organization that you must follow for this definition essay. The following are two patterns that you could use, depending on your purpose and content:

Emphasis on **examples**:
  I. Introduction*
 II. Differentiate from other
     member(s) of the same class
III. Extended example
 IV. Extended example(s)
  V. Conclusion*

Emphasis on **differentiation**:
  I. Introduction*
 II. Differentiate from A
III. Differentiate from B
 IV. Extended example(s)
  V. Conclusion*

(*thesis statement)

Your thesis statement should provide a crisp definition of the term; you could lead with it in the introductory paragraph, or if you want the paper to develop it as it unfolds, you could include it in your conclusion.

Appendix B

"Jocks"

Jocks; the self revered cool kids of the school systems and society. The qualities of these shallow minded narcissistic people barely qualify them as human beings rather than the barbaric people they are. You may have been introduced to this classification of people in your high school by way of wedgies and noogies as opposed to the more civilized handshake. Naylor says "Words are innocuous; it is the consensus that gives them true power" (489). Well these people are the consensus; they are the bullies of society, the quarterback who knocks your books out of your hands in the hall, making you late for class while he stands there with his friends laughing and pointing as you pick up the scattered mess that represents their intelligence. Seeking to boost their self esteem by attacking people they view to be physically inferior. Their varying displays of approval and affection to one another borderline homoerotic and a self proclamation to being cool; with their chest bumps, touché slaps, and intricate high five celebrations.

Self declared to be the epitome of masculinity, jocks are driven by egos and their constant desire to be accepted by the likes of their own kind. All choices they make are based on the desire to maintain and proving their egos is gist. They are fueled by one desire; to obtain physical perfection, thus the mass consumption of protein shakes and bars, meat and energy drinks or anything that helps their testosterone levels function at an optimum are necessary. They travel in pack formation, usually consisting of members of the sports teams they are affiliated with. Jocks, meatheads, or roid ragers are some of the slang used to refer to these people. Their main form of communication is the bro format; "What's up bro, I got wickedly crunked at a party this weekend doing keg stands where afterwards I bench pressed the empty keg with three cheerleaders sitting on it."

Jocks attire consists of anything typically to glorify or draw attention to them. Whether it be sports jerseys, school letter jackets adorned with emblems and symbols signifying the accomplishments made in the sports participated in, to the under armor gear they wear to show off their physiques or any attire that shows their dedication to the life of being "EXTREME!"

The places where you can find these handicapped barbaric meatheads can be at the gym, performing rigorous activities to help get in physical in shape, or as you may have heard one say; "Bro, I'll be meet you at the gym, where we will get our swoll on." They can also be found at a gymnasium or fields where athletic competitions are held, or spotted at the school pep rally. They'll be the shirtless chest pounding maniacs with jersey number painted on bare skin yelling quotes from the movie 300 by Frank Miller, "This is SPARTA!"

Regardless of your affiliation in life; be it nerd, emo, red-neck, skater, yo-boy, you are viewed as an outsider to these people and have probably been ridiculed by jocks. If you are not one of their kind you will not be accepted and if you are nerdy especially; the jocks are to you as kryptonite is to Superman.

Appendix C

"Creativity"

Creativity is perhaps most commonly attributed to paintings or writing. After all, we have all been told at some point in our lives that we need to be creative, perhaps for an upcoming essay or an abstract painting in a past art class. Learning how to be creative is important, our creativity is what makes these projects shine, but one's creativity can be found in far more than just his or her writing or painting. Creativity is used in forming ideas, concepts, and even in invention and problem solving. It is not than just originality and the uniqueness of one's work or idea, but also the cleverness of its design.

Creativity is perhaps at its best when used in sharing an idea, concept, or work of art that provokes thought. There are several ways in which something may be thought provoking; one way is to offer someone another's prospective. Such an example would be an American journalist interviewing native Iraqis on their opinions and the Iraq war. Another way is to provide a moral dilemma, exposing the grey areas in our morality.

Although creativity is a skill normally seen as important to the entertainment industry and the media, it is also an important skill used by entrepreneurs and inventors. An ambitious entrepreneur must not only be unique but also must stand out among others providing the same product or service. It will be that entrepreneur's creativity in advertising as well as the product or service being provided that will lead to his or her ultimate success. Many inventors today are also entrepreneurs. Inventors rely on their creativity and ingenuity to create a product that not only has defined niche, but is also simple to use and useful to everyone.

"Thinking outside the box" is a term often used for when somebody uses their creativity and ingenuity to answer a tough question or provide a previously unknown point of view on a subject. Thinking outside the box doesn't necessarily require someone to critically analyze a given situation or examine it in detail; thinking outside the box is focusing on something that others overlook, for example, a frozen food company looking to save money on expenses may have a clever employee who realizes that removing the plastic barrier which separates the chicken from the mashed potatoes can save the company millions.

When art, ideas, inventions, or businesses are creative, they are not just unique, but also clever, witty, and intriguing. Every detail, no matter how large or small, has a purpose. But creativity cannot exist without one very important thing: creative people.

Works Cited

Anderson, Lorin W., and David R. Krathwohl. *A Taxonomy for Learning, Teaching, and Assessing.* New York: Addison Wesley, 2001. Print.

Anson, Chris. "Reflective Reading: Developing Thoughtful Ways to Respond to Students' Writing." *Key Works on Teacher Response: An Anthology.* Portsmouth: Heinemann, 2006. Print.

Broad, Bob. *What We Really Value: Beyond Rubrics in Teaching and Assessing Writing.* Logan: Utah State UP, 2003. Print.

CLAQWA Online: Building Your Thinking and Writing Skills. "CLAQWA Rubric and Resources: Cross-Disciplinary." Beta 5.0.0 2010. Web. 25 May 2012.

Condon, William, and Diane Kelly-Riley. "Assessing and Teaching What We Value: The Relationship between College-Level Writing and Critical Thinking Abilities." *Assessing Writing* 9 (2004): 56–75. Print.

Elbow, Peter. "Voice in Writing Again: Embracing Contraries." *College English* 70.2 (2007): 68–88. Print.

Facione, Peter. "Executive Summary: The Delphi Report." *Critical Thinking: A Statement of Expert Consensus for Purposes of Educational Assessment and Instruction.* Millbrae: California Academic, 1990. Print.

Facione, Peter, and Noreen Facione. "Holistic Critical Thinking Scoring Rubric." *Insight Assessment.* California Academic Press, 1994. Web. 24 Jun 2011.

Fanetti, Susan, Kathy M. Bushrow, and David L. DeWeese. "Closing the Gap between High School Writing Instruction and College Writing Expectations." *English Journal* 99.4 (2010): 77–83. *ERIC.* Web. 15 Sept. 2011.

Huot, Brian. "Toward a New Theory of Writing Assessment." *College Composition and Communication* 47.4 (1996): 549–66. Print.

Lujan, Alfredo Celedon. "The Salem Witch Trials: Voice(s)." Sullivan and Tinberg.

Lunsford, Ronald F., John Kiser, and Deborah Coxwell-Teague. "Advanced Placement (AP) English and College Composition: A Comparison of Writing at the High School and First-Year College Levels." Sullivan, Tinberg, and Blau.

Martins, David. "Scoring Rubrics and the Material Conditions of Our Relations with Students." *Teaching English in the Two-Year College* 36.2 (2008): 123–37. Print.

Shafer, Gregory. "Living in the Post-Process Writing Center." *Teaching English in the Two-Year College* 39.3 (2012): 293–305. Print.

Stroutholopoulos, Chris, and Janet L. Peterson. "From Rigidity to Freedom: An English Department's Journey in Rethinking How We Teach and Assess Writing." *Teaching English in the Two-Year College* 39.1 (2011): 43–62. Print.

Sullivan, Patrick. "What Is 'College-Level' Writing?" Sullivan and Tinberg.

Sullivan, Patrick, and Howard Tinberg, eds. *What Is "College-Level" Writing?* Vol. 1. Urbana: NCTE, 2006. Print.

Sullivan, Patrick, Howard Tinberg, and Sheridan Blau, eds. *What Is "College-Level" Writing?* Vol. 2: Assignments, Readings, and Student Writing Samples. Urbana: NCTE, 2010. Print.

Thaiss, Chris, and Terry Myers Zawacki. *Engaged Writers and Dynamic Disciplines: Research on the Academic Writing Life.* Portsmouth: Heinemann, 2006. Print.

Wilson, Maja. *Rethinking Rubrics in Writing Assessment.* Portsmouth: Heinemann, 2006. Print.

Integrating Reading and Writing

Learning to Read as Continuing Education

David A. Jolliffe

In this excerpt from David Jolliffe's wide-ranging and often humorous review essay about reading and composition studies, the author concludes that even though formal instruction in "reading" tends to drop out of the school curriculum at about grade 8, many students at two- and four-year colleges need instruction in reading, especially in the close, careful, critical reading of academic prose that is essential for success in college.

At every college and university where I have taught in the past twenty-five years—and this list includes four state universities, a private liberal arts college, and a large Catholic university—the talk about student reading is like the weather: Everybody complains about it, but nobody does anything about it.

We've all heard, and perhaps contributed to, local bellyaching about student reading: Substantial numbers of students come to class apparently without having read the assigned material; many of those who do attempt to complete the assigned reading seem incapable of grasping its meaning and complexities; students readily admit that they often

From *College Composition and Communication*, 2007, vol. 58, no. 3, pp. 470-79.

don't need to read the course material because the professor will "cover" it in lectures and let them know "what's going to be on the test." The official, data-driven discourse about student reading at the national level in both high school and college is equally discouraging. The most consistently cited barometer of student reading at the high school level, the National Assessment of Educational Progress (NAEP), regularly depicts a secondary school population deficient in the critical reading abilities necessary for college success. The 2005 NAEP report shows that the average score for eighth-grade readers dropped one point, from 263 to 262 on a 500-point scale, in the past two years. A reader performing at this national average level would be able, for example, to "recognize the significance of an article's central idea" but unable to "provide supporting details to explain [an] author's statement." NAEP has delayed the release of the 2005 scores for twelfth-grade reading (one wonders why), but the 2003 results had the average high school senior scoring 287 on the 500-point scale. That reader would, for example, be able to "apply text information to a hypothetical situation and explain" but be unable to "provide support for [a] judgment" ("Nation's Report Card"). While no comparable study examines reading achievement levels among college students, the National Survey of Student Engagement (NSSE) does provide a window into their attitudes toward reading. The most recent NSSE report (2005) reveals that "less than one-fifth of first-year students expect to spend more than 25 hours per week studying, the approximate amount of time faculty say is needed to do well in college" and "by their own admission, three of ten first-year students do just enough academic work to get by" (12).

The problems inscribed in these discourses, local and national, are particularly pertinent for the college composition class, the one course in nearly every first-year student's schedule where he or she should expect that careful, critical reading is vital for success. I suspect the days are past when students could write all their compositions solely on the basis of their own ideas, observations, and experiences, without referring to texts. In college composition, students rarely take examinations, so they can't depend on the professor to tell them what's on the test. They need to read the assigned books, articles, essays, and chapters (don't they?) because their compositions involve their interacting with these texts in some way (don't they?). If you wonder why I'm questioning my own argument in parentheses, it's this: As either the writing program administrator or a faculty member at all six of the institutions where I've taught, I've heard time and again the same complaints about student reading in composition courses—students often come to class without having read the material and are therefore incapable of "participating in a discussion" (whatever that phrase means); when they do complete the reading, many students cannot understand the assigned texts with a level of insight that goes beyond the transparent and superficial.

It's unfortunate that composition instructors and program administrators complain about student reading but don't do anything about it, because they could do something about it if they chose to. In this essay, I ruminate on what they could do toward building a challenging, serviceable, teachable model of reading for their courses. First, I examine a handful of stumbling blocks—conceptual, attitudinal, and pragmatic—that impede instructors' and students' giving critical reading its due in college composition courses. Then I assay a handful of relatively new books that suggest how the best college instructors—of composition and other fields—can think about themselves as teachers of reading in ways they can live with and that show how high school students could be taught to read in courses in all content areas. I hope to convince readers that college composition instruction can capitalize on (and improve) students' high school reading experiences if instructors and program administrators think carefully about where their students are starting as readers, where they want them to get by the end of the course, and how to help them get from *incipit* to *finis*.

"You Mean I Have to Teach Reading?" Issues Impeding a Productive Attitude

Let's face it: If we're going to do something about the aforementioned problems with student reading, we're going to have to teach students something about reading, but first we'll have to deal with a substantial handful of stumbling blocks that get in the way of our doing so. We should acknowledge the most stark and visceral of these roadblocks from the outset. The very thought that they ought to teach reading sticks in the craw of many college-level instructors. Shouldn't students in traditional, mainstream (not to mention honors or advanced) writing courses have mastered careful, critical reading by the time they get to college? The answer to this question, I'd guess, is yes, no, and maybe. Yes, high school students should have had more experience learning how to read texts, particularly nonfiction prose, carefully and critically in high school. But, no, it's not reasonable to expect they have "mastered" the process by the time they come to college, simply because the material they're now reading demands that they modify, ratchet up, and rethink the ways they read the material they're assigned. And maybe our assumptions about whether students should have mastered careful, critical reading actually occlude a consideration of other factors that affect student reading in college courses. At any rate, I'd argue that the "Do I really have to teach reading?" question represents dead-end thinking. You teach the students you have in front of you. You teach them what you think they ought to know no matter what you think they ought to have "mastered" before they got to you.

I'd also maintain that it's easier to get around the "Do I really have to teach reading?" roadblock if you consider carefully the aforementioned "other factors" that influence the position critical reading has in college curriculums and courses. With some of these factors, the problems derive from educational practice prior to college. With others, the fault lies not in the schools but in ourselves.

A quirky wrinkle in the traditional secondary school curriculum makes it difficult even for high school teachers to accept that they ought to teach reading, let alone college-level instructors. By the time students are graduating from high school, the course called "reading" has been absent from the curriculum for at least three or four years, having usually made its last appearance in the eighth grade, at the latest. By the time they come to college, then, students haven't had a course called "reading" for five or six years. Oh, to be sure, some of their high school teachers might have tucked something resembling reading instruction into courses or units labeled "critical thinking" or "study skills," and college students may have a class called "first-year seminar" or "first-year experience" that takes a stab at helping students cope with the reading demands of college. But by the time students come to college, it's been a long time since students have had any instructor say to them, "Okay, let's work on how to read this text."

Moreover, while the notion of taking a "reading class" has dropped off the radar screen for most first-year college students, the very thought of what a "reading class" might be at the post-secondary level has never quite coalesced. To put it starkly: reading as a concept is largely absent from the theory and practice of college composition. The program of the 2005 Conference on College Composition and Communication, for example, mentions the word *reading* only thirty times in the titles of papers given in the four-hundred-odd concurrent panels and special sessions. . . . Marguerite Helmers claims that "the act of reading is not part of the common professional discourse in composition studies" (4). In other words, no clear, salient theory of what reading is or does prevails in college composition, even though an anthology of readings sits at the center of many, if not most, college writing courses. Students have to read in college composition, but rarely does anyone tell them why or how they should read. As a result of this ill-defined perspective on reading, when college composition instructors (and administrators and textbook authors) actually do take up reading as a curricular or pedagogical focus, they often do so at diametrically opposite ends of a continuum of complexity.

At one end of this continuum, students and their instructors find oversimplified, mind-numbing, reductive curriculums and pedagogies. When students (particularly in two-year colleges but also at many four-year institutions) are placed in developmental, "remedial" reading courses, usually on the basis of their ACT or SAT verbal scores, they predominantly encounter instruction in what often gets labeled "study skills." In such courses, students supposedly learn how to explain word meanings through the use of contextual clues, morphological structure, and dictionaries; identify main and supporting ideas in brief texts; recognize an author's purpose and point of view; draw inferences; understand their own "learning style"; practice skimming and scanning; and so on.

Courses dominated by such instruction send a clear message about what reading is and does. Reading is a search-and-capture strategy, an exercise in which the author's meaning is a fixed entity that the students are somehow unable to "get." They are led to believe they lack the ability to crack the secret code that's in the text, and, as a result, they can't take advantage of the sole function of reading in college: to fill their minds with the information, data, and perspectives that they're expected to comprehend as this material is "covered" in their courses. There's precious little interactivity in this largely passive kind of reading instruction, almost nothing that urges students to bring their ideas, experiences, and resources to bear in reading the text, and virtually no motivation for them to do so. Comprehending the main idea is what "the man" says to do.

At the other end of the complexity continuum are writing courses that openly embrace a reading-enriched curriculum dominated by complicated and challenging analytic and interpretive strategies. A signal representative of such courses would be one based on David Bartholomae and Anthony Petrosky's groundbreaking book, *Ways of Reading*. Bartholomae and Petrosky also send a clear message about what they believe reading is and does. Reading is an active, constructive process that calls for the reader to juggle nimbly the following tasks: accepting a text's emergent meaning, resisting any pat formulation of the central idea, and assimilating the text's ideas in one's own view of the world. Reading in such a fashion, Bartholomae and Petrosky believe, assimilates students into the kinds of conversations that constitute the essence of postsecondary education.

Now in its seventh edition, *Ways of Reading* teaches students to engage in what Bartholomae and Petrosky call "strong reading," a complex, constructivist practice of building a mental framework for interpreting experience, but then continuously testing, resisting, and revising the framework as they read. A strong reading boldly proceeds in the face of any "doubts and hesitations" (8) a reader might experience. Indeed, a strong reading embraces uncertainties as generative. (Note the difference here from the traditional remedial pedagogy, which sees "doubts and hesitations" as missteps to be avoided en route to capturing the author's meaning.) A strong reading reads "with the grain" of an author's text — students are urged "[t]o read generously, to work inside someone else's system, to see your world in someone else's terms." But it also operates "against the grain" — students are encouraged "to turn back against" the author's project, "to ask questions" that "might come as a surprise," to "look for the limits of her vision, to provide alternate readings of her examples, to find examples that challenge her argument, to engage her, in other words, in dialogue" (11).

As admirable as their method and rigor might appear, however, courses that promote "strong reading" à la *Ways of Reading*, whether they actually use this textbook or not, ultimately cannot represent the reading experience, either ideal or real, of students in mainstream college composition courses for two reasons. The first has to do with a problem of ethos, with a mismatch between the character of instructors in such courses and the persona they expect students to assume. Bartholomae and Petrosky, for example, present themselves as experienced, embedded, connected readers for whom the pieces in *Ways of Reading* play a major role in their intellectual lives. Writing about Susan Griffin's "Our Secret" and John Edgar Wideman's "Our Time," Bartholomae and Petrosky offer the following:

> We carry these essays with us in our minds, mulling over them, working through them, hearing Griffin and Wideman in sentences we write or sentences we read; we introduce the essays in classes we teach whenever we can; we are surprised, reading them for the third or fourth time, to find things we didn't see before. (5)

Later, when Bartholomae and Petrosky explain the kinds of questions they raise when they read a challenging essay for the second time, they note that these questions seem "natural to us; they reflect our habitual way of reading and, we believe, the general habits of mind of the academic community" (12). To be sure, one of the goals of *Ways of Reading* seems to be to lead students to be the kinds of readers who reread essays as a matter of course, who "carry" texts with them and internalize what they read, who can connect what they read in essays for their composition course to pieces they read for other classes or texts they read as part of their burgeoning new lives as young adults. This idealization is a tough sell with our students, who take four or five courses at a time, schedule in bits of time during their busy weeks to get their reading done (maybe!), and consider themselves both fortunate and prepared if they have read the assigned work once before they come to class to "discuss" it or write about it. For our students, reading essays for composition class is not really reading—it's doing homework.

The second problem with assuming that a Bartholomaic/Petroskyite position might support reading instruction in college writing courses has to do with the position's limited perspective on what students in college actually do read. Bartholomae and Petrosky assume that the primary fodder for college students' reading consists of challenging essays that actually invite a strong second (or third or fourth) reading. With such pieces, they write, "[t]he meaning . . . is determined by what you do with the essay, by the connections you can make and your explanation of why those connections are important" (8). What such an assumption fails to take into consideration, I maintain, is that very little (for a great many college students, almost none) of the first-year or general education experience actually offers students reading experiences that invite them to make these connections. A typical first-year college student is taking, say, introductory psychology, first-year writing, a calculus course, a science course with a lab requirement, and perhaps something like World Civilization, introduction to art history, or a foreign language. Filling up his or her plate evenly from this scholarly bounty, our student reads textbooks, does problems and labs, takes tests, and writes papers occasionally. He or she might encounter discursive essays that warrant a strong reading only in first-year writing. But first-year writing is just one course of four or five that our students take. What can students learn about the nature of reading in college — its definition and its purposes — if three-quarters or four-fifths of their academic lives are dominated by texts that do not openly invite a strong reading?

Between these two extremes on the complexity continuum — between "read-to-get-the-gist" instruction and "read-to-complicate" instruction — one finds a great, gray middle. In most college composition courses, reading plays some role — students read, analyze, discuss, and write about texts — but no one is very clear about what reading is or does in such courses. Three functions of reading seem to occur in this middle space, but none seems actually to dominate. First, instructors assign texts that are supposed to stimulate the students' own thinking and writing on an issue. I call this the "bounce off" function. Consider, for example, an assignment that would ask students to read King's "Letter from Birmingham Jail" and then write about a situation in their own lives that would lead them to participate in civil disobedience. They could write about the situation without reading King's text, but the latter provides them a springboard into their own composition, which might not take off without the impetus the primary text provides. My friend David Lindstrom at Colorado State University refers to the most tepid student responses that emanate from such assignments as "floating descants." They seem to sing a melody above the tune provided by the primary text and only rarely, if at all, drop down to interact with the actual text itself. Second, instructors ask students to read texts and then use their organizational patterns in an original composition. This is the "reading-to-imitate-development" approach. Consider the well-known assignment of the comparison/contrast essay: Students are asked to read Bruce Catton's "Grant and Lee," a frequently anthologized essay demonstrating the point-by-point method of organizing comparison/contrast (in contrast to the block-by-block method) and then write their own composition, comparing and/or contrasting two entities (for example, high school education and college education, network TV and cable TV, college sports and professional sports, and so on) using the model provided by Catton's text. Third, some assignments call upon students to capture the gist of a primary text (or more than one) and then to use that gist as evidence in support of a position the student has taken. I call this the "digest-to-incorporate" method. Say, for example, a student is writing an argumentative essay on some aspect of capital punishment. He or she might read a handful of position statements on the issue and then write a composition that agrees with those that favor his or her stance and find flaws with the ones that do not.

Each of these approaches to incorporating reading in writing instruction adheres, at least tacitly, to the capture-the-authorial-message stance embodied in traditional remedial reading courses, and each is problematic, primarily because those who promulgate them rarely consider carefully what reading is or does in each approach. At each of the six colleges and universities where I've worked, I have found instructors who designate "discussing" a set of readings as an appropriate instructional task for one or more days on the course syllabus. "What exactly does that mean?" I would ask myself (and frequently these instructors, if they worked in the composition program I directed): What does it mean to "discuss" a text in composition class? What exactly is the relationship between the reading you're asking students to do, the "discussions" they have about the readings during class time, and the texts the students themselves are expected to compose?

Some of these instructors might have said to me, "Oh, I'd like my students to read King's letter so that they will think more fully about the potential for civil disobedience in their own life and society." Some of these instructors might have admitted to me, "I'd really like my students to write a comparison/contrast essay that resembles Catton's as completely as possible," but not many; I'm pretty sure that the purely modal approach to writing instruction that this assignment represents is on the wane. I can't imagine an instructor saying to me, "Well, I hope they read several essays, chapters, and books to find support or refutation for their thesis." But I would hope that most of these instructors (and many of them fulfilled my hope) would say to me something like this: "I want my students to read so that they will understand how readers and texts work together to create meaning, accomplish purpose, and achieve effect in many different intellectual communities. I want my students to read so that they will see how the form of a text—its organization, structure, diction, syntax, imagery, and figurative language—is completely consonant with its function, with its invitation for readers to create meaning, accomplish purpose, and achieve effect. I want my students to read so that they will understand how their own texts must constitute an invitation for this meaning/purpose/effect creation to take place within the intellectual community with which they want their text to 'do business.'"

The problem for these instructors would be that most mainstream composition curriculums and pedagogical strategies aren't designed to help students achieve these goals. And, because the topic of reading lies outside the critical discourse of composition studies, these instructors would not have access to ample resources to help them think about a model of active constructive reading in their courses or about strategies for putting that model into play.

So what can instructors and writing program administrators do? Four things. First, we need to acknowledge the materiality of reading in college courses and in arenas beyond college. If one of the goals of college composition is to teach students how to read constructively and actively in all corners of their lives, then a model for reading instruction in college writing courses needs to accommodate the fact that college students read lots of textbooks, and productive, working adults read lots of reports, manuals, memoranda, and so on — all texts that do not readily call forth a strong reading. I would never want to suggest that students in college composition not be exposed to challenging, complex essays that call upon them to read "with the grain" and "against the grain." I hope that the textbook market continues to generate wonderful books like *Ways of Reading*. But I would suggest that we need to teach our students to be constructive, connective, active readers of *all* the material that comes their way — textbooks, reports, memoranda, and so on, as well as complicated, discursive essays. Second, we need to develop a model of what reading ideally is and does in our programs and classrooms. We need to start with our outcomes and teach backward from them. Assuming we have a sequential curriculum that culminates with the most difficult and challenging piece of work students do in the course, we should take a close look at the final assignment and ask ourselves, "What exactly is the ideal relationship between reading and writing in this assignment? If the best student does this assignment exactly as it's meant to be done, what will reading be and do in the assignment? What must the best student do with his or her reading to complete the assignment effectively and successfully?" The Council of Writing Program Administrators has provided an initial step toward achieving this goal by developing its "Outcomes Statement for First-Year Composition." Most of that document, sensibly, deals with student knowledge and behavioral outcomes for writing, but the relatively brief section on "Critical Reading, Thinking, and Writing" offers two outcomes that college composition administrators and instructors should unpack further: "By the end of first year composition, students should use reading and writing for inquiry, learning, thinking, and communicating," and "Faculty in all programs and departments can build on this preparation by helping students learn the interactions among critical thinking, critical reading, and writing" (60). What precisely might it mean, we should ask ourselves (and teach to our students) to "use reading for inquiry, learning, and thinking?" How, exactly, should we teach students what "critical reading" is, and then teach them about "the interactions among critical thinking, critical reading, and writing?" Third, equipped with our statements of outcomes for reading, we should ascertain where our students are as critical, constructive, active readers at the beginning of our courses and programs. Every composition program I've ever been affiliated with has required instructors to begin every course with a "diagnostic" assignment, designed to determine a student's strengths and weaknesses as a writer. Should we not do the same with reading? What, I wonder, would an appropriate, valid reading diagnostic for a college writing course look like? Finally, we need to think carefully about what it will take to get students from their starting points to the outcomes: What do students need to know about what reading is and does in our program and our courses? What techniques and strategies for effective reading in college and beyond do we need to explain, model, demonstrate, and evaluate their practice of? How do we move our students from start to finish?

Fortunately, there are some very smart people thinking and writing about these issues on both sides of the high school–college divide. Their work could help us determine what appropriate reading outcomes for a college writing course might be and show us how students in the best high schools are being taught to read—and, by implication, whether students are coming to college ill-equipped to deal with the reading demands a first-year program and a general education curriculum place on them. With the perspectives these books provide, we can think more consciously as a profession about meeting our incoming students as readers and moving them toward our outcomes.

Works Cited

Bartholomae, David, and Anthony Petrosky. *Ways of Reading*. 7th ed. Boston: Bedford/St. Martin's, 2005.

Catton, Bruce. *Grant Takes Command*. Boston: Little, Brown, 1968.

Helmers, Marguerite, ed. *Intertexts: Reading Pedagogy in College Writing Classrooms*. Mahwah, NJ: Lawrence Erlbaum Associates, 2003.

King, Martin Luther, Jr. "Letter from Birmingham Jail." 31 Jan. 2006 http://www.nobelprizes.com/nobel/peace/MLK-jail.html.

National Survey of Student Engagement, Annual Report 2005. 31 Jan. 2006 http://nsse.iub.edu/pdf/NSSE2005_annual_report_pdf.

The Nation's Report Card. 31 Jan. 2006 http://nces.ed.gov/nationsreportcard.

"WPA Outcomes Statement for First-Year Composition." *WPA: Writing Program Administration* 23 (1999): 59–66.

A Framework for Rereading in First-Year Composition

Dan Keller

In reference to this selection, author Dan Keller notes that "my reason for writing the essay was to fill a much-needed gap in composition scholarship on the teaching of reading. Although textbooks offer reading strategies and assignments, I believe that teachers need stronger frameworks for connecting the acts of reading and writing. In this essay, I offer a framework that focuses on rereading activities. I argue that teachers should reduce the number of assigned readings in a course to make curricular space for practicing three kinds of rereading: metacognitive, intertextual, and imitative. By rereading the same essays in these different ways, students learn how to approach a text with strategies that encourage them to be more thoughtful and engaged readers and writers."

In her 2010 essay "How Do We See What We See?" Jennifer Rich reflects on why students failed to achieve a particular kind of critical reading with an advertising assignment. Although the students analyzed some aspects of the assigned texts, they did not produce the analysis specified by the assignment. Students could not see the texts—could not read them—in the same way the teacher could. Instead of focusing on the students' failure, Rich turns toward pedagogical blind spots, the unexamined assumptions teachers possess about themselves, their students, and the critical activities of the classroom. Rich's reflection leads to important questions about pedagogical blind spots that get to the heart of what makes teaching so difficult:

> What are the critical skills that are invisible to me—because of my training, because of my experience, because of (fill in the blank)—that I take for granted in the students? Am I not, in some way, failing to read myself and my teaching as rhetorical events—constituted by specific contexts, with a specific audience and purpose in mind? And if I fail to do so, am I not in some sense dooming my students to failure by placing these expectations—my own reading of the act of reading—under erasure, hindering the students in their own quests for meaning making? (182)

Rich's questions are worth quoting at length because they express clearly the concerns and frustrations that many composition teachers must feel. The questions also offer a direction for exploring the tensions between our expectations of students' critical reading skills and the

From *Teaching English in the Two-Year College*, 2013, vol. 41, no. 1, pp. 44-55.

effectiveness of our scaffolding of those skills. I agree with Rich that we need to "decode ourselves" (182), to more closely examine our practices and expectations and how those might be articulated more clearly to students.

An area of composition pedagogy that needs further examination is reading (Jolliffe; Salvatori and Donahue). When discussing readings for the first time with a class, I tend to hear two kinds of responses from students: the gist and the personal response. When students respond to the "gist" of the reading, they reduce the reading to a generalization, or they take one particular moment as representative of the entire reading. The personal response tends to involve how the students feel about the reading—whether they like it or not, whether they agree or disagree, or what it reminds them of from their own experience. It is rare when students point to specific ideas in a text, consider its audience and context, examine ideas from different perspectives, or reflect on how they processed it as an unfolding event. Much like Rich, I do not want to blame students for their initial responses or see them as signs of reading failure. After all, it is likely that these kinds of responses have been effective in other situations. Indeed, many students have told me that the "gist strategy" works well for quizzes and tests, and the personal response works well when teachers want to get students involved. However, if reading is not being enacted in ways expected or hoped for in college classrooms, then it is vital that writing teachers examine how reading pedagogy is positioned in first-year composition.

Composition teachers are also reading teachers, but it is probably safe to say that we are more comfortable teaching writing. We have more theoretical and practical resources to turn to as we assign, respond to, and discuss writing. Reading is obviously connected to writing, but composition has not given it as much attention. Linda Adler-Kassner and Heidi Estrem note a lack of reading pedagogy resources for training graduate teachers and conducting program development: "at the same time as instructors ask for more explicit guidance with reading pedagogy, that pedagogy is rarely included in composition research, graduate composition courses, or first-year writing program development materials" (36). Certainly, we have textbooks with strategies and assignments, but reading pedagogy should involve more than a collection of strategies and assignments. Given this lack of depth in our reading pedagogy, how can writing teachers "decode" expected reading practices for students? What I want to offer in this essay is a framework for integrating reading into first-year composition in a way that promotes clearer articulations of reading practices. First, I argue for assigning fewer readings so that teachers and students can engage in rereading, returning to texts to emphasize different purposes and strategies that also give students a more sustained experience with individual texts. Making this space for rereading provides opportunities to articulate, model, and practice the reading we expect in composition.

Then, I detail how rereading can promote three types of reading: meta-cognitive, intertextual, and imitative.

Making Curricular Space for Rereading

If we want to help students grow as attentive, critical readers, then we should examine how reading fits into composition's curricular space, which means asking questions about how many texts we assign as readings. Consider a brief illustration of how students experience writing in a composition classroom. Instead of writing numerous essays that they never see again, students write fewer essays that they revise—literally, re-see—multiple times. We structure curricular space to make room for students to compose drafts, receive feedback, and revise in response to that feedback and their own re-seeing of their writing. This structure that brings feedback and revision to the forefront of multiple class activities reinforces the message that academic writing can bene-fit from practice, feedback, and revision. Compare this to the likely sce-nario with assigned readings, which includes numerous texts that are rarely—if ever—seen again; interpretations of those texts that receive little feedback; and the absence of revised interpretations. What kind of message about reading is reinforced with this model? Teachers want students to read critically and to revisit readings, but how can we ex-pect such activities if our courses are structured to move on to more and more texts? In my first-year composition course, I typically assign nonfiction readings; these texts demand sophisticated rhetorical read-ing of tone, audience, argument, and context. On some days, discussion stalls as we spend time addressing a misunderstanding of content or context; even at the end of a productive discussion, it can seem as if we barely touched upon certain aspects of the text. Such days led to ques-tions about how reading has been structured in the class: What if stu-dents were assigned fewer texts, asked to return to those texts, and given different reading approaches to apply to those same texts? Could rereading give students more practice with and insight regarding the values and forms of academic reading?

One of the obstacles to engaging students in rereading is curricular overload. Thomas Newkirk has argued against "educational clutter—the piling on of objectives and requirements—that makes any form of sustained work difficult" (11). Instead, teachers should create space where "there is time to explore, there is the tolerance of silences, there is the deliberate buildup to an activity, there is the feeling of mental space to work in" (11). When I consider Newkirk's description of the "deliber-ate buildup" and the "feeling of mental space," I reflect on how the first-year composition class is crowded with objectives and assignments, with each jostling for attention and curricular space. Time for explora-tion and effective scaffolding often gets compressed—and sometimes crushed. Every course syllabus is a negotiation of curricular necessities with available space; every course ends with a look back at how many objectives and requirements did not receive sustained attention. A cluttered course can prevent the kind of scaffolding teachers need to build to help students understand and practice expected ways of reading and writing.

Other obstacles to engaging students in rereading include textbook size and teachers' beliefs about reading. As textbooks pack in more readings and increase in cost, teachers may feel compelled to assign more readings to justify the expense paid by students. There is also the viewpoint that students will read and write better if they read more; that is, exposing students to a larger page count of readings will improve their confidence and familiarity with reading. Although I understand the logic behind such a view, I question the expected outcome. Assigning more readings probably leads to scaffolding each of them less. We assign fewer pieces of writing because we want students to work through and experience how a piece of writing can develop. This pedagogy should be mirrored in how we teach reading, providing the curricular space to slow down, focus, and achieve a sense of expertise with a few texts. In the three sections that follow, I give detail to how rereading can promote metacognitive, intertextual, and imitative reading. I focus on these three forms of reading for two reasons. First, metacognitive reading is vital in how it prepares students for reflective, controlled reading. Second, the two other forms of reading make explicit connections to writing, which must be a central concern as we consider how to merge reading and writing assignments in a course that has writing as its primary responsibility.

Metacognitive Reading

Writing pedagogy stresses metacognition, the reflection on and awareness of the thinking process. Teachers engage students in metacognitive writing strategies to help them gain more insight into how they write and revise. Students are asked to write about their writing in a variety of ways: composing an early reflection on how they plan to write an essay, a middle-stage reflection on what they've written so far, and a cover letter that describes strengths, weaknesses, and revision possibilities on an essay about to be submitted. Having students write a lot is not enough; the hope is that becoming aware of how one thinks through writing will lead to more control over writing practices in the future. Although these reflections are sometimes not as deep as we would like, they contribute to our goal of students' becoming more self-aware, self-sufficient writers. To achieve this goal, teachers not only provide time for such reflective activities, but we also talk to students about how to think about writing; through these discussions about writing, we offer a language for conceptualizing writing and provide opportunities to understand the values embedded in academic writing. These pedagogical moves that involve concepts and values are important because they reveal to students at least some sense of what matters and what is expected of them when it comes to writing. These moves make academic writing a little less mysterious to students. When we teach writing in these ways, we attempt the kind of "decoding" activity that Rich calls for in her essay (182). How might we pursue metacognitive reading strategies that make academic reading a little less mysterious?

Modeling a reading experience can give students a language for thinking about reading and a sense of what we value when reading in college. Jeff Sommers has written about the benefits of performing his reading process in front of students. He felt the need to demonstrate his reading process after recognizing the passive ways in which students were reading assigned texts; he also wanted to improve their confidence. Based on students' written responses to how they were reading, Sommers reached the conclusion that students "felt guilt about their reading skills" (302). For the read-aloud, he selected a text with which he was unfamiliar, and he gave an unstudied demonstration of his surprises, confusions, and observations. Sommers not only demonstrated the close attention to the text that he expected from the students, but he also eased the students' doubts about their own reading skills by showing how an expert reader struggled with an unfamiliar text (304). I regularly perform the kind of modeling described by Sommers, and students seem to benefit from the demonstration. However, the demonstration can also be misleading; after all, even with an unfamiliar text, I would apply knowledge of the genre and the historical context to ask questions and interact with the text in ways beyond most students' capabilities. In more recent read-alouds, I add two specific questions that I ask at least once on every page: What is my understanding of this part of the text? What are important ideas in the context of this class? I provide and model these questions because they are generic enough to encourage metacognitive reading for any text. The two questions invite readers to think about how they are making sense of the text. For example, in a popular culture–themed course, I ask students to practice the questions on the following passage from Dustin Kidd's essay "Harry Potter and the Functions of Popular Culture," a dense passage that students tend to rush past without reflection:

> The exact norms that any particular culture consumer will internalize will depend on the consumer's social location and social roles, which is why popular culture is an important dynamic in the creation and maintenance of social boundaries. The clothing we wear, the music we listen to, and the television we watch not only constitute our identities but also help to separate our identity categories from others'. (76)

Kidd's first sentence is the kind that students admit to "sleepwalking" through as they read: they move their eyes over it, produce little meaning from it, and do not recall reading it by the end of the page. I use that sentence to help students practice the question "What is my understanding of this part of the text?" When students struggle with making sense of the sentence, I suggest that they break the sentence into two or more parts and to paraphrase each part. Students linger on the phrase "depend on the consumer's social location and social roles," and they often construct a meaning that leads to concrete examples, such as how a person's gender or age can become attached to some norms instead of others. If they struggle with "the creation and maintenance of social boundaries," I point out that reading the next sentence may make it clearer, which it does; they gather that "social boundaries" involve how we see ourselves as belonging to some groups and not to other groups. Practicing this question, then, can offer two strategies that advanced readers draw upon to resolve a lack of comprehension: paraphrasing and reading for context clues.

The second question—"What are important ideas in the context of this class?"—can help students focus on the ideas that are central to the class, moving beyond like/dislike reactions and "I couldn't relate to it" responses. Although it may seem like an obvious question, students tell me that it is a useful reminder that they should regard each text as a part of the larger, ongoing conversation of the course. The question also promotes making connections among readings, which is integral to intertextual reading, the focus of the next section. In the context of my course's pop culture theme, students respond to this question by situating the Kidd passage within the concerns we've addressed by that point in the course. They talk about how this passage reinforces the idea that what people value in pop culture—the music they like, the film and TV characters with whom they identify—goes beyond mere personal preference and involves how people see themselves in relation to others. Both of these questions provide opportunities to keep students focused on the text and to think about how they are building meaning from it.

Having some experience with these metacognitive strategies, students can then be asked to return to a reading, focusing on aspects that did not seem important the first time or attempting to figure out parts that did not make sense. This metacognitive reading task challenges students to be more aware of how they are reading as they make sense of what previously eluded them. What is the problem they encounter when reading this part of the text? How can they resolve that problem? How do they perceive the text as a whole after rereading this difficult part of the text? This task reinforces the idea that first readings are especially prone to partial, rushed responses; it suggests the value of wrestling with and resolving challenging elements of texts. An alternative activity asks students to reread a text, focusing on specific parts—introduction, conclusion, a significant example or argument—and thinking about how these parts can be connected to the larger purpose of the text. Not only does this activity ask students to reflect on how they read, but it also gives them practice with reading to connect parts to the whole. Metacognitive reading can help students see reading as an active process that involves making decisions about how to approach and interpret a text. Engaging students in these practices can provide a foundation for the forms of reading that I discuss next: intertextual and imitative reading.

Intertextual Reading

My view of intertextual reading is that it is the intentional act of reading one text in juxtaposition to another; it involves the building of meaning through an interactive consideration of texts.[1] The ability to read texts in light of other texts is a vital part of effective writing, particularly in research assignments that expect students to make connections among sources and create the sense of a conversation. In their research on how students write from sources, Rebecca Moore Howard, Tricia Serviss, and Tanya K. Rodrigue observe that students' engagement with sources seems to be minimal; they drew this conclusion based on how students typically quoted individual sentences from sources and did not present summaries of those sources. These results lead Howard, Serviss, and Rodrigue to "ask not only whether the writers understood the source itself but also whether they even read it" (186). As they note, their "preliminary inquiry suggests that we have much more to learn" about how students read and use sources (189). I imagine the results of their study are familiar to most writing teachers; research papers are already difficult, time-consuming assignments due to the teaching of research databases, citation systems, and the options and rules for paraphrasing, summarizing, and quoting material. Teaching how to read for research purposes is another layer of difficulty. Ideally, students put sources into a conversation when they write a research paper, integrating and interacting with the ideas and words of other writers to create a particular perspective on a topic. However, the result is often the superficial engagement described by the study above; instead of being part of an integrated, interactive conversation, the sources that students incorporate are often separated from each other, briefly engaged with as the student moves from one source to the next. The rushed, cluttered curriculum—and how reading pedagogy fits into it—may contribute to students' superficial engagement with sources.

Rereading may improve students' attempts to make more sophisticated intertextual connections, which can then lead to deeper engagement with writing from sources. For instance, in my thematic first-year composition course, "Literacy and Technology," students read only five nonfiction pieces, which allows curricular space for returning to those readings in various iterations: one or two readings earn a complete rereading, some get revisited in pieces as we practice a different strategy or make connections between texts, and all are briefly returned to in a class discussion that prepares students for the research paper. For their seven-page research assignment, students incorporate at least two sources from class and two from research they conduct through library databases and popular search engines. As a result of this limited scope of readings, students are urged to go beyond superficial engagement with each reading; it is difficult to move from source to source quickly when fewer are available.

The thematic readings provide one level of connection, and rereading them provides an opportunity to slow down and focus on particular moments that might be connected to conversations with other texts. For instance, students recognize that Nicholas G. Carr's "Is Google Making Us Stupid?" and Steven Johnson's "Dawn of the Digital Natives" both address concerns about the effects of digital reading; Carr's view is negative, and Johnson's is defensive. Beyond such general connections, though, students have difficulty putting the two into conversation without reading and writing exercises that work toward such integration. As students reread each piece, I ask them to locate what they think are significant ideas offered by the authors; even if the students cannot articulate a direct connection, they should be alert to instances in which the writers are discussing similar objects, events, or ideas. From Carr's article, students often select this excerpt:

> When the Net absorbs a medium, that medium is re-created in the Net's image. It injects the medium's content with hyperlinks, blinking ads, and other digital gewgaws, and it surrounds the content with the content of all the other media it has absorbed. A new e-mail message, for instance, may announce its arrival as we're glancing over the latest headlines at a newspaper's site. The result is to scatter our attention and diffuse our concentration.

As we examine this excerpt, I ask students to write about it in three ways: first, connect it to the larger point Carr makes in the essay, which urges students to make connections between part and whole; second, write a paragraph in which they build on Carr's ideas, supporting his statement with examples and ideas of their own; third, write a paragraph in which they challenge Carr's ideas, raising skeptical questions and considering alternative explanations. This responsive writing engages students in critical thinking about the writer's claims. It also encourages them to see source material as something to work with and respond to instead of as inert material to quote as information. Students tend to move beyond agree/disagree in these writings, offering their own complaints and problems with online distraction as they support Carr's ideas; they also challenge Carr's negative view of scattered attention, considering how online reading can lead to beneficial comparisons of sources through tabbed browsing and the instant availability of information. The students end up articulating specific advantages and disadvantages of online reading.

Having established their own conversation with Carr, they see a slight connection with this part of Johnson's article in which he responds to criticisms of digital reading: "Odds are that you are reading these words on a computer monitor. Are you not exercising the same cognitive muscles because these words are made out of pixels and not little splotches of ink?" Writing to support and challenge this statement by Johnson comes easily after having expressed general agreement with Carr's criticism of online reading distraction. They ask skeptical questions about Johnson's suggestion that people use "the same cognitive muscles" when reading a page and reading a screen; they wonder whether people have to think differently when reading through different media. As they support Johnson's statement, they move toward the idea that it might be a good thing to exercise different "cognitive muscles," that each form of reading—print and digital—may offer advantages and disadvantages, opportunities and challenges. By the end of this exercise, students have written material that responds to and connects the ideas of each author. They also have a model for approaching intertextual reading and making explicit connections in their writing.

Imitative Reading

I imagine many writing teachers engage students in some form of imitation, the use of models that students study and draw from to experiment with the shapes that exist for writing. However, in recent decades, composition's relationship to imitation has become uncertain. Frank M. Farmer and Phillip K. Arrington note that imitation has a long history in rhetoric and had been a popular activity in composition classrooms; however, by the 1990s, it became a less common topic in scholarship, which they regard as composition's "largely *tacit* rejection of imitation" (12). The rejection could be traced to a conflict with the practices of the process movement. To imitate would mean to focus on someone else's product, not the process of creating one's own piece of writing. Indeed, writing in the early 1970s, Edward P. J. Corbett argues for the use of imitation but observes that the "present mood of education theorists is against such structured, fettered training. The emphasis now is on creativity, self-expression, individuality" (249). Additionally, some of the resistance to imitation probably involved how such reading positioned the student writers in relation to the expert writers they were studying. After all, imitative reading demands close attention to the choices made by the writer: What did the writer intend? How did the writer construct that sentence? Reading in ways that focused on another writer might have seemed counterproductive to inspiring creative, self-expressive writing.

If resistance to imitation remains, I think it has more to do with the idea of "structured, fettered training" to which Corbett referred and less to do with self-expression. As a writing teacher, I am constantly trying to balance direct instruction with the ideal goals of process writing, providing activities and assignments that help students learn about and through writing without giving them step-by-step instructions or exact models. A problem of supplying students with models is that they might be followed too closely; the alternative of offering no models risks leaving some students without much support. Mixing directive and nondirective instruction means being vigilant to when teaching that acknowledges the complexity of writing might slip into teaching that further shrouds writing in mystery. In my experience of teaching on an open-enrollment campus, I find that students less familiar with academic reading and writing benefit from practice with imitative reading and writing. One of the expectations of academic reading and writing is to pay close attention to language: as readers, students are expected to examine the discursive choices made by writers; as writers, students are expected to think carefully about the discursive choices they make. Imitative reading can support students in fulfilling these expectations.

As a form of rereading, imitative reading promotes metacognitive, playful reading by moving students away from informational reading and asking them to consider possibilities: What might be some reasons for these writerly choices? What are some of the possible effects of such choices? This playful form of reading helps students study and appreciate another writer's skill, but not in an unattainable and intimidating way. Reading for imitation can reduce the mystery of writing, holding prose under a light and dissecting it to understand the parts that make it a whole. Students often tell me that it gives them more control over how they read by not letting the words happen to them; as they consider the choices made by the writer, they also see that the writer could have made different choices—an important realization for their own development as writers.

When rereading, students can be asked to focus on particular segments of text and read them in specific ways. To prepare students for imitative reading, I provide questions and a language for conceptualizing levels of attention for studying models. I supply the following questions: Why did the writer choose that word? Why that specific example or detail? How does the sentence length affect us? What are some possible effects? I then describe attention as consisting of three levels of focus: fragment, which involves a microscopic attention to a word or a phrase; link, which involves a "zooming out" to related, connected details such as words and sentences; and whole, which involves how the smaller fragments and links contribute to an overall effect. After supplying this frame for reading, we return to a piece we have already read so that we can focus on language choices. As an example, here is the introduction from *Time* magazine's "Getting Real about the High Price of Cheap Food" by Bryan Walsh:

> Somewhere in Iowa, a pig is being raised in a confined pen, packed in so tightly with other swine that their curly tails have been chopped off so they won't bite one another. To prevent him from getting sick in such close quarters, he is dosed with antibiotics. The waste produced by the pig and his thousands of pen mates on the factory farm where they live goes into manure lagoons that blanket neighboring communities with air pollution and a stomach-churning stench. He's fed on American corn that was grown with the help of government subsidies and millions of tons of chemical fertilizer. . . . And when the rains come, the excess fertilizer that coaxed so much corn from the ground will be washed into the Mississippi River and down into the Gulf of Mexico, where it will help kill fish for miles and miles around. That's the state of your bacon—circa 2009.

Turning to the questions I have provided, students pick up on specific phrases like "curly tails," "manure lagoons," "American corn," and "stomach-churning stench," explaining how they might influence readers; for instance, "curly tails" creates a cute, sympathetic image of the pigs, and "American corn" suggests a sense of national responsibility. As students point out specific parts of the text, I continuously remind them of the question "What are some possible effects?" to push them from observation to interpretation. After paying attention to how individual sentences function alone and together, they get the sense of how the paragraph moves them from a confined pen to the Gulf of Mexico, seeing how Walsh's writing spirals out in a chain of cause and effect, of local choices to global effects. They note how the blunt, final sentence is achieved by both its brevity and its placement after a long sentence. I then ask students to imitate the model's chain-of-events structure in an introduction on any topic; after this, I supply students with other introductory models to examine on their own.

Composition teachers also have the rich resource of rhetorical figures to draw upon for imitation. Imitating rhetorical figures can further remind students that they are writing for the ear and the eye. In this example, Sarah Vowell uses anaphora—phrase repetition at the beginnings of clauses—as she describes how she will one day fulfill her father's request to have his ashes shot out of a nineteenth-century replica cannon that he built:

> I will have my father's body burned into ashes. I will pack these ashes into paper bags. I will go to the mountains with my mother, my sister, and the cannon. I will plunge his remains into the barrel and point it into a hill so that he doesn't take anyone with him. I will light the fuse. But I will not cover my ears. Because when I blow what used to be my dad into the earth, I want it to hurt. (24)

Using the imitative reading questions, students pick up on the pattern of "I will," and we discuss how it functions to emphasize the drama of the situation. They also note the subversion of the pattern with "But I will not" and how it calls attention to the touching conclusion. After the class has examined this example of anaphora, I ask students to write their own series of sentences using the example's structure. We then discuss how anaphora might be used in their own essays, and students often suggest that anaphora might be too "flashy" for the body of an essay but appropriate for an introduction or conclusion.[2] Following imitative reading with immediate practice in imitative writing sends a strong signal about the connectedness of reading and writing. With repeated practice, this combination of reading and writing—I hope—can become a set of tools for students to use in future writing situations.

Conclusion

Although I think there are clear benefits to reducing the number of readings to create curricular space for guided rereading, I want to reflect on a persistent problem and how it resonates with composition as an anomalous experience for students. Even when a rereading is structured with a clear purpose that pushes students to read it differently, some students are frustrated and bored by the very notion of returning to a reading. These reactions remind me of the praise students give my nonwriting courses for "doing something new every day." They remind me that many of their first-year courses are nothing like first-year composition. Many other courses are structured with lectures, note taking, and tests; if students write an essay for a class, they write it once and receive a final grade (or have an option—not a requirement—to revise). Much of their first-year experience involves forward motion, moving on to the next lecture, the next chapter, the next test. The recursive learning situation of first-year composition is an anomaly. That point may seem obvious, but it is also a situation that becomes natural and forgettable as time goes on. We would do well to remember that we are asking students to read and write in unusual, unexpected ways.

When I take this perspective and reread Jennifer Rich's concerns that open this essay, I have two reactions. First, I consider her question, "Am I not, in some way, failing to read myself and my teaching as rhetorical events—constituted by specific contexts, with a specific audience and purpose in mind?" (182). This wider perspective reminds me that first-year composition is an unusual rhetorical situation for students; they are being asked to adopt a very different role as audience. To some degree, I find this comforting. It reminds me why the rhetorical event of teaching writing (and reading) is so difficult. Then, my second reaction is to underscore the importance of examining the expectations, values, and practices of first-year composition. As I have articulated in this essay, a model for pursuing that examination involves removing curricular clutter to slow down and focus on particular aspects of reading and writing that need more elaboration and guidance in the classroom.

Notes

1. David Bloome and Ann Egan-Robertson provide an overview of different definitions and approaches to intertextuality.
2. Other scholars have written about the pedagogical value of rhetorical figures (Butler; T. R. Johnson), and many online resources have compiled examples of figures.

Works Cited

Adler-Kassner, Linda, and Heidi Estrem. "Reading Practices in the Writing Classroom." *Writing Program Administration* 31.1/2 (2007): 35–47. Print.

Bloome, David, and Ann Egan-Robertson. "The Social Construction of Intertextuality in Classroom Reading and Writing Lessons." *Reading Research Quarterly* 28.4 (1993): 304–33.

Butler, Paul. *Out of Style: Reanimating Stylistic Study in Composition and Rhetoric*. Logan: Utah State UP, 2008. Print.

Carr, Nicholas G. "Is Google Making Us Stupid? What the Internet Is Doing to Our Brains." *Atlantic* July–Aug. 2008: n. pag. Web. 24 Jan. 2010.

Corbett, Edward P. J. "The Theory and Practice of Imitation in Classical Rhetoric." *College Composition and Communication* 22.3 (1971): 243–50. Print.

Farmer, Frank M., and Phillip K. Arrington. "Apologies and Accommodations: Imitation and the Writing Process." *Rhetoric Society Quarterly* 23.1 (1993): 12–34. Print.

Howard, Rebecca Moore, Tricia Serviss, and Tanya K. Rodrigue. "Writing from Sources, Writing from Sentences." *Writing & Pedagogy* 2.2 (2010): 177–92. Print.

Jolliffe, David A. "Who Is Teaching Composition Students to Read and How Are They Doing It?" *Composition Studies* 31.1 (2003): 127–42. Print.

Johnson, Steven. "Dawn of the Digital Natives." *Guardian* 7 Feb. 2008. Web. 5 Jan. 2012.

Johnson, T. R. *A Rhetoric of Pleasure: Prose Style and Today's Composition Classroom*. Portsmouth: Boynton/Cook, 2003. Print.

Kidd, Dustin. "Harry Potter and the Functions of Popular Culture." *Journal of Popular Culture* 40.1 (2007): 69–89. Print.

Newkirk, Thomas. *Holding On to Good Ideas in a Time of Bad Ones: Six Literacy Principles Worth Fighting For*. Portsmouth: Heinemann, 2009. Print.

Rich, Jennifer. "How Do We See What We See? Pedagogical Lacunae and Their Pitfalls in the Classroom." *Teaching English in the Two-Year College* 38.2 (2010): 177–83. Print.

Salvatori, Mariolina Rizzi, and Patricia Donahue. "Stories about Reading: Appearance, Disappearance, Morphing, and Revival." *College English* 75.2 (2012): 199–217. Print.

Sommers, Jeff. "Illustrating the Reading Process: The In-Class Read-Aloud Protocol." *Teaching English in the Two-Year College* 32.3 (2005): 298–306. Print.

Vowell, Sarah. *Take the Cannoli: Stories from the New World*. New York: Simon & Schuster, 2000. Print.

Walsh, Bryan. "Getting Real about the High Price of Cheap Food." *Time*. 21 Aug. 2009. Web. 18 Nov. 2011.

Thoughts on Selecting Readings

Katie Hern

According to author Katie Hern, "The following guidelines were developed in 2011 for the California Acceleration Project's (CAP) extended faculty development program. This program supports a move away from the traditional, multisemester approach to remediation and offers, instead, an accelerated pathway for underprepared students. In English, this involves creating rich, thematic courses that engage students in college-level reading and writing experiences, within a highly supportive classroom environment. Discrete skills instruction is replaced with extensive reading and meaning-making about relevant topics, with just-in-time remediation embedded along the way as needed (e.g., organizational guidance, sentence-level issues). A detailed discussion of CAP instructional design principles can be found in Toward a Vision of Accelerated Curriculum & Pedagogy: High-Challenge, High-Support Classrooms for Underprepared Students *(LearningWorks, 2013). As of 2016–17, faculty from more than eighty-five California community colleges will have worked with CAP to implement accelerated approaches to English and math."*

What will you have your students read? This might be the most important decision you'll make as an English teacher. A good choice means engaged students who integrate the texts in their own writing and produce stronger essays. A poor choice means suffering all semester—low energy in the classroom, frustrated students not doing the reading, essays that are heavy on generalities and light on evidence.

The following discussion is informed by the English curricular philosophy at Chabot College, where developmental students practice the same kinds of reading, thinking, and writing they'll be required to do at the college level. Developmental students read full-length texts— usually nonfiction—and they write argument-based essays about the issues raised in those texts. The principles and examples below come from my own experience teaching Chabot's accelerated developmental course, a 4-unit integrated reading and writing class that is one-level-below college English and open to any student (no minimum placement score or prerequisites).

From 3CSN Statewide Acceleration Initiative, California Acceleration Project, 28 May 2011 (http://cap.3csn.org/files/2012/01/ThoughtsOnChoosingReading.pdf).

A Few Key Principles

1. Don't skimp on volume

A lot of students leave high school having done very little real reading. They boast about earning A's on papers without having opened the book, "BS-ing" their way through and plugging in quotes. This is particularly true for students who had early struggles with reading due to dyslexia, interrupted schooling, or other issues. If they are already insecure about their reading, and they read something they don't understand, they will often just stop reading. It's hard to sustain motivation when doing something that makes you feel stupid. ("I'm in college. I should get this.") It's also hard to admit that you're having trouble reading.

But the only way to become a stronger reader is to *read*. That means students in accelerated courses need to do some substantial reading. A few short articles on a theme aren't going to be enough for them to really develop their academic literacy. Students need exposure to different topics, writing styles, levels of challenge; they need texts they work on closely during class and texts they process on their own. In my own accelerated course, students read 500–600 pages from different nonfiction books, articles, and websites during the semester.

2. Go for nonfiction about relevant issues

One of the reasons students arrive at college under-prepared for the reading is that they haven't been apprenticed to be effective readers across the disciplines. High school English courses often focus heavily on literature—fiction, poetry, plays—not the kinds of texts students will see in college level sociology or political science courses. And teachers in other subjects often develop ways to cover their content without relying on students' independent reading (e.g., lecturing, providing detailed outlines before tests). Developmental college students need sustained practice and guidance with nonfiction texts—texts that introduce them to key questions and concepts from different academic disciplines, texts that give them the chance to join the conversation.

It helps *a lot* if students are interested in what they're reading. I try to pick topics that have some direct relevance to students' lives. A few years back, I had a lot of success with books that examined the social and moral implications of our everyday economic choices—my best pairing was *Fast Food Nation* with *The Wal-Mart Effect*. Right now, my accelerated students read three psychology books, exploring issues like *How reliable are our memories? What causes addiction? Are human beings sadistic by nature? Do we have free will, or is everything we do caused by conditioning?* When the class is going well, students start *wanting* to read, a new experience for many of them.

3. Evaluate the balance of narrative, information, and argument

For me, an ideal accelerated English text has both accessibly written narrative components and more expository/argument-based discussions of social or political issues. Ann Fadiman's book *The Spirit Catches You and You Fall Down* is a great choice in this regard. The chapters alternate between the story of one family—Hmong immigrants in Merced, California, whose young daughter has epilepsy—and the larger forces shaping what happens to them, including the Hmong spiritual worldview, the U.S.-Vietnam war, and the ethnocentrism and cross-cultural breakdowns that occur between the family and their U.S. doctors.

I have considered, but not adopted, books that felt too heavy on narrative and too light on broader issues. Two that fit into this category for me are *Enrique's Journey* and *The Immortal Life of Henrietta Lacks*. Both books tell the story of one family, and both touch larger social issues (immigration and the ethics of medical research, respectively). However, the larger issues were treated as a brief journalistic prologue or epilogue, and the majority of the book involved simply telling the individual story. If I were to use these books, I would likely assign them for students to read independently and focus class time on engaging other resources that go more deeply into the broader issues and debates.

One book I've used successfully that is heavy on the information/argument and lighter on narrative is George Lakoff's *Don't Think of an Elephant*. He uses easily accessible language and examples to explain the American political landscape and the basic differences between conservative and progressive positions. It is a fantastic way to introduce students to these concepts, especially if paired with readings students can use to concretely apply Lakoff's broad principles (e.g., having students select and research current political issues).

4. Evaluate the density of unexplained references and terminology

A while back I was looking for a good book to pair with *Fast Food Nation*, and I happened upon *The Lexus and the Olive Tree: Understanding Globalization* by *New York Times* writer Thomas Friedman. My book order was overdue, and it looked decent when I skimmed through it on Amazon. It wasn't until the book arrived that I realized I'd made a terrible mistake. The first chapter starts out folksy and accessible—"What was it Forest Gump's mama used to say?"—but then becomes very rapidly mired in a web of unexplained allusions. One paragraph on page 7 refers to the Cold War, the Iron Curtain, communism, autarky, capitalism, détente, non-alignment, perestroika, the hammer and sickle, and the second Industrial Revolution. Luckily, there was still time to cancel my order.

The problem is not the presence of unexplained references or unfamiliar vocabulary—indeed, some instances of these are desirable because students get practice navigating them as readers (e.g., becoming aware of what is throwing them off, using context clues, seeking out background information).

However, when a book is *too* heavy with these, it is difficult to keep students engaged and motivated, and you need to devote significant portions of class time to unpacking the reading together. This is what happened the semester I used *Our Media, Not Theirs* by media scholars Robert McChesney and John Nichols. The book is full of important ideas about the economics of the corporate news industry, but students need to be introduced to that industry more fully than the authors provide for. A chapter of this book might be good as a short excerpt, deliberately chosen for the extra reading challenge, but as a whole book, it's probably better suited for a college-level course than a developmental one (and even then, it would need a lot of setup and unpacking).

Quick Summary: Katie's Reading Picks for Accelerated Developmental English

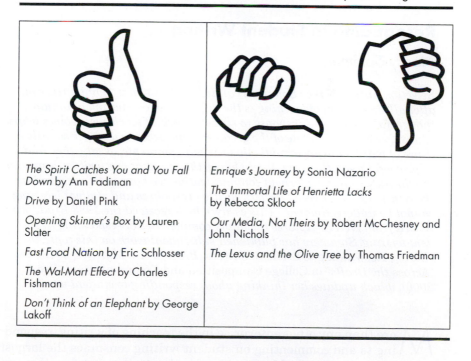

The Spirit Catches You and You Fall Down by Ann Fadiman	*Enrique's Journey* by Sonia Nazario
Drive by Daniel Pink	*The Immortal Life of Henrietta Lacks* by Rebecca Skloot
Opening Skinner's Box by Lauren Slater	*Our Media, Not Theirs* by Robert McChesney and John Nichols
Fast Food Nation by Eric Schlosser	*The Lexus and the Olive Tree* by Thomas Friedman
The Wal-Mart Effect by Charles Fishman	
Don't Think of an Elephant by George Lakoff	

10

Responding to Student Writing

Responding to Student Writing

Nancy Sommers

Selection author Nancy Sommers candidly admits that "what strikes me after all these years of teaching is the difficulty of composing a humane, thoughtful, and useful response to student work. If teaching involves leaps of faith, responding is one of the greatest leaps because we have so little evidence of what students actually do with our comments, or why they find some useful and others not. We do know, though, that our written responses are the most enduring form of communication we have with our students—the relationship between teachers' written responses and student learning cannot be underestimated." This essay, which received the 1983 Braddock Award from NCTE, explores the many complexities of responding to student writing. Sommers has published subsequent work on this topic, including Responding to Student Writers *(Bedford/St. Martin's, 2012) and* "Across the Drafts" in College Composition and Communication *(Dec. 2006), which updates her thinking about responding to student work.*

More than any other enterprise in the teaching of writing, responding to and commenting on student writing consumes the largest proportion of our time. Most teachers estimate that it takes them at

From *College Composition and Communication,* 1982, vol. 33, no. 2, pp. 148-56.

least 20 to 40 minutes to comment on an individual student paper, and those 20 to 40 minutes times 20 students per class, times 8 papers, more or less, during the course of a semester add up to an enormous amount of time. With so much time and energy directed to a single activity, it is important for us to understand the nature of the enterprise. For it seems, paradoxically enough, that although commenting on student writing is the most widely used method for responding to student writing, it is the least understood. We do not know in any definitive way what constitutes thoughtful commentary or what effect, if any, our comments have on helping our students become more effective writers.

Theoretically, at least, we know that we comment on our students' writing for the same reasons professional editors comment on the work of professional writers or for the same reasons we ask our colleagues to read and respond to our own writing. As writers we need and want thoughtful commentary to show us when we have communicated our ideas and when not, raising questions from a reader's point of view that may not have occurred to us as writers. We want to know if our writing has communicated our intended meaning and, if not, what questions or discrepancies our reader sees that we, as writers, are blind to.

In commenting on our students' writing, however, we have an additional pedagogical purpose. As teachers, we know that most students find it difficult to imagine a reader's response in advance, and to use such responses as a guide in composing. Thus, we comment on student writing to dramatize the presence of a reader, to help our students to become that questioning reader themselves, because, ultimately, we believe that becoming such a reader will help them to evaluate what they have written and develop control over their writing.[1]

Even more specifically, however, we comment on student writing because we believe that it is necessary for us to offer assistance to student writers when they are in the process of composing a text, rather than after the text has been completed. Comments create the motive for doing something different in the next draft; thoughtful comments create the motive for revising. Without comments from their teachers or from their peers, student writers will revise in a consistently narrow and predictable way. Without comments from readers, students assume that their writing has communicated their meaning and perceive no need for revising the substance of their text.[2]

Yet as much as we as informed professionals believe in the soundness of this approach to responding to student writing, we also realize that we don't know how our theory squares with teachers' actual practice—do teachers comment and students revise as the theory predicts they should? For the past year my colleagues, Lil Brannon, Cyril Knoblauch, and I have been researching this problem, attempting to discover not only what messages teachers give their students through their comments, but also what determines which of these comments the students choose to use or to ignore when revising. Our research has been entirely focused on comments teachers write to motivate revisions. We have studied the commenting styles of thirty-five teachers at New York University and the University of Oklahoma, studying the comments these teachers wrote on first and second drafts, and interviewing a representative number of these teachers and their students. All teachers also commented on the same set of three student essays. As an additional reference point, one of the student essays was typed into the computer that had been programed with the "Writer's Workbench," a package of twenty-three programs developed by Bell Laboratories to help computers and writers work together to improve a text rapidly. Within a few minutes, the computer delivered editorial comments on the student's text, identifying all spelling and punctuation errors, isolating problems with wordy or misused phrases, and suggesting alternatives, offering a stylistic analysis of sentence types, sentence beginnings, and sentence lengths, and finally, giving our freshman essay a Kincaid readability score of 8th grade which, as the computer program informed us, "is a low score for this type of document." The sharp contrast between the teachers' comments and those of the computer highlighted how arbitrary and idiosyncratic most of our teachers' comments are. Besides, the calm, reasonable language of the computer provided quite a contrast to the hostility and mean-spiritedness of most of the teachers' comments.

The first finding from our research on styles of commenting is that *teachers' comments can take students' attention away from their own purposes in writing a particular text and focus that attention on the teachers' purpose in commenting.* The teacher appropriates the text from the student by confusing the student's purpose in writing the text with her own purpose in commenting. Students make the changes the teacher wants rather than those that the student perceives are necessary, since the teachers' concerns imposed on the text create the reasons for the subsequent changes. We have all heard our perplexed students say to us when confused by our comments: "I don't understand how you want me to change this" or "Tell me what you want me to do." In the beginning of the process there was the writer, her words, and her desire to communicate her ideas. But after the comments of the teacher are imposed on the first or second draft, the student's attention dramatically shifts from 'This is what I want to say," to "This is what you the teacher are asking me to do."

This appropriation of the text by the teacher happens particularly when teachers identify errors in usage, diction, and style in a first draft and ask students to correct these errors when they revise; such comments give the student an impression of the importance of these errors that is all out of proportion to how they should view these errors at this point in the process. The comments create the concern that these "accidents of discourse" need to be attended to before the meaning of the text is attended to.

It would not be so bad if students were only commanded to correct errors, but, more often than not, students are given contradictory messages; they are commanded to edit a sentence to avoid an error or to condense a sentence to achieve greater brevity of style, and then told in the margins that the particular paragraph needs to be more specific or to be developed more. An example of this problem can be seen in the following student paragraph:

wordy - be precise *which Sunday?* *comma needed*

Every year [on one Sunday in the middle of January] tens of millions of

word choice

people <u>cancel</u> all events, plans or work to watch the Super Bowl. This

wordy

audience includes [little boys and girls, old people, and housewives and

Be specific - what reasons?

men.] <u>Many reasons</u> have been given to explain why the Super Bowl has

and why *what spots?)*

become so popular that commercial (spots cost up to $100,000.00.

awkward

One explanation is that <u>people</u> like to take sides and root for a team.

another what? *↓ spelling*

<u>Another</u> is that some people like the pageantry and excitement of the

too colloquial

event. These reasons alone, however, do not explain a happening as big as

the Super Bowl.

you need to do more research

This paragraph needs to be expanded in order to be more interesting to a reader.

In commenting on this draft, the teacher has shown the student how to edit the sentences, but then commands the student to expand the paragraph in order to make it more interesting to a reader. The interlinear comments and the marginal comments represent two separate tasks for this student; the interlinear comments encourage the student to see the text as a fixed piece, frozen in time, that just needs some editing. The marginal comments, however, suggest that the meaning of the text is not fixed, but rather that the student still needs to develop the meaning by doing some more research. Students are commanded to edit and develop at the same time; the remarkable contradiction of developing a paragraph after editing the sentences in it represents the confusion we encountered in our teachers' commenting styles. These different signals given to students, to edit and develop, to condense and elaborate, represent also the failure of teachers' comments to direct genuine revision of the text as a whole.

Moreover, the comments are worded in such a way that it is difficult for students to know what is the most important problem in the text and what problems are of lesser importance. No scale of concerns is offered to a student, with the result that a comment about spelling or a comment about an awkward sentence is given weight equal to a comment about organization or logic. The comment that seemed to represent this problem best was one teacher's command to his student: "Check your commas and semi-colons and think more about what you are thinking about." The language of the comments makes it difficult for a student to sort out and decide what is most important and what is least important.

When the teacher appropriates the text for the student in this way, students are encouraged to see their writing as a series of parts—words, sentences, paragraphs—and not as a whole discourse. The comments encourage students to believe that their first drafts are finished drafts, not invention drafts, and that all they need to do is patch and polish their writing. That is, teachers' comments do not provide their students with an inherent reason for revising the structure and meaning of their texts, since the comments suggest to students that the meaning of their text is already there, finished, produced, and all that is necessary is a better word or phrase. The processes of revising, editing, and proofreading are collapsed and reduced to a single trivial activity, and the students' misunderstanding of the revision process as a rewording activity is reinforced by their teachers' comments.

It is possible, and it quite often happens, that students follow every comment and fix their texts appropriately as requested, but their texts are not improved substantially, or, even worse, their revised drafts are inferior to their previous drafts. Since the teachers' comments take the students' attention away from their own original purposes, students concentrate more, as I have noted, on what the teachers commanded them to do than on what they are trying to say. Sometimes students do not understand the purpose behind their teachers' comments and take these comments very literally. At other times students understand the comments, but the teacher has misread the text and the comments, unfortunately, are not applicable. For instance, we repeatedly saw comments in which teachers commanded students to reduce and condense what was written, when in fact what the text really needed at this stage was to be expanded in conception and scope.

The process of revising always involves a risk. But, too often revision becomes a balancing act for students in which they make the changes that are requested but do not take the risk of changing anything that was not commented on, even if the students sense that other changes are needed. A more effective text does not often evolve from such changes alone, yet the student does not want to take the chance of reducing a finished, albeit inadequate, paragraph to chaos—to fragments—in order to rebuild it, if such changes have not been requested by the teacher.

The second finding from our study is that *most teachers' comments are not text-specific and could be interchanged, rubber-stamped, from text to text*. The comments are not anchored in the particulars of the students' texts, but rather are a series of vague directives that are not text-specific. Students are commanded to "Think more about [their] audience, avoid colloquial language, avoid the passive, avoid prepositions at the end of sentences or conjunctions at the beginning of sentences, be clear, be specific, be precise, but above all, think more about what [they] are thinking about." The comments on the following student paragraph illustrate this problem:

↓ Begin by telling your reader
what you are going to write about.

In the sixties it was drugs, in the seventies it was rock and roll. Now in

avoid - "one of the"

the eighties, one of the most controversial subjects is nuclear power. The

elaborate

United States is in great need of its own source of power. Because of

environmentalists, coal is not an acceptable source of energy. [Solar and

be specific

wind power have not yet received the technology necessary to use them.]

avoid - "it seems"

It seems that nuclear power is the only feasible means right now for ob-

taining self-sufficient power. However, too large a percentage of the

be precise

population are against nuclear power claiming it is unsafe. With as many

problems as the United States is having concerning energy, it seems a

Thesis sentence needed

shame that the public is so quick to "can" a very feasible means of power.

Nuclear energy should not be given up on, but rather, more nuclear

plants should be built.

Think more about your reader.

One could easily remove all the comments from this paragraph and rubber-stamp them on another student text, and they would make as much or as little sense on the second text as they do here.

We have observed an overwhelming similarity in the generalities and abstract commands given to students. There seems to be among teachers an accepted, albeit unwritten canon for commenting on student texts. This uniform code of commands, requests, and pleadings demonstrates that the teacher holds a license for vagueness while the student is commanded to be specific. The students we interviewed admitted to having great difficulty with these vague directives. The students stated that when a teacher writes in the margins or as an end comment, "choose precise language," or "think more about your audience," revising becomes a guessing game. In effect, the teacher is saying to the student, "Somewhere in this paper is imprecise language or lack of awareness of an audience and you must find it." The problem presented by these vague commands is compounded for the students when they are not offered any strategies for carrying out these commands. Students are told that they have done something wrong and that there is something in their text that needs to be fixed before the text is acceptable. But to tell students that they have done something wrong is not to tell them what to do about it. In order to offer a useful revision strategy to a student, the teacher must anchor that strategy in the specifics of the student's text. For instance, to tell our student, the author of the above paragraph, "to be specific," or "to elaborate," does not show our student what questions the reader has about the meaning of the text, or what breaks in logic exist, that could be resolved if the writer supplied specific information; nor is the student shown how to achieve the desired specificity.

Instead of offering strategies, the teachers offer what is interpreted by students as rules for composing; the comments suggest to students that writing is just a matter of following the rules. Indeed, the teachers seem to impose a series of abstract rules about written products even when some of them are not appropriate for the specific text the student is creating.[3] For instance, the student author of our sample paragraph presented above is commanded to follow the conventional rules for writing a five-paragraph essay—to begin the introductory paragraph by telling his reader what he is going to say and to end the paragraph with a thesis sentence. Somehow these abstract rules about what five-paragraph products should look like do not seem applicable to the problems this student must confront when revising, nor are the rules specific strategies he could use when revising. There are many inchoate ideas ready to be exploited in this paragraph, but the rules do not help the student to take stock of his (or her) ideas and use the opportunity he has, during revision, to develop those ideas.

The problem here is a confusion of process and product; what one has to say about the process is different from what one has to say about the product. Teachers who use this method of commenting are formulating their comments as if these drafts were finished drafts and were not going to be revised. Their commenting vocabularies have not been adapted to revision and they comment on first drafts as if they were justifying a grade or as if the first draft were the final draft.

Our summary finding, therefore, from this research on styles of commenting is that the news from the classroom is not good. For the most part, teachers do not respond to student writing with the kind of thoughtful commentary which will help students to engage with the issues they are writing about or which will help them think about their purposes and goals in writing a specific text. In defense of our teachers, however, they told us that responding to student writing was rarely stressed in their teacher-training or in writing workshops; they had been trained in various prewriting techniques, in constructing assignments, and in evaluating papers for grades, but rarely in the process of reading a student text for meaning or in offering commentary to motivate revision. The problem is that most of us as teachers of writing have been trained to read and interpret literary texts for meaning, but, unfortunately, we have not been trained to act upon the same set of assumptions in reading student texts as we follow in reading literary texts.[4] Thus, we read student texts with biases about what the writer should have said or about what he or she should have written, and our biases determine how we will comprehend the text. We read with our preconceptions and preoccupations, expecting to find errors, and the result is that we find errors and misread our students' texts.[5] We find what we look for; instead of reading and responding to the meaning of a text, we correct our students' writing. We need to reverse this approach. Instead of finding errors or showing students how to patch up parts of their texts, we need to sabotage our students' conviction that the drafts they have written are complete and coherent. Our comments need to offer students revision tasks of a different order of complexity and sophistication from the ones that they themselves identify, by forcing students back into the chaos, back to the point where they are shaping and restructuring their meaning.[6]

For if the content of a student text is lacking in substance and meaning, if the order of the parts must be rearranged significantly in the next draft, if paragraphs must be restructured for logic and clarity, then many sentences are likely to be changed or deleted anyway. There seems to be no point in having students correct usage errors or condense sentences that are likely to disappear before the next draft is completed. In fact, to identify such problems in a text at this early first draft stage, when such problems are likely to abound, can give a student a disproportionate sense of their importance at this stage in the writing process.[7] In responding to our students' writing, we should be guided by the recognition that it is not spelling or usage problems that we as writers first worry about when drafting and revising our texts.

We need to develop an appropriate level of response for commenting on a first draft, and to differentiate that from the level suitable to a second or third draft. Our comments need to be suited to the draft we are reading. In a first or second draft, we need to respond as any reader would, registering questions, reflecting befuddlement, and noting places where we are puzzled about the meaning of the text. Comments should point to breaks in logic, disruptions in meaning, or missing information. Our goal in commenting on early drafts should be to engage students with the issues they are considering and help them clarify their purposes and reasons in writing their specific text.

For instance, the major rhetorical problem of the essay written by the student who wrote the first paragraph (the paragraph on nuclear power) quoted above was that the student had two principal arguments running through his text, each of which brought the other into question. On the one hand, he argued that we must use nuclear power, unpleasant as it is, because we have nothing else to use; though nuclear energy is a problematic source of energy, it is the best of a bad lot. On the other hand, he also argued that nuclear energy is really quite safe and therefore should be our primary resource. Comments on this student's first draft need to point out this break in logic and show the student that if we accept his first argument, then his second argument sounds fishy. But if we accept his second argument, his first argument sounds contradictory. The teacher's comments need to engage this student writer with this basic rhetorical and conceptual problem in his first draft rather than impose a series of abstract commands and rules upon his text.

Written comments need to be viewed not as an end in themselves—a way for teachers to satisfy themselves that they have done their jobs—but rather as a means for helping students to become more effective writers. As a means for helping students, they have limitations; they are, in fact, disembodied remarks—one absent writer responding to another absent writer. The key to successful commenting is to have what is said in the comments and what is done in the classroom mutually reinforce and enrich each other. Commenting on papers assists the writing course in achieving its purpose; classroom activities and the comments we write to our students need to be connected. Written comments need to be an extension of the teacher's voice—an extension of the teacher as reader. Exercises in such activities as revising a whole text or individual paragraphs together in class, noting how the sense of the whole dictates the smaller changes, looking at options, evaluating actual choices, and then discussing the effect of these changes on revised drafts—such exercises need to be designed to take students through the cycles of revising and to help them overcome their anxiety about revising: that anxiety we all feel at reducing what looks like a finished draft into fragments and chaos.

The challenge we face as teachers is to develop comments which will provide an inherent reason for students to revise; it is a sense of revision as discovery, as a repeated process of beginning again, as starting out new, that our students have not learned. We need to show our students how to seek, in the possibility of revision, the dissonances of discovery—to show them through our comments why new choices would positively change their texts, and thus to show them the potential for development implicit in their own writing.

Notes

1. C. H. Knoblauch and Lil Brannon, "Teacher Commentary on Student Writing: The State of the Art," *Freshman English News,* 10 (Fall, 1981), 1–3.
2. For an extended discussion of revision strategies of student writers see Nancy Sommers, "Revision Strategies of Student Writers and Experienced Adult Writers," *College Composition and Communication,* 31 (December, 1980), 378–388.
3. Nancy Sommers and Ronald Schleifer, "Means and Ends: Some Assumptions of Student Writers," *Composition and Teaching,* 2 (December, 1980), 69–76.
4. Janet Emig and Robert P. Parker, Jr., "Responding to Student Writing: Building a Theory of the Evaluating Process," unpublished papers, Rutgers University.
5. For an extended discussion of this problem see Joseph Williams, "The Phenomenology of Error," *College Composition and Communication,* 32 (May, 1981), 152–168.
6. Ann Berthoff, *The Making of Meaning* (Montclair, NJ: Boynton/Cook Publishers, 1981).
7. W. U. McDonald, "The Revising Process and the Marking of Student Papers," *College Composition and Communication,* 24 (May, 1978), 167–170.

Conversing in Marginal Spaces: Developmental Writers' Responses to Teacher Comments

Carolyn Calhoon-Dillahunt and Dodie Forrest

In this selection, Carolyn Calhoon-Dillahunt and Dodie Forrest describe the results of an empirical study they conducted in an effort to bridge two significant research gaps: two-year college basic writers and students' responses to teacher feedback. Using two key questions—How do developmental writing students react to teacher comments? and What do they do with those comments?—Calhoon-Dillahunt and Forrest studied students' responses to pre- and postsurveys and questionnaires, conducted interviews, and analyzed student drafts and revisions. They discovered that developmental writers did, indeed, read and appreciate teacher commentary and found suggestions and end comments to be the most helpful. Their results also suggested that throughout the course, students were becoming more autonomous writers and more aware of global issues in their writing. This study reminds us that teacher feedback plays an important role not only in teaching and learning but also in creating a personal connection with student writers, which ultimately can help retention efforts in all levels of writing instruction, but perhaps especially in developmental writing courses.

From *Teaching English in the Two-Year College,* 2013, vol. 40, no. 3, pp. 230-47.

As writing instructors, we spend hours "talking back" to our students through written comments on their drafts. But how do student writers receive our comments, and what do they *do* with this feedback? Teachers invest so much time and energy in our responses to papers. How do we know what gets through, what makes sense to our students?

These questions certainly aren't new. Composition scholars such as Sommers, Brannon and Knoblauch, Connors and Lunsford, Straub and Lunsford, and Anson, to name a few, have probed all kinds of interesting issues within the murky waters of teacher comments. However, the impetus for our own research surfaced at the 2005 CCCC Convention in San Francisco when Nancy Sommers shared the results of a four-year longitudinal study of Harvard student writers. One of the most compelling conclusions Sommers reached in her study was that "feedback, more than any other form of instruction, shapes the way a student learns to write. . . . [F]eedback, more than any single factor, contributed to their sense of academic belonging or alienation" (*Across the Drafts*). Sitting in the upper reaches of the packed auditorium, we viewed Sommers's short film *Across the Drafts* and heard insights, such as that of first-year student Tiffany Threadcraft: "Sometimes you've got to start over, even if you think it's a really cool idea. [Feedback has] given me the validation that revision really is necessary and not just something that someone made up, which is kind of the place that I was in before I started my writing course." How uplifting to hear a student writer express her understanding and appreciation of the connection between feedback and revision.

Afterward, we felt inspired to conduct our own empirical study of student response to teacher feedback, one that focused on community college writers, specifically developmental writers. What would *these* students, in some ways the very antithesis of Harvard students, have to say? Would *our* students at Yakima Valley Community College — many of them first-generation students, academically underprepared, ethnically diverse, and most holding down jobs or raising families or both while attending school in the most economically challenged area of Washington State — value feedback as a resource for revision and personal writing growth as Harvard student Tiffany Threadcraft did?

Following Our Curiosities

While Sommers's presentation motivated us and provided some direction, we further realized, after listening to educator Judith Wootten describe the "crisis of confidence" first-generation students experience when they run up against academic discourse, that teacher comments may greatly influence our developmental writers' confidence and ability to be sustained in the college environment. However, our follow-up research revealed that few studies focused on *students'* responses to teacher comments, and those fairly dated studies largely concentrated on first-year college students in a university setting (Straub). Rather, much of the research focused on methods and models of comments *teachers* might make on student papers. And until Sommers and Saltz's recent work examining the role of writing in freshman writers' development, even fewer studies looked at student writing in context. As Sommers notes, "[I]n our professional literature about responding, we too often neglect the role of the student . . . and the vital partnership between teacher and student, by focusing, almost exclusively, on the role of the teacher" ("Across" 249). While significant studies have taught us much about what teachers do when they comment and what types of comments may be the most effective, a research gap persists between what teachers do when they "talk back" on the pages of student papers and how students react to that feedback. Given the rich variety of student identities in addition to the range of experiences and perceptions formed within a single writing course, it is easy to imagine the complexities in which students navigate teacher comments. Consequently, the student-teacher partnership of which Sommers speaks (and continues to research, most recently at Bunker Hill Community College) might be heightened if more of us observed the ways students in an array of writing courses and academic settings process responses to their writing.

As we planned our study, we anticipated our results would likely differ from those that Sommers reported at the 2005 CCCC Convention. Our students are not Harvard students, after all. They are not simply novices to academic writing; the average student at Yakima Valley Community College begins his or her college writing experience in a developmental writing course. Knowing this, we believed our students would have poor attitudes about writing, perhaps because of poor past experiences with writing. We also expected that our developmental writers' sense of autonomy would be less than that of college-level writers, that they would want and need more directive feedback from teachers and would show greater deference to an instructor's commentary.

Our Process

To begin to answer our most important questions—*How do developmental writing students react to our comments? What do they do with our comments?*—we needed a fairly large sample of students and a variety of tools. We began our pilot study in fall 2005. Since our campus is on the quarter system, fall quarter draws the most first-time college students to campus, students we wanted to target. In addition, our college offers two developmental courses below college-level composition, with the greatest enrollment in English 075, the course that directly precedes English 101 (college composition). Our developmental writing faculty emphasizes process writing, making English 075 an ideal course to study how developmental writers think about and use instructor comments.

We selected five sections of English 075 from among faculty volunteers, approximately half the sections offered on campus that fall. Instructors in three of the five sections used portfolio assessment, enabling us to examine students' revision process after teacher commentary. The other two instructors provided summative comments and grades without allowing further revision. We imagined a pool of 100 students, since each class had an enrollment cap of 20; however, between class attrition and students who opted out, we began the study with 86 students.

To ascertain students' attitudes toward teacher feedback, both the types of feedback they found helpful and their reactions toward their own teacher's commentary, we created two questionnaires. While questionnaires used in earlier studies have asked students to rate preferences of teacher comments on a sample student paper (Straub), we were curious about students' reactions to receiving written comments on their *own* papers. The first survey was administered at the beginning and end of the quarter with a range of open- and closed-ended questions designed to gauge students' affective responses toward and general preferences for teacher feedback and, especially, to note any changes in their attitude during the writing course, which was often their first experience with writing instruction in the college setting (see appendix). The second questionnaire was a "Thinking about Instructor Feedback" form with a series of questions designed to elicit students' reactions to the specific comments they received from their writing teacher on each writing project (see Figure 1).

In addition to surveying participants, we interviewed about one-fourth of the students, exercising Elizabeth Hodges's "talk-aloud protocol" on a draft from each student with whom we consulted, to better grasp how students understood and reacted to their teachers' comments. Hodges's study focused on the crossroads of teacher written

Figure 1. Thinking about Instructor Feedback Form

1. Before you read your instructor's comments, describe what you are feeling right now.
2. Now read your instructor's comments. What are your reactions to the comments you received?
3. Which comments make the most sense to you and/or which comments do you find the most helpful? (Explain why.)
4. Which comments do you find confusing and/or which comments do you find the least helpful? (Explain why.)
5. Do you have any questions or comments about the feedback you received from your instructor?

response and student reception of those responses, allowing her to "see when teachers and students are having or not having the same conversations" (Hodges 78).

Finally, to examine changes students made in their texts as a result of teacher comments, we collected drafts and revisions from students who had the opportunity to revise one or more drafts over the quarter, in other words, those students who were enrolled in portfolio-based classes. We were able to study revision attempts from about half the total students in our study. Those participants submitted copies of their early drafts with teacher comments along with their final, revised drafts, and we highlighted the changes between drafts. Comparing drafts and revisions allowed us to see which comments students responded to and how they used the comments to revise.

Our Discoveries

How Students Felt about Teacher Commentary

To examine students' affective responses, the pre-/post-questionnaire included a section with questions about the sorts of feedback methods to which students had been exposed previously as well as a series of open-ended questions about feedback methods students found helpful and not, memorable comments they had received, and what they believed teacher comments should do. The final section of the questionnaire included a series of twenty statements on which students, using a Likert scale, indicated the extent to which they agreed with each statement. For example, "Comments help me understand how I am doing as a writer"; "Seeing comments on my essay makes me feel frustrated/anxious"; and "Reading teacher comments makes me think more deeply about my ideas and how I express them."

As we tabulated the results, to our surprise our developmental writers' attitudes did not exactly match our expectations. Ultimately, the developmental writers we surveyed, like the Harvard students in Sommers's study, read and appreciated teacher commentary and found "suggestions/constructive criticism" to be the most helpful. In fact, the writers we surveyed believed suggestions and constructive criticism are the very purpose of teacher commentary, as one student noted, "[Comments should] [h]elp guide you on your paper without telling you what to do." Another student added that teacher comments should "[h]elp you improve your writing in the future. Let you know your strengths and weaknesses." The developmental writers we studied wanted the same type of commentary—honest, specific, and constructive—that college-level students did in many previous studies, including formal work by Straub and Sommers as well as informal classroom surveys of community college students by Mitchler (447).

Past studies do not paint a consistent picture of student writers' reactions to praise. For instance, Burkland and Grimm noted that in their survey of nearly 200 freshman composition students, "[s]tudents expressed a strong preference for criticism and an ambivalence about praise" ("Motivating" 242). Land and Evans's surveys of high school and college students also found that students are "less enthusiastic about this strategy [praise] than are many authorities on writing pedagogy" (114). Our findings corroborate Burkland and Grimm, who noted that students liked praise but didn't really see it as "useful" ("Students' Response" 14). Although the developmental writers in our study said they appreciated praise, in their view, praise seemed to serve more as a relationship builder with their instructor, a self-esteem booster ("It made me feel more confident about my writing"; "I felt a sense of accomplishment"), or a motivator ("It made me want to keep writing") than a tool to help students improve their written products.

That said, overwhelmingly the comments that students *remembered* were positive comments that complimented the students' work, effort, or improvement. A few students remembered only negative comments, however, and their remarks were heartbreaking to read: "[I]t was a bad comment something to the effect of you will never be able to write anything good"; "One teacher crossed out a section and wrote 'No.' This was memorable because it didn't give any reason to why it was crossed out so it lowered my self-esteem for writing papers instead of boosting confidence"; "I suck at writing. Never have gotten praise." Comments like these, though rare in the survey, reflected the attitudes we assumed most of our developmental writers would have; they also deliver a sobering reminder of the impact our words may have on student writers.

Student participants displayed some surprising attitude shifts at the end of the quarter compared to the beginning. Most notable were changes in what students said they wanted or found helpful from teacher commentary. We initially expected developmental writers to prefer directive commentary, such as corrections or explicit instructions about what to change—and certainly some research suggests that students do indeed prefer and better apply directive commentary (Jackson, Carifio, and Dagostino; Ziv). However, the developmental writers in our study showed greater autonomy than we anticipated, especially by the end of the term. Results of the post-questionnaire revealed the following:

- Fewer students appreciated corrections/cross-outs at the end of quarter.

  There are a lot of ways to say the same thing but to say my way is wrong and theirs is right takes away my freedom of expression.

  This made me feel that my hard work was insignificant and discouraged me on my next drafts.

- Somewhat fewer students found directive comments helpful at the end of quarter.

    I find that directions telling me how to change my writing are the least helpful because they take away my freedom in my own writing.

- Fewer students found marginal comments helpful, and more students found end-of-essay comments helpful, suggesting students in the study preferred more "global" feedback on their writing.

    [End comments] helped me more because it felt like [the instructor] was talking to me.

    I found end of the essay comments more helpful. Because you are able to read through your paper . . . [and] at the end get the big picture on what you did right or wrong.[1]

While in both the pre- and post-questionnaires the vast majority of students indicated that teacher comments should "help students improve," the number of students who indicated that teachers' comments should "fix" the writing or show students what's "right" and "wrong" decreased from 16 responses (out of 86 surveyed) to 4 by the end of the term. We found this shift to be especially encouraging. Perhaps the changes in attitude favoring end comments over directive comments suggest a growing sense of authority as writers; students in the study appeared to be considering their work more holistically and to be less concerned with correcting surface errors only. These findings also suggest that our developmental writers are much like the "novice writers" Sommers and Saltz described in "The Novice as Expert: Writing the Freshman Year": the feedback they receive appears to affirm them as writers and as college students.

Further attitude shifts appeared in response to five Likert scale statements (see Figure 2). When students were asked if they understood what the instructor is trying to communicate with his or her comments, more students at the end of the term agreed or strongly agreed that they understood the comments. Similarly, fewer students agreed or strongly agreed with the idea that they were often confused by the comments their instructors make on their papers. By the end of the quarter, only 10 percent of the students in the study felt that having extensive comments on a paper indicated a worse paper. And fewer students agreed with the idea that the purpose of teacher comments is to tell them what to "fix" to get a better grade on an essay. All of these trends suggest the students were becoming more self-directed writers with a growing sense of awareness and appreciation of comments that addressed global concerns. Only one significant attitude shift seemed troubling: fewer students at the end of the quarter indicated that they

Figure 2. Notable Attitude Shifts toward Instructor Feedback at Beginning and End of Quarter

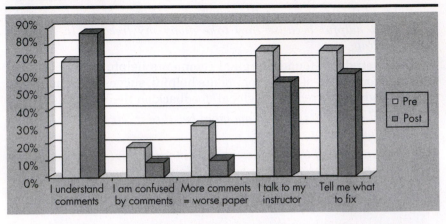

talk to their teacher if they don't understand the commentary. A variety of reasons may account for this shift: students largely may have felt they understood the commentary; students may have developed other support systems to help them process feedback; students may not have experienced a comfortable rapport with their particular instructor; or students may have believed it is unimportant to seek out teacher help for every item that confuses them. Overall, in response to statements about reading and using teacher feedback, students consistently agreed or strongly agreed that they read (96.5 percent) and used (93 percent) their teacher's comments, suggesting instructors' late night commenting is indeed noticed and appreciated.

Another way we tried to gauge students' attitudes toward and understanding of teacher feedback was with the "Thinking about Instructor Feedback" form. Each time students received an essay back from their instructor with markings and comments, we asked that the instructor take about fifteen minutes of class time to have the students read their comments and respond in writing to the five questions on the form.

Student responses to the first prompt—"Before you read your instructor's comments, describe what you are feeling right now"—were sometimes entertaining. Most students seemed to understand that we were looking for an emotional characterization, but a few shared physical complaints, like being cold, hungry, or tired, and a few described outside stresses. On the whole, most students described a negative feeling, such as being nervous or afraid, as they anticipated their instructor's feedback. While some students did feel eager or confident about the feedback they were about to receive, we were struck by how much anxiety students expressed before having their essays returned. Such anxiety affirmed our impressions of the "insecure" developmental writers we had imagined prior to our study. Fortunately, once the students actually read the instructors' comments, most recorded favorable responses to the feedback. When asked about their reaction to their teachers' comments, for instance, the vast majority used words such as "encouraged," "pleasantly surprised," "reassured," and "relieved" to express how they felt about the feedback they received. Most often students indicated that they found the teacher comments helpful and appreciated their instructor's effort. Many students remarked that the comments showed the instructor carefully read and was interested in their work ("It felt like she was really trying to understand what I was saying rather than just grading me"). Even those students who received feedback telling them that more revision was needed tended to agree with the instructor, finding that the instructor's comments actually confirmed their own impressions of their text ("I knew I was struggling with MLA"; "I knew I hadn't edited well"; "She nailed the comment about my conclusion. I need to work on that"; "I agreed with her comments. They were what I was expecting").

Nevertheless, the last couple of questions on the feedback form provided the deepest insight. Students were first asked which comments on their paper they found most helpful, and nearly all students referenced a particular comment the instructor made, though some talked about comment types, like "end comment," "corrections," "MLA format," and so forth. However, when asked which comments students found least helpful or most confusing, we found a whole list of English-teacher lingo, words and phrases such as "polish," "develop," "think about," "flesh out," "tweak," "analyze," "use your own words," "dig deeper," "relevance," and "show," as well as grammar terminology, such as "shifts," "comma splice," and "active vs. passive." (Confusion over this lingo became even more apparent when we looked at the textual changes students made after receiving their teacher feedback.) Additionally, student participants indicated that they struggled to understand symbols, markings, and abbreviations, and even their instructors' handwriting or use of fragmented expressions. Some of the developmental writers further expressed uncertainty about teachers' personal reactions to ideas in their drafts. The students did not know if or how they were supposed to apply these comments as they revised. In a survey of students in two of her end-of-sequence composition courses, Sharon Mitchler found similar results with her more experienced writing students: students reacted negatively to vague comments, cryptic marks, instructors "taking over" students' work, grades without commentary, instructors offering personal opinions, and illegible handwriting (448). Even though many previous studies suggest these sorts of comments are not helpful to students (Hayes and Daiker; Land and Evans; Sommers; Dohrer; to name a few), it is clear from our study that composition instructors still may not fully consider the needs of their audience when writing comments to students. As a student quoted in Sommers's "Across the Drafts" suggests, "Too often comments are written to the paper, not to the student" (250). Greg Giberson provides another important distinction in the way too much teacher jargon can disrupt the student-teacher partnership in learning: "When teachers respond to texts with cookie-cutter words and phrases such as 'awkward,' 'avoid cliché,' or 'elaborate,' we are not responding to the text we are reading, but to the ideal text that we have in our minds" (413).

How Students Understood Teacher Commentary

As the end of the quarter neared, we arranged interviews with as many student participants in our sample as we could, about 20 students, all of whom were enrolled in courses using portfolio assessment. We largely modeled these interviews after Hodges's "talk-aloud protocols"— personal interviews that invite student writers to talk through their thought processes as they read aloud their instructor's written comments. As writing center directors, we know the value of talk in creating meaning, so including some interviews not only offered us direct, personal access to the student participants, but it also gave us a more complete picture of how students engage (or disengage) with written teacher comments. We scheduled interviews to coincide with a time when the instructor had returned a draft for revision. We asked students to bring a copy of that draft to their appointment and assumed they had read their instructor comments before meeting with us. In each interview, we began by asking students to tell us about their writing project. Then we asked students to read their drafts aloud, pausing wherever they saw a mark or margin note and reading the comment aloud as well. Students were instructed to respond to each comment after they read it, but we also prompted students for response, asking "What do you think that means?" or "Tell me what you are thinking now." When students reached the end of their essays, they were asked to read aloud and respond to their instructor's end comment. We concluded the interviews with questions 3–5 from the "Thinking about Instructor Feedback" form (Figure 1).

As the students read their papers aloud, we noted several striking patterns. First, while students indicated that they had read and understood most or all of the instructor's comments at the beginning of the interview, as they read the comments aloud, the students showed less understanding than they had initially claimed, sometimes even asking one of us for clarification about a notation or comment. Moreover, we were surprised by *how* the students read the marginal comments. As instructors, we tend to respond to student writing in context, making marginal notes near the area where we have a question or concern about or praise for what the student has written. We may even pose questions or offer personal replies as if we are having a conversation with the student on the page. However, the students we interviewed tended to read the instructor margin comments as though these comments were separate and distinct from the portions of student text to which the feedback corresponded. In fact, students often had to be pressed to read the comments where they occurred and to think about what each comment might mean in relation to their own words. Anecdotally we had observed this behavior in students in our own classes, who busily read our comments when we returned an essay, but seldom *reread* their own paper to make sense of what we wrote. However, in the "talk-aloud protocol," this behavior—and its impact on students' ability to process, understand, and make use of the comments—was even more pronounced. In most interviews the students seemed to be reading the comments in context of their own writing for the very first time. In doing so, many had "aha!" moments as they talked through their thinking about what the comment meant and their reaction to that comment. While feedback used as a dialogic has long been an established part of composition pedagogy, our experience with the "talk-aloud protocol" suggests that students need far more coaching in how to read and make use of written instructor comments before they may fully benefit from the conversation many of us are trying to have with them on the page.

What Students Did and Did Not Do with Instructor Comments

The final and perhaps most challenging portion in our pilot study centered on analyzing how students used teacher commentary when revising their papers. Because our methodology involved comparing drafts with revisions and looking for evidence of applied teacher feedback, we could examine only essays from classes in which students submitted revised essays *after* receiving teacher commentary. Not all of the volunteer instructors required such revisions. Consequently, for this portion of the study, we were left with a reduced sampling of work from 46 student participants, each of whom submitted two drafts with written teacher comments from two distinct writing assignments along with subsequent revisions. In all, we analyzed 92 pairs of papers (drafts with teacher comments and corresponding revisions). As we spent time highlighting the changes students made in their revisions, however, we quickly realized that the data we collected did not give us a clear or complete picture of what changes students made and why.

After identifying the revisions, we tried to match changes to specific instructor feedback. Incidentally, we were intrigued by the variation in instructor markings, ranging from extensive end comments with few marginal notes or editing marks to commentary that was almost exclusively editing marks, corrections, and directive suggestions. The variation was not unexpected, as we had not asked participating instructors to change or standardize their commenting styles. Nevertheless, our goal was to better understand how the developmental writers in our study interpreted and used the comments they received, regardless of the instructor's commenting preferences. Consequently, we decided not to count the number of individual comments, but whether drafts contained each *type* of comment—editing, marginal, or end. We also defined comment types as follows: editing comments included notes, marks, or corrections; marginal comments included any substantial question, suggestion, or observation written beside the student's text in conversation with the writer's ideas; and end comments provided holistic feedback, a global comment students could use for revising that particular draft.

In the 92 essays we analyzed, 86 percent had at least one editing comment, 95 percent included at least one marginal comment, and 79 percent included an end comment. Although all drafts had some sort of end note from the instructor, on several drafts the instructor's ending comment simply referred students back to the marginal comments or made a general, encouraging remark, such as "Good start," and we did not consider those remarks to be global commentary a student could use for revision. Despite the variances in number and types of commentary, all students had some suggestions from their instructors to guide their revisions.

Our next step was to find out whether the instructor comments stimulated any revision attempt from the student participants. After all, isn't the connection between feedback and revision what motivates instructors to spend hours responding to a stack of essays, the idea that our comments create a "teachable" moment for our students? First, we examined the changes that students made in response to their instructors' comments. Again, we chose not to count the total number of attempts but rather focused on which *types* of comments elicited a revision attempt from students. Figure 3 compares the number of teacher comment types made on the 92 drafts to the number of times students attempted to address at least one comment of each type. We should note that, in our analysis, we counted *any* attempted changes that could be attributed to a teacher comment regardless of its success, and in many cases the changes did not, in our view, improve the students' texts. In the revised student essays, 86 percent revealed students had responded to one or more editing comment; likewise 86 percent of the revisions indicated students had responded to one or more marginal comment. Yet only 52 percent of the revisions showed evidence of students attempting to address one or more issues raised in the end comment (see Figure 3). This last statistic was most noteworthy to us because it directly conflicted with what we found in our questionnaires gauging students' affective and attitudinal reactions to teacher feedback. While we had felt encouraged that more students claimed to value end comments in the questionnaires, the textual reality of their revisions suggested that students only used global comments about half the time.

Figure 3.   Student Attempts to Address Various Instructor Comments

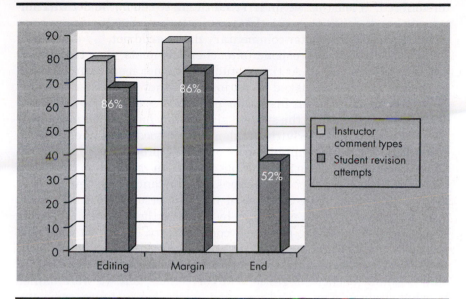

Perhaps the discrepancy between these developmental writers' expressed appreciation for end comments and their use of them (or lack thereof) indicates a growth in attitude not yet fully realized in their actual revisions. Students simply may like the end comment "genre," which often speaks directly to the student (as opposed to the text) in a conversational tone, perhaps emulating audio comments, which, as Susan Sipple found, tend to personalize the commenting process, strengthening the student-teacher bond (28). Yet student participants may have opted not to address the end comment because it requires more time and effort than they allotted or could give. Holistic end comments require a different level of intellectual energy on the part of any writer. Re-envisioning ideas on a global scale often calls for the writer to imagine some new approach and determine a location in the text for incorporating the changes, steps that may not be mapped out specifically for the writer. As a result, students must risk more to revise in a way that addresses end comments, and they may feel less certain about attempting such changes. Another possibility may be the problems with the genre of the end comment itself; its often predictable form can reduce its pedagogical effectiveness, pushing teachers' commentary toward generic conventions rather than authentic dialogue (Smith 266).

Students' rhetorical responses to feedback generated some additional surprises. While nearly all students made at least some attempt to revise their essays after teacher commentary, their revisions did not always correspond to a teacher comment. Students made a number of textual changes independent of suggestions or corrections their instructors offered, at least as we understood them. We do not know what inspired the students to make those revisions or what they may have perceived in the instructor commentary that we did not.

When students did respond to teacher comments, sometimes their revisions were off track. At times, students did not seem to understand what they were being asked to do, just that they needed to do something. For instance, if an instructor prompted a student to add more analysis or explanation, the student simply may have added more summary or examples. Clearly, the student understood he or she was supposed to *add,* but the additions were often inappropriate or ineffective. Some students also made inexplicable changes in response to comments that didn't provide precise directions. For instance, in a few cases, a teacher asked a genuine question or made a personal comment in the margin, and the student responded by omitting the passage altogether, a revision attempt that appeared contradictory to the intent of the comment.

What students elected to change was also a mystery. No student addressed all teacher suggestions or corrections, but we were baffled by what students chose to address and ignore. For instance, some students corrected one error, say a comma splice on the first page, but overlooked the same comment on the same type of error later in the paper. Similarly, there was no pattern indicating which marginal suggestions a student opted to respond to or disregard. We noted a curious echo in the revisions, however: students whose instructors made few editing marks on the page tended to address few or none of the limited corrections their instructors offered, while students whose teachers frequently provided corrections tended to address the corrections, but only when errors were actually marked by the teacher; these students did not attempt to correct unmarked errors on their own. Such responses to the text suggest that the teacher's commenting style spoke volumes to students about what was important in the teacher's evaluation and perhaps in the teacher's pedagogy. For instance, we wonder if the students who ignored an instructor's infrequent editorial marks recognized that the lack of corrections on the draft meant editing was not a prominent part of their teacher's instruction or grading. We wonder, as well, if students who attended to instructor corrections were more or less dependent on their instructor to act as editor of their drafts without the students actually learning to identify and correct an error pattern on their own.

Reflections

In retrospect, we recognize that many of our early expectations of the developmental writers we studied, namely that they would want more directive feedback, have a lesser sense of autonomy, and would show greater deference to an instructor's comments, fit the marginalized status of "basic writer" as "other," defined by DeGenaro and White. Admittedly, we saw these students as different from other writers: as "basic" or "developmental" first and writers second. Given our years of experience and expertise teaching basic writers, we were a little chagrined to discover that our expectations reflected more of our own biases than truths about developmental writers. While developmental writers may indeed lack in experience and skill, we learned that the student participants in our study did have a similar attitude as Tiffany Threadcraft, the Harvard student in Sommers's film who said feedback validated the revision process for her. The students in our study likewise valued instructor feedback as a tool to help them improve as thinkers and writers even though they struggled to apply that feedback. While they attempted to address editing and margin comments to a greater degree, a result that may hint at some deference toward localized, in-text feedback, their growing preference for the end comment is a sign that a broader based, personally composed response to their ideas is what they care about. The end comment, then, may be one of the most important places on the page for them to receive affirmation that their ideas were heard and considered, perhaps even influencing their continued growth as academic writers beyond the paper they attempted to revise.

Listening to the developmental writers in our study, we came away more mindful of how important audience awareness is when we're commenting. While jargon and code may be efficient for us, especially when we must respond to a dizzying number of essays in a fairly short amount of time, our student participants told us what other studies also have found: these comments do not communicate clearly to the students we are trying to reach, nor do they support students as they revise. Additionally, while our students did not seem as fragile as we imagined, many of them preferring suggestions and constructive criticism to praise, our comments do more than simply provide guidance for improvement; our comments can promote confidence and may even communicate to students that they "belong" in college. Given the vulnerability of this student population, we instructors should choose our words thoughtfully.

Our interviews revealed that students do not intuitively see marginal comments as "conversation" on the page, results that also were confirmed in our review of students' revisions. Written comments certainly can and should play that role, but our findings helped us realize that reading comments and using them to revise must be taught, like other aspects of the writing process. As a result, each of us has altered our teaching practices to allow time in class for students to review their papers marked with our comments and have the opportunity to process comments with us, by asking questions or getting additional advice. We continue to use the feedback form we developed for the study in our own classrooms to better understand how students receive and understand our comments. In addition, we both talk with our students about *how* to read our comments and what different types of comments (editing, margin, or end) may try to accomplish.

Ultimately, this study left us with more questions than answers, questions that would require different research methodology to try to answer. That said, we learned a lot from this pilot study about ourselves as writing teachers, about classroom-based research, and about our assumptions. Moreover, we came away from our study with a deep appreciation for our colleagues and their students, who so generously gave of themselves and enabled our research. We also are reminded of the complexity of this work we do as composition instructors. Despite the misfires and miscommunications, the space we share in the margins is cherished space—often our only one-to-one contact with students. Writers want to be read, want a response; for developmental writers, particularly, this connection is often what helps support and retain them in a place where they may not always feel they belong.

Appendix

Name:

Pilot Study Questionnaire

Part I:

1. What methods have your teachers used to mark or comment on your papers?

    A. **Marginal comments** (comments in the margins of your paper). *Check all that apply.*

    ☐ Abbreviations or codes that identify errors or problems with the text

    ☐ Questions

    ☐ Dialogue: a conversation/discussion (vs. corrections) about the ideas/content of your piece

    ☐ Praise/positive remarks

    ☐ Criticism/negative remarks

    ☐ Suggestions/constructive criticism

    ☐ Directions: tells you what to do to change your writing

    ☐ Other (Please describe in space below):

    B. **In-text comments** (comments in/on top of your writing). *Check all that apply.*

    ☐ Abbreviations, editing marks, or other codes that identify errors in your writing

- ☐ Cross outs/actual corrections to your writing (rewriting portions of text for you)
- ☐ Questions
- ☐ Dialogue: a conversation/discussion (vs. corrections) about the ideas/content of your piece
- ☐ Praise/positive remarks
- ☐ Criticism/negative remarks
- ☐ Suggestions/constructive criticism
- ☐ Directions: tells you what to do to change your writing (but doesn't fix it for you)
- ☐ Other (Please describe in space below):

C. **End of essay comments**. *Check all that apply.*
- ☐ Explanation of grade
- ☐ Suggestions to improve essay
- ☐ Suggestions to improve writing in the future
- ☐ Praise/positive remarks
- ☐ Criticism/negative remarks
- ☐ Specific directions for revision (tells you what to change/how to change it)
- ☐ Other (Please describe in space below):

D. **Other marking/commenting methods.** *Check all that apply.*
- ☐ Scoring Grid/Rubric/Check sheet (standardized comments or evaluation criteria on a separate sheet of paper attached to essay)
- ☐ Grade only/no comments
- ☐ Conferences (one-on-one meetings with oral discussion/comments)
- ☐ Other (Please describe in space below):

2. Which commenting/marking methods did you find the most helpful? Why?

3. Which commenting/marking methods did you find the least helpful? Why?

4. What was the most memorable comment you ever received on a piece of writing? Why?

5. In your opinion, what should teachers' comments do?

Part II:

Please indicate the level with which you agree or disagree with each of the statements below.

    0 = not applicable/no basis for judgment

    1 = strongly disagree

    2 = disagree

    3 = neutral—neither agree, nor disagree

    4 = agree

    5 = strongly agree

1. I read all instructor comments on my essays.   0 1 2 3 4 5
2. I feel I understand what the instructor is trying to communicate to me with the comments.   0 1 2 3 4 5
3. I use instructor comments to improve my essay.   0 1 2 3 4 5
4. Teacher comments point out my weaknesses/ show me what I am doing wrong.   0 1 2 3 4 5
5. I am often confused by comments the instructor makes on my papers.   0 1 2 3 4 5
6. Teacher comments motivate me to improve my writing.   0 1 2 3 4 5
7. Without comments I wouldn't know how good my writing is.   0 1 2 3 4 5
8. Having teachers respond to my writing makes me feel like my ideas are worthwhile/important.   0 1 2 3 4 5
9. Comments help me know what my teacher wants.   0 1 2 3 4 5
10. Seeing comments on my essays makes me feel frustrated/anxious.   0 1 2 3 4 5
11. I look for a grade first and then skim the comments.   0 1 2 3 4 5
12. I assume the more comments an instructor writes, the worse my paper is.   0 1 2 3 4 5
13. I talk to the instructor if I don't understand a comment.   0 1 2 3 4 5

14. I generally don't read or use teacher comments.　　0 1 2 3 4 5
15. Reading teacher comments makes me think more　　0 1 2 3 4 5
deeply about my ideas and how I express them.
16. I often disagree with what my teacher says about　　0 1 2 3 4 5
my writing.
17. I like knowing what my teacher thinks about my　　0 1 2 3 4 5
writing.
18. I have difficulty reading or understanding what　　0 1 2 3 4 5
the comments say.
19. Comments help me understand how I am doing　　0 1 2 3 4 5
as a writer.
20. Teacher comments should tell me what to fix, so I　　0 1 2 3 4 5
can get a better grade.

Note

1. These student comments, which were freewritten without an opportunity
for editing by the students, have been proofread, with typos corrected to
focus attention on the content.

Works Cited

Across the Drafts: Students and Teachers Talk about Feedback. Harvard Expository Writing Program, 2005. DVD.

Anson, Chris M. "Reflective Reading: Developing Thoughtful Ways to Respond to Students' Writing." *Evaluating Writing.* Ed. Charles R. Cooper and Lee Odell. Urbana: NCTE, 1999. 302–24. Print.

Brannon, Lil, and Cy Knoblauch. "On Students' Right to Their Own Texts: A Model of Teacher Response." *College Composition and Communication* 32.2 (1982): 157–66. Print.

Burkland, Jill, and Nancy Grimm. "Motivating through Responding." *Journal of Teaching Writing* 5.2 (1986): 237–47. Print.

———. "Students' Response to Our Response, Parts I and II." Proc. of Conference on College Composition and Communication, 29–31 Mar. 1984, New York. *ERIC.* Web. ED 245241. 25 Aug. 2010.

Connors, Robert J., and Andrea A. Lunsford. "Teachers' Rhetorical Comments on Student Papers." *College Composition and Communication* 44.2 (1993): 200–223. Print.

DeGenaro, William, and Edward White. "Assessment and the Basic Writer." *Teaching Basic Writing.* McGraw-Hill, 2004. Web. 1 June 2006.

Dohrer, Gary. "Do Teachers' Comments on Students' Papers Help?" *College Teaching* 39.2 (1991): 48–54. Print.

Giberson, Greg. "Process Intervention: Teacher Response and Student Writing." *Teaching English in the Two-Year College* 29.4 (2002): 411–17. Print.

Hayes, Mary F., and Donald A. Daiker. "Using Protocol Analysis in Evaluating Responses to Student Writing." *Freshman English News* 13.2 (1984): 1–4, 10. Print.

Hodges, Elizabeth. "Negotiating the Margins: Some Principles for Responding to Our Students' Writing, Some Strategies for Helping Students Read Our Comments." *Writing to Learn: Strategies for Assigning and Responding to Writing Across the Disciplines.* Ed. Mary Deane Sorcinelli and Peter Elbow. San Francisco: Jossey-Bass, 1997. 77–89. Print.

Jackson, Ina, James Carifo, and Lorraine Dagostino. "The Effect of Diagnostic and Prescriptive Comments on Revising Behavior of Community College Students." US Dept. of Ed. 1998. *ERIC.* Web. ED 417449. 25 Aug. 2010.

Land, Robert E., Jr., and Sandra Evans. "What Our Students Taught Us about Paper Marking." *English Journal* 76.2 (1987): 113–16. Print.

Mitchler, Sharon. "Writing Back." *Teaching English in the Two-Year College* 33.4 (2006): 446–54. Print.

Sipple, Susan. "Ideas in Practice: Developmental Writers' Attitudes toward Audio and Written Feedback." *Journal of Developmental Education* 30.3 (2007): 22–31. Print.

Smith, Summer. "The Genre of the End Comment: Conventions in Teacher Responses to Student Writing." *College Composition and Communication* 48.2 (1997): 249–68. Print.

Sommers, Nancy. "Across the Drafts." *College Composition and Communication* 58.2 (2006): 248–56. Print.

Sommers, Nancy, and Laura Saltz. "The Novice as Expert: Writing the Freshman Year." *College Composition and Communication* 56.1 (2004): 124–49. Print.

Straub, Richard. "Students' Reactions to Teacher Comments: An Exploratory Study." *Research in the Teaching of English* 31.1 (1997): 91–119. Print.

Straub, Richard, and Ronald F. Lunsford. *12 Readers Reading: Responding to College Student Writing.* Cresskill: Hampton, 1995. Print.

Wootten, Judith, et al. "The First Two Years: Spaces for Change." Featured Sess. Conf. on Coll. Composition and Communication. Chicago. 23 Mar. 2006. Presentation.

Ziv, Nina Dansky. "The Effect of Teacher Comments on the Writing of Four College Freshmen." *New Directions in Composition Research.* Ed. Richard Beach and Lillian Bridwell. New York: Guilford, 1984. *ERIC.* Web. ED 203317. 25 Aug. 2010.

Teaching Academic Literacies

The Myth of Transience

David Russell

"About 30 years ago" says author David Russell, *"I hatched the ideas in this introductory chapter—and the idea for the whole book—while I was teaching nights at two community colleges in Oklahoma City, and tutoring Tuesdays and Thursdays in the University of Oklahoma writing center (then located, as is so often the case, in a musty basement). All this while my wife was working the graveyard shift, and three kids not yet in school. I had students from all walks of life, as happens in community colleges. And it struck me, day after day, that Mike Rose was right that there is what he called the 'myth of transience' in American higher education—the notion that writing is a 'problem' that will someday go away. And this myth really hurts people. Too many students are told they aren't good enough. Too many teachers from all disciplines look down on students for their writing 'problems' rather than having the pleasure of helping their students learn a field through writing. I wanted to understand how we got to this point. And I wanted hope for a way out. In the 30 years since then, the WAC movement has grown to the point that I have hope that the myth of transience will finally be put to rest—if we take the long historical view, and keep working day by day to begin where students are with their writing and learning."*

From *Writing in the Academic Disciplines: A Curricular History*, 2nd ed. Southern Illinois University Press, 2002, pp. 3-10.

W*riting in the Academic Disciplines* is a history of writing instruction outside general-composition courses in American secondary and higher education, from the founding of the public secondary school system and research universities in the 1870s through the spread of the writing-across-the-curriculum movement in the 1980s. The vexed history of general-composition courses, especially freshman composition, has been told often and well by James A. Berlin, Wallace W. Douglas, Albert R. Kitzhaber, Robert J. Connors, and many others upon whom I often draw in this account. But my task here is to examine the ways writing has been taught—directly or indirectly—in the wider curriculum or, to be more precise, in the myriad curricula that make up the differentiated structure of secondary and higher education in modern America.

As surprising as it may seem to us today, there was no systematic writing instruction per se past the elementary school in America until the advent of mass education and the formation of discrete academic disciplines in the last third of the nineteenth century. Advanced instruction in vernacular language dates from antiquity, of course, and from the eighteenth century American colleges and preparatory academies taught rhetoric in the vernacular. But before the 1870s, writing was ancillary to speaking. Because the whole curriculum and much of the extracurriculum was based on public speaking (recitation, declamation, oratory, debate), there was little need for systematic writing instruction.

The Triumph of Specialization

For a speaker, writing was merely an aid to memory; for a reader, it was merely a substitute for a present speaker (private oral reading was still common well into the nineteenth century). The leadership roles which graduates of the old college commonly assumed—"the pulpit, the senate, and the bar"—also made writing ancillary to public speaking. Thus, formal writing instruction essentially amounted to training in handwriting, the mechanical process of transcribing sound to visual form. Literacy meant knowing one's ABCs. Once these orthographic conventions were mastered, "correct" writing was an ordinary outcome of being raised a gentleman or gentlewoman who spoke "correct" English, which is to say the language of the upper class. As Susan Miller has persuasively argued, writing was so embedded in the everyday orally based practices of that class that it was largely transparent and required little or no instruction beyond the elementary school.[1]

By the 1870s, however, the role of writing in education and in the wider culture had begun to shift in subtle but profound ways. America created a host of new professions whose members communicated primarily through texts that were never meant merely to be substitutes for oral communication: the myriad reports, memoranda, specifications, scholarly articles, and so on, which modern society developed. Professionals in and out of academia now used writing to manipulate texts as objects, to be silently studied, critiqued, compared, appreciated, and evaluated. With the revolution in print technology (the modern pen, Linotype, vastly improved presses, typewriter, duplicating machines, vertical files, etc.) and the parallel revolutions in industry (systematic management of far-flung enterprises) and in academia (disciplinary specialization), writing became central to organizing production and creating new knowledge,[2] Writing was now embedded in a whole array of complex and highly differentiated social practices carried on without face-to-face communication. The new professionals (academic or otherwise) increasingly wrote not for a general reader (that is, for any member of the educated class) but rather for specialized audiences of colleagues who were united not primarily by ties of class but by the shared activities, the goals, and—this is crucial—the unique written conventions of a profession or discipline. With this enormous expansion of specialized knowledge and discourse, writing became, as Miller puts it, "a way of thinking, not just a way of preserving thinking for speech" (64).

Unfortunately, the new mass-education system America created to train this cadre of professionals failed to adjust its concept of writing to account for the fact that both writing and education had been transformed. In the new print-centered, compartmentalized secondary and higher-education system, writing was no longer a single, generalizable skill learned once and for all at an early age; rather it was a complex and continuously developing response to specialized text-based discourse communities, highly embedded in the differentiated practices of those communities. Nor was academia any longer a single discourse community but a collection of discrete communities, an aggregate of competing professional disciplines, each with its own specialized written discourse. Moreover, the system of secondary and higher education, once confined to the preparatory academy and the liberal arts college, now widened to include a whole spectrum of differentiated institutions (land-grant universities, technical institutes, public high schools, business schools, trade schools, etc.) preparing and credentialing students for a host of social roles. Each discipline, each kind of institution, developed its own "literacy," its own tacit expectations about how its members (and its students) should write.[3] Despite these profound changes, the mass-education system tenaciously clung to the outmoded conception of writing as transcribed speech and to the vanishing ideal of a single academic community, united by common values, goals, and standards of discourse. Operating together, these misconceptions had profound consequences for writing instruction.

One important result was a conceptual split between "content" and "expression," learning and writing. If writing was an elementary, mechanical skill, then it had no direct relation to the goals of instruction and could be relegated to the margins of a course, a curriculum, an institution. Knowledge and its expression could be conceived of as separate activities, with written expression of the "material" of the course a kind of adjunct to the "real" business of education, the teaching of factual knowledge. From very early in the history of mass education, writing was primarily thought of as a way to examine students, not to teach them, as a means of demonstrating knowledge rather than of acquiring it. Though a few reformers struggled to overcome this false distinction, they never had widespread success, and academia never made writing a central part of teaching in the disciplines.

Another, more visible result of these misconceptions is a 120-year tradition of complaint about student writing (which Harvey Daniels has amusingly chronicled in *Famous Last Words*).[4] Because academics and other professionals assumed that writing was a generalizable, elementary skill and that academia held a universal, immutable standard of literacy, they were constantly disappointed when student writing failed to measure up to the local, and largely tacit, standards of a particular social class, institution, discipline, or profession by which they were in fact judging that writing. Educators produced report after report lamenting the "crisis" in student writing, secure in their assumption that writing was simply a form of talking rather than a complex and developing response to a community's discourse—a mode of learning, in other words. In 1892 one of the first Harvard committees charged with the task of "solving" the "writing problem" thought it "a little less than absurd to suggest that any human being who can be taught to talk cannot likewise be taught to compose. Writing is merely the habit of talking with the pen instead of the tongue."[5] Over the next century, committees of faculty and business leaders repeatedly expressed similar frustration that students had not "learned to write" by the time they reached high school or college or graduate school or career. But the complaints rarely addressed the central issue: standards of literacy were no longer stable; they were rising and, more importantly, multiplying. Thus, Miller concludes,

> our natural tendency to inform contemporary education with this still-active aspect of an oral residue is also an implicit source for laments for what is curiously always thought of as the recently lost excellence of student discourse. But such nostalgia does not acknowledge . . . [that] literacy must, because of multiplied fields of writing, be relearned in new contexts throughout educational processes and later. We never get "beyond" writing to oratory as the ancients did in their educational sequence, nor can we stabilize writing's conventions and merely reapply school writing in new settings [66].

The assumption that writing was "talking with the pen," an elementary transcription skill, mistakenly led educators to look for a single solution to a specific educational problem when they actually needed a whole new conception of the role of writing in learning, one that would take into account the modern organization of knowledge through written communication. They persisted in holding on to what Mike Rose has called the "myth of transience." "Despite the accretion of crisis reports, the belief persists in the American university that if we can just do *x*, or *y*, the problem [of poor student writing] will be solved—in five years, ten years, or a generation—and higher education will be able to return to its real work."[6] Because writing seemed to be independent of content learning, the many solutions proposed over the years tended to marginalize writing instruction and reinforce the myth of transience by masking the complexities of the task.

The first and most common "solution" was a general-composition course. When late-nineteenth-century educators cast about for ways to solve the "problem" of students' writing, they eventually settled on a single freshman course of about fifteen or thirty weeks (successor to a very different rhetoric course in the old liberal curriculum). Though it was taught in many ways to students of every kind, freshman composition almost always treated writing as a generalizable elementary skill, independent of disciplinary content. The course focused on mechanical skills: correct grammar, spelling, and usage necessary for transcribing preexisting, fully formed speech or thought into correct written form. The teaching of rhetoric, so central to the old oratorical tradition, gradually faded, though not without a fight, to be replaced by general composition. Writing instruction was denied disciplinary status, compartmentalized into freshman composition, and housed in English departments, where it competed (unsuccessfully) with the new professional discipline of literary study. In time, freshman English became ubiquitous, nearly always the only institutionwide requirement for writing instruction (or writing) in higher education. And with systematic writing instruction thus marginalized, there arose an implicit assumption that general-composition courses should teach students from any background to write correct and coherent expository prose for any purpose in any social or disciplinary context—and that a student's failure to do so was evidence of the need for more elementary training or *remediation,* as it came to be called.

When general-composition courses did not succeed in this impossible task (despite countless experiments and reforms), institutions sometimes tried curriculumwide schemes. Though the phrase *writing across the curriculum* is relatively new, dating from the mid 1970s, the idea of sharing responsibility for writing instruction forms a recurrent theme throughout the history of American secondary and higher education. Like so many other educational reform movements, cross-curricular writing instruction was accepted in principle ("Every teacher should teach writing" is one of the oldest saws in American education), but in practice, reforms were absorbed and transmuted by the system they resisted. In this way reformers' ideas lost their power for change and instead merely reinforced the myth of transience, a process educational historians have long noted in other areas.[7]

There have been literally hundreds of cross-curricular writing programs since the turn of the century at institutions of every type. Indeed, each generation has produced its own versions of cross-curricular writing programs, yet none, except perhaps the last, has made a permanent impact on the modern university curriculum or on literacy in America. Sooner or later these programs were marginalized for many of the same reasons general-composition courses were. Because administrators and faculty did not perceive the central role of writing in modern academic disciplines and professional work, they tended to make writing instruction an adjunct to a course or program rather than an integral part of it. When they did require writing as part of regular courses in the disciplines, that writing was less likely to be integrated into the activity of the course or program and more likely to be seen merely as a favor to the English department or the institution, as a way of enforcing standards of correctness or reinforcing general-composition courses, or as a means of evaluation.[8] The most mechanical aspects of writing received the most attention: "grammar across the curriculum," as C. W. Knoblauch and Lil Brannon have termed it.[9] Even disciplines that took responsibility for writing instruction tended to marginalize writing in special departmental writing courses (e.g., business writing, agricultural writing). Thus, the conceptual split between content and expression found its curricular embodiment not only in remedial or general-composition courses but also in discipline-specific writing courses taught by those outside the discipline (usually trained in English departments).

In the rush to find a single comprehensive solution, academia never systematically examined the nature of writing or its potential for improving learning. The myth of transience masked deep conflicts in the mass-education system over the nature of writing and learning: what is academic writing and how is it learned? What is an academic community and who should be admitted? America has never come to terms with the submerged conflicts that underlie its attitudes and approaches to advanced literacy. And this continuing failure to confront those conflicts kept writing instruction on the margins of the curriculum rather than at its center. As Rose concludes, "Wide-ranging change will occur only if the academy redefines writing for itself, changes the terms of the argument, [and] sees instruction in writing as one of its central concerns" (359).

These deep conflicts emerge as themes in my account of America's century-long flirtation with writing instruction in the disciplines. And [here] I outline four of these conflicts as a framework for the story which follows. The first two have to do with the nature of writing and its acquisition: writing as a single elementary skill, a transparent recording of speech or thought or physical reality, versus writing as a complex rhetorical activity, embedded in the differentiated practices of academic discourse communities; and writing acquisition as remediation of deficiencies in skill versus writing acquisition as a continuously developing intellectual and social attainment tied to disciplinary learning. The second two conflicts center on the relation between language and the structure of mass education: academia as a single discourse community versus academia as many competing discourse communities; and disciplinary excellence versus social equity as the goal of writing instruction. By bringing these long-submerged conflicts into the light of historical analysis, it may be easier to see the enormity and complexity of the task that American mass education set for itself in teaching students "to write."

Notes

1. For the following analysis, I am deeply indebted to Susan Miller, *Rescuing the Subject: A Critical Introduction to Rhetoric and the Writer* (Carbondale: Southern Illinois UP, 1989) chap. 2.
2. On the expanding role of writing in industrial management, see JoAnne Yates, *Control through Communication: The Rise of System in American Management* (Baltimore: Johns Hopkins UP, 1989).
3. From the mid nineteenth century to the late twentieth, definitions of adult literacy rose from the ability to write one's signature or recognize letters to the ability to read and write at a twelfth-grade level. On increasing standards of literacy in response to industrialization, see Jeanne S. Chall, "Developing Literacy . . . in Children and Adults," in *The Future of Literacy in a Changing World*, ed. Daniel A. Wagner (Oxford: Pergamon, 1987): 65–80.
4. Harvey Daniels, *Famous Last Words: The American Language Crisis Reconsidered* (Carbondale: Southern Illinois U P, 1983); see also Leonard A. Greenbaum, "A Tradition of Complaint," *College English* 31 (1969): 174–78.
5. "Report of the Committee on Composition and Rhetoric," no. 28 in *Reports of the Visiting Committees of the Board of Overseers of Harvard College*, 1902, 155 (HUA).
6. Mike Rose, "The Language of Exclusion: Writing Instruction at the University," *College English* 47 (1985): 355.
7. For studies of the appropriation of progressive ideas, see David B. Tyack, *The One Best System: A History of American Urban Education* (Cambridge, MA: Harvard UP, 1974); Michael B. Katz, *Class, Bureaucracy, and Schools* (New York: Praeger, 1971); and Roderic C. Botts, "Influences in the Teaching of English, 1917–1935: An Illusion of Progress," diss., Northwestern U, 1970.
8. See, for example, Christopher Thaiss, "The Future of Writing Across the Curriculum," in *Strengthening Programs for Writing Across the Curriculum*, ed. Susan H. McLeod (San Francisco: Jossey, 1988) 94; Tori Haring-Smith, "What's Wrong with Writing across the Curriculum?" CCCC Convention, Atlanta, Mar. 1987.
9. C. W. Knoblauch and Lil Brannon, "Writing as Learning through the Curriculum," *College English* 45 (1983): 465–74.

Works Cited

Botts, Roderic C. "Influences in the Teaching of English, 1917–1935: An Illusion of Progress." Diss. Northwestern U, 1970.

Daniels, Harvey. *Famous Last Words: The American Language Crisis Reconsidered*. Carbondale: Southern Illinois UP, 1983.

Greenbaum, Leonard A. "A Tradition of Complaint." *College English* 31 (1969): 174–78.

Haring-Smith, Tori, ed. *A Guide to Writing Programs: Writing Centers, Peer Tutoring Programs, and Writing Across the Curriculum*. Glenview, IL: Scott Foresman, 1987.

Katz, Michael B. *Class, Bureaucracy, and Schools*. New York: Praeger, 1971.

Knoblauch, C. W., and Lil Brannon. "Writing as Learning Through the Curriculum." *College English* 45 (1983): 465–74.

McLeod, Susan H., ed. *Strengthening Programs for Writing Across the Curriculum*. San Francisco: Jossey, 1998.

Miller, Susan. *Rescuing the Subject: A Critical Introduction to Rhetoric and the Writer*. Carbondale: Southern Illinois UP, 1989.

Rose, Mike. "The Language of Exclusion: Writing Instruction at the University." *College English* 47 (1985): 341–59.

Thaiss, Christopher. *Language Across the Curriculum in the Elementary Grades*. Urbana, IL: NCTE, 1986.

Tyack, David B. *The One Best System: A History of American Urban Education*. Cambridge: Harvard UP, 1974.

Yates, JoAnne. *Control Through Communication: The Rise of System in American Management*. Baltimore: Johns Hopkins UP, 1989.

Community College Teachers as Border Crossers

Howard Tinberg

The selection that follows is the introduction to Howard Tinberg's book Border Talk. *According to the author, "Community colleges reside 'between places,' between K–12 and four-year colleges, and, since many students are either working or planning to go directly into a job after taking community college courses, between school and the workplace. Rather than this being problematic, community colleges might exploit their position and become 'border-crossers,' able to bridge the gap between generalized and specialized knowledge, between one discipline and another, and between academic and workplace literacies. This excerpt serves as an introduction to an ethnographic account of a three-week summer workshop in which community college faculty from varied disciplines met to discuss what they valued in student writing. In so doing, these faculty members were able to cross*

From *Border Talk: Writing and Knowing in the Two-Year College*, NCTE, 1997, pp. vii-xiii.

departmental and programmatic lines to share their expertise. These exchanges yielded a set of shared values regarding student writing even as they revealed meaningful differences."

Crossing the border evokes ambivalent images. . . .

—Ruth Behar

To teach at a community college is to be "in translation" or between places. With their mission to provide vocational training and to prepare students for transfer to colleges and universities, community colleges have always had a complex purpose (Cohen and Brawer 1982). That complexity colors instruction at all times. What we teach and how we teach must reflect the diverse needs of our students, the needs of those who plan to transfer to four-year institutions and the needs of those who intend to enter the workplace immediately upon graduating from the community college; the needs of traditionally aged students and the needs of so-called returning students, who have spent years out of school. A poem, for example, must be read and taught to suit the complexities of the community college classroom. How will their histories shade students' readings?

The task of tailoring instruction to students' histories and needs has become even more complex as students' numbers increase. The expansion of community college enrollment since the 1960s has been well documented. As of 1988, when the Commission on the Future of Community Colleges published *Building Communities*, nearly half of all undergraduates in the United States attended community colleges (*Building* 1988).

It is hardly surprising, given the range and complexity of our task, that community college faculty are perceived as overworked. But what usually follows is an assumption that community college faculty are teaching drones, burned-out husks of what we once were, with little time and inclination to stay up-to-date on current scholarship and research. In one recent study, two researchers of the community college scene declared that community colleges were everywhere experiencing an "academic crisis," their faculty facing the prospects of little promotion and doomed to teach the same courses year after year (McGrath and Spear 1991). Two-year college faculty, they assert, simply have little opportunity to engage in dialogue with colleagues even down the corridor, let alone in other institutions. They spend more and more class time teaching basic or remedial skills, not the college-level courses that they thought they would be teaching when they began. That picture would seem to be supported by a profile done of a single community college during the 1970s, in which faculty member after faculty member testified to the hindrances to teaching (London 1978). "Sometimes they make life a little difficult," says a math teacher of her students:

and they come in not having read the chapter that was assigned for the week, not even having tried the home work. Then I usually just go back, give a brief lecture, and then we talk our way through the chapter. Sometimes most of them come in unprepared. (117)

While they describe real problems facing community college teachers, such studies yield very little information about the reflection that accompanies the teaching that two-year college faculty do. We rarely see or hear faculty theorizing about their discipline or their teaching (trying to solve, for example, the problem of why students are not reading their texts). In short, we see very little of community college teachers at work—preparing lessons, adjusting to the classroom moment, engaging in thoughtful reflection and dialogue.

The image of community college faculty as workhorse teachers is reinforced in a survey done by the Carnegie Foundation. More than 90 percent polled said that they were more interested in teaching than in research. The question was phrased, "Do your interests lie primarily in research or in teaching?" (Boyer 1990, 44). Given the either/or option, the faculty responded in a way that could be hardly surprising. The problem is that the question perpetuates the illogical separation of teaching and research.

In recent years, certain calls have gone out that we reconsider the nature of research and scholarship, and their relationship to teaching (Boyer 1990; Vaughan 1994; Tinberg, "Border-Crossings" 1993). Ernest Boyer, an influential voice, has called for a "scholarship of teaching" (1990, 23). Some have actually argued that we see classroom activities as the fit subject of research in [their] own right. In composition studies, methods borrowed from fields such as psychology and anthropology—the case study, the oral history, the ethnography—have had an important impact (Kantor, Kirby, and Goetz 1981; Calkins 1985). With the renewed emphasis on teaching (as opposed to research) and on cross-disciplinary learning, such classroom research has inspired a tremendous amount of interest in a short time (Angelo and Cross 1993; Goswami and Stillman 1987; Daiker and Morenberg 1990; Ray 1993).

But such calls have the net effect of further segregating teaching from another, more privileged form of research and scholarship (which Boyer renames "the scholarship of discovery" [17]). Classroom research runs the danger, in my view, of being the things that teachers do when they can't do the "right" kind of research.

More interesting and more profound have been attempts to engage in, to use Henry Giroux's metaphor, "border crossings" (Giroux 1992). By that Giroux means excursions between distinct disciplines and between distinct ways of knowing. The old walls, the old borders between one field and another, simply have lost their usefulness. Giroux argues for a pedagogy centered on "new languages capable of acknowledging the multiple, contradictory, and complex positions people occupy" (21). "Central" to this new pedagogy, he writes, "is the importance of challenging, remapping, and renegotiating those boundaries of knowledge" (26). What this remapping involves is viewing our own disciplines through the lens of another: to wear the difference, as it were, and, in the process, achieve some common ground.

To remap the terrain of knowledge—as ambitious as that might sound—ought to be the goal of teachers who want to engage in scholarship and research. To discover a language that partakes of "border talk" ought to be the means and the end of our inquiry. By "border talk" I mean a language that has currency across the divides between disciplines and institutions, between the local and the global, the practical and the theoretical, the private and the public, the two-year college and the research university. The walls remain, but the translation between becomes the thing.

The work that follows is an attempt at translation, a translation of the work and talk that teachers do. I intend to report what I observed when several colleagues from a variety of disciplines at my community college, along with a group of peer tutors, came together in the summer of 1994 to talk about writing, reading, and knowing. After serving during the previous semester as staff for our college's writing lab, we could now reflect on what we had learned and what we had yet to learn.

My mode of discourse will be as mixed as the border talk heard during those sessions: narratives, journals, and interviews will complement the traditionally academic analysis and argument. The personal will complement the public. As Mary Louise Pratt informs us, personal narratives are as much part of the ethnographic tradition as so-called "objective . . . practices" and much is to be gained from the mingling of the two (1986, 32). Indeed, postmodern ethnographers derive their authority from being part of the picture rather than outside of it (Rosaldo 1993). The truths that emerge from such work, argues James Clifford, are "inherently *partial*—committed and incomplete," but nonetheless authoritative (1986, 7). As I have argued elsewhere, teachers—no matter the institution or discipline—are implicated in their classroom narratives (Tinberg, "Border-Crossings," 9). Decisions that they make—from text selection and syllabi to the arrangement of seats in a circle—influence what happens in their classrooms.

The account that follows will contain many voices, the voices of those engaged and thoughtful colleagues who shared their time and their concerns during our summer sessions. They talked frankly about teaching in their disciplines—and did so with an informed expertise that was truly impressive.

Community college faculty are in a prime position to initiate such an exchange across borders because we live on the borders, as it were. We work in the space between the schools and the universities. In our teaching, we traverse the middle ground between the needs of those who will transfer to the university and those who will enter the working world directly from our classes. Many of us, indeed, have partaken of both the academic and the workaday worlds ourselves. Jerry, from our college's mathematics department, recalled to me the days he drove a truck for a living:

> I drove a truck and made deliveries. These guys called me "teach" even back then, because I had a high school education. Some of them were totally illiterate. By the way, the tags on the bags were color-coded so they could load the right things on the truck.

It is an experience that he continues to draw on as a way to engage his students who are

> out working in machine shops, driving a truck, out on fishing boats. If you can understand the problems that these people are facing right now—and I did it all the way through college, working fifty to fifty-five hours a week when I was in college—if they can understand that you care, they will get something from you. They will understand that your experience is the same as theirs and that you have gone beyond them and that you have something to offer them.

Marlene, a historian, recalls vividly her days working in a factory, which was an attempt to understand the very workers whose lives she was committed to improving. Raised in the upper-middle-class community of Shaker Heights, Ohio, Marlene noted that her father was a high school dropout who had been forced to go to work during the Depression. She observed that she and her family never quite "fit in" in what she called the elitist community where she was raised. The tumultuous political movements taking place in the 1960s showed her that others shared her experience and provided the catalyst for her desire to improve the lot of others.

In a certain sense, we community college faculty are quintessentially postmodern. We possess no single identity, but rather have shifting and blurred identities. Like the subject of postmodern anthropology, we move in a variety of worlds. We are the educational "mestizas," the translatable teachers. I am reminded of what the anthropologist Ruth Behar observes about writing as a woman ethnographer (who happens also to be a Cuban-born Jew):

> The feminist ethnographer is a dual citizen, who shuttles between the country of the academy and the country of feminism. She's an odd kind of bilingual woman. To her subjects she speaks in a tongue bristling with seductive promises that she will not be able to keep. To her colleagues, she must speak in a way that will persuade them that "working" on another woman is a contribution to the discipline she has vowed to serve; they will ultimately judge her work on the basis of how well she can translate the other woman's tongue into a language they can understand. (1993, 297–98)

My goal, in the ethnography to follow, is to shuttle between places in an "odd kind of bilingual" dance—between theory and practice, between teaching and research, between one discipline and another. We will hear discussions ranging from the theoretical question of how we know what we know to the more grounded terrain of what we must do in our classrooms and in our writing centers to improve student writing.

As I sit here at my computer . . . , I am thinking back on what it is like to occupy the space between. A Ph.D. steeped in literary theory and trained in the traditional canon, I strain here and in my classroom to find a language that has currency for theorists as well as for practitioners. I publish, I give papers at professional conferences, and I teach. I work to connect all these activities; I try to translate them across borders. In my professional writing, I try to strike a balance between the public and the private, the academic and the expressive, the abstract and the classroom-based. In my teaching, I seek to use theory as guide to my practice and look to practice to engender theory.

But in bringing theory to discussions of classroom practice at my community college, I run the risk of being seen as "too good" for this place, too high-powered, too Ph.D. (I have actually been told by colleagues that it was only a matter of time before I "moved on.") And as a community college teacher who writes often about my classroom experiences I often run the risk of not seeming scholarly enough to pass muster in professional journals. As I struggle along the borders, I see myself as occupying a "contact zone," the place where, according to Pratt, cultures interact and influence each other. The language that emerges from such a zone "interlock[s] understandings and practices" (1992, 7).

Looking back at our summer workshop, I now see that we were straining to produce that very kind of language ourselves. It was not simply that we were looking to find a common language with which to talk about writing and knowing (as generalists, we felt quite comfortable with the notion). We were also attempting to see whether we could translate to one another the differences that defined us as teachers of psychology, nursing, dental hygiene, literature, history, business, mathematics, and ESL. In my mind, that was the greater challenge.

Essentially, we were to focus, during the workshop, on three questions: What does it mean to write and know in the disciplines? How do we respond effectively to the writing our students do in our courses? And, finally, what do we need to say and do when tutoring students outside of the classroom (when they visit our writing lab)? In answering these questions, we hoped to produce two important documents (which we called "communiqués"): a revised statement of "primary traits" or what constitutes "good writing" at our college (building on the statement generated by colleagues at a similar workshop held the previous summer), and a tutoring protocol describing ways to facilitate student learning in a tutoring session.

It was an open question as to whether we would be comfortable talking about discipline-specific ways of writing and knowing. After all, here we were, committed to the community college mission, committed to the mission of general education. Although we were trained to teach our own specialized subject areas, we also saw ourselves as giving students reading, writing, and thinking skills to enable them to flourish in the workplace as well as in academic settings. Does a specialized view of knowledge and knowledge-making truly apply to teaching at the community college? we asked ourselves. Are we interested in promoting this specialized view of knowledge or a more generalized or transferable view? "Everything that rises must converge," wryly observed Peter, from the English department. His point was that disciplinary knowledge, if it is to be humane and useful, must offer common ground. And yet, as we talked among ourselves and drew from our own disciplinary perspectives, we asked whether there were disciplinary boundaries or categories that define the work we do, boundaries or categories that perhaps we should make explicit to our students. Marlene, a historian, and Chris, from the psychology department, had the following exchange on the matter:

> *Marlene:* Students will ask, "What do you mean, 'define the Renaissance'?" Well, was it the same for the peasants as it was for the elite? The more I talk the more I elaborate but I am also letting out the choices for them. . . . I don't have a concept of where I want them to arrive.

> *Chris:* I think you did, from what you were just saying. What you wanted them to do was bring class analysis to answer that question. An economic analysis of the question of the Renaissance. That's actually one of your categories. One of the lenses through which you want your students to see history.

Although class analysis does not belong solely to the study of history, it is for Marlene an important "lens" through which *she* views history. The question for Marlene as an instructor becomes whether she is willing and able to articulate that perspective to her community college students, to lay it out there from the start. Marlene, for her part, construes the act of "giving" her students this kind of information as somehow restricting their choices. She operates from an instinct that most community college teachers have, which is to teach in a way that does not exclude—to produce, in essence, generally educated students. And yet her expectations of students' responses to that assignment seem to be shaped by a class or economic perspective.

Articulating disciplinary ways of knowing, Judith Langer tells us, is no simple or easy task (1992, 83). I might add that it becomes especially challenging at the community college. Not only must we be able to view and understand our discipline's conceptual categories but we must then render them in a language that is useful in the classroom. But even beyond these considerations—as intimidating as they are—is the concern that Kathy, our ESL specialist, raised: "At the two-year college level, how many of our students are actually being asked to write as a historian writes? or asked to write like a psychologist? How much of this is going to be practical at the two-year college?" The need to be "practical," to focus on what works for our students and for the careers and lives they face outside our classrooms, becomes the driving force for a great many of us who teach at the community college. The question then becomes this: Can we at the community college offer knowledge that is *both* specialized and generally useful?

Works Cited

Angelo, Thomas A., and K. Patricia Cross. 1993. *Classroom Assessment Techniques: A Handbook for College Teachers*. San Francisco: Jossey-Bass.

Behar, Ruth. 1993. *Translated Woman: Crossing the Border with Esperanza's Story*. Boston: Beacon.

Boyer, Ernest L. *Scholarship Reconsidered: Priorities of the Professoriate*. 1990. Princeton: Carnegie Foundation for the Advancement of Teaching.

Building Communities: A Vision for a New Century. 1988. Washington, DC: American Association of Community and Junior Colleges, National Center for Higher Education.

Calkins, Lucy M. 1985. "Forming Research Communities among Naturalistic Researchers." In Ben W. McClelland and Timothy R. Donovan, eds. *Perspectives on Research and Scholarship in Composition*. New York: Modern Language Association. 125–44.

Clifford, James. 1986. "Introduction: Partial Truths." In James Clifford and George E. Marcus, eds. *Writing Culture: The Poetics and Politics of Ethnography*. Berkeley: University of California Press. 1–26.

Cohen, Arthur M., and Florence B. Brawer. 1982. *The American Community College*. San Francisco: Jossey-Bass.

Daiker, Donald, and Max Morenberg. 1990. *The Writing Teacher as Researcher: Essays in the Theory and Practice of Class-Based Research*. Portsmouth, NH: Boynton/Cook.

Giroux, Henry. 1992. *Border Crossings: Cultural Workers and the Politics of Education*. New York: Routledge.

Goswami, Dixie, and Peter Stillman, eds. 1987. *Reclaiming the Classroom: Teacher Research as an Agency for Change*. Upper Montclair, NJ: Boynton/Cook.

Kantor, Kenneth J., Dan R. Kirby, and Judith P. Goetz. 1981. "Research in Context: Ethnographic Studies in English Education." *Research in the Teaching of English* 15:293–309.

Langer, Judith A. 1992. "Speaking of Knowing: Conceptions of Understanding in Academic Disciplines." In Ann Herrington and Charles Moran, eds. *Writing, Teaching, and Learning in the Disciplines*. New York: Modern Language Association. 69–85.

London, Howard. 1978. *The Culture of a Community College*. New York: Praeger.

McGrath, Dennis, and Martin B. Spear. 1991. *The Academic Crisis of the Community College.* Albany: State University of New York Press.

Pratt, Mary Louise. 1986. "Fieldwork in Common Places." In James Clifford and George E. Marcus, eds. *Writing Culture: The Poetics and Politics of Ethnography.* Berkeley: University of California Press. 27–50.

———. 1992. *Imperial Eyes: Travel Writing and Transmigration.* London and New York: Routledge.

Ray, Ruth E. 1993. *The Practice of Theory: Teacher Research in Composition.* Urbana, IL: National Council of Teachers of English.

Rosaldo, Renato. 1993. *Culture and Truth: The Remaking of Social Analysis.* 2d ed. Boston: Beacon.

Tinberg, Howard B. 1993. "Border-Crossings: Shaping the Academic Conversation." *Advanced Composition Forum* 5:8–11.

Vaughan, George B. 1994. "Scholarship and Teaching: Crafting the Art." In Mark Reynolds, ed. *Two-Year College English: Essays for a New Century.* Urbana, IL: National Council of Teachers of English. 212–21.

PART FOUR

Rethinking "Business as Usual"

Because writing pedagogy has always evolved, the last several decades have produced significant changes for our discipline, particularly in relation to the two-year college. Some of these shifts have been research-driven, as scholarly developments in writing studies and education, along with changing literacy technologies, have reshaped teaching approaches at all types of institutions. Other shifts have been policy-driven. The Obama administration's initiatives to increase the percentage of Americans with postsecondary degrees, for example, have led to a dramatic surge of interest in community colleges among higher education researchers and policy makers. This sudden attention has created new opportunities as well as new pressures and demands for two-year college English faculty. In Part Four of this book, we highlight the different ways that two-year college teacher-scholars can engage with emerging research, theory, and policy to rethink "business as usual" in their writing classrooms and programs.

The first chapters in this section focus on two aspects of writing pedagogy that have undergone serious reconsideration in recent decades: genre and grammar instruction. Chapter 12 focuses on the five-paragraph essay. In "My Five-Paragraph-Theme Theme," a pastiche of the five-paragraph essay, writing assessment theorist Ed White highlights the rhetorical and intellectual limitations of this timeworn assignment type. We follow this with Michelle Tremmel's overview of the history of the five-paragraph essay, "What to Make of the Five-Paragraph Theme: History of the Genre and Implications." Tremmel describes the five-paragraph essay as a "pseudogenre" (p. 354 in this volume) that has had a negative impact on student learning and writing. Tremmel suggests that we eliminate the five-paragraph essay from our curriculum and replace it with more problem-based, "rich-task" writing experiences for students (p. 363). Tremmel's proposals align with recent developments in genre and transfer of learning theory.

Chapter 13 takes on an even more challenging and often poorly understood scholarly issue: the teaching of "grammar." In recent years, language diversity and language-level writing instruction has received renewed attention within the field of composition (Matsuda), and this is a particularly important pedagogical issue for teachers of writing at two-year colleges. In "Why Our Students Need Instruction in Grammar, and How We Should Go about It," Mark Blaauw-Hara synthesizes several decades of scholarship on grammar instruction demonstrating that decontextualized discussions of grammar "rules" have little or no impact on students' actual writing. While Blaauw-Hara concurs with the scholarly consensus that notions of grammatical "error" or "correctness" are ideologically constructed, he notes that there are important socioeconomic benefits to familiarity with the conventions of "standard" written English, and that two-year college students deserve access to the "linguistic landmarks of the culture of power" (p. 371). In this article, Blaauw-Hara presents a series of practical strategies for teaching grammar as a matter of rhetorical choice.

The theoretical trajectory that Blaauw-Hara traces in his work anticipates the pedagogical approach articulated by Debra Myhill, Susan Jones, Annabel Watson, and Helen Lines in their recent essay, "Playful Explicitness with Grammar: A Pedagogy for Writing." While their study was conducted with secondary-age students, the principles these scholars advocate have important implications for post-secondary writing instruction as well:

> Sams (2003) has argued that both traditional and in-context approaches to the teaching of grammar fail because "they treat grammar as something that exists apart from and outside of the writing process itself" (57): what we offer here is a role for grammar, coherently theorised within a pedagogy of writing, underpinned by metalinguistically aware teaching and learning, and framed by exploration, playfulness, and experimentation. (p. 397)

Taken together, these essays suggest that the question of grammar instruction in the writing classroom is not binary—do we or don't we?—but rather a matter of *how*, *why*, and *when*.

Finally, Chapter 14 focuses on the developmental education reform movement that has been reshaping writing instruction in two-year colleges across the country. This movement has been spurred by a series of influential studies emerging from the Community College Research Center (CCRC) at Columbia University's Teachers College. In a 2009 article that helped launch this movement, "Challenge and Opportunity: Rethinking the Role and Function of Developmental Education in Community College" (available online), Thomas Bailey surveyed an array of evidence and concluded that "developmental education as it is now practiced is not very effective in overcoming academic weaknesses" (12). Although controversial among educators, his call for "a major and much-needed effort to strengthen and rethink developmental education" (28) has been answered by a wave of reform initiatives nationwide. In some cases, this reform movement has created opportunities for faculty-led efforts to reimagine developmental literacy instruction at their colleges.

The scholarship featured in this chapter highlights recent work from two-year college teacher-scholars in our ongoing efforts to improve developmental education. Perhaps the most prominent example of this kind of innovative work is the curriculum developed at the Community College of Baltimore County. In "The Accelerated Learning Program: Throwing Open the Gates"—included here—Peter Adams, Sarah Gearhart, Robert Miller, and Anne Roberts present their Accelerated Learning Program (ALP) model, which has been adopted by colleges across the nation. ALP is distinguished by its faculty-driven ethos and grounding in disciplinary expertise, as well as its documented record of enhancing student success (Cho, Kopko, Jenkins, and Jaggars).

We follow this essay with the recent Two-Year College English Association (TYCA) "White Paper on Developmental Education Reforms," which offers a comprehensive portrait of the current state of developmental education reform and how it is affecting curricula, work conditions, and faculty professional authority in two-year colleges around the country. In some cases, state legislatures are mandating across-the-board reform measures that faculty must implement, sometimes with few resources and little opportunity for research or reflection. As readers will see, these policy developments are often spearheaded by philanthropists and higher education leaders who fail to take two-year college faculty perspectives and disciplinary expertise into account. For more on faculty-driven efforts to assert disciplinary authority over placement assessment at two-year colleges, see TYCA's 2016 "White Paper on Writing Placement Reform" (available online at http://www.ncte.org/tyca/positions).

We close this chapter with an excerpt from Mike Rose's *Back to School: Why Everyone Deserves a Second Chance at Education* (2012). Rose has had a long career as a teacher, scholar, writer, and activist, and he has been a vocal champion of the two-year college. The excerpt we present here provides historical, sociological, and political context for the current state of developmental education. Rose concludes by suggesting that

> we need to take basic-skills instruction out of the hinterland of higher education, liberate it from the academic snobbery and bankrupt assumptions about teaching and learning that profoundly limit its effectiveness. . . . This is not just a subject matter or institutional issue, but a civic and moral issue as well. (p. 439)

Two-year college writing instructors are deeply engaged in this civic and moral enterprise, and they have been at the forefront of efforts to develop theoretically sound, evidence-based pedagogical approaches to developmental education and basic writing since the 1960s. Clearly, any attempt to design and implement more socially just educational structures for the nation's increasingly diverse postsecondary student population must include the input and expertise of two-year college teacher-scholars.

There are, of course, many other aspects of writing instruction — some specific to two-year colleges, some that transcend institution type — that are currently undergoing significant rethinking, far more than we could fit into this chapter. These include the integration of multimodal and digital literacies into writing pedagogies; the growing awareness of our need to engage in "translingual work" in the writing classroom (Lu and Horner); the recognition and inclusion of diverse codes and language varieties into academic writing; and evolving models for writing program administration in two-year colleges. We invite readers to explore these issues through the rich discussions unfolding in TYCA-affiliated forums.

Works Cited

Bailey, Thomas. "Challenge and Opportunity: Rethinking the Role and Function of Developmental Education in Community College." *New Directions for Community Colleges*, vol. 2009, no. 145, 2009, pp. 11-30.

Cho, Sung-Woo, Elizabeth Kopko, Davis Jenkins, and Shanna Smith Jaggars. "New Evidence of Success for Community College Remedial English Students: Tracking the Outcomes of Students in the Accelerated Learning Program (ALP)." CCRC Working Paper No. 53. December 2012. Web.

Klausman, Jeff, et al. "TYCA White Paper on Writing Placement Reform." *Teaching English in the Two-Year College*, vol. 44, no. 2, 2016, forthcoming.

Lu, Min-Zhan, and Bruce Horner. "Introduction: Translingual Work." Translingual Work in Composition. Special issue of *College English*, vol. 78, no. 3, 2016, pp. 207-18.

Matsuda, Paul Kei. "It's the Wild West Out There: A New Linguistic Frontier in US College Composition." *Literacy as Translingual Practice: Between Communities and Classrooms*, edited by Suresh Canagarajah, Routledge, pp. 128-38.

Rethinking the Five-Paragraph Essay

My Five-Paragraph-Theme Theme

Ed White

The old guy who asked me to write about why I like the five-paragraph theme—and then went on to say all kinds of stuff criticizing what I wrote—has asked me now to write a headnote for it for this book. I'm doing it for the following three reasons. First, because he is me way in the future and he can make me do it whether I want to or not. Second, his take on education is way different from what we think in high school nowadays. And third, lots of people have read my article since I wrote it and they like it a lot, so it must be good, whatever he thinks.

The first reason just means he has the power and I don't. As one of my friends likes to say, you can make me write but you can't make me think. I write to pass tests and I almost always get an A. End of story.

The second reason is that I'm a busy guy and I don't have the time for all that outside reading and other opinions he wants me to think about. My friends and I, we know what's what and that's enough for us.

And third, that article you are going to read is pretty good. It has complete sentences, no spelling or grammar errors, and all five paragraphs stick together like they should. Each paragraph deals with one idea and shows it to be right.

From *What Is "College-Level" Writing?* Volume 2: *Assignments, Readings, and Student Writing Samples*, ed. Patrick Sullivan, Howard Tinberg, and Sheridan Blau NCTE, 2010, pp. 137–41.

In conclusion, this theme has shown that my essay is worth your time to read, since it's short and on topic, well-written, and popular. And you can skip all that analysis at the end if you have better things to do.

—Ed White, *the author imagined at age 17*

Since the beginning of time, some college teachers have mocked the five-paragraph theme. But I intend to show that they have been mistaken. There are three reasons why I always write five-paragraph themes. First, it gives me an organizational scheme: an introduction (like this one) setting out three subtopics, three paragraphs for my three subtopics, and a concluding paragraph reminding you what I have said, in case you weren't paying attention. Second, it focuses my topic, so I don't just go on and on when I don't have anything much to say. Three and only three subtopics force me to think in a limited way. And third, it lets me write pretty much the same essay on anything at all. So I do pretty well on essay tests. A lot of teachers actually like the five-paragraph theme as much as I do.

The first reason I always write five-paragraph themes is that it gives me an organizational scheme. It doesn't matter what the subject is, since there are three parts to everything you can think of. If you can't think of more than two, you just have to think harder or come up with something that might fit. An example will often work, like the three causes of the Civil War or abortion or reasons why the ridiculous twenty-one-year-old limit for drinking alcohol should be abolished. A worse problem is when you wind up with more than three subtopics, since sometimes you want to talk about all of them. But you can't. You have to pick the best three. That keeps you from thinking too much, which is a great time saver, especially on an essay test.

The second reason for the five-paragraph theme is that it makes you focus on a single topic. Some people start writing on the usual topic, like TV commercials, and they wind up all over the place, talking about where TV came from or capitalism or health foods or whatever. But with only five paragraphs and one topic you're not tempted to get beyond your original idea, like commercials are a good source of information about products. You give your three examples, and zap! you're done. This is another way the five-paragraph theme keeps you from thinking too much.

The last reason to write this way is the most important. Once you have it down, you can use it for practically anything. Does God exist? Well, you can say yes and give three reasons, or no and give three different reasons. It doesn't really matter. You're sure to get a good grade whatever you pick to put into the formula. And that's the real reason for education, to get those good grades without thinking too much and using up too much time.

So I've given you three reasons why I always write a five-paragraph theme and why I'll keep doing so in college. It gives me an organizational scheme that looks like an essay, it limits my focus to one topic and three subtopics so I don't wander about thinking irrelevant thoughts, and it will be useful for whatever writing I do in any subject. I don't know why some teachers seem to dislike it so much. They must have a different idea about education than I do.

I wrote this little *jeu d'esprit* while flying back to Arizona from Florida after serving as a table leader for the 2007 Advanced Placement English test. I had been part of an army of readers scoring about 280,000 exams, each containing three impromptu essays written by high school students—many of them trained to write five-paragraph essays in order to pass writing tests. I had been disheartened by how many good writers I saw writing badly. It was clear that this training in producing five-paragraph essays often had little to do with writing as a form of discovery and reflection, not to speak of developed argument. But what else can we expect of high school seniors writing an impromptu essay in forty-five minutes? Many of these 280,000 students had obviously been trained to write five-paragraph themes, and who can blame either the teachers or the students for that? Still, I was troubled: Why did so many of the AP essays show so little of what we teach in first-year writing courses, despite the obvious competence of the students in the techniques of essay production?

I know that there is much to be said for teaching the five-paragraph theme, from the teacher's as well as the student's perspective, and I tried to have my theme enumerate them. Though a formula, it is an organizational scheme—and it is better to have some organization than none at all. We know that an essay needs to be built around assertions and that some kind of evidence for these assertions is necessary. The writer of this five-paragraph theme doesn't appear to have any sense that writing could encourage reflection or discovery; the formula doesn't exactly prohibit it, though this writer appears to be among the many who feel it renders such matters unnecessary. Above all, this writer appears to know that the five-paragraph theme allows every student to turn out something "that looks like an essay," and this important fact meets our obligation as teachers to get as many of our students as possible through the incessant testing of writing. It is even possible, as a few AP students demonstrated, to use that formula to turn out some real writing, and I'm sure some very good English teachers have used the five-paragraph formula to help students get started. But by and large, formulas don't much engender thinking; indeed they actively discourage it.

Finally, what troubled me most as I wrote this five-paragraph theme was what happened to me as a writer when I knew the only purpose I was writing was to pass a test. I organized my thoughts, such as they were, edited my work carefully, even imagined the teachers who would be grading my work. Would I have passed the test? Probably. And yet most of what I value about writing is missing here: reflection, understanding of the issues, awareness of other perspectives on the topic, and an understanding of the relation of writing to thinking.

We see plenty of students like this in our first-year composition classes, whether the college is a "selective" one or not. Our job is to make sure students like this have "a different idea about education" by the time they leave our class. That is not only a pedagogical problem embedded in the curriculum of most such courses but an issue that rhetoricians for the last two thousand years have wrestled with. How can we teach the rudiments of an organized argument without trapping our students in a limited formula? The five-paragraph theme is the most recent version of writing from models, learning through copying formats, developing templates—a concept with a long pedagogical history. Used well, this form of rote learning teaches important skills that students learn to use in many different ways; used badly, it dries up the imagination, substitutes form for substance, and teaches that writing is not a matter of discovery or thought but just a matter of filling in the blanks.

If we choose to use the five-paragraph theme to teach the concept of organization and development of ideas we need to be sure that competing heuristics with the same goals are also part of what we teach. Thus, we should also spend some time with narrative structures that respond to assignments calling for telling about a personal experience and what it means to the writer—and, possibly, the reader. The first draft of such a paper will have a simple chronological structure, detailing the experience. But revisions will find ways to open with the reasons the experience mattered, include those ideas throughout the narrative, and conclude with some suggestion that readers should be interested in the writer's reflections, which are not merely personal.

Or we could present, as another alternative, the structure required by a comparison/contrast assignment, derived from two readings: In what respects do these writers differ or agree, and what conclusions on the topic do you draw from that comparison? Now we need a structure that allows the writer to discuss each reading in some detail, then moves to another section describing their agreement, another on their differences, and finally a developed argument about what matters about the two positions and where the writer has come to stand on the topic.

Such an expanded idea of organization needs to deal with the exigency that calls forth the writing—that is, some reason besides getting a grade for producing a text. Only then can we approach formats and formulas that might help with organizing ideas. I was lucky enough to find such a teacher in first-year composition, and he turned me into a writer—and changed my life. I'd like to think that college-level writing will continue to offer such challenges and opportunities to all the students passing through our classes.

Powerful formulas help students get going and often help them to pass tests—but at the cost of creativity or really thinking about what they say. I would like to argue here that formulas—and especially the five-paragraph essay formula—should be regarded by teachers as a way station on the path to more real writing. This formula should be used only to meet short-term goals. Unfortunately, I think most students are happy to stop with the formula, so teachers should avoid it whenever possible.

What to Make of the Five-Paragraph Theme: History of the Genre and Implications

Michelle Tremmel

In this essay, Michelle Tremmel surveys our discipline's long engagement with the five-paragraph essay. Busy two-year college instructors will, perhaps, be most inspired by ideas Tremmel offers on authentic composing problems, especially those informed by "new literacy," like the Life Stories project at Kirkwood Community College. As Tremmel noted in correspondence with us about this essay, "If we can learn from the history of current-traditionalism and the five-paragraph theme and change our practices based on that knowledge, this will help us make greater connections between classroom writing and the world outside of school."

"How do *you* feel about the five-paragraph theme?" I have posed this question as a conversation starter on the topic of theme writing over the past two years to first-year college writers, along with elementary and secondary English teachers, two-year and four-year college instructors, and others interested in literacy instruction who have attended conferences sponsored by the Conference on College Composition and Communication and the Iowa Council of Teachers of English. Using a circular or star-shaped sticker, 127 respondents have recorded their feelings on a Likert-type continuum drawn on a blue, five-foot poster and decorated with three familiar depictions of the template.

From *Teaching English in the Two-Year College*, 2011, vol. 39, no. 1, pp. 29-42.

What the continuum reveals is a lack of consensus about this uniquely "North American species" of "pseudogenre," a formula that puzzles those who teach writing elsewhere in the world (Pirie 75): Assessments range from "very positive" on the left side to "very negative" on the right, and at least one sticker occupies almost every point on the continuum, creating a balanced range of responses from strong approval to strong disapproval. Moreover, the diverse views represented in this informal poll mirror the opinions and feelings about theme writing published by more than thirty different journals across nearly 300 articles over the last one hundred years—including 253 focused specifically on the five-paragraph theme. Since about 1907 with the *Atlantic Monthly*'s publication of "The Daily Theme Eye" (about essayist Walter Prichard Eaton's theme-writing experience at Harvard), the professional literature has repeatedly taken up the topic of daily themes, weekly themes, biweekly themes; 50-, 250-, 500-, or 1,000-word themes; themes in all manner of subject; and, by the late 1950s, the five-paragraph theme.

My analysis of this professional conversation indicates that a majority have argued by a ratio of about five to one against theme writing, in general, and by about three to one against the five-paragraph theme, in particular, as sound approaches to teaching composition, while at the same time teachers have consistently assigned (five-paragraph) themes to their students. In light of such tension between opinion and practice, I intend in this article to bring together various voices on theme writing across time along with some key bits of the history of current-traditional rhetoric (in which theme writing is embedded) so that already overburdened teachers of writing have, in one place, information that might help them make choices about how they prepare writers to meet the demands of twenty-first century communication. I see this article as a conduit to historical research that, though not new, remains unknown to many practitioners, as well as a call for a serious shake-up in the way writing gets taught. History teaches that such a shake-up is difficult because education "breeds conservatism . . . a preference for stability, and a cautious attitude toward change (Cuban 18); the structure of schooling at all levels (with myriad external pressures, including intense standardized testing) helps perpetuate the traditional; and the systemic status quo of educational practice consistently attempts to use logic to cut up complex processes into the manageable chunks thought to be easily disseminated to novices. In particular, this problematic thinking applied to composition teaching over the last 120 years has led many to believe that applying "a merely cognitive grasp of the principles of writing" will cause significant improvement in student writing (Stewart, "Advanced" 199) and that the five-paragraph theme is the perfect vehicle.

From a twenty-first-century perspective, however, continuing to emphasize the five-paragraph theme (now spread even into upper elementary school) seems completely misguided, and teachers would do well to abandon its teaching, a decision predicted almost thirty years ago (Withey 24) that has yet to happen. In so arguing, I recognize that others might say the genre's staying power must mean that it works. Isn't that why it persists? Even though teachers have opposed the use of themes to teach writing since the early twentieth century (see, for example, H. Davis 328) and even though since the early 1970s many have consistently denigrated the five-paragraph theme specifically (see, for example, Williamson 132; Hairston 52; Sitler 24; Hillocks, "Fighting" 70; Miller 99),[1] doesn't its continued presence in our writing classrooms signify effectiveness? The literature on theme writing and the experience of many teachers and students suggests the answer to this question is "No, the five-paragraph theme hurts more than it helps."

For those who teach college composition courses (including me), an even more important consideration than whether they believe the five-paragraph theme's persistence in precollege writing instruction equals effectiveness is what to do when students come ready to deploy it. The decision is not whether it belongs in writing pedagogy or whether instructors should introduce it—that horse is already out of the barn—but whether they should disrupt or reinforce it. Of course, this quandary assumes that those who teach college writing recognize the genre's limitations—an assumption, I need to acknowledge, that has limitations in light of conversations I have had with first-year-writing instructors who vehemently defend their teaching of the five-paragraph theme. Before I talk further about this decision and the qualities of better approaches teachers might take to help students develop as writers, I want, first, to examine how the profession has been "wedded intellectually to" the five-paragraph theme (Stewart, "Some History" 136) through "current-traditionalism," an approach to writing instruction, based on positivism, that emerged during the mid-nineteenth century "in response to the new scientific curriculum of the modern American university" (Berlin 9). This connection between current-traditionalism (C-T) and the five-paragraph theme is important because it suggests that teachers cannot move away from the latter without radically rethinking the former, something that has proven difficult.

Current-Traditionalism and Why the Five-Paragraph Theme Seems Sensible

A number of influences—well documented by others (see, for example, Berlin; Crowley; Kitzhaber)—helped shape and have sustained current-traditional rhetoric over the last 125 years. Of these, Petrus Ramus's early contribution plays a particularly important role in the evolution of the five-paragraph theme (Crowley 135). During the sixteenth century, Ramus took a common approach to philosophical inquiry, used for *generating* knowledge, and restricted its use to *arranging* knowledge (36).

This advent of "methodical memory," as Sharon Crowley names it, shifted the use of structured heuristics for *inventing* material for discourse (long a staple of rhetoric) to a drafting approach that conflated invention and arrangement. Three centuries after Ramus, his conflated "method" informed the "nested" composing that current-traditional writing instruction adopted (134). Its bottom-up approach, which moves from words, to sentences, to paragraphs, to multiparagraph compositions—as though the structures of one translate to the structures of those up the food chain—contributed to C-T's focus on "patterns of arrangement and superficial correctness [as] the main ends of writing instruction" (Berlin 9). This thinking first took hold as universities reworked traditional rhetoric programs (based primarily on oral declamation) into written composition designed to accommodate large numbers of "nontraditional" students (women and Civil War veterans, for instance).

Such was the general context in which Barrett Wendell "invented" the daily theme at Harvard in 1884 (Kitzhaber 210) to give students focused, sustained (some might say unrelenting) practice in the sacred current-traditional trinity of "unity," "mass," and "coherence" (Wendell 96). Wendell's daily theme and other loosely conceived versions of the "school theme," used primarily for writing practice and examination (and consistent with C-T's emphasis on stylistic and grammatical correction), evolved over the next fifty years into the reified five-paragraph template circa 1959 when Victor Pudlowski articulated its components in the *English Journal* article "Compositions—Write 'Em Right." This "right" way of writing fit perfectly into the C-T pedagogy of the time and continues to do so fifty years later in many programs that rely on "nested" practices of composing and the five-paragraph theme because their apparently logical, orderly, efficient, and systematic approach fits neatly into writing-lesson compartments. And even if college writing instructors eschew C-T pedagogy, including the five-paragraph theme, it has a negative impact on their teaching when students come to them with views about how writing works and how to organize ideas in writing gleaned from programs that find C-T such "a compelling paradigm" that it is "impossible for them to conceive [of writing instruction] in any other way" (Berlin 9).

Within a neat C-T writing system, the five-paragraph theme has been appealing, championed in professional journals as a widely applicable organizational "building plan," "building block," or "map" (Wiseman 9; Smith 17; Parker 82)—or even, paradoxically, as a promoter of creativity that gives "student writers a set of conventions to break away from" (Perrin 312). For struggling writers (for example, second-language learners or special needs students), in particular, proponents of the five-paragraph theme have characterized it positively as a "stepstool" (Brown 60), "training wheels" (Nunnally 70), or "scaffolding" (Carignan-Bellville 57–58), claiming its benefit as a default structure to "g[et] started" (Knutson 53), pass a curricular checkpoint, or achieve a proficient "cut score" on a high-stakes test, a major reason for the genre's intensified emphasis in the era of "No Child Left Behind."[2]

In the "objective" scope of C-T thinking, the five-paragraph theme seems inherently sensible to teachers and students alike and fits seamlessly into a tidy, sequential approach that appeals to a certain Western love of orderliness and efficiency. And for students it feels safe. Let me give an example. Several years ago, I taught a very logical thinker, whom I will call Becky, in an honors section of what many colleges call Composition II. As a high school student, Becky had attended a small academy within her district, which, on the one hand, offered intellectually stimulating courses, such as Advanced Placement courses, but on the other, leaned heavily on the five-paragraph theme in its writing program. Becky had mastered the genre, and that mastery had served her well. There was just one problem: her adherence to it was crippling her writing in college, making it perfunctory if mechanically perfect. Until Becky could abandon the seeming logic of the five-paragraph theme, she could not cultivate the two habits of mind Nancy Sommers and Laura Saltz identify as crucial to growth over time in college writers: an acceptance of "themselves as novices in a world that demands 'something more and deeper' from their writing than high school" (134) and the adoption of an attitude toward writing assignments in which they "begin to see writing as a transaction, an exchange in which they can 'get and give'" and in which they see "a larger purpose" (139).

Why the Five-Paragraph Theme Doesn't Work

The kind of intense drilling and emphasis on correctness promoted by the five-paragraph theme that stunted the quality of Becky's writing also stunts the "interest *for* writing" that novices at all levels need in order to care enough to "set effective goals, make use of helpful strategies, and seek feedback as they work with writing tasks" (Lipstein and Renninger 79). My students' experiences with the five-paragraph theme bear this out; they consistently report that it demoralizes them and turns them off to writing, telling me that it blocks idea invention and makes them give up because they never seem to get it right. And they often complain more harshly about the formula than I ever would (even putting me in the position of defending their overworked teachers, who, I know, as a former secondary teacher myself, try hard to teach writing of any kind under the burden of too many students and too much grading and testing).

To illustrate, I offer two examples of what my students tell me (with the qualifier that I have not conducted a rigorous human-subjects study of contemporary student voices on the five-paragraph theme). First, several of them, when asked what they found less than helpful in their precollege writing experiences, have indicated that training in the genre unproductively forces attention away from the ideas of their writing onto the formula. One student's comment is representative:

> Much of my junior year was spent writing 5 paragraph essays. . . . No matter what we wrote about, whether it was a research evaluation or a minor reflection, everything was to consist of 5 paragraphs. This was not helpful because it didn't allow ideas to flow together. It added more structure than was necessary . . . which greatly inhibited the creativity of my writing.

A second, particularly passionate student summed up the sentiment in a plea to high school teachers: "Can we please stop teaching the 5-paragraph paper? It's so confusing to get used to [and] worse [in college] than using Wikepedia." What such student comments indicate, along with the bulk of the literature I reviewed, is that instruction in the five-paragraph theme builds neither interest in the *act* of writing nor strategies that help students develop ideas in writing. Instead, the rigid structure becomes the point and focus of writing, creating a barrier to growth.

As opponents of the formula have analogized, the genre is an uninspired and uninspiring "neurotic activity" (Emig 99) or "army-camp" approach to teaching composition (Strenski 139), which offers a "cookie-cutter" (as one of my students characterized it); a "jug" to "fill up" (Naff and Schnaufer 103); a "Procrustean formula" (Anderson 302; Bamberg 426); or other crutches like "water wings" (qtd. in Rex et al. 777) or a "paint-by-number" set (Nelson 58) that teaches "nothing about real painting" (Pirie 77). Such metaphors, along with my students' comments, suggest that the strictly controlled practice of the five-paragraph theme has problems in that, like the props to which it has been compared, mastering the formula causes novices to over-rely on it, slowing writing progress (Pirie 77). Like too-comfortable training wheels, the formula is so seductive that students struggle to unlearn it when increasingly sophisticated writing tasks require increasingly sophisticated organizational strategies. As one of my students said, "I wanted to write with this style [the five-paragraph theme] every time I sat down to write a paper. I had to constantly think about not [doing that,] and I think that made me focus less on the content of the papers." For him and other writers, knowing the template too well stunts rather than supports development as they struggle to deal with difficult and complex composing processes. Its persistence, despite a general turn in the last forty or so years to other approaches that promise *more* for writing (process, rhetorical, social-constructivist, collaborative, and so on), is particularly troublesome when, in an inappropriate hybridizing of the five-paragraph theme with incompatible approaches, the genre "straightjackets" those pedagogies, subsuming them *within* the current-traditional paradigm, which can harmfully truncate idea-discovery and result in a quick race to a central thesis and a tightly structured but often illogically "elaborated" piece of writing (Hillocks, "Focus" 245–46). What is involved here is not a choice between "product" and "process." In fact, that false dichotomy has been a major distraction in debates about writing pedagogy. Instead, the *product* of the five-paragraph theme is really a *process* all its own that clashes with and subverts other processes, countermanding richer and more educative ones that can serve our students better when, as John Trimbur puts it, they answer the "call to write" in situations beyond composition courses. Lessons in the five-paragraph theme and accompanying C-T principles twist those other approaches and rob teachers of precious time needed to create experiences in which students can wrestle with the messiness of composing. They prevent writers from moving around organically and recursively between idea invention and idea arrangement in shaping their thoughts into discourse for particular and changing rhetorical genres and contexts.

As much as teachers and students might *want* the five-paragraph theme to provide a rich composing experience, it simply cannot. Rather than form following function, the formula of the five-paragraph theme precedes function—and is often a-rhetorically and inappropriately grafted onto function—in ways that derail composing. Further, I do not think we can blame students or teachers for this, as though the template were perfect, like a Platonic ideal, degraded and vulgarized in novices' or ineffective instructors' hands—nor do I think that changing the number of body paragraphs makes any positive difference. Instead, the formula itself precludes *meaningful* thinking and organizing, as Edward White's well-known satire of the genre demonstrates (p. 349 in this volume).[3]

What Decisions Writing Teachers Have to Make about the Five-Paragraph Theme

If all of this brings increased clarity to the issue of the five-paragraph theme, what needs to happen next, I think, is for writing teachers to consider carefully the conflicts and tensions with which the field of composition has struggled for a hundred years and to thoughtfully examine both the intellectual and emotional relationships they have with current-traditionalism and the five-paragraph theme. To begin, they could interrogate their teaching decisions in light of their own histories and, potentially, uncover how both the current-traditional approaches they saw their teachers use (Cuban 254) and the "pragmatic and experience-based structure" of five-paragraph-theme teaching "lore" (North 24) have shaped their attitudes and approaches. When I do the kind of examination I am suggesting, two conflicting feelings give me pause. On the one hand, my teacher-self is convinced intellectually and experientially that the five-paragraph theme harms student writers. On the other hand, my former-student-self fondly associates the formula with a favorite English teacher whom I highly admired and who firmly believed that the way to prepare me to write for college in the 1970s was via the five-paragraph theme.

Reflecting on my ambivalent feelings has enlightened my understanding of the relationship I have with the five-paragraph theme and its effect on my teaching. In such reflection I have asked myself, "What part did the genre play in the way I learned to write and think about writing?" "Was it safe and automatic once I mastered it?" "Did I please my teacher and have grade success by performing the five-paragraph theme?" "Did I reach a high score or rank on a writing assessment by using it?" "What effect did following the formula have on risk-taking, messiness, and hard thinking for me?" "What problems has it caused or resolved for me *as a writer*?" "How does my experience with the genre relate to my students' experiences?" "What problems has it caused or resolved for me *as a teacher of writing*?" And so on. Answering such questions and talking with others about similar self-analyses can be useful in dispassionately examining the costs and benefits of the five-paragraph theme in a time when intense pressure to improve student writing immediately often causes programs to turn to it as a quick fix.

If teachers resist succumbing to that pressure, what should they do instead? I could offer some stopgap measures ("fix-it" strategies, as a reviewer of an earlier version of this article called them) on how to "unteach" the five-paragraph theme or how to teach organization in writing differently than by that container genre. I do have ideas about that from my own teaching and from the more than sixty suggestions published by others who have written about theme writing and the five-paragraph theme over the past ninety years. However, doing so really is beside the point. Those who avoid current-traditionalism and the five-paragraph theme already know them, and those who do not can feel free to contact me if they want to start small in abandoning C-T practices. Not providing them here will probably bother some readers, like the conference attendee who, after hearing the history of the genre and my arguments for letting it go, pressed me for concrete replacements, or the *English Journal* author who counseled those who tell teachers to abandon the five-paragraph theme, "If you're going to take away what some of us believe in, please offer something else in its place. And be specific" (Lockward 34).

"Fix-it" approaches can work in limited ways, but both the articles in my historical study and the disparate responses on my five-paragraph-theme poster suggest that the profession has not managed to rid itself of the genre and other vestiges of current-traditional rhetoric by distracting itself with stopgap measures. What both teachers and students of writing need more is a resolve to fight for whole-scale change that rejects current-traditionalism, to cultivate a trust in productive uncertainty that includes both a tolerance for and belief in orderly chaos in writing processes, and finally to invest the time that less "efficient" approaches, nurtured within a community of writers, require to show results.

Young writers "want to write" when they enter their first classrooms, Donald Graves argues in his groundbreaking study *Writing: Teachers and Children at Work*: "They want to write the first day they attend school. This is no accident. Before they went to school, they marked up walls, pavements, newspapers, with crayons, chalk, pens or pencils . . . anything that makes a mark. The child's marks say, 'I am'" (3). Children do not need a formula. They do not come to school needing or loving the five-paragraph theme. What Graves's seminal research illuminates, instead, is "that children need time to process their thoughts and 'rehearse' before writing, and that their best writing flows from their deepest interests" (Slover). And student writers are not well served by teachers who attempt to motivate by telling them, as I recently heard a teacher say (true to current-traditional thinking), that they will earn two points for an opening sentence and four points for two body paragraphs—or to cajole them into writing by promising they *have* to write *only* two hundred words.

Instead, what writers of all ages need in order to gain increasingly sophisticated skills and grow in their writing is to stay interested in the pursuit of writing. That interest for engaging in the writing act is a key issue of motivation that needs more attention. Even though I am quite certain that most of my students will not become professional basketball players, those who have a strong interest in basketball think nothing of standing at a free throw line and honing their skills by shooting a thousand free throws a day. Conversely, when it comes to writing, these same students want to get that act over with as soon as possible and be efficient about it. The C-T approach and the five-paragraph theme, because these avoid—seemingly at all cost—the messiness of composing, have taught students to think differently about writing than they do about basketball or other activities in which they are invested. It is school that conditions students to an avoidance and efficiency view of writing, but it does not have to. As an administrator recently said about local school reform, "We need to find a different way. We need to go back and look at the system itself" (Dooley 4B). So, too, those who teach writing, including me, need to challenge the educational systems in which they operate to build programs that help students care enough about writing (even though many will not become professional writers) to want to develop "critical thinking skills" and twenty-first-century communication strategies.

Where We Should Go from Here:
"Renewal" Rather than "Reform"

To give American society these competencies it purports to value, writing programs must give up a systemic addiction to formulas like the five-paragraph theme and the rigid composing steps of current-traditionalism and instead offer students authentic composing *problems* to solve. However, teachers can only move forward in an expansive and meaningful way if they take the first step of every successful recovery program: acknowledging and accepting the counterproductive and, indeed, detrimental effects of clinging to C-T thinking. Different paths exist, but teachers will not get far in overcoming a current-traditional addiction if they try to forge these paths in isolation. Many have tried this from at least as early as 1917, when William Davis argued a simple idea that the profession has yet to accomplish in any whole-scale way: We need to "mak[e] the study [of composition] seem valuable and important" to students, to offer a genuinely "impelling motive," and to "make sure of [their] desire to communicate something" (293) to someone for a rhetorical purpose besides earning a grade or passing a test.

Working together, writing teachers need to embrace a "mission" not of "reform" but of "renewal" and to "take a long view" of intellectual growth, as Ann Foster, executive director of the National Network for Education Renewal, recently argued about educational change. They need *new* "formal structures" for "reciprocal partnerships" (among, for example, schools, colleges, and communities) in order to have an impact on long-entrenched formal structures of schooling. Thinking about "renewal" in terms of writing programs suggests that even if educators can make the case that C-T rhetoric and the five-paragraph theme work for a range of students in the short term, deploying that pedagogy undercuts essential long-term goals that programs should have for encouraging novice writers to care enough about what they write, how they write, and for whom they need and want to write to develop the skills they need to do so.

For renewing writing pedagogy, educators should embrace some key practices:

- Put curricular formation in the hands of practitioners, along the lines of Japanese Lesson Study (Stigler and Hiebert), which trusts the knowledge and professionalism of teachers;

- Reject efficiency and deficiency models of education;

- Give learner-writers more control over their own writing and learning;

- Pay as much attention, in pedagogical decision making, to building a continuing interest in the act of writing as to building skills;

- Connect writing classes and authentic rhetorical situations beyond school; and, most important and integral to the others,

- Postpone writing tests and grading long enough to allow students to grapple with the complexity and confusion that is writing as they work toward competency and beyond (via, for example, a locally appropriate portfolio assessment program).

Getting down to particulars, a litmus test for a program (or, to start small, an assignment) that exemplifies these qualities of renewal is what the Australian New Basics Project calls a "rich task," defined as a "transdiciplinary," "problem-based," "integrated intellectual, linguistic, social, and cultural practice . . . represent[ing] an education outcome of demonstrable and substantive intellectual substance and educational value" and "connect[ing] to the world beyond the classroom" (Queensland 7).

To embrace the qualities of renewal and "rich tasks," teachers need only look around at the many places where they already exist. For instance, James Moffett offers an early and detailed vision of these in *The Universal Schoolhouse*, a vision that others have actualized in a wide variety of interpretations: at Nancie Atwell's twenty-year-old Center of Teaching and Learning ("About"), in the forty-four-year-old "Foxfire Approach to Teaching and Learning" ("What"), at National Writing Project sites, and in community-based literacy programs like "TEEN Group: Writing as Social Action" (Schaafsma). In first-year composition and other college-level writing courses, rich tasks are going on, as well. These occur in stand-alone assignments like long-term multigenre composing projects (Davis and Schadel; Mack; Romano). They also happen in specialized thematic or learning-community sections of composition courses, linked to students' academic interests and programs (for example, the English 250 sections "Speaking in Place," "Design Exchange," and "Newspaper Physics" that Iowa State University offers).

Specifically at the community college, "new literacy" projects like "Life Stories" also exist. Integrated into a five-credit college writing course (English 120), this academic and service-learning project pairs local senior citizens with Kirkwood Community College students in Cedar Rapids, Iowa, in a semester-long collaboration that involves students interviewing their partners, researching topics related to seniors' lives, and writing in a variety of genres. As the culmination of this "life stories" work, students create multimedia presentations, including digital audio recordings, which they publish beyond the classroom on a CD they present to their partner for sharing with family and friends (Myers-Verhage).

What all these approaches have in common—and what is important about them—is that their "rich tasks" leave no room for the five-paragraph theme but, instead, foster process recursivity and skill building in meaningful contexts. Further, they offer models of "renewed" (rather than "reformed") writing pedagogy for dissemination efforts that the profession should pursue to make such work not special but the norm.

No doubt, educators are experiencing increasing pressure to break up complex educational processes, like writing instruction, into smaller, more discrete bits that they must frequently test in order, ostensibly, to achieve a better quality whole. In the history of American education this is not new, and writing teachers who have felt the frustration of trying to pound the square peg of current-traditional rhetoric into the round hole of real writing know this approach is not up to the task. In a 180-degree reversal on educational reform, former assistant secretary of education Diane Ravitch points out that "[o]ur educational problems [despite at least one hundred years of reform cycles] are a function of our lack of educational vision" (225), and those reforms "are diminishing [public education's] quality and endangering its very survival" (242). That lack of vision is also complicit in the perpetuation of the current-traditional approach to teaching writing, pioneered by Barrett Wendell and evolving into instruction in the five-paragraph theme. However, even Wendell himself, a hundred years ago, rejected current-traditionalism after devoting his whole professional life to it (Kitzhaber 69). I believe writing programs can serve student writers better if they also commit themselves to a widespread abandonment of current-traditional methods and the five-paragraph theme, embracing instead approaches shaped by a vision of "renewal" and embodying the characteristics of "rich tasks." Will writing instruction in the United States take that more fruitful path and not continue to doom itself to repeating its history? If so, the profession will have learned from its long relationship with theme writing, and I can put my poster aside because its question, "How do you feel about the five-paragraph theme?" will cease to matter.

Notes

1. Of the 127 articles I found in which writers come out clearly against the five-paragraph theme, these are representative and show the persistence of opposition across five decades.
2. Even though, according to Nancy Glazer of Educational Testing Services, the five-paragraph theme is a "neutral" aspect of writing in large-scale assessments like the SAT and scorers are told, "Do not reward or penalize for the five-paragraph essay," many teachers *perceive* the genre is required and thus drill their students in it.
3. In a 2010 *Chronicle of Higher Education* "Point of View" piece, Rob Jenkins launches a defense of the five-paragraph theme, suggesting, like other proponents since at least 1966 (see Nichols 908), that its value lies in its flexibility (like an "accordion") and its practice potential for apprentice orga-

nizers, who, like medical students, should not be allowed to dissect human cadavers (deal with real organizing problems) before working on "frogs" (mastering the five-paragraph theme). Jenkins and I agree that choosing the five-paragraph-theme does not hinge on the product vs. process duality; however, we differ in our view of the harms vs. benefits of choosing the genre to teach the basic writing concepts of beginning-middle-end, rather than using richer approaches like reading-as-a-writer text analysis.

Works Cited

"About the Center for Teaching and Learning." *Center for Teaching and Learning*. Center for Teaching and Learning, 2010. Web. 27 Dec. 2010.

Anderson, Chuck. "A Comment on 'On Going Home: Selfhood in Composition.'" *College English* 47.3 (1985): 300–302. Print.

Bamberg, Betty. "Coherence and Cohesion: What Are They and How Are They Achieved?" *College Composition and Communication* 34.4 (1983): 417–29. Print.

Berlin, James A. *Rhetoric and Reality: Writing Instruction in American Colleges, 1900–1985*. Carbondale: Southern Illinois UP, 1987. Print.

Brown, Dorothy S. "A Five-Paragraph Stepstool." *College Composition and Communication* 28.1 (1977): 58–60. Print.

Carignan-Belleville, Lynne. "Jason's Story: Motivating the Reluctant Student to Write." *English Journal* 78.3 (1989): 57–60. Print.

Crowley Sharon. *The Methodical Memory: Invention in Current-Traditional Rhetoric*. Carbondale: Southern Illinois UP, 1990. Print.

Cuban, Larry. *How Teachers Taught: Constancy and Change in American Classrooms, 1880–1990*. 2nd ed. New York: Teachers College P, 1993. Print.

Davis, H. W. "Intolerance in the Teaching of English." *English Journal* 11.6 (1922): 323–30. Print.

Davis, Robert L., and Mark F. Shadel. *Teaching Multiwriting: Researching and Composing with Multiple Genres, Media, Disciplines, and Cultures*. Carbondale: Southern Illinois UP, 2007. Print.

Davis, William Hawley. "The Teaching of English Composition: Its Present Status." *English Journal* 6.5 (1917): 285–94. Print.

Dooley Sheena. "Longer School Year Debated." *Des Moines Sunday Register* 3 Oct. 2010, central ed.: 1B+. Print.

Emig, Janet. *The Composing Processes of Twelfth Graders*. Urbana: NCTE, 1971. Print.

Eaton, Walter Prichard. "The Daily Theme Eye." *Prose Patterns*. Ed. Arno L. Bader, et al. New York: Harcourt, Brace, 1933. 83–86. Rpt. of *Atlantic Monthly* Mar. 1907. Print.

Foster, Ann. Partnering for Student Success: A School and University Conference on School Partnerships. Iowa State U at Ames. 14 Sept. 2010. Address.

Glazer, Nancy. "One of Many Myths: Does the Five-Paragraph Essay Sink or Swim in Large-Scale Writing Assessment?" Conference on College Composition and Communication Annual Convention. San Francisco. 12 Mar. 2009. Presentation.

Graves, Donald H. *Writing: Teachers and Children at Work*. Exeter: Heinemann, 1983. Print.

Hairston, Maxine. "Using Carl Rogers' Communication Theories in the Composition Classroom." *Rhetoric Review* 1.1 (1982): 50–55. Print.

Hillocks, George, Jr. "Fighting Back: Assessing the Assessments." *English Journal* 92.4 (2003): 63–70. Print.

———. "The Focus on Form vs. Content in Teaching Writing." *Research in the Teaching of English* 40.2 (2005): 238–48. Print.

Jenkins, Rob. "Accordions, Frogs, and the Five-Paragraph Theme." *Chronicle of Higher Education* 21 Feb. 2010. Web. 10 Feb. 2011.

Kitzhaber, Albert R. *Rhetoric in American Colleges, 1850–1900.* Dallas: Southern Methodist UP, 1990. Print.

Knutson, Roslyn L. "A Formula for Generating a Literary Thesis." *English Journal* 69.9 (1980): 51–53. Print.

Lipstein, Rebecca C., and K. Ann Renninger. "Interest for Writing: How Teachers Can Make a Difference." *English Journal* 96.4 (2007): 79–85. Print.

Lockward, Diane. "An Open Letter to Writing Conference Speakers." *English Journal* 74.5 (1985): 33–34. Print.

Mack, Nancy. "The Ins, Outs, and In-Betweens of Multigenre Writing." *English Journal* 92.2 (2002): 91–98. Print.

Miller, Jeanetta. "Persistence of the Five-Paragraph Essay." *English Journal* 99.3 (2010): 99–100. Print.

Moffett, James. *The Universal Schoolhouse.* San Francisco: Jossey-Bass, 1994. Print.

Myers-Verhage, Shelby. Telephone interview. 29 Dec. 2010.

Naff, Bea, and Thiela Schnaufer. "Global Issues: Rhetoric Reconsidered—Here and Abroad." *English Journal* 86.6 (1997): 102–3. Print.

Nelson, G. Lynn. "Writing beyond Testing: 'The Word as an Instrument of Creation.'" *English Journal* 91.1 (2001): 57–61. Print.

Nichols, Duane C. "The Five-Paragraph Essay: An Attempt to Articulate." *English Journal* 55.7 (1966): 903–8. Print.

North, Stephen M. *The Making of Knowledge in Composition: Portrait of an Emerging Field.* Upper Montclair: Boynton/Cook, 1987. Print.

Nunnally, Thomas E. "Breaking the Five-Paragraph-Theme Barrier." *English Journal* 80.1 (1991): 67–71. Print.

Parker, Chauncey G. "Jettisoning the Five-Paragraph Essay: Mistaking the Cure for the Disease." *Teaching English in the Two-Year College* 17.2 (1990): 80–82. Print.

Perrin, Robert. "10:00 and 2:00: A Ten-Paragraph Defense of the Five-Paragraph Theme." *Teaching English in the Two-Year College* 27 (2000): 312–14. Print.

Pirie, Bruce. *Reshaping High School English.* Urbana: NCTE, 1997. Print.

Pudlowski, Victor. "Compositions—Write 'Em Right." *English Journal* 48.9 (1959): 535–37. Print.

Queensland Government. *New Basics—The Why, What, How, and When of Rich Tasks.* Brisbane, New Zealand: New Basics Branch, 2001. PDF file.

Ravitch, Diane. *The Death and Life of the Great American School System.* New York: Basic Books, 2010. Print.

Rex, Lesley A., et al. "Teachers' Pedagogical Stories and the Shaping of Classroom Participation: 'The Dancer' and 'Graveyard Shift at the 7-11.'" *American Educational Research Journal* 39.3 (2002): 765–96. Print.

Romano, Tom. *Blending Genre, Altering Style: Writing Multigenre Papers.* Portsmouth: Boynton/Cook, 2000. Print.

Schaafsma, David. "TEEN Group: Writing as Social Action." National Council of Teachers of English Annual Convention. Detroit. 22 Nov. 1997. Presentation.

Sitler, Helen Collins. "What College Writing Instructors Expect and Why You Should Join the Resistance." *English Journal* 82.6 (1993): 21–25. Print.

Slover, Kimberley. "The Write Way." *UNH Magazine*. U of New Hampshire, Winter 2005. Web. 5 Oct. 2010.

Smith, Kerri. "In Defense of the Five-Paragraph Theme." *English Journal* 95.4 (2006): 16–17. Print.

Sommers, Nancy, and Laura Saltz. "The Novice as Expert: Writing the Freshman Year." *College Composition and Communication* 56.1 (2004): 124–49. Print.

Stewart, Donald C. "An Advanced Composition Course That Works." *College Composition and Communication* 25.2 (1974): 197–200. Print.

———. "Some History Lessons for Composition Teachers." *Rhetoric Review* 3.2 (1985): 134–44. Print.

Stigler, James W., and James Hiebert. *The Teaching Gap*. New York: Free P, 1999. Print.

Strenski, Ellen. "Disciplines and Communities, 'Armies' and 'Monasteries,' and the Teaching of Composition." *Rhetoric Review* 8.1 (1989): 137–46. Print.

Trimbur, John. *The Call to Write*. 5th ed. Boston: Wadsworth, 2011. Print.

Wendell, Barrett. *English Composition*. New York: Charles Scribner's Sons, 1903. Print.

"What Is Foxfire?" *Foxfire*. Foxfire Fund, 2010. Web. 13 Dec. 2010.

Williamson, Richard. "The Case for Filmmaking as English Composition." *College Composition and Communication* 22.2 (1971): 131–36. Print.

Wiseman, Nell. "Writing Assessment." *English Journal* 93.2 (2003): 9. Print.

Withey, Margaret M. "The Computer and Writing." *English Journal* 72.7 (1983): 24–31. Print.

13

Rethinking "Grammar"

Why Our Students Need Instruction in Grammar, and How We Should Go about It

Mark Blaauw-Hara

In this article, Mark Blaauw-Hara argues for the necessity of language-level instruction in two-year college writing classrooms and presents a series of practical suggestions for doing so effectively. He reviews the scholarly conversation about grammar instruction in the writing class-room, acknowledging the importance of honoring students' home languages and questioning notions of absolute "correctness." Nonetheless, Blaauw-Hara views proficiency in the conventions of "standard" written English as an economic necessity for many students. He points out the extensive evidence that decontextualized discussions of grammar have little impact on students' actual writing, arguing instead for seven key strategies for teaching grammar in context: address grammar rhetorically, teach writing as a process, focus teacher-student interaction on talking and listening, work on grammar in students' own writing, encourage careful re-reading, provide models of good writing, and assign agency to the student.

Six years ago, the writing program at my community college instituted a portfolio assessment in three of our writing courses—a developmental course and the first and second semesters of our first-year composition sequence. All students submit portfolios containing sev-

From *Teaching English in the Two-Year College*, 2006, vol. 34, no. 2, pp. 165-78.

eral essays, which are read by two instructors in the writing program and assessed according to a common rubric. The rubric is simple: basically, a list of our course outcomes, with spaces to rate the student's demonstration of achievement in each outcome as poor, adequate, or fluent. After six years of assessment, we've seen that in each of the three courses, the outcome that consistently garners the fewest "fluents" and the most "poors" is the one dealing with grammatical and mechanical conventions.

This wasn't really a surprise. Here at the community college, our student population consists of many students who never thought they were candidates for higher education; most didn't take high-school courses considered "college-prep," and, unfortunately, their writing skills tend to be poor across the board. We writing teachers have our work cut out for us, and most of us find it much more enjoyable to teach other aspects of writing—development, adherence to a thesis, personal engagement—than we do grammar. Certainly, few of us were drawn to English by, say, an irrepressible desire to master the subjunctive. And the so-called "larger issues," such as teaching students to construct essays that delve into a topic at depth, really are necessary if students are not only to produce quality, college-level writing, but also to learn how to engage with and manipulate ideas with the sort of fluency required in college and the work world.

But students also need fluency in standard written English, and, unfortunately, I think many of us rationalize our avoidance of grammar with arguments about how it should come last in the writing process (it should), or how constructing a well-crafted paragraph is more important than knowing whether or not to put a comma before the "and" that precedes the final item in a series (it is). However, shunting grammar to the periphery ensures it doesn't get engaged in the way it merits. Despite how we may feel politically and emotionally about valuing students' native dialects and the desirability of myriad patterns of speech and writing, the work world—and, indeed, most of the world of higher education not directly involved in language studies—that awaits our students upon graduation or transfer does not share such values. In addition to the ability to engage with, shape, and develop ideas productively in their writing, our students *need* to be able to adhere to standard English to succeed in their other classes and to get jobs at the end of their schooling, and it's our responsibility as writing teachers to help them in this task.

A few years ago, the Council of Writing Program Administrators drafted several outcomes for first-year composition. The sections are rhetorical knowledge; critical thinking, reading, and writing; processes; and knowledge of conventions. Under the last one, they state that students should learn formats, develop knowledge of genre conventions, learn documentation, and "control such surface features as syntax, grammar, punctuation, and spelling" ("WPA" 325). Around the same time this was published, Larry Beason examined the reactions of business-people to common grammatical errors—things like fragments, misspellings, word-ending errors, fused sentences, and quotation marks—and found that such errors led to adverse judgments about the writers. A communications instructor at our college and her class performed a similar study and reached similar conclusions ("Business"). And all writing instructors probably have had the experience of being stopped in the hall by teachers in other disciplines and regaled with stories of students who have taken first-year composition and yet still "can't write" (read: "They use 'poor' grammar").

Something must be done. However, I don't think the answer is to devote fourteen weeks a semester to whole-class grammar instruction. Nor is it to ignore the issue, or to focus only on educating the public on discourse communities and dialect. At least at our college—and, I strongly suspect, at others—students have clearly demonstrated a need to improve their command of standard written English, and we writing teachers must decide how to meet that need. In this essay, I'll highlight some problems with traditional whole-class grammar instruction, advocate some productive ways to conceive of grammar and correctness, and lay out several specific strategies supported by research to help our students build fluency in standard English.

Problems with Traditional Grammar Instruction

It appears that teaching grammar in the way most of the public visualizes it—the teacher lectures on grammatical concepts, diagrams sentences on the board, gives a quiz, etc.—does not work. In fact, it appears to *hamper* students' writing abilities. In *Explorations in the Teaching of English*, Steven Tchudi and Diana Mitchell argue that a "direct focus on skill instruction proves generally fruitless because it fails to concentrate on language users and their needs. The net effect of skill-building programs is often to inhibit the skill users, crippling their natural language ability and blunting their desire to do anything new with words" (248). They cite a 1966 review of empirical research whose authors, Neil Postman and Charles Weingartner, found that "training in formal grammar did not transfer to any significant extent to writing or to recognizing correct English" (249). Similarly, educational theorist James Moffett writes that "parsing and diagramming of sentences, memorizing the nomenclature and definitions of parts of speech, and otherwise learning the concepts of traditional, classificatory grammar [. . .] do not reduce errors" (164). Other teachers and scholars argue much the same thing (Harris 119–20; Shaughnessy 155; Tarvers 71). In "Grammar, Grammars, and the Teaching of Grammar," Patrick Hartwell quotes a report whose authors found that "in view of the widespread agreement of research studies based upon many types of students and teachers, the conclusion can be stated in strong and unqualified terms: the teaching of formal grammar has a negligible or, because it usually displaces some instruction and practice in composition, even a harmful effect on improvement in writing" (Braddock, Lloyd-Jones, and Schoer; qtd. in Hartwell 370). And Mina Shaughnessy writes, "It is [. . .] important to remember that the student who is not at home with standard English has most likely had several doses of grammar already and it hasn't worked" (155).

Unfortunately, these assertions leave most of us at a loss. Our students need to be able to write using standard English, but the research seems to suggest we can't (or shouldn't) teach it to them. We seem to have a problem with no solution—unless we change the ways we conceive of and teach grammar.

Productive Ways to Conceive of Grammar and Correctness

According to William DeGenaro, the historical mission of the junior college was "to socialize the new working-class student body into a bourgeois sensibility" (130). A key place this happened was the writing classroom. Tchudi and Mitchell describe another historical mission for writing instructors: "Language instruction has been consistently linked to morality," they write, "with English teachers perceived as defenders of the language against the onslaughts of 'barbarians,' including their students" (8). While most of us would resist a job description that centered on socializing a group into a "bourgeois sensibility," there are undeniable class dynamics at play in today's community-college writing classroom, and our students, while perhaps not barbarians, are often violently resistant to grammar instruction. Such resistance is understandable: even though our goal is to teach them the linguistic landmarks of the culture of power, thereby enabling them to chart a safe passage through it, when we frame our discussion of grammar in terms of correct and incorrect—with students' natural ways of expression tending to fall in the latter category—it can sure feel to them like socialization by force. It may be possible to diffuse at least part of their resistance, though, by reconceiving grammar and grammar instruction, and by letting our students in on that reconception.

For instance, it appears that an understanding of grammar as absolutely "correct" or "incorrect" is inaccurate. Over the past few decades, new ways have emerged of looking at what we talk about when we talk about grammar. Hartwell outlines several layered "grammars," and begins his discussion by citing three described by W. Nelson Francis: Grammar 1, which is the internal grammar we acquire through interactions—it's unconscious, and our understanding of it is the only way we can communicate; Grammar 2, which is a set of codified rules that imperfectly describe Grammar 1; and Grammar 3, which is really "linguistic etiquette" (374–75), and usually has a pejorative attached—e.g., bad grammar and good grammar. To these, Hartwell adds Grammar 4, or the grammar taught in school, and Grammar 5, or grammatical concepts taught for the purpose of improving style (375).

According to Hartwell, the rules of Grammar 2, while useful in describing our language, "are simply unconnected to productive control over Grammar 1" (380), and those of Grammar 4 are helpful and make sense to students only if they have already acquired them in Grammar 1 (385). In other words, if they already know the rule but can't put words to it, grammar instruction helps them in that it gives them an explanation for what they already know. However, if they don't already know the rule, they aren't going to learn it from grammar instruction. They may memorize it, but it won't make sense on a deep enough level to produce a fundamental change in their writing. And, according to Hartwell, Grammar 5 isn't of much use to developing writers, either, for it distracts them from the process of "manipulating language in meaningful contexts [. . . and from] language activity that enhances the awareness of language as language" (390).

The problem is, we need to figure out some way to access and (let's face it) change the rules in students' versions of Grammars 1 and 3. Especially confusing to community college students is Grammar 3 — linguistic etiquette—which doesn't have so much to do with "correctness" in terms of whether a sentence makes sense but more to do with appropriate usage. For instance, when a student writes "I seen three deers the other day," we understand perfectly what he means; although we might say the sentence is "incorrect," there is nothing wrong with it from a communicative perspective. Instead, the problem lies in the fact that the student has violated a rule of etiquette: he's not writing in a way appropriate to the academic community.

Similarly, Tchudi and Mitchell argue that what is "correct" depends on sociological context, and that we should teach students to think in terms of dialect, shifting the objective from learning to write correctly to acquiring an "academic" dialect (255). They stress that rather than devaluing students' native dialects with notions of correct and incorrect, we need to make the benefits of learning an academic dialect plain, and then provide students with the resources (individualized instruction, handbooks, models, etc.) to acquire it (256–57). Moffett also defines "correctness" as "conformity to the particular grammar of standard dialect" (156), and cautions us to remember that we're asking a student to prefer how *we* talk to how everyone else she knows talks. He argues that when there are socioeconomic differences between the student and the teacher (as there generally are at the community college), "corrective grammar teaching assumes that a speaker of the non-standard dialect should write in standard English even though he is barred from association with speakers of standard English. Actually to preserve his own sense of integrity, he has a powerful motive not to adopt this alien grammar" (157).

Shaughnessy addresses this point as well, cautioning writing teachers to remember that a student's trouble adhering to standard English arises "from his mastery of one language or dialect [which corresponds to Hartwell's Grammars 1 and 3], and that changing to another often involves at certain points a loss or conflict of meaning and therefore difficulty in learning, not because he is stubborn or dumb or verbally impoverished but because he expects language to make sense" (155). For instance, if a student has grown up with everyone around him using "lay" when they should use "lie," the rule for differentiating between them seems incredibly abstract and slippery, and the only reinforcement comes in school; when he goes back home, his father will still tell the dog to "go lay down"—and when even the dog understands what is meant, who can blame the student for continuing to confuse the two, and resisting learning the rule over which his teacher gets so inexplicably worked up?

Still, the student has an incentive to learn such rules: we know that grammar and usage serve as socioeconomic markers and can influence how others perceive us (Lynch-Biniek; Moffett). As Tchudi and Mitchell write, "correct" grammar can "provide students with access to higher social levels" (253). This gives us a rationale for teaching it, and it provides reasons for learning it students can understand—if they learn to influence readers positively, it can pay off with better grades, a better job, and a general improvement in socioeconomic status.

Many authors advocate such a shift in how we think and talk about grammar, from a view focused on absolute correctness to one based on the effects of grammatical choices on readers—a more rhetorical understanding of grammar. In his article on how businesspeople react to error, Beason argues for defining errors "not just as textual features breaking handbook rules but as mental events taking place outside the immediate text" (35); in other words, the problem with errors isn't that they're essentially wrong, but that they inspire undesirable reactions in readers. Similarly, in "The Phenomenology of Error," Joseph Williams suggests we think of error less as a violation of a rule and more as a "social error," or something that matters only because we give it meaning. He argues that we "shift our attention from error treated strictly as an isolated item on a page, to error perceived as a flawed verbal transaction between a writer and a reader [. . .]. The matter of error turns less on a handbook definition than on the reader's response" (163–64). In fact, sometimes "errors" work better rhetorically than "correct" sentences—after all, professional writers frequently break rules when it serves their purposes.

Perhaps what is called for is a way to teach students how to understand the rhetorical reasons behind grammatical guidelines, so they can make their own informed decisions about when and when not to follow them. Donna Gorrell writes that rather than "leaning on correctness" (394), we should teach our students to compose consciously and develop their own individual styles; John Dawkins states that "the secret [. . .] is for student writers to do what good writers of nonfiction do:

use meaning as a basis for decision making, not grammar-based rules" (156–57). And it is important to remember that as students experiment with gaining fluency in the academic dialect and developing their own styles, they will make mistakes. Rather than reacting negatively, we should, as Tarvers argues, see some of those mistakes as "a sign of growth"—i.e., our students are attempting new things in their writing, and they won't get it perfect the first time (71).

Specific Strategies

So how do these ideas translate to what we should do on Monday in English 101? To answer this question, I've generated seven suggestions—based both on research and on my own classroom experience—which can help us move from the theoretical to the practical.

Address Grammar Rhetorically

As I stated above, we need to move from viewing grammar in terms of absolute correctness to viewing it as being correct in context. We also need to help our students begin to see it that way, because if we talk about it in the same way they've heard it before—i.e., by implicitly devaluing their native dialects and the social and economic worlds they inhabit, and with no acknowledgment of grammar's context-dependent, rhetorical nature—we will almost surely get the same results as students' former teachers. We have an advantage in that our students *want* to be successful in the academic and work worlds; we need to help them understand—and believe—that a command of standard written English can help them achieve that success.

I attack this goal from an argumentative standpoint, assuming an audience that, while (I hope) not hostile to me, is certainly hostile to my thesis (that they need to put a priority on improving their command of grammar and editing). Early in the semester, I share an anecdote about the airline losing my luggage—including my suit—before a job interview. I tell them how I frantically cobbled together a motley collection of dress clothes from the local shops still open when I got into town, and how, despite the new clothes, I stayed awake out of nervousness until the airline dropped off my recovered suit at three in the morning. We have a chuckle as we picture this, and then I ask them why they think it mattered to me what kind of clothes I had on when what I had in my head—the things I would say in the interview—was exactly the same regardless of what I wore. They have no problem listing why I cared: a negative first impression, a distracting appearance, a lack of confidence, etc. And although we agree that such negative results would be unfair—it wasn't my fault my luggage got lost—we can also agree that those results would be no less likely for their lack of fairness. From there, it's an easy transition to a discussion of how one's competence as an editor can have real bearing on how one's writing is read, and how one is perceived, regardless of whether the ideas are solid or not.

Next, I share research—a greatly abridged version of the research I shared earlier in this article—detailing how others in the business world or academe react to what they see as grammatical incompetence. I stress again that the issue isn't whether it's fair or unfair; it's just reality. Their chemistry teacher will teach them the science required for the term paper; she wants the grammatical know-how already to be present. Similarly, their employers will tell them the contents of the letters they are to write to all clients; the sentence structure, however, will be up to them, and for their job security, they'd better get it right. I talk about how grammar isn't even close to the most important thing in writing—to return to my anecdote, I could have been well-dressed but devoid of ideas, and that would be far worse than to be missing a suit—and I tell them I'm not asking them to write or speak in standard English all the time, but that I want them to learn it and become fluent in it so they can, essentially, put on suits when they need to.

Finally, I lay out a plan for them to achieve such fluency, or at least to take the first steps on the path to doing so. That plan has several components, which correspond to the sections below.

Teach Writing as a Process

One of the key things we can do is teach students that there are several stages to a successful writing process, and that editing comes last. Unfortunately, unskilled writers tend to focus on achieving correctness as the paramount goal in writing (Harris 120), and frequently focus on avoiding errors from the start (Bissex 37). We can help by showing the normal, messy evolution of a piece of writing. In my classes, I emphasize process by sharing drafts of pieces I'm currently working on. For instance, during a unit on synthesis in my recent research writing class, I shared my drafts of this article, including an annotated bibliography, an "idea map" where I had organized the research by topics and suggested strategies, and an initial draft. For a creative writing class, I shared several drafts of a poem, talked about why I'd made the changes I did, and even shared the rejection letter and annotated copy of the poem from the editor at the first place I'd submitted it. Throughout these discussions, I emphasized that I was providing a window into my writing process. I talked about the value each stage had in the creation of my pieces, and we discussed how they might find a process that worked for them.

Despite my nervousness at sharing my own work—especially work that was unfinished, messy, and not quite right—my students were engaged in discussing these drafts and were willing to ask questions about my choices; several came up to me after class and told me how much the experience helped them—both in terms of providing a model for their own writing process and in simply seeing me step down from my teacher's pedestal and share my own confusions and challenges. None said they respected my feedback on their own writing less now that they'd seen that great writing didn't leap from my head fully formed.

In addition to demonstrating a solid writing process, we should also do what we can to make sure our grading systems and the structure of our courses treats writing as a process. Edwina Helton and Jeff Sommers suggest we find "a way to integrate grading and responding in a manner that promotes learning through revision," and that rather than use grades, we initially mark essays according to where they seem to fall in the writing process—early, middle, or late (157–58). Students would not work on editing issues until their drafts fell in the later stage.

Several years ago, I adopted a similar technique and switched from assigning a grade to each essay to grading by portfolio. Once a grade is put on a paper, students tend to treat it as finished. I didn't want students to finish a paper in the fourth week of the course; instead, I wanted them to keep coming back to it, to look at it with new eyes enriched by the knowledge they'd gained in the intervening weeks. Basically, I wanted to encourage revision. So, I divided their final grade into two parts: process and product. The process portion is determined by the day-to-day work in the course—whether they have a draft on time, whether they do their homework, and the like—and the product portion is entirely based on the final portfolio, which contains three essays of their choice. They produce five essays in the course, and in my comments I focus on identifying areas for revision, asking questions, and offering ideas. On a rubric similar to one suggested by Peter Elbow (195), I mark several areas on each essay as strong, OK, or weak. Students can resubmit their essays as many times as they want. To encourage better initial submissions, I give an incentive for their process grade if the majority of their essays fall at an OK level or above, but I emphasize that some holes are fine; the focus should be on selecting three essays to rework extensively for the final portfolio. The process requires quite a bit of both written and oral feedback to allay student worries that I will hit them with a surprise failing grade at the end of the course, but such feedback is pleasurable—instead of crafting my comments to head off arguments about paper grades, I can focus on helping them identify what works and what could be revised.

Focus Teacher-Student Interaction on Talking and Listening

Another strategy we can employ to improve students' grammatical skills is to concentrate on dialogue and questioning. Some authors assert that targeted questioning will enable the teacher and student to identify problems and fix them together. Jeff Brooks advises we "ask questions as often as possible," and use that dialogue to develop small tasks for the student to work on independently (86). Muriel Harris also advocates using questioning to target instruction on only what the student needs to hear (120), as does Kathryn Evans, who also cautions that quite a bit of teacher response tends to be context-free—i.e., the same regardless of student or paper—and of limited value (293). And Linda Boynton argues for regular individual conferences in developmental writing classrooms, stating that such conferences "help students find a 'voice' that truly makes them a part of the academic community" (391).

Many of us have students write targeted reflections on the processes they followed after each essay, and technology has offered us some new ways of continuing the dialogue outside the classroom, such as threaded discussions and even online chat-room office hours. However, I haven't found anything I like so much as the face-to-face writing conference. Perhaps it's because I was a writing center consultant before I was a teacher. The techniques used by most peer tutors—reading papers aloud, minimizing the amount of writing one does on someone else's paper, asking lots of questions—work wonders in the classroom setting as well. And conferences allow us to address complex ideas such as the rhetorical nature of error in a much more relaxed setting than the classroom.

In addition, at the community college, we often work with nonfluent writers, and it can be difficult to understand the richness of the meaning they're trying to get across from just their written words. Through conversation, we can access that richness. Then, together, we can develop strategies to help the writing improve. Conferences are especially helpful for grammatical issues; chances are, a student has had several teachers in the past write "frag" next to the many fragments in her writing, and the handbook definition hasn't helped. Enormous progress can be made in a relatively short time if that time is highly focused. But it's necessary to talk with the student, to question, and to work intensively with the student's own work in order to pinpoint exactly what the student's thought process is that's resulting in the error and to develop an individualized strategy for success.

It is always difficult to find time for such conferences, of course. Writing centers and learning-support labs can help, and so can peer-response groups (although I have had mixed results with those on grammatical problems; they seem to be better at content-level issues). I find that both the students and I get so much out of our one-on-one interactions, though, that I build my courses around them.

Work on Grammar in Students' Own Writing

Connected to the need to base grammar instruction in a conversation between teacher and student is the necessity of using students' own writing as the medium for instruction. As Harris puts it, when we teach grammar in the context of the student's own writing, "we are no longer merely working on formal grammar, grammar in the abstract, but working with the student on his or her own prose structures" (119–20).

Josephine Tarvers states that students learn best by "having their writing diagnosed, keeping an error log, and learning to predict where errors may occur so they can check carefully for them" (71). One promising strategy comes from Helen Collins Sitler, who identifies one of her goals as helping her students develop awareness of their own patterns of error and shares a strategy she has had good results with: "fix-it pages," in which she marks down the errors in a student's final draft "that most detract from the writer's conveying a meaningful message" (73). The page has columns for how the student should fix it, where the rule is in the handbook, and if it is changing in the student's writing— the students fill those out themselves. In future assignments, students use their own fix-it pages to remind themselves to check for errors they tend to make. It's important to note that the column about how to fix the error isn't just a restatement of a rule; it's where students note the detailed strategies they've devised to make sure they get it right in the future. I plan to use this technique in the fall.

Encourage Careful Rereading

Brooks argues that "if we can get students to reread a paper even once before handing it in, in most cases we have rendered an improvement" (84). Likewise, Ann Berthoff suggests that "any writing assignments that encourage students to look and look again will be teaching critical reading and critical thinking" (48).

One of the most common strategies writing teachers (including me) seem to use to get students to slow down and pay attention to what is actually on the page is to have them read their papers aloud. Hartwell writes that students who are asked to read their papers aloud will correct most of their errors themselves (386). I have found reading aloud to be most effective in addressing typos, forgotten words, and mistaken word endings, most commonly in the context of peer-response groups; I've had less success using it alone to remedy larger issues such as sentence fragments, or especially tricky ones like comma placement and colon use. For more difficult issues, students tend to need more help from me in conference before they can recognize such errors.

Provide Models of Good Writing

It seems intuitive that in order for students to improve as writers, they need to be immersed in good writing and asked to write imitatively, thereby stretching their command of written language in much the same way young children stretch their oral communication skills by talking with adults. Moffett tracks language acquisition in kids and points out that they naturally learn most of the fundamental rules of oral communication through conversation and observation. Assuming our students decide to commit themselves to learning standard English, Moffett suggests we teach it by immersing students in it to allow them to acquire the rules naturally (158, 163). (This might be seen as a way of directly expanding Hartwell's Grammars 1 and 3.) Bonnie Devet also suggests imitation—give students great sentences from great authors, she writes, and have them try to write similar sentences—while Glenda Bissex stresses the necessity of providing students with models, with the goal of making the writing techniques inherent in the models their own.

I think it's important to provide students with excellent models about subjects they care about, not just adequate models. Like many teachers, I use essays from past students as models for specific essays I'd like students to write, and as springboards to a discussion of what the authors did well and what they could have done better. However, I think most readings should be truly excellent—as in professional. (For instance, I teach annotation and active reading on the first day of class using a few paragraphs from Mike Rose's *Lives on the Boundary*; I've taught structure and punctuation by analyzing a *New Yorker* article by Elizabeth Kolbert on global warming.) Not only does this give us a chance to see how writing functions in the real world, and to discuss things like audience and the rhetorical choices the author made, but it lets students see what can be achieved with writing in much the same way a high-school basketball player who watches the pros sees the potential of her sport realized. Many of my students rarely read more than they are required to; how can we expect them to understand the power and pleasure of the written word without providing them with excellent examples?

In many cases, students complain, at least initially, about the complexity of the readings. Especially in the first and last few weeks, it is necessary to check in some way to make sure they're actually reading them. However, I think requiring students to read complex (albeit understandable, with some effort) pieces is not only valid, but necessary. As Moffett writes, "[T]he final answer to linguistic elaboration [i.e., adept construction of complex sentences] lies beyond language, in general cognitive development, and [. . .] intellectual stimulation is far more likely to accelerate syntactic growth than grammar knowledge" (163). In other words, we should give students excellent readings to show them not only great writing, but great thinking as well.

Assign Agency to the Student—Don't Correct

One common theme in current research is that correcting grammatical problems in a student's paper actually undermines our goals as writing teachers. Instead, we should focus on talking and listening, drawing the student's attention to key elements in the paper, and giving him or her support. Greg Giberson cautions that "common types of response in which teachers cross out sentences or phrases and rewrite them for the student can have the effect of appropriating ownership of the text from the student" (411). In other words, if our purpose is to teach students skills to succeed in future writing situations in which there may or may not be teachers present—in short, if we aim to produce successful, self-reliant writers—we will target our response to encourage those traits.

In "Minimal Marking," Richard Haswell describes an error-marking strategy that is extremely noninvasive and, based on an empirical study he performed, effective. The only thing Haswell does to indicate error is put a check mark in the margin next to the line in which the error occurs (167). He marks multiple checks for multiple errors. Papers are returned fifteen minutes before the end of class, and students find and correct the errors. He works with students individually to make sure the corrections are actually correct. Haswell has found that, on their own, students will correct 60 to 70 percent of their errors; "carelessness and not stupidity" is generally the source of the error (167).

I use a variation on minimal marking in my own classes. I've had good results with a version of focus correction areas (FCAs) ("Focused"); basically, I've identified eight or nine grammatical concepts I'd like my students to master by the time the semester ends. For each polished essay, we focus on two or three of them. Along with each essay assignment, I hand out a sheet that details those areas, provides examples and explanations, and indexes the pages in our handbook that discuss those concepts. I talk about them very briefly when I hand them out, and then we don't mention them (unless they ask me to) for the next couple of weeks. As we get closer to the essay's due date, I teach microlessons on the FCAs, assign students to write paragraphs about readings, and then have them correct or modify the paragraphs for whatever grammatical concepts we're working on. I collect these paragraphs and give them feedback targeted on our current FCAs; I don't grade them. These microlessons are designed primarily to position editing at an appropriate spot in the writing process (the end), to increase awareness of the grammatical concepts right before essays are due, and to give me a chance to provide individualized, targeted feedback.

On my students' formal essays, I follow Haswell's practice of check marks in the margin. Like Haswell, I've found that students tend to be able to find and correct simple errors on their own once I draw their attention to the lines in which the errors occur; if they can't, I have them ask me, and if it's a pattern of error, I usually suggest an individual conference. Especially in the case of students I have for both first- and second-semester composition, I notice a marked improvement in their ability to identify and correct errors on their own over the course of our time together.

Conclusion

At our college, and surely at others, students have demonstrated a need for a greater command of standard written English. Our responsibility as writing instructors isn't to address only those aspects of writing with which we feel comfortable; instead, it is to identify areas in which we can help our students and to respond. The teaching of grammar is a problematic task, but with an awareness of current research, coupled with a spirit of openness and flexibility in the classroom, it may be possible to teach grammar effectively. Let's hope it is. As instructors, we must move beyond what hasn't been working and find what will.

Works Cited

Beason, Larry. "Ethos and Error: How Business People React to Errors." *CCC* 53.1 (Sept. 2001): 33–64.

Berthoff, Ann E. "A Curious Triangle and the Double-Entry Notebook; or, How Theory Can Help Us Teach Reading and Writing." *The Making of Meaning: Metaphors, Models, and Maxims for Writing Teachers*. Montclair, NJ: Boynton, 1981. 41–47. Rpt. in Wiley, Gleason, and Phelps 45–49.

Bissex, Glenda L. "Growing Writers in Classrooms." *Language Arts* 58 (1981): 785–91. Rpt. in Wiley, Gleason, and Phelps 34–39.

Boynton, Linda. "See Me: Conference Strategies for Developmental Writers." *TETYC* 30.4 (May 2003): 391–402.

Braddock, Richard, Richard Lloyd-Jones, and Lowell Schoer. *Research in Written Composition*. Champaign, IL: NCTE, 1963.

Brooks, Jeff. "Minimalist Tutoring: Making the Student Do All the Work." *Writing Lab Newsletter* 15.6 (1991): 1–4. Rpt. in *The St. Martin's Sourcebook for Writing Tutors*. Ed. Christina Murphy and Steve Sherwood. New York: St. Martin's, 1995. 83–87.

"Business Communication and College Curriculum: North Central Michigan College Employer Survey 2001." Unpublished study, 2001.

Dawkins, John. "Teaching Meaning-Based Punctuation." *TETYC* 31.2 (Dec. 2003): 154–62.

DeGenaro, William. "Social Utility and Needs-Based Education: Writing Instruction at the Early Junior College." *TETYC* 28.2 (Dec. 2000): 129–40.

Devet, Bonnie. "Welcoming Grammar Back into the Writing Classroom." *TETYC* 30.1 (Sept. 2002): 8–17.

Elbow, Peter. "Ranking, Evaluating, and Liking: Sorting Out Three Forms of Judgment." *College English* 55.2 (Feb. 1993): 187–205.

Evans, Kathryn A. "Rethinking Self-Assessment as a Tool for Response." *TETYC* 28.3 (Mar. 2001): 293–301.

"Focused Editing." Collins Educational Associates. 2004. 13 June 2006 http://www.collinseducationassociates.com/FCAs.htm.

Francis, W. Nelson. "Revolution in Grammar." *Quarterly Journal of Speech* 40 (1954): 299–312.

Giberson, Greg A. "Process Intervention: Teacher Response and Student Writing." *TETYC* 29.4 (May 2002): 411–17.

Gorrell, Donna. "Style and Identity: Students Writing like the Professionals." *TETYC* 32.4 (May 2005): 393–402.

Harris, Muriel. *Teaching One-to-One: The Writing Conference* Urbana, IL: NCTE, 1986.

Hartwell, Patrick. "Grammar, Grammars, and the Teaching of Grammar." *College English* 47 (Feb. 1985): 105–27. Rpt. in *The St. Martin's Guide to Teaching Writing* Ed. Robert Connors and Cheryl Glenn. 3rd ed. New York: St. Martin's, 1995. 370–93.

Haswell, Richard. "Minimal Marking." *Teaching Writing: Theories and Practice* Ed. Josephine Koster Tarvers. 3rd ed. New York: Harper, 1992. 166–70.

Helton, Edwina L., and Jeff Sommers. "Repositioning Revision: A Rhetorical Approach to Grading." *TETYC* 28.2 (Dec. 2000): 157–64.

Kolbert, Elizabeth. "The Climate of Man—1." *New Yorker* 25 Apr. 2005: 56–71.

Lynch-Biniek, Amy. "Bemoans, Belittles, and Leaves," *Teaching English in the Two-Year College* 33:1 (September 2005): 29–37.

Moffett, James. *Teaching the Universe of Discourse*. Boston: Houghton, 1983.

Postman, Neil, and Charles Weingartner. *Linguistics: A Revolution in Teaching*. New York: Dell, 1966.

Rose, Mike. *Lives on the Boundary: A Moving Account of the Struggles and Achievements of America's Educationally Underprepared*. New York: Penguin, 1990.

Shaughnessy, Mina P. "Some New Approaches toward Teaching." *Journal of Basic Writing* 13 (1994): 103–16. Rpt. in Wiley, Gleason, and Phelps 149–56.

Sitler, Helen Collins. "Solutions to Mechanical Errors in Writing: Usage Scans and Fix-It Pages." *TETYC* 29.1 (Sept. 2001): 72–76.

Tarvers, Josephine Koster. *Teaching Writing: Theories and Practice*. New York: Harper, 1992.

Tchudi, Steven, and Diana Mitchell. *Explorations in the Teaching of English*. 3rd ed. New York: Harper, 1989.

Wiley, Mark, Barbara Gleason, and Louise Wetherbee Phelps. *Composition in Four Keys: Inquiring into the Field*. Mountain View, CA: Mayfield, 1996.

Williams, Joseph M. "The Phenomenology of Error." *CCC* 32 (1981): 152–68. Rpt. in Wiley, Gleason, and Phelps 163–75.

"WPA Outcomes Statement for First-Year Composition." *College English* 63.3 (Jan. 2001): 321–25.

Playful Explicitness with Grammar: A Pedagogy for Writing

Debra Myhill, Susan Jones, Annabel Watson, and Helen Lines

As Debra Myhill, Susan Jones, Annabel Watson, and Helen Lines, the authors of the selection that follows, note, "The research team at the Centre for Research in Writing at the University of Exeter, UK, have been investigating writing processes and the teaching of writing for many years. Most recently, they have been considering the contested issue of grammar teaching, adopting an inter-disciplinary theoretical perspective. In particular, they have argued that an appropriate pedagogy for writing should include grammar teaching which draws writers' attention to the linguistic choices and possibilities available to them. A randomized controlled trial, conducted by the team, has indicated a beneficial effect on writing outcomes when adopting this approach, at the same time as highlighting the importance of teachers' subject knowledge of grammar. This chapter outlines this pedagogy and the theoretical ideas it draws on, and is significant in illustrating that teaching grammar is not about errors and accuracy but is fundamentally about supporting young learners in accessing a repertoire of infinite possibilities."

Introduction: Grammar and Writing

The contested history of the role of grammar in an English or literacy curriculum has been well rehearsed, indeed repeatedly rehearsed, over time (Braddock et al., 1963; Locke, 2009; Myhill and Jones, 2011; QCA, 1998) and it is a debate that stems from fundamental epistemological disagreements about the value of knowledge about grammar. The abandonment of grammar teaching in most anglophone countries in the 1960s and 1970s followed the Dartmouth Conference of 1966 in the United States and the widespread view that formal grammar teaching had no part in an English curriculum, or worse, that learning grammar was damaging to children's language development (Elbow, 1981), with a *harmful effect* upon writing improvement (Braddock et al., 1963, p. 37). However, whilst terms such as 'abandonment' may reflect a dominant perspective, they do not reflect the inevitable variety of practices and diversity of beliefs that characterise English classrooms around the world, and grammar has always been taught in some classrooms. Moreover, notionally at least, in England, grammar has been a mandatory part of the curriculum since the introduction of the National Curriculum (DES, 1990), with a more prescriptive outline of required grammar in the 1995 version (DfE, 1995), and considerable emphasis upon

From *Literacy*, 2013, vol. 47, no. 2, pp. 103-11.

grammar in the English/Literacy component of the National Strategies that followed in 1998. What remains true, however, is that at policy and professional levels, there is ambiguity and ambivalence about the role of grammar in the curriculum.

This ambivalence is particularly keen in relation to the impact of learning about grammar on other aspects of language performance, especially writing. There have been repeated studies or reviews that have shown no evidence of a positive impact of teaching grammar on children's writing (Andrews et al., 2006; Elley et al., 1979; Hillocks, 1984; Wyse, 2004). However, these studies have largely investigated whether teaching a discrete grammar course improved writing attainment, and frequently the "non-grammar" group had additional opportunities to write. There have been no large-scale studies that investigated the benefit of creating an integration of writing and grammar, where relevant grammar was meaningfully introduced at appropriate points in the teaching of writing. The study (Myhill et al., 2012) that informs this article set out to address this gap: in this article, we seek to articulate the theoretical thinking underpinning the pedagogy adopted for the study and caution against policy mandates which ignore the importance of principled pedagogical understanding.

Grammar for Writing: The Research Study

Conceptualising Grammar

One challenge confronting any researcher of grammar is the multiplicity of meanings and connotations that the word evokes. Everyone knows what grammar is, including Joe Public and Percy Politician, and everyone has a view: indeed, many have their own *bête noire* of grammatical impropriety. And here is where the problem begins. Contemporary linguistics consistently conceptualises grammar descriptively, the study of language as it is used, in different contexts and in different social settings. In contrast, the public, and even at times the professional, view of grammar is prescriptive, specifying how language should be used. Prescriptive views of grammar are "often social rules that are believed to mark out a speaker or writer as educated or as belonging to a particular social class" (Carter and McCarthy, 2006, p. 6). At a policy level, grammar becomes inexorably conflated with moral propriety and combating "dark social forces" (Cameron, 1995, p. 96), whether that be Norman Tebbit connecting grammar with street crime (Cameron, 1995, p. 94) or the *Evening Standard* reporting that the London riots in 2011 could be attributed to the fact that young people did not know how to speak properly (Johns, 2011). From an educational perspective, grammar has been cast as an antidote to all things bad, where "strong doses of English grammar" will act as "a cure for some of our educational ills" (Elley et al., 1979, p. 3). Certainly, a dominant educational view of grammar is that it is about the avoidance or remediation of error: it is about accuracy, correctness, and "proper" English. This stance is likely to result in grammar teaching characterised by learning grammar rules, undertaking decontextualised exercises and drills, and feedback which corrects grammatical errors.

In our study, therefore, we began by clarifying our theoretical conceptualisation of grammar in order to develop appropriate pedagogical practices through which to make connections between grammar and writing. We adopted Carter and McCarthy's definition of grammar as being "concerned with how sentences and utterances are formed" (2006, p. 2), incorporating the structure of sentences, syntax, and the structure of words, morphology. We also included within the umbrella of this definition the structure of texts, discourse. It is a fully descriptive view of grammar, interested in developing learners' knowledge about how language works in different contexts. Carter and McCarthy usefully distinguish between grammar as *structure*, how words, sentences, and texts are constructed, and grammar as *choice*, the range of possibilities open to a language user. They argue that "the grammar of choice is as important as the grammar of structure" (2006, p. 7) and in the study reported here, the focus was upon the grammar of choice. It is essentially a rhetorical view of grammar, interested in how language choices construct meanings, and recognising that "the grammatical choices we make, including pronoun use, active or passive verb constructions, and sentence patterns—represent relations between writers and the world they live in" (Micciche, 2004, p. 719). This links well with the idea of writers as designers (Myhill, 2011a; Sharples, 1999), which sees writers as agentive, creative shapers of meaning, designing texts in terms of ideas, layout, voice, and including grammatical choice. It encourages a playful attitude towards language, exploring the possibilities and limits of what language can achieve. Working from the premise that grammar serves as a semiotic mediating tool, to develop knowledge about language means to become metalinguistically aware and to be able to think grammatically about language (Williams, 2004, 2005). Likewise, Vygotsky (1962) argues that what learners will develop as mediational means for future activities is influenced by what they have become aware of in language. He described writing as the "deliberate structuring of the web of meaning" (1962, p. 100). Accordingly, our goal was not to teach about "correct" ways of writing, but to open up for young writers a repertoire of infinite possibilities for deliberate structuring and authorial decision-making.

The Intervention

The study informing this article is reported more fully elsewhere (Jones et al., 2012; Myhill, 2011b; Myhill et al., 2012). In a nutshell, the study involved one Year 8 class drawn from 32 schools in the Midlands and the South-West. Following a test of teachers' grammatical knowledge, the teachers were matched for strength of subject knowledge, then half the classes were randomly allocated to a comparison group and the other half to an intervention group.

The intervention involved the teaching of three writing units, addressing fictional narrative, argument, and poetry writing. Each unit lasted for 3 weeks of lessons (approximately three 1-hour lessons per week) and one unit was taught in each term of the school year. Learning objectives for each unit were selected from the Framework for English (DfES, 2001), which at that time was the curriculum document informing teaching in English secondary schools—in this way, the learning outcomes were wholly compatible with national expectations. A detailed set of teaching materials was devised for each writing genre in which grammar features relevant to the writing being taught were integrated: for example, looking at how noun phrases can support effective description of settings in narrative. The teaching focus of each unit was writing, not grammar, and the creation of the teaching materials was informed by the theoretical conceptualisation outlined above. The comparison group addressed the same learning objectives, the same medium-term plan, and produced the same written outcomes, but they did not receive the detailed lesson plans with the embedded grammar.

The Results

Students' improvement in writing as a consequence of being in the intervention or comparison group was determined through the use of a pre- and post-test of writing, mirroring the national writing test for 13–14-year-olds (Key Stage 3), and designed and marked by Cambridge Assessment who were formerly the test developers and markers for the national writing test at Key Stage 3. The statistical analysis indicated a statistically significant positive effect for the intervention group: over the year, students in the intervention group improved their writing scores by 20 per cent, compared with 11 per cent in the comparison group. The analysis also showed that the embedded grammar teaching had greatest impact on able writers. This finding may be attributable to the absence of improvement in able writers in the comparison group, who barely improved over the year, whereas the weaker writers in the comparison group did make some improvement over the year. Finally, the statistical analysis also signalled the crucial role played by teachers' own grammatical knowledge as this was a significant factor mediating the success or otherwise of the intervention.

Having outlined briefly the key design and outcomes of the research study, the remainder of this article will outline the pedagogical principles that underpinned the intervention, and illustrate both the theoretical grounding and practical classroom examples that exemplify the approach.

Framing the Pedagogy: Key Teaching Principles

Drawing on this theoretical conceptualisation of writing as design and a rhetorical view of grammar, focusing on grammar as choice, we began creating the teaching materials by first devising a set of pedagogical principles that acted as guides framing the design. These pedagogical principles were as follows:

- grammatical metalanguage is used, but it is always explained through examples and patterns;

- links are always made between the feature introduced and how it might enhance the writing being tackled;

- discussion is fundamental in encouraging critical conversations about language and effects;

- the use of "creative imitation" offers model patterns for students to play with and then use in their own writing;

- the use of authentic examples from authentic texts links writers to the broader community of writers;

- activities should support students in making choices and being designers of writing;

- language play, experimentation, risk-taking, and games should be actively encouraged.

Through the incorporation of these pedagogical principles into the teaching units, the intention was to develop students' metalinguistic understanding through making visible and explicit the authorial choices, the repertoire of possibilities, available to them. The specific theoretical thinking informing each of the principles and examples of how each one could be realised in practice is elaborated in more detail below.

Grammatical Metalanguage Is Used, but It Is Explained through Examples

Although some have argued, such as Robinson (2005, p. 39), that "the role of metalanguage is highly significant in the ongoing development of pupils' language abilities," there has been relatively little purposeful discussion of the place of grammatical terminology in the writing curriculum for first language speakers. Whilst there is an evident precision in being able to use appropriate metalanguage to discuss language, there is always a danger that the terminology obscures the learning focus of the lesson, or indeed becomes the learning focus. At its worst, terminology could become a barrier to learning. As Fearn and Farnan observed, simply being able "to define and identify grammatical labels is not related to writing skills" (2005, p. 2) and our goal was to develop the metalinguistic understanding of the way language was being used, to see how language works. The work of Williams (2004, 2005) in Australia is significant in this respect as he demonstrated that children at an early age are able to cope with the demands of formal linguistic features when grammar forms a purposeful part of textual study. In the light of this, the use of grammatical metalanguage was actively built into lessons, since hearing the terminology used in relevant contexts is likely to support later acquisition of the metalanguage. The decision to use a particular grammatical term was not serendipitous, but purposeful, and was only used "if the term was necessary or useful in helping students understand and discuss the chosen language content" (Mulder, 2010, p. 65). However, the grammatical metalanguage was never the core focus of an activity: examples and patterns were always used alongside the metalanguage to allow students to access and play with a particular structure and discuss its effect even if they did not remember the grammatical name. Keith argued that students needed to explore the metalinguistic concept first before moving into labelling: "grammatical concepts come first, then the terminology" (1997, p. 8). In the classroom example illustrated in Table 1, the term "modal verb" is used, but the prior exploration of modal verbs in famous speeches and the support of a resource simply listing the modal verbs enable students to access the activity, even if their grammatical understanding of modal verbs is limited.

Table 1. Classroom Example of Using Grammatical Metalanguage through Examples

Context: writing a persuasive speech

Learning Focus: how modal verbs can express different levels of assertiveness or possibility in persuasion

Resource with modal verbs listed: *can; could; may; might; must; shall; should; will; ought to* following an activity exploring modal verbs in famous speeches

Task:
- Imagine that you are Roy Hodgson talking to the England team before the penalty shoot-out in the Euro 2012 match against Spain. Write a short 'pep talk,' arguing that it is still possible to win, using some of these modal verbs to predict what *might/can/ will* happen in the shoot-out.
- **You could start:** "We can win a penalty shoot-out."

Links Are Always Made between the Feature Introduced and
How It Might Enhance the Writing Being Tackled

Given that historically, earlier studies on the grammar–writing relationship had established little impact of discrete grammar courses on
students' writing, it was crucially important for this study that teaching made connections for learners between a particular grammar feature and its potential meaning-making effect. Indeed, two small-scale
studies in the United States that investigated the impact of grammar
on writing provide some earlier evidence of the benefits of establishing
these connections for learners. Fogel and Ehri's study (2000) focused on
supporting learners in recognising the difference between American
Standard English and Black Vernacular English (BVE), because their
students were too frequently writing in BVE. Using grammar as the
tool, they "clarified for students the link between features in their own
non-standard writing and features in Standard English" (Fogel and
Ehri, 2000, p. 231). More recently, Fearn and Farnan (2007) undertook
an intervention study where they taught students sentence grammar
in the context of writing and found a positive outcome. Whilst it is not
clear that their approach sought to explore the rhetorical and meaning-
making potential of grammar, what they did do was to argue that "grammar instruction influences writing performance when grammar and
writing share one instructional context" (Fearn and Farnan, 2007, p. 16).
For our study, given that the goal in embedding attention to grammar
within a writing curriculum was to support writing development, not to
learn grammar, considering and discussing grammatical constructions
in textual contexts was critical. Considering how grammatical structures
create meaning in specific contexts reinforces the importance of context, and understanding the different effects that different structures can
create is part of beginning to understand the writer's craft and the possibilities open to a writer.

In this way, establishing links between a grammar feature and a
writing context supports development of students' metalinguistic understanding. As noted previously, whilst the use of grammatical metalanguage was not avoided, the focus of the teaching was not on grammatical
labelling. Here, there is an important distinction between declarative
knowledge of grammar terms, and procedural knowledge, or knowledge-
in-action (Gombert, 1992, p. 191). Without this connected procedural
knowledge, there is always the danger that the grammar component in
a writing lesson is reduced to teaching the "normative structures and
grammatical labels in isolation from meaning" prefigured by Derewianka and Jones (2010, p. 14). In the policy context of England, making
meaningful connections between writing and grammar avoids redundant learning, such as believing that complex sentences are good sentences or that opening a sentence with an adverb is good practice (Myhill, 2011b, p. 265) (see Table 2).

Table 2. Classroom Example of Making Connections between a Grammatical Structure and a Writing Context

Context: writing fairy tales

Learning Focus: the simplicity of noun phrases in fairy tales

Connections between grammar and writing:
Through discussion and guided textual analysis, the teacher draws out the following characteristics of noun phrases in fairy tales:
- Fairy tales draw on oral narratives and written versions retain many of the patterns of oral language. These helped listeners to follow and remember the story. Nouns and adjectives are often used very simply.
- Repetition of adjectives, for example, *long, long ago; far, far away; a dark, dark wood.*
- Short noun phrases with just one adjective, for example, *wicked stepmother; enchanted forest; handsome prince; golden apple.*
- Predictable 'stock' of nouns and adjectives, for example, *beautiful; evil; castle; king; forest; princess.*

Discussion Is Fundamental in Encouraging Critical Conversations about Language and Effects

If making connections between grammar and writing is significant in developing learning about writing, then talk is a key mechanism through which this learning is achieved. The deliberate incorporation of multiple opportunities for students to discuss the grammar points being introduced is founded upon theories of learning that emphasise the importance of talk in fostering effective learning. The talk encouraged by the intervention was exploratory talk (Alexander, 2004; Barnes et al., 1986; Mercer, 2000), where the teacher is not the authority in possession of the right answer, but where the students explore the possibilities of language and discuss their interpretations of effects. For both Barnes et al. (1986, p. 81) and Mercer (2000, p. 55), exploratory talk supports learners in making connections between their learning experiences. It is also important in enabling real learning to occur, in "a collaborative endeavour in which meanings are negotiated and some common knowledge is mobilized" (Mercer, 2000, p. 6), rather than rote or superficial learning transmitted by the teacher. This is perhaps especially relevant in terms of developing metalinguistic understanding about writing, where it is all too easy for teachers to establish formulaic approaches to writing, often driven by the high-stakes testing climate in England (Myhill, 2011b; Myhill and Jones, 2011, p. 265). Talk, therefore, may be the key to moving students from superficial learning about grammar (e.g., add adjectives to create description) to deep learning (e.g., some adjectives are redundant because the noun is de-

Table 3. Classroom Example of a Discussion Task to Stimulate Critical Conversations about Text

Context: writing fictional narrative

Learning Focus: how short sentences can create tension in narrative

Task:

In pairs, read the extract from Peter Benchley's *Jaws* and find the three shortest sentences he uses. Discuss why he might have chosen to make these three sentences so short? What part do they play in the narrative structure of this incident? What effect might they have on the reader?

scriptive). Kellogg (1994) argued that writers needed metacognitive knowledge to generate *a model of their audience* and to reflect *on rhetorical and content probabilities,* and stressed that teaching writing is as much about teaching thinking as it is about teaching writing (p. 213). The role of the teacher is to act as a "discourse guide . . . using language for thinking collectively" (Mercer, 2000, p. 170) and to facilitate discussion about linguistic choices, possibilities, and effects. Through this kind of exploratory talk, students are given ownership in making writerly decisions, and are enabled to "make informed judgements about language," questioning rather than compliantly accepting "socially defined notions of 'good grammar'" (Denham and Lobeck, 2010, p. 230) (see Table 3 above).

The Use of "Creative Imitation" Offers Model Patterns for Students to Play with and Use in Their Own Writing

In contemporary classrooms, imitation is frequently a pejorative term, signifying a low level of unoriginal activity, perhaps copying or rote-learning. But imitation, or *mimesis,* has a long history in creative art, drawing on the thinking of Aristotle in particular. Aristotle, in his *Poetics* (1996), considered the relationship between life and art, arguing that it is intrinsic to human nature to be imitative and that we learn through imitation. Although much of Aristotle's thinking in relation to mimesis is about how the audience of creative art is stimulated to understand life and emotions better through the representational imitation of art, it is also about how the artist creates art forms through "perception and understanding of their representational content and structure" (Halliwell, 2002, p. 199). Halliwell suggests that we learn through active experimentation "with story patterns, metrical forms, stylistic registers" (2002, p. 175), and the concept of imitation was central to the study of rhetoric in Western thought. Conscious imitation of artistic role models was advocated and "poets actively sought to imitate

Table 4. Classroom Example of Using Imitation to Support the Use of Model Patterns in Writing

Context: argument writing

Learning Focus: how using an imperative opening sentence followed by an emotive narrative can act as an effective hook for a persuasive argument which follows

Task:
Use the following opening of a fund-raising campaign leaflet against animal cruelty as a model for writing the opening paragraph of your own argument.

Picture the scene. There are dogs running wild around a courtyard littered with muck and machinery. There are dogs rammed in cages, noses pressed against the bars. There are dogs whose fur is hanging in great clumps, with bare skin and running sores. The noise of barking and yelping is deafening, but in one cage a golden labrador lies silent, head on its paws, looking at the yard with melancholy eyes.

exemplary forerunners and the artistic conventions they made authoritative" (Potolsky, 2006, p. 50).

The use of textual models as scaffolds for young learners in writing is much more familiar, through the work of the genre movement in Australia (Martin, 1985; Rose, 2009) and Lewis and Wray's work (1997) on non-fiction writing in England. In essence, the use of models encourages imitation in order to support initial learning about a text. The same principles of support apply to imitation at sentence or phrase level: imitation is a scaffold that allows students to try out new structures and play with new ways of expressing something. Whilst the precise grammatical metalanguage may be used to describe the pattern, the use of imitation allows the writer to practise and manipulate the structure without necessarily being able to label it grammatically. Such imitation may also be a powerful learning tool in helping to embed new structures cognitively within the student's writing repertoire. Paraskevas encourages her students "to imitate artful sentences, to practise writing their own well-crafted model sentences" (2006, p. 66) arguing that this process enables the internalisation of the patterns imitated, and that "imitation is the first step toward giving writers choices that reflect their stylistic and rhetorical competence" (2006, p. 66). And, of course, creative imitation may be a first step in generating wholly original combinations (see Table 4 above).

The Use of Authentic Examples from Authentic Texts Links Writers to the Broader Community of Writers

There are two important reasons for using authentic texts as models and exemplars in the writing classroom. Firstly, using authentic texts avoids the pitfalls of examples artificially created to exemplify a gram-

Table 5. A Classroom Example of Using an Authentic Text to Link Writers to the Community of Writers

Context: writing poetry

Learning Focus: how punctuation and syntax can reinforce meanings

Activity:
Using Wilfred Owen's *Dulce et Decorum Est*:

Pairs/Fours:
Give out copies of the poem with punctuation prompt questions. Students annotate the poem with comments on the relationship between the punctuation and the meaning, and the effect Owen might have been trying to create.

Teacher:
Using the teacher-annotated copy of the poem and prompts, take feedback and support students' understanding of the effects on meaning of different punctuation and different sentence lengths. Note, for example, the final stanza is a single sentence with two long subordinated clauses, building towards the main clause, which is the meaning kernel in the poem.

---

mar point which have no resonance of truth. Traditional school grammar books frequently rely on sentences created, devoid of context, to exemplify neatly a grammatical point, and at worst they can be unconvincing and implausible. In the sample materials published for the forthcoming national test of grammar, punctuation, and spelling for 11-year-olds in England (DfE, 2012), the passive is exemplified with the sentence, "A biscuit was eaten by Sam," which, although grammatically correct, is not a sentence which it is easy to imagine ever being used in an authentic context. Using authentic texts offers students encounters with language-in-action, rather than language-for-demonstration: as Paraskevas argues, "students must be given clear, linguistically accurate information about the structure of their language, information they can use to analyse any real language text—not the simplistic sentences that often appear in some handbooks" (2004, p. 97).

A second reason for using authentic texts is that one goal of an explicit focus on grammar in writing is to help young writers to explore what real writers do and the choices they make in order to nurture their own repertoire of possibilities as authors. It helps to connect writers in classrooms to the broader community of writers beyond the classroom and opens up the opportunity that texts themselves might teach about writing, what Ehrenworth describes as "an apprenticeship relation with great authors, even at the level of sentence structure" (2003, p. 92). In other words, using authentic texts makes meaningful links between being a reader and being a writer. It also recognises that writing is a cultural and social practice, and that classrooms are "framed communities in which children learn to manipulate the semiotic resources available to them in order to make meaning" (Andrews and Smith, 2011, p. 24) (see Table 5 on the previous page).

Activities Should Support Students in Making Choices and Being Designers of Writing

Integral to the purpose of embedding grammar within a pedagogy for writing is the nurturing of students' ability to make informed choices in their writing and to see the process of writing as a process of design (Myhill, 2011a). The underlying idea of design derives from new literacies research that sees literacy as a transformational meaning-making process in which the resources available are re-combined and re-articulated to create a new design (Cope and Kalantzis, 2000, p. 22). In a multimodal world, the notion of design is often equated with visual or layout features, but design choices operate at every level of text production, from choices about the content and ideas and the macro-structure of a text to choices about words, images, and syntactical structures at a micro-level. The rich potentiality of syntactic shaping as a design tool is often ignored — the subtle shifts of meaning and emphasis which can be created by inverting the syntax of a sentence so that the subject comes at the end; by choosing to place adjectives after the noun rather than before the noun; by using a verbless sentence and so on. This is the grammar of choice at play.

Encouraging thinking about choices and design fosters ownership and authorial responsibility. It makes the writing process more visible, illustrating concretely that writing is a complex act of metalinguistic decision-making, as writers strive to make their writing match their rhetorical intentions. This kind of sophisticated decision-making is a marker of development in writing. Young writers tend towards thinking about what to say and then writing it down, what Bereiter and Scardamalia (1987) call "knowledge-telling"; as writers develop, they are better able to make choices about how to represent their ideas in text and are "knowledge transforming." Mature writers are able to shape "what to say and how to say it with the potential reader fully in mind" (Kellogg, 2008, p. 7). Moreover, encouraging writers to become aware that choices are available to them supports the development of a repertoire of possibilities, and gives greater autonomy to the writer. A reduced reliance on teacher-led recommendations may help to avoid the tendency towards formulaic writing, accompanied by checklists of techniques where inclusion of particular techniques is more important than writerly decision-making (see Table 6).

Language Play, Experimentation, Risk-Taking and Games Should Be Actively Encouraged

The notion of playfulness, reflected in the title of this article, is directly counter to the deficit model of grammar, characterised by prescriptive, rule-bound views and an emphasis on accuracy and error remediation.

Table 6. A Classroom Example of an Activity
Supporting the Making of Design Choices

Context: writing argument

Focus: how sentence length and sentence structure can be used to create rhetorical effect in the closing of a persuasive argument

Task:

Students are given the sentences from the final paragraph of a persuasive speech, each sentence on a separate strip of paper. They are given two sets of the same sentences. In pairs, they create two versions of the ending of the argument and discuss the different ways the two versions work. Finally, they choose and justify the choice of their preferred version.

Playfulness and experimentation help writers to see the elasticity of language, the possibilities it affords and what language can do, rather than what writers must not do. Originality in writing is underpinned by linguistic playfulness: indeed, "creativity requires risk-taking and there is no innovation without creativity" (Sahlberg, 2010, p. 343). Although creativity is not a permissive free-for-all, and "creative education involves a balance between teaching knowledge and skills, and encouraging innovation" (NACCCE, 1999, p. 6), it is possible that in the context of writing we have overemphasised skills at the expense of playful innovation. The pedagogical approach described in this article offers explicit guidance and development of metalinguistic knowledge, but this is overlaid with playful activities that allow exploration and experimentation with new knowledge. Philip Pullman rather beautifully describes this kind of playfulness as fooling about:

> . . . fooling about with the stuff the world is made of: with sounds, and with shapes and colours, and with clay and paper and wood and metal, and with language. Fooling about, playing with it, pushing it this way and that, turning it sideways, painting it different colours, looking at it from the back, putting one thing on top of another, asking silly questions, mixing things up, making absurd comparisons, discovering unexpected similarities, making pretty patterns, and all the time saying "Supposing . . . I wonder . . . What if. . . ." (Pullman, 2005)

Ironically, the admonishment of fooling about is a more typical discourse in many classrooms. However, if students are to be allowed to fool around with language, they need classroom environments that recognise the value of constructive "failure," which understand that a playful, unusual attempt to write in a different way may not be successful, and which "helps young people learn how to cope with failure" (Rolfe, 2010, p. 13). Learning through unsuccessful attempts is rich and productive, but only if students are not censured for their "failure." It is

Table 7. A Classroom Example of a Playful, Experimental Writing Task

Context: writing poetry

Focus: how varying sentence structure and sentence length can create different emphases in poetry

Task:
Using an exploded version of Sylvia Plath's *Mirror* presented alphabetically as a word grid, students are asked to generate pairs of sentences, experimenting with the possibilities outlined below:
- Beginning with a non-finite verb, adverb, or prepositional phrase
- Using a short verbless sentence
- Using a one-word sentence
- Using repetition of a single word or short phrase

also likely that competitive, performative educational cultures, characterised by high-stakes testing regimes, lead to a standardisation of learning, rather than divergent or creative thinking (Sacks, 2000). Indeed, it is significant that in our study, the able writers in the comparison group did not improve over the year of the research. This lack of improvement may be because able writers often play safe and avoid trying out new ways of writing: having mastered repertoires of writing which secure a grade A, they may be reluctant to develop their repertoires by testing out new ways of writing for fear of an impact on their grades, or because of a fear of appearing to be strange or wrong (Sahlberg, 2009). To counteract this kind of safe, strategic compliance requires teachers who are themselves "courageous, risk-taking, playful and intuitive" (Goouch, 2008, p. 99) (see Table 7 above).

Discussion

The long-running debate about the role of grammar in the curriculum has always tended to focus on grammar as content, a body of knowledge to be acquired, accompanied by unresolved and contested arguments about the educational purpose and value of that body of knowledge. In contrast, the conceptualisation of grammar at the foundation of this study is a descriptive grammar, focusing on the grammar of choice: in essence, then, we are advocating not a content grammar, but a grammar of process. It is based upon the key principle that "knowing grammar is knowing *how* more than knowing *what*" (Cameron, 1997, p. 236) and leads to "a pedagogy which orients learners to thinking about the effects of grammatical patterning in texts so that their meanings can be uncovered" (Clark, 2005, p. 45). For young writers, such an emphasis on grammar as choice and process should support metalinguistic development and foster the ability not only to make explicit choices in writing but also to articulate an authorial justification for those choices. This explicitness enables young writers to exercise "conscious control and conscious choice over language which enables both to *see through* language in a systematic way and to use language more discriminatingly" (Carter, 1990, p. 119). At the same time, becoming attentive to grammatical patterns and structures and understanding how different linguistic choices subtly shade meanings in different contexts may lead to internalised writer knowledge, which can subsequently be used without conscious choice. In other words, contextualised grammar teaching, grammar as choice, helps young writers to become more metalinguistically aware.

However, this approach to the teaching of grammar and writing requires metalinguistically aware teaching. The most effective teachers in our study were confident in making meaningful connections between grammar and writing for the students in their own classes, and they had sufficient metalinguistic knowledge themselves to encourage active discussion about authorial choices in writing. Their lessons exhibited the characteristics of description, exploration, engagement, and reflection identified by Svalberg as the *"salient features"* of metalinguistically aware teaching (2007, p. 296) and experimental playfulness was evident. In contrast, where teachers struggled with the demands of the intervention, difficulties were attributable to the challenge posed by the grammatical knowledge required and a tendency to try to control students' language choices. The complementary counterpoint to exploratory discussion of language is the habit of explicitness. Metalinguistically aware teachers were able to make "appropriate and strategic interventions" in order to make *"implicit knowledge explicit"* (Carter, 1990, p. 117): they were able to draw out students' implicit knowledge of language, derived from their in-school and out-of-school literacy experiences and make it explicitly available to them as a meaning-making resource.

In many ways, the academic, professional, and political debate about the role of grammar in the curriculum has been an impoverished one, rarely rooted in theoretical thinking, robust empirical evidence, or authentic classroom practice. The study reported here is not a definite answer to a perennial problem. Rather it foregrounds the importance of articulating and enacting a principled rationale for grammar that can inform classroom practice. Sams (2003) has argued that both traditional and in-context approaches to the teaching of grammar fail because "they treat grammar as something that exists apart from and outside of the writing process itself" (p. 57): what we offer here is a role for grammar, coherently theorised within a pedagogy of writing, underpinned by metalinguistically aware teaching and learning, and framed by exploration, playfulness, and experimentation.

References

Alexander, R. (2004) *Towards Dialogic Teaching: Rethinking Classroom Talk*. Cambridge: Dialogos.

Andrews, R. and Smith, A. (2011) *Developing Writers*. Milton Keynes: Open University Press.

Andrews, R., Torgerson, C., Beverton, S., Freeman, A., Locke, T., Low, G., Robinson, A., and Zhu, D. (2006) The effect of grammar teaching on writing development. *British Educational Research Journal*, 32.1, pp. 39–55.

Aristotle (1996) *Poetics* (translated with an introduction and notes by M. Heath). London: Penguin.

Barnes, D., Britton, J., and Torbe, M. (1986) *Language, the Learner and the School*. London: Penguin.

Bereiter, C. and Scardamalia, M. (1987) *The Psychology of Written Composition*. Hillsdale, NJ: Lawrence Erlbaum Associates.

Braddock, R., Lloyd-Jones, R., and Schoer, L. (1963) *Research in Written Composition*. Urbana, IL: National Council of Teachers of English.

Cameron, D. (1995) *Verbal Hygiene*. London: Routledge.

Cameron, D. (1997) Sparing the rod: what teachers need to know about grammar. *Changing English: Studies in Reading and Culture*, 4.2, pp. 229–239.

Carter, R. (Ed.) (1990) *Knowledge about Language*. London: Hodder and Stoughton.

Carter, R. and McCarthy, M. (2006) *Cambridge Grammar of English*. Cambridge: Cambridge University Press.

Clark, U. (2005) Bernstein's theory of pedagogic discourse: linguistics, educational policy and practice in the UK English/literacy classroom. *English Teaching: Practice and Critique*, 4.3, pp. 32–47.

Cope, B. and Kalantzis, M. (2000) *Multiliteracies: Literacy Learning and the Design of Social Futures*. London: Routledge.

Denham, K. and Lobeck, A. (Eds.) (2010) *Linguistics at School*. Cambridge: Cambridge University Press.

Derewianka, B. and Jones, P. (2010) From traditional to grammar to functional grammar: bridging the divide. *NALDIC Quarterly*, 8.1, pp. 6–15.

DES (1990) *English in the National Curriculum*. London: HMSO.

DfE (1995) *English in the National Curriculum*. London: HMSO.

DfE (2012) *English Grammar, Spelling and Punctuation Test*. London: DfES. Available at http://media.education.gov.uk/assets/files/pdf/e/english%20grammar%20spelling%20and%20punctuation%20test%20%20%20sample%20materials.pdf (accessed 20 July 2012).

DfES (2001) *Framework for Teaching English: Years 7, 8 and 9*. London: DfES.

Ehrenworth, M. (2003) Grammar—comma—a new beginning. *English Journal*, 92.3, pp. 90–96.

Elbow, P. (1981) *Writing with Power: Techniques for Mastering the Writing Process*. New York: Oxford University Press.

Elley, W. B., Barham, I. H., Lamb, H., and Wylie, M. (1979) *The Role of Grammar in a Secondary School Curriculum: Educational Research Series No 60*. Wellington, New Zealand: New Zealand Council for Educational Research.

Fearn, L. and Farnan, N. (2007) When is a verb using functional grammar to teach writing. *Journal of Basic Writing*, 26.1, pp. 1–26.

Fogel, H. and Ehri, L. C. (2000) Teaching elementary students who speak black English vernacular to write in standard English: effects of dialect transformation practice. *Contemporary Educational Psychology*, 25, pp. 212–235.

Gombert, J. E. (1992) *Metalinguistic Development*. Chicago, IL: University of Chicago Press.

Goouch, K. (2008) Understanding playful pedagogies, play narratives and play spaces. *Early Years: An International Journal of Research and Development*, 28.1, pp. 93–102.

Halliwell, S. (2002) *The Aesthetics of Mimesis: Ancient Texts and Modern Problems*. Princeton, NJ: Princeton University Press.

Hillocks, G. (1984). What works in teaching composition: a meta-analysis of experimental treatment studies. *American Journal of Education*. November, pp. 133–170.

Johns, L. (2011) Ghetto grammar robs the young of a proper voice. *Evening Standard*, 16 August.

Jones, S., Myhill, D. A., and Bailey, T. C. (2012) Grammar for writing? An investigation into the effect of contextualised grammar teaching on student writing. *Reading and Writing*, Online Sept 2012.

Keith, G. (1997) Teach yourself English grammar. *The English and Media Magazine*, 36, pp. 6–10.

Kellogg, R. T. (1994) *The Psychology of Writing*. Oxford: Oxford University Press.

Kellogg, R. T. (2008) Training writing skills: A cognitive developmental perspective. *Journal of Writing Research*, 1.1, pp. 1–26.

Lewis, M. and Wray, D. (1997) *Extending Literacy: Children Reading and Writing Non-fiction*. London: Routledge.

Locke, T. (2009) "Grammar and writing: the international debate," in R. Beard, D. Myhill, M. Nystrand, and J. Riley (Eds.) *International Handbook of Writing Development*. London: Sage, pp. 182–193.

Martin, J. (1985) *Factual Writing*. Geelong, Victoria: Deakin University Press.

Mercer, N. (2000) *Words and Minds*. London: Routledge.

Micciche, L. (2004) Making a case for rhetorical grammar. *College Composition and Communication*, 55.4, pp. 716–737.

Mulder, J. (2010) "Supporting the teaching of KAL in Scottish Schools," in K. Denham and A. Lobeck (Eds.) *Linguistics in Schools*. Cambridge: Cambridge University Press, pp. 62–75.

Myhill, D. A. (2011a) "Grammar for designers: how grammar supports the development of writing," in S. Ellis, E. McCartney, and J. Bourne (Eds.) *Insight and Impact: Applied Linguistics and the Primary School*. Cambridge: Cambridge University Press, pp. 81–92.

Myhill, D. A. (2011b) "The ordeal of deliberate choice: metalinguistic development in secondary writers," in V. Berninger (Ed.) *Past, Present, and Future Contributions of Cognitive Writing Research to Cognitive Psychology*. New York: Psychology Press/Taylor Francis Group, pp. 247–274.

Myhill, D. A. and Jones, S. M. (2011) "Policing grammar: the place of grammar in literacy policy," in A. Goodwyn and C. Fuller (Eds.) *The Literacy Game*. London: Routledge, pp. 45–62.

Myhill, D. A., Jones, S. M., Lines, H., and Watson, A. (2012) Re-thinking grammar: the impact of embedded grammar teaching on students' writing and students' metalinguistic understanding. *Research Papers in Education*, 27.2, pp. 139–166.

National Advisory Committee on Creative and Cultural Education (NACCCE) (1999) *All Our Futures: Creativity, Culture and Education*. London: Department for Education and Employment.

Paraskevas, C. (2004) Learning about grammar. *International Journal of Learning*, 11, pp. 93–99.

Paraskevas, C. (2006) Grammar apprenticeship. *English Journal*, 95.5, pp. 65–69.

Potolsky, M. (2006) *Mimesis*. New York: Routledge.

Pullman, P. (2005) Common sense has much to learn from moonshine. *The Guardian*, 22 January. Available at http://www.guardian.co.uk/education /2005/jan/22/schools (accessed 22 January 2010).

QCA (1998) *The Grammar Papers; Perspectives on the Teaching of Grammar in the National Curriculum*. London: Qualifications and Curriculum Authority.

Robinson, M. (2005) Metalanguage in L1 English-speaking 12-year-olds: which aspects of writing do they talk about? *Language Awareness*, 14.1, pp. 39–55.

Rolfe, H. (2010) *Learning to Take Risks, Learning to Succeed*. London: NESTA.

Rose, D. (2009) "Writing as linguistic mastery: the development of genre-based literacy pedagogy," in R. Beard, D. Myhill, J. Riley, and M. Nystrand (Eds.) *International Handbook of Writing Development*. London: Sage, pp. 151–166.

Sacks, P. (2000) *Standardized Minds: The High Price of America's Testing Culture and What We Can Do to Change It*. Cambridge, MA: Perseus Books.

Sahlberg, P. (2009). Creativity and innovation through lifelong learning. *Lifelong Learning in Europe*, 14.1, pp. 53–60.

Sahlberg, P. (2010) "The role of education in promoting creativity: potential barriers and enabling factors," in E. Villalba (Ed.) *Measuring Creativity*. Luxemburg: OPOCE, pp. 337–344.

Sams, L. (2003). How to teach grammar, analytical thinking, and writing: a method that works. *English Journal*, 92.3, pp. 57–65.

Sharples, M. (1999) *How We Write: Writing as Creative Design*. London: Routledge.

Svalberg, A. (2007) Language awareness and language learning. *Language Teaching*, 40, pp. 287–308.

Vygotsky, L. S. (1962) *Thought and Language*. Cambridge, MA: Massachusetts Institute of Technology.

Williams, G. (2004) "Ontogenesis and grammatics: functions of metalanguage in pedagogical discourse," in G. Williams and A. Lukin (Eds.) *The Development of Language: Functional Perspectives on Species and Individuals*. London: Continuum, pp. 241–267.

Williams, G. (2005) "Grammatic in schools," in R. Hasan, C. Matthiessen, and J. Webster (Eds.) *Continuing Discourse on Language*. London: Equinox, pp. 281–310.

Wyse, D. (2004) Grammar. For writing? A critical review of empirical evidence. *British Journal of Educational Studies*, 49.4, pp. 411–427.

14

Rethinking Developmental Education

The Accelerated Learning Program: Throwing Open the Gates

Peter Adams, Sarah Gearhart, Robert Miller, and Anne Roberts

The Accelerated Learning Program (ALP) has doubled the percentage of basic writers who succeed in their basic writing course and in first-year composition at almost 200 colleges, mostly two-year. In this article, Peter Adams, Sarah Gearhart, Robert Miller, and Anne Roberts, four faculty members at the Community College of Baltimore County, describe their experience in developing and then offering the first sections of ALP. At a time when it seems as if most of the impetus for change comes from outside higher education—from state legislatures, foundations, and nonprofits—it is refreshing to read how this important, nationally embraced curriculum redesign originated with a group of two-year college faculty.

Historical Context

I n 2001, Mary Soliday, then at CUNY's City College, observed that in the early days of open admissions at the City University of New York, two groups favored basic writing courses for quite different reasons.

From *Journal of Basic Writing*, 2009, vol. 28, no. 2, pp. 50-69.

The first group saw such courses as paths to success, courses that would help students who were weak in writing to conform to the conventions of the academy. The second group supported basic writing for quite a different reason, seeing it as a gate to keep unqualified students out of college-level courses and, thereby, maintain standards in those courses ("Ideologies" 57–58). Bruce Horner and Min-Zhan Lu have referred to these odd bedfellows as "the binary of political activism and academic excellence" (*Representing* 14).

In the 1990s, at what was then Essex Community College and is now the Community College of Baltimore County (CCBC), Peter Adams, then coordinator of the writing program, worried about the program. He recognized that an effective basic writing program might serve as a gate for students until they were ready to succeed in first-year composition and a path to college success as soon as they were ready. But he wanted to make sure that these developmental courses were more path than gate, leading students to success rather than barring them from it.

In Adams's first attempt to evaluate the program, he used data he had been compiling on an Apple IIe computer for four years. He had entered the placement results and grades in every writing course for students assessed since Fall of 1988. Using the 863 students who took the upper-level developmental writing course, ENGL 052, in academic year 1988–1989 as the cohort he would study, Adams calculated the pass rate for ENGL 052 as well as the pass rate for students who passed that course and took first-year composition (ENGL 101) within four years. Charts 1 and 2 display these data.

The pass rate of 57% in the developmental course didn't look too bad, and the whopping 81% pass rate in ENGL 101 was even higher than the rate for students placed directly into the college-level course.

Chart 1. Success Rates for Students Who Took ENGL 052 in 1988–1989

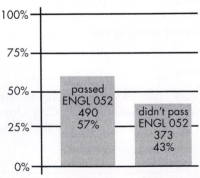

Chart 2. Success Rates for Students Who Took ENGL 101 after Passing ENGL 052 in 1988–1989

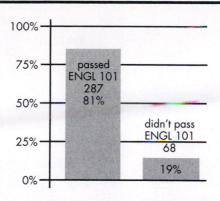

At first glance, it appeared that our basic writing course was doing a good job. In fact, developmental programs in writing, reading, and math have often pointed to such data as evidence that traditional approaches are working. As reassuring as these data looked, however, Adams worried that somehow they didn't tell the whole story, and when he undertook a more detailed, longitudinal study, he learned that his worry was justified.

Looking at success rates for one course at a time masks the true picture. When Adams looked at the longitudinal experience of students who attempted ENGL 052 and ENGL 101, he discovered an alarming situation. Two-thirds of the students who attempted ENGL 052 never passed ENGL 101. The problem was not that basic writers were attempting first-year composition and failing; the problem was that they were giving up before they ever reached that course, a fact hidden when he had simply looked at the pass rates for the small number of students who did make it into regular composition.

Chart 3 presents the number and percentage of students who passed each milestone during the four years from 1988 to 1992.

The students represented in Chart 3, like those in Charts 1 and 2, were followed for four years. When we say 57% passed ENGL 052, we mean they passed within four years, not necessarily the first time they attempted the course. A significant number took the course more than once before passing. When we say 43% didn't pass ENGL 052, we mean they didn't pass within four years; many of them attempted the course more than once.

As Chart 3 reveals, instead of the 81% success rate that we saw in Chart 2, only about a third of students who began in ENGL 052 succeeded in passing ENGL 101. Our basic writing course was a path to

Chart 3. Longitudinal Data on Students Who Took ENGL 052 in 1988–1989

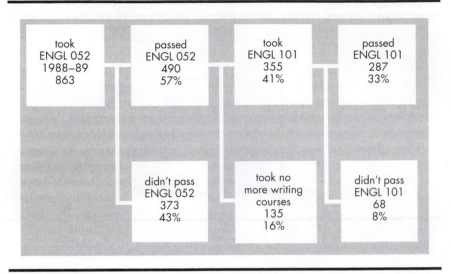

success for only one-third of the students enrolled; for the other two-thirds, it appears to have been a locked gate.

We have come to conceptualize the situation represented in this chart as a pipeline that students must pass through to succeed. And we have concluded that the longer the pipeline, the more likely there will be "leakage" from it—in other words, the more likely students will drop out before passing first-year composition. Because the database we compiled in the early 1990s included data only for writing courses, we had no way of knowing whether these students dropped out of the college altogether, but we did know when they stopped taking writing courses. Further, since they could not achieve any degree or certificate at the college without passing ENGL 101, we knew that they didn't achieve any credential. Although our original intention in collecting these statistics was to help us enforce our placement system, we soon learned that it also helped us evaluate our writing program by allowing us to calculate the percentage of students who succeeded in passing each milestone in the program.

Then, in Fall of 1992, it became useful in another way. At that time, Peter Adams was chairing the Conference on Basic Writing (CBW), which led to his organizing the fourth national conference on basic writing, to be held at the University of Maryland in October of 1992. Things were moving along smoothly; David Bartholomae had agreed to give the keynote address, registrations were rolling in, and it looked like our carefully crafted budget was going to be adequate. And then, several weeks before the conference, Adams realized that he had a serious problem. Although the conference officially began on Friday morning, the organizers had planned an optional dinner on Thursday evening for those who arrived early . . . and more than a hundred people had signed up for that dinner. But we had not arranged nor budgeted for a dinner speaker.

Having already committed every cent in the budget, Adams realized that he would have to speak at the dinner since he couldn't afford to pay an outside speaker. He decided to report on the data his college had been collecting and analyzing on its basic writing students. The only problem was that the data were so discouraging that it hardly seemed appropriate for the opening session at a national basic writing conference.

For several days, Adams tried to think of a positive spin he could put on these data . . . without success. Finally, he fixed on the idea of suggesting some positive action basic writing instructors could take in response to the discouraging implications of the data. What would happen, Adams asked, if instead of isolating basic writers in developmental courses, we could mainstream them directly into first-year composition, while also providing appropriate support to help them succeed?

Most of Adams's talk that Thursday night was about how using a database to evaluate his college's writing program had revealed quite low success rates for the developmental program; only the last ten minutes or so were devoted to his very tentative idea that the success rate for basic writers might improve if they were "mainstreamed" into first-year composition. The lengthy and heated discussion that followed this talk was completely focused on the "mainstreaming" idea. Finally with most of the audience still suffering from jet lag, the conference participants more or less agreed to disagree, and adjourned for the evening.

Adams knew the title of David Bartholomae's keynote address scheduled for the next morning, "The Tidy House: Basic Writing in the American Curriculum," but he had no idea what Bartholomae was actually going to talk about. As he sat in the audience listening, an odd feeling crept over him. He heard Bartholomae suggest that

> . . . in the name of sympathy and empowerment, we have once again produced the "other" who is the incomplete version of ourselves, confirming existing patterns of power and authority, reproducing the hierarchies we had meant to question and overthrow, way back then in the 1970s. ("Tidy House" 18)

David Bartholomae, starting from a very different place, was arriving at a conclusion similar to the one suggested by Adams the evening before. At that point, Bartholomae and Adams were probably the only two people in the room who didn't think this coincidence had been carefully planned. The fact that articles representing their two talks ended up next to each other in the Spring 1993 issue of the *Journal of Basic Writing* (Bartholomae, "Tidy House"; Adams, "Basic Writing Reconsidered") only heightened everyone's assumption that they had conspired to question the essential nature of basic writing at a conference on basic writing. They hadn't, as they both insist to this day, despite the fact that few have ever believed them.

In the years since that 1992 conference, a number of institutions have adopted various versions of the mainstreaming approach that was suggested at the conference. Arizona State University, with leadership from Greg Glau, developed the well-known "stretch" model, which allows developmental students to be mainstreamed directly into first-year composition, but into a version that is "stretched out" over two semesters ("*Stretch* at 10"). Quinnipiac University pioneered the "intensive" model, which has basic writers take a version of first-year composition that meets five hours a week instead of three (Segall 38–47). A few years later, Rhonda Grego and Nancy Thompson devised the "studio" approach at the University of South Carolina. In this model, students in first-year composition and sometimes other writing courses can also sign up for a one-hour-per-week studio section. There they meet with students from other classes to talk about "essays in progress" (6–14).

Many other schools developed variations on these approaches in the late 1990s and early 2000s. Our college was not one of these. Instead we endured a turbulent dozen or so years as three independent colleges were merged into one mega-college: the Community College of Baltimore County. In the process, fierce battles were fought, one chancellor received a vote of no confidence, tenure was abolished, and many faculty members devoted much of their energy to "aligning" the programs, courses, and policies of the three schools that had merged. By 2005, the worst of these struggles were over, and faculty were ready to return to more productive work. In the Fall of 2006, the English Department of the newly merged Community College of Baltimore County turned to the question of the low success rates in our basic writing courses.

In the meantime, many others were noticing the very low success rates for developmental programs nationwide. In a national study, Tom Bailey of the Community College Research Center at Columbia University found similarly alarming leakage in all developmental courses, including reading and math:

> How many students complete the sequences of developmental courses to which they are referred? The first conclusion to note is that many simply never enroll in developmental classes in the first place. In the Achieving the Dream sample, 21 percent of all students referred to developmental math education and 33 percent of students referred to developmental reading do not enroll in any developmental course within three years.
>
> Of those students referred to remediation, how many actually complete their full developmental sequences? Within three years of their initial assessment, about 42 percent of those referred to developmental reading in

the Achieving the Dream sample complete their full sequence, but this accounts for two-thirds of those who actually *enroll* in at least one developmental reading course. These numbers are worse for math—only 31 percent of those referred to developmental math complete their sequence. (4–5)

In "Outcomes of Remediation," Hunter Boylan and Patrick Saxon have observed that "[a]n unknown number but perhaps as many as 40% of those taking remedial courses do not complete the courses, and consequently, do not complete remediation within one year." Reviewing large-scale studies from Minnesota, Maryland, and Texas, Boylan and Saxon conclude that "[t]he results of all these studies were fairly consistent. In summary, about 80% of those who completed remediation with a C or better passed their first college-level course in English or mathematics." Just as we at Essex Community College discovered when we began to look at longitudinal data, success rates for individual courses conceal a serious problem, for "[i]t should be noted . . . that not all of those who pass remedial courses actually took college-level courses in comparable subject areas. An Illinois study, for instance, reported that only 64% of those who completed remedial English and reading in the Fall of 1996 actually completed their first college-level courses in those subjects within a year."

So the problem we had discovered on the local level in 1992 appears to mirror similar problems nationally: too many students simply leak out of the pipeline of the required writing sequence.

Development of the Accelerated Learning Program

At an English Department meeting in January of 2007, several CCBC faculty members proposed that we pilot some form of mainstreaming to see if we could improve the success rates of our basic writing students. After considering several different models, we settled on what we now call the Accelerated Learning Program (ALP) as having the greatest potential. While we were not among the pioneering schools that developed mainstreaming approaches in the 1990s, we have benefited greatly from those programs. ALP has borrowed the best features of existing mainstreaming approaches, added some features from studios and learning communities, and developed several new features of our own.

Of course, the program we eventually developed reflected the realities of our existing approach to teaching writing. The writing sequence at CCBC includes two levels of basic writing and two levels of college composition. To graduate, students must pass any required basic writing courses and then pass two semesters of college composition, both of which are writing courses. Only the higher-level college composition course satisfies the composition graduation requirement when students transfer to most four-year schools.

Here's how ALP works. The program is available, on a voluntary basis, to all students whose placement indicates they need our upper-level basic writing course. Placement is determined at CCBC by the Accuplacer exam. Students may retest once and may also appeal by a writing sample. In addition, all sections of writing courses require students to write a diagnostic essay the first week of classes; when this essay indicates students should be in a different level course, they are advised, but not required, to move to that course.

A developmental student who volunteers for ALP registers directly for a designated section of ENGL 101, where he or she joins seven other developmental students and twelve students whose placement is ENGL 101. Apart from the inclusion of the eight ALP students, this is a regular, three-credit section of ENGL 101, meeting three hours a week for one semester. We think the fact that the basic writers are in a class with twelve students who are stronger writers, and perhaps more accomplished students, is an important feature of ALP because these 101-level students frequently serve as role models for the basic writers.

Equally important, we avoid the sometimes stigmatizing and often demoralizing effects of segregating basic writers into sections designated as just for them by fully integrating them into a college-level course and then providing additional support in the form of a second course. The eight developmental students in every ALP section of ENGL 101 also take what we call a companion course with the same instructor who teaches them in ENGL 101. In Maryland, state regulations bar the awarding of credit toward graduation for "remedial" courses; since this companion course is currently conceived of as a basic writing course (remedial, by the state's terminology), students may not receive credit for it. The companion course meets for three hours a week for one semester. In this class, which meets immediately after the 101 section, the instructor provides additional support to help the students succeed in composition. The class may begin with questions that arose in the earlier class. Other typical activities include brainstorming for the next essay in 101, reviewing drafts of a paper, or discussing common problems in finding a topic to write about. Frequently, instructors ask students to write short papers that will serve as scaffolding for the next essay or work with them on grammar or punctuation problems common to the group.

Gaining Administrative Support

After the English Department agreed it wanted to pilot ALP, meetings were set up with the Dean of Developmental Education and the Vice President for Instruction. At first, the Vice President declared the college simply could not afford to fund classes with only eight students, but a last-minute compromise was suggested: faculty could teach the companion course that met three hours a week with only eight students for two credits of load instead of three. The Vice President agreed, reluctantly. But would the faculty?

As it turns out, they did. After all, the companion course would have only eight students, and, while it would meet three hours a week, it would not really require a separate preparation. It's more like a workshop for the ENGL 101 class. Most importantly, as faculty began teaching the course, they found that ALP was often the most rewarding teaching they had ever done. As Sandra Grady, one of the earliest ALP instructors, declared at the end of the first semester, "That was the best teaching experience I've ever had," and Professor Grady has been teaching more than thirty years. All of us who have taught ALP courses have found having a class small enough so that we can get to know each student and pay attention to their individual needs provides a kind of satisfaction that is rarely possible with classes of twenty or more. Peter Adams, Robert Miller, and Anne Roberts, co-authors of this article, began teaching in that first semester, and Sarah Gearhart joined us in the second semester.

Results

As of the summer of 2009, the Community College of Baltimore County has offered thirty sections of ALP over two years to almost 240 students. The results, while preliminary, are extremely encouraging.

Chart 4 displays the results for a comparison group of students who took the *traditional* upper-level basic writing course in Fall of 2007. The data represent the results at the end of the Spring semester of 2009, so all of these students have had four semesters to pass their writing courses. Note that 21% of the original group have never passed ENGL 052. While it looks as though this group of students "failed" the course, in fact, many of them didn't actually "fail." For a variety of reasons, they simply gave up and stopped coming to class. Some became discouraged; others became overwhelmed. For some, events outside school demanded too much of them; for others, their personal lives required their attention. For these reasons, it would not be accurate to say that 21% failed. In addition, the 19% who passed ENGL 052 but didn't attempt ENGL 101 have clearly dropped out. This attrition rate of 40% is of great concern, as it was when we studied developmental students back in 1992.

Chart 5 presents the results for all the students who have taken ALP since the program began in Fall 2007, up to and including the Spring semester of 2009. While the first semester's cohort of 40 students has had four semesters to complete their writing courses, the remaining students have had fewer semesters. The most recent group, approximately 80 students who took ALP in Spring of 2009, has had only one semester. Despite this shorter time for most of the students,

Chart 4. Success Rates of Students Who Took Traditional ENGL052 in Fall 2007

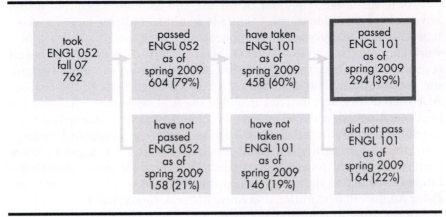

Chart 5. Success Rates of Students Who Took ALP052 from Fall 2007 to Spring 2008

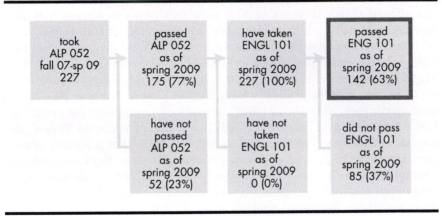

the ALP success rates are significantly higher and the drop-out rates significantly lower than for the comparison group. The boxes outlined in black in Charts 4 and 5 show the success rates for the two groups.

Why ALP Works

As we came to realize that ALP was producing striking improvement in student success, we began to speculate about why. What was it about ALP that contributed to those successes? We have identified eight features of ALP that we think are responsible for most of the gains in retention and success. Half of these are features we borrowed from earlier innovative programs.

Mainstreaming

Over the past fifteen years, a number of schools like Arizona State University, SUNY New Paltz, and City College (CUNY) have adopted models that mainstream basic writers into credit-bearing writing classes (see Glau; Rigolino and Freel; Soliday and Gleason). We think mainstreaming has a powerful psychological effect for basic writers. When students placed into basic writing are allowed to go immediately into first-year composition, their sense that they are excluded from the real college, that they are stigmatized as weak writers, and that they may not be "college material" is greatly reduced.

Cohort Learning

Each ALP student takes two courses, ENGL 101 and its companion course, in a cohort with seven other basic writers and the same instructor, an arrangement that owes much to the concept of learning communities. Vincent Tinto has argued that leaving college often "arises from isolation, specifically from the absence of sufficient contact between the individual [student] and other members of the social and academic communities of the college." He adds the observation that "membership in at least one supportive community, whatever its relationship to the center, may be sufficient to insure continued persistence" (55–61). As Faith Gabelnick and her co-authors have reported, learning communities, in which students take two or more courses with the same cohort of students, provide just such a community: "Learning community students value knowing other students in classes and realize an immediate sense of belonging" (67). Rebecca Mlynarczyk and Marcia Babbitt have observed similar results at Kingsborough Community College (71–89). In the ALP program, among the eight basic writers who spend six hours a week together in a cohort with the same instructor, we are finding similar increases in bonding and attachment to the college. The students begin to look out for each other in a variety of ways—calling to check on students who miss class, offering each other rides to campus, and, most importantly, helping each other to understand difficult concepts they encounter in their academic work.

Small Class Size

We have found the small class size of the companion course, only eight students, to be an essential feature of ALP. We arrived at the conclusion that the sections would have to be small by reading the work of Rhonda Grego and Nancy Thompson, who developed the concept of studios, "where a small group of students . . . meet frequently and regularly . . . to bring to the table the assignments they are working on for a writing course" (7). We knew we wanted the ALP students to comprise less than half the students in the 101 sections, where class size at our school is twenty, so we proposed a class size of eight for the companion course. We have concluded that many of the benefits of ALP derive from this small class size. Students are less prone to behavior problems when they are in a small group. The bonding mentioned earlier is more likely to occur. And the conversation can be focused on each individual's questions much more easily.

Contextual Learning

Both learning communities and studio courses credit some of their success to the fact that students are learning about writing in a meaningful context. Grego and Thompson point out that the conversations in studio sessions often explore the context for a writing assignment or for a teacher's comments on a student's essay (140–42). Similarly, learning communities, especially those that match a writing course with a "content course" such as history or psychology, tap into the advantages of contextual learning. The writing instruction seems more meaningful to the students because it is immediately applicable in the content course. In ALP, the ENGL 101 class provides a meaningful context for the work students do in the companion course. In more traditional basic writing classes, instructors frequently find themselves saying, "Now pay attention. This will be very helpful when you get to first-year composition." We don't have to say this in the ALP classes; our students are already in first-year composition. What we do in the companion course is immediately useful in the essays the students are writing in ENGL 101.

Acceleration

In the longitudinal studies we conducted, we discovered that many students never completed the sequence of required writing courses because they gave up at some point in the process. And the longer the course sequence, the more opportunities there are for such "giving up." Most startling to us was the nearly 20% of our students who actually passed the traditional basic writing course, but then gave up without ever even attempting ENGL 101. We have concluded that the longer the "pipeline" through which our basic writers must move before completing their writing sequence, the greater the chances they will give up and "leak" out of the pipeline. ALP shortens the pipeline for basic writers by allowing them to take their developmental writing and first-year composition courses in the same semester. This acceleration is one of the features we developed at the Community College of Baltimore County.

Heterogeneous Grouping

Another feature of ALP that was developed by CCBC is heterogeneous grouping. In most of the earlier mainstreaming models, basic writers were placed in first-year composition, but in sections populated only by other basic writers. Each group of eight ALP students takes ENGL 101 in a section with twelve 101-level writers who can serve as role models both for writing and for successful student behavior. We also find that the stigmatizing and demoralizing effects of placement in a course designed just for basic writers are greatly reduced by this feature.

Attention to Behavioral Issues

A third locally developed feature of ALP is our conscious and deliberate attention to behavioral issues. We believe that not understanding the kinds of behavior that lead to success in college is a major factor in some basic writers' lack of success. We work hard to help our students understand the type of behavior that will maximize their chances for success in college. For example, many of our basic writers have taken on more responsibilities than they can possibly fulfill. We ask students to create a timeline that accounts for everything they must do in a given week, an exercise that sometimes leads them to make changes in their lives to increase their chances for success. Some students discover they need to cut back on their hours at work; others realize that they have registered for too many courses.

Behavioral problems often result from attitudinal problems. In class we talk about what we call the "high school attitude" toward education: the attitude that it isn't "cool" to appear interested in class, to be seen taking notes or raising one's hand to answer a question. Using humor and sometimes even a little mockery, we lead students to realize that the "high school attitude" toward "coolness" isn't "cool" in college.

And then there are the recurring problems with cell phones and Facebook, with arriving late or falling asleep, with not buying the required text or not completing the required assignment. ALP instructors are aware that these kinds of issues will need more conscious attention, and the small class size makes such attention possible.

Attention to Life Problems

A fourth feature of ALP we developed at CCBC is to encourage instructors to pay deliberate attention to problems in the students' lives outside of school. Many students who give up on our courses do so, not because of any difficulty with the material in the course but, primarily, because of circumstances in their lives outside of college. They are evicted from their apartment, their children become ill, their boss insists they work more hours, they find themselves in abusive relationships, or they experience some other overwhelming life problem. ALP faculty recognize the need to address these life issues. They find time to ask students how their lives are going. They frequently refer students to sources of outside support for such concerns as financial aid, health issues, family problems, and legal problems. When several students in the same class have a similar problem, instead of sending them to see an advisor, we have the advisor visit the class. We have assembled a roster of resource people who are willing to visit our classes and work with students on life problems.

Costs

Regardless of its success rates, ALP may appear to be prohibitively expensive, as our Vice President for Instruction had initially thought. But careful analysis reveals that ALP actually costs less per *successful student* than more traditional approaches.

To see how this could be the case, consider a hypothetical group of 1,000 students who show up in September needing developmental writing. Under the traditional model, we would need to run 50 sections of basic writing to accommodate them (our class size for writing courses is 20). Since the actual cost of these 50 sections would vary depending on the salary levels of the instructors, we'll make this calculation in terms of faculty credit hours (FCHs). Since faculty are compensated with 3 FCHs for teaching our upper-level basic writing course, the cost for those 1,000 students would be 150 FCHs.

Because only 60% of students taking our traditional upper-level basic writing course ever take ENGL 101, we would need to accommodate just 600 students in ENGL 101, which would require 30 sections. At 3 FCHs per section, the ENGL 101 costs for 1,000 students would be 90 FCHs, and the total for ENGL 052 and 101 would be 240 FCHs.

To accommodate those same 1,000 students in an ALP program would require 125 sections (class size for the ALP classes is 8). Because of the small class size and because the companion course is not really a separate preparation, faculty receive 2, not 3, FCHs for a section of the companion course. The 125 sections would, therefore, cost the college 250 FCHs.

Since all 1,000 students would take ENGL 101, we would need 50 sections to accommodate all 1,000 students. At 3 FCHs per section, the 101 portion of the ALP program would cost 150 FCHs, and so the total cost for the ALP model would be 400 FCHs.

Before deciding which model is more expensive, however, it is not enough to consider just the costs; it is also necessary to consider the outcomes. Under the traditional model, 39%, or 390 students, will pass ENGL 101. Under ALP, 63%, or 630 students, will pass ENGL 101. As a result, the cost *per successful student* for the traditional model (390 students divided by 240 FCHs) would be 1.625 FCHs. For the ALP model, the cost (630 students divided by 400 FCHs) would be 1.575 FCHs per successful student. ALP actually costs less per successful student than the traditional model.

In sum, for basic writers, ALP doubles the success rate, halves the attrition rate, does it in half the time (one semester instead of two), and costs slightly less per successful student. When these data are presented to administrators, the case for adopting the ALP model is compelling.

Plans for the Future

ALP has produced very promising results. For each of the past four semesters, it has resulted in success rates at least double those for our traditional basic writing course. Having achieved these preliminary successes, our plans for the future include continued and expanded study of the program, improvements in the program to make it even more effective, scaling up of ALP at CCBC to 40 sections per semester in Fall 2010 and to approximately 70 sections per semester in Fall 2011, and dissemination of ALP to other colleges.

First, we want to insure the validity of our preliminary data, which has indicated such dramatic improvement in success rates for ALP students over students in the traditional program. We are concerned about two possible threats to the validity of that data: the possibility that students who volunteer for ALP are not representative of developmental writing students at CCBC, and the possibility of instructor bias in grading the ALP students in ENGL 101.

To address the possibility that students who volunteer for ALP are not a representative sample, we have formed a partnership with the Community College Research Center at Columbia University. CCRC is conducting multivariate analyses of the effects of participating in ALP on student pass rates in English 101 as well as on other measures, including rates of persistence and passing college-level courses in subjects other than English. This study will make use of "matched pairs," selecting a student who has taken the traditional ENGL 052 to be matched with an ALP student on eleven variables: race, gender, age, financial aid status, full- or part-time status, prior college credits, grades in prior college courses, placement scores, program, high school attended, and high school diploma status.

We are also concerned about the possibility of unconscious instructor bias in favor of the ALP students. The English Department has developed rubrics that describe a passing essay for the basic writing course and for ENGL 101. However, considering the close relationships that naturally develop between ALP faculty and the eight ALP students with whom they meet for six hours a week, it is possible that occasionally instructors unconsciously pass an ALP student in ENGL 101 whose performance was slightly below passing level. To investigate this possible bias, we will be following the ALP students into ENGL 102, the next course in the writing sequence, comparing their performance there with that of students who took traditional ENGL 052. ENGL 102 instructors will not have formed any kind of bond with the students and, in fact, will not even know that they were in ALP.

Also, we will be conducting a blind, holistic scoring of essays from ENGL 101 classes to compare the quality of the writing of ALP students who passed the course with the quality of the writing of 101-level students. If we determine through this study that some ALP students are being passed in ENGL 101 even though their performance is below the passing level, we will investigate other ways of making the pass/fail decision for these sections. We may, for example, decide to have final portfolios graded by someone other than the student's own instructor.

In addition to investigating any threats to the validity of our data on success rates of ALP students in ENGL 101, we will be investigating whether higher percentages of ALP students, compared to students who take the traditional basic writing course, continue to reach various milestones such as accumulating 15, 30, and 45 credits, one-year persistence, completion of certificate and degree programs, and successful transfer to four-year institutions.

Finally, we want to attempt to understand exactly what it is about ALP that leads to its successes and which features contribute most to the improved performance of ALP students. Using pre- and post-semester surveys, focus groups, and faculty reports, we will attempt to determine which of the eight features of ALP contribute most to student success.

We are fairly confident ALP works well in our context, so we look forward to learning if it works as well at other colleges. To this end, we organized a conference on acceleration in June of 2009. Forty-one faculty from twenty-one different schools attended. After a spirited two-day conversation with lots of give and take and very good questions from participants, four schools agreed to pilot ALP on their campuses in the coming year: CUNY's Kingsborough Community College (New York), El Paso Community College (Texas), Patrick Henry Community College (Virginia), and Gateway Technical and Community College (Kentucky). We eagerly await their results. In addition, we are hopeful that other schools will adopt the ALP model in coming years. On June 23–25, 2010, we will be holding an expanded version of the Conference on Acceleration at CCBC.

ALP has benefited greatly from the work our colleagues at other institutions have done since that Conference on Basic Writing back in 1992. We have developed a model for developmental writing that shows great promise, and we are certain that others will improve on our model in coming years.

We are also convinced that this work is extremely important given the present climate for higher education. The country has begun to pay attention to basic writing and developmental education more broadly in ways both negative and positive. There is a growing realization that the programs we began so hopefully during those early days of open admissions have not performed nearly as well as we had hoped. Some would conclude from these low success rates that our budgets should be reduced or even that our programs should be eliminated. Susanmarie Harrington and Linda Adler-Kassner observe that we are working in "an educational environment in which basic writing and remedial programs are under attack" (8). Mary Soliday points out that "Outside the academy, critics of remediation waved the red flag of declining standards and literacy crisis to justify the need to downsize, privatize, and effectively restratisfy higher education. By blaming remedial programs for a constellation of educational woes, from budget crisis to low retention rates and falling standards, the critics of remediation practiced an effective politics of agency." That is, they attributed the blame for these growing problems to the developmental students and "the 'expensive' programs designed to meet their 'special' needs" (*Politics of Remediation* 106). In 2005, Bridget Terry Long, writing in *National Cross Talk*, observed that "this debate about the merits of investing in remediation, which has an estimated annual cost in the billions, has intensified in recent years. There are many questions about whether remediation should be offered in colleges at all." Long goes on to take a close look at how we determine the success of "remedial" programs and to demonstrate that with appropriate measures—comparing students with similar economic and educational backgrounds—remedial programs do indeed seem to help students do better in college.

Despite the positive implications of more nuanced research such as that conducted by Long, the criticism of basic writing programs is not likely to diminish in the near future. And in the field of basic writing itself the realization that many basic writing programs are falling short of the kind of results we had hoped for in the early days—a realization that first surfaced at the basic writing conference in Baltimore in 1992—is leading to the development of improved and innovative programs. In "Challenge and Opportunity: Rethinking the Role and Function of Developmental Education in the Community College," Tom Bailey notes that there has been "a dramatic expansion in experimentation with new approaches." Major funding agencies, both governmental and nongovernmental, are beginning to see developmental education as an area of interest. However, if we are not able to improve our success rates, if we continue to serve as a gate, barring large numbers of students from receiving a college education, those who argue for a reduction or elimination of basic writing could prevail. That is why it is so important at this crucial time that we look for ways to make basic writing more effective. The very survival of our programs could be at stake. But there is an even more important reason for continuing to improve our effectiveness: the success of our programs is of life-changing importance to our students.

Works Cited

Adams, Peter. "Basic Writing Reconsidered." *Journal of Basic Writing* 12.1 (1993): 22–36. Print.

Bailey, Thomas. "Challenge and Opportunity: Rethinking the Role and Function of Developmental Education in the Community College." *New Directions for Community Colleges* (2009): 11–30. Web. 30 July 2009.

Bartholomae, David. "The Tidy House: Basic Writing in the American Curriculum." *Journal of Basic Writing* 12.1 (1993): 4–21. Print.

Boylan, Hunter R., and D. Patrick Saxon. "Outcomes of Remediation." League for Innovation. Web. 30 July 2009.

Gabelnick, Faith, Jean MacGregor, Roberta S. Matthews, and Barbara Leigh Smith. *Learning Communities: Creating, Connections Among Students, Faculty, and Disciplines*. New Directions for Teaching and Learning. San Francisco: Jossey-Bass, 1990. Print.

Glau, Greg. "*Stretch* at 10: A Progress Report on Arizona State University's Stretch Program." *Journal of Basic Writing* 26.2 (2007): 30–48. Print.

Grego, Rhonda, and Nancy Thompson. *Teaching / Writing in Third Spaces*. Carbondale, IL: Southern Illinois UP, 2008. Print.

Harrington, Susanmarie, and Linda Adler-Kassner. "'The Dilemma That Still Counts': Basic Writing at a Political Crossroads." *Journal of Basic Writing* 17.2 (1998): 3–24. Print.

Horner, Bruce, and Min-Zhan Lu. *Representing the "Other": Basic Writers and the Teaching of Basic Writing*. Urbana, IL: NCTE, 1999. Print.

Long, Bridget Terry. "The Remediation Debate: Are We Serving the Needs of Underprepared College Students?" *National CrossTalk*. The National Center for Public Policy and Higher Education, Fall 2005. Web. 20 Dec. 2009.

Mlynarczyk, Rebecca Williams, and Marcia Babbitt. "The Power of Academic Learning Communities." *Journal of Basic Writing* 21.1 (2002): 71–89. Print.

Rigolino, Rachel, and Penny Freel. "Re-Modeling Basic Writing." *Journal of Basic Writing* 26.2 (2007): 49–72. Print.

Segall, Mary T. "Embracing a Porcupine: Redesigning a Writing Program." *Journal of Basic Writing* 14.2 (1995): 38–47. Print.

Soliday, Mary. "Ideologies of Access and the Politics of Agency." *Mainstreaming Basic Writers: Politics and Pedagogies of Access*. Ed. Gerry McNenny and Sallyanne Fitzgerald. Mahwah, NJ: Erlbaum, 2001. 55–72. Print.

———. *The Politics of Remediation: Institutional and Student Needs in Higher Education*. Pittsburgh: U of Pittsburgh P, 2002. Print.

Soliday, Mary, and Barbara Gleason. "From Remediation to Enrichment: Evaluating a Mainstreaming Project." *Journal of Basic Writing* 16.1 (1997): 64–78. Print.

Tinto, Vincent. *Leaving College: Understanding the Causes and Cures of Student Attrition*. Chicago: U of Chicago P, 1986. Print.

TYCA White Paper on Developmental Education Reforms

Two-Year College English Association Research Committee

Responding to the wave of developmental reform initiatives sweeping the United States, the TYCA Research Committee was charged with providing TYCA members with a comprehensive national portrait of this movement and examining its impact on conditions for two-year college faculty and students. In the resulting white paper, the committee reports on its findings. This committee concluded that developmental education reform has been a decidedly "mixed bag" for the advancement of literacy education grounded in disciplinary theory and research—and for faculty professional authority. This document also provides TYCA's current official position on developmental education reform, offering recommendations for administrators, legislators, and national disciplinary professional organizations. The committee members included Joanne Giordano, Holly Hassel, Jeff Klausman, Margaret O'Rourke, Leslie Roberts, Patrick Sullivan, and Christie Toth.

Executive Summary

Reform movements aimed at improving success and completion rates of underprepared students at America's two-year colleges are sweeping the country. Legislatures from Florida to Washington, from Connecticut to Colorado, are mandating reform. The Two-Year College English Association (TYCA) offers this white paper to provide an overview of this current reform movement, highlight some of the potential problems, and offer recommendations. Overall, TYCA expresses reservations about legislative imperatives to reform developmental reading and writing instruction in postsecondary education, particularly those efforts that exclude two-year college faculty from the public discourse and ignore the academic and material realities of two-year college students' lives.

Current Reform Movements

Current reform movements revolve around several interconnected areas: admissions to four-year colleges, placement in developmental or college-level courses, curriculum and program design, and support programs. In some states, four-year state colleges are no longer allowed to offer developmental coursework, which pushes students into already overburdened two-year colleges. Placement into degree-credit courses is also being mandated. In some states, a single test is being

From *Teaching English in the Two-Year College*, 2015, vol. 42, no. 3, pp. 227-43.

implemented across all colleges, regardless of best practices. In other states, more welcome reforms are offered, such as multiple measures of placement, including high-school GPA. At the same time, certain category-based exemptions from readiness assessment—high-school diploma holders, veterans—raise serious questions. Curricula and program designs are also being legislatively mandated, too often without attention to local context and without appropriate faculty training and input.

Concerns

Two-year college faculty are frequently charged with implementing these initiatives and asked to make decisions about program redesign with little time for study and without training or compensation. Moreover, legislative reforms routinely overlook the varying institutional structures that reflect deep divides in training, pedagogy, and theoretical perspective among faculty and different disciplines. All or any of these may seriously undermine the effectiveness of reform efforts.

TYCA also raises questions that the reform movement too often misses. For example, what constitutes success at a two-year college? It may well be different from what constitutes success at most colleges and universities. Similarly is high school graduation indicative of college readiness? And what does "college-level literacy" really mean and how is it measured? Perhaps most importantly, if these reforms lead to closing off postsecondary access to some groups of students, will we be engaging in class- and race-based "tracking" that perpetuates occupational and professional segregation?

Recommendations

English faculty at two- and four-year campuses, administrators at these colleges, and the legislative bodies involved in reform share common goals: preparing students to be successful in college, supporting students' efforts to fulfill their own educational goals, and helping institutions more effectively achieve their missions. To that end, TYCA offers these recommendations for administrators and legislators:

1. Involve developmental education instructors, including contingent faculty, in reform design and implementation;

2. Initiate localized research-based pilot programs rather than statewide changes;

3. Prioritize evidence from local assessments and research on student success;

4. Use multiple pieces of evidence, including student writing, to assess student needs and abilities;

5. Replace multiple-choice exit exams with local assessment of student work;

6. Fund and develop strong academic support systems for students;

7. Support ongoing professional development for all developmental educators;

8. Support two-year college English faculty partnerships with area high school teachers.

TYCA offers these recommendations for national disciplinary organizations:

1. Establish a standing developmental education advocacy group or task force that can represent the organization's expertise;

2. Encourage more Research I and PhD-granting universities to provide graduate preparation for two-year college teacher-scholars who are equipped to engage these issues at institutional, state, and national levels.

Introduction and Purpose

Many people are aware of President Obama's "ambitious completion agenda." To further this agenda, the president has set a new national goal: by 2020, America will "once again have the highest proportion of college graduates in the world" (White House). Responding to the reality that college education is increasingly important for economic stability and mobility, more and more high school graduates are electing to pursue postsecondary education, and growing numbers are choosing to begin that education at a two-year college. However, as recent data from the Community College Research Center (CCRC) show, just one-third of students who start at a community college earn a credential within six years (Community College Research Center). Compared with overall graduation rates of 50–80% at selective four-year and research institutions (the average six-year graduation rate at four-year public colleges is 58.1%), the completion rates at community colleges certainly seem dismal ("College Completion"). Concerns about these statistics— often framed as an issue of return on public investment—are driving state-level postsecondary education reform initiatives across the country, many of which focus on developmental/remedial education.

One assumption underlying these reform movements is that the community college "completion problem" is caused in large part by underprepared students and institutions' ineffectiveness at moving such students through degree programs efficiently. In order to help underprepared students become ready for credit-bearing courses more quickly, many two-year colleges have been redesigning their developmental education programs, and many others are feeling mounting pressure to do so. Faculty are frequently charged with expediting such reform and are often asked to make decisions about program redesign with little time for study and reflection. Complicating this issue are the varying institutional structures for delivering remediation. In some two-year colleges, developmental reading and writing courses are taught within the English department, and English faculty routinely teach both developmental and college-level writing courses; at other colleges, developmental reading and writing are housed within a separate developmental education unit, and these courses are taught by an entirely separate faculty (see Perin and Charron). Within such organizational structures, "developmental" and "college-level" faculty may have disparate disciplinary identities, professionalization experiences, and pedagogical orientations. Regardless of their institutional structures, two-year college faculty who are charged with implementing reforms are often asked to do so without additional resources for faculty development or compensation for increased workload. Substantial research suggests that greater student-faculty interaction increases student success and retention (Glau, "Stretch Program" 82).

The Two-Year College English Association (TYCA) expresses reservations about legislative imperatives to reform developmental reading and writing instruction in postsecondary education, especially those efforts that exclude two-year college faculty from the public discourse and ignore the academic and material realities of two-year college students' lives. In "Measuring 'Success' at Open Admissions Institutions: Thinking Carefully about This Complex Question," Patrick Sullivan questions graduation rates as a "standard benchmark for success at most institutions of higher learning" (p. 42 in this volume). Sullivan points out that many students at open-admission campuses require academic remediation and experience a host of extra-academic factors that make their transition to higher education more difficult than "repeat-generation" students and students from socially affluent backgrounds. In light of these realities, Sullivan asserts that it is worth reexamining what constitutes "success" for such institutions, stating, "We must develop a definition of 'success' that acknowledges the unique complexities, challenges, and material conditions that typically come into play for students who attend open admissions institutions" (p. 54). As professionals with unique expertise regarding these student populations and their learning needs, two-year college faculty should play a key role in defining "success" at such institutions beyond simplistic measures of completion.

Legislative mandates regarding completion, and particularly developmental education reform, raise important questions about how such changes might limit students' opportunities in higher education:

- Is every high school graduate in America ready for the reading and writing demands of college?

- What are the goals and objectives of college-level literacy instruction, and how is students' "success" in these areas being measured?

- What might students who do not earn credentials be gaining from their accumulated credits and learning experiences?

- If we close off postsecondary access to some groups of unprepared students, are we essentially engaging in class- and race-based "tracking" that perpetuates occupational and professional segregation?

These questions reflect our concern that policymakers often misunderstand community colleges and the diversity of students who attend open-admissions institutions. Many policymakers routinely compare the completion rates of open-admissions institutions with those of traditional selective admissions institutions without considering the distinctions between their missions and student populations.

Given these diverse contexts and questions, then, the purpose of this white paper is manifold. We aim to provide an overview of the issues surrounding developmental education reform and to provide an overview of the range of programmatic options currently being implemented to shorten the amount of time students spend in developmental courses and prepare students for credit-bearing coursework. To achieve these purposes, we look at a case study of faculty in Florida who have responded to legislative interventions regarding developmental education. We then offer an overview of some of the current legislative interventions into developmental education that are affecting two-year college faculty and students, followed by a national snapshot of alternative approaches to developmental literacy programming that have emerged in response to reform movements. Lastly, we offer recommendations on behalf of the professional organization for faculty, administrators, and legislative bodies who share common goals: preparing students to be successful in college; supporting students' efforts to fulfill their own educational goals (whether that be additional education, skills, or attainment of a two- or four-year credential); and helping institutions more effectively achieve their missions.

Case Study: Florida's Senate Bill 1720

When legislators institute broad statewide reforms to developmental education, it is often two-year college faculty who are responsible for determining how to implement such mandates at the institution level. An illustrative example is Florida's Senate Bill 1720, passed in 2013, which exempts recent Florida high school graduates and active-duty military personnel from mandatory placement testing and developmental education and requires all public postsecondary institutions to offer incoming students at least two remediation options other than traditional sixteen-week developmental courses. Individual colleges have been charged with developing advising procedures for exempt students and devising multiple developmental support options that students can complete concurrently with college-level courses.

During the 2013–2014 academic year, faculty across the state scrambled to put in place more extensive advising and first-week diagnostic assessments that would help them identify and counsel exempt students who were likely to need additional writing support (Cherry et al.). Likewise, although they had relatively little time for research or reflection, colleges quickly developed and implemented a variety of remediation options to meet the needs of their student populations within their given institutional contexts. These options included a range of alternative models that have emerged or gained traction in the context of developmental reform movements: intensive "boot camp" or "bridge" programs prior to the start of the semester (in which students take compressed "refresher" courses); accelerated learning courses based on Baltimore Community College's model (Adams et al.); contextualized learning courses that paired writing instruction with required courses in the social and behavioral sciences; and modularized courses targeting specific literacy-related learning needs (for more on these models, see "Snapshot of Program Design Options" below). Campus learning centers also began facilitating supplemental writing instruction using online products like Pearson's MySkillsLab and MyCompLab. In their classrooms, Florida faculty are preparing to respond to greater variation in student preparation levels without a reduction in class sizes or teaching load (Cherry et al.), counter to recommendations by the Conference on College Composition and Communication (Horning).

Although faculty in Florida colleges have been responding to SB 1720 in thoughtful and innovative ways — often with few or no additional resources — many have expressed concerns about how the law is affecting students. Faculty worry that some students' needs are not being met, particularly those who are working and/or have families and make their decisions about support options in the context of competing demands on their schedules and finances. For some of these students, the most expedient options may not meet their actual learning needs, leaving them underprepared for the kinds of writing they are expected to undertake in credit-bearing courses. Faculty are particularly concerned about students' opportunities to prepare for college reading under these program reforms, as well as the integrity of the credit-bearing composition curriculum as the range of student preparation in these courses widens (Cherry et al.).

Florida faculty members are also concerned about how SB 1720 will affect working conditions in their colleges. In addition to the uncompensated labor involved in mandated program redesign and the added challenges of meeting a wider range of student preparation levels in the course sections, faculty worry that changes to the structure of developmental education may disproportionately affect adjunct faculty, who teach the majority of developmental reading and writing courses.

As part-time instructors, these faculty have few or no administrative responsibilities, and are therefore the least involved in departmental and institutional decisions about how to address the legislature's mandates. Adjunct faculty also have little job security, and reductions in the number of developmental courses may leave some of these instructors out of work (Cherry et al.).

Finally, SB 1720 threatens to undermine the professional status of two-year college faculty, highlighting the need for support from disciplinary professional organizations. Many faculty feel frustrated and powerless in the face of a legislature that makes decisions about higher education with little regard for their professional expertise but, at least in some instructors' view, appears quite responsive to lobbying by for-profit colleges and other corporate interests (Cherry et al.). Several college writing programs in Florida have been sharing resources and institutional responses to SB 1720 through professional organizations like the Florida English Association (FEA) and TYCA Southeast. However, presenters at the 2014 TYCA Southeast conference report little overlap in the membership of FEA and the Florida Developmental Education Association, the other major state-level professional organization representing two-year college developmental faculty (Cherry et al.). The current reform movement provides an opportunity for professionals in different organizations to collaborate for students' best interest.

Legislative Interventions and Program Responses

While Florida's SB 1720 is a particularly dramatic case study, legislative interventions have been made across the country in several areas of developmental education: admissions, initial placement of students into courses, and program design and curriculum. In this section, we provide an overview and illustrations of the types of state-mandated reforms for which many two-year colleges have become responsible.

Admissions

Two-year colleges are traditionally open-admission institutions; however, as developmental education is being scaled back or eliminated at many public four-year institutions, two-year colleges are feeling pressure to reform their programs, resulting in questions not only about *how* they will serve students, but also about *which* students they should serve at all. In California, the Early Start initiative requires students who need developmental education to begin their pre-college-level studies at a two-year college before enrolling at a California State University; these students are not required to complete their developmental education prior to enrollment but must remain co-enrolled until they have reached college level (California Department of Developmental Services). Similarly, students in Louisiana must "cross-enroll" in two-year colleges to take required developmental education courses. Joining Louisiana and California, the states of Ohio, Missouri, and Colorado have eliminated or drastically reduced or redesigned developmental education on their four-year college campuses. The result is a rethinking of the very purpose of developmental education at two-year colleges and the mission of two-year colleges in general. For example, two-year college faculty in Missouri are responding to a state bill requiring "best practices" in developmental education by considering whether they can or should continue to serve all students who seek enrollment. Should they admit students whose reading assessments place them so far below college level that they have virtually no chance of ever reaching credit-bearing courses? If not, where should these students go? Ultimately, the very existence of the open-admissions two-year college is thrown into question by state-mandated developmental education reform initiatives.

Placement

One of the fundamental functions of a writing program is administering locally appropriate placement procedures. Who is better equipped to determine which students are most likely to succeed in which classes than the faculty who teach those classes and students, provided those faculty are informed and have time to examine the local context in a larger frame of understanding? Placement is complex, and reform is needed: while some of the state-mandated reforms are welcome, others are more troubling because they are not derived from theoretically and empirically grounded practices or supported with necessary resources and faculty training.

Many English educators support placement processes that move beyond single test scores and support legislation that responds to mounting evidence that standardized placement tests do not provide accurate placement for students. Shanna Smith Jaggars and Michelle Hodara, for example, have shown that standardized placement tests "are only weakly predictive of student success and do not provide a diagnosis of each student's particular strengths and weaknesses" (7). Clive Belfield and Peter M. Crosta have shown that standardized placement tests like ACCUPLACER and Compass have "severe error rates," misplacing approximately 3 out of every 10 students (39; see also Hodara, Jaggars, and Karp). In fact, a student's high school GPA appears to be a better predictor of college success than standardized placement test scores (Belfield and Crosta 17–18).

However, some state legislatures bypass faculty input and appear to engage in political rather than research-based decision making. Florida's changed placement procedures in SB 1720 offer a case in point. By signing the bill into law, the Florida governor mandated what might be considered a version of directed self-placement, declaring some students exempt from mandatory placement assessment and giving most students who are assessed as needing developmental instruction multiple remediation options (see "Case Study" above). The law also radically redefines "college ready" by decreeing that a Florida high school diploma for anyone who has been enrolled since the ninth grade earns automatic placement into college-level courses, regardless of other indicators. Finally, Florida is implementing a single placement test with a single cutoff score established by the state board, which ignores differences in student populations in different parts of the state and the varying curricular and institutional programs at different colleges (Florida Senate). All of these state-mandated reforms ignore local faculty expertise and well-documented best practices in writing placement assessment ("Writing Assessment").

Other legislatures are also considering or have implemented state-mandated placement processes that do not necessarily reflect disciplinary knowledge of best practices. In Washington (as well as many other states), a student's score on the assessment associated with the Common Core State Standards, put together by the Smarter Balanced consortium, will be used to place students into college-level courses; though the test itself has not yet been implemented, cutoff scores for placement into college-level writing have already been established by policymakers. The Virginia Placement Test (VPT), which places students into a class without offering faculty a test score or any diagnostic information, has been implemented statewide. The results differ from college to college: some are seeing more students than before placed into developmental courses while others are seeing more students placed directly into first-year writing. In the latter colleges, the success rate in first-year writing has dropped significantly (Spiegel). However, these changes are not consistent with national position statements that assert the importance of writing assessment that is based on multiple pieces of evidence from student writers.

Some legislative mandates, however, have drawn from best practices outlined in the position statements and disciplinary best practices. For example, Connecticut's Public Act 12-40, a legislative bill passed in 2012 commonly referred to as PA 12-40, mandated a placement procedure using "multiple measures." All state colleges are required by Board of Regents policy to use multiple measures for placement, including ACCUPLACER. North Carolina has mandated multiple placement measures, most notably using high school GPA to place students into classes. State colleges in Connecticut—including the twelve community colleges in the system—are now experimenting with or piloting additional multiple measures for placement.

Program Design and Curriculum

Some state legislatures are also dictating changes to program design (for in-depth descriptions of many of these alternative program types, see "Snapshot of Program Design Options" below). Connecticut has mandated "accelerated" courses and embedded support while limiting developmental education for students to one semester. Moreover, Connecticut has mandated that state colleges and universities build remedial education into credit-bearing courses, requiring "just-in-time" support, possibly including tutoring. In legislation related to but not included in PA 12-40, the Connecticut legislature also established a "floor" for developmental students. This legislation sought to remand students who test at or below the eighth-grade level in reading or math starting in the fall 2014 semester to "regional remediation centers." After considerable public outcry, this idea has been dropped, and regional "transition strategies" are currently being developed for Connecticut's most underprepared college students (Connecticut Association for Human Services).

Other states, such as Indiana and Washington, are requiring high schools to identify those students who may need developmental education and offer them remedial work in the twelfth grade. In Washington, that determination will be made in the eleventh grade after the student has taken the Smarter Balanced test one time (it is unclear whether test preparation will be part of that "remedial" work). In Colorado, the state government has authorized public universities and colleges to offer developmental education on their own campuses, reversing a trend that began when California relegated all developmental education to the community college system. Colorado colleges and universities are now reforming their programs to include small-group study classes as co-requisites to first-year writing courses and stretch-model first-year writing courses as an alternative for some students (Parker). Similar alternatives are required in Florida (see "Case Study" above).

One consequence of state-mandated program redesign is the impact on faculty. In some colleges, for instance in Florida and Virginia, developmental English faculty, particularly adjunct and part-time, have been laid off and others reassigned due to the redesign of their programs. Beyond the professional cost to individual faculty, the loss of trained, seasoned instructors deprives developmental students of opportunities for personal contact with expert, caring practitioners that Gregory R. Glau sees as instrumental to their retention and success (Glau, "Stretch Program").

Finally, state governments are also dictating curricula. North Carolina has mandated that integrated developmental reading and writing be designed and offered statewide. This legislation requires faculty training but does not offer additional funding. Elsewhere, such as in Colorado, accelerated learning models and studio models are being required (see "Snapshot of Program Design Options" below). While these are proven approaches to developmental education, they have been mandated without providing additional support for faculty development.

These interventions demonstrate that state legislatures are willing and able to involve themselves in developmental policy and program design, often with little or no input from two-year college faculty. Furthermore, the events in Florida and Connecticut show that such legislation can leave faculty with the task of overhauling their programs on short notice and with few or no additional resources. Even when state legislatures are not directly involved, two-year college faculty are increasingly faced with institutional or system-wide pressures to reform their developmental programs to address concerns about student completion. As the practice of legislative intervention expands, TYCA hopes to a) develop a national voice for faculty who are charged with implementing changes and b) provide resources and recommendations for program reform. In the following section, we offer an overview of the alternative developmental program design options that have emerged in response to reform movements over the last two decades, including the available evidence for and against each model.

Snapshot of Program Design Options

The goal of most developmental education reform is to *accelerate* students' movement through developmental coursework and/or place students into college-level writing courses sooner. These two goals are not always one and the same, as some acceleration programs do away with separate developmental courses altogether. Nikki Edgecombe of the CCRC writes that the term *acceleration* can still mean two different things to college administration and faculty: either rethinking both content and time devoted to courses and sequences, or the reorganization of curriculum and instruction so that students are required to meet the same number of contact hours but in a less traditional sequenced course delivery. There are six major programmatic alternatives to traditional developmental courses that two-year colleges have been adopting in the context of developmental education reform: mainstreaming, studio courses, compression, integration/contextualization, stretch courses, and modularization. As the Florida case study demonstrates, colleges often adopt multiple models in an effort to meet a range of student needs.

Mainstreaming: In "mainstreaming" options, cohorts of students who have been identified as needing additional writing support enroll in first-year college-level composition with other nondevelopmental students but also attend a mandatory supplemental companion class or lab, sometimes on the same day or days, with the same instructor. Baltimore County Community College, led by Peter Adams, is perhaps the best known of these accelerated-learning program (ALP) models. One of the primary benefits of acceleration via mainstreaming is increased persistence: students complete college composition for college credit sooner than those on a traditional developmental course path. The most obvious drawback at the community college level is that not all students are ready to be placed in an ALP course even with the additional support (i.e., a supplemental class or lab) or to balance multiple college courses with their other responsibilities, as is the case for many part-time students and returning adult students. In "Re-Modeling Basic Writing," Rachel Rigolino and Penny Freel at the State University of New York at New Paltz describe their Supplemental Writing Workshop (SWW) Program for basic writing students, developed in response to public pressure to discontinue non-degree credit writing courses at baccalaureate institutions. The SWW alternative offers students additional hours of support with integrating first-year writing and tutoring sessions, and students earn degree credit over the course of the year for the two-semester writing sequence (51). For institutions that are facing administrative or economic pressure to eliminate basic writing and/or non-degree writing courses, the SWW model may provide an alternative.

Studio Courses: Another approach to acceleration is "studio" courses, often modeled on the work of Rhonda Grego and Nancy Thompson at the University of South Carolina. In the studio model, all first-year students enroll in freshman composition, and in the first week of the course students engage in writing exercises, including a writing self-assessment. These texts are used to identify which students might benefit from studio support; participating students sign up for small peer groups that meet weekly with an experienced writing instructor to support their work in the writing course (Grego and Thompson 63–64). Such models provide intensive, individualized writing instruction designed to help students develop as writers and succeed in the composition course.

Compression: In "compressed" courses, the content of an existing course or courses in a sequence is condensed into fewer weeks while maintaining the same number of instructional/contact hours. For example, a traditional sixteen-week course might be compressed into an eight-week course that meets for four rather than two hours per week. This enables a student to move through a two-course sequence in a single semester. The compressed developmental sequence in Community College of Denver's FastStart Program, for instance, has resulted in higher completion rates for both the developmental course and college composition (Edgecombe et al.).

Integration or Contextualization: Integration (sometimes called *contextualization*) provides developmental content in the context of other general education, technical, or vocational courses, often through team co-teaching. Integration can include "paired" courses: the Washington State Community College's I-BEST program (sometimes referred to as "bucket" courses) is one well-known example. John Wachen, Davis Jenkins, and Michelle Van Noy found that the advantages of integration with contextualization included institutional and student cost savings, higher pass rates, and increased credit-earning potential (26). Reading and writing integration is also at the heart of the California

Acceleration Project (CAP), developed at Chabot College by Katie Hern, which offers a one-semester compressed course that combines the two-semester, pre-college-level English course into a single semester (see Hern, "Accelerated English" and "Exponential Attrition"). Integrated reading, writing, and reasoning curricula are part of all developmental and degree-credit English courses in CAP.

Stretch Courses: Devised at four-year institutions tasked with dismantling stand-alone basic/developmental writing, stretch courses expand the first college-level writing course from one to two semesters. Students who would otherwise be placed into a traditional developmental writing course enter directly into the first college-level writing course but complete the composition requirement with more time and support (Glau, "*Stretch* at 10," "Stretch Program"). Describing Boise State University's "stretch" course, Thomas Peele states, "The most successful aspect . . . may be the simple fact that it allows students and faculty to spend more time together by pairing students with the same instructor for a full year . . . provid[ing] faculty with additional time to identify and address individual student needs" (51).

Module Courses: Module courses divide specific "skills" into units or modules rather than integrating them into courses, a structure that advocates claim allows students to focus on only those areas in which they have specific weaknesses. Thad Nodine et al. report that most modularization has taken place in developmental math, and that few studies have been done to really show if students receiving modularized support have enough context to apply what they learn, whether they persist in modularized programs, or if the process actually accelerates student progress (Edgecombe 11). Sullivan's "Just-in-Time" model ("Just-in-Time") offers a version of modularization in which advanced developmental students engage in flexible and clearly delineated assessments tied to key competencies in the first-year writing course, allowing them to earn degree credit while still technically enrolled in developmental courses (123).

Researchers and program administrators in writing studies have devoted significant intellectual effort and institutional resources to developing innovative ways to equip underprepared students for college-level work and to assessing the effectiveness of the programs they devise (see Glau, "Stretch Courses"). However, the flurry of legislative interest in the failures of existing programs and demands for new models speaks to the political and social dissatisfaction with the results of our current effort—as well as the challenges two-year college faculty face in helping students from diverse backgrounds develop the academic skills and social capital required to navigate the complex cultural system that is higher education.

While policymakers are enacting developmental education reform in order to serve the public interest, they typically have little awareness of our field's rich theorizations of language, literacy, and learning, which are essential to designing effective programs. Likewise, policy-makers have consistently failed to recognize the professional expertise and authority of the two-year college English faculty who will be tasked with implementing such legislation. With a rich disciplinary and scholarly foundation of research, evidence-based recommendations, and position statements available through the National Council of Teachers of English, the Two-Year College Association, and the Conference on College Composition and Communication, educators in postsecondary writing have a robust body of resources to draw from in making this disciplinary knowledge available to policymakers and administrators.

Recommendations and Paths Forward

Most two-year colleges are institutions of access that serve an extraordinarily broad range of learners. Nearly all two-year college English instructors work on a daily basis with students who are underprepared for college-level reading and writing in their first semester and who often require ongoing academic support throughout their college experience. Developmental education courses and placement processes play an important role in determining student success across all English courses in the two-year college curriculum. For this reason, institutional, state, and national policies that shape developmental education can have a profound effect on the working lives of all two-year college English faculty, regardless of whether they themselves teach developmental reading and writing. More importantly, such radical changes to developmental education do not fully consider the impact on our most vulnerable student populations, including potentially closing off access to higher education altogether.

It is essential, then, that two-year college English educators take part in public and institutional conversations about how to define college readiness, provide academic support to students who are underprepared for college reading and writing, and preserve the access that has traditionally been a hallmark of most two-year colleges' missions. TYCA, then, offers recommendations for both disciplinary groups and for educators and administrators at institutions who are re-examining their developmental education programs.

Recommendations for Institutional Administrators and Educators

Two-year college administrators and educators can join national, state, and institutional conversations about developmental education by advocating for the following practices:

1. *Include developmental education instructors*—including contingent faculty and part-time instructors—in decision-making pro-

cesses that affect policies, programs, and funding for developmental education at two-year colleges.

2. *Initiate improvement to developmental education programs and courses through research-based pilot programs that include rigorous assessments of student outcomes* rather than mandating large-scale statewide or institutional changes. Make developmental education policy decisions based on systematically collected data about the academic needs of the student populations that a college serves in relation to its institutional mission. Identify what is and is not working in developmental education by thoroughly assessing the effectiveness of practices and programs for specific student populations within locally situated contexts.

3. *Prioritize evidence from local assessments and research on student success.* Avoid drawing conclusions about effective strategies for developmental education based solely on research at institutions with different student populations, admissions standards, institutional missions, funding structures, academic support services, and/or working conditions for instructors. Support research based in open-admissions institutions with at-risk and underprepared students, research that will build a stronger body of empirical and theoretical work for basic/developmental writing instructors.

4. *Assess students' need for developmental education and readiness for credit-bearing courses based on multiple pieces of evidence, including student writing.* Eliminate the practice of using standardized tests as stand-alone measures for assessing students' readiness for college-level learning and determining placement in developmental English courses. Where at all possible, encourage directed self-placement, rather than undirected self-placement, as a part of the placement process.

5. *Eliminate developmental education exit tests that determine readiness for credit-bearing courses based on multiple-choice exams.* Instead use instructor or departmental assessments of the work that students complete for their developmental courses to provide students with multiple opportunities to develop and then demonstrate the academic literacy skills required for first-year college courses.

6. *Fund and develop strong academic support systems to help students make a successful transition* from developmental to credit-bearing courses and to provide them with continued support throughout their college careers, including tutoring centers, supplemental instruction, and studio courses.

7. *Support ongoing professional development for developmental educators*, especially for contingent faculty and part-time instructors who often have the most contact with underprepared and at-risk student populations.

8. *Support English departments at two-year colleges to establish part-nerships with area high schools* in order to facilitate articulation and alignment across institutional boundaries and smooth the transition to college for more students.

Recommendations for National Disciplinary Organizations

- *Establish a standing developmental education advocacy group or task force* — a group of two-year college professionals who can join committees, be consulted by legislatures and government agencies, and bring a deep knowledge of current research to discussions of developmental education reform. Such a committee may participate in a national agenda in multiple ways: visit campuses, for example, and provide professional development opportunities, advocate for thoughtful and research-based decision making (like the Community College Research Center), serve as a political action committee, created at least in part to help guide future legislative action (on the state and federal level) and resist any action that might be ill-advised.

- *Provide support, encouragement, and incentive* for more Research I and PhD-granting universities (as the places resourced to produce and disseminate research as well as tasked with preparing future faculty) to provide appropriate graduate preparation, professionalization, and ongoing professional development opportunities for two-year college teacher-scholars (across English studies) who are equipped to engage these issues at institutional, state, and national levels; such educators will be better able to assert their professional authority and advocate for students.

Educational policymaking, as well as institutional and individual faculty responses to mandates around developmental education, will affect the quality of life and the quality of our democracy for decades to come. Let us do the work of reforming developmental education with great resourcefulness, care, and thoughtfulness and with a fuller understanding about how much is at stake.

Works Cited and Recommended Readings

Adams, Peter, Sarah Gearhart, Robert Miller, and Anne Roberts. "The Accelerated Learning Program: Throwing Open the Gates." *Journal of Basic Writing* 28.2 (2009): 50–69. Print.

Baldwin, Patty, Helen Gillotte-Tropp, Sugie Goen-Salter, and Joan Wong. *Composing for Success: A Student's Guide to Integrated Reading and Writing.* Boston: Pearson Custom Publishing, 2007. Print.

Belfield, Clive, and Peter M. Crosta. "Predicting Success in College: The Importance of Placement Tests and High School Transcripts." *Community College Research Center*. Teachers College, Columbia U. CCRC Working Paper no. 42. Feb. 2012. Web.

Bradburn, Norman M., and Robert Townsend. "Higher Education's Missing Faculty Voices." *Chronicle of Higher Education* 2 June 2014. Web.

California Department of Developmental Services. "Early Start Home Page." *California Department of Developmental Services*. 2014. Web. http://www.dds.ca.gov/earlystart/.

Cherry, Tammy, Marilyn Metzcher-Smith, Elizabeth Cobb, Jennifer Paquette, and David Hurner. "Florida College's Responses to Bill 1720." Two-Year College English Association Southeast Annual Conference. Hilton Hotel, Tampa. 28 Feb. 2014. Panel.

"College Completion." *Chronicle of Higher Education*. 2010. Web. http://college completion.chronicle.com/table/.

Community College Research Center. "Community College FAQs." *Community College Research Center*. Teachers College, Columbia U. N.d. Web. http://ccrc.tc.columbia.edu/Community-College-FAQs.html.

Connecticut Association for Human Services. "Developmental Education at Connecticut Community Colleges: A Key to Economic Recovery." Hartford: Connecticut Association for Human Services, 2011. Print.

Edgecombe, Nikki. "Accelerating Academic Achievement of Students Referred to Developmental Education." *Community College Research Center*. Teachers College, Columbia U. CCRC Working Paper no. 30. Feb. 2011. Web.

Edgecombe, Nikki, Shanna Smith Jaggars, Elaine DeLott Baker, and Thomas Bailey. "Acceleration through a Holistic Support Model: An Implementation and Outcomes Analysis of FastStart@CCD." *Community College Research Center*. Teachers College, Columbia U. Feb. 2013. Web.

Florida Senate. "CS/CS/CB 1720: Education." *Florida Senate*. Bill Summary, Education Committee. 2013. Web. http://www.flsenate.gov/Committees/bill summaries/2013/html/501.

Glau, Gregory R. "*Stretch* at 10: A Progress Report on Arizona State University's *Stretch* Program." *Journal of Basic Writing* 26.2 (2007): 30–48. Print.

———. "Stretch Courses." *Council of Writing Program Administrators*. WPA-CompPile Research Bibliographies no. 2. Feb. 2010. Web.

———. "The 'Stretch Program': Arizona State University's New Model of University-Level Basic Writing Instruction." *WPA: Writing Program Administration* 20.1 (1996): 79–91. Print.

Goen-Salter, Sugie. "Critiquing the Need to Eliminate Remediation: Lessons from San Francisco State." *Journal of Basic Writing* 27.2 (2008): 81–105. Print.

Grego, Rhonda, and Nancy Thompson. "Repositioning Remediation: Renegotiating Composition's Work in the Academy." *College Composition and Communication* 47.1 (1996): 62–84. Web.

Hassel, Holly, and Joanne Baird Giordano. "First-Year Composition Placement at Open-Admission, Two-Year Campuses: Changing Campus Culture, Institutional Practice, and Student Success." *Open Words: Access and English Studies* 5.2 (2011): 29–59. Web.

Hern, Katie. "Accelerated English at Chabot College: A Synthesis of Key Findings." *California Acceleration Project*. 2011. Web.

————. "Exponential Attrition and the Promise of Acceleration in Developmental English and Math." *Chabot College*. June 2010. Web.

Hodara, Michelle, Shanna Smith Jaggars, and Melinda Mechur Karp. "Improving Developmental Education Assessment and Placement: Lessons From Community Colleges across the Country." *Community College Research Center*. Teachers College, Columbia U. CCRC Working Paper no. 51. Nov. 2012. Web.

Horning, Alice. "The Definitive Article on Class Size." *WPA: Writing Program Administration* 31.1/2 (2007): 11–34. Print.

Humphreys, Debra. "What's Wrong with the Completion Agenda—And What We Can Do about It." *Liberal Education* 98.1 (2012). Web.

Jaggars, Shanna Smith, and Michelle Hodara. "The Opposing Forces That Shape Developmental Education: Assessment, Placement, and Progression at CUNY Community College." *Community College Research Center*. Teachers College, Columbia U. CCRC Working Paper no. 36. Nov. 2011. Web.

Lindsey, Brink. "The Education Dividend." *Chronicle of Higher Education* 15 Oct. 2012. Web.

Nodine, Thad, Mina Dadgar, Andrea Venezia, and Kathy Reeves Bracco. "Acceleration in Developmental Education." *WestEd*. 2013. Web.

Parker, Jessica. Email to Jeff Klausman. 27 May 2014.

Peele, Thomas. "Working Together: Student-Faculty Interaction at the Boise State Stretch Program." *Journal of Basic Writing* 29.2 (2010): 50–73. Web.

Perin, Dolores, and Kerry Charron. "'Lights Just Click on Every Day.'" *Defending the Community College Equity Agenda*. Ed. Thomas Bailey and Vanessa Smith Morest. Baltimore: Johns Hopkins UP, 2006. 155–94. Print.

Radford, Alexandria Walton, Lutz Berkner, Sara C. Wheeless, Bryan Shepherd, and Tracy Hunt-White. "Persistence and Attainment of 2003–04 Beginning Postsecondary Students: After 6 Years; First Look." *U.S. Department of Education*. National Center for Education Statistics, Institute of Education Sciences. Dec. 2010. Web.

Rigolino, Rachel, and Penny Freel. "Re-Modeling Basic Writing." *Journal of Basic Writing* 26.2 (2007): 51–74. Web.

Royer, Daniel, and Roger Gilles. *Directed Self-Placement: Principles and Practices*. Cresskill: Hampton P, 2003. Print.

Shapiro, Doug, Afet Dundar, Mary Ziskin, Xin Yuan, and Autumn Harrell. "Completing College: A National View of Student Attainment Rates." *National Student Clearinghouse Research Center*. 16 Dec. 2013. Web.

Spiegel, Cheri Lemieux. Personal interview with Jeff Klausman. 30 May 2014.

Sullivan, Patrick. "'Just-in-Time' Curriculum for the Basic Writing Classroom." *Teaching English in the Two-Year College* 41.2 (2013): 118–34. Print.

Wachen, John, Davis Jenkins, and Michelle Van Noy. "How I-BEST Works: Findings from a Field Study of Washington State's Integrated Basic Education and Skills Training Program." *Community College Research Center*. Teachers College, Columbia U. Sept. 2010. Web.

White House. "Higher Education." Education: Knowledge and Skills for the Jobs of the Future. *White House*. N.d. Web.

"Writing Assessment: A Position Statement." Conference on College Composition and Communication Committee on Assessment. *National Council of Teachers of English*. Nov. 2006 (rev. Mar. 2009). Web.

A Learning Society

Mike Rose

In his book Back to School: Why Everyone Deserves a Second Chance at Education, *renowned literacy scholar Mike Rose presents an enthusiastic defense of open access to higher education, community colleges, and adult education programs. Based on observations and conversations with students, teachers, and staff, Rose argues for the importance of "second chance" educational institutions and the contributions they make to American social mobility and civic engagement. Rose also suggests that policy makers, colleges, and even teachers themselves sometimes undermine meaningful access for students who seek to change their lives through education. In this passage from the conclusion to this book, Rose situates our current educational policy moment in broader historical context and argues for rethinking the instrumentalist assumptions about learning, labor, and class that underpin many of today's educational reform initiatives.*

> The farmer, the mechanic, the manufacturer, the merchant, the sailor, the soldier . . . must be educated.
>
> —Philip Lindsley, *president of the University of Nashville, 1825*

Since the early days of the Republic, adult Americans have been seeking ways to further educate themselves after their (successful or unsuccessful) formal education is over. The motives vary and combine—intellectual stimulation, social benefit, or occupational advancement through the learning of specific job skills—but the bottom line is that we as a people seem driven toward self-improvement and have created a staggering number of ways, both superficial and substantial, to achieve it: from self-help books to correspondence courses to continuous incarnations of mutual-improvement societies (lyceums, mechanics' institutes, chautauquas) to classes in university extension.

Unions such as the Knights of Labor and farmers' political organizations, most notably the Grange, had considerable educational programs. There was the public-library movement and agricultural extensions and experimental colleges for working people. Private occupational or proprietary schools arose and grew. The public community college began in 1901 and expanded rapidly through the mid-twentieth century, and the GI bill opened two- and four-year colleges to a remarkable number of returning veterans, changing the nature of American higher

From *Back to School: Why Everyone Deserves a Second Chance at Education*. New Press, 2012, pp. 183–89.

education in the process. There are literacy programs and workforce development initiatives and adult schools that offer everything from basic education to courses on local geography, French cooking, and navigating the Internet. As historian Joseph Kett put it in *The Pursuit of Knowledge Under Difficulties*, a sweeping account of this multistrand tradition, in the same way that "democracy seems only to whet appetites for more democracy," so too "each advance in educational opportunity" sparks a desire for more education. The people we've met in this book are the newest participants in this tradition.

As we've seen, many of the reasons this new generation needs to pursue a second chance are deeply troubling: inadequate K–12 schools, limited youth programs, unemployment, and the effects of poverty on neighborhoods and families. Furthermore, the sheer numbers of people involved strain an already overloaded system; yet the system has to respond, because there is a lot riding on their success, for them and for our economic and social structure. Especially in these recessionary times, the influx of all these students — many in need of academic remediation and other services — is a source of great consternation to policy makers and educational administrators. Just about everything I've read or heard on the topic frames it as a problem.

While acknowledging the significant budgetary and institutional challenges involved, it is also possible, shifting to the historical perspective provided by Joseph Kett, to view the swelling enrollments in a positive light. This new population is more diverse — especially by race and ethnicity — than most of those who have participated in nontraditional American educational movements and institutions in the past. People like those in this book represent an advance in educational opportunity, an example of educational democracy whetting the appetite for more access, more possibility, more of a chance to learn new skills, master new bodies of knowledge. As one of the students we met earlier put it, she wants to be able to take tests and write essays "like it is part of my life."

To realize the promise of a second-chance education for this new population, we will need to do a number of things. The first few of these won't cost much at all, but might be among the most difficult to realize, for they call for a shift in ways of thinking. The good news is that multiple examples of these shifts in thinking are already occurring in classrooms and programs around the United States, exemplars that we can learn from, that can open up our educational imagination.

Let us begin with first principles. While acknowledging the importance of the economic motive for schooling, our philosophy of education — our guiding rationale for creating schools — has to include the intellectual, social, civic, moral, and aesthetic motives as well. If these further motives are not articulated, they fade from public policy, from institutional mission, from curriculum development. Without this richer philosophy, those seeking a second chance will likely receive a bare-bones, strictly functional education, one that does not honor the many reasons they return to school and, for that matter, one not suitable for a democratic society.

We'll also need to fundamentally rethink the divide between the academic and vocational courses of study, an arbitrary but quite consequential way of separating kinds of knowledge. This rethinking will of necessity involve scrutiny of the long-standing Western separation of physical from mental activity and the beliefs about intelligence and the social order that accompany that separation.

We need to take basic-skills instruction out of the hinterland of higher education, liberate it from the academic snobbery and bankrupt assumptions about teaching and learning that profoundly limit its effectiveness. To do this does not signal complacency about the conditions that lead to academic underpreparation but acknowledges the fact that we've never had a period in our history when remediation has been unnecessary—so we had better get good at it if we want to maintain educational opportunity. This is not just a subject matter or institutional issue, but a civic and moral issue as well.

Two other efforts are necessary to realize this recasting of basic-skills instruction, and these will cost money. First, the need for substantial professional development is overwhelming. I've seen so many committed, hard-working teachers using reductive skills and drills curricula because that's what was given to them, and that's all they know. Because basic-skills instruction is held in such low regard, and its cookbook, scripted curriculum is so transportable, it's assumed that anyone can teach it. The second point concerns the use of computer technology in basic-skills instruction. The technology holds great promise, but we must keep in mind that any technology is only as good as the thinking behind it and the use made of it. If computer technology, as sophisticated as it can be, is used in ways that simply reflect the same old reductive beliefs about cognition and remediation, then it won't move us forward at all. Changing both beliefs and practices in remedial education and creating good technology and meaningfully integrating it into curriculum will require human and fiscal resources.

To think clearly about the debate over college for all versus occupational training—and thus to come to a fruitful path beyond the debate—we'll need to be mindful of several things. Part of the problem is that our society does not provide a range of options after high school for young people to grow in productive ways, to learn about the world and about their talents and interests. We lack, for example, a robust system of occupational apprenticeships or a comprehensive national service program. The deep-rooted divide between the academic and vocational courses of study—and the social-class biases reflected in that divide—also complicate the debate. We won't be able to create more imaginative postsecondary options for young people until we address this divide. Another issue to consider is this: It took a long time and a good deal of effort to initiate a cultural shift so that a wider sweep of our population began to see college as a possibility. We need to be alert to the unintended consequences of altering that cultural shift. Finally, we have to be aware of the fact that this debate is not simply an economic one but one that is taking place against a backdrop of discrimination. The debate about who should be educated and to what end has powerful legal, social, and civic dimensions to it.

The relationship between poverty and academic achievement is a long-standing issue in K–12 education, and, unfortunately, in some recent school-reform debates the relationship has devolved into an unproductive binary. One position claims that poverty so devastates students' lives that achievement is virtually impossible. The other holds that if schools are run well, poverty is not a barrier to learning. Variations of this simplistic rendering play out in discussions of adult and postsecondary education as well—and the results are just as counterproductive.

Poverty does provide a rationale for some instructors and administrators to avoid challenging curricula and programs, to not push either themselves or their students toward excellence, to perpetuate an institutional culture of resignation. Conversely, a simplified view of poverty and achievement—a radically individualist model of mobility—flies in the face of common sense. Zip code might not be destiny, but it does correlate with stability of housing and employment, with health care, with environmental threats, with three square meals a day—all of which affect the time students have to attend classes, study, get assistance, concentrate, even just see clearly the print on the pages of their textbooks. To realize the promise of a second-chance education, we'll need to create the best programs we can and provide adequate financial aid, support services, and a social safety net to enable people to attend and thrive in them.

There can be a conflict between access—removing barriers to participation in school—and standards. There is no easy resolution to this conflict, but what we can do is keep both goals equally in sight, committing to both admitting people and educating them well. And when a standard is put in place that has the potential to enhance the quality of education for some—for example, increasing the literacy and mathematics content of the GED examination—we also have to create opportunities for those whose knowledge is not yet at the level of the new exam.

Institutions that serve a primarily second-chance population have to orient themselves as best they can on all levels—from physical layout, to guidance and counseling, to curriculum design, to professional development—to the populations they serve. Many such institutions claim to do this already, and some do so masterfully. But, in line with my observations about poverty and achievement, this orientation needs to be one that both meets people where they are *and* moves them forward to fulfilling their goals—and possibly opens up new goals for them.

There is much talk in our time of the United States becoming a "learning society." Management consultants write about "organizational learning," and adult development experts champion "lifelong learning." The focus of this talk tends to be on professionals and managers and people with a baccalaureate degree and beyond—mostly members of the middle and upper-middle classes. But if we're serious about our country being a learning society, then we need to include all of its members, "the farmer, the mechanic, the manufacturer. . . ."

Diverse Student Populations

One of the great joys of teaching at a two-year college is the variety of students you meet—from all walks of life, from every conceivable background, and from around the world, often in the same class. This diversity is one of the strengths of two-year colleges, and it is also one of the reasons these institutions have been described as "the people's college." Because of the demographics they serve, two-year college teacher-scholars have been major innovators in our discipline's efforts to meet the needs of diverse students. They also have an important responsibility to help create classrooms, departments and institutions, and a professional community that promotes social justice rather than reproduces structures of inequality.

As we might expect, the diversity of two-year college students presents unique challenges and opportunities for writing teachers. The readings in this section offer approaches to creating successful learning environments for students from a wide range of backgrounds. While there is much valuable work in our discipline on this subject, we have chosen to foreground essays written by teacher-scholars at open admissions institutions about two-year college contexts. The essays in this section of our book focus on many different forms of diversity, including students' socioeconomic status, academic preparation, race, ethnicity, language background, gender, age, and veteran status.

For many people across the United States, two-year colleges have become the most affordable and accessible means of pursuing postsecondary education. Students from low-income or working-class backgrounds are frequently in the majority at these institutions. Many have full- and part-time jobs as well as family responsibilities. The most recent Community College Survey of Student Engagement, for example, reports that 47.8 percent of students at two-year colleges worked more than twenty hours per week; 41 percent spent six or more hours a week caring for dependents; and 26 percent spent six or more hours a week commuting to and from classes. These socioeconomic realities also intersect with issues of race, ethnicity, gender, and language(s) in ways that affect students' learning experiences. Many of the essays we include in this chapter examine these important intersections.

Most two-year colleges enroll students with a wide range of prior academic experiences, and writing faculty at these institutions often become specialists in working with students who have been institutionally constructed as "underprepared." While issues of academic preparation are central to much of the scholarship featured in this collection, Chapter 15 highlights two classic essays that can help instructors understand such students' own perspectives on their educational experiences. Smokey Wilson provides a moving, richly detailed case study of one of her students, Darlene, who was labeled a "slow learner" early in her academic career. Likewise, Marilyn Sternglass offers a longitudinal portrait of one of her students, Joan, who faced many academic, socioeconomic, and physical challenges during her time in college but eventually earned her bachelor's degree. Instructors preparing to teach basic/developmental writing for the first time are likely to find these essays enlightening and inspiring.

A large number of students from historically underrepresented racial, ethnic, and language backgrounds begin their postsecondary education at two-year colleges (Cohen, Brawer, and Kisker). Indeed, faculty at these colleges have been at the forefront of developing responsive pedagogical approaches for these cohorts of students. While it is impossible to address the complexities of these issues fully in a single chapter, or even a single book (and we believe there is a pressing need for more scholarship on these critical issues), in Chapter 16 we offer a selection of essays that highlight pedagogical approaches developed in and for two-year college writing classrooms that move toward being culturally relevant and sustaining (see Ladson-Billings; Paris). In "Teaching English in a California Two-Year Hispanic-Serving Institution," Jody Millward, Sandra Starkey, and David Starkey reflect on their efforts to serve Latina/o and Chicana/o students at their institution. In "Dialects, Gender, and Writing," Greg Shafer describes how he invites his students, many of whom are African American, to grapple with the ideologies surrounding language diversity, race, and gender that have shaped their perceptions and identities as writers. Finally, Kristen di Gennaro's essay offers conceptual tools and pedagogical insights for addressing multilingual students' experiences and identities at the programmatic level. Together, these essays offer a set of preliminary critical tools for discussing the locally specific interrelations of race, ethnicity, language, socioeconomic status, and schooling experiences that shape literacy learning in two-year colleges.

Finally, Chapter 17 examines the diversity of age and life experience in many two-year college classrooms. In addition to "traditional" students (those between the ages of eighteen and twenty-four), these institutions also enroll many older and returning students. As Michelle Navarre Cleary suggests, such students often bring a wealth of motivation and experience with them to our classrooms, along with anxieties and competing responsibilities from other areas of their lives. At the other end of the spectrum, the growth of dual and concurrent enrollment programs in many states means that two-year college English faculty are increasingly teaching courses that include high school students. In "(Re) Envisioning the Divide: The Impact of College Courses on High School Students," Kara Taczek and William Thelin offer a rich case study of the challenges of teaching "college-level writing" with an age group that historically has not been present in college classrooms. The final selection in this chapter examines a population of students garnering increasing attention among two-year college teacher-scholars: military veterans. For a variety of reasons, including geographical accessibility, the limitations of GI bill benefits, and, in some cases, (dis)ability-related issues, two-year colleges have become a popular entry point for veterans pursuing postsecondary degrees, and these students often bring distinctive experiences, resources, and needs to the writing classroom. Galen Leonhardy's essay "Transformations: Working with Veterans in the Composition Classroom" focuses specifically on the writing experiences of veterans in two-year colleges.

Of course, there are many other dimensions of diversity that bear on two-year college writing classrooms: student and instructor LGBTQ+ identities; religious or spiritual beliefs; (dis)ability and neurodiversity; and differences between rural, suburban, and urban contexts, to name just a few. We hope the selection of essays presented in this section offers instructors a useful starting point for thinking about the relationships between various forms of diversity and writing pedagogy in their local institutional contexts.

Reflecting on the profound and often painful insights in Taiyon J. Coleman, Renee DeLong, Kathleen Sheerin DeVore, Shannon Gibney, and Michael C. Kuhne's recent article "The Risky Business of Engaging Racial Equity in Writing Instruction"—published just as this volume was going to press—we also hope to work with readers to create the conditions by which faculty whose identities and experiences have been marginalized can contribute to *and be heard within* institutional, professional, and scholarly conversations. This work is likely to require an embrace of multilingualism (Bawarshi, Guerra, Horner, and Lu), familiarity with critical race theory (Delgado and Stefancic), and perhaps even a reassessment of critical thinking itself (Fox).

Works Cited

Bawarshi, Anis, et al., editors. *Translingual Work in Composition*. Special issue of *College English*, vol. 78, no. 3, 2016.

Cohen, Arthur, et al. *The American Community College*. 6th ed., Jossey-Bass, 2014.

Coleman, Taiyon J., et al. "The Risky Business of Engaging Racial Equity in Writing Instruction: A Tragedy in Five Acts." *Teaching English in the Two-Year College*, vol. 43, no. 4, 2016, pp. 347-370.

Community College Survey of Student Engagement. "2011 Cohort: National Frequency Distributions for All Students." University of Texas at Austin, Community College Leadership Program, 2011. http://intranet.shoreline.edu/institutional-assessment/documents/surveys/ccsse2011-allstu-freq-cohort.pdf

Delgado, Richard, and Jean Stefancic. *Critical Race Theory: An Introduction*. 2nd ed., New York University Press, 2012.

Fox, Catherine. "The Race to Truth: Disarticulating Critical Thinking from Whiteliness." *Pedagogy*, vol. 2, no. 2, 2002, pp. 197-212.

Ladson-Billings, Gloria. "Toward a Theory of Culturally Relevant Pedagogy." *American Educational Research Journal*, vol. 32, no. 3, 1995, pp. 465-91.

Paris, Django. "Culturally Sustaining Pedagogy: A Needed Change in Stance, Terminology, and Practice." *Educational Researcher*, vol. 41, no. 3, 2012, pp. 93-97.

Underprepared Learners

What Happened to Darleen? Reconstructing the Life and Schooling of an Underprepared Learner

Smokey Wilson

This essay, a classic on the experiences and potential of basic writing students at community colleges, presents the story of Darleen, a Hispanic student who entered college nearly two decades after dropping out of the school system that had tracked her into special education courses. Smokey Wilson examines Darleen's childhood education and family experiences from multiple perspectives, then traces her literacy learning over several years of "basic skills" instruction at a community college. Wilson describes how Darleen constructed a sense of herself as a student, arguing that her success derived from both personal determination and a keen ability to develop social relationships at the college that supported her learning. As a sympathetic and clear-eyed portrait of the experiences of a student dismissed by many educators—including, initially, Wilson herself—this essay is a testament to learners' possibilities and the enduring importance of the open-access mission.

From *Two-Year College English: Essays for a New Century*. NCTE, 1994, pp. 37-53.

As an open-admissions institution, the community college has offered its instructors the opportunity to work with those who, as Mike Rose says, got lost in our schools and who return to college to repair fractured educations. In the late 1960s and early 1970s, teachers took to heart Mina Shaughnessy's admonition to "dive in," and began to find ways to engage adults in reading and writing tasks that enabled them to acquire the skills and knowledge they needed to live and work in some ascendant way. In the 1990s, urban learners face even more difficult situations in school: violence, drugs, teenage pregnancy. School failure for minority groups is with them, and us, today. Students who have suffered these ills will be ready for the community college in the year 2000.

If we are to be ready for them, we need to learn more from the students who currently sit in our classrooms, students like Darleen. Darleen is forty-one. After quitting high school at the end of ninth grade, she returned four years ago to the urban community college where I teach. She represents many other adults: no longer young, unskilled, haunted by self-doubt, and yet paradoxically optimistic about the power of education to rekindle a sense of self-worth. In a sense, Darleen is a worst-case scenario: placed in special education classes as a girl, a school dropout, pregnant at fifteen, unable to read, write, or calculate as an adult, habitually silent. She scarcely seems a promising candidate for college work. Yet (and this contradiction raises a central question of this paper) she is also a best-case scenario: after basic skills work, she is headed toward an AA degree. What happened to Darleen which accounts for the movement away from school as a youngster and then back into school twenty years later?

Talking to Darleen offered a starting point for understanding her change in direction. She has a keen sense that a personal connection with teachers and tutors played a key role in her learning—and in her failure to learn. Taking up Darleen's theme from a theoretical position, I suggest that we need to integrate Darleen's emphasis on the importance of a personal connection in terms of our changing ideas about how learning in school takes place. When Darleen was first in school, remember, teachers thought of all learning, especially learning to read and write, as a solitary activity. Students were expected to study independently; to work together was cheating. Now, twenty years later, we have come to understand that literacy is socially constructed. We question the notion of solitary authorship and see writing as a collaborative enterprise. In looking back on her school experience, Darleen intuits what researchers are just discovering: that learning to read and write depends on the connections between expert and novice, and that failure to take in literacy lessons is also created by breakdowns in these connections, by misconnections.

The Story the School Records Tell

Darleen's cumulative records, which span the years from entry into kindergarten to "dropping out" at the end of ninth grade, show how these misconnections are made. The movement for her was always in one direction: a distancing from school barely noticeable in primary school, escalating rapidly in middle school, becoming irreparably wide by junior high. This image of a child slipping away from school emerges the way buckets fill up under a leaky roof: no single drop seems to make the discernible difference.

On the pupil identification form, there is no special hint of a dismal outcome: Last name, Ramos; first name, Darleen. (This is, by her request, not a pseudonym.) Birth date: 12/20/51. Her address is listed at a street on the fringes of the inner city, her apartment, "downstairs." Father, Felipe; home address, above; occupation: Mechanic; Mother, Maria; home address, above; Hwfe—Cannery. These few words conjure up a vision of the routine that guided the lives of this family, an understanding based, in my recollection, of a time when manufacturing was the staff of life in this city: the big Del Monte factory down near the freeway, the giant truckloads of tomatoes that poured into town from the Central California Valley in July and August, the smokestacks that poured out white steam every afternoon, the pressure and bustle of double shifts that ended and poured everybody home again, the seasonal work ending in October. Now the cannery is closed permanently; the child is middle-aged. With one last note—Brothers and sisters: Angelo and Kathleen—Darleen was assigned to "A.M. kgn," Room 2.

The record speaks again one year later, when Darleen's teacher made comments about her for the school nurse; these phrases call her "anemic-looking," a "mouth breather." The following year's teacher again commented on her mouth breathing. Adenoids? Bad tonsils? The school record made no detour into rumination or hunches. In 1962, the nurse recommended a vision exam for prescription glasses. The last entry regarding her vision reported, "Nothing done re: eyes." As we try to understand the forces that helped shape an adult who did not learn to read or write well enough to meet the expectations of school or employers, the lack of essential health care at the right time must not be left out of the accounting. When I asked her what she remembers about learning to write, she said that she learned "mostly by watching other kids"; she could not see the blackboard from her seat.

The next sheets in Darleen's cumulative record are teachers' progress reports, spaces about a half-inch square for each area in the curriculum for each semester. During her three semesters in kindergarten, nothing is inscribed in the "reading experience" column. Nothing with print? Nothing? Throughout her elementary school years, one theme that stands out in Darleen's education is a dearth of books.

Another theme is the repetition of the few texts she was given. All told, by the end of her elementary school experience, she had read, twice each, the three pre-primers, *Fun with Dick and Jane*, *Many Surprises*, and *Our Town*. According to the record, these books, along with copies of *Weekly Reader* and two or three library books, constituted what the teacher counted as Darleen's world of print in school until she was twelve.

Like the books Darleen read, the comments her teachers wrote about her are conspicuous either by their absence or by their repetition. Until she was nine years old, no teacher wrote anything in the "special abilities, accomplishments, and interests" column, when someone commented that she was helpful; the following year, she was noted as "desirous of learning." However, in the "learning difficulties" column, there is no such scarcity. She was termed "very shy" in kindergarten. The next year she was pegged as "very slow," immature, poor at writing, apt to daydream. The following year saw these comments repeated, plus the addition of "unable to comprehend new facts."

But the most damning comment, I think, occurs at the end of her second year in first grade, when the teacher wrote, "doing the best that she is able to do." Although this teacher assigned a final grade of S for satisfactory in both conduct and achievement, the year's comment seems, in retrospect, ominous. Although her movement from one grade to the next had been slow, the record assigned her to a graded classroom; at the end of six such grades, of course, one "completes elementary school." But at the end of this year, Darleen's record became oddly nonsequential as she was no longer assigned a grade level, but only to "Sp" (for special education classes), which effectively removed her from clear and definite progress toward graduation.

From this point on, her progress is noted yearly, in June, rather than semester by semester. The box for "promotion" is left empty. Ditto marks repeat the "doing the best that she is able to do" comment from previous years, and additional notes signal a student in distress, mentioning attitudinal difficulties associated with her efforts to learn. She is described as "upset easily when criticized" and "very nervous when she learns new concepts." Scientific-sounding terms—"ocular-motor poor"—lend a note of medical authority to the teachers' observations.

The classroom teachers' comments have their source, I suspect, in the specialists' comments and test scores that are also a part of Darleen's cumulative folder. The year she was placed in special education, a Stanford-Binet estimated her mental age at 5.0 years and chronological age at 8.0. This test score is in the same vein as the teachers' comment from that year: "doing the best that she is able to do." Six years later, when she was fifteen, a Wechsler Intelligence Scale for Children (WISC) score of 64 was described by the examiner as "well below average." The longer she stayed in school, the further her mental age lagged behind her actual age; one year later, a Stanford-Binet estimated that the sixteen-year-old Darleen had a mental age of eight. On the basis of these tests, the testing specialist outlined the following vocational implications:

> a very sheltered work situation. Her concentration is too shallow for making judgments, and she has significant perceptual difficulties which further hinders [sic] judgment . . . The examiner suggests that Darleen could satisfactorily handle sorting jobs (like sorting and folding laundry, or

something similar) which would require only gross motor coordination and minimal perceptual judgment.

Reflections: Reconstructing the School's Role

I have been pondering the record for several months now, trying to figure out how Darleen slipped away from her teachers. It doesn't seem a mystery, at first. After all, the English of school was foreign to her. She was, naturally enough, quiet. The materials that the school offered Darleen—*Fun with Dick and Jane, Our Town*—were not likely to lead her to recognize her family or the urban center she called "Her Town." But the ideology, the reasons her teachers attended to her deficiencies and neglected her potential, is anything but transparent. We can say that she went to school in an institution where the deficit model held sway, surrounding her like water surrounds a fish. Submerged in teachers' and testers' minds, this model probed her knowledge of vocabulary or Block Design tasks, looking for certain cognitive structures. Not finding these structures, her performance on the tests justified their low expectations for her: "doing the best she is able to do"; "concentration too shallow for making judgments"; "requires a very sheltered work situation."

But there are contradictions that belie a simple interpretation of this girl as a "slow learner," indications that the staff selected out the negative rather than the positive elements she brought to school. Side by side with evidence of "superficial concentration" during the IQ test is an examiner's note about her persistence on task. Darleen's verbal IQ scores exceeded her performance scores—and this in spite of the fact that her reading tests suggested a limited ability to decode or comprehend text. Apparently these contradictions raised no significant questions about the accuracy or the appropriateness of the labels she had acquired. And without invoking the big generalizations, like institutionalized racism, it is difficult to understand how what happened to Darleen was viewed as right, just, and inevitable—which is the stuff ideologies are made of.

But whatever the issues her schooling raises for us, elementary school ended for her in 1964, when she was thirteen. At last there is a mark in the "promotion" box: junior high, special class. The following year, comments on the cumulative folder are replaced by junior high and high school transcripts which contain only grades: C's in all courses, including English 1, English 2, arithmetic, and science. One A in student work experience. No F's or D's.

The IQ tests also explain her mediocre grades. F's, it seems, are reserved for students who "could do better." C's, the no-comment grade of the five-point scale, say essentially that she was doing the best that she could do. The testing was completed in the spring of her ninth-grade year. In October of the following semester, she left school; the last note in her file says "DROPOUT" in capital letters. Apparently, three years later, she returned to school for one month, but was asked to leave because she was too old.

The Story Darleen and Her Family Tell

Just as the school does not seem to have a particularly sharp image of her, Darleen has a consistently hazy recollection of her school experience. Her recollections of what she did in school after third grade are nonexistent; of the first two years, she has written: "[W]e would write the alphabets, read stories, draw out ourself on the floor" (i.e., one child would draw an outline of the other's body on a piece of paper, an activity often used to foster self-image in the primary grades).

She describes feeling what appears to be rather vulnerable, mystified—perhaps "powerless" is the current term that applies. Her elementary school memories of the world of print are even narrower than her cumulative record reported: she recalls not the basal readers, but only several Dr. Seuss books and a story about a "Little Red Schoolhouse," and she remembers these books, apparently, because they were associated with trips to the school library where someone read them aloud. Though she checked one book out each time, she cannot recall doing anything with these books when she got home.

She cannot remember the name of a single teacher in her grade school. Her only sharp and spontaneously reported recollection was of a second-grade teacher who locked her in a closet in the classroom and then forgot to let her out at the end of the school day. What behaviors resulted in this punishment, or why it was so harsh, are difficult to follow as she describes them. The circumstances are, like so many in her school life, unclear.

She characterizes herself as "very quiet—I stood to myself." She had no friends because she was, she says, "afraid to open up," She was afraid "they were laughing behind my back." She reports that what she feared was that others would discover her difficulty with writing: "If someone asked me to sign their yearbook, I would not." She maintained this distance without change, apparently, until leaving school, except that from these years she recalls one teacher by name, Mrs. Dudley, with whom she felt personally close. While she can't remember what classes this woman taught, she felt she could ask her anything she wanted to. She remembers Mrs. Dudley as an inspiration. Darleen says that, "In those days, if you were pregnant, you couldn't go to school [but] on the sad day I gathered together my things, this teacher said that I should never give up my dream of an education."

She says she never did give up on her education, but school certainly took a back seat after the birth of her two children. Her family circle widened to include her husband and baby, her parents, and her brothers and sisters. She apparently worked at odd jobs, doing a paper route, serving food in the school cafeteria, helping her landlord. While her children were growing up, she took care of them while her husband worked as an auto-body repairperson, a security guard, a carpenter.

Darleen is vague about the reasons for her difficulties in school. She speaks with some bitterness about the way she was treated in school since, as she says repeatedly, "I always did my work." She does not remember her mother giving the school permission to place her in special education classes. Sometimes Darleen seeks an explanation for school problems in her family life. They were "never there for me." Her family did not help her get glasses. No one read to her. As we try to understand the forces that pushed Darleen out of school, we must consider how home and school interacted.

My first visit with Darleen's mother yielded the family's official version of the school story: Darleen was a good girl who never missed school, was never any problem. She was shy, a loner. If there were problems, Darleen never told her family about them. The mother's story, like the school's, does little to dispel the image of a child whom adults did not know very well, a youngster left to fend for herself against siblings and peers who were unkind, who called her names like "stupid" and made her the butt of hurtful pranks.

But if this constitutes a kind of neglect, it must be seen in the context of the mother's other stories, which she told in subsequent conversations — stories of what it took to keep this household together. There were aunts, uncles, grandmothers, mother and father, and six children to support. With immense drive, Darleen's family undertook this task. Her father worked for many years for a transit company. Her mother labored first in the fields — "picking currants was the worst" — and then on jobs washing Pullman cars, doing industrial laundry, and pipe fitting. She finally started at the cannery, first on the line, then was promoted to "floor lady," and finally to supervisor. She summed up her attitude toward life, the one which she recommended that her child "pound onto herself: If you want it bad enough, you could *do* it; just say you know you could do it, and before you know it, you could do it. Just say, You're goin' to make it!'" Encoded in these phrases is her belief in personal power, a determination that "It can be done — *Si, se puede*." How, then, did this family play into the scenario of Darleen's failure in school as a girl, when, as an adult, she has become a successful college student?

Reflections: Reconstructing the Family's Role

The answer is not a simple one. John Ogbu (n.d.) has argued that the origins of competence — the general and specific skills needed to get along in the world — lie in the nature of adult cultural tasks. As he puts it: "Insofar as most adults in the population perform their sex-appropriate tasks competently . . . it follows that most children grow up to be competent men and women" (n.p.). Minority groups living within but separate from mainstream middle-class culture develop alternative skills for coping with life. Of all the children, only Darleen's brother did, in fact, graduate—not only from high school, but from San Jose State University. It is tempting to imagine, then, that Darleen—daughter in a family within a cultural group in which women were historically not expected to "need" education—faced fewer educational opportunities because of who she was: poor, Hispanic, female.

By fifteen, Darleen had moved out of the sphere of academic influence and into the adult patterns of women in her culture. She had a baby, and she and her husband pursued alternative means of economic survival by taking on casual or menial jobs and by participating in mutual exchange with their family and friends. Darleen built a stable, if economically precarious, life for herself, her children, and her children's children, following the models her parents passed on to her.

But to say only this is to ignore the spirit of that family. Along with the *"Si, se puede"* determination to survive and succeed, which she took in from her mother and father, a respect for education remains one of Darleen's central values. I would echo Mike Rose's (1989) comment that, for people like her, schooling, learning to read and write, is more than just a chance at a better job—it is "intimately connected with respect, with a sense that they are not beaten, the mastery of print revealing the deepest impulse to survive" (p. 216). She speaks proudly of her children's graduation from high school, and proudly of her own efforts to complete her education. As she wrote (and I reproduce her text exactly), "I used to baby sit but now I go to school and I hope to get my G e d someday."

If we were to fault the school for Darleen's failure, it would be only to say that they (like we) were victims of theory: they practiced the best that was known at the time. That residual framework of "cultural deficit" thinking, sunk deeply into the assessment and instructional processes of the sixties, guided teachers and testers to select certain features of Darleen's character ("slow," "apt to daydream") as a basis for decision making, and to ignore other features ("persistence on task," "desirous of learning"). If we were to fault the family—but wait. The point is not to find fault, but to uncover the multiple forces that pushed Darleen always in one direction: out of school. Only by appreciating the massive nature of these obstacles is it possible to acknowledge what Darleen had to overcome to create a new self-image—a student self.

The Story of an Underprepared Learner in College

At thirty-seven, Darleen entered community college. She did it in the face of her fear about that IQ score, of not belonging and being called stupid, of exposing her scant command of written language. Few educational settings would welcome those kinds of scores, that kind of history. Yet it is precisely such reconstructive work with underprepared learners that community college basic skills programs, under open-admission policies, set as one of their priorities. So here we are looking not only at the forces that fracture an education, but also at those that can repair it, how students like Darleen can, if they wish, rebuild studenthood.

Piri Thomas (1972 [1967]) has written that, for a poor Hispanic child in urban America, "if you ain't got heart, you ain't got *nada*" (p. 37). It was heart, *corazón*, courage—those qualities which translate into persistence on task which early school teachers and counselors had generally overlooked—that put Darleen back on the road to becoming a student. On the first day Darleen arrived at the community college, courage seemed less than adequate equipment. Her thick magnifying lenses in enormous brown frames and wispy hair almost hid her eyes as she waited on the cement bench in the courtyard by my office. The day was hot and she was sweating in new school clothes. The fall semester had begun two weeks before, and my classes had no room for her. I remember my quick and unkind judgment, not different from that of other teachers who had helped to shape the figure I saw in front of me. Late enrolling, barely able to read, she almost exuded ineptitude. I told her my classes were full and probably—because students in this course had to take several classes at once—too demanding. "Come back next semester," I said, figuring I had done her, and myself, a favor. I did not expect to see her again, but the next semester she returned to my class.

She says that she would never have tried again, except that she met a tutor as she left, who said, "Oh, don't worry. We have lots of people here who have trouble with reading. You'll learn." At that time she read only single-syllable words and could not fill out the one-page college application form without help. This invitation remained central in her mind.

Like all Darleen's previous teachers, I had my biases. A study of Freire's notions of centering instruction in the needs of students had led me to a determination to teach to strength and not to weakness. I had long before been taken by Vygotsky's (1978) notion that a teacher works in the "zone of proximal development"—not with those cognitive structures a learner has in place already but with those ready to develop, with the assistance of expert tutelage, that learning precedes development rather than the other way around. I have written elsewhere about how these pedagogical notions enabled me to work with Darleen as a reader (Wilson, 1990) and that the road was full of interactive pitfalls and pratfalls. Here, I will focus on how these notions informed the instruction which led her to develop writing for the academic literacy that she would need for community college work.

For students like Darleen, the academic invitation must be extended through the pedagogy teachers use. One of the richest resources of the community college is the opportunity it affords teachers to teach in new ways. The student-centered classroom for developmental writers offers a particularly rich opportunity to design experimental writing tasks. Free from demands for specific kinds of writing products, teachers can offer challenging composing tasks and learn much about students' writing processes by observing how learners approach these tasks. Although instructive research is now being done on the logic of errors made by underprepared students (Hull & Rose, 1990), how these students learn, over time, to match their writing with assigned tasks has been less often examined. And as we mark out four stages of Darleen's writing development over a two-year period, a time in which she worked with various teachers in a variety of courses, we see that the overriding accomplishment is a continually improving ability to hit the target the teachers' tasks set up.

Upon entering her first reading class in the community college, Darleen was off base in just about every way—except that she adhered to the essential minimum: she tried, diligently, to do the work. I observed this initial writing behavior as she worked on an assignment called "Beautiful Words." My own purpose in giving this assignment was to discover whether or not students could develop metalinguistic awareness, an awareness of "word-as-object." The students' task was to select a number of words that conjured up rich sensory images or were sonorous. The lesson was introduced with a poem by Laurie Duesing, which I read somewhere a few years ago, called "I ask them to choose five beautiful words." The poem begins:

> My students give me sanctuary and refuge, olive, and lime
> Offer flourish, pristine, divine. . . .
> Their choices show they already know the joy of green, yellow, and black.

The class read the poem aloud and talked about these words—the way they evoked particular images, the way each one sounded. The assignment asked students to think of words which they thought of as "beautiful," to select magazine pictures to illustrate them, and to explain what they found beautiful about the words. When the assignment came in, it was clear that Darleen had not registered the word-as-object notion. Instead, she produced a list (characteristic of many writers in the earlier stages of literacy) in which she collected words—like "time," "marriage," "shopping," "television," "school," "romance," "soap," "baby"—words which asserted her values, the "beauty" of the words aside. As I now read back through her booklet of words, I can see that it bears her indelibly personal imprint. "Soap," for example, suggests her pride in cleanliness; she defines the word by using it in the following sentence (again reproduced as she wrote it): "I use a lot of soap wish my colthes." She explains its importance to her in terms of other key values ("without soap we would not have clean clothes to where to school"). She had missed the teacher's point, but what she did is characteristic of many underprepared learners who do not always have the framework from which to identify what is important to the teacher, or even to recognize the possibility that what she did was not what the teacher meant. The list of words, each one explained in one or two sentences and replete with errors in conventional correctness, marks the first stage of Darleen's writing that I observed.

A second phase appeared the following summer, when she enrolled in another semester of basic reading. In this class she was encouraged to keep a dialogue journal in the reading class. In this journal, the teacher's task was apparently an easier target for Darleen to hit: it asked only that students write about topics of personal interest to them, which lent itself to something Darleen had already shown a predisposition toward. She quickly became adept at this, her writing becoming progressively lengthier, more fluent, and with fewer unconventional spellings. By the end of the summer semester, her writing had doubled in length, and she had apparently also begun to regard writing as a form of direct communication with the teacher. In this sample from her journal, she began with "Well," a familiar topic marker in ordinary conversation, and the narrative she told suggested an ongoing exchange with her respondent:

> Well yesterday when my Granddaughter came over and she was crying my cat ran out of the room to see what was going on, he is so funny sometimes I think that he is a real person because he likes to watch TV he very playful when I am down he make me happy, my cat is black and wite and his name is Sylvester and he is two month, he like to sleep at the end of my bed and wake me up in the morning, he is like a little kid the one thing I like is that he dose not ask for anything money.

By the end of the summer, Darleen began to develop a new branch in her writing; still in the context set up by the dialogue journal, these entries introduced topics not drawn from personal experience. In her work's earliest form, she copied bits of writing she enjoyed reading, with no attribution of ownership. In one, she wrote: "You Know You're Getting Old When (1) Everything Hurts and what Doesn't Hurt Doesn't Work 2) Your Knees Buckle, and your Belt Won't." She records twenty-two such aphorisms. Copying at various points became problematic for Darleen, and only a bit at a time did she begin to figure out what teachers regarded as "her own independent work." But copying instructed her in the conventional marks of print (apostrophes, capital letters, and indentations for paragraphs) as well as line formats that were new to her. Though copying is proscribed from earliest school (Hull & Rose, 1990), it marked the beginning of something new in her writing.

In the next phase (and the last one to be considered here), Darleen produced "academic prose" at its most elemental level. She came closer to producing what teachers call "an essay" by blending the two previous composing practices she had acquired—copying and descriptions of personal experience—into a single unit. But this was not accomplished without great struggle—in fact, Darleen was almost to the point of turning away from "her dream of education." As witness and coach, I charted closely how Darleen forged this new procedural knowledge about "how to write."

Darleen had moved into a more advanced level of basic skills courses in the community college, one of them a sociology class. By March, the tasks were becoming increasingly difficult. In this assignment, students selected a poem and applied it to circumstances in their own lives. The work was to be done as an in-class essay, and Darleen, the teacher reported afterward, wrote only a few words. "Maybe she just isn't ready," the teacher mused. The sociology instructor returned the paper to Darleen and told her to work more on it. Later, Darleen was alternately depressed and angry: "I don't have anything to say about what Langston Hughes is talking about. I'm not black! She's mean!" were just two of the barriers I remember she threw up for herself to ward off her concern that here, finally, was the point at which she "just didn't have it."

While she was sitting outside my office, at the same concrete bench where she had waited for me that first day, just two years before, I spoke to Darleen, trying now to get her to stay, to try. It wasn't easy. The weight of all those buckets of spillover from early failures sat squarely between us, and it took what delicacy I could muster to launch discussion of the idea. She might, I suggested, have had some experiences not too far away from "being made to stay in the kitchen when company comes." The bonds made during the previous semesters stretched taut, then held. She relaxed as we talked about growing up Hispanic in white America; we rehearsed verbally what she could write down later, a method which I had studied earlier as a step on the road to assisting students like Darleen in developing written compositions (Wilson, 1988). When she was calm, when she had, in words, experiences that she could connect to the assigned reading, she went at once to a quiet desk and wrote the following piece. I quote a longish portion of this first draft to illustrate this blending of voices—Langston Hughes's and her own. I have italicized the portions she quotes directly from Hughes's piece:

This is what Epilogue means to me

As a Puerto Rican I learn to deal with a lot of the outside problem as well but I, too, laugh and eat well and grow strong because I, too, am an American. And being an American I know what it means to have freedom, and I know we are gods children we deserve to eat in the same restaurant or ride on the same bus. As American I am not ashamed of who I am or what I can and Cannot do, and I don't care who is ashamed of me *I too sing America.*

I am the darker Brother
They send me to eat in the kitchen
When company comes.

This line says to me that if someone was to send me in the kitchen I would feel not wanted, or there is something wrong with me. This line says to me that even though they may be ashamed of me I will grow strong.

What the essay lacks as college material is not difficult to see. But what the essay contains, we teachers must train our eyes to look for. It is a weaving of two voices, a polyphony which reminds us, as Shirley Brice Heath (1990) calls to our attention, that conversation and essay form have common roots and shared histories. It is easy to overlook Darleen's achievement. She has just talked through this essay with someone; she has not digested the poet's voice. And I would agree—but here, in this work, for the first time, Darleen is writing about her own experience through words of a poet distant from her in both space and time. In this composition, we see the underpinnings of the essay form so familiar to secondary and college teachers: the multivoiced layering that includes in its most sophisticated form the writer's persona, the supporting authority's voice, and the readers' implicit voices—of agreement and dissent—as well. Like any complex practice, it had to be constructed. Darleen came to the practice of copying and the practice of writing about herself; she used them separately for nearly two years. Then, in response to a new and more difficult context, she momentarily lost and then recovered her heart, and then fused for the first time these written practices. And we see again what Darleen lost in her first try at schooling, when she failed to develop the literate dialogue with teachers from which so much can later grow.

Almost two years later, four years after her first day of returning to school, she was finally "promoted" out of remedial classes in the community college. She took (and passed with A's) an English composition class one level below the transferable course in composition, "Ethics and Human Values," child psychology. She is now taking a college-level course in speech and continues to struggle with the math that prepares her for elementary algebra. Darleen's college career has begun in earnest.

Reflections: Issuing the Academic Invitation

I do not want to draw conclusions from this story about Darleen, a story constructed by many participants and reconstructed here from various perspectives. Instead, I want to use it to point to the various windows it opens on the learning process and on the role of the community college in fostering this process.

Darleen's case leads us to reconsider the old conflict between nature or nurture, the question of whether "you are born with it" or "your culture gives it to you." As I tried to make sense of what happened in Darleen's school career as a girl, it seemed that the school measured her "nurture" with a middle-class yardstick and reasoned (illogically, I now think) from their results to her "nature." What these tests did not measure was another aspect of the human condition which is also significant: the determination expressed by Darleen's mother when she said that she "pounded it on them: you can do anything you want bad enough." It was this persistence, along with some impulse that she could not ignore, that led Darleen to and sustained her in a re-entry into school. But this does not account for the kind of "operative skill" she brought to the community college. The mechanism by which she began to master at forty what she had failed to grasp at fourteen lies in her ability to use a social intelligence to assist her in achieving her educational goal.

She had set a prodigious task for herself. School demands multiple specialized kinds of literacy, from writing lab notes in biology to composing essays for English. She was the rankest beginner at all of it. How was she going to get the opportunities she needed to learn? From the first day she returned to school, she showed that she understood that some web of relationships formed the heart of the new social group to which she wanted to belong, and she set about tying into this network. She made immediate friends with the tutor who had spoken to her when she arrived; she maintained telephone contact with college staff over several months to assure a place in the basic skills program she wanted to enter. She used these politically powerful links for her learning—a tutor can offer extra help with homework; a teacher can provide additional information during office hours. Once admitted to the basic skills classes, she offered to do small favors like stuffing fliers in envelopes in the office; in exchange, she had the chance to listen to teachers and other students chat from a more "intimate" position. She provided snacks or soft drinks to those working late. She formed alliances that could serve her. By dint of this effort, she broke into the academic community that she wanted to join, and the community college teachers and instructional aides opened their ranks to her.

Intelligence tests do not measure this kind of intelligence, this social intelligence, which Darleen seems to have had. And here, in reconsidering the record of Darleen's early school and family life, I am struck again by the implications of her silence: her inability to use her intelligence to connect into social networks at her school—perhaps it was that, above all else, that pushed her out between the cracks. Like so many underprepared adults in basic skills programs, Darleen had long been shut out of networks with those more literate than herself, networks of membership that would have allowed her possibilities to unfold. Working within these networks allowed this development. Although her literacy achievement was low, Darleen's ability to develop literacy with a more experienced teacher was high. Literacy is contagious—you catch it from a teacher. The complexity of the learning network needed to foster this development, the painstaking connections that must be built between what the student brings and what the teacher offers, must become more widely recognized by teachers, researchers, and administrators.

Other concerns that Darleen's story highlights are questions current in the field of rhetoric and composition: Are texts ever "autonomous"? They are, as Louise Wetherbee Phelps suggests (1989), created in response to teachers' assignments, to suggestions for revision, to various readings and rereadings. Through this process, it is possible to see that written language is produced no less collaboratively than are conversations. We can't read Darleen's story without coming, in a new way, to questions about the nature of literacy as it has been, and is now, taught and used in schools.

And finally, Darleen opens a new view on the situation of the underprepared learner in the community college. Once cheerfully open-admission schools, many of these institutions have become anxious — often pressured by Federal Financial Aid mandates — to set up entrance standards and maximum time limits for those in remedial classes. Yet urban two-year colleges, if they are to realize their mandate to provide academic and vocational education for their communities, must recognize, as they make policy, the complexities students like Darleen present. Could a student so fragile have successfully routed herself first to a library literacy program staffed by volunteers, then to adult basic education, and finally arrived at the community college ready to write the college essay? Unless some pretty careful links are put into place among all these institutions — links which are not in place as we face the year 2000 — I doubt it.

If the community college has taught Darleen much that she needed to redefine herself as a student, the community college stands to learn a great deal from students like her. Students like Darleen will not go away, and if we offer them what they need, they can become a rich resource in this generation and the next. In times of cutbacks, naysaying, and exploding technologies that threaten to leave out large segments of our society from the work of the twenty-first century, it is a long shot at best. But in the spirit of Darleen's persistence, her *corazón*, let teachers pass on to teachers, to researchers, to administrators, to state and federal policymakers, what has been learned in the last generation.

Works Cited

Heath, S. B. (1990). The essay in English: Readers and writers in dialogue. In M. Macovski (Ed.), *Textual voices, vocative texts: Dialogue, linguistics, and literature* (pp. 72–93). Cambridge: Oxford University Press.

Hull, G., & Rose, M. (1990). Toward a social cognitive understanding of problematic reading and writing. In A. Lunsford, H. Moglen, & J. Slevin (Eds.), *The right to literacy* (pp. 235–245). New York: Modern Language Association of America.

Ogbu, J. (n.d.). On the origins of competence. Manuscript. University of California: Berkeley.

Phelps, L. W. (1989). Images of student writing: The deep structure of teacher response. In C. M. Anson (Ed.), *Writing and response: Theory, practice and research* (pp. 37–68). Urbana: National Council of Teachers of English.

Rose, M. (1989). *Lives on the boundary.* New York: Free Press.

Thomas, P. (1972 [1967]). *Down these mean streets.* New York: Alfred A. Knopf. Rpt. in J. Durham, L. Graham, & E. Glaser (Eds.), *Directions 1 Anthology* (pp. 37–42). Boston: Houghton-Mifflin.

Vygotsky, L. S. (1978). *Mind in society: The development of higher psychological processes.* M. Cole, V. John-Steiner, S. Scribner, & E. Souberman (Eds.). Cambridge, MA: Harvard University Press.

Wilson, S. (1988). *Relations between teacher-student interaction and written compositions.* Diss. Berkeley: University of California.

Wilson, S. (1990). Between teacher and student: The making of texts by adult new readers. In K. P. Joy & J. Staton (Eds.), *Writing our lives: Reflections on dialogue journal writing with adults learning English* (pp. 36–45). Englewood Cliffs, NJ: Prentice-Hall.

Wilson, S. (1991). Becoming centered in the students: What a teacher can do for underprepared learners. In L. Cook & H. Lodge (Eds.), *Expanded vision: English teaching in today's classrooms.* Urbana: National Council of Teachers of English.

Students Deserve Enough Time to Prove That They Can Succeed

Marilyn S. Sternglass

This article, part of a larger longitudinal study of basic writing students' development presented in Marilyn Sternglass's celebrated book Time to Know Them, *offers the case study of Joan, a disabled African American student from a troubled family who was initially deemed underprepared for college writing. Sternglass follows Joan over the course of her six-year college career. Despite challenges, occasional setbacks, and intermittent struggles with writing assessments and assignments, Joan eventually completed her degree and secured employment that allowed her to draw on her own family history with substance abuse to serve others recovering from drug addiction. Written in overt defiance of scholars and policy makers who would declare students like Joan unworthy of entering higher education, Sternglass's essay makes a compelling case for the importance of taking a long view of the educational experiences of basic writing students.*

From *Journal of Basic Writing*, vol. 18, no. 1, 1999, pp. 3-20.

Teaching in areas of language development is often a frustrating enterprise because the time frame for an individual instructor is frequently very short, most often one semester, occasionally a year. Because we know that language development is a long-term enterprise, we chafe over not knowing what will happen to our students when they leave our classrooms. We also want to know what kind of instructional support we can offer in their first-year writing classes that will be most useful to them in meeting the academic demands that will be made on them in succeeding years. A six-year longitudinal study that I recently completed at The City College of City University of New York can encourage us that under proper instructional conditions of support, our students can transform their potential for success into actual success.

In my book, *Time to Know Them: A Longitudinal Study of Writing and Learning at the College Level*, I bring together aspects of composition research not duplicated in any previous studies: (1) examining writing and learning from a true longitudinal perspective; (2) studying a multicultural urban population; (3) investigating the relationship between writing and learning by examining papers written over time for regularly assigned academic courses across a range of disciplines; and (4) taking into consideration non-academic factors that influence academic performance. The book presents an argument that, given sufficient time and support, students who start at basic writing levels have the potential to succeed and do succeed.

It is fitting but sad in a way that my book has been awarded a prize bearing Mina Shaughnessy's name by the Modern Language Association because my book makes essentially the same argument that *Errors and Expectations* made 22 years ago, that students who begin at basic levels of writing instruction do have the potential and the capability to succeed at their academic tasks. That we all have had to continue to fight this battle for such a long time reflects the resurgence of conservative educational and political policies that were so evident in the criticism of open admissions at City University of New York in the early 1970's.

Since that time, an extraordinary amount of evidence has accumulated that demonstrates that the open admissions students were successful not only academically but professionally and personally, but it took more than the conventional four-year time slot for the students to complete their studies. In a retrospective study of the first cohort of students admitted under the open admissions policy at CUNY in 1970, Lavin and Hyllegard found that "[n]early half [of the students] needed more than four years to complete their bachelor's degree, 10 percent needed more than five years, 8 percent took more than seven years, and 5 percent went beyond nine years" (57). Lavin and Hyllegard went on to emphasize that ethnic differences in the length of time required to graduate were striking. "Among the senior college-entrants, only 15 percent of whites but almost 40 percent of blacks and a third of Hispanic graduates needed more than five years. . . . Among open-admissions students, . . . one quarter of Hispanic degree holders and almost a fifth of blacks went beyond nine years, compared with 7 percent of white open-admissions graduates" (57).

In 1998, Bowen and Bok cited research that 26 percent of all BA recipients and 32 percent of African American BA recipients earned their BAs more than six years after matriculation (Nettles and Perna, 277 cited in Bowen and Bok, 56).

The students in my study, carried out between 1989 and 1995 at City College, followed a similar trend. As of December 1996, of the 53 students who started in my study, with two-thirds enrolled in basic writing classes, 17 (32%) had graduated, 10 (19%) had transferred to other colleges, 18 (34%) had dropped out, and 8 (15%) were still enrolled in the college, seven years after they had begun their studies. What these somewhat dry figures reveal is that after seven years, 66% of the students in my study had either graduated or were continuing in higher education. Too often, students who transfer to other colleges are lumped together with the true dropouts, thus inappropriately inflating the dropout figure.

The significance of these extended years of matriculation is that they strongly suggest that a combination of factors slowed students' progress: beginning in basic level classes in reading, writing, and/or mathematics; changing majors, especially, for example, as frequently happened at City College when students discovered they did not have the requisite mathematics background for engineering or the sciences; and having to work from 4 to 40 hours per week, as the students in my study did, thus requiring more part-time study for students who were both economically and academically disadvantaged when they began their college careers. Recently, Wallace and Bell pointed out that an implicit form of racial discrimination occurs "if the educational experience offered to African American students in primary and secondary schools results in these students not being as well prepared for the demands of higher education as are other students" (313). Similarly, "the financial requirements of higher education may pose a greater problem for minority students who come from low-income households or who are first-generation college students" (312). This is the reality for most students who begin their studies at City University of New York and many other public institutions of higher education.

In 1989, when I began my study, I felt that it would be essential to document precisely the ways in which students use the time frame to gradually acquire the skills they need to succeed academically. It was already clear to me in 1989, as Lavin and Hyllegard pointed out in their 1996 book, that increasing educational attainment and narrowing ethnic inequalities were not current priorities in the nation's agenda (240). And, clearly, the proposed educational policies for CUNY that eliminate remediation or limit it to one semester will most harshly impact the students who benefit from an extended time frame to demonstrate their capabilities.

For my study, I decided to teach three sections of composition in the fall of 1989, one section of English 1 (the lower level of basic writing), one section of English 2 (the second level of basic writing), and one section of English 110 (the freshman composition course). I asked the students in these sections if they would be willing to participate in my study, to let me interview them twice each semester, to collect or make copies of papers they wrote in all their classes, and to allow a research assistant to observe one of their classes each semester. I also collected copies of their transcripts each semester and copies of their attempts to pass the Writing Assessment Test and the Proficiency Test required of all graduates of City College. Of the 53 students in the classes who initially agreed to participate, 21 identified themselves as African-American, 26 Latino, 4 Asian, and 2 White. Thirty were males and 23 were females. Twenty-five were born outside the continental United States, including 3 born in Puerto Rico. At the end of the six years of the study, I had complete data for nine students and partial data for the others.

There are two issues I would like to consider in this paper: the development of complex reasoning skills, but not in a neat, linear pattern, and the importance of appropriate instructional support at key moments in a student's academic journey. I think it will be best to examine these issues through the experiences of a real student as she encountered the demands of the academic setting. You will see from the case study I present that I am not arguing that the students in my study achieved the highest academic levels; what I am arguing is that they achieved sufficient expertise to become productive, contributing members of the society, and they acquired the self-esteem they deserved from their extraordinary efforts.

In his infamous book, *City on a Hill*, James Traub documented what he perceived to be a hopeless but well-meaning cause at City College, true educational attainment by students who started with extreme educational disadvantages. One of the chapters in his book was titled, "A Miraculous Survivor," and it was about one of the students in my study, an African-American woman I called Joan, who started in the English 2 class. (Traub had access to the work of the first four years of Joan's six years at the college.) Joan was truly disadvantaged in many ways: she had had a poor educational preparation for college studies; she was visually disabled, having lost 70% of the vision in her left eye as a result of an accident when she was two years old; and she was the youngest child in a single-parent household where most of her older siblings were addicted to either alcohol or drugs. She had not been taught how to take notes in high school, and her writing tasks had been mainly creative ones. In her college writing, Joan's papers were not laden heavily with grammatical errors, but she initially lacked depth in her responses to the academic demands, depending heavily on definitions and regurgitation of received knowledge. Traub denigrated her achievements in his book, stating that by his standards, Joan had not become an "educated person"; she had not developed "intellectual discrimination and she certainly knew virtually nothing of philosophy and history" (132). Some of his accusations may ring true from his Harvard-educated perspective, but Traub failed completely to recognize that as Joan gathered more knowledge in her major field, psychology, she became able to make connections between the insights of that field and other discipline areas and to apply her insights to real-world problems. Although she continued to struggle with abstract areas such as philosophy, she developed the capability to bring significant understandings from her own experience to the needs of others. Joan's writing over the years revealed that she learned from the instruction she received and she was able to apply new insights to both academic and practical problems. Joan's troubled family background gave her "empathy," in her words, with the people who came to the methadone clinic where she first had an internship and then a permanent position after she graduated.

Joan told me in her first semester at the college that she found the college demands extremely different from the high school requirements "which made things a little difficult to adjust to, but I can say it was a challenge for me." She had not been asked to do much writing in junior high school. In high school, in her English classes, she had written summaries but not much else. She received 90's for her work. This led her to believe that she had been properly prepared for writing demands when she came to college. "But I really wasn't," she said.

In her writing placement test, Joan presented a traditional organizational pattern, an introduction, two paragraphs of development, and a conclusion. The best guess for the reason for failure, and her placement in English 2, was that there were a few grammatical and punctuation errors. Missed by the readers were Joan's thoughtful comments on the topic of whether students should be expelled from courses if they are late more than three times. Joan noted that students become disadvantaged when they are late because "most lessons given by teachers or college professors are started out with an aim which sometimes revolves around the lesson itself. By the student being late, he or she is totally lost because they have missed the whole meaning of the lesson which could be the beginning of the end for a student." Although the idea is not stated as clearly as it might have been, Joan had identified an important reason why students should be prompt in attendance, one unmentioned by most takers of the Writing Assessment Test (WAT). Joan easily passed the WAT at the end of her first semester.

In the English 2 course that first semester, Joan wrote several drafts of a paper comparing her experiences with those of an anthropologist in a foreign country. In her final draft, she wrote: "As I walked through the college doors, I began to feel more and more uncomfortable because I was surrounded by many people who were much different than me. . . . People sensed my fear as soon as I walked through the doors. They knew that I was a freshman who know nothing about college life." Reminiscent of the stage of "silence" in Belenky and her colleagues' *Women's Ways of Knowing*, Joan seemed strongly intimidated by the college environment. But, in an earlier draft of the paper, she had included a section suggesting a hope that she might be able to overcome these fears: "At City College, I also became angry and frustrated because I felt a sense of isolation and self-consciousness in the college atmosphere. Also I felt very afraid and lost. But, later on, I began to realize that as I learn a little more about college life at City College, it will be much easier to adjust." A pattern began to emerge in her writing that suggested that she dealt more fully with ideas and emotions in early drafts than in final papers. Perhaps she felt constrained to deal more narrowly or neatly with ideas in her final papers.

Admitted into the freshman composition course the next semester, Joan found the course not very helpful to her. She felt that too much time was spent on grammar rather than on discussion of the assigned readings. She also had difficulty understanding the comments made on her papers by her instructor, an adjunct in the English Department who at that time had little preparation for the teaching of composition. Although her instructor made copious comments on her papers, he used terms that were either too "jargon-laden" and complex for her to follow or that failed to lead her to develop the necessary insights. For one paper, students were assigned to revise the summary of an essay by J. Black on Kafka. Joan wrote: "'A Report to an Academy' by Franz Kafka is about an ape who wanted to become a human." The instructor wrote in the margin: "Why did either Kafka or Black state the ape's first wish was to become human?" This "why" question was a good comment, and if left alone for emphasis, it would have been useful to Joan. Joan's paper continued, supplying some reasons as follows: "Along with this, he wanted freedom The ape did not want to be caged up. In order to become successful at being human, he had more steps to follow." The instructor's next comment was as follows: "You could take the first sentence of this, remove one, and by fiddling a bit with punctuation, transition words (conjunctions and conjunctive adverbs), sentence length (perhaps combining 2), and most of all sentence order, make this opening make sense. Try." The advice in reworking these introductory sentences was far too complicated for her to follow. At the minimum, the instructor might have rewritten these sentences to provide a model for Joan and to show her the possibilities. As a summary comment, the instructor wrote, "Overall, you really don't get at the essential problems with Black's essay in terms of the reasoning, though you do smooth out his grammar in some places." Extensive as the instructor's comments were, they did not address the specific places in the paper where Joan's analysis of Black's reasoning was lacking.

At the beginning of her second year, Joan told me that in the previous year she had learned to use writing to better understand the material in her courses by "taking notes in all classes, taking out the important terms from those notes, and using them as the basis for study." She underlined definitions and important terms in her books. This strategy of referring carefully to authorities was also implemented in her writing, where she underlined key terms. She had cut back her working hours to 13 per week so that she could try to get better grades.

In the writing in her sociology course, Joan's papers were full of definitions, with authorities for each carefully provided. Although this approach was initially successful for her, in examinations her instructor wanted more analytical responses, particularly when differences between concepts were asked for. Received knowledge could not carry her very successfully when analysis was required. She received a "D" in this course. Citing authorities, providing definitions, and discussing causes of problems were more successful for her in her psychology class that semester. Joan liked the readings and found the class discussions helpful in clearing up ideas presented in the lectures. She received a "C" in this course. By the end of that semester, Joan felt that writing helped her remember ideas much more, the first phase of using writing as a way of learning. She said: "If I write when I'm reading, it sinks in more." Her work load had increased and she was working double shifts from 7:15 AM to 11:30 PM three days a week. "I'm tired," she said. She had learned the importance of planning ahead, and she "liked it when teachers gave a syllabus and advance notice." Clearly, such materials help students like Joan, who have time-consuming outside commitments, to handle the planning of their academic work in a better way.

Joan had more difficulty with courses that required multiple choice exams than those in which she could write papers. She found multiple choice exams difficult because the answers were "debatable" and she had difficulty choosing among the options. She was starting to plan ahead more for her courses and beginning necessary research sooner than she had in the past.

In the spring semester of her second year, Joan was taking a psychology course, an art course, a speech course, and the world civilization course for the second time. (She had dropped this course during an earlier semester.) The psychology course was the hardest one and she found the language "very technical with difficult words." She was concerned that she was having so many problems in understanding and carrying out the assignments since this was her major field, but she passed the course with a "C."

By the end of her second year at the college, Joan had passed three psychology courses, had started to fulfill the core course requirements of the college, and, of the three skills assessment tests in reading, writing, and mathematics, she still had the Reading Assessment Test and the Math Assessment Test looming before her. She had learned how to use periodicals for research, and she was committed to continuing at the college with a major in psychology.

In the fall semester of her third year, Joan felt that her writing in her psychology courses was improving. She was able to apply insights from a psychologist's model of child development to observations of a particular child, and the instructor approvingly wrote "very good" or "good" five times on her paper. She received a "B+" on this paper and the instructor remarked at the end, "Your thinking is rather scientific and systematic," an acknowledgment of the approval that received knowledge garners. But Joan was having problems with her world civilization and French courses. Having failed the first two pop quizzes in the world civilization course (multiple-choice and objective questions), Joan finally asked for the official designation of "disabled" that she had avoided for so long. She realized that she needed to take more time for the reading in the world civilization course, and she was troubled because she "forgets what [she] is reading" and her "mind wanders in class." She managed to pass both courses with "C" grades, but she received a "D" in French the next semester and eventually asked for exemption from the final required fourth semester French course on the basis of her disability.

Joan's predilection toward presenting "received knowledge" in her papers prevented her from accomplishing her professors' demands for more analytic writing. In the second level world civilization course, Joan wrote a paper on a novel by Chinua Achebe. The instructor commented on the paper that she had "recounted much of the novel rather than analyzing it."

By the end of the semester, Joan said that having to work long hours had made her sluggish, and she was not eating well. The day before our interview, she had worked from 7 AM to 5 PM, getting up at 4 AM to fulfill all her responsibilities. But she had become more committed to her psychology major.

In the spring semester of her third year, Joan was writing papers in her abnormal psychology course that her professor liked, commenting, "Terrific job," at the end of one of them and giving her a "B+" on the paper. But her grade in the course was dragged down by her performance on the two examinations that counted for two-thirds of the course grade, and she received a "C" in the course. Once again, where exams were weighted more heavily than papers, students who benefited from the reflection provided in writing were disadvantaged. The major writing assignment for the course was the review and analysis of pertinent articles in the field of abnormal psychology. Students were expected to apply theories learned in the course to the situations described in the articles. Joan's paper for the course presented a variety of cases with psychological interpretations grounded firmly in research that she had studied. In her analysis of the first case of a doctor who inseminated his patients with his own sperm, Joan described this condition as "an individual having a superiority complex about his/herself. These individuals believe that they are so perfect that he or she has no thoughts or consideration of others. These individuals suffer from low self-esteem and may go through great lengths to demonstrate their self-worth by making themselves the center of attention." Joan had clearly understood the parameters of this assignment and was capable of fulfilling them.

At this stage, Joan recognized that writing helped her understand where she stood "with theories and materials as well as grades." She felt that exams do not show everything without writing assignments. She told me, "In a writing assignment, a teacher can point out problems and misunderstandings." In other words, she could learn from the responses of her instructors to the writing. In exams, students only found out whether they were right or wrong but not always why.

That same semester, Joan was enrolled in the first level world humanities course. She was very much impressed with the professor, describing her as a "warm and worldly woman." Although there were stringent reading requirements, eight books during the semester, Joan did not complain about these assignments. There were no papers required for the course; the only writing was essay questions on the final examination. Joan said that she had learned to define a word in a sentence to help a reader understand her meaning. This professor appeared to become a serious role model for Joan. She received an "A" in the course.

Thus, at the end of her third year at the college, Joan had acquired a certain kind of academic competence. She could take insights from research and theory and apply them to individual psychological cases. She felt that responses to her writing assignments were much better guides to increasing her understanding of the materials she was working with. Simultaneously, her relationships with her professors had grown in the spring semester, and this had had a very positive impact on her.

In the fall semester of her fourth year at the college, Joan was taking courses in biology, psychology, the third level of world civilization, and the second level of world humanities. She felt that her most difficult course was the world humanities class, and she was having problems "shifting from one type to another type of reading." In a paper for this course, for the first time, Joan began to build relationships between what she was learning in one discipline to another. She applied concepts from psychology to her analysis of Voltaire's *Candide*. She wrote: "Pangloss inspired Candide's Optimism because he attributed what we would call in Psychology, a Halo-effect to every experience in life, meaning there is good in everything and everyone." In another paper, on whether Nora was entitled to divorce her husband in *A Doll's House*, Joan began a thoughtful analysis of the relationship. "Torvald not only stripped Nora of her pride and dignity as a person, but he also assisted in the degrading of her character by taking advantage of her child-like ways." The instructor admired this insight and wrote "nice" in the margin. Joan had moved to the second stage of using writing as a way of learning, the analytic stage.

Joan had an acute sense of what she could pick up from her professors that would help her. She learned to use transition words from listening to her professors. She had discovered that professors love it when students mimic them. Because her psychology professor said "moreover" and "in that," Joan learned to use these terms in her writing. She also applied this insight to papers she wrote in other courses. She told me, "I understand something when I write it. I like writing because it gives me a chance to elaborate on a subject, not being limited in any way." Again she reiterated to me that she felt she was better able to explain and elaborate in writing than on multiple-choice tests, where she felt it was more difficult for her to show what she had learned.

At the end of the semester, Joan told me more about her family life. She and her mother (who was disabled and received supplementary Social Security funds) lived in public housing. Joan received assistance for books from the SEEK program at the college, a Pell grant to help cover her living expenses, and tuition support from the Tuition Assistance Program. Any spending money she needed, she had to earn. Clinical psychology had started to attract Joan, and she thought she would like to help troubled teens, especially those addicted to narcotics. She had promised herself that she would never turn out like her brothers and sisters. "Being at college is my life," she said. "I will not let anyone take it away from me."

The next semester, the spring semester of her fourth year, Joan was taking a required astronomy course, two psychology courses, and a course on U.S. society. Her first paper for a psychology course on theories of personality was not very successful, but the teacher's comments and suggestions provided the kind of help that Joan needed in order to improve her papers, evidence of the learning she felt could take place in response to writing that did not occur with short answer examinations. In the paper, Joan had attempted an analysis of a young man suffering from what she called "anti-social personality disorder." Joan had written that the subject's behavior "is demonstrated by this individual many times in the many schools and facilities where he was placed." Her instructor cited specific details from the case study that Joan should have considered and analyzed more carefully (e.g. "information that this [moving around] should have explained some of the truancy and misbehavior and alerted them to get the mother in and interview her carefully"). From these comments, Joan could see that she had not used the evidence from the case study to provide the required in-depth analysis.

Joan's next paper in the course was more productive, as she speculated on the causes of the behavior of the individual she was analyzing. In a paper titled, "The Man in the Shell," she combined her former predilection for citing authorities with her own analysis of the subject's problems. She wrote: "Here is a man with many negative thoughts, a slim build, and extremely low self-esteem. One does not need a scholar to figure out that this individual has an intense phobia or fear of people, activity, and/or pleasure." She followed this with a series of speculative questions about how the subject might behave in situations not described in the case study data, in conditions that she postulated. Even though the instructor had a different view from the one expressed by Joan, Joan was not punished for taking a risk. She received a grade of 8 out of a possible 10 on the paper, and the instructor wrote "good" beside the grade marking. Whereas in the past, Joan had talked about writing primarily as a means of helping her remember the material better, now she saw writing as giving her an opportunity to elaborate on ideas and to give her personal opinion. She was also moving toward the third stage of using writing as a way of learning, the creation of new knowledge, new to the learner even if not new to the discipline.

In Joan's other psychology class that semester, Introduction to Human Development, the class observation revealed the instructor helping the students prepare for the mid-term examination that they would be taking at the next class meeting. The professor offered advice about how the students could best learn for the exam: "First read the introduction, second the summary, then, the chapter. Never read the whole chapter at one time. At the end of the chapter, take notes. Reading alone does not work." This was the only time in the 74 classroom observations made in 20 disciplines in this study that a professor explicitly recommended to students that they combine writing with reading as a way of learning.

By the end of her fourth year, Joan had finally passed all the Skills Tests required by the college. She had passed the Writing Assessment Test easily at the end of her first semester. She was given extra time to take the Reading Assessment Test after she received the designation of being disabled, and she passed that in her third year. But the Math Assessment Test had continued to bedevil her. She had a tutor for three weeks and she reviewed previous tests carefully. When she took the actual test, she managed to finish the questions five minutes early. Thus, at the end of her fourth year at the college, Joan would now be permitted to register as a Junior and would be removed from the "Skills Assessment Test-Warning" designation. It is all too obvious that if the proposed policies on passing the Skills Assessment Tests at CUNY are implemented, requiring students to have passed all the Skills Tests by the end of their first semester, students like Joan will never have the opportunity to proceed this far.

When asked in what ways she felt she was now a different person from the one she was when she started at City College, Joan said that she was really starting to understand that "business is business. . . . Now I am into concrete things that the college offers, like films, or things that will help me get extra credit for my classes." She knew that she had to get her grade point average up. She said, "I'm really here to obtain a degree and get a job. I started to wake up in '91 [her third year at the college]. My GPA was higher at first, but now I'm taking more difficult courses."

Recognizing that her visual disability slowed her down in undertaking complex writing tasks, Joan had learned by the fall of her fifth year at the college, when I collected a writing profile from her, that she had to try to start her assignments a week before the due date. If she needed to do research for the paper, she went to the library. If she already knew something about the topic and she was interested, she would do an outline and introduction. With what she called these "easier" papers, she wrote one draft and then made corrections. But if the paper was on a more technical topic, she found all the information she could and took from it what she needed. She then wrote one or more rough drafts. In these more technical papers, she had to be sure of the facts. These papers continued to reflect a strong reliance on outside authorities. Joan said that the writing process became distressing if she could not find the necessary information; she did not want to write from hearsay.

Joan wrote her papers at a night stand in her mother's room where the lighting was bad, using a blue ball-point pen. She said, "Black is blah and makes me uncomfortable." She used paper with big lines, probably because of her vision problems, but she said the "college ruled paper makes me feel cramped and prevents me from loosening up." She took her handwritten draft to a computer at the college and typed it in. She noted that as she was typing, "something may not sound right or I find a better way to say it. I do some changing at the computer or type in different stuff." So, although Joan may not formally call this process revising, this is what was occurring.

Although she had passed the Math Assessment Test, Joan found the required statistics course in her psychology major her most difficult course in the fall of her fifth year. In her world arts course, Joan talked with another student in my study who had also been in her English 2 class, Delores. Delores, a Latina student from the Dominican Republic, had been very successful at the college and had been accepted into the combined BA/MA program in psychology. Delores offered to tutor Joan in statistics. Joan managed to pass the statistics course with a "D" and her philosophy course with a "C," having made a conscious decision not to argue with the instructor when she found her own beliefs questioned. During this semester, she was working three days a week in an internship at a health center, doing counseling and clerical work.

Joan recognized that writing served to alert her as to how well she understood the material in her courses. She said, "I fear that if I don't get writing, I don't have a grasp of where I'm going in the course. I have had more trouble with courses that don't require writing." She was using mapping, a strategy she had learned in her basic skills reading course, to help her with her writing. She said, "Mapping helps me find my thoughts. I use one word and look for another word that relates to it."

In her writing during this semester, Joan once again drew on her knowledge of psychology to assist her in the analysis of materials. In a paper on the film version of *The Joy Luck Club* for her world arts course, Joan wrote: "The filmmaker wants us to empathize with the mother, by observing her, not as an antagonist, a victim of the circumstances, as she had no choice but to abandon her children, hoping that someone would have the heart to return them." Had Joan taken this world arts core course earlier in her academic program, she would not have had these psychological terms and perceptions to assist her in her analysis. Her instructor was pleased with this insight and wrote "good" in the margin of the paper.

In the spring of her fifth year, Joan took the next level of world humanities required by the college. This course focused on Black American studies. Her professor, a woman, talked about slavery and stereotypes in the course. Joan had read a good deal in this field, so she did not find the course difficult. In one of her papers, Joan asserted a prime value of education for herself: "In closing, reading *The Narrative of the Life of Frederick Douglass*, one can conclude, education was, and still remains, the key element involved in overcoming oppression. One should never forget that knowledge is the one tool that can be used to overpower the white man." Inside Joan, not evident in her quiet demeanor, resided the pride that had carried throughout the difficulties of her personal life and her college life to this point of achievement, within grasp of earning her undergraduate degree in the next year.

Joan came to another realization about the role of writing during this spring term. She said, "Writing helps me put ideas into my own words—makes me think how things can be put more simply than in textbooks sometimes." This conscious realization of the value of putting ideas into her own language was a crucial insight for Joan. It was an insight mentioned by most of the students in my study, although the insight occurred at varying times in the students' academic experiences.

Thus, by the end of her fifth year, Joan had successfully completed most of the required core courses. She was passing her courses with "B's" and "C's." She had missed the final in her French course when she developed a throat and eye infection at the end of the semester, and she failed this course. Writing had become the way she kept her grades up, as she continued to experience difficulty with short-answer examinations. She was increasingly able to apply the insights from her psychology classes to readings and concepts in other courses.

In order to graduate, Joan needed to pass the English Proficiency Test, another writing test similar to the WAT but requiring higher writing standards. She took this examination in the fall of her sixth and last year at the college. One of the options of the test allowed students to pick up a reading which would serve as a basis for some of the topics on the test. Students could select a question based on the reading or one of the other questions presented "cold" to them as had been the questions on the WAT. Joan selected a topic about the hardships facing arrivals in a new country either as immigrants or students. She wrote an outline, including in the introduction the three aspects she would develop in the paper. In her outline, she set out in the second section to consider why these were hardships, a significant cognitive move for her. This would be followed by a conclusion. In the exam paper, Joan focused on the hardships of Asian immigrants, drawing from the reading she had been supplied with. In each paragraph of development, she stated the point she wanted to make, established its significance, using words like "because" and "in order that," and concluded with an example to illustrate her point. These points were followed by a summary paragraph. Despite her difficulty with comma use and an occasional verb-form lapse, the organization and content of Joan's exam carried her to a successful conclusion. She had waited until her senior year, her sixth year at the college, to take this exam, and her exam book noted on the cover that she was a "graduating senior."

Passing the proficiency test was an omen of the generally good semester Joan was having. Although she was under a lot of pressure, she told me that she "didn't feel extra anxious." She said, "I go through motions one day at a time. I see other people with problems." During that semester, she was working 2 to 3 days a week in 4-hour stints at her internship in the drug and alcohol unit of the hospital that eventually hired her full-time. In the internship, she conducted group therapy sessions and she felt very dedicated to her field work. She was also working 10 to 14 hours a week at Radio City Music Hall. She was enjoying courses in family psychology and speech. In the latter course, she was polishing up her diction and articulation. She found it interesting to give presentations and the experience was useful to her when she had to speak to groups of individuals with drug and alcohol addictions in her internship.

By the time I saw Joan again at the end of the fall semester, Traub's book, *City on a Hill,* had been published. When Joan first read the chapter Traub had written about her, she was deeply depressed. Joan told me that first she had worried about her family's reaction to his dismissive comments about her achievements, but, she said, "they didn't have much of a reaction." She felt that her degree was confirming for her that she was capable of doing what she wanted to do. The most important thing she had learned from her experience with Traub was, "You can't just be nice to everybody. You can't trust everyone." She had been surprised by the book, apparently expecting a more sympathetic treatment of her experiences and accomplishments. Furthermore, she told me that Traub had been inaccurate in some of the things that he reported about her life. Since the book was published so close to the time that Joan would be graduating, it probably had less of an effect on her than it might have had had it been published earlier. She had gained enough pride in her accomplishments that she could rather quickly overcome the immediate distress she felt when she first read the book.

In her last year, Joan was more conscious than ever of the ways in which writing had helped her to learn. She said, "I used to have trouble getting my thoughts together—how to get away from paraphrasing and putting thoughts into my own words. I stick to my concepts; it helps keep the thoughts well organized, in a structure. When I write papers, it helps me get better grades. I might have a mid-term 'C+,' but a paper gives me a chance to develop my own thoughts and prove myself more." This constant reiteration by the students in my study of how writing gave them an opportunity "to prove themselves" reinforced the significance of including writing opportunities that allowed students, first of all, to learn for themselves and, second, to demonstrate their knowledge and understanding to others.

In her last semester at the college, Joan struggled with the required experimental psychology course, in which use of statistics was essential. The course was evaluated on the basis of short laboratory reports and final examination. With a great deal of help from her professor and the laboratory assistant who corrected and commented on the lab reports, Joan passed the course with a "D."

Joan had not come to City College as a very confident student. Burdened with complex physical, family, and economic problems, she slowly strengthened her resolve to complete her academic studies successfully. In her early years of study, she depended on authoritative knowledge to support her assertions. While this approach brought her enough success to pass many of her courses, she increasingly found a demand for thinking that was more analytic. Like other students who had started in basic skills classes, Joan found that writing gave her better opportunities to demonstrate the learning she had achieved than did short-answer examinations. When given the opportunity to write research papers, Joan became able to apply psychological principles and theories not only to cases presented in her psychology classes, but also to literary works she was asked to interpret. Quantitative studies plagued her throughout her years at the college, and she struggled to pass required college skill tests and academic courses like astronomy, statistics, and experimental psychology. Because she had to work many hours at outside jobs to earn spending money, Joan forced herself to bring better planning skills to her commitments and to organize the time needed to fulfill her academic assignments more carefully. Over time, she came to see her professors as her allies, and she became comfortable seeking out their help. Writing became an essential means of learning, as she recognized that reading alone was not an adequate tool for understanding the complex materials she was encountering.

So, here was Joan, graduating after 6 years, hired as a full-time counselor in a methadone clinic, reveling in her achievements after long and difficult years of stress and hardship. She told me in a telephone conversation in September 1995 that she was earning $25,753.36 (she knew this amount to the last penny) in a union job with full benefits, including 20 days' vacation, 12 sick days, 8 holidays, and 4 personal days. After 90 days, she expected to get a raise, and she would get annual raises after that. Her brother helped her realize that she was "making more money than anyone else in the family has." She would be using the money to move her mother out of the projects and, for the first time, she said she would have "a room of my own."

After six years of arduous school responsibilities, work responsibilities, and family responsibilities, Joan was not a "miraculous survivor" as Traub had called her. There was no miracle that accounted for her success. Her accomplishments stemmed from hard work and dedication, her most important trait, tenaciousness, and the support and encouragement she had received from her instructors over the years. She has become a contributor to the society through her own efforts.

And that is exactly one point of this long retelling. Students like Joan are willing to put in the extraordinary effort to overcome the difficulties imposed by their poor academic preparation, and their difficult family and economic conditions. They do not want to become drains on the society; they want to become contributors. We must join together to persuade the political forces who want to deny such opportunities to students like Joan that it is in their interests, as well as the individuals' interests, to support CUNY and other institutions of higher education in their efforts to help students reach their full potential as contributing citizens.

Another point of describing this student's experience is to illustrate the benefits that can be derived from longitudinal research that combines in-depth interviews and analyses of written work to follow the conceptual development that occurs over the entire period of the undergraduate education. Such research emphasizes the critical role that writing plays in developing complex reasoning processes that allow students to bring personal experience and knowledge to bear on their assessment of "accepted" knowledge to foster a critical stance that incorporates their perspectives and that leads to re-thinking and re-shaping this "accepted" knowledge.

Longitudinal research is not easy to undertake nor does it lead to quick rewards or frequent publication. By its very nature, longitudinal research requires patience and persistence, but the understandings gained from it cannot be replaced by any other methodology. For example, only through such an approach is it possible to document the growth in complexity of thinking and analytical reasoning that occurs over the college years. Instructors of basic writing courses and/or freshman composition often feel frustrated as they are confronted with the demands of teaching purpose, organization, audience, sentence structure, grammar, and revision in a one- or two-semester course. To this is added the requirement to analyze complex texts so that readings are frequently incorporated into the writing classes. That excellence in all of these areas cannot be achieved in such a short time frame is evident, but the demand is placed there by the instructors in other disciplines as well as by the institutional tests that judge students' abilities to progress to advanced levels. When our field has enough longitudinal studies of students' experiences of different backgrounds and from different kinds of instructional institutions we will be better able to make the argument that these writing abilities develop over time and under the appropriate instructional prodding. Such demands imply that at all levels of instruction, whatever the format — sequences of basic writing classes, mainstreamed classes, or freshman composition — students should be practicing analysis of complex reading materials just as they are practicing the conventions of essay writing.

Seeing the students mature and develop increasing self-confidence over the years reinforced my view that it was essential to take a long-term perspective to evaluate the potential that they have for academic success. It seems appropriate to ask if this type of research is particularly meaningful for the perception of minority students and second-language students? My answer would be yes, because it shows how students who may not have had the requisite academic preparation when they began their college studies have the potential to succeed and do succeed when they are given the appropriate time and support. Competence does not occur instantaneously, especially for those who have not had the appropriate preparation, but over time students do reach their true potential. Research over time is an important way to validate that success.

There is a concerted effort at the present time to reduce the possibility of students who need basic level instruction to succeed at the college level through eliminating what have been called admissions preferences and then, in a more insidious policy, making it less likely that those who are admitted have the possibility of succeeding and continuing on with their education. Much of this latter policy is directed at the first semester or the freshman year as a make-it or break-it time. What I hope is that my research and the research of others that will follow will demonstrate that the freshman year should instead be looked upon as the first step in a succession of steps over the full years of a college education. That first year should provide the opportunity for those students who have been inadequately prepared for the college experience to begin to acquire the skills and knowledge they need that will grow as they continue their studies. In order to demonstrate that this growth will and does occur, we must have more longitudinal studies that will provide the evidence needed to persuade the decision makers — administrators and politicians — to provide the financial and educational resources the students deserve. Time is on the students' side, but they need to be given the requisite time.

Works Cited

Belenky, Mary F., Beth Clinchy, Nancy Goldberger, and Jill Tarule. *Women's Ways of Knowing: The Development of Self, Voice, and Mind*. New York: Basic Books, 1986.

Bowen, William G. and Derek Bok. *The Shape of the River: Long-Term Consequences of Considering Race in College and University Admissions*. Princeton, NJ: Princeton University Press, 1998.

Lavin, David E. and David Hyllegard. *Changing the Odds: Open Admission and the Life Chances of the Disadvantaged*. New Haven: Yale University Press, 1996.

Nettles, Michael T. and Laura W. Perna. *The African American Education Data Book: Higher and Adult Education*, Vol. 1. Fairfax, VA: Frederick D. Patterson Research Institute of the College Fund/UNCF, 1997.

Shaughnessy, Mina P. *Errors and Expectations: A Guide for the Teacher of Basic Writing*. New York: Oxford University Press, 1977.

Sternglass, Marilyn S. *Time to Know Them: A Longitudinal Study of Writing and Learning at the College Level*. Mahwah, NJ: Lawrence Erlbaum Associates, 1997.

Traub, James. *City on a Hill: Testing the American Dream at City College*. Reading, MA: Addison-Wesley, 1994.

Wallace, David L. and Annissa Bell. "Being Black at a Predominantly White University. *College English* (January 1999): 307–327.

Racially, Ethnically, and Linguistically Diverse Students

Teaching English in a California Two-Year Hispanic-Serving Institution: Complexities, Challenges, Programs, and Practices

Jody Millward, Sandra Starkey, and David Starkey

*David Starkey, a four-year scholar and a relatively new hire at Santa Bar-
bara City College (SBCC), found himself engaged by SBCC Multicultural
Transfer Program's monthly meetings. Faculty spent their time at these
meetings contextualizing and adapting the work of two- and four-year
scholars to their own classrooms and students. Faculty shared pragmatic information about what worked and what didn't, and they also discussed ways to rethink and revision assignments. As a four-year hire to a
community college and a published writer and scholar, Starkey believed
these discussions should be shared. When Cristina Kirklighter issued a
call for articles on pedagogy at Hispanic-serving institutions, he proposed
interviewing two faculty who had leadership and teaching experience in
this program, which was designed to promote the success of Hispanic students in a community college English sequence. In doing so, he gave voice
to two teacher-scholars who did not often choose to publish. This article
exposes the hidden tensions in truly multicultural classrooms, how*

From *Teaching Writing with Latino/a Students: Lessons Learned at Hispanic-Serving
Institutions*, edited by Cristina Kirklighter, Diana Cárdenas, and Susan Wolff Murphy.
SUNY Press, 2007, pp. 37-59.

*marginalization affects student performance, and how a multicultural
classroom affects white students who often instinctively rely on privilege.*

David Starkey: Jody and Sandy, you have dedicated your careers to
the working poor. Given the racialization of poverty in California
(and Santa Barbara), that means primarily Latinos/as. You have directed programs, collaborated in state and national conference presentations, and promoted teacher training on local, state, and national levels with a comprehensive booklet that includes theories and principles
of multicultural pedagogy and an anthology of assignments. I would
like to draw on your experience to frame the issues that two-year college teachers address at Hispanic-Serving Institutions (HSIs) such as
Santa Barbara City College (SBCC).

Your key commitment has been to SBCC's Multicultural English
Transfer (MET) program, which offers a designated strand of reading-
writing courses from two levels below transfer through transfer composition. Our faculty sequences classroom and writing assignments within
each course and across course levels based on principles we have identified that help underrepresented students succeed. Briefly, these include
building a classroom community, linking students to campus resources,
promoting student participation within the academic community, and
encouraging students to build bridges between the academy and their
familial, cultural, and linguistic communities. We meet monthly to discuss pedagogies that encourage individualized instruction and student
success. With a 27.8 percent Latino/a enrollment, SBCC is designated an
HSI. How would you describe our students?

Jody Millward: When I think of our students, I picture a concentric
circle with the student in the middle. Then I picture the family and local
community in the next circle, the academic community in the next, and
the political and economic context in the outer circle. I realize that at
times our students feel those circles collapsing in on them. I often do
this as an exercise in my classes, having students write their individual
characteristics of each circle, and then we do a joint diagram. Patterns
emerge, and we begin to realize the many challenges each student faces
and, thus, our pedagogical challenges. Our students do not operate in a
vacuum, and while the complexity of their lives can (and does) enrich
their classroom contributions and writing, those very complexities can
derail them.

David: And these challenges may be invisible to instructors who
have never faced them in their own academic careers.

Jody: Right. Let us adapt the diagram and put the two-year college
instructor in the center. She or he would define the self in terms of age,
gender, ethnicity, family structure; the next circle would be the classroom—number of classes, total number of students, student characteristics. Many teachers view each student as an individual and believe each

class has its own personality. Of course this is true. Still, we can identify patterns and develop strategies that will allow us to provide individualized instruction. I have just finished the "2005 TYCA Two-Year College Facts and Data Report" as part of a CCCC's Research Initiative grant.[1] The demographic information warns that we cannot afford to hang on to notions of the traditional college student. Nearly 90 percent of the two-year population has a nontraditional marker.[2] In 2003, community colleges enrolled nearly 60 percent of all Hispanics and Native Americans and nearly half of all blacks and Pacific Islanders nationwide.

Given California's location (bordering Mexico and on the Pacific Rim), we can predict that our classes will not be "traditional." A 2005 study shows that nearly half of all California ninth graders are low income and will not complete four-year university entrance requirements. As an additional risk factor, Latinos/as comprise nearly half of the English Language Learners in the K–12 population (Beachler et al. 2005, 3). As Beatrice Méndez Newman notes, 42 percent of all HSI Latino/a enrollment is in California. Peter Schrag reports that "80 percent of all California Latino[as]" enroll in a community college, "four times as many [as in] UC, CSU, and all California private colleges combined" (2004, 2). Sandy's research indicates that we will have ESL, bilingual, and Generation 1.5 Latinos (students whose native language is not English, but who have been educated in the American K–12 system) in our classrooms, and the linguistic challenges differ drastically. That may be why Hispanics are "over-represented in basic skills courses" (Beachler et al. 2005, 6).

Sandra Starkey: The major challenge for two-year college teachers is the diversity of students in foundational (i.e., developmental) composition classrooms. We have students with vastly different needs and expectations: reentry students, international students, immigrant English Language Learners, Generation 1.5, special needs students, local students with family responsibilities, parents, the "traditional" 18-year-old high school graduate financially dependent on his or her parents and, yes, the "unmotivated" community college student—with a variety of goals (certificates, AAs, transfer). Teachers wonder: What is the best text and curriculum? How strict should my attendance policy be? How much group work or conferencing should we do? How much should I focus on grammar? What benefits one group may disadvantage another. While we may know that every community college student needs a great deal of individualized attention, our SBCC full-time course load for at least one semester a year is minimum 100 students (all foundational courses), maximum 144 students (all transfer level). I have become an informal counselor, advising students on required classes and what majors they may pursue and informing them of financial aid opportunities. Nothing in graduate school prepares us for these multiple roles, and not all teachers are willing to take them on. For example, we all feel more comfortable advising the English major. Now consider the realities for most Latinos: many feel they must pursue careers that will support their families (both immediate and extended), and many Latinos/as have underestimated their ability to transfer. We cannot ignore the fact that a certificate or an AA could provide them with emotionally and financially fulfilling careers. But as teachers of students we fear we underserve; we all want to increase the transfer rate of Hispanics.

A handout about Latino/a students, brought back from the 2004 conference sponsored by UCLA's Student Transfer Outreach and Mentor Program and circulated by our president to faculty, students, and community members, rightfully caused quite a stir. According to this report, in California, of 100 Chicano/Latino students enrolled in elementary school, 46 graduate from high school. Of those 46, 26 pursue higher education; 17 will attend community college; 9 a four-year school. Of the 9 at the four-year university, 9 stay. Of the 17 who choose a community college, only one will transfer. The fact that the UC schools are better at retention is, I think, in part because they have more material resources (mentors, peer tutors, etc.), researchers who dedicate time to the subject, and admissions criteria that tend to eliminate students with multiple risk factors (linguistic, class, and family responsibilities). But these data show that Hispanic students need to be made aware that transfer is, indeed, an option.

Jody: And now we are addressing the outer circle of my original diagram—the political, cultural, and economic. National media now celebrate two-year colleges as the locus for retraining displaced workers and as an economically sound way to prepare students to transfer to a four-year university. But nationally, and in our own state—despite the fact that the California Community College system enrolls more students than any institution of higher learning—2004 budget cuts meant that we could not offer classes critical to job enhancement (in ESL, certificate, and associate programs), and so California community colleges turned away an estimated 175,000 students (Hayward et al. 2004). And this is a national trend. In 'The Silent Killer of Minority Enrollments," Jamilah Evelyn warned that the "threat" to diversity is state budget cuts, which "fall disproportionately on minority students." In 2003, Mark Drummond, chancellor of Los Angeles CC District, a district that enrolls more than three times the number of Latinos/as than all UCs combined, estimated that his district would turn away "some 6,000 Hispanic students—more than five times the number of [UCLA] Hispanic freshmen" (quoted in Evelyn 2003, 2). This community college district enrolls more than three times the number of Latinos than all UCs combined.

Our students succeed despite the current political, economic, and cultural climate—not because of it. They understand the politics behind citizenship laws, immigration laws, profiling, the cuts to financial aid and scholarships, English only in K–12, the revised transfer requirements of UC and CSU, and the funding discrepancies between four-year schools and two-year colleges. Students of color—especially Latinos/as, given the legislation adopted in the last decade—are sent a message that education is not meant for all. If students stumble or fail, it is not because of lack of money or resources for them or their teachers, but because they—as individuals—cannot cut it, while others obviously can. Clearly, we have a lot of data. What we do not have is a clear analysis of what happens as these forces intersect and how to change our pedagogy in ways that will enable students to realize their academic promise.

David: As a university hire and a scholar in comp theory, I wanted the information you talk about here. At the universities where I taught, I was used to low drop rates and high retention. At SBCC, I saw immediately that what I had been told about CC students' low "skills level" was not true. So I knew I had to pay attention to the affective factors. I also discovered that incorporating these issues of dropout rates and retention as topics for class analysis allowed students to situate themselves. Defining shared personal and political challenges allows them to address those challenges. I am thinking, Jody, of your brainstorming assignment, "What can't be changed or chosen after birth?" Students respond with time and place of birth, family structure, class, gender, ethnicity, and genetic makeup. They fill in specifics for a cluster of these items and predict something about that "person"; then they change at least three of those elements for a second cluster and predict something. This exercise generates discussion about the intersections of class, ethnicity, gender, status, and so on. Students also agree that not everyone born in a similar time with similar circumstances will have the same "fate" and talk about choices, challenges, and the interplay between the self and "outside forces."

Yet if we are going to talk about students in communities, we need to identify the differences between the four-year and two-year academic cultures. The University of California, Santa Barbara (UCSB), like many four-year institutions, provides first-year students with the multiple benefits of dorm life. Resident assistants serve as mentors who can provide immediate assistance, linking students to campus services when financial or academic challenges arise. In the dorms, peers share information on tests, teachers, financial aid, clubs, and on-campus jobs, and they often form informal study groups. Most importantly, they are in a culture that says academics come first. Twenty-four/seven, students are studying on campus—in the dorms, library, and computer labs. Our students come to campus, drive to a job, go and pick up a child or a sibling, and rarely have a "room of one's own" for thought and reflection. Our two-year college libraries and labs have limited hours. While it is difficult to bring these benefits to students through classroom assignments, in conjunction with teaching critical thinking, computer literacy, reading, writing, and research, students give high marks to those types of assignments in course evaluations. In a sense, we are giving them the tools they need to decode academia.

We must acknowledge that these cultural differences affect student performance. In the three years I taught at UCSB, I noticed that students in their Writing 1 (the equivalent of our Fundamentals of Composition) course had a much stronger sense of the consequences of not completing their assignments. The UCSB students had been trained in high school to get the work done, turn it in on time, show up for class, and so on. Clearly they possessed study and time-management skills that many two-year college students have never learned. Consequently, the "remediation" their writing required was much easier to accomplish, because they understood most of the codes needed to successfully negotiate the institutional requirements.

Similar to the students Méndez Newman teaches, SBCC students often use a different calculus to determine priorities as they juggle their personal and academic lives. I need to remind myself that going to work to make enough money to pay the rent or the electricity bill may, indeed, at least in the short term, appear more pressing than handing in Essay #3 the day it is due. Although, of course, when they do have time for reflection—whether it is through class discussions or essay assignments—our students are as intellectually incisive, if not more so, than their four-year counterparts.

Jody: At UCSB, I taught full-time in a program designed to promote the success of underrepresented students (now called A.C.E.). I rarely lost a student, maybe one or two in an academic year. In my first semester at SBCC, I lost three in the Fundamentals course alone. They just stopped coming. Like you, I found their skill sets were not that different from those of students at four-year schools. As a teaching assistant at UCSB, I had two Latinas from an inner-city Los Angeles high school in my Writing 1 course. Their scores, in the language of the time, defined them as "borderline." Their high school English teacher attended a welcome function and celebrated their preparation. When I received their first essays, I was astonished by her characterization. However, within two quarters (students in this program could choose to stay with the same teacher), I used the same glowing language in their recommendation letters. They caught up. Our students do, too, but it takes longer because often they interrupt their comp studies. Some "take a break from English" because they perceive comp and math as work intensive and as gatekeeper classes. Others dip in and out during the semester because they are sideswiped by life or, as the semester wears on, realize that while their outside responsibilities have not lessened, their work in classes has intensified—particularly in disciplines that rely on a few major tests or one long paper to assess student knowledge of a specific subject. Given the sequential nature of our classes, students with multiple responsibilities find meeting every deadline nearly impossible. They can "catch up" and get the work done but miss the benefits of the recursive nature of the writing process. The MET faculty have experimented with ways to build flexibility into the course structure (e.g., permitting one late paper, no questions asked, or accepting the final draft at the end of the assigned week). I accommodate those with emergencies by letting them complete portions of the course online. One woman finished the course work early and brought her newborn in on the last day for all of us to meet. But perhaps we could do more. Given the realities of students' lives, how do we incorporate prewriting, live peer response to drafts, metacognitive assessments of writing process, and so on? Is offering the course traditionally while working online with individual students doable (given our workloads) or good pedagogy, since the MET faculty view composition courses as a pathway into the campus community and craft assignments to help students integrate multiple social identities?

Sandra: If I may, that goes back to an early point I made. There is little research into this critical issue. While four-year college students often enter with a history of success and nurturing and have some knowledge of how to decode academic conventions, our students (particularly first-generation with linguistic and cultural differences and mixed experiences of success in K–12) enter with very different attitudes. Some believe knowledge is self-achieved and assume, "I must be able to do it all—work, family, and a full-time load—or I'm not college material." Others think they will test the waters and any failure confirms they are not "college material." This viewpoint is a key difference. Yet the literature does not address how these beliefs affect both individual performance and classroom dynamics. Jim Cummins's (2001) "Empowering Minority Students" shows that school failure among minority groups has much to do with the relation of that group to the "majority" group. If the minority group is viewed as a low-status one in the larger society, then failure rates, not surprisingly, are much higher. An oft-quoted study involves Finnish students, defined as "low status" in Sweden, who had high failure rates in comparison to Finnish students in Australia, where they were viewed as "high status" (53). When a person's language and culture are devalued by the culture in power, the impact is tremendous. That is why we need to pay attention to the cultural, economic, and political forces affecting our Latino/a students.

David: Having taught in Finland, I find that a particularly telling example. From the average American's perspective, both groups are "Scandinavians," basically indistinguishable from one another. And yet there is a marked tension between Swedes and Finns, particularly among the working classes. Yet I am aware of no research focusing specifically on two-year college Latinos/as in terms of who succeeds and why and what role composition courses play. Instead, we find ourselves gleaning what we can from four-year studies or localized examples of two-year college successes. Both types of research view students through the lens of a particular community—ethnicity, class, first generation. But how do we help individualize instruction for our Latino/a majority with their varied linguistic and cultural backgrounds?

Jody: What comes to my mind is Ann M. Penrose's (2002) study on first-generation students. She provides valuable information on how home and academic cultures diverge by identifying the commonalities of First Generation college-goers (FG) that differentiate them from their peers:

- discontinuity between home and school culture, beween the norms of the neighborhood or family and those of the academy

- sensitivity to social and academic factors that will distinguish them from their classmates

- more likely to notice distinctive features of academic discourse

- significant differences between literacy practices at home and school

- contrast between intuitive models of literacy and formalized expectations of academia

- tension between the personal, emotional voice and the dispassionate language of academic analysis

Penrose notes, "By virtue of their decision to attend college, these students have not only entered alien territory but distanced themselves from the understanding of family and friends" (2002, 439), and she suggests that because "literacy practices enact the values and customs of a community, they represent a critical site of vulnerability for those who are uncertain of their membership." Penrose concludes that "FG students do not bring . . . insecurities with them to college," but develop them afterward (2002, 457).

Yet reports of students and faculty in the MET program challenge these assumptions. In general, first-generation two-year college students tend to be tentative upon entry; as they experience success, however, they blossom. Latinos/as in particular see that they can recover and pick themselves up when they fall, an experience they often feel was denied them in high school. In the last three years, many of my Latino/a students have transferred, with mixed success, in their first semesters. Just off the top of my head: to UCSB, Juan in computer science, Eduardo and Napoleon in business; to Cal Poly in San Luis Obispo, Jose and Miguel in engineering, Leah in landscape architecture, and Denova in nutrition; to UCLA, Ernesto in premed and Margaret (whose major I do not know). And currently, Antonia, Jorge, Bianca, and Lily are in graduate schools. I knew these students well. When they graduated from SBCC, each saw bilingualism as a strength; several had drawn their families and neighborhood friends into their study time. Two women convinced their mothers, Mexican immigrants, to enroll at SBCC. When I went to their graduations, I met their extended families. Some had traveled from Mexico. These students were proud and confident. Rather than developing insecurities during their two-year college experience, they developed great confidence.

A 2002 study of "high-risk" two-year college students and recent transfer reports confirm this anecdotal information. A study of high-risk two-year college students found that while students are "more likely to find their exams challenging," they are

> much less likely to come to class unprepared, are more likely to ask questions and participate in class discussions, [and] are more likely to prepare two or more drafts of a paper or assignment before turning it in. They are more dedicated to studying despite the number of hours they work (79% . . . work more than 30 hours per week compared to 6 percent in the low-risk group [and] devote as much time to preparing for class as their lower-risk classmates do). (Penrose 2002, 9)

That is great news, important news. It suggests that many first-generation and/or reentry students do not underestimate the time and effort that success will take or undervalue the pride and confidence that such success brings.

On the other hand, four-year colleges tend to underestimate the burdens our transfer students carry. I just had lunch with one of my former students who graduated from UCLA within two years of transfer while working forty hours a week to support herself. The senior survey she received asked students to check hours a week worked—forty hours was not an option. On the upside, she was personally proud of her accomplishment and confident that because she had done what UCLA apparently believes is inconceivable, she can handle anything. On the downside, this is a clear example of how elite institutions render many students invisible. As we often ask in MET, are opportunities limited for students with several high-risk markers? This, too, is the type of research that needs to be pursued.

Sandra: I have had that experience—the experience of watching confidence, particularly for Latinos/as, increase as they build bridges between their home and academic cultures. Yet I fear we are so focused on transfer, we sometimes forget to ask, "What happens to them once they get there?" I have been working with a UCSB outreach group that involves the university, the two-year college, and local high schools, and I have learned a lot about the preconceptions and biases university faculty have toward these students. The leap from the two-year college to the university is almost as traumatic as the leap from high school, yet the university is just starting to put into place the orientations and community building for transfer students that is so integral a part of the freshman experience. Starting a dialogue and maintaining connections between these three institutions is so important to our mission.

Jody: We also have some hard data: nationwide, transfer students have an 80 percent persistence rate; but we also know that while 35 percent of upper-class and 21 percent of middle-class students transfer, only 7 percent of the working poor do so (Millward 2005, 8). As you noted earlier, the racialization of poverty in states such as California makes Latino students woefully underrepresented in transfer. Cross-institutional partnerships are key. For me, the paucity of such programs nationwide shows the conservative nature of the academy. Embedded within academia is the cultural norm of the "traditional" college student, a mere 27 percent of the national college population (Millward 2005, 5). In this model, a financially independent college student, living on campus, completes the bachelor's degree within four years and then enrolls in another institution for graduate work. This certainly does not honor the very real family and economic responsibilities of many "nontraditional" two-year students who have obligations that keep them local. A formal collaboration, programs with articulated goals, would provide two-year college students with the support and expectations they need for success within their local communities through the bachelor's degree and beyond.

Sandra: In the meantime, we need to adapt four-year research and create a pedagogy that allows students to integrate their home culture into every level of their academic experience from the moment they enroll in a two-year college. English classes are uniquely situated to help them do just that.

David: MET does just that. For example, we know retention rates go up when students feel connected to the campus community. But we do not have a multicultural center, and often students feel they do not have time to participate in tutoring much less join campus organizations and clubs. Sandy, your "treasure hunt" assignment directly addresses student awareness of campus resources. You provide hypothetical case studies of students whose challenges affect their ability to focus on school. Working in collaborative groups, they research which agency on campus would best assist that student, report back to the class, and then write a paper on a friend or peer and provide advice to that student incorporating what they have learned. For me, that stands as a model (among many) of what the MET faculty have done over the years. You get students into the offices, talking to faculty, staff, and fellow students, and then place them in a position of authority and give them a context of helping someone else. That makes the writing authentic. The end result is that students realize services and networks can save them time and money by helping them resolve issues that may cause them to underperform or drop a class.

Sandra: You are right, David. MET has made a difference. As someone who has taught in the program for over a decade, what I most value are the monthly faculty discussions. We have at least ten faculty (more in the last few years) volunteering for the program. Hearing challenges, assignments, research, and insights from part timers, new teachers, and senior faculty provides the support we need to experiment. Instructors have the right to share what did not work. We do not discuss personalities or self-defined "failed experiments" outside of our meetings.

We are, I think, constantly striving to provide what Méndez Newman calls for—adjusting our pedagogy rather than defining students by the deficit model. The cornerstone program principle, "No student comes to SBCC hoping to underperform, fail, or drop out," drives our classroom efforts. As a faculty, we practice what we preach to students: pause, assess, ask for help, and regroup. We all rely on each other.

Jody: MET's frank exchanges help mitigate the isolation that two-year college teachers often feel when facing the multiple challenges of their classrooms. As David was talking about how we as teachers adapt assignments to our population, I thought about the career assignment, something I (like many others) used over a decade ago at UCSB. Louis Attinasi's (1989) study shows that choosing a major is a key retention factor: students who discover they do not like their majors are at risk, and those who do not choose a major miss a path into the academy. Four-year students seem to have the confidence to experiment and change majors and the family support when they do so. It is not necessarily pleasant and can make them feel at sea, but their strategies for addressing this core issue are, in general, effective. But first-generation students do not have a full understanding of the range of majors available. For example, I had a Latino who designated computer science as his major because only one member of his family, a cousin, had gone to college and that is what he had done. But he hated the field, got poor grades, and was thinking about dropping out. If we had not had career assignments in our sequence, I know he would have dropped. The assignments gave him a way to analyze his choice. When I started here, only MET transfer classes [devoted] time to the major. Now MET pretransfer reading classes have students do collages, pretransfer composition courses have them do interviews with those working in the field or career center research, and then we have the transfer-level paper that incorporates interviews and research requiring students to "translate" the bureaucratic language of the database and the informal language of the interview into an "I-search" paper. If an understanding of the college culture and confidence inspires Latinos who chose a certificate or an associate's path to set higher goals as studies suggest (Hochiander, Sikora, and Hom 2003, 13, 15–16), then it is critical to show students their options.

Sandra: Yet this assignment is particularly difficult for Latino/a students, even as we attempt to celebrate the languages, dialects, and personal heritage they bring to the classroom. For example, students with a rich language history who engage in "code switching" are performing a complex linguistic task that can enrich their writing. Many Latinos/as have a difficult time controlling the voices that emerge in the database information and the interview language of practitioners who often are Spanish speakers. We must, though, be teaching them the language of the "academy," and we will disadvantage them if we do not make this code explicit, as Lisa Delpit (1988) points out. We really cannot afford an either-or approach; we need to give students the tools they need to gain access into four-year universities, and we need to do so by building on the literacies they bring into our classrooms. Yet consider the linguistic diversity within our classrooms. We have Generation 1.5 and immigrants from different states (and thus dialects) of many different Spanish-speaking countries. In addition, we have students who are highly literate in their native language but have had only two or three years of ESL instruction; and we have students who speak both languages but have little formal instruction in either language.

Jody: Few of us have the linguistic training we need. Knowing Spanish may help, but we need more training to better identify the varied patterns students rely on when they frame an essay, choose a level of diction, construct a voice, and wrestle with sentence-level issues. Some of what I have read has helped—in particular with how students structure an essay, oral markers, conflating formal and informal diction—but I suspect that student linguistic patterns differ based on how the factors Sandy identified are combined.

Sandra: This has got to be our biggest challenge, and my sabbatical project on Generation 1.5 shows there is no magic bullet. It does confirm, however, that the diversity of the students' language experience/background mandates that we work with each student individually.

David: You are saying that the one-to-one conference on an essay draft, which we already know to be an essential part of any basic writing course, is even more crucial in linguistically diverse classes.

Sandra: Yes. My sabbatical has shown me the value of individualized, detailed linguistic profiles. For example, many of our older, reentry, or fairly recent immigrant students have problems with verb tense, agreement, articles, and idioms. These students, whose primary language is Spanish, have problems producing the U.S. deductive "academic" essay, since Spanish has a very different discourse pattern. Yet many 1.5 students use English as their primary language. They speak Spanish only at home and in a limited fashion with their peers, and they may feel increasingly unable to communicate complex feelings in Spanish, which can be very painful. This inability can create unconscious or conscious ambivalence about gaining proficiency in academic English. The students, as we know, may use various dialects, including Spanglish, Chicano English, Chicano Spanish, and mixtures of these. But many times they are actually more proficient in English than in Spanish, although they may identify themselves as "bilingual." Often the problems will be with word choice and clarity as the students reach beyond their common oral language to an "academic register." We will also see run-ons and fragments, typical markers of the oral style. As Maria Montano-Harmon (1991) reminded us in our MET training session some years ago, code switching—going back and forth from an informal, oral style to a more academic (or an attempt at an academic) register—generates such errors. Of course, we also have Latino/a students who do not speak Spanish at all. We have to be very careful about making assumptions. We need to know the linguistic background/profile of each student.

Pedagogy, both classroom activities and writing assignments, can make a difference. In each course of our sequence, we focus on language registers. In my pretransfer level, for example, I have students identify a conflict they are having either at work, in college, or in a group where they volunteer. They write a letter to a friend describing the challenge, write a letter to the person responsible for change in the group, and then analyze the differences between these registers. Jody and I have both used Tan's "Mother Tongue" and then had students identify the different languages they use in academic, work, family, and peer communities. And I have used Jody's assignment, where she gives students the option of translating a poem and then analyzing the choices they made in doing so and why. That way we have students themselves subvert the notion that speaking two languages is a disadvantage, and we try to have monolingual students see that they too have several codes by virtue of the registers they choose to use.

Jody: In my second-semester transfer course (lit and composition), I teach a series of poems about language learning. Students love Pat Mora's *Elena*. On the surface, it is a simple poem about a mother from Mexico who is trying to learn English. Her husband speaks only Spanish and does not want her to learn the new language. Her children speak more and more in English, and, like the neighbors and storekeepers, they laugh at her attempts to speak English. She ends up locking herself in the bathroom to study privately to avoid the tensions in the house. This literature allows us to discuss the cultural assumptions her children have absorbed—the fact that those who speak Spanish are less intelligent. We analyze her husband's view; he faces that attitude every day in the work world and so feels that English provides his family with a way to separate from (even look down upon) him. Students may interview friends or family who immigrated here about their experiences to determine which cultural assumptions remain and which have changed since the poem was written. They also can survey students who grew up in homes where English was not the first language to determine when they speak which language and why and what their attitudes are. These assignments allow them, I think, to gain a broader perspective on the issue. It is interesting how many write in their journals about their personal feelings when they see their parents dismissed in stores, doctor's offices, and so on.

Such assignments also allow us to discuss the causes and functions of student silence. The early studies about the silence of minority students in the classroom remain relevant: Students fear being misunderstood because they speak with an accent and may fear that asking a question or having their responses challenged will confirm for themselves and others that they do not belong in college (Saufley et al. 1983, 48). Culture has a marked influence too. Despite my encouragement, I had a young Latino who first spoke in the last third of our second, eighteen-week semester together. He later told me that his father had forbidden him to talk in a class, because "only God and the Norteamericanos know." Now I incorporate readings, research, and the option to write on this theme of student silence. Students can see that silence is often tied to cultural beliefs. They see that in the United States (as the popularity of talk shows confirms) "everybody has a right to their own opinion and to express it," while other cultures may find our behavior rude or arrogant.

David: While all of us in MET require classroom participation, we have developed ways to lower the risk level for students beyond group presentations. For example, students can present each other's work, design the way the audience is seated, use technology to remove the focus from the speaker, or even sit to the side while a peer writes the main points of the presentation on the board. This flexibility allows students to assert authority while providing them with the safety they need to do so.

Sandra: We have made tremendous progress in this area, but it is an issue we need to address in every class, and it reflects the importance of building bridges between the home and the academic cultures. When we do that, students will more likely take risks in terms of the topics they choose and the depth of their analyses and will focus more on their writing (including word choice and grammar). For our Latino/a students, family is a support system that often carries multiple responsibilities. For example, the majority of four-year freshmen will not be called upon to interpret for their parents on a daily basis, to advise and take care of their younger brothers or sisters, and/or monitor their siblings' elementary and high school educations. First-generation students often serve as role models but cannot ignore the family responsibilities they had when in high school. Additionally, some Latinas/os face other cultural expectations: pressure to marry or lack of spousal support. On the one hand, some feel pressured to succeed in order to please the family; some feel pressured to place family above academics. The key is to show students how to negotiate between their different communities—their different linguistic, familial, class, and cultural identities. We use assignments that allow them to see that the skills or talents they develop in one arena can support their success in another. We also suggest ways to address what may seem to be competing or conflicting responsibilities between home and school. For example, we suggest that students recruit siblings or parents or spouses to help with their homework (memorization, flash cards, creating study aids, etc. and to serve as interview sources). This practice accomplishes several things at once: child care (of siblings or offspring) becomes shared study time; the students send the message that they value the history and intelligence of all members of their families; and students become active role models, sending a message that they expect children to follow in their footsteps.

David: So much of this depends upon building a safe classroom environment. Yet we do not teach in a vacuum, and racism inevitably emerges in our classrooms. We talk about this a lot in our faculty meetings. It is so damaging.

Sandra: When our students place into a pretransfer course, they know they are being defined by our state and our college as "remedial." Some white students enter the classroom, see students of color, and hear accents and immediately think, "I am in the wrong class. I wasn't assessed right." They adopt a resistant pose—sit in the back of the room and "eye roll." I will also hear comments during peer editing, or students will ask me directly, "Why should this person read and comment on my paper? They barely even speak English!" This is very troubling and definitely damaging. We try to elevate students who speak more than one language by talking about the advantages of being bilingual or multilingual, but some of our white students have absorbed the cultural stereotypes and fear that their placement in English affirms that they, unlike their high school friends, are not "college ready." They shut down or lash out.

Jody: I agree. It is an unresolved, almost under-the-radar issue. And it is complicated. Because we cannot support the racism reflected by their passive or overt resistance and because we find it personally offensive as well, it is difficult to keep intellectual distance and to parse what is behind such behavior. I believe Mike Rose (1989) gets to the heart of it when he warns, "The danger [is that students] might not be able to separate out their particular problems with calculus or critical writing from their own image of themselves, as thinkers, from their intellectual self-worth" (173).

Sandra: MET faculty speak individually to the student who makes a covert racist statement and discuss overt racist statements with the class as a whole. However, as Jody says, it is difficult at times to do this without humiliating or losing the student who made the comment. But the worst thing is for teachers to turn a blind eye because they fear confronting a student. We know of the powerful effect negative stereotyping has on student performance, and we need to determine how best to eradicate such stereotyping in our classrooms.

Jody: What is also troubling is that these resistant students who do not change their attitude end up underperforming or dropping the class when they realize it is not going to be an automatic easy "A," and that the reading, writing, and research requirements demand commitment to risk taking and growth. This stance is sometimes a defense for mainstream students, especially those who may have had advantages in place but did not gain university admission. It is usually a maturity issue. Given the realities of tracking, these students transition from high schools with little experience of diversity. Often they do not understand that college compositions demand revision, and so they do not revise. They do not understand the success of 1.5, immigrants, or other non-native speakers who welcome the opportunity to revise.

While we have developed many strategies for building community and addressing the limits and powers of stereotyping and intervene when we can define and name such bias, the systemic racism imbedded in our culture undercuts our efforts. The majority of whites do not voice or act on these biases, but the few who do affect classroom climate and hurt themselves. I would like to see more about this in the literature, but it is a touchy subject because of the complexities mentioned. How do we help students understand that their actions reflect an unconscious absorption of stereotypes that can derail them as easily as they derail students of color? They too hear the public voices claiming that high schools do not provide quality education, and that test scores suggest students are not as well prepared as past generations. In California, these debates include the suggestion that immigrants and English language learners are lowering the scores. This suggestion leads some white students to believe they should be stronger in English than their multilingual classmates, and when scores suggest they are not, they hear the message that they did not perform well enough in high school because they are not "college material." How do we shift the paradigm from community colleges enrolling second-class students to one that promotes the notion that integral to the college-going experience is mastering a set of lifelong learning skills that are at the heart of the two-year college open-missions statement? Simply put, students must develop the ability to assess their own weaknesses, commit to improvement, and change perspective when the result will be personal growth and a more productive contribution to community.

David: Yet we must be careful not to mask a critical component of the multicultural dynamic, that is, the complexities of teacher-student race relations. We know those disaffected students often suggest that Latino/a and African American faculty have "an agenda" where topics on race are raised, while they seem to assume that white faculty must address these issues as part of the college curriculum. We may get some resistance to the topics, but it is not personalized. That has to make us wonder not if but how much our students of color censor what they say, especially in classrooms with white faculty. But the reality is, while students of color make up a large percentage of our classrooms, a small percentage of our faculty is Latino/a, African American, Pacific Islander, or Native American. It is imperative, then, for us to develop a pedagogy that serves our students well.

Sandra: The hiring of Latinos in HSIs must be the top priority. Sadly, though, in Santa Barbara, we just are not seeing those candidates. Teaching K–12 and at the two-year college offers little money and practically no prestige. Many Latinos/as planning to transfer want careers that offer more. Mentoring Latino/a students and making sure our institutions recruit candidates of color help. In the meantime, as you have said, all two-year or four-year HSI teachers (or any/teacher for that matter) should be shocked and disheartened by the transfer rates for Latinos/as and should be actively searching for solutions within their own classrooms, among their peers, in their institutions, and in their fields of study. That is our responsibility as teachers.

Jody: The need for more teachers of color in composition class-rooms—especially Latinos/as, given our high Latino/a population—is critical. What bell hooks (1990) identified in *Yearning: Race, Gender, and Cultural Politics* still holds true. And my experience in CAP has confirmed the difference that role models can make. For the past five years, I have cotaught a course with a Latino math faculty (first Ignacio Alarcon, now Monica Dabos). Our enrollment is over 80 percent Latino. We focus on the math and English sequences of required courses because transcripts reveal that students tend to focus on completing one sequence or the other, and this process delays degree completion and/or transfer. Two key elements of the program are student mentors (who attend the course and hold individual weekly meetings with their assigned peer groups) and faculty-student meetings to discuss goals, progress, and any need for assistance (academic or personal). We do not force students to disclose information but provide opportunities to discuss, in confidence, anything that interferes with academic progress. Our goal, like MET's, is to help students revision "conflicting demands," help them build bridges between their home and academic cultures, and help them construct an integrated sense of self.

Latino/a student mentors and faculty role models make all the difference. While my working-class background, large family, and strong family ties provide common ground with some students, my first line of information is always the mentors. When a problem arises and the student is invited to speak to a program coordinator, Latino/a students most often choose Monica. A well placed "I know you are having a difficult time right now. If there is anything I can do, just let me know"—without any judgment implied—gives them the confidence they need to come to me for assistance, and the dynamic shifts. Students choose the faculty member with whom they feel most comfortable, or the one who is available.

I think connections to faculty are vitally important. If we do not have enough Latino/a faculty members, then students must be aware that they can turn to other faculty and that they have the right to do so. Interacting with a faculty member begins dialogue. Some Latinos/as are reluctant to discuss family issues with outsiders.

David: Do you think the political debates about affirmative action contribute to this dynamic? And do you believe that this may be a dynamic that cuts both ways? That is, white students must assume a sense of superiority when they find themselves in classes where there are a significant number of students of color and Latino students may feel that programs designed with them in mind suggest they are not able to make it on their own and that knowledge or, more specifically, a college education should be an individual accomplishment.

Jody: Definitely. When I was working with the cofounders to design MET (Mark Ferrer) and the College Achievement Program (CAP) (Ignacio Alarcon), I was heavily influenced by Rachel T. Hare-Mustin's and Jeanne Marecek's (1988) analysis of the ways ignoring difference (in culture, resources, etc.) supports the status quo; denying an unequal playing field ensures those with power will keep power (1998, 456). On the other hand, emphasizing difference and creating separate but equal programs also support the status quo as these programs do not receive equal resources, recognition, or access, and lead to an "exaggeration of differences" (1988, 456–57). We had many discussions about how to avoid building either bias into the programs.

Sandra: MET is open to all students, and many sign up simply because the time is more convenient. When we are asked what is different about our classes by those students who simply "find" themselves in the program, we emphasize that MET is committed to recreating the multicultural demographics of our county in our classrooms and to preparing students for success in a multicultural environment. We stress that this includes access to and experience with technology (as our MET classes have guaranteed computer classroom time), a focus on transfer options, assignments that link students to the academic and local community, and so forth.

David: And while we have discussed those Latinos/as who are reluctant to seek help and those disaffected white students, in general, the collaborative projects and presentations work to build an effective, productive community. The classroom becomes a relatively safe place to explore and acknowledge difference and to work together on shared goals. And, in the final analysis, each student is individually responsible for his or her work in the classroom.

Jody: In CAP, we do not focus on economic need or ethnicity. We focus on what the literature defines as risk factors for student retention and success. The peer groups are often multiethnic: whites, Latinos/as, Asians, blacks, and those of mixed backgrounds are all working more hours than they should while attending school; the parents' group pulls in men and women from different ethnicities; first-generation students will often include those from different cultures, as well as first-time collegegoers who live at home. The peer group structure, like the collaborative projects in MET, makes it safe to explore difference and serves as a support system for those with similar challenges. A core focus of the class is learning how to build networks. Significantly, students accept as leaders anyone who has demonstrated competency in math, English, or other academic areas where they are struggling. So this too affirms individual achievement. The collaboration of mentors and coordinators reinforces the notion that we all should seek help when we need it. I think if these programs focused solely on ethnicity, we might not achieve the success rates we do. And we have made a substantial difference: our retention rates hover around 90 percent for the class; our students' GPAs are consistently equal to, if not higher than, the general population; if a CAP student fails an English or math course, she or he is more likely to reenroll in that course the following semester than are students in the general population; and our students are more likely to move from part-time to full-time status than is the general population.

David: CAP has built-in structures and a great support network of Latino/a students to help address some of these issues. How do we work toward that ideal in our composition classrooms? Does it help, for example, if I share that I grew up in a working-class neighborhood in Sacramento, and that most of my friends chose to enter the workforce rather than to enroll in college? Am I conveying that I may have a clearer sense of my students' backgrounds than someone who grew up surrounded by privilege? Or, to cite another example, my Spanish is weak and that makes me sympathetic to second-language learners. Should I work on bringing it up to a passable level? If I were more fluent, would I use Spanish in class? In conferencing? Do Latino/a students see white teachers' attempts to use Spanish as somehow insulting—implying that the students are incapable of adequately communicating in English?

Sandra: I do tell my students that as a teenage parent, I chose to attend SBCC, yet I do not imply that I faced exactly the same challenges. I explain that I went through college with two babies while working part time, and I would be happy to share strategies that helped me succeed. I think it has really helped me reach out to young mothers (many of whom are Latinas). Maybe some students are thinking inwardly, "Oh, come on, another middle-class white woman who's trying to say she had it so tough." But I am willing to take that risk because I feel volunteering the information helps my students. Hopefully, I do not alienate too many others. No one has ever said so.

Jody: I believe it can help. Sandy has the highest enrollment and success rates of women with children (including single mothers) in MET and the composition program. This fact suggests that students have an effective underground network, as semester after semester her classes have a higher percentage of mothers, particularly Latinas. When I have these students in the next course, mothers and women who know they want both a family and career ask me if I knew Sandy was a mother when she went to school.

I too use my job and language acquisition history when appropriate. For example, I tell them—either in individual conferences or if it comes up in relation to a story—I was a maid, an all-night waitress, that I sold doughnuts, and that my father, a coal miner, never went to high school. They correct my Spanish pronunciation, and I admit that although I studied for years and can read Spanish, I gave up trying to speak because my accent is so horrible. Often, native speakers cannot understand me. I was too embarrassed to take the risk, and to voice my regret because "the mark of a true intellectual has always been the ability to speak two or more languages." But like the two of you, I never suggest that my experiences are the same or more difficult than theirs. They know, and I acknowledge, if they do not voice what they know, that I could afford not to risk speaking Spanish; they have to take risks in English.

My ideal is that all teachers would receive training in cultural, class, gender, sexual orientation, and learning styles differences. I would also like to see a pedagogy that allows all students to acknowledge how ethnicity, class, gender, sexual orientation, and/or different abilities contribute both to individual identity and to shaping a community. This, of course, could be interpreted by conservatives as a way to justify the denial of class and race, and on the left as my attempt to erase cultural identity because I am white. But the reality is, our students will not be (and have not been) exposed to a power structure that privileges any ethnicity but white. We have to keep teaching, acknowledge our privilege, and learn how to draw upon the strengths that diversity offers—for all of our students' sakes and our own. And students must feel free to call upon faculty for support. Otherwise, the power dynamic remains unchanged, and underserved students remain underserved.

David: It seems when there is sufficient funding for programs such as SBCC's Transfer Achievement Program, MET, and CAP, student success rates rise dramatically, particularly for Latinos/as in those programs. An extensive support network of counselors and tutors to step in and help when the instructor is overwhelmed gives us real reasons to be optimistic. But in bad budget times, that support network develops some big holes. Usually the first cuts are to professional development opportunities—sabbaticals, travel, research for program development, and pedagogy. It makes our challenge of trying to balance research with full teaching loads even more problematic. And our district is in relatively good financial shape. My question is, what is being lost in other districts and nationwide, and what can we do about it?

Sandra: I understand why this happens, but how can we keep moving forward if our faculty cannot do the research necessary?

Jody: The stopgap answer is that we do what we can in our own classrooms, in our own institutions, in our own states, and in our national political contexts because those are the outside forces that circumscribe what we can do in terms of practice and research. But I would also go back to Sandy's point about crossinstitutional partnerships. Our four-year colleagues in rhetoric and composition studies do not want to speak for us (I have heard that said in several conversations when I suggested that they focus research efforts on two-year colleges), and that is understandable. But it also renders us invisible, because we do not have the funding for professional development and research that our four-year colleagues do, and our promotion and tenure do not depend on research. Research happens despite the political, economic, and cultural context. Two-year faculty committed to research and program development focused on increasing the success of their nontraditional students often must do this work in addition to teaching heavy comp loads. In addition, working mothers and faculty of color are asked to represent their students on their campuses and in their local communities (and not all of these requests are scholarly). I remind myself (à la hooks) that I am white, now middle class, without children, a woman who can afford to volunteer time and energy to the national TYCA and CCCCs and to research. Two-year college faculty just are not there because they have high teaching loads, commitments to their students on campuses, and obligations to their local communities and families.

More importantly, the study of rhetoric and composition must include two-year college students. Journals in our field include articles on multicultural education, workplace writing, beginning writers, and so on. Two-year colleges teach an estimated 50 percent of all freshman and 70 percent of all "developmental composition," and our student demographics offer scholars (including graduate students) new areas and angles of research. My ideal, of course, would be that we were consulted in terms of what needs to be examined to promote student success in composition, and that four-year scholars would build into their grants, and so on, ways to include two-year college teachers (such as buying out some of their teaching time). A few have. But if we are to increase Latino/a student access and success, we need to be realistic. The majority of Latinos/as enroll in two-year colleges. The majority of two-year college faculty does not have the professional support needed to investigate challenges and share successes. And the data suggest that despite our best efforts, we continue to fail some Latino/a students.

David: So you would, in fact, permit, four-year college folks to speak for you?

Sandra: I would happily give my sabbatical research to anyone who could influence scholarship or political legislation that would help our faculty increase the success and transfer rates of the 1.5 generation of Latinos/as — of all underrepresented students.

Jody: And there we are. We do and share what we can in our classrooms, in our states, and within our professional hierarchy. We, like two-year college teachers in every state, desperately want our California students — the majority of whom are Latinos/as — to succeed. And that takes articulation, money, time, and research networks that cross institutions. It takes coalitions for pedagogical and political advocacy to reverse the trends of low funding, transfer obstacles, and lack of support for underrepresented students. We cannot afford to have successful Latino/a transfers remain the exception to the rule. We just cannot afford it.

Notes

1. "The Two-Year College English Association (TYCA) identifies and articulates the best theories and practices, and pedagogy in teaching English in the two-year college through regional and national conventions and a journal, *Teaching English in the Two-Year College (TETYC)*" (NCTE 2006). The TYCA is a constituent organization of the National Council of Teachers of English (NCTE).
2. Nontraditional markers include delaying enrollment into college, working over thirty-five hours a week, having dependents other than a spouse, being financially independent, being single parents, and/or not having high school diplomas; 64 percent of those with three or more of these markers attend a community college. High-risk students have one of these markers or are first-generation students or academically underprepared; community college students are three to four times more likely to fit this profile than their four-year peers. Over half of our students are first generation; 60 percent attend part time, 34 percent spend at least eleven hours a week caring for dependents (Millward 2005, 6, 5).

Works Cited

Attinasi, Louis C. 1989. "Getting In: Mexican Americans' Perceptions of University Attendance and the Implications for Freshman Year Persistence." *Journal of Higher Education* 60:3: 247–77.

Beachler, Judy, Deborah Boroch, Robert Gabriner, Craig Hayward, Edward Karpp, Kenneth Meehan, and Andrea Serban. 2005. "A Summary of Key Issues Facing California Community Colleges Pertinent to the Strategic Planning Process." *Center for Student Success, Research and Planning Group for California Community Colleges.* (June): 1–10.

Cummins, Jim. 1990. "Empowering Minority Students: A Framework for Intervention." In *Facing Racism in Education*, ed. Nitza Hidalgo, Ceasar McDowell, and Emilie Siddle, 58–60. Cambridge, MA: Harvard Educational Review.

Delpit, Lisa D. 1988. "The Silenced Dialogue: Power and Pedagogy in Educating Other People's Children." *Harvard Educational Review* 58:3: 280–98.

Evelyn, Jamilah. 2003. "The 'Silent Killer' of Minority Enrollments." *Chronicle of Higher Education* 49:41 (June 20). Rpt. *The Chronicle of Higher Education: Government and Politics*, 1–7. http://chronicle.com/weekly/v49/i41/41a0l70l.htm (accessed June 21, 2005).

Hare-Mustin, Rachel T., and Jeanne Marecek. 1988. "The Meaning of Difference: Gender Theory, Postmodernism and Psychology." *American Psychologist* 43: 455–64.

Hayward, Gerald C., Denis P. Jones, Aims C. McGuinness, Jr., and Ailene Timar. 2004. "Ensuring Access with Quality to California's Community Colleges." Executive Summary. National Center for Public Policy and Higher Education. http://www.highereducation.org/reports/hewlett (accessed June 2005).

Hochiander, Gary, Anna C. Sikora, and Laura Horn. 2003. "Community College Students: Goals, Academic Preparation, and Outcomes." Postsecondary

Descriptive Anaylsis Report. National Center for Education Statistics (June). http://www.nces.ed.gov/pubs2003/2003164.pdf (accessed June 17, 2005).

hooks, bell. 1990. *Yearning: Race, Gender, and Cultural Politics*. Boston: South End Press.

Millward, Jody. 2005. "2005 TYCA Two-Year College Facts and Data Report." (September). http://www.ncte.org/library/files/Related_Groups/TYCA/TYCA _DataReport.pdf (accessed December 8, 2005).

Montano-Harmon, Maria. 1991. "Contrastive Rhetoric and Dialect." Presentation, Linguistic Research Minority Project, UC Santa Barbara, July.

National Council of Teachers of English. 2006. "Mission and Goals of TYCA." http://www.ncte.org/groups/tyca/about/110654.htm (accessed July 21, 2006).

Penrose, Ann M. 2002. "Academic Literacy Perceptions and Performance: Comparing First-Generation and Continuing-Generation College Students." *Research in the Teaching of English* 36:4: 437–61.

Rose, Mike. 1989. *Lives on the Boundary: The Struggles and Achievements of America's Underprepared*. New York: Penguin.

Saufley, Ronald W., et al. 1983. "The Struggles of Minority Students at Predominately White Institutions." In *Teaching Minority Students*, ed. James H. Cones, 40–49. San Francisco: Jossey-Bass.

Schrag, Peter. 2004. "California's First-Generation Students." *San Diego Union-Tribune* (May 6). Rpt. SignOnSandiego.com. http://www.signonsandiego.com /uniontrib/20050506/news_lzle6schrag.html (accessed June 5, 2005).

Dialects, Gender, and the Writing Class

Greg Shafer

In this article, Greg Shafer describes a first-year writing course focused on the social, cultural, and political dimensions of language, including language diversity, gendered discourse, and race. This course was designed to encourage students who speak a range of dialects to question their own beliefs — internalized from the broader society's language ideologies — about decontextualized notions of "correctness." Shafer discusses lessons and assignments that invite students to think about the relationships between language and identity, social structures of power, and the politics of resisting Standard English ideologies. Making language the subject of sustained critical inquiry, Shafer argues, fosters an appreciation for diverse experiences, complex ethical reasoning, and a more nuanced understanding of the rhetorical dimensions of language.

I never liked writing. I just don't do it well.

—A student's autobiography

From *Teaching English in the Two-Year College*, vol. 35, no. 2, 2007, pp. 169-78.

I've avoided this class for two years. I guess it's time to be reminded what a bad writer I was in my last writing class.

—A student's opening day statement

Comments like these are a common part of my first day of English composition. Invariably, in writing their opening day personal autobiographies, students unleash a torrent of reasons why writing scares them. Most, of course, focus on reasons that have little to do with the craft or complexities of great writing. There are concerns about commas and sentence structure, spelling, and semicolons. Others worry about their speech, suggesting that their home dialect is the reason for their inability to flourish in past language classes. Numerous students bemoan their use of "substandard" English, thinking that their ways with words create a deficit rather than a difference.

What emerges from too many of my students—and I think this is a concern for many other instructors—is a curious mixture of fear and ignorance about language in general and writing in particular. Despite the incredible range of registers they use in speaking with friends and college faculty—and their efficacy in adjusting their speech to the linguistic context—most students are convinced that they cannot write and that their use of language is deficient because they have not been taught enough proper English rules. Equally unfortunate is their belief that composition is the place where they will be taught the single, "correct" way to craft a paper, erasing years of bad habits and undisciplined excursions into creative nonsense. "I just mess around with poetry," wrote a student in writing about her past language experiences. "I guess it's time to get serious."

It was based on such comments—and the general mentality that radiates through them—that I chose to base my freshman composition class on correctness, dialects, and the complex world of language. More than anything, I thought it was essential that anachronistic myths about language be challenged and explored and that minority students be told that their dialects are not substandard or sloppy but simply a different form of discourse—one that is eminently appropriate in many contexts. I wanted to eliminate the angst and expose students to the myths of language that often make them feel that their ways with words are inferior, placing them in the role of pariah in class. Most important, I thought it was critical that students understand the social and political aspects of language, to see that all of us speak a dialect and that it is a part of who we are and says much about our view of society.

Linguist John Baugh suggests that the dynamics of language use in and out of the classroom are important in understanding race, power, and the perceptions students have of themselves: "While educators may recognize the vital role of Standard English to future success, the demands in out-of-school contexts may be quite different" (67). Baugh goes on to describe the dynamics of his life as a black child and the perception among his peers that kids who spoke Standard English were "usually called sissies or worse" (67). Those who chose to embrace the English of white teachers and students were "held in low regard and those students who rejected Black speech in favor of the standard were accused of being Uncle Toms" (68). Indeed, language is not simply about right and wrong—about correct and incorrect—and it is essential that our students comprehend the cultural significance of language and our approaches to teaching them language.

Such a class seems increasingly relevant. With questions of diversity and immigration forever swirling around our society—and with new movements to create "English-only" ballots in response to illegal immigrants—students need to appreciate the ideological aspects of language. They need to know that everyone speaks a dialect and that diversity is not only helpful but essential in navigating one's way through a world of linguistic enclaves and regional and social dialects. Women need to know that there is a venerated and growing school of scholars who study language and gender and suggest that language is often used to oppress them—that language is political. "Women remain outsiders, borrowers of the language," writes Dale Spender in her classic *Man Made Language* (50). In the same way, African Americans need to know that their dialects are rule-governed and poetic—and often used to establish solidarity and community—despite the ignominious legacy of treating African American Vernacular English (AAVE) as a sloppy alternative to Standard English.

Introducing the Unit on Language

I begin the class with a short examination of the political and social components that pervade every aspect of language. We begin with a look at the way different discourse communities use the language and the values placed on those styles. Because it is so close to their personal experience, I like to begin by presenting the students with a series of headlines from popular magazines, asking them to identify the kind of person the headline is targeting and what this says about the language different groups use. For instance, in my last class, I gave them the following list of phrases from men's and women's magazines and asked them to identify the discourse community based on the kind of language used:

"Gorgeous Eye Looks"

"So-pretty Summer clothes"

"What Are You Dying to Know About?"

"Laugh at Danger"

"Lose Your Gut"

After presenting the class with the list, I asked them simply to place the phrase with the correct gender and discourse community. Is it addressed to men or women? Boy or girl? Is this designed for a specific economic class? Race? How is language intertwined in solidarity between certain groups of people? How is the language of women distinctive from that targeting men?

In virtually every case, students are able to tell me that the first three phrases were placed in a women's magazine like *Cosmopolitan*, *Redbook*, or *Better Homes and Gardens* and that the last two were part of *Men's Health*, *Maxim*, or another male-oriented periodical. "What can we learn about language by categorizing these phrases?" I ask them. "Is language not only about right and wrong but also about identity? Do we use a particular discourse as part of personal pride and cultural autonomy? Is language a part of who we are?"

Such questions propel the class into a better appreciation of how language functions in their lives and how critical it is to their self-perception. It also reveals disquieting questions about how language is not only created by us but also used to shape and limit who we are by gender and other classifications. "I guess I never realized how childish the language is that women's magazines use," said Sally, a student in my class. "It seems to make us infantile when we want to be taken seriously."

Such comments lead us into a discussion of past scholarship on language and women. I like to introduce them to Betty Friedan's classic *The Feminine Mystique* and her premise that language was once used to limit and shape an entire population of women. In this case, the class does not have to read the entire book to appreciate the essence of Friedan's powerful contentions concerning women and media discourse. Instead of asking them to read the entire work, I usually mix quotations from and about the work with commentary on the time. Sheila Tobias's *Faces of Feminism* captures much of the book's themes when she argues that "Friedan was able to trace a general shift in society's view of woman from active participant in all aspects of life to specialist in the home" (66). This "feminine mystique," as Friedan described it, was "an artificial construct made up by manufacturers, in cooperation with advertisers and the media, to sell to the American public an ideal woman constantly available for shopping" (Tobias 66). In the end, Tobias suggests that "Friedan concluded, the feminine mystique was the result of a conspiracy" (66).

Examining magazines aimed at women allows students to ruminate on the question of language, gender, and power. It permits them to consider language from a critic's point of view, reflecting on the words used to appeal to women and the language that tends to define female discourse. It invites them to contemplate theories of language as a political instrument. It helps them to see that language is never a neutral medium but a construct that seems to be orchestrated by men or other groups that wield influence. I include quotations from Dale Spender's classic *Man Made Language* and her argument that language has long been a way to keep women in the position of subjugation because symbols and words are controlled by men. Spender uses the example of *motherhood* to show how women have been given certain values through language and the words that are venerated. Motherhood, writes Spender, is considered the zenith of one's life as a woman, but only because men have carefully crafted the way the word is perceived in society.

"The society in which many of us have been reared has a legitimated meaning for *motherhood* which means feminine fulfillment, which represents something beautiful, that leaves women consumed and replete with joy" (54), argues Spender. But what if women don't want such a word—and its concomitant set of values—to represent the apogee of their lives? What if words like *profession*, *vocation*, *education*, and *success* were words that women wanted to embrace as central to their existence? What if women do not want to be defined by a word like *mother*? Spender suggests that language shapes women to be mothers, and to pursue certain avocations that undermine serious careers. Women remain silent and muted, unable to break the long chain of male-dominated language. Again, I like to provide a synopsis of Spender's ideas, mingle them with Friedan's, and include quotations like the following:

> It is through the silence of women that male knowledge of motherhood—and of numerous other events—goes unchallenged. The male version of reality can be perpetuated, and even strengthened, because it remains unquestioned. (Spender 57)

Looking at magazines and listening to the lyrics on CDs also allows students to survey the sprawling array of divergent dialects and registers that are used to attract a certain audience. Within a few minutes of our discussion, we begin to recognize the importance of context in using language. "If I want to communicate with someone, I have to know what language is appropriate for that situation, for that setting," I said after considering a magazine written for African Americans. "If I don't speak their language, I am not part of their group and am considered an outsider."

From magazines, I like to give students the following quotation from actor and activist Ossie Davis, who has written provocatively about the use of language to perpetuate a racist agenda. In his essay "The Language of Racism," Davis argues, "The English language is my enemy. It is one of the primary carriers of racism from one person to another" (73). How, I ask my students, can language be used to limit certain language users and how can it make success and even society unfair? Is school and its emphasis on a Standard English unfair to speakers of minority dialects? How do we make claims to being a democratic classroom and still tell African Americans their dialect is substandard or sloppy?

Before we devote too much time to an answer, I include the essay from Geneva Smitherman's book *Talkin that Talk*. Especially edifying about this work is Smitherman's deft and comprehensible examination of AAVE and her clear explanation of how this dialect is rule-governed and as sensible and erudite as any form of communicating. Many students come to our classes with the notion that there is a single way to communicate and that English is a place where that one discourse is practiced and refined. They are incredulous when they are introduced to Smitherman's quotation concerning dialect use and the English language:

> Ebonics is emphatically not broken English, nor sloppy speech. Nor is it merely "slang." Nor is it some bizarre form of language spoken by baggy-pants-wearing Black youth. Ebonics is a set of communication patterns and practices resulting from African appropriation and transformation of a foreign tongue during the African Holocaust. (19)

Smitherman's words tend to galvanize the class and induce provocative questions about the language that is most important for our society and the place of school in educating students in communication. Rather than approaching English as a prescriptive set of monolithic rules that must be learned before one is considered educated, students begin to appreciate the complicated and forever political aspects of language. Further, they begin to appreciate the importance of context to expression. I often juxtapose Smitherman's quotation with a quotation from David Bartholomae's "Inventing the University," where Bartholomae suggests that the purpose of the composition class is to teach students to mimic the academy and write like their educated—and usually white—professors. "They must learn to speak our language" (273), he argues early in his essay. Such suggestions, we agreed as a class, would limit the kinds of expressions that are used and accepted. Would it also limit the vision we all have of what good communication is? So what should we be doing in class and what kind of English is most important for our growing and diverging world?

An additional point to make is the presence of dialects and the fact that we all speak one. Equally important is for students to appreciate the fact that visions of dialects reflect visions of the people who speak them. I often ask students to consider the various regional and social dialects they hear and comment on their impressions. Students tend to react to southern voices with responses that echo their impressions of people who live in the southern part of the United States. Some see them as earthy, honest, and homespun, while others use words like racist, redneck, and uneducated. Much of the same is true when my students are exposed to dialects from the Northeast or from New York. "We all have opinions of dialects based on the people who speak them," summarized one of my students.

In examining dialects and our subjective opinions of their worth, students quickly realize that language is a very political act—that it cannot be extricated from visions of what good English is and how it should be enforced on people who do not speak as those in power think they should. "It just never occurred to me that using a double negative or omitting parts of speech could ever be correct," said one student. "But I guess correctness depends on the audience and the situation." Argued another student, "when you correct someone's speech, you're telling them that their culture and history is wrong. That doesn't seem right."

Another illuminating essay that I often share with students is Signithia Fordham's article on how students frequently use language as a way to combat a linguistic system that they see as unfair and undemocratic. According to Fordham, in her essay "Dissin' the Standards: Ebonics as Guerilla Warfare at Capital High," students use Standard English in the classroom but only in designed ways and with the clear knowledge that it is part of an alien dialect—one that is not part of their heritage. Outside of class, adds Fordham, the students use the dialect of their friends and a discourse community that is far removed from the classroom. In short, argues Fordham, students are very aware of the politics of language and use it as a way to maintain their cultural and racial identity while still succeeding in school. "Dissin' the standard is at the core of the guerilla warfare at the school and is fundamentally revealed in both the student's refusal to discontinue their use of Ebonics as the language of conversation while at or in school and their wholesale avoidance of the standard dialect in most other contexts" (272), writes Fordham. Later, she adds, "language is a, or perhaps the basic medium of group identity, welding disparate individuals into a closely knit, bonded social group" (274).

The linguistic phenomenon is personified in the experiences of linguist John Baugh, who describes his own childhood as a constant balancing act between the Standard English that he knew he must learn and the AAVE that was part of his community. Baugh's dilemma helps depict the authentic, real-life dilemmas of language users and helps move students beyond simplistic ideas of language as being monolithic and free of ideology. Early in his book *Beyond Ebonics*, Baugh asks:

> What then was I to do? Should I use Standard English to the exclusion of African American vernacular speech norms, and risk ridicule or social rejection from my black peers? Or should I resist my parent's Standard English advocacy and suffer the domestic consequences of open linguistic rebellion at home? (6)

Such questions—and the entire idea of "linguistic rebellion"—help galvanize the class around the notion of language as a complex political and cultural issue. As students begin to see the way language acts to validate and alienate, they begin to appreciate the inexorable place of ideology and power in the linguistic life of each user. Success and identity are inextricably mingled with our language choices and our personal self-worth is forever on display in how and with whom we talk.

Of course, my class is also assiduous in addressing the question of standards in a world that often has little patience for or knowledge of other dialects. After discussing the uses of language to create identity and solidarity, we devote time to the conflict between family language and the world of business. Often I share an essay by educator Ernie Smith, who chronicles his tortuous struggle to come to terms with his AAVE and the way the world of power used it against him. For Smith, it was essential that he stay "real" in terms of his identity and dialect while also navigating his way through a world that expected linguistic versatility. What is perhaps most moving about Smith's essay is his journey from being punished for his Ebonics—and his life as a "player and hustler"—to expanding his language to become a successful graduate student and antiwar speaker. Along the way, Smith learns that his vernacular is essential to who he is, while also learning that it is only one of many registers we use in a complex linguistic world. "Linguistic competence" gets Smith through the world of "slum hustling," and later is polished to make him a successful teacher.

In discussing Ernie Smith, my students are quick to see the importance of context for language use. It was wrong for teachers to label Smith a "verbal cripple" (17), but it underscores the importance of context, linguistic flexibility, and the living, dynamic character of language. Discourse changes with the context and those who are to be effective must adjust and adapt, blending their registers to stay in rhythm with their participants. "I don't speak to friends in the same way that I speak to my teachers or boss and I don't speak to my mom like I do to my girlfriend," said Brad. "Language classes need to look at the many ways we use English to be successful and the attitudes people have toward different discourses."

Topics for Research

Research papers for my language class revolved around various conundrums that had been broached as we explored dialects, gender, and the dynamic world of language. Some students wanted to delve into the issue of education and language correctness, while others investigated the rules of AAVE. And then there were others who sought to answer vexing questions about the impact of language on the way we are shaped as men and women. One of the most explosive papers written in my class looked at the world of men and language, arguing that English used in popular culture tends to make men into the kind of slobs and "dudes" that we see often in pop culture. "The language we read and hear in popular culture," wrote Bart, a student in my class, helps shape the male identity to be an underachiever and a "slacker." In the same way that girls are not supposed to sound tough or aggressive, men are never supposed to sound smart or scholarly. It tends to make their discourse community ostracize them as "effeminate," Bart argued in his introduction.

In writing this fascinating essay, Bart looked at magazines and popular media, highlighting the way men use language and their discourse practices with women and other men. "In commercials and in magazines, men are portrayed as 'boys' or as adults who just can't grow-up or have intellectual interests. In other cases," Bart argued, "they are aggressive in both their actions and the language that they use." As an example, Bart looked at some of the popular men's magazines that, as a rule, tend to feature a combination of scantily dressed women and advice on sex and body building. In doing his research, Bart found that language in these magazines was distinctive and emblematic of a macho, sometimes misogynistic perspective. Bart looked at various *Maxim* magazines, which feature soft pornography with articles on looking good and having a better sex life. It is an incredibly popular new genre and has spawned other magazines that present a provocatively dressed woman on the cover and various invitations to adventure into the magazine itself to gawk at women and get tips on performing better in athletics and in the conquest of a woman.

Bart referred to the language and made associations to the sexist attitudes that many of his friends have. "In the May 2006 edition of *Maxim*," he explained, the cover had a feature on "Meat Beat Manifesto" and gave a list of phrases for masturbation. The June edition of *Maxim*, he continued, had features on "The Most Badass Car You've Never Heard of," and another on "They'll Make You Puke." In the July edition, there were articles on "Beach Pickup Lines," and "Poker Mouth."

As a collection, Bart concluded in writing his essay, it is easy to see how different—how crass and bombastic—the language is. Nobody would ever use such crude language in a women's magazine because language helps define who we are as men and women. The language in women's magazines is softer, less forceful, more tentative, and even apologetic. Bart also discussed the implication of this language, the tendency of men to be more violent and aggressive. "Is this a part of our natural development as men or is it conditioned by the language we are subjected to?" he asked in one of the most provocative parts of his paper.

"What if I said that the sunset was 'lovely'?" he asked in a paragraph of his paper. He answered the question by suggesting that his girlfriend would think he was more sensitive while his guy friends would wonder if he were gay. Bart's paper looked at the diction of gender and the implications for society. He referred to the names given to men and women, reminding the class that girls are named after flowers (Rose, Violet, Daisy) while men are named after warriors and leaders such as *Neil*, which means "champion," *Raymond*, which means "wise protection," and *Rex*, which simply means "king." His paper concluded with pungent questions about language and the impact it has on our perceptions.

A second paper examined the language of AAVE and its appropriation into the mainstream culture. Greg, an African American man, discussed how words that originate in the African American community are becoming mainstream as it becomes increasingly fashionable to incorporate such phrases and words into our pop culture. "I am troubled," he wrote, "when I hear two White kids calling each other 'dog' and asking each other 'what up?'" Greg argued that such phrases are a part of AAVE—its diction and syntax—and are simply being used as a language of rebellion. "Kids today want to break away from their White parents and the safe suburbs they live in, so they decide to talk like a Black man, never knowing its history or what this does to the image of Black people."

Greg's paper became especially interesting as he argued that the deletion of the verb in "what up" is used as a rule-governed part of AAVE, but when used by white kids, it is seen as just a nonstandard form—a weapon of revolt. "This prevents people from seeing my dialect as a legitimate language," he continued to argue. "It trivializes the validity of this dialect and the people who use it as part of a race." Greg went on to discuss some of the words and phrases used by African Americans and the way these words have been adopted by pop culture as a way to create a rebellious counter culture. "I hear white kids using double negative and deleting the verbs and I know it's coming from their desire to be like the rapper they listen to. It's their way of rebelling."

But, as Greg argued, AAVE is not the domain of rappers and white kids who want to seem subversive. "They are taking our language—its rules and diction—and making it into some kind of lower, more crass, less disciplined language. Our dialect is being stolen by pop culture."

Greg also included words that have become part of the young Americans diction, such as *bling-bling* and *dog*. "These words have a history," he argued. "If you can insult someone, it signifies a level of friendship, of trust. I think this gets lost in the large scale marketing of my dialect." Greg mentioned the use of pronouns. "When my Momma says 'they should do it theyselves' she is speaking from a historical tradition. It's the same when she uses a double negative or the use of the same verb to signify past and present tense as in 'The car pass me by twice last week.' If we are to respect this distinctive language, we need to prevent it from becoming the language of the MTV dude," Greg remarked at the end of his paper.

Greg's look at the history of AAVE included a short discussion of how African Americans came to this country speaking a variety of different languages and cleverly used special words and phrases to communicate surreptitiously with their fellow slaves. Slaves who arrived from West Africa gradually assimilated their languages to their masters, creating a pidgin and eventually, as it spread to more slaves, a creole. Greg quoted Smitherman in explaining the deletion of *to be* among African Americans, telling us that "West African languages allow for the construction of sentences without a form of the verb *to be*" (5). "Thus," Smitherman continues, "we get a typical African-English pidgin sentence such as 'He tell me he God,' as spoken by Tituba, a slave from the British West Indies, and recorded by Justice Hathorne at the Salem witch trial in 1692" (*Talkin and Testifyin* 5).

In short, then, Greg's argument was that AAVE has a history that is grounded in oppression and the struggle for solidarity and freedom. It should not be appropriated or trivialized by pop culture and fashioned to appear to be the language of crime, white teens, or media giants. "In this way," he argued, "we lose the historic significance, since these people are using it without reverence or understanding. They are imposters."

Such papers engendered incredibly sophisticated discussions about language use and the cultural and political ways it is used and appropriated for various agendas. It helped us transcend the monolithic statements about "good English" that often are bandied about by politicians and language critics. It helped my students to see that language is never as simple as the rules of a book and has much to do with who we are and how we see ourselves. In many ways, our study of language helped us to transcend the ordinary and trite so students could make moral and intellectual decisions about their own lives. It made them active, reflective thinkers. As teachers, we must never forget that it was only four decades ago that many who taught English thought that linguistic difference was tantamount to linguistic inferiority. Perhaps it is also important to recall the 1974 policy statement by the Conference on College Composition and Communication, arguing that students have a right to their own language and that "the claim that anyone's dialect is unacceptable amounts to an attempt of one social group to exert its dominance over another" (CCCC).

Maxine Green suggests that educators must "engage their students in the process of demystification as they must work with them to interpret what is presently happening with regard to education and to school" (108). This notion of moving beyond what is given to us as "correct" is what makes a study of language so invaluable. Students are able to transcend monolithic platitudes about correctness and see language for its dynamic and political self. In the process, they are able to examine themselves and their place in their linguistic world.

Works Cited

Bartholomae, David. "Inventing the University." *Perspectives on Literacy*. Ed. Eugene R. Kintgen, Barry M. Kroll, and Mike Rose. Carbondale: Southern Illinois UP, 1988. 273–85.

Baugh, John. *Beyond Ebonics*. New York: Oxford UP, 2000.

———. *Out of the Mouths of Slaves.* Austin: U of Texas P, 1999.

Conference on College Composition and Communication. "Students' Right to Their Own Language." Special Issue of *College Composition and Communication.* 25.3 (Fall 1974), 1–32.

Davis, Ossie. "The Language of Racism." *Language in America.* Ed. Neil Postman, Charles Weingartner, and Terence P. Moran. New York: Bobbs Merrill, 1969. 73–82.

Fordham, Signithia. "Dissin the Standards: Ebonics as Guerilla Warfare at Capital High." *Anthropology and Education Quarterly* Spring (1999): 272–93.

Friedan, Betty. *The Feminine Mystique.* New York: Norton, 1997.

Green, Maxine. *Landscapes of Learning.* New York: Teachers College P, 1978.

Smith, Ernie. "Ebonics: A Case History." *The Skin That We Speak.* Ed. Lisa Delpit and Joanne Kilgour Dowdy. New York: The New Press, 2002. 15–30.

Smitherman, Geneva. *Talkin That Talk.* New York: Routledge, 2000.

———. *Talkin and Testifyin.* Boston: Houghton Mifflin, 1977.

Spender, Dale. *Man Made Language.* Boston: Routledge, 1981.

Tobias, Sheila. *Faces of Feminism.* Boulder, CO: Westview, 1997.

The Heterogeneous Second-Language Population in US Colleges and the Impact on Writing Program Design

Kristen di Gennaro

The community college student population includes many second-language (L2) English learners, ranging from students who have recently arrived in the United States to those who have resided here for most of their lives (the latter are also referred to as Generation 1.5). Some researchers and practitioners have proposed subdividing L2 students into distinct groups and offering different writing courses for each. This article reviews theoretical frameworks for classifying L2 learners and summarizes empirical research comparing learners' writing ability and instructional needs, with a particular focus on Generation 1.5. Despite the diversity among L2 students, instructors may find common ground in terms of students' academic writing needs.

To effectively address the needs of second language (L2) learners in college writing courses, many postsecondary institutions, especially those located in cities with high concentrations of immigrants, offer college-level courses for L2 students. Such courses include noncredit

From *Teaching English in the Two-Year College*, vol. 40, no. 1, 2012, pp. 57-67.

English language courses in an intensive English program, developmental or basic writing courses created with native speakers in mind, and credit-bearing first-year and advanced composition courses designed specifically for L2 students. The existence of a variety of course options for L2 writers signals recognition by writing programs of the varying needs that L2 students may have; determining which courses are most suitable for certain L2 learners, however, remains a complex issue. In fact, in recent years several practitioners working with L2 writers have called into question the custom of treating all L2 learners as one group, defined primarily by their non-native speaker status. Indeed, anyone who has taught classes with large numbers of L2 learners can attest to the great deal of heterogeneity within the L2 population in US writing programs. For example, students in composition courses may range from immigrants educated primarily in the United States to international students who have achieved advanced degrees in other countries and languages, as well as to students who have learned English for academic purposes in former British colonies.

Given the diversity of L2 learners in US postsecondary education, writing program administrators are currently grappling with several pressing questions:

> Should L2 US high school graduates be placed into special ESL courses?
>
> Can an intensive English program, with courses designed to address international students, address the needs of US high school graduates?
>
> Does the writing ability of L2 high school graduates resemble that of L2 students arriving from overseas?
>
> Does the diversity within the L2 population potentially warrant separate courses for different types of L2 learners?

Based on these concerns, some practitioners have moved toward the creation of separate courses for different types of L2 learners, while others point to L2 learners' similarities as reasons for not dividing them into subpopulations. For example, in "Creating an Inter-Departmental Course for Generation 1.5 ESL Writers," Christine Holten details the successful creation of a course especially for resident ESL writers at the University of California, Los Angeles. In contrast, Paul Kei Matsuda's chapter "International and U.S. Resident ESL Writers Cannot Be Taught in the Same Class" included in a book concerning myths in second language instruction, cautions that given the difficulties identifying and placing resident ESL writers, the best solution may be to rethink all second language writing courses to better address the needs of all multilingual writers. While a body of research investigating differences among various types of L2 learners has begun to emerge (see Harklau, Losey, and Siegal; Roberge, Siegal, and Harklau), there remains a very limited amount of empirical evidence supporting the need for separate courses for different L2 learners.

In this discussion piece, I begin by reviewing various terms and descriptions that have been used extensively in the literature to categorize different types of L2 learners. I then summarize several studies that have empirically investigated differences within the L2 population, based (somewhat loosely) on these frameworks. I conclude by noting the need for more empirical research supporting—or refuting—the subdivisions of L2 learners into separate writing courses and suggestions as to what writing program administrators can do in the meantime.

Review of Theoretical Frameworks

EFL and ESL Learners

Perhaps the most prominent distinction, historically, between different types of L2 learners has been that between English as a Foreign Language (EFL) and English as a Second Language (ESL), with the former term typically used to describe the teaching and learning of English in a country where English does not have recognized status outside the classroom, and the latter used in countries where English is one of the primary languages of the nation. Though often used interchangeably within applied linguistics today, some researchers have rejected the labels EFL and ESL as categorical distinctions for learners of English, given the lack of empirical evidence supporting such a distinction, as well as the inadequacies of a binary framework for describing a complex sociolinguistic situation. For example, to replace the EFL-ESL distinction, Braj Kachru ("World English") has proposed the tripartite model of Inner Circle, Outer Circle, and Expanding Circle speakers, corresponding roughly with native speakers, ESL speakers, and EFL speakers, respectively. P. Bhaskaran Nayar, in "ESL/EFL Dichotomy Today," believes that the implicit differences between the EFL speakers in Kachru's Outer Circle and the ESL speakers in an immigrant-oriented monoglossic society are large enough to warrant very different labels, and thus proposed adding the term *English as an associate language* alongside EFL and ESL, yet such terminology has not been widely adopted by the applied linguistics community. In short, the terms EFL and ESL, as they were originally used, drew attention to the different environments in which English is taught and learned, and thereby suggested that EFL and ESL learning differs somehow. While many applied linguists currently downplay the importance of such differences by using the terms EFL and ESL interchangeably, others have attempted to highlight the differences by proposing alternative dichotomies or distinctions.

Elective and Circumstantial Bilinguals

Another well-known framework for distinguishing L2 learning environments and, therefore, L2 learners is that proposed by Guadalupe Valdés in "Bilingual Minorities and Language Issues in Writing." Valdés views the distinction between different types of L2 learners from the perspective of societal bilingualism. Specifically, Valdés first distinguishes between *elective* and *circumstantial* bilinguals. Elective bilinguals are those who, after having spent most of their lives in a society where their first languages (L1s) have majority status, have opted to learn an L2 through immersion into an L2 society. Circumstantial bilinguals, conversely, are those who have been forced into the L2 environment as immigrants, refugees, or citizens of postcolonial states, all cases where their L1s may lack prestige. Circumstantial bilinguals are further subdivided into *incipient* bilinguals, who are still in the early stages of L2 acquisition, and *functional* bilinguals, who have had a great deal of experience with the L2 yet remain clearly non-native. According to Valdés, incipient bilinguals will probably benefit from continued L2 instruction and exposure, while functional bilinguals may have reached a plateau in their L2 learning, rendering some types of language instruction less effective for them.

Eye and Ear Learners

Focusing on L2 learners in the United States in particular, Joy Reid uses the terms *eye learners* and *ear learners* to highlight the language strengths and weaknesses of international students and US resident students. Eye learners, according to Reid, are international students who have chosen to attend postsecondary schools in the United States. Having completed secondary education in their home countries, they are literate in their L1s, and their learning of English has been primarily through book learning (i.e., eye learning) in an EFL classroom setting. As a result, they tend to perform better in tasks focusing on reading and grammatical rule learning than on listening and speaking tasks or on other tasks requiring extended production. Ear learners, by Reid's framework, are those who tend to be orally fluent in their L1s, but who have not reached advanced levels of L1 literacy. Given their acquisition of English through immersion in US society, ear learners tend to perform better on oral and aural tasks than on written tasks, and they form grammatical and vocabulary rules based on how they have heard the L2 spoken.

International L2 and Generation 1.5 Learners

Most recently, several researchers have focused on the differences between students who attend US colleges and universities after having completed secondary education in their home countries and students who enter US colleges as long-term US residents, often having arrived as immigrants while still in kindergarten through twelfth grade. The former are considered international L2 learners of English who may have studied English for many years, but in their home countries in an EFL environment. Their exposure to English may have been limited, as their instruction was predominantly in their L1s. The latter type of students, who have received much, or even most, of their precollege education in English, have come to be known as *Generation 1.5 learners* (using terminology from immigration scholars Rubén Rumbaut and Kenji Ima's study "The Adaptation of Southeast Asian Refugee Youth"), given their similarities with both first- and second-generation immigrants. Unlike international L2 learners, Generation 1.5 learners have acquired most of their English not through EFL classes but from living in an English-speaking environment. Consequently, Generation 1.5 students have been exposed to a greater quantity of English than international L2 learners, as the instruction they received in US schools was in English.

In sum, several frameworks noting distinctions within the L2 population have been proposed (e.g., Kachru; Nayar; Reid; Valdés), suggesting that certain background characteristics may influence L2 learners' language abilities and writing performance and, therefore, the types of instruction that would benefit them most. Many of the theoretical frameworks regarding specific differences among L2 learner groups have been based on anecdotal, impressionistic evidence, yet a limited but growing body of research has emerged (see below) in which differences across L2 learners with varying background characteristics have been investigated empirically. In the following section, I summarize several of these studies, noting their main findings and implications for practitioners and writing program administrators.

Empirical Studies Comparing Different Types of L2 Learners

One of the earliest studies to examine differences across groups of L2 learners with different backgrounds is Susan Bosher and Jenise Rowekamp's investigation of the relationship between certain factors and L2 students' success in US higher education. The fifty-six L2 learners in their study were divided into two groups: those who had completed high school in their home countries and those who had completed high school in the United States. The researchers then collected data regarding participants' length of residence in the US, their years of schooling in the US versus in their home countries, and their scores on three sections of the Michigan English Language Assessment Battery (MELAB), a standardized test commonly used to assess L2 learners. Results showed that participants who had completed high school in their home countries scored significantly higher on the objectively scored (i.e., written multiple choice) section of the MELAB, while those who had completed high school in the US scored significantly higher on the listening section. Interestingly, there were no significant differences in composition scores across the two groups. In a comparison of participants' GPAs after their first, second, and third years of college, the number of years of schooling in the home country produced high positive correlations with participants' first-, second-, and third-year GPAs. Conversely, years of schooling and length of residence in the US produced significant negative correlations with participants' college GPAs. Such findings suggest that L2 learners who have received the majority of their formal education in their home countries may perform better in US higher education than those L2 learners who have been educated primarily in US schools.

In a similar study, Dennis Muchinsky and Nancy Tangren also compared participants' scores on Michigan language tests and included a comparison of performance on a thirty-minute composition component as well. As with Bosher and Rowekamp's study, standardized test results favored the US high school graduates only in the listening section of the test. Analyses of participants' compositions revealed that the essays by the US-educated students were longer than the other group's essays, but the internationally educated group had the highest overall essay scores. These findings seem to support the view that Generation 1.5 learners are typically fluent language users, but not necessarily well prepared in the language of academic writing.

Adopting Valdés's model of incipient versus functional bilinguals, Jan Frodesen and Nancy Starna examined linguistic features in L2 learners' writing in an attempt to distinguish students at different stages in their acquisition of L2 proficiency. Specifically, they examined detailed linguistic profiles of two students who had completed at least part of their high school education in the United States before going on to college. One student's writing displayed few, yet systematic, errors at the sentence level similar to those still made by advanced L2 learners, such as incorrect verb tenses, verb forms, word forms, and use of idiomatic expressions. Given the systematicity of this student's linguistic errors, Frodesen and Starna concluded that he was a functional bilingual who would benefit from a mainstream English composition course. The other student's writing displayed a wide variety of errors, such as word forms, verb forms, verb tenses, subject-verb agreement, articles, word choice, noun plurals, and sentence structure problems. Based on this range of errors, especially the errors with word choice and sentence structure, Frodesen and Starna considered this second student to be an incipient bilingual who would benefit from taking ESL courses in college. Though not highlighted in their study, it is worth noting that the student whose writing displayed fewer, yet systematic, errors had started attending high school in the US at the age of sixteen after having studied EFL in his home country, while the student whose writing included many error types had attended school in the US since 8th grade at the age of thirteen after virtually no EFL preparation in his home country. In other words, an earlier age of arrival did not seem to place the second student at an advantage when it came to college academic writing ability, suggesting that educational background may have been the primary difference between the two learners in this study.

Most recently, several dissertations have appeared in which the writing ability of various L2 learner populations has been rigorously and extensively investigated. Elisabeth I. Levi, for example, carefully analyzed linguistic and rhetorical features in the writing of 140 participants constituting three different groups: those educated fully in their home countries, L2 students who had graduated from US high schools, and monolingual English basic writers. Writing samples from all participants were analyzed in three categories: grammatical features, lexical features, and overall writing quality. Grammatical, lexical, and rhetorical errors were compared across groups using logistic regression, and MANOVA (multivariate analysis of variance) was used to compare writing scores. Findings were mixed, showing that in some respects the US-educated L2 learners' writing ability was more similar to that of their monolingual US peers, yet in other respects it was more similar to that of the L2 group educated overseas. Specifically, results showed that the US-educated L2 group differed more from the overseas-educated L2 group than from the monolingual English basic writers in terms of most types of morphosyntactic and rhetorical features coded, yet they differed more from the monolingual writers than from the overseas group in terms of the numbers of morphosyntactic errors and lexical usage. Based on her results, Levi concluded that US-educated L2 learners' writing is sufficiently distinct from the other two groups' writing, and thus such learners might benefit from courses designed with their specific needs in mind.

Following Levi, Stephen Martin Doolan's dissertation also compared Generation 1.5 learners' writing to that of international L2 learners and native speakers of English, but he added a dimension of writing level. Doolan compared students at the developmental and first-year composition levels. Doolan analyzed participants' writing for specific morphosyntactic and textual features in an attempt to determine to what extent Generation 1.5 learners' writing is distinct from that of traditional L2 and native English-speaking writers. As in Levi's study, findings were mixed, indicating significant differences between Generation 1.5 and L2 students on holistic writing scores and various types of errors at both proficiency levels examined. Significant differences were also found between Generation 1.5 and native-speaker texts at the developmental level. Such results led Doolan to conclude that Generation 1.5 writers resemble native speaker writers more so than has been previously reported in the literature, and thus that Generation 1.5 students may be best served by placement into mainstream, rather than ESL, writing courses.

Employing procedures from corpus linguistics and discourse analysis, Mary Connerty examined both quantitative and qualitative data comparing groups of Generation 1.5, international L2, and native speakers of English. Focusing on learners' representation of self, Connerty found that the Generation 1.5 learners tended to rely more on personal experiences as sources for content in their writing than either the international L2 or native English-speaking groups did. Connerty also noted, however, that her native speaker group overused certain nonacademic elements in their writing, such as first-person singular and second-person pronouns, more so than the other two groups. Such a finding serves as a reminder that native speakers, too, are still learners of academic writing. In fact, Connerty concluded by suggesting that courses for Generation 1.5 learners include explicit instruction of rhetorical patterns and register differences thereby raising students' awareness of how they project themselves in their writing while also providing them with more choices for self-presentation.

In my own dissertation (di Gennaro), I adopted a mixed-methods research design examining international L2 and Generation 1.5 learners' writing from both quantitative and qualitative perspectives. Unlike other quantitative studies, where researchers used descriptive or inferential statistics to compare holistic essay scores or frequencies of individual linguistic features (such as morphosyntactic errors and personal pronouns), I employed a multifacet Rasch measurement model to compare participants' scores in five different components of writing, as well as their overall writing performance. More specifically, participants' writing was evaluated according to five rubrics, each describing a different aspect of writing ability: grammatical, cohesive, rhetorical, sociopragmatic, and content control. Multifacet Rasch measurement then recalibrated raters' raw scores for each participant onto an equal-interval scale, which allowed for more meaningful comparisons both within and across the two groups of participants as group averages, individual participants' scores, and component difficulty levels all had the same frame of reference. Findings from the quantitative stage revealed that, as a group, the international L2 learners performed better than the Generation 1.5 learners, and that, separately, the two groups were shown to have opposing strengths and weaknesses in two components of writing ability: the international learners performed best in grammatical control yet poorly in sociopragmatic control, while Generation 1.5 learners performed best in sociopragmatic control yet poorly in grammatical control.

The quantitative analyses also made it possible to identify ten participants (five from each group of learners) with equivalent overall writing ability, based on their converted scores. Writing samples from these ten participants were then analyzed qualitatively, with particular focus on the forms and meanings associated with participants' grammatical errors and the contexts surrounding participants' use of certain sociopragmatic markers. Findings from this stage suggested that the Generation 1.5 group's grammatical errors reflected a lack of awareness of the type of grammar preferred in academic writing contexts, and that the international L2 group's use of sociopragmatic markers reflected a preference for personal opinions and non-academic sources (e.g., proverbs, famous people's opinions) for support. In other words, both groups of learners revealed difficulties within different aspects of academic writing, suggesting that both groups, despite their different backgrounds, could benefit from instruction focused on the academic nature of writing in post-secondary institutions.

Discussion and Conclusion

Paradoxically, it seems that as more results from empirical studies investigating differences across Generation 1.5 and international L2 learners emerge, it becomes increasingly difficult to state with precision the types of writing difficulties each group will exhibit. For example, while Bosher and Rowekamp's analysis detected no significant differences in holistic composition scores across the two populations, the international L2 learners in Muchinsky and Tangren's study had the highest overall essay scores. The apparent contradictory findings from these two studies suggest that holistic essay scores alone may not be sufficient for detecting differences across the two groups' writing ability. In Frodensen and Starna's in-depth analysis of learners' writing, the writing produced by their late-arriving L2 learner exhibited few yet systematic errors, while the writing produced by their early-arriving L2 learner exhibited numerous and wide-ranging error types. Such findings draw attention to the fact that long-term US resident L2 learners may struggle with grammatical correctness in their writing as much as, if not more than, international L2 learners.

In Levi's statistical analyses of learners' grammatical, lexical, and rhetorical errors, both US-educated (Generation 1.5) and overseas-educated (international L2) learners committed numerous errors in their writing, yet the types of errors displayed by each group differed significantly. Doolan, as well, found significant differences between the two groups of learners according to the types of errors included in their writing. Finally, while Connerty found that her Generation 1.5 learners relied more on personal experience in their writing than did international L2 learners, my qualitative analysis of learners' use of sociopragmatic markers revealed the opposite (see di Gennaro).

In sum, the growing empirical evidence comparing Generation 1.5 and international L2 learners' writing depicts a much more complex picture than that suggested by the theoretical frameworks described above. While contradictory findings are certainly due, in part, to differences in the investigative methods employed, as well as parameters used for defining Generation 1.5 and international L2 learners, such findings also highlight drawbacks to attempting to dichotomize different types of L2 learners in an effort to confirm or refute certain theoretical frameworks. Furthermore, despite both theoretical and empirical studies, definitive answers to the many questions that writing program administrators and practitioners currently face remain elusive. For example, while Levi believes her findings support the creation of separate courses for Generation 1.5 learners, Doolan suggests that Generation 1.5 learners are similar enough to native speakers that they would benefit from mainstream writing courses. Throughout the course of my own research and teaching experience, I have shifted from insisting that Generation 1.5 learners need their own courses, separate from international L2 learners, to rejecting such an idea, given the many commonalities among L2 writers as a whole, despite the noted differences across various subgroups. This debate recalls earlier discussions (see Silva) distinguishing L2 writers from L1 (basic) writers, and whether the observed differences between the two groups warranted the creation of separate composition sections for L2 writers. At the time, Silva concluded that placing L2 writers into mainstream or basic writing courses was the least desirable option, the "sink or swim option" (38). As an alternative, Silva endorsed the creation of separate L2 composition courses, or cross-cultural sections with equal numbers of both L1 and L2 writers taught by instructors "sensitive to L2 writers' needs" (41).

Currently, I would suggest using caution before subdividing or dichotomizing L2 learners any more than has already been done in the literature. That is, before writing program administrators and practitioners working with L2 learners in postsecondary education endorse distinct pedagogical programs for different L2 learners, more research is needed confirming that such distinctions are actually beneficial for students. Furthermore, any noticeable differences among groups of L2 learners are likely to change as the demographics of the Generation 1.5 population change and as international students gain increased access to information about US linguistic and cultural norms (Matsuda). One certainty, however, is that the L2 population in US postsecondary education is growing, and that such growth is due, in part, to more L2 learners graduating from US high schools, but also, in part, to increased recruitment of international L2 students (Bartlett and Fischer). Thus, rather than focusing exclusively on differences, which often leads to a focus on deficiencies (see Friedrich), it may be helpful for future studies to note the similarities among various types of L2 learners in an effort to design courses addressing both their strengths and their needs.

To conclude, various theoretical frameworks and empirical studies suggest that the L2 population in US postsecondary education comprises a heterogeneous group of learners. While results from recent studies differ in terms of specific findings and recommendations, one point at which much of the research converges is the need for L2 learners of all types to learn features of academic writing and to note how such writing differs from other forms of language interaction. Thus, rather than design courses addressing different L2 learners' putative deficits, it may be more valuable for writing program administrators to ensure that courses for all learners include explicit instruction in features of academic writing.

Acknowledgments

I would like to thank Monika Ekiert, who read early drafts of this article, and the reviewers for this special issue of *TETYC*, who provided valuable suggestions for the final version. I would also like to thank The International Research Foundation (TIRF) for supporting my research with a doctoral dissertation grant.

Works Cited

Bartlett, Tom, and Karin Fischer. "The China Conundrum." *New York Times* 3 Nov. 2011. Web.

Bosher, Susan, and Jenise Rowekamp. "The Refugee/Immigrant in Higher Education: The Role of Educational Background." *College ESL* 8.1 (1998): 23–42. Print.

Connerty, Mary. "Variation in Academic Writing among Generation 1.5 Learners, Native English-Speaking Learners and ESL Learners: The Discoursal Self of G1.5 Student Writers." Diss. U of Birmingham, 2009. Print.

di Gennaro, Kristen. "An Exploration into the Writing Ability of Generation 1.5 and International Second Language Writers: A Mixed Methods Approach." Diss. Teachers College, Columbia U, 2011. Print.

Doolan, Stephen Martin. "A Comparison of Generation 1.5, L1, and L2 Tertiary Student Writing." Diss. Northern Arizona U, 2011. Print.

Friedrich, Patricia. "Assessing the Needs of Linguistically Diverse First-Year Students: Bringing Together and Telling Apart International ESL, Resident ESL, and Monolingual Basic Writers." *Writing Program Administration* 30.1–2 (2006): 15–35. Print.

Frodesen, Jan, and Nancy Starna. "Distinguishing Incipient and Functional Bilingual Writers: Assessment and Instructional Insights Gained through Second-Language Writer Profiles." *Generation 1.5 Meets College Composition: Issues in the Teaching of Writing to U.S.-Educated Learners of ESL*. Ed. Linda Harklau, Kay M. Losey, and Meryl Siegal. Mahwah: Lawrence Erlbaum, 1999. 61–80. Print.

Harklau, Linda, Kay M. Losey, and Meryl Siegal, eds. *Generation 1.5 Meets College Composition: Issues in the Teaching of Writing to U.S.-Educated Learners of ESL*. Mahwah: Lawrence Erlbaum, 1999. Print.

Holten, Christine. "Creating an Inter-Departmental Course for Generation 1.5 ESL Writers: Challenges Faced and Lessons Learned." *Generation 1.5 in College Composition: Teaching Academic Writing to U.S.-Educated Learners of ESL*. Ed. Mark Roberge, Meryl Siegal, and Linda Harklau. New York: Routledge, 2009. 170–84. Print.

Kachru, Braj. "World English and Applied Linguistics." *RELC Anthology*. Ed. M. L. Tickoo. Vol. 26. Singapore: SEAMEO Regional Language Centre, 1991. 178–205. Print.

Levi, Elisabeth I. "A Study of Linguistic and Rhetorical Features in the Writing of Non-English Language Background Graduates of U.S. Schools." Diss. U. of Pennsylvania, 2004. Print.

Matsuda, Paul Kei. "International and U.S. Resident ESL Writers Cannot Be Taught in the Same Class." *Writing Myths: Applying Second Language Research to Classroom Teaching.* Ed. Joy Reid. Ann Arbor: U of Michigan P, 2008. 159–76. Print.

Muchinsky, Dennis, and Nancy Tangren. "Immigrant Student Performance in an Academic Intensive English Program." *Generation 1.5 Meets College Composition: Issues in the Teaching of Writing to U.S.-Educated Learners of ESL.* Ed. Linda Harklau, Kay M. Losey, and Meryl Siegal. Mahwah: Lawrence Erlbaum, 1999. 211–34. Print.

Nayar, P. Bhaskaran. "ESL/EFL Dichotomy Today: Language Politics or Pragmatics?" *TESOL Quarterly* 31.1 (1997): 9–37. Print.

Reid, Joy. "'Eye' Learners and 'Ear' Learners: Identifying the Language Needs of International Students and U.S. Resident Writers." *Second-Language Writing in the Composition Classroom: A Critical Sourcebook.* Ed. Paul Kei Matsuda, Michelle Cox, Jay Jordan, and Christina Ortmeier Hooper. Boston: Bedford/St. Martin's. 2006. 76–88. Print.

Roberge, Mark, Meryl Siegal, and Linda Harklau. *Generation 1.5 in College Composition: Teaching Academic Writing to U.S.-Educated Learners of ESL.* New York: Routledge, 2009. Print.

Rumbaut, Rubén G., and Kenji Ima. "The Adaptation of Southeast Asian Refugee Youth: A Comparative Study." San Diego: San Diego State University (ED 299 372), 1988. Print.

Silva, Tony. "An Examination of Writing Program Administrators' Options for the Placement of ESL Students in First Year Writing Classes." *Writing Program Administration* 18.1–2 (1994): 37–43. Print.

Valdés, Guadalupe. "Bilingual Minorities and Language Issues in Writing: Toward Professionwide Responses to a New Challenge." *Written Communication* 9.1 (1992): 85–136. Print.

Nontraditional Students

Anxiety and the Newly Returned Adult Student

Michelle Navarre Cleary

*Many adults come to college initially more anxious about school in general —
and writing in particular — than their younger peers. This anxiety is one
reason adult students are more likely to drop out in their first year back in
school. That reality raises a difficult question for writing teachers: How do
we reduce writing anxiety while also challenging adult students to develop
as writers? In this selection, Michelle Navarre Cleary provides a number of
practical suggestions to address this problem, while also challenging some
common wisdom for working with adult learners.*

> It's a challenge, especially the writing. Pretty much just getting back into it.
>
> —Jessica

> Yeah, I had mouth sores.
>
> —Sam

J essica and Sam were two of twenty-five newly returned adult students
whom I spent over sixty hours interviewing in the fall of 2008.[1] Twenty-
three of these students expressed significant anxiety about writing for

---

From *Teaching English in the Two-Year College*, vol. 39, no. 4, 2012, pp. 364-76.

school. Like Sam, some had anxiety so intense it produced physical symptoms like mouth sores and muscle spasms. The main sources of their anxiety were not knowing what to write because they had a hard time imagining the university and not knowing if they were writing well enough because they had a hard time imagining themselves in the university. As David Bartholomae has pointed out, "every time a student sits down to write for us, he has to invent the university for the occasion" (60). Because adult students are less likely to have the academic currency and cultural capital of their younger peers, inventing the university can be particularly challenging. As Sam put it, "I don't fit in here; I don't know what I'm supposed to do." Focusing on Jessica and Sam, this essay shows the sometimes unexpected ways in which teaching decisions did and did not reduce students' writing anxiety.

I focus on Jessica and Sam for two reasons. First, of the twenty-five students, Jessica is one of seven who graduated within three years, while Sam is one of four who dropped out before completing a year back in school. Second, both took the same introductory class in the fall of 2008, but they had different teachers who made different teaching decisions. At the end of the quarter, Jessica felt assured that she could write for school, while Sam did not. In this essay I show how Sam's anxiety increased because of the ways she was and was not invited to use her prior experience, while Jessica's anxiety decreased as a result of writing and receiving feedback on multiple low-stakes assignments. Together, Sam and Jessica demonstrate that, because of their rich histories, the ways adult students respond to teaching decisions is highly individualized and not always predictable. Thus, helping them get beyond writing anxiety requires understanding and responding to each student.

Why Worry about Anxiety?

Adult students are less likely to persist than younger students (McGivney 35; Murtaugh, Burns, and Schuster 355; Swail 18–19) and most likely to drop out in their first year back in school (Choy 17). Writing is one reason they fail to persist. As one student said, "I mean there were points where I was like, oh I'm just ready to give up. I don't think I can do this. . . . it wasn't the reading, it wasn't the class participation, but it was the writing of the papers" (Angelina). Angelina is not alone. Anna Zajacova, Scott Lynch, and Thomas Espenshade found that nontraditional students at CUNY ranked "writing term papers" as the most stressful of twenty-seven tasks (686), where "[s]tress has generally been found to have a negative influence on GPA and on staying enrolled" (696). Adults just returning to school have substantially higher anxiety about school in general and writing in particular than younger students (Krause, "Supporting" 208; Navarre Cleary 115–19; Sailor ix). Gretchen Starks showed that adult women at a rural community college "felt writing was a barrier to their ability to continue in college" (3). To help remove this barrier, we need to understand how our teaching decisions affect adults' anxieties about writing.

Research Methods

The students I interviewed attended a college for those aged twenty-four and older that is part of a large, private, urban midwestern university (Midwest). Their average age was thirty-nine, and they ranged in age from twenty-six to fifty-five. Forty percent identified themselves as persons of color. Sixty percent did not have a parent who had completed college. All but two were attending school part-time, and most worked full-time in jobs as varied as administrative assistant, business owner, exotic dancer, trainer, and landlord. While diverse, my sample does not represent the full diversity of the adult college student population in the United States. Of these twenty-five students, only six were male and two Latino/Latina.[2] Many, but not all, were more financially secure than the adults I previously taught at a local community college. My goal is not to make generalizable claims about how anxious adult students respond to specific teaching methods, but rather to show the complexity of how two students responded to well-intentioned associate professors who understood that adults are often anxious about school in general and writing in particular.

All of the students were enrolled in one of three sections of Foundations of Adult Learning (Foundations) taught by my colleagues at Midwest. Although not a writing class, this course does require writing, including an eight- to twelve-page research paper with an annotated bibliography. This assignment is required in every Foundations class, and all students receive the same assignment with a detailed outline for it in the common handbook. However, each teacher approaches the class differently. For example, both Jessica's and Sam's teachers required multiple drafts of this research paper, but only Jessica's teacher assigned a series of low-stakes writing assignments leading up to the high-stakes research paper.

Tamsin Haggis argues that adult learning theories fail to account for the diverse, complex, and sometimes contradictory learning experiences of adults. To better understand these experiences, she calls for more studies of how adults describe their learning (209). With Haggis's call in mind and with the goal of gaining a more nuanced understanding of how teaching practices can impact the writing development of adult students, I conducted these semistructured interviews as part of an IRB-approved study tracing the writing development of returning adult students. I interviewed students for roughly an hour at the start, in the middle, and at the end of the quarter. In these interviews, students frequently expressed anxiety about writing, particularly when asked about how they were doing, their writing processes, and teacher feedback. An initial reading and subsequent coding of the transcripts confirmed my observation that anxiety was a prominent theme.

Sam and the Perils of Prior Experience

Sam's story shows the limits of a central tenet of not just writing instruction for adults, but more generally of adult education: namely, that recognizing and building upon adults' experiential knowledge increases confidence and helps adults learn by encouraging them to connect what they already know to new learning (see, for example, Brookfield; Knowles; Kolb). Sam demonstrated that asking adults to write about what they know can sometimes increase rather than decrease their anxiety.

Sam grew up in a working-class Texas family. From her parents, who owned a laundry and several other businesses, she gained her entrepreneurial spirit and her lack of confidence in her verbal abilities. As she says, "I'm not afraid of change or anything new." In fact, she sought it out, getting bored easily. A former professional ballet dancer, she became a real estate broker and ran construction and insulation companies with her husband. From making several hundred dollars selling candy to her grammar school classmates to financing the start of her construction business with credit cards, Sam was a confident risk-taker: "I just assume I'm going to be successful." However, Sam was not sure she could be successful in college because she lacked confidence in her verbal abilities. Growing up with a taciturn father and a quiet mother, she turned to dance to express herself: "That's why I became a dancer. I didn't have to say anything." Sam excelled at ballet, earning a full scholarship to a performing arts boarding high school in Florida where "[t]here was very little concern for academics." As a result, when Sam decided to return to school, "the idea of reading and writing a paper scared me to death."

Although willing to face her fear of writing, Sam was ambivalent about being a student. Dancing quite literally brought Sam to campus at the same time as it taught her to equate "higher education with failure." Unlike most first-generation college students, Sam "always participated in the university" because she "had grown up in their dance department." However, in the dance world, college is the consolation prize for those who cannot make it professionally. Sam did succeed as a professional dancer, but not before being told she should go to college because she was too tall and ten pounds too heavy to dance professionally. As a result, she had "been resistant to school in the past." Although she came to value education, she also recognized that she had internalized "this ridiculous idea" that college is for those who have failed, so "even today I find myself in limbo because I have that written in my head . . . people who are educated . . . are those that couldn't make it." In addition, because of her dance background, Sam privileged expression over analysis. She struggled with analytic writing, which she equated with the work of critics who could never understand dance because, for Sam, the understanding comes in the doing.

In sum, Sam's writing anxiety stemmed from her sense of alienation from the academic. This alienation was rooted in her belief that she was not well prepared for academic literacy at home or school, in the early messages that school means failure, and in her grounding in creative expression rather than analysis. Theresa Lillis demonstrates that academic literacy excludes nontraditional students and that traditional methods of teaching writing take the conventions of this literacy for granted, further perpetuating this exclusion (53–77). Sam's experience demonstrates a student struggling to understand these unarticulated conventions while also feeling that they challenged some of her core values. Sam realized that academic writing was "a whole other idea of even thinking for me. So I am concerned about my writing skills."

Her anxiety increased when she was asked to write about her dance experience without the scaffolding she needed. The assignment followed best practices for teaching adults in that it attempted to build upon Sam's experiential knowledge. For example, Kathleen Cassity found that the adult women she studied "each demonstrated that finding some way to connect to academic course material through personal experience was one of the primary techniques she used for breaking through anxiety" (290). Thus, assignments in which adults can write about what they know (such as narrative, expository, and community or work-based problem-solution essays) should help reduce anxiety and facilitate their transition into academic writing.

Sam's assignment did attempt to scaffold her writing with a series of questions asking her to identify a learning experience, describe it, reflect upon it, and generalize about it. The question designed to help her generalize asked about the "theories, ideas, concepts, or principles" informing her experience. Her teacher told her to "write a full paragraph. This is where you have to talk about the theory behind dance." However, Sam had no idea what was meant by "theory": "I don't even know what those theories are. I don't even know what they're talking about." As a result, Sam was frustrated that her lack of academic knowledge kept her from being able to express her expertise: "I wrote the show must go on as a theory. And then I was like, oh gosh, I don't really know how to think of dance. And, in kind of like an academic paper form."

Sam did have definite ideas about dance. For example, she was passionate that art is in the doing and can only be understood by the artists, not by observers. However, when called upon to write in "an academic paper form," Sam reached for the readily available, if not appropriate, commonplace that the show must go on. David Bartholomae argues that students use commonplaces to establish their authority when they have none: "When a student is writing for a teacher, . . . [t]he student, in effect, has to assume privilege without having any. . . . The student defines as his own that which is a commonplace . . . this act of appropriation constitutes his authority" (67, 72). In Sam's case, she was the authority on dance. It was the mismatch between her expertise as a dancer and her understanding of academic writing that left Sam less, rather than more, confident when she tried to write about what she knew. Sam's experience was too rich to make prompts like "Describe your experience as a dancer" meaningful. She needed questions that invited her to think more specifically, such as, "What performance stands out in your mind most vividly? Why?" "What do you think people most misunderstand about classical ballet?"

Not only was Sam unsure how to write for school, but she also found her method of learning called into question. Scholars recommend having adults write about their prior writing education to uncover and address anxiety from negative experiences (Gillespie; Gillam 12–14). Sam demonstrates the importance of learning not only what students have learned about writing but also how they have learned to learn. As a dancer, Sam had learned by copying models. Back in school, she actively sought out models to help navigate academic conventions. She used the models on the Purdue OWL to learn how to do citations and an annotated bibliography, both writing tasks she had not previously encountered. For her final research paper assignment, the one that "gave me mouth sores," she asked to see samples. When her teacher refused her request, Sam was flummoxed: "I think by copying or I had . . . a whole career based upon . . . seeing something and then replicating it. So, so and he was like no. But I need to see something." She pointed out that when she was learning dance, "they were happy to show, and I was happy to copy." Sam was frustrated that the rules of learning seemed to have been changed on her. Not only was it not okay to copy, but her previous learning was devalued when she got the message that copying was something she should not be happy to do. Although this was a class in which students are asked to explore their learning styles, Sam's instructor did not connect her request for a model to the learning style of a dancer until we discussed her request much later. Like Sam, he was reasoning from his prior experience. While her experiences taught her the value of models, he stopped considering models because he found students "slavishly imitated" them. Giving students a diverse selection of models and discussing with them the writers' decisions can avoid this imitation.

The value of learning through models was another way in which Sam found her professional training as an artist, which focused on expression, conflicting with the demands of her academic work, which focused on analysis. Perhaps because she had mastered so many other domains from dance to real estate, Sam was confident that once she understood the "formula" for academic writing, she could do it. To gain that understanding, she needed explicit instruction on academic writing conventions. Models can be one form of explicit instruction; feedback on low-stakes writing is another. Unlike Sam's teacher, Jessica's professor assigned six low-stakes writing assignments prior to the first-draft of the high-stakes research paper. His feedback on these assignments, while brief, general, and almost entirely positive, turned out to be just what Jessica needed.

Jessica and the Power of Positive Feedback

Jessica grew up in public housing on the South Side of Chicago, with parents who encouraged her to be the first in her family to graduate from college. When her friends started getting into trouble, Jessica distanced herself from them and got more involved in school. She was one of the success stories at her high school, where only about a third of the students graduated. Jessica finished fourth in her class with a 3.3 GPA and a track scholarship to a regional state university. However, she gave up the scholarship when she got pregnant at the end of high school. She tried going back to school a year later, but found it too hard to take care of her child, work full-time, and attend school, so she dropped out after three quarters. Jessica worked her way up from temporary jobs to a position as a receptionist at a bank where her co-workers urged her to return to school. At age twenty-nine, she did just that. Despite the challenges of being a single mother, full-time worker, and part-time student, Jessica had a positive attitude and a deep determination to be successful: "I'm not going to start something that I'm not going to finish." She enjoyed being back in school but also felt "overwhelmed" with "all of the writing."

Jessica's response to the feedback she received qualifies some of the conventional wisdom about what constitutes useful feedback — sometimes a few encouraging comments are exactly what a student needs. Nancy Sommers has argued that students "overwhelmingly" want specific feedback and that "constructive criticism, more than encouraging praise, often pushes students forward with their writing" (251). In a meta-analysis of studies of feedback, John Hattie and Helen Timperly argued that adult students distrusted praise: "older students perceived praise after success or neutral feedback after failure as an indication that the teacher perceived their ability to be low" (97). In fact, positive feedback was not always enough for some students in my study. When they received only positive feedback, particularly when that feedback was general, four students reported getting more rather than less anxious. Sarah, for example, wanted feedback that would help her improve as a writer. Instead of constructive criticism, she just heard that everything she wrote was "all great." Sarah left Midwest after two quarters.

For Jessica, the few general and overwhelmingly positive comments her instructor provided on her initial writing assignments (see Table 1) rekindled her confidence and liberated her to learn. This positive

Table 1. Feedback on Jessica's Six Low-Stakes Writing Assignments.

Assignment	In-Text Comments	Other In-Text Marking	Summative Comments
Reading response 1	"Excellent!"	3 key words circled 1 comma correction 1 comma circled 1 word change of "till" to "until"	"Good job! See last page" "I appreciate your writing style — Excellent grasp of concept — good summary of the articles — Some good reflective insights embedded in your paper — I urge you [to] think more about how these articles may impact your goals. Well done!"
Reading response 2			"Well done, Jessica! Clearly you 'get it' and will do well at [Midwest] + beyond!"
Reading response 3			"Good job!"
Reading response 4	"and can share w/ others"	Opening sentences of first 2 paragraphs underlined	"Good job!" "Clearly you 'get it'"
Interview report		1 underline of key information	"Excellent! Would she make a good P.A.?"
Article summary			"Good! Was this a peer reviewed article?"

feedback, particularly the feedback that directly addressed Jessica's anxiety about not being good enough to succeed, built her confidence. Jessica internalized her teacher's assurance that she "gets it," telling me later on in the interview that she had less "frustration . . . with my anxiety" because "*I'm getting it*, okay I'm not going to do so bad" (emphasis added). Because returning to school requires a significant sacrifice of time and money for Jessica and many other adults, "Positive response to their writing, writing which has often been made possible by neglecting other duties, convinces students that their efforts are worthwhile" (Fredericksen 119). Positive feedback allowed Jessica to move past self-doubt: "I felt more confident of my writing. I felt more confident of myself and my thoughts." With this confidence, she then set herself up for success by getting started earlier on her papers and so giving herself time to revise.

Timely feedback on early assignments was particularly important to the students in my study. Jessica used feedback on her initial assignments to understand what she was being asked to do. When her teacher wrote, "I urge you [to] think more about how these articles may impact your goals," Jessica realized that "I had left out . . . what I was getting in the reading." This feedback, while critical, increased Jessica's confidence because it helped her understand what was expected: "I know what to do now. And I stopped second guessing myself." When she received feedback that identified what she was doing well, Jessica was able to recognize a strength she could use for other writing tasks. For example, before receiving feedback that she had "excellent examples of life experiences," Jessica had not thought of examples from her experience as a strength of her writing. Jessica continued to seek out and appreciate feedback throughout the quarter. When she was confronted with a new writing task, the research paper assignment, she was eager for initial feedback to know if she was "headed in the right direction" as she worked to understand this more complex assignment.

Most of the students I interviewed reported being less anxious about their writing by the end of the quarter. They attributed their decreased anxiety to one or more of the following: learning to use writing process strategies; having a number of low-stakes writing assignments that gave them practice writing for school; and receiving early and frequent teacher feedback on their writing. Of these three, teacher feedback had the greatest impact on their writing anxiety. Without it, they remained lost; with it, they were liberated to learn. Feedback that clarified expectations and gave specific suggestions for improvement helped students understand what to do. Feedback that engaged with their ideas and praised their strengths gave them the confidence that they belonged back in school. For some, like Jessica, a little feedback went a long way, while for others too little, too general, or too positive feedback only increased their anxiety.

Recommendations for Reducing Anxiety

The examples of Sam and Jessica highlight some, but not all, of the most common recommendations for reducing the anxiety of adult composition students. Composition scholars who work with adults most often recommend the following practices:

> Encouraging students to write about their experiences and their prior learning (Cassity 293; Fredericksen 119–20; Gillam 12–14; Gillespie; Hurlow 66; Morrison 33–34; Pies 14; Sommer 120–33, 214–15)

> Creating collaborative learning opportunities (Fredericksen 117; Krause, "University" 159–60; Miritello 7; Morrison 32–35; Sommer 66–73, 212; Wiant 58–60)

Demystifying academic writing with explicit instruction (Krause, "University" 163; Lillis 53–77)

Assigning frequent, low-stakes writing and teaching writing as a process with multiple drafts (Fredericksen 117–18; Morrison 35; Pies 14–15, 18; Sommer 209–12, 215–16)

Providing feedback on drafts that is focused and formative, praises strengths, and offers constructive criticism that helps students develop ideas (Fredericksen 117–19; Pies 18; Sommer 134–50)

However, as Sam and Jessica make clear, teachers who wish to help returning students move beyond their anxiety need to understand the complex and sometimes surprising ways in which students respond to these teaching practices. Happily, many strategies for learning how students are making sense of our teaching are also ways to reduce their anxiety.

Four strategies I have found particularly effective are *exploring prior learning*, *discussing writing anxiety in class*, *conferencing*, and *assigning low-stakes writing*. As an initial assignment, I have students describe their prior writing experiences and also what they have learned about themselves as writers and as learners. Their responses let me know who depends upon outlining, who thinks good writing is a matter of correct spelling, and who will be helped by models. Second, class discussions about writing anxiety engage both young and old students, all of whom have plenty to say on this topic. Simply learning that other students are anxious helps reduce the anxiety of returning students (Miritello 7; Morrison 32). For this discussion, I have students read Anne Lamott's "Shitty First Drafts," which has the advantage of being short and funny and introducing the idea of writing process methods as a way to manage writing anxiety. Third, conferencing helps establish a personal connection with students. Often previously silent students will talk freely in a conference about their writing anxieties. When I have not been able to meet with students individually, conferencing with them in small groups has also been effective. Finally, besides giving students low-stress writing practice, low-stakes writing allows me to "check in" with students throughout the term. Thomas Angelo and K. Patricia Cross, John Bean, and Peter Elbow recommend several ways low-stakes writing can be used to assess students' understanding and concerns. I have ended classes by having students write on the "muddiest point" and have started classes asking them to write what they remembered from the previous class. Jessica's teacher had students write short, weekly papers summarizing a reading. Another teacher had students write a one-page response to each class. Each of these strategies helps teachers learn about and be able to respond to the particular learning experiences, assumptions, and anxieties students bring to their writing assignments.

Conclusion

Tamsin Haggis states: "A focus on the uniqueness of learning experience, rather than on 'adults' as a general category, has wide-reaching implications. It suggests a need to find out more about the complexity of real, situated learning experiences" (210–11). In this article, I focus on the "real, situated learning experiences" of two first-generation students, one of whom recently graduated while the other dropped out after taking two more classes. Sam's and Jessica's unique histories shaped their responses to their learning in fall 2008 in ways that sometimes challenged expectations. For Sam, writing about prior learning, but not being able to use prior learning methods, only increased her anxiety and made new learning more difficult. For Jessica, positive feedback successfully reduced her anxiety and enabled learning. Although incoming adults have higher anxiety than younger students, research indicates that adults improve their writing more quickly than younger students (Krause, "Supporting" 209), and adults who persist have no more writing anxiety than younger students (Elias 40–41). The risk is that returning students give up before they gain confidence in their writing. Sam's and Jessica's experiences suggest that more adults could be retained through their first year if they received writing instruction that responded to their individual needs. As Mary Kay Morrison says, "What it all comes down to is a willingness to be flexible and individualized in our approach" (32).

Notes

1. I use the term *adult student* to refer to college undergraduates who are twenty-four years old or older. However, as more younger students work to finance their education, they increasingly share many of the needs and interests of older students.
2. In 1983, Merle O'Rourke Thompson found that returning women had higher anxiety than younger students, but that older men had significantly less writing anxiety than either older women or younger students. This result might indicate an unexplored gender differential given that the research on writing anxiety and returning students is based largely upon female subjects. Women account for about 60 percent of the adult student population ("Table 191"), but they are overrepresented in the research literature. For example, only 9 percent of Thompson's subjects and 24 percent of mine were returning men.

Works Cited

Angelo, Thomas A., and K. Patricia Cross. *Classroom Assessment Techniques: A Handbook for College Teachers.* San Francisco: Jossey-Bass, 1993. Print.

Bartholomae, David. "Inventing the University." *Writing on the Margins: Essays on Composition and Teaching.* Boston: Bedford/St. Martins, 2005. 60–85.

Print. Rpt. from *When a Writer Can't Write: Studies in Writer's Block and Other Composing-Process Problems*. Ed. Mike Rose. New York: Guilford P, 1985. 134–66.

Bean, John C. *Engaging Ideas: The Professor's Guide to Integrating Writing, Critical Thinking and Active Learning in the Classroom*. San Francisco: Jossey-Bass, 1996. Print.

Brookfield, Stephen. *Understanding and Facilitating Adult Learning: A Comprehensive Analysis of Principles and Effective Practices*. San Francisco Jossey-Bass, 1986. Print.

Cassity, Kathleen J. "Bringing Lived Cultures and Experience to the WAC Classroom: A Qualitative Study of Selected Nontraditional Community College Students Writing Across the Curriculum." Diss. U of Hawai'i, 2005. *ProQuest*. Web. 9 Dec. 2006.

Choy, Susan. *Nontraditional Undergraduates*. U.S. Department of Education, National Center for Education Statistics. 2002. Web. 1 June 2010.

Elbow, Peter. "High Stakes and Low Stakes in Assigning and Responding to Writing." *Writing to Learn: Strategies for Assigning and Responding to Writing Across the Disciplines*. Ed. Mary Deane Sorcinelli and Peter Elbow. San Francisco: Jossey-Bass, 1997. 5–14. Print.

Elias, Rafik Z. "An Examination of Nontraditional Accounting Students' Communication Apprehension and Ambiguity Tolerance." *Journal of Education for Business* 75.1 (1999): 38–41. *Informa World*. Web. 30 Dec. 2010.

Fredericksen, Elaine. "Silence and the Nontraditional Writer." *Teaching English in the Two-Year College* 25.2 (1998): 115–121. *ProQuest*. Web. 4 Dec. 2006.

Gillam, Alice M. "Returning Students' Ways of Writing: Implications for First-Year College Composition." *Journal of Teaching Writing* 10.1 (1991): 1–20. Web. 23 June 2011.

Gillespie, Marilyn. "Research in Writing: Implications for Adult Literacy Education." *The Annual Review of Adult Learning and Literacy* 2.3 (2001). National Center for the Study of Adult Learning and Literacy. Web. 25 Sept. 2005.

Haggis, Tamsin. "Exploring the 'Black Box' of Process: A Comparison of Theoretical Notions of the 'Adult Learner' with Accounts of Postgraduate Learning Experience." *Studies in Higher Education* 27.2 (2002): 207–20. *EBSCO*. Web. 2 Feb. 2009.

Hattie, John, and Helen Timperly. "The Power of Feedback." *Review of Educational Research* 77.1 (2007): 81–112. *ProQuest*. Web. 27 Oct. 2009.

Hurlow, Marcia. "Experts with Life, Novices with Writing." *Dynamics of the Writing Conference: Social and Cognitive Interaction*. Ed. Thomas Flynn and Mary King. Urbana: NCTE, 1993. 62–68. *ERIC*. Web. 29 Dec. 2010.

Knowles, Malcolm. *The Adult Learner: The Definitive Classic in Adult Education and Human Resource Development*. Amsterdam: Elsevier, 2005. Print.

Kolb, David A. *Experiential Learning: Experience as the Source of Learning and Development*. Englewood Cliffs: Prentice Hall, 1984. Print.

Krause, Kerri-Lee. "Supporting First-Year Writing Development Online." *Journal of General Education* 55.3/4 (2006): 201–20. *Project Muse*. Web. 27 Dec. 2010.

———. "The University Essay Writing Experience: A Pathway for Academic Integration during Transition." *Higher Education Research and Development* 20.2 (2001): 147–68. *Carfax*. Web. 18 May 2010.

Lamott, Anne. "Shitty First Drafts." *Bird by Bird: Some Instructions on Writing and Life.* New York: Anchor Books, 1994. 21–27. Print.

Lillis, Theresa M. *Student Writing: Access, Regulation, Desire.* London: Routledge, 2001. Print.

McGivney, Veronica. "Understanding Persistence in Adult Learning." *Open Learning* 19.1 (2004): 33–46. *Academic Search Premier.* Web. 18 May 2010.

Miritello, Mary. "Teaching Writing to Adults: Examining Assumptions and Revising Expectations for Adult Learners in the Writing Class." *Composition Chronicle: Newsletter for Writing Teachers* 9.2 (1996): 6–9. *ERIC.* Web. 31 Aug. 2007.

Morrison, Mary Kay. "'The Old Lady in the Student Lounge': Integrating the Adult Female Student into the College Classroom." *Two-Year College English: Essays for a New Century.* Ed. Mark Reynolds. Urbana: NCTE, 1994. 26–36. Print.

Murtaugh, Paul A., Leslie D. Burns, and Jill Schuster. "Predicting the Retention of University Students." *Research in Higher Education* 40.3 (1999): 355–71. *JSTOR.* Web. 18 May 2010.

Navarre Cleary, Michelle. "What WPAs Need to Know to Prepare New Teachers to Work with Adult Students." *WPA: Writing Program Administration* 32.1 (2008): 113–28. Print.

Pies, Timothy. "Reducing Anxiety in the Adult Writer." *Adult Learning* 5.3 (1994): 14–15, 18. Print.

Sailor, Susan Hardee. "The Effect of Peer Response Groups on Writing Apprehension, Writing Achievement, and Revision Decisions of Adult Community College Composition Students." Diss. U of Florida, 1996. *UMI.* Web. 29 Dec. 2010.

Sommer, Robert F. *Teaching Writing to Adults: Strategies and Concepts for Improving Learner Performance.* San Francisco: Jossey-Bass, 1989. Print.

Sommers, Nancy. "Across the Drafts." *College Composition and Communication* 58.2 (2006): 248–57. *ProQuest.* Web. 20 Feb. 2009.

Starks, Gretchen. "Perceptions of Writing by Exceptional Cases of Adult Returning Women in a Rural Community College: Differences between Persisters and Leavers." Annual meeting of the American Educational Research Assn. San Francisco. Mar. 1989. *ERIC.* Web. 17 Mar. 2007.

Swail, Watson Scott. *Graduating At-Risk Students: A Cross-Sector Analysis.* Washington: Imagine America Foundation, 2009. *Education Policy International.* Web. 18 May 2010.

"Table 191. Total fall enrollment in degree-granting institutions, by sex, age, and attendance status: Selected years, 1970 through 2018." *Digest of Education Statistics, 2009.* National Center for Education Statistics. 18 Dec. 2010. Web.

Thompson, Merle O'Rourke. "The Returning Student: Writing Anxiety and General Anxiety." *Teaching English in the Two-Year College* 10.1 (1983): 35–39. Print.

Wiant, Fredel Marie. "A Study of Collaborative Writing Response Groups and Writing Anxiety among Female Community College Re-Entry Students." Master's thesis. U of Colorado, 1997. Print.

Zajacova, Anna, Scott M. Lynch, and Thomas J. Espenshade. "Self-Efficacy, Stress, and Academic Success in College." *Research in Higher Education* 46.6 (2005): 677–706. Web. 18 May 2010.

(Re)Envisioning the Divide: The Impact of College Courses on High School Students

Kara Taczak and William H. Thelin

Authors Kara Taczak and William Thelin note that "We typically only ever hear the success stories about dual enrollment, and we can sometimes forget that there's another side: what happens when students don't 'succeed' in dual enrollment, and in fact, what happens when students just aren't ready for this type of learning? How can we slow down this race toward adulthood and allow young students to be young students, and thus, allow them to mature to a point of being ready for college courses? We explore this 'other side of the story' in this essay."

High school students taking college courses that simultaneously fulfill high school requirements and give general education credit toward a bachelor's degree have become more of a presence on college campuses across the nation. The purpose behind these programs appears to be the belief that dual enrollment (also known as "concurrent enrollment") provides students with momentum toward degree completion. According to Clifford Adelman, students who earn fewer than twenty credits by the end of the first calendar year of college enrollment tend to experience a "serious drag" on their attempts at completion, so a "transition process" is necessary at the high school level (5). Furthermore, the National High School Center finds that the programs also reduce the amount of remediation at the college level, help gain access to education formerly reserved for top-performing students only, and offset some of the high tuition costs of university education (7).

This essay examines the effects of a dual enrollment program on teaching and learning in one particular section of English composition taught by an instructor we will call Professor Foley. Using data generated from qualitative research, we suggest that the cognitive capabilities of some dual enrollment students have not developed enough to handle effectively the challenges of the contemporary conception of composition. We believe that this furthers a regressive view of composition in the eye of the public, a view that does not take into consideration the research in the field and that focuses on current-traditional precepts to guide its perceptions.[1]

Background

Nearly every state offers some form of dual enrollment, and at least eighteen of those states now mandate that the opportunity for dual enrollment be extended to high school seniors. Whether offered through

From *Teaching English in the Two-Year College*, vol. 37, no.1, 2009, pp. 7-23.

distance learning (Bodmer), in conjunction with certified high school teachers on site at the high school (Farris), or on the actual college campus, administrators and instructors have struggled with questions about the effectiveness of such programs. The High School Leadership Summit, sponsored but not necessarily endorsed by the U.S. Department of Education, suggests that policymakers need to address problems concerning equal access to these dual enrollment opportunities, financial arrangements equitable to all involved, collaborations between secondary and postsecondary schools, and the maintenance of college-level rigor in these courses (3). Quantitative studies have attempted to link dual enrollment to both short-term and long-term success. In a study of Florida's statewide program (3), Karp et al., for example, found strong correlation between participation in dual enrollment programs and students' likelihood of earning a high school diploma, enrolling and staying enrolled in college, and maintaining high GPAs. Although not as consistently as in the Florida sample, Karp et al. discovered that dual enrollment participants in career and technical education programs also profited (4–5). Bodmer, however, relates qualitative evidence concerning composition curriculum being censored by high school principals, leading to a review from administrators and other faculty in determining what was appropriate for a composition course (122–24). Furthermore, Tom Miller's research at the University of Arizona found that dual enrollment students failed the college writing assessment at a rate a third higher than that of other students, although this result was partly attributed to the fact that students started with lower verbal SATs and high school GPAs (Yancey 203). Overall, however, little is known about the effects of dual enrollment on students (Bailey and Karp 21).

Our study examines a different type of dual enrollment. During the summer of 2007, six high school sophomores walked into a college composition classroom at a Midwestern state university, poised to complete a college-level course. The students were part of the Strive Toward Excellence Program (STEP) that was established by the university in 1988 to help middle school and high school students prepare for and understand college. The intention behind STEP, according to the university's website, is to provide "students with the attitude, skills, support, and financial assistance to pursue and successfully attain a college degree." The six students were admitted into Professor Foley's class as part of a STEP pilot to determine whether a group of fourteen- and fifteen-year-old students could, indeed, succeed alongside other college students and, if so, perhaps achieve the equivalent of an associate's degree by the time that they were finished with high school. The students were handpicked by STEP, based on their previous success and their ACT scores (which needed to fall in the range of 16 to 26).

Bailey and Karp's review of existing literature on "credit-based transition programs" produced a taxonomy from which to understand STEP (although STEP is not specifically mentioned in the article). AP programs, for example, are called "singleton" programs because they are stand-alone college courses. STEP appears to be a mixture of what Bailey and Karp term a "comprehensive program" and an "enhanced comprehensive program." Comprehensive programs include a majority of students' junior and senior high school courses, sometimes on the college campus, sometimes not. No social preparation is given. Bailey and Karp differentiate the Enhanced Comprehensive Programs by this social aspect, describing them as seeking to prepare students for college — not only through rigorous academic instruction, but also by offering a wide range of activities such as counseling, assistance with applications, mentoring, and general personal support. They aim to address all elements of the secondary-postsecondary transition and encompass the majority of the students' high school experiences (12).

Bailey and Karp add that these programs seem best suited for students who are not traditionally on the college track (12). The programs look for socially or economically disadvantaged students and locate their courses on the college campus, usually in an embedded high school on the campus. STEP focuses on middle school students whose parents do not have college degrees. Therefore, the students, as young as fourteen, become first-generation college students. Yet, unlike most of these programs, in STEP the students take some courses with other students, and the program looks for academically inclined students. The instructors are regular college lecturers and professors. The curriculum is supposed to be the same as offered to other first-year students.

For our purposes, we insist that STEP is a hybrid program and thus avoid easy comparisons to other dual enrollment programs. Yet, despite this hybridity — or perhaps because of it — the results of our study might inform many instructors teaching dual enrollment courses because, as stated earlier, we argue that, for the teaching of composition at least, students need more maturity and the chance to develop cognitively in order to succeed. On top of that, we demonstrate the negative impact that these students had on both the traditional students in the class, ages eighteen to twenty-one, and the nontraditional students, over the age of twenty-one. We also demonstrate the loss of pedagogical rigor and standards, resulting from instructor efforts to negotiate differing maturity levels. However, signs of progress did emerge in at least one of the STEP students examined.

We used a participant-observation methodology to glean information from these students, as well as from the other students in the class. A team of four participant-observers attended class on a daily basis and took detailed notes, interviewed the students and the instructor outside of class three times during the term, collected all classroom materials, and reviewed student writing for signs of growth. The STEP students were part of a broad focus of research that aimed to see the effects of particular pedagogical techniques on a diverse group of students. The team also wanted to uncover student reaction to the espoused commitment of the professor to critical pedagogy. The team leader had to make an amendment to the IRB form, in order to interview minors, and eventually secured permission from the parents of four of the six STEP students to include those students in the study. Each STEP student who participated in the study was interviewed three times during the five-week session: the first week, the third week, and the week after the class concluded. They were also given an exit survey, which they turned in at the same time as their final portfolio.

Two important variables to consider include teacher preparation and the term in which the course took place. Foley had no knowledge that the STEP students would be a part of the course until a coordinator from STEP greeted him at the classroom door, minutes before the first session was to take place. Such a lack of communication between university units is consistent with some of the discoveries that Farrell and Seifert document about failures in dual enrollment programs (75–76); it paved the way for what could have been a "blunder," as Thelin and Tassoni describe it, in a critical classroom (1–3).

Foley's classroom already had nineteen students in it, ranging in age from fourteen to thirty-eight. The Midwestern university where this research took place is a comprehensive school where nontraditional students are common: thirteen of the students were older than eighteen, four were mothers with multiple children, and six were eighteen-year-old first-year students. At least one of the students had failed the previous composition class. Into this mix of students came the six STEP students. The STEP coordinator gave Professor Foley instructions not to modify any of his materials or his approach to the class for the STEP students, because the program encouraged the students to experience college-level instruction and expectations unfiltered. Yet, Foley found it impossible to proceed with the curriculum as he had planned, given the unexpected diversity of the students.

The second variable might account for his reactions—the course took place over an accelerated summer term. As Foley noted in all of our interviews, summer sessions move too quickly for already-admitted students. The experience of the STEP students must have been especially trying, because they had a limited understanding of what the course would entail. The four students in the study, all of them female, came into the classroom seemingly eager to learn and ready to develop writing skills. However, one student, named Juliet, understood skills as "closing sentences on paragraphs" or "spelling," whereas another student, Shannon, hoped that this class would prepare her for an education degree so that she would be able to "write letters home to parents or to other faculty in the school." Another student, CeCe, stated that she wanted "to further [her] education . . . to get ahead of the regular classes in high school."[2] The students did not recognize composition as encompassing more than grammar or preparation for other tasks. According to the university's website, one of the goals of STEP is "assist[ing] students to develop identifiable skills in writing, mathematics, and analytical thinking, which will enable them to enroll in the appropriate college-prep courses." Therefore, the students most likely assumed that obtaining skills was the only appropriate goal for them to have as well. Certainly, the STEP students might have benefited from having more time in a fifteen-week term to adapt to the expectations of the course, as well as to the contents and methods of the critical pedagogy that Foley envisioned.

Keeping these variables in mind, however, we believe that our data raise some important issues for educators and administrators to consider. The creation of this particular dual enrollment program was characterized by good intentions, which could be seen in the actions of the support staff throughout the term. Yet, did this program have a positive impact, socially and academically, on these students?

Foley's Classroom

Foley follows the democratic methods of critical pedagogy that Paulo Freire and Ira Shor have defined. Foley promotes a student-centered classroom that frontloads the students' needs and backloads his own, as well as encouraging an analysis of common precepts that ultimately challenge the status quo. Often Foley had to adjust to the needs of the students, especially the STEP students, when it came to some fundamental understanding. Early on, after two of the STEP students had misunderstood an assignment, he had to explain that an essay consisted of an introduction, a body, and a conclusion. Furthermore, he had not planned on teaching any grammar classwide, wanting to reserve such discussions for one-on-one conferences based on patterns that he uncovered in individual student papers.[3] However, Foley had to replace planned activities with two grammar instructional sessions, each lasting twenty to thirty minutes, because of the STEP students' need to learn basic terminology and the reasoning behind sentence combining and comma placement.

Critical pedagogy encourages a democratic classroom where students have a voice. Therefore, Foley also had the students negotiate and vote on things such as classroom rules, grading contracts, and essay topics. The students created a uniform grading contract on the first day of class that generated a list of criteria that needed to be met in order to get an A, B, or C. Four of the STEP students signed an A contract initially; the other two signed a B contract. As the weeks progressed, Foley met with the students to discuss whether or not they had a realistic chance to meet their contracts, and two of the STEP students had to rework their contracts twice, each negotiating for a lower grade.

The research team rotated in shifts to cover all course hours, but at times all four participated in the class. The observers noted that, from the first day, the students broke themselves into "pods" or cliques that were segregated based on age and gender. One class member responded to the pod issue by stating that the students got into "the cliques depending on how they [we] act" and felt that cliques were a part of life. She qualified this by saying, "I think you can grow with the clique. Some of the people I already knew from school. But if I saw someone outside class, I would probably talk to them." The STEP students broke themselves into groups, with the two boys staying together. CeCe, a fourteen-year-old, offered an explanation for this division:

> Because you feel comfortable working with them after you work with them once. You base yourself off of a group of people in that classroom. And that is the group that you want to continue to work with because if you don't work with them then you feel like your paper is not done right or something like that.

Foley led discussions on audience awareness, critical analysis, and organization, approaching these issues through subject matter that ranged from environmental issues, to drunk driving, to appropriate and inappropriate public displays of emotion, which gave the students the opportunity to share their differing experiences. The pedagogy that he implemented also allowed the students the opportunity to listen and engage with students from different backgrounds. One of the nontraditional students was a breast cancer survivor, which seeped into her conversation often; another was on probation from a mixup with a friend's ATM card. One STEP student mentioned in an interview that she liked the diversity of the class because it allowed her to see different types of people. However, she did note that "some people older than me might have a problem with it because you know teenagers are usually chatty and we aren't used to being in a college class, so we just talk anyway."

The STEP students had regular tutoring, and one member of the observation team, who was also an instructor at the midwestern university, volunteered to tutor them once a week. They were enrolled in two other classes; one was a library instruction class, the other bowling. The library instruction class helped these students with the final essay assignment, which dealt with human relationships with animals. The other three essay topics, however—stereotyping, public displays of emotion, and the difference between aspirations and dreams—did not involve a research component. For the purpose of this article, we present three case studies of the STEP students: one who was a high performer, one a middle performer, and one a lower performer.

Shannon

Shannon, a fourteen-year-old, participated in class regularly and seemed to be eager and willing to work. In her profile, an assignment from the first day of class, she demonstrated an awareness of the world around her that the other STEP students lacked. Shannon voiced concerns about the environment and the war in Iraq, suggesting that more recycling must be implemented and that the fighting had been going on for too long.

This awareness, however, did not manifest itself in deep critical analysis. Shannon could explain a problem and show some of the subtle consequences, but she did not develop her writing beyond pat conclusions. For example, she understood that stereotyping presented a problem to society and gave examples about how it could limit or intimidate people. However, her conclusion—despite the fact that Foley gave her the opportunity to revise multiple times—never moved beyond "the world would be a better place for everyone if we stop stereotyping each other." Although Foley commented that just saying "Don't do it" does not take into account the complex reasons that stereotyping exists, Shannon did not dig deeper, even when given examples and parallels. Her final paper on the extinction of jaguars relied solely on lightly paraphrased research and did not answer the assignment question about weighing the beliefs of those who believe in "human destiny" against those who believe in animals' innate right to exist. Despite Foley's coaxing, Shannon never submitted a revision that showed effort at tackling the complexity of the issue. Shannon excelled only on the third paper topic, about aspirations, probably because it did not ask her to extend her analysis above and beyond herself. Overall, her writing showed proficiency in sentence structure and organization, but she had difficulty developing examples and did not incorporate lessons on analysis, anticipating audience needs, and thesis development into her essays.

Shannon projected a positive attitude throughout the term. She liked the differences in students:

> The kids obviously, the students in class, are a lot different from being in a class with people strictly your age. People are *married* in our class; so the maturity level is a little better in this class than it would be in high school. But then again I know I go to a private Catholic school so everyone's pretty mature there, too. It's still different.

She understood that the older students might have more direct experience on issues, and she acknowledged during her last interview that some of the political issues that surfaced did not hold her interest because of her age. She said that when a topic made her uncomfortable, she contented herself with listening and did not feel slighted.

Even though her interviews show that she maintained some of the expectations of high school—instructors should call on students, groups should be assigned, etc.—she also liked what she considered the more "laid back" atmosphere of the college course. She noted the more mature themes of assigned reading and enjoyed the emphasis on papers as opposed to testing and memorizing, believing that writing essays taught her more. Very interestingly, by her last interview, she came to regard Foley as "a member of the class" who gave his opinions as freely as others. She had trouble seeing herself as a knowledge-maker and did not feel that she learned more about herself through writing, but she seemed to have been able to change her opinion of the instructor—as the sole authority to one who shared authority with the students. She remarked especially about the considerable input that Foley encouraged students to give on topic selection and assignments.

Shannon appears to have taken away from the class, at the least, a level of comfort with the pedagogy and with her responsibility as a student. In this way, she benefited from dual enrollment. However, when she discussed what she had learned, Shannon had difficulty articulating concepts. She still spoke of her revision process as "fixing [and] deleting." Although she mentioned the need to incorporate more analysis into her writing process, she did not define this need in such a way that we could determine whether she had a firm grasp of what analysis entails.

Juliet

Juliet, a fifteen-year-old, participated regularly in class, although, as with many maturing teenagers, she often spoke before thinking through the issue and thus answered with responses that did not pertain to the questions. However, she asked many questions if she did not understand something and voiced a willingness to work hard. Her profile suggested some obstinacy in considering the ideas of others. She called herself a "very opinionated person" and tied it to the need "to have someone speak the truth regarding world issues," but she did not mention any interest in national or international affairs. She stated emphatically that she says what she feels and means it.

This obstinacy presented itself in her writing. She seemed very sensitive to criticism, and, although she submitted several revisions, she often did not take into consideration comments from her peers or from Foley. Foley eventually settled on having her work through internal inconsistencies. For example, in Essay #1, she stated that stereotypes are "assumptions made of someone by . . . first sight." Foley pointed out that her description in this essay of her father being stereotyped by his friends as a "computer whiz" did not fit this definition, because, according to Juliet, he had gained this reputation because of his talent with computers, not by anything that could be seen at first sight. Juliet still did not revise to clear up such contradictions, making deletions and changes to her experiences and observations that often compounded the problem.[4] Foley pointed out larger issues, showing her that her paper on public displays of emotion did not confront the key question of the effect of suppressing public emotion, and he urged her to renegotiate her contract so that he could concentrate on basic issues of focus and correctness.

Juliet's final essay still contained multiple sentence-level errors, and she showed no signs of understanding the needs of an audience, connecting a body to a thesis through explicated analysis, organizing effectively, or incorporating relevant, specific detail. Her prose was coherent, but she seemed to lack control. Even though Foley gave her a B on her aspirations paper, he did so with hesitancy, explaining that he was going to allow her to move on despite her not having attended to the sentence-level errors from the first draft. The other papers, which had required Juliet to use her experiences and observations to explore larger issues, never rose above the C level.

Juliet seemed inconsistent from one interview to the next. As stated in her profile, she viewed herself as a "very opinionated" person, and when presented in class with a different opinion, she appeared to resist listening. She would look away, fidget, and talk to the student sitting next to her. She sensed that Foley disagreed with her stance on same-sex marriage and gave this response in the interview:

> I think it is my stance and where I stand on it and where he stand on it because we have two different opinions that could affect the way I think and act about it because my opinion is completely different from his and he wants to make sure that he proves his point so that I could maybe change my way I think.

Later, she said that the discussion could be "politically controversial but it doesn't matter" to her. The research team's field notes document several occasions during class when Juliet visibly shut herself off to others' opinions before she gave herself the chance to understand them fully. One example of this occurred during peer workshop, when others had critiqued her second paper. Her face grew red, she shook her head while averting her eyes, and she said sarcastically, "Okay, what else?" without writing down the comments or engaging the other students in dialogue.

Juliet also had a hard time deciding on what a teacher's role in the classroom should be. In her first interview, she stated that Foley created a comfortable atmosphere, saying that he "doesn't pressure and make people talk," but in her next interview she stated, "a teacher is just a teacher to me . . . ones that are good quality (they) made things easy for us . . . a bad teacher is someone who is controversial, opinionated." When asked if Foley could improve his teaching, she explained that when he provided sample essays, there were "mistakes" in them. She wanted him to give essays to use as examples that had no "mistakes." Foley's purpose, however, was to present the class with writing of his own—at the drafting stage—to model for the students some effective methods of responding to writing and ways for a writer to incorporate peer responses into revision strategies. Julie wanted Foley to represent a teacher that she had envisioned in her mind—a teacher who gave a "perfect" example of writing. Understandably enough, she did not know how a college professor's approach to a class might differ from that of a K–12 teacher, but Foley did not match the ideas that she had in mind.

In her interviews, Juliet seemed hesitant in her answers, often asking for the question to be repeated in a simpler manner and then ending her response with "Was that ok?" or "I'm trying to think of it [her answer] to help you." She wanted to learn and wanted to do her best in her interviews, but her lack of experience showed with the inconsistencies in her answers. Even though she acknowledged that age plays a part in learning, later in the same interview, she stated she had not learned anything about herself through this classroom experience, but then she said that experience can be a form of knowledge. This shows that she did not push her surface reactions with further analysis. Juliet wanted to do well and wanted to learn, but her lack of experience kept her from opening up to learn from others, including from Foley.

CeCe

Fourteen-year-old CeCe resisted the classroom from the beginning, explaining during her first interview that she found Foley "boring." She rarely paid attention in class, hiding her constant text messaging from Foley (but not from the research team) and chatting with Juliet and others about extracurricular matters during small group work. She enjoyed fashion and could critique clothes lines and jewelry for their quality, but her writing did not reflect this ability to critique, because she did not follow assignment requirements to analyze in a way that put her experiences into a larger context. She had severe sentence-level difficulties and stated in her profile and several times thereafter that she hated English. Although Foley met with her one-on-one several times to help her, she appeared incapable or unwilling to use his suggestions and examples. According to Foley, she lost patience with the close scrutiny that he would give to her papers during these conferences and she would leave prematurely, telling him that she got it now and could do the rest on her own. Her papers did not reflect this understanding.

CeCe was caught plagiarizing twice. Although the composition program had a strict disciplinary policy connected with plagiarism, Foley chose to work with CeCe's STEP advisors rather than enforce the policy, which would have resulted in her receiving an automatic F for the course. After recognizing CeCe's attempts at plagiarizing on the first essay, Foley coached her to take "one step at a time," suggesting that her many errors needed to be addressed after she settled the content issue. He had hoped that, with encouragement, CeCe would understand that she could write an essay that was all her own. Yet, CeCe failed to address these major content issues. For her essay on public displays of emotion, CeCe responded to the assignment in a way that showed a misunderstanding of the prompt: her essay dealt with the effects of growing up without a father. She did not relate a story about having to suppress emotion and left unanalyzed the experience that she did talk about. Unlike Shannon's or Juliet's, CeCe's third essay was her weakest. This essay's topic was aspirations, and she wrote about wanting to be a barber and a race-car driver. She plagiarized information from the Internet about Dale Earnhardt Jr. and Jennifer Tumminelli, saying that she loved to watch them race, but then, according to Foley, she admitted in conference that she had never even seen them. Foley noted that her paper hinted at the way gender impacted aspirations, but although CeCe added some details about her motivations for being a barber, she did not submit a revision that attempted to analyze further the effects of gender. Rather, she added statements such as, "With my personal determination, personality, hard work, and openness, I will prove the society wrong, and women are just as good in these two male dominated fields." Her final paper of the term, however, seemed to show improvement in sentence structure and organization, but the paper, about bald eagles, was largely plagiarized from multiple Internet sources, including the website of a fourth grader who had put his school project online. Therefore, our research could not track any improvement over the course of the semester. She showed little, if any, understanding of the rhetorical concepts stressed throughout the term.

CeCe appeared more defensive in her response to learning alongside older students, saying that

> people that are like forty have way more experience, through like . . . like he telling us to write a paper on aspirations and emotions. I don't know what my aspiration is yet. They been knew that. Like they been knew what they wanted to be and that is not an equal balance as far as the topics go. Like the animal paper, I agree with the animals, because that is like a neutral thing. You don't have to have experience.

For CeCe, it seemed as if her lack of experience did more than hold her back in her writing; it held her back in discussions as well. She believed that the discussions were "dead." She continued by saying, "No one talks and everyone just sits there and listens to him talk all day long with the same voice. No one smiles. No one does anything. Everyone just sits there." Although the sessions varied in response levels and excitement, the observers' in-class notes do not indicate that no one smiled or talked. Most class sessions had a mixture of small and whole-class group work. Foley did not rely on lecture except to introduce concepts. CeCe's impressions probably have more to do with her discomfort with participating in discussions.

Although other STEP students seemed to benefit from the diversity of the classroom, CeCe rejected it. Many of her responses to her interviews were one-word answers, and those that were longer were negative. When asked if she thought she had learned anything in class, she responded, "Besides that I suck at writing? No." She also felt that Foley did not "talk about . . . nothing to do with English or writing." She believed that composition dealt with grammar, so when asked again if she learned anything in class she said, "I basically learned some grammar and how to expand some papers, you know. Pretty much it."

CeCe's immaturity, even more so than Juliet's, limited her learning experience. She had difficulty opening herself up to new or differing perspectives and approaches to learning, dismissing what was not already in her repertoire with disdain. It did not appear that she attempted to analyze, to question, or to scrutinize. She tried to do the bare minimum to get by; consequently, this led to her ending the session with the belief that she had learned little and gained nothing from the experience.

The Class Reacts: Overall Atmosphere

Given the diversity of the class, other students felt that the STEP students' lack of experience held the class back. Several of the students noted in their interviews that the "kids" seemed immature and not ready for college. Some questioned why the STEP students had enrolled in a college class. It created an unequal classroom dynamic that was divided by the third day, according to the observers' notes. The STEP students never attempted to venture into another "pod," and the traditional students never attempted it either. The older students often felt frustrated with the younger students and sometimes even appeared to refrain from joining the classroom discussion. This frustration was evident in their interviews. One student, Marisa, had a particularly harsh reaction to the STEP students:

> most of the time, this particular classroom, it was just too much noise, trying to do writing assignments, trying to focus or concentrate, and constantly having noise in the background, not just basic noise from people moving around, but just constant talking and bickering and that was so very annoying.

She continued by saying that the class "seemed kind of elementary, but then at the same time it's [the students] a distraction." Samantha, a mother of six, agreed with this by stating that the classroom felt "kind of high-schoolish. A lot of whispers that go on and we have to go over a lot of things over and over again because the younger kids just don't have the knowledge and the experience to understand." These two were the most outspoken in the class, but many of the other students experienced similar emotions. The research team often sat with the nontraditional students outside on breaks, and many times these students voiced concern and frustrations over class and the discussion. The students' general reaction to the STEP students was that they held the class back from fully realizing its potential, and the students felt that they would have learned more about writing if the STEP students had not been in the class.

According to many of the students interviewed, both traditional and non-traditional, the STEP students lacked life experiences, so the problematic classroom behavior was not entirely their fault. They were just young; thus, some of the older students suggested the impossibility of the STEP students responding to situations in the same way that adult students could. The STEP students' lack of experience held the discussion back, but it could not be helped because of their age. One student, Elizabeth, felt that the STEP students responded to this with fear: "Oh, I think with the younger kids it's a fear of the age, of fitting in, mutual interests I'm sure." The fear led to a discomfort in the classroom, making it hard for the STEP students to adjust. Elizabeth believed that fourteen- and fifteen-year-old students are more concerned with "fitting in" to the situation and not as concerned with learning. She felt this was a typical response because high school is a different setup than college, and in high school the maturity that comes with experience is not the same as in college. Students learn different life experiences at different ages, and certain experiences can only be learned at a specific age.

Some of the non-STEP students did respond well to the diversity. These students believed that age gaps showed different sides of an experience and brought a new perspective to the discussion. They also felt that the STEP students would benefit from older students because it allowed them to be a part of a mature experience, which could lend itself to a new understanding and appreciation for education. However, only three students out of nineteen offered this positive feedback about the STEP students' presence.

No heated arguments took place within the class or during breaks from class. The observers linked this to the traditional students feeling that such confrontation was not worth the effort. However, Marisa did address the students one day in class. During an interview, she recalled what she had been thinking before the in-class scolding unfolded:

> we had to do a writing assignment about our thought process while we had a five-minute quiet time, and well you know I started not to say it but even during that five minutes of trying to be quiet it was still noise coming from that same area, and I'm like even when it's time to be quiet, they'll find a way to make noise and that was just so annoying to me.

She was not harsh in her manner, but she attempted to get the students back on track. The students' reactions to her were to be quiet for a bit, but once the activity was over, they picked back up with the whispering and noise. Marisa felt that Foley should have separated the

STEP students from each other at the beginning of the session, feeling that this might have helped the situation: "He never did say too much. He was just kinda, you could see that he was irritated, but sometimes he would wait awhile before he would finally say or he would just say the person's name in the process of you know explaining something to us to get their attention." Foley responded once to the disruptive behavior by attempting to put the STEP students into different groups; however, by the end of the session, none of the other students wanted to work with them, stating that they did not feel their work was being properly evaluated by fourteen-year-olds.

Marisa, along with some other students, walked away from the class with a negative attitude toward writing, mentioning in her final interview that she was unhappy with the progression of the class. The observers wondered how much of this was attributed to the STEP students' presence. Although the final interviews were not definitive on this issue, ultimately neither the STEP students nor the traditional and nontraditional students appeared to benefit from one another, because no pod ventured willingly into other pods during any of the group activities (including peer response groups).

Rigor and Standards

As noted, Professor Foley changed class lessons to accommodate the STEP students. More importantly, however, his expectations clearly lowered as the term progressed. Although several of the other students in the class demonstrated abilities that Foley could have tried to elevate, he appeared to relent, telling students that papers had fulfilled their contracts, even when more issues could have been addressed. Consistently, the research team analyzed the quality of essays as lower than Foley did, especially for the students who had more talent.

During several discussions with Foley, he pointed to the STEP students as a factor. Essays from other students who had potential looked better than they perhaps were in comparison to the STEP students, and Foley did not ask for further revisions. He lingered on the topic of maturity during our interviews with him. For example, he thought Alicia's experience as a server gave her more insight into public displays of emotion than the grade school experiences used by the STEP students. The older students' ability to reflect, draw out meaning from their words, and put observations into a larger context stood in stark contrast to the fourteen-year-olds in the STEP program. Even though he had not realized that he was inflating grades at first, by the time he assessed their portfolios, he knew that work he had accepted for A contracts was not as strong as it could have been. However, he justified the higher grades to an extent, indicating, perhaps, that he knew earlier that he had lowered standards. The STEP students occupied much of his time. The STEP students' supervisor would line up all six students at his office for his scheduled hours, preventing other students from discussing their writing with him on several occasions. Foley had tried to steer students to the writing center, but its hours were limited during the summer, and the tutors there also had ended up being overwhelmed by the STEP students using their facilities because the students had taken many of the available appointment slots. Foley mentioned that he felt bad for several of the non-STEP students because he had not given them the attention that they needed. He might have raised grades as a way of making up for this lack of attention.

Foley lamented that he had had no previous experience teaching K–12 students; he felt that he could not measure which cognitive demands in his pedagogy exceeded the normal abilities of a fourteen-year-old. As noted earlier, the STEP program administrators had not consulted with him prior to putting the students in his course, and the supervisors—not K–12 specialists themselves—offered no training or mentoring. When deciding on grades, he felt that he could not, in all fairness, judge the STEP students by collegiate standards. He gave an A to two STEP students when he normally would have given a B mark. He even felt that an F for CeCe was too harsh, so he gave her a D instead. Therefore, the STEP students received grades for college credit in English composition that were not awarded on the basis of their performance, but on the basis of Foley's best estimation of a fair standard for young adolescents taking a college course. It seems that rigor and standards suffered on all fronts.

Conclusion

Our study indicates that taking a college-level course did not serve the STEP students in this dual enrollment program. On the one hand, the STEP students had the opportunity to become better-rounded as students, gain more knowledge than a normal high school student, and become better prepared to enter college. The STEP students believed that by taking college classes while still in high school, they would gain information that they could apply to high school and later on in college. In their interviews, some STEP students stated that the class experience had been worth it because they learned the "skills" of writing. On the other hand, they appeared to have overlooked the larger mission of the writing course; they misunderstood the goals of the class, so the application to later courses, civic participation, and employment opportunities might be limited.

No easy solution presents itself. This study is small and perhaps if it were replicated to consider dual enrollment students during a regular term, the results would be different. If Foley or another teacher had had the opportunity to prepare for the STEP students, the curriculum might have unfolded differently and yielded greater returns. But as they are, our results suggest a conflict between the conception of knowledge that motivates a college instructor like Professor Foley and the growth of dual enrollment. The work of developmental psychologists Robert Kegan and William Perry Jr. informs our analysis. Both researchers divide cognitive development into stages with strong associations to age. The stages progress from egocentric outlooks on life to more nuanced reflections on one's position in the world—or roughly, a range from childlike attitudes to mature perspectives. Although Doug Hunt believes that watching composition students working on a problem that catches them in a transitional stage of development gives "some insight into the way people in this culture cross the threshold of adulthood" (36), what happens when the students are four years away from what this culture now deems adulthood? In other words, if prepubescent and pubescent students are, by virtue of age, in the natural state of what Perry calls "dualism" or are moving toward the first substage of "multiplicity" (66–80), we cannot reasonably expect the vast majority of them to respond to the challenges found in a progressive composition classroom.

This conclusion should hardly startle any educator. Yet, dual enrollment programs are rapidly changing the landscape of college campuses. Clearly, there must be a view of education in the minds of administrators and state legislators—an epistemological ideology—that does not value composition as a knowledge-generating discipline. In fact, knowledge under this scenario must be a static collection of information that can be memorized and regurgitated, not something applicable and relevant.

We could explore the implications of our research for dual enrollment programs and suggest ways to make them more effective. Perhaps fourteen- and fifteen-year-olds are simply too young for this experience, and programs should wait for the junior and senior years of high school to start this transition. Maybe isolating the students from the general population would allow instructors to focus on more appropriate topics for the students' maturity levels. It is possible, also, that instructors could benefit from more exposure to K–12 research and translate or transform best practices for this population into the college classroom. But finding ways to fix dual enrollment is akin to helping students find ways to fix their papers. Just as we want the writer to learn about writing, we should want administrators of dual enrollment programs to understand the flaws in the grand narrative about composition instruction. We remain convinced that the solution to the problem lies in shaping better messages about writing instruction.

Linda Adler-Kassner identifies a four-step process from which to enact change in this way: identifying an issue and a goal for change, identifying what we know and need to know to achieve the goal, identifying audiences/shaping messages, and assessing work toward the next steps (131–61). Certainly, for this particular issue, the outreach has to be to high school administrators and teachers, a historically difficult bridge to cross. Yet, if we are to shape a consistent, strong, effective message, we cannot ignore this collaboration. Once we speak the same language as K–12 educators, we can start conveying a message about writing instruction that is based on research, not lore, and reach another target audience—parents and the public at large. If we can change perceptions of education and writing instruction in particular, we can better argue for slowing down this seeming race to adulthood and allow children to be children. We must write this story.

Notes

1. The authors wish to thank Peggy Richards, Patricia Kincaid, and Brandon Sloan for their work as part of the research team that collected the data for this article.
2. All students' names have been changed.
3. Our review of Foley's commenting on student papers revealed a system meant to help students learn how to use the course handbook. Foley would put an "x" next to sentences with surface-level errors and write down the page numbers of the handbook that explained the appropriate rules. He expected students to refer to the book and ask him questions when he conferred with them.
4. At one point, Foley had to confront her on issues of honesty, pointing out to her that she had changed details and facts from the same personal experiences and observations she had used in earlier drafts so that it would appear to answer marginal questions of logic and consistency.

Works Cited

Adelman, Clifford. "The Toolbox Revisited: Paths to Degree Completion from High School through College." United States Department of Education (Executive Summary) 2 March 2006. 11 August 2008 http://www.ed.gov/rsch stat/research/pubs/toolboxrevisit/index.html.

Adler-Kassner, Linda. *The Activist WPA: Changing Stories about Writing and Writers*. Logan, UT: Utah State UP, 2008.

Bailey, Thomas, and Melinda Mechur Karp. "Promoting College Access and Success: A Review of Credit-Based Transition Programs." *The Progress of Education Reform* 6.3 (May 2005) 1–36. 20 July 2008 http://www.ed.gov /about/offices/list/ovae/pi/cclo/crdbase.pdf.

Bodmer, Paul. "Is It Pedagogical or Administrative? Administering Distance Delivery to High School." *Delivering College Composition: The Fifth Canon*. Ed. Kathleen Blake Yancey. Portsmouth, NH: Boynton/Cook Publishers, 2006. 115–26.

Farrell, Patricia L., and Kim Allan Seifert. "Lessons Learned from a Dual-Enrollment Partnership." *New Directions for Community Colleges* 139 (2007): 69–77.

High School Leadership Summit. "Dual Enrollment: Accelerating the Transition to College." United States Department of Education. 19 June 2008 http:// www.ed.gov/about/offices/list/ovae/pi/hsinit/papers/dual.pdf.

Hunt, Doug. *Misunderstanding the Assignment: Teenage Students, College Writing, and the Pains of Growth*. Portsmouth, NH: Boynton/Cook, 2002.

Karp, Melinda Mechur, et al. "Dual Enrollment Students in Florida and New York City: Postsecondary Outcomes." *CCRC Brief* 37 (Feb. 2008). http://ccrc .tc.columbia.edu/Publication.asp?UID=578.

Kegan, Robert. *The Evolving Self: Problem and Process in Human Development*. Cambridge, MA: Harvard UP, 1983.

National High School Center. "Findings from the Early College High School Initiative: A Look at Best Practices and Lessons Learned Regarding a Dual Enrollment Program." American Institute for Research. March 2007. ERIC. 20 July 2008 http://www.eric.ed.gov/ERICDocs/data/ericdocs2sql/content _storage_01/0000019b/80/3d/79/8a.pdf.

Perry, William Jr. *Forms of Ethical and Intellectual Development in the College Years*. New York: Holt, Rinehart, and Winston, 1970.

Thelin, William H., and John Paul Tassoni. "Blundering the Hero Narrative: The Critical Teacher in Classroom Representations." *Blundering for a Change: Errors and Expectations in Critical Pedagogy*. Eds. John Paul Tassoni and William H. Thelin. Portsmouth, NH: Boynton/Cook, 2000. 1–7.

Yancey, Kathleen Blake. "Delivering College Composition into the Future." *Delivering College Composition: The Fifth Canon*. Ed. Kathleen Blake Yancey. Portsmouth, NH: Boynton/Cook, 2006. 199–209.

Transformations: Working with Veterans in the Composition Classroom

Galen Leonhardy

Working with veterans in the composition classroom is the primary focus of "Transformations," which was originally titled "Platelets" — the common term for basic structures in both blood and clay. Accordingly, Galen Leonhardy's essay is about shaping writers and writing. To that end, he applies basic composition theory and practice to the specific task of facilitating versatility development with veterans as they progress through writing classes, though the theoretical concepts have application far beyond the scope of English classrooms and beyond the more narrow focus of veteran-specific strategies.

So, in community college no one would even know I was a vet. I had long hair and a long beard. At first, I was even accused of plagiarism because my writing skills were better than what was expected. I don't remember being allowed to write narrative, but I also don't remember being told not to. The first quarter was straight comp, doing the five-paragraph theme. The second quarter was writing about literature. I didn't learn about

From *Teaching English in the Two-Year College*, vol. 36, no. 4, 2009, pp. 339–52.

sentence combining and stuff until I was in grad school. I got my PhD when you started—mid-80s. I was in the community college in 1976 and at the university in 1977, graduating with the BA in 1979. I just wasn't seen as the vet, except in the VA office, I think.

—Victor Villanueva, July 4, 2008

In working with the veterans at Black Hawk College and other two-year and four-year institutions, I have learned that, when a vet is ready to write about a military experience, there is generally a sense of commitment to the process and the product. My comments as vets progress through their writing processes tend not to be harshly presented, even though most vets with whom I have worked resent shallow readings of their work and are not afraid of having their essays dug into. After all, boot camp helped most of us get past feelings of hypersensitivity. That is not the same in terms of ideological critique, however, which necessitates a more gradual approach. In short, the development of critical political sensitivities seems best suited to private journal writing, brief bantering, and research-based activities—research that allows entry-level vets to transform awareness by constructing contextualizing histories and then, in more advanced works, to begin seeing the global or interrelated nature of the political and historical webs of interaction that so affected their lives.[1]

That is a process that could take twenty years or so, but it is one that we can start in the composition classroom. Certainly, veterans, combatant or noncombatant, should not be dissuaded from experiencing writing as a process of reshaping service-related experiences into malleable compositions. That is not as easy as it sounds, but it is what we can do to get vets started. To make that start, composition instructors must first recognize that we have much to learn from veterans, just as we have much more to do for them. More specifically, veterans of the current wars do not have the same emotional needs as those involved in past wars, although current veterans do have cognitive needs that are similar to those of other students.

Background and Current Terrain

Veterans make up a fair number of potential students. It is important to understand them, even if we do not agree with the politics of the War on Terror, Operation Enduring Freedom (OEF), or Operation Iraqi Freedom (OIF). According to the Department of Veterans Affairs (VA), in FY 07 there were nearly 24 million living veterans, forty percent of whom were under the age of sixty-five. Of those veterans, just a bit more than 1.7 million were female. There were more than 523,000 education beneficiaries. About twenty percent were first-time recipients. About eighty percent of living vets are White; in terms of minority populations, 10.9 percent are Black, 5.6 percent Hispanic, .08 percent Native

American or Alaskan Native, and 1.3 percent other than those listed. Of OEF/OIF veterans, about thirty-four percent have been deployed multiple times. Another interesting fact, because it means that many of our veterans return to or are currently living in the districts that our community colleges serve, is that fifty-two percent are Reserve or National Guard members. At Black Hawk College this past year, there were 340 vets enrolled: 61 females and 279 males. In terms of economic support, many vets are going to school on the new GI Bill. They earned the opportunity—sometimes the hard way.

The discipline of composition theory and rhetoric has changed since Professor Villanueva finished his tour in Vietnam, left the Army, and made his way through the progression of experiences, schools, and degrees that eventually led to his authoring of *Bootstraps* and to his being of service to the countless students, teachers, and scholars for whom his work has been of influence. Vietnam vets often had to camouflage themselves within college settings. When we combine that with the complexities of minority status, the walls of racism, and the hurdles of poverty, we can begin to understand the significance of Villanueva's accomplishments and why his work offers the chance of inclusion while pointing toward liberation.

Three years after Villanueva's start at community college, Mina Shaughnessy published *Errors and Expectations*. By the time I made it to community college, Donald Murray had published *Write to Learn* and Professor Villanueva was working on his PhD. In the decade between Villanueva's college experience and mine, much had changed. Thanks to scholars like Murray, Shaughnessy, and Macrorie, among others, basic writing classes had become common. Narrative writing and sentence combining were commonly used. Writing labs had also become common. Without narrative, without sentence combining, without the additional support of basic writing or what many now refer to as prep courses, my development as a writer would have been less rewarding. At Spokane Falls Community College, I progressed through two basic writing courses and then received direct instruction from a rhetorical perspective that helped me experience narrative and research writing while also learning possibilities garnered by synthesizing the personal with larger sociopolitical realities. Composition theorists have moved on since then, but much of the theory that influenced my teachers is still practical pedagogy, even though it's no longer in vogue.

As a young former marine learning to write, I started with narrative, focusing on my West Pacific Fleet experiences in Asia. By allowing me to write about my experiences in order to make meaning of those experiences, teachers helped me learn that oppression, as framed by Paulo Freire, was malleable—a reality I could work to transform (31). The story of a teenage prostitute in the Philippines became a letter to then Speaker of the House, Thomas Foley. Through writing, the oppression that I had witnessed moved me into the civic discourse of my nation.

A political science teacher shifted my focus from Asia toward American involvement in South America and the maintenance of dependent economies. The process was gradual and connected to research-based activities: American political and historical interactions became global realities. By then, I could write and read well enough to survive and I knew where the tutors were when problems arose. In short, my knowledge of writing and my critical political sensitivities were shaped by experiences that included research and that allowed me to contemplate political and historical relationships.

And now, twenty-some years later, I am the college teacher, one who quite often has the opportunity to work with and learn from combatant and noncombatant military personnel. Unfortunately, more vets should be in basic writing classes. Like many two-year schools across the country, mine uses a computerized test that consistently places vets into college-level writing classes, even though their compositions exhibit extreme sentence-level cohesion issues, not to mention other indicators of precollege-level fluency. It is the same with non-veterans. Worse yet, the State of Illinois, like many other states, funds precollege classes as less than full-status classes.[2] The lessons garnered from the post–World War II education rush by veterans are discounted, as are the lessons of open admissions and the contributions of countless writing and assessment theorists. We are left trying to figure out how to keep vets from falling out as they shift from a context that privileges kinesthetic intelligence to a context privileging those intelligences that are required in academic investigations.

Veterans, Combat Zones, and Composition Theory

> Common sense told me to stand up and run from the German machine gun. When I was a soldier in World War II, the soldier's craft taught me that machine guns rise as they fire; it is best to stay low and run toward the firing machine gun.
>
> —Donald M. Murray

Much has happened since Murray's experiences. Nowadays there are women who write about being caught in ambushes and being involved in firefights. One multilingual (Spanish and English) Latina, the mother of a three-year-old, wrote about firing her .50 caliber at enemy positions, covering her comrades while the unit repositioned. Brown-eyed, stone-faced, systematic in her acquisition of skills, she passed the class and made it into the nursing program. Just recently, I saw her in the Testing Room at our school. She was pregnant and in a wheel chair. Refusing to accept a "C," she drove, even though she had been ordered to bed rest by the doctor. She did not ask for an extension: she just achieved the objective. Despite being multilingual, she refused to incorporate Spanish overtly into her writing. There was no room for ideological critique, a vast difference from the majority of young Latinas, most of whom find relief in learning that there is a place for their multilingual, multirhetorical skills (see Villanueva Jr., *Bootstraps*). She is a proud woman warrior, an American soldier wanting to become a nurse, gain economic stability, and raise a family (see Villanueva, "Considerations for American Freireistas").

In terms of male vets, this past semester there were six marines, one student who served in the Navy, and one who served in the Army; six were White and two were Latino. Based on sentence fluency, all six marines ought to have been placed in a basic writing course. The soldier, Don, a multilingual Latino and four-tour Army combat veteran, turned out to be a devoted student: although he could hardly create a paragraph-length series of coherent sentences when he started, his habit of going without sleep and willingness to work with English as a Second Language (ESL) tutors allowed him success. The young man who had been in the Navy was the only one with entry-level skills. He excelled until right near the end, when he had a two-week meltdown and vanished. I allowed him the opportunity to catch up on the work, which he did. On a less hopeful note, even though the semester-long class started with three weeks of sentence combining and two weeks of narrative writing, all but one of the marines dropped out. By the end of the class, only three veterans remained: the sailor, the soldier, and one devil dog,[3] two of whom were Latino.

Each veteran who passed, regardless of initial literacy, completed the sentence combining assignment and a narrative related to his military experience. Two of the three, both Latino, used our ESL writing labs, in which we have professional, caring, college-degreed tutor/instructors rather than student tutors. Don's narrative, after a significant amount of revision, included the following description of an ambush experience:

> As we drove our second of five routes patrolling, an Improvised Explosive Device (IED) struck my truck. All I remember was a high pitched ringing noise because after that, I had a ruptured left ear. I couldn't hear nor did I have my bearings. However, I was more concerned with the lives of my team rather than my own. Next thing I know I was out of the truck and attempting to check on my team when the platoon's medic stopped me and proceeded to provide first aid. He pulled me down and started to ask me questions, but soon realized that my hearing was not fully functional. I had blood down my face, but it was from my ear and the medic physically checked my wound and gave me the thumbs up. There were bullets all over the place but I couldn't hear them.

Not every veteran writes about such edgy experiences. Regardless, narratives of military experience seem important for vets who completed the course. Basic skills such as study habits and sentence construction, however, appear to be more important. Specifically, veterans who did not complete the class, all of whom were White, did not do the first assignment, the sentence combining, or any work with writing tutors. In terms of recommendations, vets need to be accurately placed with authentic forms of assessment. If vets need additional support, two-year colleges need to make the highest levels of support available. If composition teachers cannot orchestrate such change, it is our job to meet the students where they are, which is why I start with sentence combining. In terms of composition pedagogy, not much needs to be changed for the sake of veterans.

After sentence combining and narrative assignments, vets and non-vets alike can move toward increasing their awareness of rhetorical strategies and then argumentative research assignments. Summary writing, timed arguments, and learning to construct pages for works cited are part of that process. Daily journal writing, like sentence combining, is foundational in my classes. Free writing, as Macrorie points out in *Telling Writing*, liberates students to write without fear of being castigated and helps create a mental state that is conducive to remembering past experiences more fully and vividly (288). Despite a bit more complaining from generally younger non-vets, this process works for most and does not require changes for veterans.

Vets do sometimes bring traumatic military experiences to classroom interactiᵒ ᵗt then so do other students. In the same room where Don f penned his ambush experience, a twenty-two-year-old civiliar scribed in detail the story of being pulverized in front of her chil en by a former husband. "He beat me so bad that night that I had ʷo broken ribs, a hairline fracture in my ankle, a broken nose, and in both of my eyes, all the blood vessels were broken." In the end, her husband put a shotgun in his mouth and pulled the trigger.

Beyond allowing extra time on tests for physically and/or mentally wounded vets, the fact of trauma only means shifting enforced thematic content from what is obviously inappropriate. I make room in the class for undocumented trauma because I believe that combat zones are not isolated to battlefields. Accordingly, all students have extra time on tests if needed. In terms of composition pedagogy, it does not seem prudent to focus course content thematically on the war. Some vets do not want to write about it, for obvious reasons. In terms of assignments, however, the primary objective should be allowing vets opportunities to explore their military experiences and to facilitate that process if and when veterans so choose.

Inclusion, Banter, and Remembering Transformations

Said simply, vets deserve inclusion in our composition classrooms. Inclusion for vets should progress from personal to public. If they choose to write about military experiences in journals, the writing should be for their eyes only. The one-page daily entries that are required in my classes are private beyond page counting. In terms of moving from private to public, composition teachers need to keep their ears open around vets. One of the valves that opens the space between personal and public for many vets seems to be banter.

Banter is a playful and sometimes competitive, although most often good-humored, exchange of jesting. I promote, monitor, and control banter in classroom interactions because it allows students to test informally my expectations and their ideas. Banter provides brief glimpses of what vets are thinking, and some veterans use classroom banter to test material that might be used in future writing. If a veteran chooses to explore his or her experiences within the banter or writing, at that point it becomes public.

After small group interactions and within class discussions, veterans often banter competitively with me. In terms of common topics, sailors remind me that the Corps is part of the Navy. I call sailors "squids" because, when they march, squids are all arms and legs and one great big bulbous head. Banter itself is one of the rhetorical conventions used by service members to communicate serious issues while leavening emotional intensity. It can sometimes produce disquieting moments, however. One marine noted to a group of soldiers that he would not have had to go into Fallujah if the Army had done its job. The four-tour Latino soldier once joked about a mixture of aspirin (as I recall) and a cough medicine that he and his platoon members called their "ritual," a concoction that would put them to sleep and keep away nightmares.

Within such banter and subsequent discussions, there are many opportunities to present reliable information and to debunk falsehoods in relatively nonthreatening ways. For example, there is often room for the political redirection of students who are inclined to believe that Iraq was responsible for the 9/11 attacks, as well as the redirection of those students—both veterans and non-veterans—whose nationalistic and xenophobic philosophies support more restrictive paradigms. In short, if it suits the teacher, banter can open spaces for the dissemination of reliable information and support a variety of dialogic interactions. Certainly, within competitive banter, the space opens for the kind of ideological redirection that those of us who are opposed to misinformation might hope for.

The public process of reshaping experience from journaling to narrative often, but not always, leads to a gradual reshaping from narrative into argumentative research, which may include portions of original narratives or may be tangentially refocused on a topic relevant to military experience. A narrative written by a Latino marine, for example, reshaped into a research paper about the Veterans' Administration and medical benefits. For the vets who complete a narrative, connecting to researched information is often a process that takes place, as Macrorie wrote in *The I-Search Paper*, because "somebody needs to find out something or wants to satisfy an itch of curiosity as insistent as athlete's foot" (162). Memories, even though they may be the stuff of nightmares, are vital to writers. Memories, that is, shape and can be reshaped.

Beyond listening to what veterans say and providing opportunities for direct instruction and the gradual acquisition of skills, how can we best facilitate their needs in our composition classrooms? My more caring colleagues keep asking me that question. The answer has two parts. First, good pedagogy in the composition classroom is good pedagogy for all students. We do not need to change what we do, as long as our practice is supported by theory and research. In terms of working specifically with vets, however, I suggest leading by example.

We need to take the point position. One thing that helps me work with veterans and non-veterans alike is completing my own course assignments. It is common for quality composition instructors to be writers who teach. Taking a classroom assignment and creating a published work both validates assignments and allows for remembrance. Writing narratives and transforming them into argumentative research papers or publications provides opportunities to remember the work, the feelings, the mistakes, the hurdles, and the accomplishments that go with learning college-level requirements.

Last semester, students and I shared the experience of journal writing. My entries were public, an attempt to model Ken Macrorie's notion that good journals do not "speak" privately (*Telling Writing* 141). The students' entries were private, freeing them from the forced sharing of intimacies. I wrote at least two entries for every one of theirs and sometimes read short selections, which often led to interesting discussions. The essay that you are reading began as one of those journal entries and then became the source for a history assignment. I first wrote about one of my more significant military experiences — one previously denied expression. What helped most in getting that journal-based version on paper was believing that the process of writing about my military experience would help provide the insight needed for what Nancy Sommers, in "Across the Drafts," referred to as "the work of entering into our students' minds and composing humane, thoughtful, even inspiring responses" (248). It was a deeply emotional struggle, just as it is for many vets. Those entries were more rant than narrative, more a scribbled bunch of memories and condemnations. The rant was reshaped into a basic narrative about experiences as a member of the Lebanon Peacekeeping Forces, which became the foundation for the history assignment. It is my goal to lead by example, remember learning experiences, remember being a younger creatively engaged writer, and thereby, become better able to facilitate students' self-critique and problem-solving processes.

Leading by example allows me to engage a process of remembering, to patrol carefully the epistemological path of recollection that leads me through the jungle terrain of my postmilitary transformation as a writer, preemptively locating the positions of error. Remembrances can be used in lectures or in more personal settings, such as small groups or one-on-one interactions. The process of completing my own assignments also increases my empathy and provides models that help me understand more fully the difficulties, physical and mental, of pounding, shaping, and reshaping an essay. I could, but usually do not, share drafts. Instead, I keep the knowledge and empathy until it is needed, introducing veterans and non-veterans alike as gently as possible to the claylike nature of writing.

Having empathy is important as teachers prepare students to get their hands into the clay. I remember early experiences as a college writer. As it was for me, the majority of veterans in my college-level classes often have no idea of how to locate a thesis statement in a *Newsweek* or *Time* editorial. They see more what interests them rather than authorial intent. Nor do they understand well how to paraphrase or generalize. Seeing cohesion or paragraph-level focus errors in their own or peer writing is quite difficult. Many have a difficult time reading even basic narratives or understanding academic expectations. In most cases, my class provides the first real opportunity to experience the process of reshaping an essay and to consider ideological influences deeply. I understand all of that.

There are things I cannot reminisce myself into understanding, however. Some of the minority veteran students enlisted because they wanted citizenship or a bootstrap with which to pull themselves and their families up. Many returning vets have memories with which I cannot fully empathize. In such cases, the vets have to help me understand the clay with which they are working.

In terms of making the private public, most veterans understand collaboration well and can involve themselves in small group interactions that support their first tries at real revision. In peer groups, vets get to have their work read, quite often for the first time. Small groups seem to facilitate class discussions, which allow vets to establish in-group relationships and non-veterans to ask questions—questions that some students deeply long to have answered.

After a period of group work followed by classroom discussion, a nineteen-year-old female asked what many might consider a rude question. Group work had led to talk about the war in Iraq. She asked if I had personally shot at or killed anybody. The openness caught me a little off guard. She had no fear of asking. I replied that luckily I had not. She asked if I had seen anybody shooting at people, to which I said that I had seen the cruiser *Virginia*, the *John Rodgers*, the *Bowen*, and the destroyer *Radford* firing on enemy positions when I was part of the Lebanon Peacekeeping Forces. She went back to work. Many non-veterans have a deep curiosity about the war in Iraq, as well as about war in general. I consider it my duty to be honest and to support such investigations; however, asking a person if he or she has killed another person does seem to push the limits of propriety, something that teachers might want to get across to students in a way that does not stifle curiosity.

In terms of ideological redirection and classroom management, the vast majority of vets in my classes tend to be more experienced students who understand rule-based instruction. There are times when reality contradicts understanding. The teacher must maintain governance over behavior expectations. We teach students how to recognize reliable sources, even when that means challenging their emotionally laden beliefs. Most of the vets seem comfortable debating an idea adamantly while still understanding the value of reasoned evidence. For teachers who are not inclined to banter, the process of research provides opportunities to move students away from myths. Students can be referred to magazines such as *The Nation* and *The New Republic* or toward articles in *The New York Times*, as well as toward websites such as the nation.com, npr.org, and brookings.edu. In short, journals, bantering, and research-based activities allow vets access to inclusion and opportunities to understand their experiences as politically and historically interrelated.

Learning and Leading

Taking a history class on the Middle East from 1700, or at least making a study of Middle Eastern history and the religions of the area, benefits both teachers and students. Goldschmidt and Davidson's *A Concise History of the Middle East* and John L. Esposito's *What Everyone Needs to Know about Islam* provide reliable starting points for both composition teachers and students. As composition teachers, we would also do well to know a bit about European colonialism, the thinking of anticolonial theorists like Franz Fanon, and the basics of world systems theory.

The Middle East has been a land of trade and a battleground for a few thousand years. Over the millennia, millions upon millions have traded there. No small number of those folks fought for land that linked what might be defined in the world systems perspective of Eric Wolf's *Europe and the People without History* as a multiethnic web of interactions, a set of interactions linking the peoples of the Mediterranean Basin with Europeans, Africans, and Asians, as well as North and South Americans, through a series of interconnected and interdependent trade routes and other social networks. It is interesting to watch vets in my classes move toward their own understandings of global interactions and what some come to see as the abhorrence of American imperialism.

In terms of knowledge associated with taking the lead for the sake of inclusion, composition teachers need to be aware of our minority vets. Victor Villanueva's *Bootstraps* is a must-read text for instructors who are interested in more fully understanding the experiences of minority and multilingual students, non-vets and vets alike. The text offers us ways of enhancing inclusion.

In terms of leading, issues associated with ethnicity, as well as race and racism, spark discussions. Interestingly, vets in my region seldom self-introduce such topics. Instead, my experiences, used to model academically acceptable discussion conventions and topics, have been the catalyst for communication about diversity, race, and racism. For example, revealing my personal experiences in the history class that I took, the one for which I revised this essay while it was still a narrative, led to one classroom discussion. The recorded lectures for the online history class included a racialized description of the Middle East—in which the professor who lectured (not the professor who managed the online class), after giving a head nod to anthropologists who objected to such descriptions because of "so much blurring of racial lines by intermarriage over the centuries," went on to note that, in a demographic description of the Middle East, we would find "some of the Negroid race in the Sudan region, Saudi Arabia—even some in the Persian Gulf [while] you would find some Mongoloids predominantly in northeast Iran and some parts of Iraq." For the most, however, "the Middle East can be categorized as Caucasian, and, from an American perspective, if you travel there, many would not look darker skinned than what many in the West would consider to be Caucasian." According to the professor, this is a fact that shows how races have "merged to the point where they are virtually indistinguishable."

I told my writing students about the experience of listening to that lecture with my Black office partner. Both Latino veterans (a marine who served in the first Gulf War and the four-tour combat veteran) made their disapproval known, as did African American students, all female (not vets). The composition students used computers to locate and read the *American Anthropological Association's Statement on Race*. I pointed out that race does not exist, but racism does, which Professor Villanueva has been telling composition theorists for years. The class discussed racism in general and racism in their own lives, as well as the idea of racism in college contexts and the idea of racism in relation to people from the Middle East, an age-old objectification that supports dehumanization of the enemy. Vets and non-vets asked in class how I dealt with the situation. As it turned out, because I had critically challenged material in online discussions and included the *American Anthropological Association's Statement on Race* in contrast to lecture content, the professor of the class wrote a note asking me to "chill out" and commenting that there was little hope of ever healing our friendship.

Unlike the Vietnam-era vets I know, veterans of the wars in Iraq and Afghanistan remain relatively quiet about the subject of race. Vietnam-era vets, by the way, make up the largest segment of living veterans in America, a group composed of some 7.9 million service members, who can be quite outspoken advocates of civil rights (Department of Veterans Affairs). In boot camp, I was indoctrinated with the idea that there were only light-green and dark-green marines. Still, the percentage of dark-green was higher than that found in civilian populations.

Having served with marines from a wide variety of economic conditions and ethnicities, I developed a deep respect for minority marines. Most knew and many of us talked about the racism that they faced.

College readings and sociology classes later introduced the idea that the reason so many minority marines entered the service was likely a result of economic considerations. For OIF/OEF vets, a variety of editorials in local newspapers have openly contradicted such reasoning in relation to current military composition, pointing out that, in the Midwest, rurally located, White middle-class males make up the majority of current enlistees, a notion that is partially confirmed by Department of Defense FY 2006 recruitment statistics showing that enlistment in the nation's smallest cities is significantly higher than in the nation's largest cities, with 12.4 recruits per 10,000 residents in small towns versus 8.7 in the cities (Fischer). A trip to the local U.S. Marine recruiting center not too far from Black Hawk College revealed lines of mostly White faces in the Polaroid images of local enlistees. Regardless, Latinos, Latinas, and African Americans comprise a significant portion of the veteran population in my classes. Still, there is little self-initiated discussion about race or racism. That noted, when the topic is introduced, I have found that vets are interested in it.

Twenty-one years ago, the process of reading and making connections between the information garnered from research and my military experiences was a foreign task, mostly because of the difficulty associated with learning how to express those connections in my own words and how to incorporate and cite source material. Attempting to shortcut the citation process produced a litany of error patterns: citing at the end of the paragraph for all of the material within the paragraph, and using an author's words rather than my own, to name two personal embarrassments now mirrored in the attempts of current vets. I had to learn how to connect to my readers with the use of sensory description, constructions of place that made historical facts more interesting. In addition, I had to learn to transition between the information from research and my personal experiences, a process that led to both failed and successful attempts with flashbacks, excerpts used as transitions, and direct quotations, experiments that helped develop my literary imagination. I also learned how to cut personal narrative and diatribe for the sake of academic tone and length requirements. Engaging in active remembrance has helped me preemptively intervene when vets and non-vets choose to pound the claylike forms of narrative into research-based writing and to connect, more often than not, the personal to larger social realities. Certainly, these are specific and beneficial strategies that composition teachers can provide for vets.

In terms of connecting personally with vets, I must admit that the idea of telling my students about my own military experiences never really occurred to me until returning veterans started coming to my office because they heard that I had been a jarhead, and, even then, I never mentioned being off the coast of Lebanon—beyond once showing my DD214 and a map of Lebanon to a young marine, choosing to tell funny stories about the people that I served with instead of explaining the rather short list of ribbons and medals. Like Vietnam vets, my generation of service members often found themselves *personae non gratae*.

As the populations of multitour OEF/OIF student veterans increased, my own self-imposed writing assignments led to more open and honest in-class discussions explaining how lived experience can be transformed from journal entry to narrative and promoting the realization that essays are malleable structures, like clay, that can be formed and reformed before the final firing of publication. Student vets learned quickly that their experiences were valuable, malleable, and ultimately useful, like a ceramic bowl. Having endured a trial by fire, the bowl can be used to serve other people for a greater good. Scuttlebutt made its way around, and, eventually, I was invited to become the advisor for our student veterans' organization.

Adding to narrative constructions a sense of history or a sense of place—or even adding information that is relevant to other discourse communities—can create the space for veterans to transform simple narratives and, thereby, find inclusion. Having a cursory knowledge of the history of the place that was the focus of military experience allows me to facilitate and critique my vets' writing about a war that has so dominated and will likely continue to dominate their perceptions. Having written about the Middle East and having lived again one of my own significant Middle Eastern military experiences, I can better check for historic inaccuracies and more effectively critique the vets' rhetorical strategies. I can also lead vets and non-vets alike toward source material when they are writing about the Middle East. In short, composition instructors need to be informed about the Middle East and the current war if they are to lead effectively.

Composition teachers also need to be aware of the power of comments on vets' papers. The process of completing an assignment for the history class allowed me to remember what it is to submit my writing for assessment and evaluation. Four weeks into an eight-week class, the teacher returned my first paper with three comments typed in bright blue. The first was a reminder that "Navel Institute" should have been "Naval Institute" (an embarrassing error, but one common to those of us who have moved from basic writing courses to upper-level studies).[4] The second comment noted an interesting point[5] without providing commentary explaining why the content was interesting. And the third comment, with its missing period, was a sloppy salutation.[6] It was upsetting that my teacher did not check or make comments about dates, sources, content, or future possibilities—which my community college teachers did to facilitate my growth as a scholar. As composition teachers, we need to be able to help our vets by making sure that their information is accurate.

The process of molding the narrative and then reshaping it from conventions that are associated with English composition to those associated with the study of history has helped me explain processes for bridging discourse community expectations. It also allowed me to realize how frustrating it was to get superficial comments after laboring for weeks with a self-valued topic, how embarrassing it is to struggle with spelling, and how greatly I abhorred those teachers who did not care to help me grow as a scholar. And then there were the feelings of being humiliated by comments that, in their superficiality, devalued or dishonored the effort of writing about painfully important experiences—such as watching a fourteen-year-girl sell her body to military comrades or not being allowed in 1983 to return to Lebanon after the October 23rd Beirut barracks bombing. What I wanted, as a younger vet-scholar, were comments that would allow me to gain authority, comments pointing to errors in my reasoning as well as in my spelling, comments that let me tell others about my experiences in the military in ways that would allow my ideas to facilitate the creation of a better world, a place where children could be free from the horror of commodification and rape. As composition teachers, let's not devalue vets' writing in the way that my history professor did. Assigning an "A" grade does not exempt us from assessment.

Conclusion

When all is said and done, I try to do for my veterans what my community college teachers did for me. It seems apparent that allowing for inclusion and providing freedom of choice in terms of writing topics produces less resistance in veterans and non-veterans alike. The process of starting with sentence combining and moving on to narrative and then to argumentation allows me to introduce in nonthreatening ways ideas that are often quite radical. Beyond that, I have come to accept that some vets want to write about service experiences. Others do not. It is not my job to "push" a veteran to relive his or her combat experiences or any other aspect of his or her military experience. The vets write about their military experiences if and when they are ready. There is enough for inclusion and enough for the possibility of transformation in that.

Notes

1. Paul Lindholdt, Anne Bolliti, Dana Elder, and Victor Villanueva, as well as Editor Jeff Sommers and two *Teaching English in the Two-Year College* reviewers helped make the writing of this essay possible.
2. In FY07, the college received $15.78 per credit hour for what our school refers to as "developmental" courses and $19.06 for baccalaureate-level courses.
3. Marine.

4. "<SURELY YOU MEAN NAVAL> (US Navel Institute, 1984); you aren't writing about the Bellybutton institute right?"
5. "I was readying myself for a fight, and I distinctly remember wondering about the countless hundreds of thousands or perhaps millions of other fighters like me who, over the course of centuries, had readied themselves. <interesting point>"
6. "Fun read Galen. Thanks for sharing it 40/40"

Works Cited

Department of Veterans Affairs. National Center for Veterans Analysis and Statistics. 30 July 2008 http:www1.va.gov/vetdata/.

Esposito, John. *What Everyone Needs to Know about Islam.* New York: Oxford UP, 2002.

Fischer, Douglas. "Rural Areas Losing More Soldiers in Iraq." *ContraCosta Times.com* March 17, 2008. 19 June 2008 http://www.contracostatimes.com /calltoarms/ci_8601083.

Freire, Paulo. *Pedagogy of the Oppressed.* New York: Continuum, 1997.

Goldschmidt, Arthur Jr., and Lawrence Davidson. *A Concise History of the Middle East.* Boulder, CO: Westview, 2006.

Macrorie, Ken. *The I-Search Paper.* Portsmouth, NH: Boynton/Cook, 1988.

———. *Telling Writing.* New Jersey: Boynton/Cook, 1985.

Murray, Donald M. *Write to Learn,* 4th ed. Fort Worth: Harcourt Brace, 1993.

Shaughnessy, Mina P. *Errors and Expectations.* New York, NY: Oxford UP, 1977.

Sommers, Nancy. "Across the Drafts." *College Composition and Communication* 58.2 (2006): 248–56.

Villanueva, Victor Jr. *Bootstraps: From an American Academic of Color.* Urbana, IL: NCTE, 1993.

———. "Considerations of American Freireistas." *Cross-Talk in Comp Theory: A Reader*. Ed. Victor Villanueva Jr. Urbana, IL: NCTE, 1997. 621–37.

———. "Re: RE." Email to Author. 4 July 2008.

Wolf, Eric. *Europe and the People without History.* Berkeley: U of California P, 1997.

PART SIX

The Profession of English at the Two-Year College

As the essays in this volume make clear, teaching English in the two-year college is what Mark Reynolds and Sylvia Holladay-Hicks call a "distinct and significant profession" (ix). The profession is significant because approximately half of all undergraduate students in the United States take their introductory writing courses at two-year colleges, and a disproportionate number of those students are from backgrounds that have historically been underrepresented in higher education. As two-year college English teachers prepare students to become successful college readers, writers, and thinkers, they are furthering the cause of equity, access, and social justice. Two-year college faculty also have a distinct professional profile, which is the focus of Part Six of this collection.

Chapter 18 examines issues of professional identity. As Christie, Brett Griffiths, and Kate Thirolf show in their article "'Distinct and Significant,'" two-year college English faculty often experience different institutional expectations and rewards, have different patterns of engagement with scholarship and professional organizations, and possess different understandings of their own professional authority than faculty at four-year institutions. These factors contribute to unique professional identities that are still under construction as both two-year colleges and the field of writing studies evolve.

One important force shaping these professional identities is the Two-Year College English Association (TYCA). As Jeffrey Andelora documents in his important series of essays in *Teaching English in the Two-Year College* (*TETYC*), efforts to integrate two-year college English faculty into professional organizations began as far back as the 1950s. During this period, existing organizations for English teachers—the National Council of Teachers of English (NCTE) and its Conference on College Composition and Communication (CCCC)—encouraged the formation of regional organizations for two-year college faculty. The seven regional TYCAs established themselves throughout the 1960s and early 1970s. NCTE and CCCC made periodic efforts over the next several decades to foster a greater two-year college presence at their annual conventions, and in the 1990s, a movement emerged to form a robust national TYCA organization that would give two-year college faculty a voice within NCTE. As Christie observes in "Unmeasured Engagement," participation in TYCA is by no means universal among two-year college English faculty. Over the last two decades, however, the national TYCA organization has become a major forum for two-year teacher-scholars, issuing position statements, fostering research and professional development, and, more recently, analyzing policy related to two-year college English teaching.

TYCA's 2012 statement, "Characteristics of the Highly Effective Two-Year College Instructor in English," is the organization's most direct articulation of what it means to be an engaged two-year college professional. As this document asserts, highly effective two-year college English instructors:

- "are exemplary teacher-scholars" [For more on the history and practices of teacher-scholarship, see Andelora's essay on p. 579 in this volume.]

- "center their classrooms on students"

- "understand and value student diversity"

- "collaborate with full time and part time colleagues to maximize student success"

- "develop individual areas of expertise that contribute to well-rounded academic departments"

- "accept the responsibility of college and broader community leadership"

The characteristics outlined in this statement reflect the distinctive knowledge, practices, and commitments required to teach writing effectively — and to continue developing professionally — in two-year college settings.

However, such professional ideals are difficult to realize given the current labor structures in two-year colleges. In most English departments, the majority of instructors are part-time adjunct or contingent faculty, many of whom lack job security, benefits, and the time and resources to attend conferences and participate in professional organizations — a subject we turn to in Chapter 19. As Helena Worthen demonstrates in "The Problem of the Majority Contingent Faculty in the Community Colleges," these instructors often teach at multiple campuses for compensation well below a living wage, and many aspire to a full-time status that few will be able to attain. In "Not Just a Matter of Fairness," Jeffrey Klausman observes that adjunct faculty often feel marginalized within their departments and have little role in institutional decision-making. They also have fewer resources or incentives to participate in professional development opportunities. These conditions impede efforts to create coherent writing programs built around shared learning goals and sound assessment practices (Klausman, "Mapping the Terrain").

Kate Thirolf's research (see Toth, Griffiths, and Thirolf, p. 515) suggests that some two-year college writing programs do a better job than others at positioning adjunct faculty as professional colleagues. Nonetheless, these labor structures present a persistent challenge to two-year college English departments. As long as more than three-quarters of two-year college English faculty are adjuncts, it will be difficult to achieve the levels of professional engagement outlined in the "Characteristics of the Highly Effective Two-Year College Instructor of English," or to ground U.S. postsecondary writing instruction in disciplinary theory and research.

Taken together, the readings in Part Six present a nuanced portrait of the state of the profession. They offer suggestions and pose as-yet unresolved questions about what it currently means—and what it *could* mean—to be a two-year college teacher-scholar. Even as this volume goes to print, that professional model continues to develop. Both Jeffrey Andelora ("Teacher/Scholar/Activist") and Patrick, for example, have introduced the idea of the "teacher-scholar-activist," a role that encompasses teaching, scholarship, and advocacy for two-year colleges and students in the realm of public opinion and policy making (see also Two-Year College English Association "Guidelines"; Toth, Sullivan, and Calhoon-Dillahunt). Likewise, in a recent *TETYC* article, Christie and Patrick have urged teachers of English at the two-year college to move beyond an individualized notion of "the teacher-scholar" to begin cultivating local teacher-scholar communities of practice. Such communities would make ongoing engagement with scholarship an integral part of day-to-day teaching and administrative practices within two-year college English departments. We hope you will find the materials we have included in this chapter helpful to your ongoing professional development.

Works Cited

Andelora, Jeffrey. "Forging a National Identity: TYCA and the Two-Year College Teacher-Scholar." *Teaching English in the Two-Year College*, vol. 35, no. 4, 2008, pp. 350-62.

- - -. "The Professionalization of Two-Year College English Faculty: 1950-1990." *Teaching English in the Two-Year College*, vol. 35, no. 1, 2007, pp. 6-19.

- - -. "Teacher/Scholar/Activist: A Response to Keith Kroll's 'The End of the Community College English Profession.'" *Teaching English in the Two-Year College*, vol. 40, no. 3, 2013, pp. 302-7.

- - -. "TYCA and the Struggle for a National Voice: 1991-1993." *Teaching English in the Two-Year College*, vol. 35, no. 2, 2007, pp. 133-48.

- - -. "TYCA and the Struggle for a National Voice: 1994–1997." *Teaching English in the Two Year College*, vol. 35, no. 3, 2008, pp. 252-65.

Klausman, Jeffrey. "Mapping the Terrain: The Two-Year College Writing Program Administrator." *Teaching English in the Two-Year College*, vol. 35, no. 3, 2008, pp. 238-51.

Reynolds, Mark, and Sylvia Holladay-Hicks, editors. *The Profession of English in the Two-Year College.* Boynton/Cook, 2005.

Sullivan, Patrick. "The Two-Year College Teacher-Scholar-Activist." *Teaching English in the Two-Year College*, vol. 42, no. 4, 2015, pp. 327-50.

Toth, Christie, and Patrick Sullivan. "Toward Local Teacher-Scholar Communities of Practice." *Teaching English in the Two-Year College*, vol. 43, no. 3, 2016, pp. 247-73.

Toth, Christie, et al. "A Dubious Method of Improving Educational Outcomes: Accountability and the Two-Year College." *Teaching English in the Two-Year College*, vol. 43, no. 4, 2016, pp. 391-410.

Two-Year College English Association. "Characteristics of the Highly Effective Two-Year College Instructor of English." Two-Year College English Association, 2012.

Two-Year College English Association, "Guidelines for Preparing Teachers of English in the Two-Year College." Two-Year College English Association, 2016.

Professional Identities

The Teacher/Scholar: Reconstructing Our Professional Identity in Two-Year Colleges

Jeff Andelora

This landmark essay provides a comprehensive historical and theoretical overview of the "teacher-scholar" professional model among two-year college English faculty. Jeff Andelora describes the institutional, professional, and disciplinary structures that have long prevented two-year college faculty from identifying—and being identified—as scholars. Drawing on the work of many early leaders in the teacher-scholar professional movement, Andelora argues for the importance of scholarship written by and for two-year college faculty as a way to establish "professional parity," as well as to achieve greater representation of two-year college interests and intellectual work within the field of rhetoric and composition. This article provides an important synthesis of the conversations that laid the groundwork for the last decade of two-year college teacher scholarship.

> We are called the "invisible colleges" both because university researchers rarely study our programs and our students, and because two-year college departments rarely publish program and institutional-based studies of our programs and our students.
>
> —John C. Lovas

From *Teaching English in the Two-Year College*, vol. 32, no. 3, 2005, pp. 307-22.

In my experience, some of the most dedicated writing teachers teach in community colleges and public- or state-funded institutions. Public institutions have a tradition of thinking about their writing program[s] and taking the training of writing teachers much more seriously than elite institutions have in the past. Elite institutions have a lot to learn from the important work that goes on at community colleges and state-funded colleges.

—Nancy Sommers

As faculty in two-year and open-admission colleges, we occupy a somewhat tenuous position in the stratified world of higher education. One might argue that, with a one-hundred-year history and currently close to twelve hundred institutions serving as ports of entry for half of America's undergraduates, our success and status are assured. Yet two-year college faculty have long felt marginalized by our university colleagues, and evidence suggests that this perception isn't entirely unwarranted.[1] This is in large part because of the institutional culture of two-year colleges, which historically has cast faculty as teachers, not researchers or scholars. Because of our relatively heavy teaching loads and general lack of institutional support for scholarship, we have not, for the most part, participated in the scholarly activity that is vital to the professional success of faculty whose tenure and promotion require them to publish. This sense of marginalization also holds, to varying degrees, within specific disciplines. Although the field of rhetoric and composition has certainly embraced the work and contributions of two-year college faculty, Cynthia Lewiecki-Wilson and Jeff Sommers write that the contemporary narratives written about composition at open-admissions institutions "structure perceptions so that it is very difficult to see, let alone seriously consider, any possibility of satisfying intellectual work occurring between composition teachers and their students in open admissions programs" (p. 60 in this volume). If these narratives carry the day and it is believed that no "satisfying intellectual work" can occur at the two-year college, then we will be forever marginalized. Yet, as anyone who has taught composition in a two-year college knows, satisfying intellectual work does take place; what doesn't take place, however, is our successfully communicating the nature of that work to the larger disciplinary community and the world beyond the academy.

In the early 1990s, in an attempt to begin telling our story, Mark Reynolds, Howard Tinberg, and Keith Kroll called on their colleagues in the two-year colleges to defy the constraints of their institutional cultures and write themselves into the professional conversations. What began to emerge over the decade was a campaign to recast ourselves as experienced teachers of writing whose pedagogies and programs were not only worthy of study, but were, in fact, central to the discipline.

Despite the professional identities that had been constructed by and for two-year college faculty, community college English faculty sought to establish a new professional identity that would transcend the dictates of the academic culture and the dichotomy of the teacher/scholar. In short, we sought to establish ourselves as viable members of the discipline with a voice that would help shape the future of composition studies. While the field of composition has been receptive to this movement—two-year college faculty have served as chairs of CCCC and are well represented in NCTE—it has been, and continues to be, a struggle. This paper will examine the ways our professional identity as community college composition faculty has been constructed and the campaign to rewrite this identity in defiance of our institutional culture. Specifically, I will look at the two strands this reform movement has taken: one, the call by leaders in two-year college English encouraging two-year college faculty to engage in scholarship and to publish their findings; and two, the call by leaders in two-year college English to encourage university rhet/comp faculty to study, either alone or in collaboration with two-year college faculty, two-year college writing programs. It's a fascinating history, one that should be of interest to anyone in the field who is familiar with rhetoric and composition's own history and struggle for identity. And, as two-year college writing faculty and their programs continue to redefine themselves and gain more prominence within the discipline, it's a history that needs to be explored and understood.

Identity as a Construct of Academic Culture

More than a century ago, two-year colleges were born into an identity crisis. According to Arthur M. Cohen and Florence B. Brawer in *The American Community College*, the early junior colleges came from various lineages: some were born as branch campuses of state universities; others were created by states themselves and overseen by a state board; others were created by local high-school districts; and still others were created by local groups with no legal authority (3). Despite the fact that all of these two-year institutions were expected to provide a college-level curriculum, the very appellation of junior college designated them as something not to be taken too seriously, almost as if they would forever be the university's kid sibling. Even the gradual shift in terminology from junior college to community college that occurred from the 1950s to the 1970s reinforced a populist, watered-down academic image of these institutions. This question of identity spilled into the disciplines. Keats Sparrow, founding editor of *Teaching English in the Two-Year College*, described the state of two-year college English during the 1960s and early 1970s that led to the formation of the journal as a "new kind of English—neither high school nor college English and not exactly in between" (14). Two-year colleges have struggled with other conflicting perceptions as well. Advocates of community colleges, citing their open-door admissions policies, articulation agreements with universities, flexible scheduling, alternative delivery methods, appeal to nontraditional students, training of midlevel workers, and relatively low cost, have called them democracy's colleges. These colleges provide access to millions who would have been denied a university education for reasons of cost, preparation, privilege, or geographic proximity (Cohen and Brawer; Pickett, p. 11; Griffith and Connor). Critics, on the other hand, have argued that community colleges were anything but democratic; instead, they've claimed, two-year colleges were supported as part of an elitist agenda to reinforce class inequities inherent in a capitalist economy, what Ira Shor terms "educational apartheid" (52). This view holds that two-year colleges became a place to divert working-class students away from the university—thus allowing elite colleges and universities to maintain their selective admissions criteria—where they would have their aspirations "cooled" until they eventually dropped out (Clark; Zwerling; Shor). Still others have argued that while there is evidence to support both of these positions, it is at best selective, and neither argument fully explains the complexity of the community college's social function (Dougherty; Lovas, "All").

Faculty at two-year colleges have found their professional identities shaped by these conflicting perceptions. Because the community college culture has traditionally emphasized the role of faculty member as teacher and devalued the role of faculty member as scholar, it's not uncommon for faculty who spend their careers teaching in a two-year college to feel a growing sense of estrangement from their discipline. In part, this role has been constructed for them. Cohen and Brawer write, "When the liberal arts were brought from the universities into the community colleges, the ethos of academic scholarship did not accompany them. The colleges were not supportive of scholarship, and the university training that instructors received was not adequate to foster teachers who would attend to the reflections and meaning of their disciplines" (336). Hiring practices reinforced this role. During the first half of this century, the majority of faculty were hired from the secondary schools—80 percent of those teaching in the 1920s had secondary teaching experience; 64 percent in the 1950s. It wasn't until the 1970s that an increasing number began to be hired from graduate programs, other community colleges, and the trades (Cohen and Brawer 77). Additionally, because it has never been a requirement that community college faculty have PhDs—in fact, there has long been a tradition of favoring the MA over the PhD based on the claim that the specialized research degree was unsuitable for teaching large numbers of a diverse, largely underprepared student body—it's reasonable to assume that the majority of two-year college faculty had not been trained to conduct research and/or take part in the specialized scholarly activity that traditionally characterized disciplinarity. In 1991 James Palmer reported that only 12 percent of community college faculty held a PhD (70). Of course, the prevailing academic culture continues to reinforce this: a heavy teaching load, no institutional requirement or reward for research or scholarship (even occasional hostility toward those who want to conduct research), and an increasingly student-centered curriculum and pedagogy, have, for many, resulted in a dissociation from the larger disciplinary community.

It is largely because of this lack of participation in research, theorizing, and knowledge building—what Ernest Boyer calls the scholarship of discovery—that a class structure has developed. In the *Chronicle of Higher Education*, Dana Zimbleman writes of the "snobbery and bias" graduate faculty have exhibited toward the work done at the community college. She writes that applying for a job at a community college is considered the "kiss of death" if you're also applying to four-year schools. In another *Chronicle* article, Christine Gray writes that she was told by her graduate professors that spending longer than three years teaching at a community college would result in her being "discredited by those working in [her] research area." While Barbara K. Townsend and Nancy LaPaglia argue in *Community College Review* that two-year college faculty have not internalized these negative stereotypes, Howard Tinberg, editor of *TETYC*, suggests otherwise. In "Writing a Book on the (Two-Year College) Job" he writes: "On the face of it, the title of this essay seems palpably absurd. What two-year college faculty member has the time and energy to write a book?" (49). However, even though we as two-year college faculty are likely to take offense at the suggestion that our work is less valuable than that of our university colleagues, if we don't write, if we don't engage in the scholarly activity on which the discipline depends, if we don't transcend our institutional culture and take part in the discourse of our discipline, there's little hope of attaining professional parity. Tinberg poses these questions: "How did I feel when students came to my classroom thinking that they were in grade 13, an extension of high school? How did it make me feel when colleagues at four-year schools viewed my work as less significant than theirs?" (50). Angry enough to write, he asserts. But this impulse is immediately checked by doubt: "Write what? What could I do or say that would be worthy of publication?" And in expressing this doubt in himself as a scholar, Tinberg speaks for many of us. He muses that these are the very questions

> that many of us who teach at the two-year college constantly ask ourselves, in part because we have internalized a view of ourselves that others constructed for us: that we are teachers first, writers and scholars last. How else can I explain the defensiveness that I hear from colleagues when the subject of writing comes up? In my work with faculty members from the English department in our writing lab, I hear this defensiveness all the time. [. . .] When did we start separating the writing (and reading,

for that matter) from our teaching and learning? Why must talented and bright colleagues constantly sell themselves short as writers? I suspect that much of this distrust is a residue of graduate school, where, as we well know, the act of writing is almost always secondary to critique and the process of composing done under great personal duress. I also suspect that there is something in the culture of the two-year college that works against the intellectual work of written scholarship and research. Like many of our students, we may think so little of our capabilities and of the work we do that writing about accomplishments simply doesn't seem worthwhile. (50)

It's this crisis of confidence, perhaps more than any other single factor, that has prevented two-year college faculty from asserting their voices and claiming recognition for their work.

Rewriting Our Identity

I don't mean to suggest for a moment that as two-year college English faculty we lack a professional identity. The seeds for a national identity were planted in 1965 when NCTE and CCCC sponsored seven regional conferences for two-year college faculty. Other milestones soon followed. In 1967 NCTE brought representatives from these regions together for a planning meeting, and CCCC supported the formation of the National Junior College Committee (NJCC)—this was later to become National Two-Year College Committee (NTCC)—the first national group. In 1974 the first issue of *TETYC*—a journal now well into its thirty-first year—was published. In 1997, NCTE formally recognized the new Two-Year College Association, an organization that was able to provide a stronger, more unified national voice than NTCC was able to provide. NCTE voted in 2001 to place the national chair of TYCA on its governing board. Paul Bodmer, who taught community college English for over twenty years, now serves as NCTE's Associate Executive Director for Higher Education. In 2001 the MLA created a Community College Committee. Since the early 1970s, CCCC has chosen seven chairs from two-year colleges.[2] Additionally, two-year college English faculty and their programs are increasingly represented in edited collections.[3] For all intents and purposes, two-year college English faculty have established a strong national identity within the field of rhetoric and composition. However, while the growth of a national organization, a successful journal, and strong representation on national committees all indicate considerable success in forming a national presence within the discipline, a look at who actually contributes to rhet/comp journals complicates the story.

Two-year college English faculty have never had a particularly strong presence in the journals that make up our discipline. In 1990 Keith Kroll called for community college faculty to join the community of professional writing teachers. He reported that of the three journals in which community college faculty would most likely publish (*TETYC*, *CCC*, and *CE*), their participation was dismal: In 1988 only 38 percent of the articles in *TETYC* were published by community college faculty. Publication in *CCC* and *CE* fared even worse, with only one article by a community college teacher appearing in three volumes of the former. He also cited that over a one-year period (September 1985 to August 1986) only 3 percent of the submissions to *CE* came from two-year college faculty. Maureen Goggin takes a more expansive look at this phenomenon in *Authoring a Discipline*. Tracking the institutional affiliation of contributors to rhetoric and compositions journals, she reports that

> contributors from two-year colleges, although never a strong constituency, nevertheless appeared to be establishing a hold on the journals in the 1960s and early 1970s, the years of greatest growth of community colleges. By the end of the 1970s, their numbers dropped below 4%. Moreover, in journals founded after 1980, authors from two-year colleges are very rare. (They account for only 2.5% of the contributors published in *JAC* [Journal of Advanced Composition], less than 1% in *RR* [Rhetoric Review] and *WC* [Written Composition], and none in *P/T* [Pre/Text].) (162)

Yet there has been an ongoing invitation to two-year college faculty to join the professional conversations. Both Goggin and Kroll refer their readers to former *English Journal* editor Donald Gray's 1981 invitation to women and community college teachers to publish. This call, at least the part directed toward community college faculty, met with little response. The mere invitation was not enough to overcome the institutional culture that had barred two-year college faculty from writing and publishing for so long. But this was about to change. While *TETYC* editors had long solicited articles from two-year college faculty, when Nell Ann Pickett became editor in 1987, she waged a national campaign to encourage publication in the journal. In a recent e-mail Mark Reynolds recalls that she traveled to each of the regional NTCC meetings, encouraged faculty to write, and spoke about the journal as a place where they could publish.

About this same time that Pickett was traveling to regional meetings holding workshops about the importance and value of seeing two-year college faculty writing for publication, Ernest Boyer called for an expanded view of scholarship. In *Scholarship Reconsidered,* he proposed a model that would recognize the diverse talent of professors at all kinds of institutions:

> What we urgently need today is a more inclusive view of what it means to be a scholar—a recognition that knowledge is acquired through research, through synthesis, through practice, and through teaching. We

acknowledge that these four categories—the scholarship of discovery, of integration, of application, and of teaching—divide intellectual functions that are tied inseparably to each other. Still, there is value, we believe, in analyzing the various kinds of academic work, while also acknowledging that they dynamically interact, forming an interdependent whole. Such a vision of scholarship, one that recognizes the great diversity of talent within the professoriate, also may prove especially useful to faculty as they reflect on the meaning and direction of their professional lives. (24–25)

In particular, Boyer's proposed scholarship of teaching opened the door for faculty at all levels to consider teaching as a viable subject for research. This was especially relevant for community college faculty whose professional lives were not well suited for what Boyer called the scholarship of discovery, but which were very well suited for a scholarship of teaching.

Coinciding with Boyer's work and as a result of Pickett's encouragement, in 1990 a number of articles were published in *TETYC* encouraging two-year college composition faculty to join the larger disciplinary community. Howard Tinberg began by calling for two-year college faculty to reject the dichotomy of writing teachers and writing theorists in favor of a new vision that saw theory as growing out of practice. He wrote, "To the profession as a whole I am proposing that a network of writing teachers be established whose mission is to render accounts from the field. I would like to see such teachers present their findings in major journals and at national meetings so that a dialogue may begin between practitioners and theoreticians. Such a dialogue is long overdue" ("Model" 23). This move, while not addressed exclusively to two-year college faculty, was clearly an attempt to carve a space in which they could participate more actively in the professional discourse. In the very next issue of *TETYC*, Kroll, citing the paucity of two-year college faculty publishing in *CCC*, *CE*, and *TETYC* as described earlier (and acknowledging the reasons for it), called for two-year college English faculty to engage in classroom research and to establish a professional identity within the discipline by publishing their findings. Echoing Tinberg, he wrote, "Classroom research offers one feasible way for English faculty to become knowledge makers, to overcome the false dichotomy that exists between teaching and scholarship in community colleges, to establish a professional identity, and to affirm our bond with the community of professional writing teachers" (107). The next year Reynolds wrote a follow-up piece to Kroll's suggesting "[ways that] two-year college teachers can find the time for professional writing, what kinds of articles they can write and publish, and how they can get the writing done" ("Writing" 290). This was important because while many two-year college faculty might resonate with the calls to publish, they had little time and received little reward for doing so. In addition to providing a number of ideas about which two-year faculty might write, Reynolds also provided a rationale:

> Writing professionally needs to be viewed in this light—as a productive and renewing component of the total teaching process. In addition, writing teachers should write to practice what they profess, to learn the craft, to become better thinkers and writers, to expand their professional world beyond the classroom and campus, to offset burnout—much of which is boredom—and finally, to experience personal and professional satisfaction. (290)

Little more than a year had lapsed when Tinberg again called for two-year college faculty to publish our experience and to "refashion our professional selves": "Are we simply classroom warriors slugging it out in the trenches? Or are we cool and detached academics, capable of abstract and theoretical perspectives? Or are we something else, a messy and impure mélange? I think the latter, and for me that is an exciting proposition" ("Seeing Ourselves" 16). Once Tinberg took over the reins as editor of *TETYC* in 2001, he renewed his efforts. In his inaugural editorial he expressed concern that not enough two-year faculty saw themselves as scholars and researchers, so he called on veteran teachers to "show colleagues—especially those who are new to the profession—how to integrate teaching, scholarship, and research" ("Scholarship" 5–6). In the *ADE Bulletin* he writes, as Reynolds had earlier, of the "opportunity, discovery, and renewal" that comes with scholarship and publication ("Writing" 49).

One important piece remained, however. Even if faculty were inspired to write for publication, how were they to do it without institutional support? A heavy teaching load, tutoring and mentoring students, committee work—all of this left little time to write. George Vaughan, former president of Piedmont Community College and current editor of *New Directions for Community Colleges*, understood this and has been a tireless advocate of fostering a climate for scholarship in the community college. He argues that community college faculty should engage in scholarship and that their institutions should embrace this as part of their mission. Acknowledging that faculty are hired for their proven excellence in teaching and their currency in their discipline, he questions the position of institutions not supporting scholarship, the very means by which faculty would stay current. He calls for a new vision of what it means to be a teaching institution:

> [I]f community college faculty and administrators are to gain the respect they have worked so hard to earn and which they so richly deserve, they simply must begin to place more emphasis on what it means to work in an institution of higher education—for an institution of higher education with an institutional mission devoid of scholarship is a contradiction in

> terms. [. . .] To achieve its mission as a teaching institution, the community college must make scholarship one of its top priorities, for one cannot remain an outstanding teacher without a commitment to scholarship. ("Scholarship and Teaching" 220)

As had Boyer, Vaughan argues for a more expansive view of scholarship, defining it as "the systematic pursuit of a topic, as an objective, rational inquiry involving critical analysis. Scholarship involves precise observation, organization, and recording of information in the search for truth and order. It is the umbrella under which research is pursued, for research is but one form of scholarship" ("Scholarship and the Community College Professional" 5). Vaughan was not, however, simply referring to Boyer's scholarship of teaching. Under Vaughan's definition, scholarship occurs within a disciplinary community and involves activities whereby one shares one's work with others who are qualified to judge it. This can take the form of talks to local groups or at conventions synthesizing current thinking on a subject, or it could involve published works such as book reviews or annotated bibliographies. Of faculty he asks two things: make scholarship part of one's annual professional growth plan and rededicate oneself to participating in the disciplinary discourse ("Scholarship and Teaching" 218–19). The first could take the form of submitting one article a year for publication, and/or making a presentation to community college faculty at the local or national level. The latter involves attending conferences and reading or contributing to professional journals. Ultimately, if faculty stay divorced from their disciplines for too long, it becomes increasingly difficult for them to meet the needs of their students. In our own field of composition, if faculty members have not kept pace with the changes we have seen over the last thirty years, what they have to offer their students is limited.

Of course the biggest challenge lies in garnering institutional support. Among Vaughan's suggestions for academic deans and presidents are rewarding scholarly work by promotion and tenure, funding scholarship through lighter teaching loads, recognizing scholarship by holding lunches or ceremonies, and/or granting significant cash awards to those deemed outstanding scholars. Elke Matijevich reports in the Spring 2002 *ADE Bulletin* that although it appears to be the exception, "[r]ecently there have been encouraging signs that some two-year colleges may be recognizing the need to support the intellectual development of their faculty members" (60). She cites Collin County Community College in Texas, which offers reassigned time and reading grants for faculty who want to keep current in their disciplines. The Community College of Philadelphia offers summer reading grants. And Chaffey College in California releases a teacher from his or her teaching duties to research, write, and publish. A number of community colleges (including my own Maricopa Community College District) offer tenured faculty sabbaticals at varying levels of pay to conduct scholarship. Overall, however, despite the work of Vaughan, there's little evidence that community college administrators or boards of trustees have embraced scholarship as part of their institutions' mission. If two-year college faculty want to publish, the majority will likely do so without institutional support.

Calls for Collaboration

The movement during the 1990s encouraging community college faculty to publish was one strand of the effort to strengthen our national identity. But there was a parallel move on the part of the two-year college English leadership to address a larger audience, turn attention to two-year college writing programs, and encourage cross-institutional collaboration. One strand of this effort was articulated by Bertie Fearing, former editor of *TETYC* and faculty member in East Carolina University's Graduate Program for Two-Year College English Teachers, a program that offered a post-MA certificate for two-year college English faculty. In "Renewed Vitality in the Twenty-First Century," Fearing encouraged two-year college faculty to identify ways that university English departments could help them, assuring that university faculty would help in any way they could, including holding workshops or writing curricula. While ostensibly responding to the need for training two-year college faculty, her call opened the door for other kinds of collaboration: "I predict," she wrote, "that the twenty-first century will see strengthening, enriching partnerships between the two-year college and the university—and between two-year college English teachers and their university colleagues" (194). A more expansive vision of collaboration was voiced by Elizabeth Nist of Anoka-Ramsey Community College and Helon Raines of Armstrong State College in Joseph Janangelo and Kristine Hansen's *Resituating Writing*: "By fostering a shared understanding of two-year college writing programs between two- and four-year writing faculties, we hope to underline the necessity for finding the resources and opportunities to work together for stronger composition programs across the spectrum of higher education" (59). After providing an overview of community college students, faculty, and English curricula, Nist and Raines highlighted the common ground shared by university and community college composition faculty by listing the challenges they both face, among them strengthening writing instruction at all levels, responding to calls for standards and assessment, and improving articulation agreements for the easy transfer of credits between institutions (65). They listed a number of actions that the Council of Writing Program Administrators (WPA) could take to "foster a greater role for two-year colleges" in the organization (66), and that university faculty could take to foster increased collaboration with two-year colleges. They recommended that university faculty adopt texts about two-year college studies[4] for their teacher preparation courses, invite two-year college faculty to work on curriculum planning committees and to speak to or teach methods and theory classes, and encourage dissertations about literacy studies at the community college (Nist and Raines 68–69). This last suggestion would be taken up and expanded by John Lovas, who, as explained in the next section, recommended that university faculty see the community college writing programs as sites for their own research.

The Profession's Intellectual Failure

The last few years have witnessed calls for research and scholarship into the writing programs of community colleges, most notably by Lovas. Acknowledging that CCCC has a strong record addressing "issues of professional equity," Lovas claims that "our profession has an intellectual blind spot regarding knowledge building in and about community colleges" ("All" 274). Why is establishing scholarly inquiry into two-year college writing programs so important? First, it's well known that approximately half of all students take their first-year composition requirement in community colleges, yet most composition scholarship is situated in the university and takes as its subject university writing programs. While this is understandable, the unfortunate result is that the teaching of writing in community colleges, which in many cases is truly thoughtful and innovative work, is not well represented in the professional literature. In "All Good Writing Develops at the Edge of Risk," Lovas argues that "you can't generalize about composition if you ignore half of it. You can't generalize about composition if you don't know half of the work being done" (276). Second, the community colleges are heirs to a rich legacy of pedagogical experience. Consider that the majority of university writing programs are staffed largely by graduate students who may or may not have an interest in teaching composition. Even the most dedicated graduate students are, by necessity, heavily involved in their own coursework and areas of interest. They may teach a few classes, but then it's often time to move on. Additionally, although a number of dedicated university professors maintain close ties with the first-year requirement, the majority of tenured faculty show little interest in teaching first-year composition. Conversely, even though community colleges also rely heavily on part-time faculty, almost without exception full-time faculty teach a minimum of three composition courses every semester. In "Playrooms, Hodgepodges, Soulless Monsters," Lovas writes:

> Those of us who have been doing this work for some time have accumulated far more experience—and knowledge—than virtually anyone in a research university. Between us, Paul Bodmer of the NCTE and I have

taught around five hundred sections of college writing at all levels of the curriculum. It would be easy to corral fifty tenured university English professors who collectively had not taught that many sections of writing in their lives. So why should they be dominating the process of theorizing about this work? (44)

In *The Politics of Writing in the Two-Year College*, Barry Alford and Keith Kroll also point out the inequities that result from composition's being theorized without attention to community college writing programs, claiming that the work of two-year college faculty has been "invisible intellectual work, usually driven by theories and practices generated from university campuses a long way from the students and faculty at two-year institutions. Two-year college faculty often end up being gatekeepers for standards they did not create and do not control" (v). Lewiecki-Wilson and Sommers argue in *CCC* that composition at open-admissions institutions is under "extracurricular" attack and encourage rhet/comp faculty at all postsecondary institutions to "see that the 'discipline' of composition takes place in the interactions of teachers and students in open-admissions composition classes" (p. 60). They urge, "Rather than regarding it as at the 'margin' of our profession, we want you to consider the teaching of writing in open admissions sites as central to the historical formation and continuing practice of composition studies" (p. 60). This, they argue, will enable us to fend off the attacks that have the potential to "shift the material conditions of the field" (p. 60).

But perhaps the most compelling reason—and perhaps the most obvious—for scholarly inquiry into two-year college writing programs is that community colleges are such critical sites for studying composition. They function as a vortex of converging forces: community colleges articulate curriculum with universities for transfer credit; they partner with and design courses to respond to the needs of local businesses; they offer dual-enrollment courses at local high schools; they admit any and all students as part of their open-door, democratic mission; they respond to the needs of the community by increasing access through distance learning, intersessions, and weekend course meeting times; they offer basic writing courses for their vast numbers of underprepared students; and, finally, as Lovas mentions, the teachers themselves have a wealth of pedagogical experience that is probably unrivaled in the university. There is simply no other site where the issues, complexities, and politics facing the teaching of composition are so well represented, and it is for this reason that two-year college writing programs are such a rich vein for research.

Even so, two-year college writing programs remain largely invisible. Two-year college faculty often lack the time—and, arguably, the training—to theorize their own programs. Recognizing this, Lovas writes in

CCC that "there's no reason a junior professor at a university couldn't build a scholarly body of work by including studies of two-year college writers and writing programs. We need new and substantial forms of collaboration on a local and regional basis so that the quality of all writing programs can be improved" ("All" 276). In the *ADE Bulletin* he also wrote of collaboration: "To capture and transmit the body of knowledge developed in community college teaching will require new kinds of cross-institutional efforts, combining the university resources for research with the rich diversity of language learning problems and opportunities in the community colleges" ("Playrooms" 45). He also calls for graduate programs in English to recognize that a number of their graduates will go on to teach in community colleges and to "adopt practices that will develop professional attitudes toward such work. Including a couple of community college faculty members on committees planning graduate curricula would be good for everyone involved" (48). All of these recommendations would help make visible the valuable work being done in community colleges.

Conclusion

The editors of *TETYC* have long encouraged two-year college English faculty to write for their journal. The 1990s in particular witnessed a concerted effort to further the development of a professional identity for two-year college English faculty, especially in encouraging two-year faculty to write for publication and encouraging university faculty to collaborate with two-year college faculty in studying their programs. Tinberg, Reynolds, and others have argued that scholarship and publishing bring discovery and renewal and give us a voice in the discipline. Additionally, as teachers of writing, we have a responsibility to practice our craft. There is evidence that these appeals have met with some positive results. Of the eighty-six article submissions to *TETYC* during the 2002 calendar year, forty-five (52 percent) came from two-year college faculty, up 10 percent from the previous year (Tinberg, "Re: Question"). Publishing in other journals continues to be scant, however. But there's some evidence that the profile of community college faculty is changing, and that may spark changes in professional involvement. While the MA is still the minimum (and generally preferred) requirement, an increasing number of job ads for community college faculty positions are showing preference for a PhD. The English department at my institution, for example, has hired seventeen new full-time faculty in the last eight years. Of these seventeen, twelve have PhDs or are actively pursuing one. Of these twelve, six are in rhetoric and composition. If this trend continues, it is likely that a new generation of two-year college faculty will be trained to research and publish. This may not only raise the profile of two-year college writing programs, it may also help others broaden their idea of what constitutes intellectually satisfying work.

Notes

1. See Townsend and LaPaglia; Barry and Barry; Lovas, "Playrooms"; C. Gray; and Zimbleman.
2. In 1972 Elisabeth McPherson became the first from a two-year college to serve as chair of CCCC. She was followed by Lionel Sharp in 1975, Vivian Davis in 1978, Lynn Troyka in 1981, Jane Peterson in 1990, Nell Ann Pickett in 1997, and most recently John Lovas in 2002.
3. See Yagaleski and Leonard; Downing, Hurlbert, and Mathieu; Bloom, Daiker, and White; Garay and Bernhardt; Moore and O'Neill.
4. While the two-year college English canon is still in its formative stages, the collections edited by Reynolds and by Alford and Kroll would certainly fit the bill, as would Tinberg's *Border Talk*.

Works Cited

Alford, Barry, and Keith Kroll, eds. *The Politics of Writing in the Two-Year College*. Portsmouth, NH: Boynton, 2001.

Barry, Roger J., and Phyllis A. Barry. "Establishing Equity in the Articulation Process." *Prisoners of Elitism: The Community College's Struggle for Stature*. Ed. Billie Dziech and William Vilter. Spec. issue of *New Directions for Community Colleges* 78 (1992): 35–44.

Bloom, Lynn Z., Donald A. Daiker, and Edward W. White, eds. *Composition in the Twenty-First Century: Crisis and Change*. Carbondale: Southern Illinois UP, 1994.

Boyer, Ernest L. *Scholarship Reconsidered: Priorities of the Professoriate*. San Francisco: Jossey, 1990.

Clark, Burton R. "The 'Cooling Out' Function in Higher Education." *American Journal of Sociology* 65 (1960): 569–76.

Cohen, Arthur M., and Florence B. Brawer. *The American Community College*. 4th ed. San Francisco: Jossey, 2002.

Dougherty, Kevin J. *The Contradictory College: The Conflicting Origins, Impacts, and Futures of the Community College*. Albany: SUNY P, 1994.

Downing, David B., Claude Mark Hurlbert, and Paula Mathieu, eds. *Beyond English, Inc.: Curricular Reform in a Global Economy*. Portsmouth, NH: Boynton, 2002.

Fearing, Bertie E. "Renewed Vitality in the Twenty-First Century: The Partnership between Two-Year College and University English Departments." Reynolds, *Two-Year College English*, 185–95.

Garay, Mary S., and Stephen Bernhardt. *Expanding Literacies: English Teaching and the New Workplace*. Albany: SUNY P, 1998.

Goggin, Maureen Daly. *Authoring a Discipline: Scholarly Journals and the Post–World War II Emergence of Rhetoric and Composition*. Mahwah, NJ: Erlbaum, 2000.

Gray, Christine R. "Not What I Had in Mind." *Chronicle of Higher Education* 19 Apr. 2002. 19 Apr. 2002 http://chronicle.com/jobs/2002/04/2002041902c.htm.

Gray, Donald. "Another Year with *College English*." *College English* 44 (1982): 385–89.

Griffith, Marlene, and Ann Connor. *Democracy's Open Door: The Community College in America's Future*. Portsmouth, NH: Boynton, 1994.

Kroll, Keith. "Building Communities: Joining the Community of Professional Writing Teachers." *TETYC* 17.2 (1990): 103–8.

Lovas, John. "All Good Writing Develops at the Edge of Risk." *CCC* 54 (2002): 264–88.

———. "Playrooms, Hodgepodges, Soulless Monsters: Why I Can't Imagine Having a Better Job." *ADE Bulletin* 129 (2001): 43–48.

Matijevich, Elke. "Encouraging Scholarship at the Community College." *ADE Bulletin* 131 (2002): 58–61.

Moore, Cindy, and Peggy O'Neill, eds. *Practice in Context: Situating the Work of Writing Teachers*. Urbana, IL: NCTE, 2002.

Nist, Elizabeth A., and Helon H. Raines. "Two-Year Colleges: Explaining and Claiming Our Majority." *Resituating Writing: Constructing and Administering Writing Programs*. Ed. Joseph Janangelo and Kristine Hansen. Portsmouth, NH: Heinemann, 1995.

Palmer, James C. "Nurturing Scholarship at Community Colleges." *Enhancing Teaching and Administration through Scholarship*. Ed. George Vaughan and James Palmer. Spec. issue of *New Directions for Community Colleges* 76 (1991): 69–77.

Palmer, James C., and George B. Vaughan. *Fostering a Climate for Faculty Scholarship at Community Colleges*. Washington, DC: American Assn. of Community and Junior Colleges, 1992.

Reynolds, Mark. "Re: Question about Our History." E-mail to the author. 9 Jan. 2004.

———, ed. *Two-Year College English: Essays for a New Century*. Urbana, IL: NCTE, 1994.

———. "Writing for Professional Publication." *TETYC* 18.4 (1991): 290–96.

Shor, Ira. "An Interview with Ira Shor—Part 1." Interview with Howard Tinberg. *TETYC* 27.1 (1999): 51–60.

Sommers, Nancy. "Colloquy Live: Why Can't Johnny Write?" *The Chronicle of Higher Education* 6 Jan. 2003. 8 Jan. 2004 http://chronicle.com/colloquylive/2003/01/write/.

Sparrow, Keats. "The Genesis and Early Development of *TETYC*: A Silver Anniversary Reminiscence." *TETYC* 27.1 (1999): 14–19.

Tinberg, Howard B. *Border Talk: Writing and Knowing in the Two-Year College*. Urbana, IL: NCTE, 1997.

———. "A Model of Theory-Making for Writing Teachers: Local Knowledge." *TETYC* 17 (1990): 18–23.

———. "Re: Question about Our History." E-mail to the author. 12 Jan. 2004.

———. "Scholarship and Research." Editorial. *TETYC* 29.1 (2001): 5–6.

———. "Seeing Ourselves Differently: Remaking Research and Scholarship at the Community College." *TETYC* 20 (1993): 12–17.

———. "Writing a Book on the (Two-Year College) Job." *ADE Bulletin* 129 (2001): 49–52.

Townsend, Barbara K., and Nancy LaPaglia. "Are We Marginalized within Academe? Perceptions of Two-Year College Faculty." *Community College Review* 28.1 (2000): 41–48.

Vaughan, George B. "Scholarship and the Community College Professional: Focusing the Debate." *Enhancing Teaching and Administration through Scholarship*. Ed. George Vaughan and James Palmer. Spec. issue of *New Directions for Community Colleges* 76 (1991): 3–15.

————. "Scholarship and Teaching: Crafting the Art." Reynolds, *Two-Year College English*, 212–22.

Yagaleski, Robert P., and Scott A. Leonard. *The Relevance of English: Teaching That Matters in Students' Lives*. Urbana, IL: NCTE, 2002.

Zimbleman, Dana. "The Community-College Job Search." *Chronicle of Higher Education* 19 Apr. 2002. 19 Apr. 2002 http://chronicle.com/jobs/2002/04/2002041901c.htm.

Zwerling, L. Steven. *Second Best: The Crisis of the Community College*. New York: McGraw, 1976.

"Distinct and Significant": Professional Identities of Two-Year College English Faculty

Christie M. Toth, Brett M. Griffiths, and Kathryn Thirolf

This article, which appeared as part of a special issue of CCC *on "The Profession," brings together findings from three separate studies related to the professional identities of two-year college English faculty: one on participation in professional organizations, one on assertions of professional authority within institutions, and one on the organizational socialization and professionalization of part-time instructors. Taken together, these studies affirm that two-year college English faculty have a professional identity that is distinct from that of their four-year colleagues, and that they face distinctive challenges and opportunities enacting their professional identities in both institutional and disciplinary contexts. Christie, Brett Griffiths, and Kathryn Thirolf discuss the implications of these findings for the field of composition, calling for greater inclusion of the perspectives and interests of two-year college faculty in national professional organizations and graduate curricula.*

In their introduction to *The Profession of English in the Two-Year College*, Sylvia Holladay-Hicks and Mark Reynolds describe teaching English in two-year colleges as a "distinct and significant profession" (ix).[1] In the chapters that follow, veteran two-year college English faculty examine the institutional conditions and curricular functions that have contributed to their profession's distinctive trajectory. This history matters, not only because it records the influences on writing instruction in two-year colleges, but also because it presents teaching at two-year colleges as rigorous intellectual activity motivated by responsiveness to student needs. However, much of the teaching knowledge generated by two-year English faculty goes unrecognized or unincorporated within scholarly conversations in composition. This lack of recognition is due, in

From *College Composition and Communication*, vol. 65, no. 1, 2013, pp. 90-116.

part, to a lack of understanding about how these professionals take up and enact their professional identities in the context of the various social structures in which they are embedded, including their professional organizations, their institutions, and their departments.

In this article, we bring together findings from three different studies in order to highlight ways that English faculty at two-year colleges understand and enact their professional identities in different professional scenes. We begin by considering the disciplinary orientations and activities of some of the most "professionalized" two-year college English faculty: those who are highly engaged with professional organizations. Then we explore ways that full-time English faculty at three community colleges identify and assert their professional authority within their institutions. Finally, we examine the organizational socialization experiences of faculty whose professionalization is often tenuous: early-career part-time faculty. Taken together, our studies suggest that two-year college faculty experience unique challenges when enacting their professional identities in both disciplinary and institutional contexts. "Four-year-centric" models of professional participation often fail to recognize the variety and breadth of two-year faculty engagement with professional organizations. On the other hand, national and institutional policies that emphasize educational attainment and workforce readiness can position two-year college English faculty at cross-purposes with the goals of administrators, thereby limiting their autonomy as writing pedagogy experts. Furthermore, some part-time faculty's limited socialization experiences hinder their developing identities as two-year college professionals. Despite these constraints, however, two-year college English faculty also experience unique opportunities to enact their professional identities through transdisciplinary scholarly engagement, assertion of professional autonomy beyond the classroom, and professional exchange with institutional colleagues.

In making claims about the "professional identities" of two-year college English faculty, we are pairing two complex terms that have been variously theorized and warrant careful attention. First, drawing on Magali Sarfatti Larson's sociology of professionalism, we adopt four criteria to characterize *professions*: (1) a shared vision for norms and goals; (2) social recognition among members; (3) autonomy to define and measure criteria by which those members should be evaluated; and (4) a self-regulating process for socializing new members into the field (xii). We adapt our understanding of "identity" from structural symbolic interactionist theories, which seek to explain how interactions with social structures shape identities. Drawing on these theories, we use the term *identity* to refer to the ways individuals interpret and enact "the multiple roles they typically play in highly differentiated contemporary societies" (Stryker and Burke 284); this includes both how individuals act in relation to the social structures in which they are embedded and the meanings they make from those interactions. Thus, in examining the professional identities of English faculty at two-year colleges, we explore the meanings these faculty attach to their roles as professionals: how they identify shared norms and goals, how they recognize one another within a diverse and differentiated community, how they develop and enact the autonomy to define and measure criteria for evaluation within their profession, and how they socialize new members into the professional community. Some of the shared norms and goals for this profession derive from disciplinary ways of knowing in composition studies, education, and other related fields. As such, the enactment of professional identity is, at times, difficult to distinguish from disciplinary identity. Here, we have made an effort to disambiguate these identities, while recognizing throughout that engagement with disciplinary knowledge is an important component of the "professional self."

This article was born of conversations that the three of us—all doctoral students at the University of Michigan—have been having among ourselves for several years. Each of us has taught or worked in two-year colleges, and we share a long-standing interest in the important but sometimes invisible work of community college faculty, which we have often found to be poorly understood, both in the literature and by university colleagues. When we began discussing our studies with one another, our collective appreciation of the complex positioning of two-year college professionals deepened. This special issue of *CCC* was the impetus for bringing our three studies together: the result, we believe, is a uniquely multidimensional portrait of two-year college English faculty professional identities.

Professional Identity in the Two-Year College

The assertion that two-year college faculty are professionals is not uncontested. In the most recent edition of Arthur Cohen and Florence Brawer's compendium, *The American Community College*, for example, the "professionalization" of two-year college faculty is treated as an open question (107). Likewise, two-year college English faculty have themselves expressed concerns about their professional status: Keith Kroll has recently asserted that neoliberal educational policies may have already triggered the end of the two-year college English profession. Indeed, in the current policy climate, faculty at two-year colleges face mounting pressure to demonstrate the utilitarian value of their instruction (Tinberg, "Teaching English"). Such calls often come from outside the discipline and operate from a limited understanding of the pedagogical challenges and opportunities that college writing instruction presents. The uncertainty surrounding the professional status of two-year college English faculty can weaken their authority, constraining their ability to direct debates about what constitutes effective instruction within their institutions, as well as in broader national conversations about educational policy and practice. Thus, failure to recognize two-year college English faculty as professionals undermines the discipline's ongoing efforts to define writing as a complex social activity and promote locally situated, student-centered pedagogies (e.g., Writing Study Group).

Recognizing two-year college English faculty *as* professionals, we contend, requires recognizing the distinctive nature of their profession. Scholars from the Two-Year College English Association (TYCA) have described the distinctiveness of their professional roles using a range of terms, including "teacher-scholars" (Andelora, "Forging"), "knowledge makers" (Reynolds, p. 139 in this volume), and "expert generalists" (Tinberg, "Teaching English"). In this article, we seek to add to this scholarly conversation, heeding John Lovas's call for more university-based research addressing the discipline's "intellectual blind spot regarding knowledge building in and about community colleges" (274), the institutions where half of all composition courses are taught.

A number of contextual factors distinguish teaching English in two-year colleges from other postsecondary institutions, and these factors influence faculty professional identities. First, two-year colleges typically have multiple missions, including academic transfer, vocational education, adult basic education, and community enrichment (Cohen and Brawer). Because two-year colleges are access-oriented institutions, serving primarily local students with varying levels of academic preparation, most offer multiple levels of developmental coursework in core areas, including reading and writing. Furthermore, teaching is the primary scholarly activity for faculty at two-year institutions: they typically carry heavier teaching loads and attain tenure primarily through demonstration of teaching quality, rather than scholarly publication (Prager). A master's degree in rhetoric and composition, literature, creative writing, or education is the standard credential for teaching English at two-year colleges, although doctoral degrees are preferred at some institutions. Composition courses make up the largest percentage of most English departments' offerings, but departments generally offer a range of other English courses as well. As in many writing programs across the country, two-year college English departments often rely heavily on part-time faculty to teach composition courses (Worthen, p. 639).

With this context in mind, we begin by examining faculty professional identity at the disciplinary level. In the following section, Christie examines two-year college English faculty engagement with professional organizations as sophisticated enactments of identity that reflect distinctive professional roles and institutional missions.

Study 1: Professional Organizations and *Transdisciplinary Cosmopolitanism*

Engagement with professional organizations is often seen as the hallmark of professionalization (e.g., Andelora, "Professionalization"): these organizations are a key mechanism for fostering social recognition among members, establishing shared norms and goals, developing criteria for evaluation, and socializing new members into the field. My research with faculty who are highly engaged with professional organizations suggests that these professional activities involve distinctive and ongoing acts of what, following Tinberg (*Border Talk* vii), I refer to as *translation*: translation across bodies of knowledge in a range of disciplines, as well as across local, state, regional, and national scales, in order to serve their specific student populations within their institutional contexts. These acts of translation characterize a distinctive mode of professional engagement that I call *transdisciplinary cosmopolitanism*, an inclusive and pragmatic approach to accessing research and practice that is uniquely suited to two-year college English faculty's professional roles.

I apply the word *cosmopolitan* as a deliberate act of reappropriation: this term has been used by higher education researchers in ways that cast two-year college faculty as provincial in relation to their four-year colleagues. These researchers have drawn on sociologist Alvin W. Gouldner's assertion that postsecondary faculty orient themselves around one of two conceptions of professional identity: the *local*, characterized by "high organizational loyalty, low commitment to specialized skills, and the use of an inner reference group orientation"; or the *cosmopolitan*, characterized by "low organizational loyalty, high commitment to specialized skills, and the use of an outer reference group orientation" (293). These researchers have generally assumed that community college faculty are more locally oriented than their "cosmopolitan" counterparts at universities (e.g., Wright et al. 148).

This study suggests that some two-year college English faculty's patterns of professional engagement might be better understood using the more expansive definition of cosmopolitanism offered by philosopher Kwame Anthony Appiah. For Appiah, cosmopolitanism is characterized by the recognition that "you will find parts of the truth (along with much error) everywhere and the whole truth nowhere" (8). This necessitates "conversations across boundaries" (xxi): in other words, translation. Appiah's definition of cosmopolitanism offers a way of understanding how highly engaged two-year college English faculty interact with professional organizations as they translate knowledge from multiple disciplines across geographic scales. Ultimately, my study suggests that these patterns of engagement bolster faculty's professional authority and autonomy and help equip them to enact their professional identities in the context of their institutions.

This study emerged from my own questions about why two-year college English faculty remain underrepresented in NCTE-affiliated professional organizations. I wanted to know what faculty who *were* engaged in these organizations thought they gained and the extent to which they felt the organizations met their professional needs: I hoped this research would help the Conference on College Composition and Communication (CCCC) better serve our community college constituency.

The findings reported here draw on one-time semi-structured interviews with twenty-four full-time two-year college English faculty who
were active participants in either CCCC or one of the regional TYCAs
in 2011–2012.[2] I randomly selected participants from these organizations' most recent conference programs and then contacted potential
participants via email. I interviewed eleven men and thirteen women
at twenty-two colleges in seventeen states, with between two and six
participants from each regional TYCA. Most interviews lasted between
forty and fifty minutes. I analyzed the transcripts through open and
axial coding (Corbin and Strauss). All participants had the opportunity
to review an early version of this manuscript, which I revised based on
their feedback. These participants represent a relatively narrow subset
of two-year college English faculty: they were all full-time instructors
who were involved with CCCC or one of the TYCAs in 2011–2012, and
most were conference presenters. Although they were not "typical two-
year English faculty," their behaviors and perspectives provide insights
about the segment of the profession that is highly engaged with NCTE-
affiliated organizations.

The twenty-four faculty interviewed participated in professional
organizations across an array of disciplines. While composition-oriented
organizations such as the TYCAs, CCCC, NCTE, and the Council of
Writing Program Administrators were most common (perhaps because
of recruitment methods), six faculty were also involved with organizations in other areas of English, such as the Association of Writers and
Writing Programs (AWP), the Modern Language Association (MLA),
and Teachers of English to Speakers of Other Languages (TESOL).
Fifteen also participated in organizations in the field of education,
most commonly the National Association for Developmental Education
(NADE). Five participated in organizations focusing on specialized topics, such as folklore or sports literature, and fourteen were involved in
broadly interdisciplinary organizations like the Community College
Humanities Association. Although participants were recruited solely on
the basis of their engagement with either a regional TYCA or CCCC,
all but one of the faculty in the study were members of multiple organizations across several disciplines.

Like English instructors at most two-year colleges, these faculty
came from diverse disciplinary backgrounds: of the eighteen who discussed their graduate studies, five had master's degrees in English literature, rhetoric/composition, or education; two had MFAs in creative
writing; and fourteen held or were completing doctoral degrees in fields
ranging from English literature to educational leadership. Their teaching roles also required disciplinary flexibility. They had taught a wide
range of classes, including composition, creative writing, literature, ESL,
humanities, and technical writing. Furthermore, these faculty had
served in a variety of administrative roles, ranging from department
chair, writing center director, and online learning specialist to simulta-

neously overseeing developmental writing and an honors program. Their engagement with various disciplinary professional organizations often tracked shifts in their teaching and administrative roles.

Appiah describes cosmopolitans as those who recognize that knowledge is like a "shattered mirror—each shard of which reflects one part of a complex truth from its own particular angle" (8). Several faculty participants described the strengths and shortcomings of different disciplinary professional organizations in analogous terms. As one interviewee (all interviewees are referred to by pseudonyms) Lisa, explained, each discipline reflects "an important piece" of her profession, but none could "fill all of the needs" of two-year college English faculty. Although two interviewees described themselves as rooted firmly in composition, most seemed to identify first as teachers of English in two-year colleges and were less wedded to a specific disciplinary identity. In fact, two were openly critical of composition, particularly what they perceived as its "marginalization" of community college–related interests and failure to engage with other disciplines relevant to two-year college teaching. As Lisa noted:

> When I go to the Cs, for instance, or I open an English journal in the field of English . . . I just don't see any mixing of all this great scholarship that I find in the field of developmental education. . . . I was shocked to see that there was no crossover between this really great, rigorous research being done that people in community colleges use . . . to make decisions about what we're going to do at community colleges about pedagogy and about students and programs. . . . There is none of it in the field of English or composition studies.

Lisa had entered community college teaching with a background in composition, but increasingly, she found herself gravitating toward NADE, in part because she perceived two-year colleges to be at the "center" rather than the "margin" of that organization.

Although three interviewees described disciplinary friction within their departments and units—often around "developmental" versus "basic" writing pedagogies—most of the faculty who were interviewed seemed to have found ways to move productively among various disciplines to access the knowledge and construct the professional identities that fit their institutional roles and responsibilities. While ten indicated that they enjoyed engaging with "cutting-edge research" and "the big picture" at national conferences like CCCC, six expressed annoyance about the privileging of abstract theory over "on the ground" applications. Indeed, the highly local nature of the community college mission—and the influence of state and regional policy on teaching conditions—led all but one faculty participant to engage with professional organizations at multiple geographic scales: twenty-one participants were involved with at least one national disciplinary organization;

twenty-one were members of regional associations, such the TYCAs; and eighteen also participated in state-level organizations. Finally, three faculty were involved with organizations connected to institutional reform initiatives, such as Achieving the Dream (ATD) or the Accelerated Learning Program (ALP).

Two-year colleges are, by design, responsive to community needs, particularly local student demographics and regional adaptations to a globalizing economy (e.g., Levin). Because of these distinctive characteristics of two-year colleges, all but one of the participants were engaged in ongoing efforts to translate not only across disciplines but also between knowledge generated at the national level and conditions in their local institutional contexts. Such translation included, for example, expanding local constructs of writing by integrating multimodal composition assignments into the curriculum, or adapting best practices for online learning—which often came from the field of education rather than composition—to their institutions' curricula, course management systems, and student populations. Assessment was also an important area for translation. Five faculty described attempts to adapt "best practices" in writing assessment to their open-access, resource-constrained institutions. Two, for example, had implemented modified versions of directed self-placement alongside entrenched standardized placement tests. This cosmopolitan translation from national disciplinary conversations to local context reflects the distinctive professional profile of two-year college English faculty: the kinds of pedagogical and administrative knowledge required in the two-year college English profession are often highly situated and context-specific.

Participants listed numerous ways in which professional organizations benefited their professional lives, including providing them with a "sense of identity" informing their teaching practices, giving two-year colleges "a voice" in national policy conversations, and helping faculty build meaningful relationships with "like-minded professionals." Furthermore, fourteen faculty indicated that engagement with these organizations bolstered their professional autonomy. By virtue of their ability to cite both academic research and other institutions' practices, these faculty found they were able to exert greater influence over institutional decisions regarding issues like placement procedures, assessment, curriculum, and hiring criteria. Being able to marshal this kind of evidence gave them credibility with administrators who might otherwise be inclined to disregard their professional perspective. In the words of one participant:

> If we want to try to sway the administration in any direction, our opinion doesn't count, you can tell that. So the fact that we go to the conferences and come back and say, here's what they're doing somewhere else. . . . We talked to Christine [sic] Toth . . . she's doing this research and she's at this institution . . . then they're convinced.

In four cases, faculty were also able to use what they learned through their involvement with professional organizations in their work on inter-institutional committees or advisory boards to shape state-level policy regarding developmental education, articulation agreements, and faculty work conditions.

In some ways, the forms of professional engagement I call *trans-disciplinary cosmopolitanism* echo the multiple forms of scholarship Ernest L. Boyer identifies in *Scholarship Reconsidered*. While Boyer highlights the important contributions that two-year college faculty can make to the "scholarship of teaching"—a call that has been eagerly taken up by many in TYCA (Andelora, "Teacher/Scholar"; Reynolds, p. 148)—he only nods to the possibility that these faculty might also be uniquely situated to undertake the scholarship of integration (synthesis of knowledge across disciplines) and application (activities that foster interaction between theory and practice). The interdisciplinary nature of many two-year college English faculty's engagement could be understood as a form of scholarship of integration; likewise, their translation of disciplinary knowledge across geographical scales constitutes a kind of scholarship of application. However, not all two-year college faculty are highly engaged with professional organizations, and not all of those who are engaged consider such engagement to be a form of scholarship. As we see in the next section, the extent to which two-year college English faculty self-identify as scholars can have important implications for their enactments of professional identity within their institutional contexts.

Study 2: *Positioning* and *Footing* of Two-Year College English Faculty

In this section, I examine how faculty take up their professional identities within their institutions, particularly the constraints and opportunities they identify for asserting their professional authority to shape departmental teaching guidelines. I use the concepts of *positioning* and *footing* (Harré et al.) to explore the ways faculty perceive and enact their authorities in their institutions. More than a decade ago, Cynthia Lewiecki-Wilson and Jeff Sommers observed that faculty at open-admissions colleges often perceive "public pressures [to] work against good teaching practices" (p. 62). This study is motivated, in part, by a desire to understand how increased attention on two-year colleges as sites for reenergizing economic growth and increasing college attainment inform faculty's perceptions of these pressures, and how they respond to such pressures within their institutions.

This analysis comes from the first part of a three-part, semester-long study. Here, I focus on semistructured interviews with faculty, during which they described their conceptions of good teaching, identified perceived pressures on their teaching, and talked through their rationales for course design using a sample course syllabus to structure the discussion. With the help of department deans, institutional research offices, and faculty liaisons, I sent recruitment materials to all full-time English faculty at three community colleges in the Midwest. Each college served a different community in terms of population density (urban, suburban, and rural), racial demographics, educational attainment, unemployment rates, and dominant occupations. Ten instructors participated in the portion of the study addressed in this article: three from the rural community college, five from the urban community college, and two from the suburban community college. All instructors were white; six were female, four male. The professional activities of participants are summarized in Table 1. I analyzed interview transcripts thematically using open and axial coding (Corbin and Strauss). Participants had the opportunity to review an early version of this manuscript. When applicable, I have incorporated their suggestions.

The concept of *positioning* builds on contemporary theorizations of identity as socially situated and helps to facilitate analysis of the subject positions individuals assign and take up through language (Davies and Harré). Recent interpretations of positioning theory distinguish between *prepositioning*, which are the implied rights, duties, and status available to an identity; *positioning*, or the duties and statuses that individuals recognize as part of their identity roles; and *footing*, a recognized authority based on those rights and statuses that mean the individual must be "listened to" (Harré et al.). The distinction between *positioning* and *footing* helps to disambiguate the act of *identifying* as a professional (including assuming the duties, rights, and statuses within a professional membership community) from the act of asserting authority based on that identity. Like the faculty surveyed by Lewiecki-Wilson and Sommers, participants in this study described myriad pressures on their teaching—including national education initiatives, institutional emphasis on workforce readiness, and changing requirements for accreditation—that contributed to an environment in which departmental change could be slow and challenging. In the face of these pressures, faculty often perceived themselves to have limited footing.

Participants expressed ambivalence about increased attention on community colleges in national conversations about college attainment and work-force readiness. In general, national community college reform movements have incorporated little instructor expertise. For example, the only faculty member to lead a session at the 2010 White House Summit on Community Colleges was Jill Biden, the host. Thus, even as the goal of the summit was to improve student success at community colleges, faculty were positioned outside the conversation, effectively denied the opportunity to share their experiences with teaching and the perceptions of student success that their professional identities prepared them to communicate. Despite expressing some appreciation for the increased attention two-year colleges are receiving, eight of the

Table 1. Summary of Scholarly Activities for Participants in Study 2

Professional and Scholarly Activities	Number of Faculty
Publishing: Textbooks	2 (coauthors for the same book)
Publishing: Scholarly articles	2 (education, literature)
Publishing: Creative	2 (poetry)
Scholarly service	1 (textbook selection committee) 1 (community writing fair)
Institutional research	Advanced learning (2) Composition course assessment evaluation (1)
Attendance at scholarly conferences	CCC (2) ALP (1) AWP (2) MDEC (2) (Michigan Developmental Education Consortium)
Participation in teaching workshops	Katie Hern (1) Chris Anson (1) Brian Jenson (1)
Membership in professional organizations	TYCA (2) NCTE (7) CCC (4) JAEPL (1) (Assembly for Expanded Perspectives on Learning) AWP (1) MDEC (1)

ten instructors in this study described this national conversation as "limiting" and as disregarding the potential intellectual rigor offered at these institutions. As one participant, Christopher, explained:

> It's great that community colleges are getting some publicity, but the idea that . . . our goal is to train a hundred thousand people for jobs. I mean certainly there's that component, but I don't know if that's really what we're here to do. It's not necessarily just a training program.

While all instructors identified job preparation as one core mission of two-year colleges, they identified a conflict between preparing students for the workforce and preparing them as college-level writers. Seven participants indicated that emphasis on job training exerted pressures inconsistent with their teaching goals, which included encouraging students to become "lifelong writers," to understand writing as a process, and to critique the ways knowledge is constructed. As one participant, Sadie, explained,

> I am starting to feel like—that we are really in some sort of war. It feels like the people who hold the purse strings are really horrible to the folks who work for them and to some degree I want to show my students that there is more available, you know that they should dream for more. . . . I take offense at the idea that I should be supplying companies with parts.

Simultaneously, faculty perceived that their administrators' goals closely aligned with sentiments expressed in national policy conversations. Specifically, faculty described pressures within their institutions to focus on workforce readiness and to increase student completion rates, particularly those enrolled in lower-level writing courses. Instructors experienced these pressures as sources of tension within their pedagogy: they had practical obligations to meet institutional completion goals, even as they sought to remain true to their own notions of good teaching. Instructors at two of the colleges emphasized that administrators were often unaware of research on teaching and learning conducted by faculty within the institution, and made decisions without seeking input from instructors. One participant described emails from senior administrators suggesting that tenure statuses might be revoked in the absence of increased student completion rates. Another described an email from an administrator explicitly reminding faculty that the college did not acknowledge or reward teaching faculty's scholarly participation.

Faculty responded to these perceived pedagogical tensions in a variety of ways, including ignoring the conflicts, strategically adapting to them, working to change policies, and burning out. When describing their teaching goals, seven faculty said they dismissed national policy discussions as well as institutional policies that did not directly affect their classrooms. They drew, instead, on their own teaching philosophies and their graduate-level preparation to reinforce their teaching goals. Some of these goals included increasing students' awareness of and ability to critique language processes ("thinking about how language does things in the world"), empowering students to participate more capably as citizens (or at least "defend themselves from obnoxious landlords"), and enabling students to become "deeply skeptical of what's going on around them."

Nevertheless, participants indicated that it was difficult to ignore pressures from within their institutions and departments. Similar to the faculty Tinberg describes ("Teaching English"), participants reported pressures to adopt more "utilitarian" approaches to teaching writing. Despite objections from the instructors in this study, department policies at one campus explicitly required faculty to incorporate direct grammar instruction as one hour of a four-credit-hour first-year college writing course.

Other pressures were not always as explicit as emails or formal department policies. Department-adopted textbooks at two colleges implicitly institutionalized modes-based teaching, even though six out of the seven faculty participants from those institutions expressed concern that the modes were oversimplified and "outdated." Faculty explained that department tradition and the slow process of departmental change constrained their ability to alter departmental policies. Specifically, instructors described a generational quality to their colleagues' beliefs about writing, indicating that "old-fashioned" faculty employed during the "first wave of community college hiring" continued to exert influence in favor of keeping traditional grammar instruction as a core component of writing courses. Moreover, one instructor explained that past expectations for accreditation, written by the Higher Learning Commission, had shaped the current departmental focus on the quantification of grammatical errors. This had led the department to include counts of comma errors on student papers in faculty tenure evaluations, further increasing pressures on instructors to include traditional grammar instruction in their teaching. Even though the criteria for accreditation have since changed, and the counting of errors is no longer a component of tenure evaluation, the language in department policies and supporting documents—including course descriptions—has yet to evolve.

When encountering conflicts at the level of departmental policy, several instructors found ways to "get around" constraining departmental guidelines by resisting the philosophy of the guidelines at the level of the classroom. One instructor incorporated an hour of direct grammar instruction per week but did not include students' scores on grammar activities when determining students' grades. Another instructor explained,

> the course includes a thing about grammar. So when you're going through your three years of probation so you can get tenure and people visit you and observe you, for instance . . . I do have fake grammar tests that I give out on the days that I was observed to take home and bring back. And then my observing committee gets one too. Okay. Is that dishonest? You bet it is. And I'd do it again.

Additional adaptations included reinterpreting guidelines. In order to circumnavigate department textbook policies, one faculty removed textbooks from the syllabus entirely. Two other faculty members engaged in what might be considered scholarship of application (Boyer) by collaboratively writing a new textbook tailored to their institution's writing sequence.

Instructors' descriptions of their teaching goals often aligned with professional statements and legislative initiatives sponsored by professional organizations such as NCTE (i.e., "2012 Legislative Platform"). This alignment supports the assertion that faculty operate under a "shared vision for norms and goals," one of Larson's defining characteristics of professions. However, even though faculty drew on disciplinary knowledge within their classrooms, they often did not perceive themselves to have the authority—the footing—to assert their understanding of those norms and goals to effect departmental change. This perceived limitation is troubling, both because it affects faculty members' abilities to maintain and regulate the criteria for teaching excellence in their institutions, and because it can contribute to declining professional fulfillment over time. In two instances, faculty who perceived insufficient footing to steer their departments described feelings of "burning out." One explained, "It's like a bad earthquake movie where I have the fault line between my feet and I'm just going down, because this side wants that, and that side wants that, and I don't think it is something we are talking about enough."

Standing in stark contrast are the narratives of faculty members who mobilized their understanding of professional norms and goals to effect department change. One faculty member drew on a CCCC presentation demonstrating a disciplinary movement away from "modes" to spearhead the adoption of a new genre-based textbook. Another instructor collaborated with colleagues who had attended an ALP conference to implement an experimental accelerated learning program. A third instructor drew on scholarship to justify open revision in his course, a practice that department policy had previously discouraged.

These divergent cases suggest that when instructors drew on the knowledge gained through their professional activities in order to exercise authoritative footing, they were able to effect change at the departmental level. Differences in perceived footing may help elucidate instructors' diverse responses to constraints. In cases where faculty considered defining and regulating department policies to be part of their professional identity, they actively drew on their professional activities to do so. However, when faculty considered classroom instruction to be their professional identity's singular domain, even those who actively participated in scholarly and professional exchange perceived only limited opportunities to shape departmental policies.

In this section, I have described some of the ways that the structural positioning of English faculty—including national conversations about two-year colleges, institutional processes of tenure and promotion, and faculty's own perceptions of their positioning with respect to their professional identities—both constrains and enables faculty to assert authoritative footing within their institutions. Given the diverse ways in which faculty in this study identified and enacted their positions as professionals, understanding how English faculty at two-year colleges are introduced to the responsibilities of their professional roles seems crucial. The majority of two-year college English professionals are part-time faculty, but full-time faculty have the potential to help shape the experiences of contingent faculty by recognizing them as fellow professionals and helping to socialize them into professional norms and goals. In the next section, we learn about part-time two-year college English faculty's professional identities in relation to their organizational socialization experiences.

Study 3: Organizational Socialization of Part-Time English Faculty

Thus far, we have examined the profession of teaching English at two-year colleges from full-time faculty members' points of view, but our examination would be remiss if it failed to consider the experiences and perspectives of part-time faculty, who represent nearly 70 percent of all faculty at two-year colleges (AFT Higher Education 10). English departments, typically among the largest departments at two-year colleges, often have particularly high percentages of part-time faculty (Benjamin). As in the discipline of composition more broadly, the heavy reliance on part-time English faculty at two-year colleges has long been a hotly debated topic (see Klausman; Lovas). As David W. Leslie and Judith M. Gappa have argued, if colleges better support their adjunct faculty and "invest in their capabilities, instead of treating them like replaceable parts" (66), there could be great benefits—for part-time faculty, their colleges, and their students—including improved morale, teaching effectiveness, and student outcomes (Jacobs).

This study suggests that one way to support part-time faculty and foster the enactment of their professional identities is by taking steps to ensure they have positive organizational socialization experiences, especially when they first begin teaching. Organizational theorists define organizational socialization as the process by which individuals learn and acquire the knowledge, skills, values, attitudes, and beliefs needed to participate effectively in an organization (Jablin; Van Maanen and Schein). Socialization processes such as interviewing, orienting, mentoring, relationship development, and role negotiation can greatly influence how connected a faculty member feels to his or her college, department, colleagues, and, by extension, his or her profession. Because part-time faculty often do not attend professional conferences due to lack of funding and time—most adjuncts hold full-time jobs or juggle multiple part-time positions (Leslie and Gappa)—the best opportunity for part-time faculty to cultivate professional identity is locally, namely at and through their colleges. Thus, organizational socialization experiences at their colleges are critically important to shaping their professional identities.

This study examines how six part-time composition faculty members described their socialization experiences at two different two-year colleges: "North Community College" (NCC) and "South Community College" (SCC). Both are public two-year colleges; neither had a part-time faculty union at the time interviews were conducted. To identify willing participants, contacts in the colleges' English departments sent a recruitment email to part-time faculty on my behalf. I intentionally sought faculty who had fewer than three years' experience teaching English at a community college so that they could adequately remember and reflect on their early organizational socialization experiences. I asked a range of questions during interviews, including what were the types of supports and challenges they encountered as they got up to speed and became familiar with being a two-year college writing instructor and what has been most influential in shaping their professional identities thus far. Interviews lasted between one and two hours. I used open and axial coding to analyze each interview transcript (Corbin and Strauss).

Like part-time faculty in English departments across the country, adjunct faculty who participated in this study came from diverse professional backgrounds (see Table 2). All six participants had some prior teaching experience; five of the six participants had experience teaching high school English specifically. Everyone but Courtney, who had a full-time job as a medical case manager, expressly stated that they would prefer to be teaching full-time. All participants had at least one degree in English or teaching, and all participants had at least one master's degree. They ranged in age from late twenties (Courtney) to mid-sixties (Sam). All participants were white, except for Courtney, who was African American.

Overall, participants described needing much more organizational socialization support than they received. The faculty who experienced a very rushed early organizational socialization phase—where they applied for a teaching job, were interviewed, hired, and began teaching within a matter of days—encountered many challenges feeling prepared and getting comfortable in their faculty roles. This situation was particularly the case for the faculty at SCC, which had few effective processes and supports in place for their new part-time faculty. For example, the total time between when John inquired about open teaching positions to when he began teaching his first class at SCC was less than twenty-four hours, an experience he described as "a nightmare." Tiffany had a similar experience at SCC. She was asked to come in for an interview the same day she emailed inquiring about open positions. Participating in an interview before entering an organization is an important part of the early organizational socialization process (Jablin), but John and Tiffany had no time to prepare for or reflect on their new professional roles as two-year college writing faculty. While these hiring processes are likely side effects of fluctuating enrollments and access-oriented registration policies, such experiences can negatively impact part-time instructors' transitions to their new institutions and their perceptions of their new professional identities as community college writing faculty. Because John was hired so late and lacked adequate organizational socialization, he said he felt very much "on [his] own." In Larson's terms, he lacked both a connection to a shared vision

Table 2. Summary of Participant Backgrounds for Study 3

Name	College	Experience teaching at CC	Family situation	Previous teaching experience	Employment elsewhere at time of interview
John	SCC	1.5 years	Single, no children	Middle school and high school	Full-time administrative staff at nearby public university
Sherry	SCC	1 year	Married, no children	Middle school and high school; adjunct at private college and university	Adjunct at private four-year college
Tiffany	SCC	1 semester	Single, no children	Substituting at high school level; graduate school instructor	Adjunct at private university
Courtney	NCC	2 years	Married, no children	Preschool; community health education classes	Full-time medical case manager
Sam	NCC	2.5 years	Married, one grown daughter	Middle school and high school; graduate school instructor	Adjunct at private four-year university
Lynn	NCC	1 year	Married, baby on the way	Private high school, ACT tutor	Barista in a coffee shop, adjunct at private four-year college

for norms and goals and social recognition among colleagues. Without opportunities for such connection and recognition, John's and Tiffany's early organizational socialization experiences constrained their emerging professional identities as community college writing faculty.

Conversely, the faculty members at NCC described receiving adequate support—and adequate time to prepare—before their first class. In addition to hiring the faculty who participated in this study at least two weeks before classes began, their department chair made a concerted effort to ensure they received sample syllabi and course handouts and PowerPoint lectures well ahead of time—an early introduction to professional as well as institutional norms and goals. Furthermore, and more importantly, their department chair also connected them with full-time colleagues who had taught their courses before. These full-time colleagues provided the new adjunct faculty with advice and course materials, including access to online course management sites.

The part-time faculty at SCC described not receiving as much socialization support as the faculty at NCC received, but perhaps even more worrisome, the formal supports they did experience were not particularly effective or well received. For example, although SCC tried to support part-time faculty through a required mentoring program that paired them with a full-time faculty colleague in the English department, the respondents tended to agree that it was "sterile" and "a waste of time." Rather than a source of support, the mentoring program was mostly a source of frustration and had the effect of making the part-time faculty in this study feel patronized. Such mandatory "mentorship," which reinforced status differences between full- and part-time faculty, may have come into conflict with adjunct faculty's emerging sense of themselves as autonomous professionals who already possessed specialized subject-area expertise.

Participants perceived more informal and natural connections with colleagues to be much more beneficial than the required mentoring program at SCC or the college-wide part-time faculty orientations and handbooks offered by both colleges. However, these connections happened rarely, and for the faculty at SCC, often only by chance. The participants indicated they were sometimes able to connect with another faculty member who taught in the same classroom before or after them. Through these connections, they shared teaching tips, lesson planning ideas, and collegial conversations that reinforced the adjunct faculty's emerging expertise and membership in the professional community. These reports suggest that positive and productive instances of the "give and take" (Tierney 6) that occur between individuals and organizations during organizational socialization happened much more frequently during informal and natural social exchanges rather than the forced and more formal situations, like SCC's required mentoring program. Instead of feeling "on [their] own," NCC's faculty felt more connected to their college, their department, their colleagues, and thus, their profession.

One way that NCC facilitated (rather than forced) connections among faculty in its English department was to hold open "mini-conferences" at the beginning of each semester, at which different faculty would lead brief sessions ranging from grading rubrics to English skills learning games and other teaching tips. Knowledge and ideas that faculty gained from attending disciplinary conferences were brought back and shared with the department at these mini-conferences, as well as over email. Each of the NCC faculty members had good things to say about the mini-conferences they attended: these activities, which brought faculty together as colleagues to share their specialized expertise, seemed to affirm their identities as professionals. Such mini-conferences might be seen as examples of Boyer's "scholarship of integration," in that they brought colleagues together to share and synthesize knowledge across and within disciplines: they gave faculty a chance to learn about and reflect on theories of teaching and learning, language and rhetoric, and developmental education.

In summary, this study suggests that these part-time faculty members' organizational socialization experiences played an important role in shaping their faculty identities. Activities that positioned incoming adjunct faculty as professionals and colleagues fostered professionalization more than mandatory trainings and required mentoring, which gave adjunct faculty little autonomy or failed to honor the expertise they already possessed. Authentic professional sharing such as the mini-conferences, as well as informal, collegial connections with other faculty in their department—although typically few and far between—was much more affirming of part-time faculty members' professional identities. It is worth noting, however, that all but one of these relatively new adjunct faculty aspired to full-time status. Thus, we are left to wonder how these faculty's professional identities might shift or change over time if they, like so many aspiring full-time two-year college English faculty, find that they have become involuntary permanent part-timers.

Conclusions

Taken together, our studies offer several insights about two-year college English faculty professional identities. First, they affirm Holladay-Hicks and Reynolds's assertion that teaching English in the two-year college is a distinct profession. However, they also demonstrate that two-year college English faculty face distinct constraints—as well as opportunities—in enacting their professional identities. Here, we return to Larson's criteria for professions as a helpful heuristic for framing the ways instructors enact their distinct professional identities.

Across all three studies, engagement with other professionals informed how two-year college English faculty identified and enacted the norms and goals associated with their profession. For the faculty in the first study, participation in professional organizations across various disciplines and geographical scales shaped how they identified and interpreted professional norms and goals. Similarly, the faculty in the second study drew on their graduate education and experiences across disciplinary communities, such as CCCC and ALP, to identify the norms and goals for teaching within their institutions. However, faculty perceived generational disagreement regarding professional norms and goals to be slowing departmental change, sometimes at the expense of staying current with the profession. Conversely, because they were new to the profession, the part-time faculty in the third study were just beginning to identify norms and develop shared goals with their institutional colleagues.

Across these three studies, social recognition played an important role in shaping how faculty identified as professionals and how they recognized other members of their professional community. Many of the faculty in the first study identified more strongly with their professional identities as two-year college faculty than as disciplinary faculty, a perception fostered through participation in two-year college organizations like the TYCAs and, in some cases, through faculty experiences of marginalization within organizations they perceived to be dominated by four-year interests. In the second study, social recognition among faculty was more contested. Although faculty recognized their colleagues' professional expertise, perceived differences between faculty's teaching approaches sometimes presented a barrier to collaborative professional interactions. Likewise, the third study underscores how important social recognition can be in the development of faculty professional identities: participating in collegial activities with other faculty enabled part-time faculty to develop a stronger sense of themselves as professionals. These studies suggest that social recognition of shared professional identity can be facilitated both extra- and intra-institutionally, but failure to foster such recognition can be detrimental to faculty's ability to identify shared professional norms and goals at the institutional level.

In terms of professional autonomy, faculty in the first two studies described institutional and departmental challenges to their ability to instantiate professionally determined criteria for evaluation of their teaching performance. Many of the faculty in the first study were, in fact, departmental leaders, and they described using disciplinary knowledge to shape policy and practice at the department level, as well as asserting their professional expertise to influence institutional and even state-level policy decisions. Although they were not always successful, most believed that their participation in professional organizations gave them more credibility with administrators. While most of the faculty in the second study were engaged in some scholarly activity, not all were able to mobilize that engagement to assert professional autonomy and thereby fully enact their professional identities—indeed, their ability to do so hinged in part on the extent to which they recognized their own professional identities as affording authority to extend their professional autonomy beyond the classroom. At the far end of the spectrum, part-time faculty in the third study seemed to have a fair measure of autonomy in the classroom but lacked connection to or influence on policy or practice conversations at any level. Together, these studies suggest that professional autonomy is a complex construction derived not only from professional expertise, but also from the shared recognition of that expertise by departmental colleagues, administrators, and policymakers.

As the first study suggests, faculty come to this profession from a range of English- or education-related disciplines. This diversity offers generative opportunities for transdisciplinary engagement, but it also complicates the processes of self-regulation and professional socialization, as many faculty acquire their professional identities on the job, and only eventually, if they choose to do so, through their participation in professional organizations. The various degrees to which the faculty in the second study perceived their professional autonomy to extend beyond their classroom suggests that even those with shared disciplinary grounding in rhetoric and composition may not have received any socialization during their graduate training regarding the dimensions of their future professional identities outside the classroom. And the third study demonstrates the extent to which a large percentage of two-year college English faculty—part-time instructors—may be getting little or no effective socialization into the profession. This factor is where current two-year college English faculty's enactments of professional identities may unwittingly contribute to an overall weakening of professional status and authority, both within their institutions and across their scholarly activities.

We see several implications of these findings for readers of *CCC*. First, in light of the experiences of faculty who described feeling alienated by CCCC, we believe NCTE and CCCC can support two-year faculty professional autonomy by continuing to strengthen partnerships with TYCA, and by redoubling efforts to become more inclusive and relevant for the two-year constituency. NCTE, CCCC, and TYCA have the potential to play critical roles in shaping the norms and values shared by two-year professionals, but they can only serve as resources for supporting professional autonomy when members perceive their participation to be valuable (and valued).

Second, graduate programs in all areas of English studies—particularly master's programs—should do a better job of preparing their graduates for the *profession* of teaching English in the two-year college. Based on our findings, we believe that engaging with professional organizations, and learning about the rights and duties faculty can undertake to uphold professional norms and values within their institutions, should be a part of the curriculum in graduate programs preparing two-year college faculty. Given the policy climate into which new two-year college English faculty will enter, equipping them to enact their professional identities may now be more important than ever.

Finally, our studies suggest that the field should continue to address the structural problem of involuntary part-time faculty. These faculty have the most tenuous professional status of all the faculty discussed in this article. In addition to the material constraints of being contingent labor—e.g., few or no benefits, little job security—they often have the least professional autonomy, experience the least social recognition, and, as the third study shows, are not well professionalized into their colleges and departments. Given the current levels of reliance on part-time faculty at two-year colleges, the status of the profession as a whole may be bound, to some extent, on the future professionalization of these faculty.

Notes

1. Throughout this article, we follow TYCA in using the term *two-year colleges*. This designator includes community and junior colleges, as well as two-year tribal colleges, most technical colleges, and the growing number of state colleges that are primarily associate degree–granting but offer a limited number of applied baccalaureate degrees.

2. There are seven regional TYCA organizations: Northeast, Southeast, Midwest, Southwest, West, Pacific Northwest, and Pacific Coast/English Council of California Two-Year Colleges (ECCTYC).

Works Cited

AFT Higher Education. *American Academic: The State of the Higher Education Workforce, 1997–2007*. Washington: American Federation of Teachers, 2009. Web.

Andelora, Jeff. "Forging a National Identity: TYCA and the Two-Year College English Teacher-Scholar." *Teaching English in the Two-Year College* 35.4 (2008): 350–62. Print.

———."The Professionalization of Two-Year College English Faculty: 1950–1990." *Teaching English in the Two-Year College* 35.1 (2007): 350–62. Print.

Appiah, Kwame Anthony. *Cosmopolitanism: Ethics in a World of Strangers*. New York: Norton, 2007. Print.

Benjamin, Ernst. "Variations in the Characteristics of Part-Time Faculty by General Fields of Instruction and Research." *The Growing Use of Part-Time Faculty: Understanding Causes and Effects*. Ed. David W. Leslie. San Francisco: Jossey-Bass, 1998. 45–59. Print. New Directions for Higher Education, no. 104.

Boyer, Ernest L. *Scholarship Reconsidered: Priorities of the Professoriate*. San Francisco: Jossey-Bass, 1990. Print.

Cohen, Arthur, and Florence Brawer. *The American Community College*. 5th ed. San Francisco: Jossey-Bass, 2008. Print.

Corbin, Juliet, and Anselm Strauss. *The Basics of Qualitative Research: Techniques and Procedures for Developing Grounded Theory*. Thousand Oaks: Sage, 2007. Print.

Davies, Bronwyn, and Rom Harré. "Positioning: The Discursive Production of Selves." *Journal for the Theory of Social Behaviour* 20.1 (1990): 44–63. Print.

Gouldner, Alvin W. "Cosmopolitans and Locals: Toward an Analysis of Latent Social Roles I." *Administrative Science Quarterly* 2.3 (1959): 281–306. Print.

Harré, Rom, Fathali M. Moghaddam, Tracey Pilkerton Cairnie, Daniel Rothbart, and Steven R. Sabat. "Recent Advances in Positioning Theory." *Theory and Psychology* 19.5 (2009): 5–31. Print.

Holladay-Hicks, Sylvia, and Mark Reynolds. Introduction. Reynolds and Holladay-Hicks ix–x.

Jablin, Fredric M. "Organizational Entry, Assimilation, and Disengagement/ Exit." *New Handbook of Organizational Communication: Advances in Theory, Research, and Methods*. Ed. Fredric M. Jablin and Linda L. Putnam. Thousand Oaks: Sage, 2001. 732–818. Print.

Jacobs, Frederic. "Using Part-Time Faculty More Effectively." *New Directions for Higher Education* 26.4 (1998): 9–18. Print.

Klausman, Jeffrey. "Not Just a Matter of Fairness: Adjunct Faculty and Writing Programs in Two-Year Colleges." *Teaching English in the Two-Year College* 37.4 (2010): 363–71. Print.

Kroll, Keith. "The End of the Community College Profession." *Teaching English in the Two-Year College* 40.2 (2012): 118–29. Print.

Larson, Magali Sarfatti. *The Rise of Professionalism: A Sociological Analysis*. Berkeley: U of California P, 1977. Print.

Leslie, David W., and Judith M. Gappa. "Part-Time Faculty: Competent and Committed." *New Directions for Community Colleges* 118 (2002): 59–68. Print.

Levin, John S. *Globalizing the Community College*. New York: Palgrave, 2001. Print.

Lovas, John C. "All Good Writing Develops at the Edge of Risk." *College Composition and Communication* 54.2 (2002): 264–88. Print.

National Council of Teachers of English. "2012 Legislative Platform." NCTE Position Statement. National Council of Teachers of English. 2012. Web. 26 Aug. 2012.

———. Writing Study Group of the Executive Committee. "NCTE Beliefs about the Teaching of Writing." NCTE Guidelines. National Council of Teachers of English. Nov. 2004. Web. 22 Aug. 2012.

Prager, Carolyn. "Scholarship Matters." *Community College Journal of Research and Practice* 27 (2003): 579–92. Print.

Reynolds, Mark, and Sylvia Holladay-Hicks, eds. *The Profession of English in the Two-Year College*. Portsmouth: Boynton/Cook, 2005. Print.

Stryker, Sheldon, and Peter Burke. "The Past, Present, and Future of Identity Theory." *Social Psychology Quarterly* 53.4 (2000): 284–97. Web. 24 Oct. 2011.

Tierney, William, G. "Organizational Socialization in Higher Education." *Journal of Higher Education* 68.1 (1997): 1–16. Print.

Tinberg, Howard. *Border Talk: Writing and Knowing in the Two-Year College*. Urbana: NCTE, 1997. Print.

———. "Teaching English in Two-Year Colleges: A Review of Selected Studies." Reynolds and Holladay-Hicks 137–145.

Van Maanen, John, and Edgar H. Schein. "Toward a Theory of Organizational Socialization." *Research in Organizational Behavior* 1 (1979): 209–64. Print.

Wright, Mary C, Nandini Assar, Edward L. Kain, Laura Kramer, Carla B. Howery, Becky Glass, and Maxine Atkinson. "Greedy Institution: The Importance of Institutional Context for Teaching in Higher Education." *Teaching Sociology* 32.3 (2004): 144–59. Print.

Unmeasured Engagement: Two-Year College English Faculty and Disciplinary Professional Organizations

Christie Toth

This selection presents findings from a study of two-year college faculty participation in disciplinary professional organizations. Responding to the apparent underrepresentation of two-year college faculty, Christie interviewed faculty involved in professional organizations about their motivations and experiences. These conversations revealed much about the benefits faculty derive from such engagement, as well as the institutional and organizational barriers that work against greater two-year college faculty involvement. This study also showed that many two-year college faculty are overcoming these barriers in innovative and largely undocumented ways, suggesting that engagement with disciplinary organizations is more extensive than conventional measures like membership and conference attendance indicate. These findings offer a starting place for thinking about how departments, institutions, and disciplinary professional organizations might foster greater two-year college faculty involvement.

This article emerged from what seemed like a straightforward query: What percentage of two-year college English faculty participate in disciplinary professional organizations? I began trying to answer this question in the fall of 2009. I had just left an adjunct position teaching evening classes at a community college—work I loved, but which seemed unlikely to allow me to quit my day job and teach full-time—to enter a PhD program, where I planned to research writing instruction at two-year colleges. When I began thinking about professional organizations, I suppose what I really wanted to know was whether my research would make any meaningful impact on the experiences of faculty and students in two-year colleges. Would the scholarship I produced at

From *Teaching English in the Two-Year College*, vol. 41, no. 4, 2014, pp. 335-53.

a research university find its way into the hands of two-year college instructors? Even if I successfully contributed to the project of forging a composition discipline more inclusive of knowledge made in and about two-year colleges (see Andelora, p. 579 in this volume; Hassel and Giordano, p. 82; Lovas; Nist and Raines), to what extent were faculty teaching in those contexts engaging with disciplinary conversations? Participation in disciplinary professional organizations seemed like one important indicator of such engagement. And so I began seeking out quantitative measures of their participation—namely, organizational membership, conference attendance, and journal subscriptions—in the composition associations affiliated with the National Council of Teachers of English (NCTE). Ultimately, however, I found that these quantitative measures failed to capture the rich and largely undocumented forms of engagement that qualitative interviews with two-year college English faculty reveal. The narrative I present here is thus a kind of "research project manqué," one that sheds light on the complexities of two-year college faculty's relationships with the discipline of composition and its major professional organizations.

Initially, I assumed that the figures I was looking for would be readily available in the research literature. What I encountered instead was a rather conflicted theoretical portrait. In *The American Community College*, Arthur M. Cohen and Florence B. Brawer state that two-year college faculty generally have weak ties to professional organizations:

> Professional association membership [among community college faculty] is down, whether measured by disciplinary association, general faculty association, or community-college specific association. For most instructors, the longer they are at the college, the weaker their affiliation with an academic discipline becomes. (106)

Cohen and Brawer argue that heavy teaching and administrative loads at community colleges, as well as a lack of institutional incentive for engaging in scholarship and attending conferences, militate against widespread engagement with disciplinary professional organizations.

Some of the most forceful critiques of two-year college faculty connections to their disciplines have come from community college instructors themselves. More than two decades ago, Dennis McGrath and Martin B. Spear lamented what they call the "academic crisis" in community colleges, asserting that weakened ties to the discipline result in a pervasive "practitioners' culture":

> Sharing a commitment to teaching, but without a shared notion of what effective teaching might be, with strong affective ties to one another, but without the intellectual guidance and constraint provided by disciplinary cultures, faculties . . . come to undervalue intellectual exchange and

> mutual criticism, and to overvalue "sharing" as sources of professional
> and organizational development. (148)

In McGrath and Spear's estimation, such "sharing" is unmoored from
the theoretical base and empirical grounding offered by a discipline,
and the result is a kind of incoherence across the curriculum that is detrimental to student learning.

Composition scholars also identify structural barriers to faculty
engagement with professional organizations. In two-year college English departments, ties to the discipline might be weakened by the fact
that some faculty come to their positions with little formal training in
rhetoric and composition (Calhoon-Dillahunt; Hassel and Giordano,
p. 82). And, in what is likely the greatest obstacle to participation in
professional organizations, over two-thirds of two-year college instructors are adjunct faculty whose opportunities for forging and maintaining connections to the discipline are even more limited (see Toth, Griffiths, and Thirolf, p. 595). (During my own time as an adjunct, I do not
remember ever being encouraged to participate in professional organizations. Of course, like many adjuncts, my work schedule also prevented me from attending most departmental professional development sessions, but this seems to illustrate the point.) As Holly Hassel
and Joanne Baird Giordano note, the working conditions fostered by an
overreliance on part-time faculty "create a recipe for a disciplinary crisis" (p. 89). Taken together, then, this literature suggests a scattered
(and largely contingent) teaching force whose status *as* a profession, at
least insofar as that status is linked to participation in professional organizations, is open to question.

Running counter to these characterizations is the robust scholarship on professional identity by the teacher-scholars of the Two-Year
College English Association (TYCA). In his series on the history of the
TYCA and its regional associations, Jeffrey Andelora describes the determination of two-year college English faculty to forge a professional
identity that simultaneously reflects the distinctiveness of their working lives, their centrality to the discipline of composition, and their place
within that discipline's major professional organizations ("Teacher/
Scholar," p. 579; "Forging"; "TYCA: 1991–1993"; "TYCA: 1994–1997"; "Professionalization"). His studies demonstrate that there has long been a
devoted subset of two-year college English faculty who, rather than allowing their disciplinary affiliations to weaken, have pushed against
material and bureaucratic barriers to redefine the discipline and restructure NCTE to meet their needs. Indeed, two-year college faculty
have always played an important role in the Conference on Basic Writing (Otte and Mlynarczyk). In recent years, a number of scholars have
attempted to reframe two-year college English departments as writing
programs and have pushed for greater recognition within the Council
of Writing Program Administrators (see Calhoon-Dillahunt; Taylor; Nist

and Raines; Klausman, "Mapping"; Klausman, "Toward a Definition"). This literature suggests that the profession's trajectory is one of *strengthening* rather than weakening ties to the discipline and its organizations.

Perhaps the strongest statement of two-year college English faculty's commitment to disciplinary professional organizations comes in the 2004 "Guidelines for the Academic Preparation of English Faculty at Two-Year Colleges," prepared by a committee of TYCA leaders. This document "offers suggestions for both the training and philosophy that two-year college teacher-scholars of the twenty-first century need to bring to the English classroom" (6). As part of a "framework for ongoing professional development," the guidelines assert:

> A two-year college teacher-scholar of English should be an active member of English professional organizations, conducting research to enhance his or her teaching, participating actively in academic conferences and publishing opportunities, and engaging in professional and community service to further the growth of the academy. (11)

Thus, at least from the perspective of TYCA and NCTE, engaging with professional organizations and attending academic conferences are essential to being both an effective two-year college English teacher and a professional in the field.

So which is it? Are two-year college English faculty disciplinarily disengaged and largely uninvolved with the professional organizations that would otherwise keep them connected to current scholarship and research? Or are McGrath and Spear's observations out of date, and are Cohen and Brawer perpetuating the kinds of stereotypes about two-year college faculty that too often emanate from a higher education literature dominated by administrator perspectives? Or, as seems most likely, does the reality lie somewhere—or in multiple locations—in between? Faced with the contradictions in the literature, I set out to compile the figures on two-year college faculty participation in NCTE-affiliated organizations for myself.

Participation in NCTE-Affiliated Professional Associations: A (Sketchy) Quantitative Portrait

At the outset of this project, the professional organizations most closely associated with the discipline of composition seemed to be the most logical sites to examine two-year college faculty engagement. In late 2009, and then again in the spring of 2011 and 2012, I asked NCTE administrative staff how many two-year college faculty were registered NCTE members, as well as how many had attended the most recent NCTE and CCCC annual conventions. I also requested numbers on how many two-year faculty, departments, and institutions held subscriptions to the major NCTE-affiliated composition journals. Finally, I contacted officers at each of the seven regional TYCA organizations and requested attendance figures for their 2009, 2010, and 2011 conferences.

As it turns out, however, NCTE's data on two-year college faculty are quite limited. As of 2012, only a third of postsecondary members had completed the profile fields on their membership form indicating the "scholastic level" with which they were affiliated, which means that the primary institution type of the majority of these members is unknown (K. Suchor, personal communication, May 21, 2012). While the national conference figures I present here are the best numerical portrait available, they should be understood as provisional (the regional TYCA attendance figures, however, are sound). Furthermore, NCTE is not able to reliably tally journal subscriptions by subscribers' institution type. Thus, I am unable to provide any quantitative discussion of faculty's engagement with disciplinary journals—such data might have been misleading in any case, given how many faculty report accessing articles through academic databases and digital files shared by colleagues rather than personal or institutional subscription.

According to the Bureau of Labor Statistics (BLS), there are 29,280 "junior college" English faculty across the United States. Two-year college faculty thus constitute more than 40 percent of the nation's 72,680 postsecondary English instructors. If we limit these figures to composition instructors, two-year college faculty undoubtedly make up well over half the teaching force. To what extent, then, does the percentage of two-year faculty in national professional organizations correspond to their numerical dominance in the field? As of May 2012, 10,492 of the approximately 30,000 members of NCTE (35 percent) had reported their scholastic level on their member profile. Of those reporting members, 7,447 (71 percent) were focused primarily on postsecondary instruction, and 976 (13 percent) of those postsecondary members indicated that they were affiliated with a two-year college. It would appear, then, that two-year college faculty are quite underrepresented within the postsecondary membership of NCTE, at least among those who report their institutional affiliations.

And what about national conference attendance? The NCTE Annual Convention invites participation from English educators across all sectors. As Howard Tinberg notes, two-year colleges are situated at the "border" between secondary and postsecondary sectors (x), and that border has become even more porous given the recent growth of dual enrollment programs (Tinberg and Nadeau). Because of this unique position, Eric Bateman argues that two-year college faculty have much to offer and much to gain from the conversations that take place at NCTE each fall. However, as Table 1 shows, two-year college faculty make up just a small fraction of the attendees at that conference—even if only a third of two-year college conference-goers reported their institutional affiliation, they probably made up less than 10 percent of attendees

Table 1. NCTE Annual Convention Attendance, 2009–2011

Year	2-year faculty attendance	Total convention attendance	Reported affiliation with 2-year colleges (%)
2009	187	6900	2.7
2010	40	5263	0.8
2011	72	6038	1.2

during the best year. This showing is much smaller than their actual role in the literacy education landscape.

Of course, given the constraints on their time and travel resources, many two-year college English faculty likely forgo NCTE in favor of the national conference that focuses primarily on postsecondary writing instruction: the Conference on College Composition and Communication (CCCC) Annual Convention. Thanks to the efforts of TYCA leaders, this conference has developed a strong two-year college presence, including a dedicated strand in the program and a suite of special interest groups and events. Given that the two-year college English profession makes up more than half the composition instructors in the United States, we might expect these faculty to constitute a large percentage of the attendance at CCCC. However, even if we assume that only a third of the two-year college attendees reported their institutional affiliations, they have probably not made up more than about 15 percent of CCCC conference-goers over the last several years (see Table 2).

In comparison to the national conventions, the seven regional TYCA conferences are easier to get to and focus specifically on the needs and interests of two-year college English faculty (Laster and Fatherree). They might therefore offer the most promising portrait of two-year college faculty engagement with professional organizations. The size of these conferences varies, both by region and by year. However, when total attendance across all seven regions is combined, the percentage of the nation's two-year college English faculty attending TYCA regional conferences has not exceeded 3.5 percent (see Table 3).

To put these various figures in perspective: if none of the faculty who attended either NCTE or CCCC went to their regional TYCA conference—and interviews with faculty suggest that there is, in fact, a lot of crossover—then even during the year with the highest two-year college faculty attendance rates (2009), it is likely that fewer than 7 percent of two-year college English faculty in the United States went to any of these NCTE-affiliated conferences. Perhaps due to unusually high community college enrollments and the onset of recession-related

Table 2. CCCC Annual Convention Attendance, 2009–2012

Year	2-year faculty attendance	Total convention attendance	Reported affiliation with 2-year colleges (%)
2009	128	3562	3.6
2010	98	3359	2.9
2011	109	3346	3.3
2012	157	3265	4.8

Table 3. TYCA Regional Conference Attendance, 2009–2011

TYCA Region	2009	2010	2011
Pacific Coast (California)	163	—	130
Midwest	190	195	201
Northeast	196	148	128
Pacific Northwest	90	117	70
Southeast	175	143	201
Southwest	90	65	60
West	86	57	82
Total	**990**	**725**	**872**
Total 2-year college English faculty nationwide (%)	**3.5**	**2.5**	**3.0**

state budget cuts, this figure may have dipped to less than 5 percent in 2010 and 2011.

These numbers are, frankly, depressing if taken at face value because they suggest that Cohen and Brawer and McGrath and Spear may be right about two-year college faculty's general level of disengagement with the discipline. Further, they might imply that the standards laid out in the "Guidelines for the Academic Preparation of English Faculty at Two-Year Colleges" are much more aspirational than descriptive, calling into question the extent to which two-year college English teaching has actually achieved the kind of professionalization that TYCA leaders set out to accomplish. These numbers also raise several questions: Why are two-year college English faculty participation rates in disciplinary professional organizations so low? What are the barriers—personal, professional, and institutional—preventing two-year college faculty engagement? Given the barriers, what motivates the faculty who *do* participate in professional organizations? And what can all of us—both within the institutions where we work and the organizations of which we are a part—do to improve participation rates? The only way to answer these questions, I decided, was to talk with two-year college faculty themselves.

Engagement with Professional Organizations: A Qualitative Portrait

Between fall 2011 and spring 2012, I conducted one-time semistructured interviews with twenty-four full-time two-year college English faculty, all of whom had attended at least one CCCC or regional TYCA conference in the past year. Focusing exclusively on full-time faculty was not a decision I made lightly. I believe adjunct faculty participation in professional organizations is vitally important; in fact, I share Hassel and Giordano's view that the future of the discipline depends on their inclusion. However, my early conversations with TYCA-goers, as well as my own experiences as an adjunct, convinced me that the disciplinary engagement of part-time instructors is shaped by a distinct set of material, institutional, and professional factors. Their engagement warrants its own study, one that foregrounds adjunct faculty voices, and I hope to collaborate with part-time colleagues on such a study in the future. Gaining a better understanding of full-time faculty's patterns of engagement, as I have attempted to do in this study, is a necessary precursor to such research.

These faculty interviews took place in three phases. First, I conducted face-to-face interviews with five attendees at my own regional TYCA organization. Then, I conducted a combination of face-to-face and telephone interviews with five faculty who attended the CCCC Annual Convention. Finally, I conducted fourteen additional interviews, either via telephone or online video [conference], with two to three faculty from each of the six remaining regional TYCA organizations. With the exception of two opportunistic interviews with acquaintances during the pilot stages of the study, I identified all potential participants by randomly selecting names from the most recent CCCC and TYCA conference programs and contacting those instructors via email. In total, I interviewed eleven men and thirteen women from seventeen different states. Most of these interviews lasted between forty and fifty minutes, and all were audio-recorded and then transcribed and analyzed through an iterative process of open and axial coding (see Corbin and Strauss). All faculty who participated in the study had the opportunity to review a draft of this article, which I revised based on their feedback.

Of course, there are a number of limitations that result from this methodology. First and foremost, the faculty I interviewed represent a relatively narrow subset of two-year college English faculty: full-time instructors who are actively engaged with NCTE-affiliated professional organizations, many of whom hold organizational leadership positions or regularly present their work at conferences. Thus, the findings I discuss here cannot be extended to the population of two-year college English faculty as a whole. Rather, these are the perspectives of individuals who generally reflect the "teacher-scholar" identity advocated in the "Guidelines for the Academic Preparation of English Faculty at Two-Year Colleges." As such, they provide rich insight into the benefits that highly engaged faculty feel they derive from participating in professional organizations, the barriers they believe prevent their colleagues from becoming more engaged, and how they have overcome those barriers in their own institutional contexts. Perhaps most importantly, these faculty's perspectives reveal distinctive and largely unmeasured forms of engagement with disciplinary professional organizations that undercut the disappointing portrait painted by the quantitative data on membership and conference attendance.

It is important to note that, despite being a select sample, the faculty in this study are also quite diverse. They come from a range of academic backgrounds and prior career experiences, teach in two-year colleges of varying sizes with varying organizational structures and student populations, and serve rural, suburban, and urban communities. Likewise, departmental cultures and levels of institutional encouragement for engaging with professional organizations vary widely among the interviewees, and every regional TYCA organization has its own distinct character, as well. Thus, no single perspective presented here should be taken to reflect the views or experiences of all faculty in the study.

Benefits of Participation

Unsurprisingly, the faculty in this study—all of whom were actively engaged with professional organizations—identified many benefits to their involvement. Some of these benefits were personal. Six noted that the organizations gave them a sense of professional or disciplinary "identity." Several faculty also indicated that attending conferences allowed them to get away from the "tunnel vision" of their own classrooms and administrative roles to "reconnect with the discipline," enjoy "intellectual stimulation," or see their colleges' experiences in broader state, regional, and national context. For some, the rewards were as much emotional as intellectual: eight stated that they came away from their professional organizations feeling "rejuvenated," "recharged," or "renewed." One instructor described his regional TYCA in terms reminiscent of religious revival: "What I get out of TYCA is rebirth . . . I'm born again once a year."

For many, the greatest rewards came from the opportunity to meet with colleagues and enjoy the company of other "like-minded professionals." As one long-time regional TYCA member rhapsodized:

> The networks that we have created as a result of, it's been 20, over
> 20 years since I've been coming to this conference, and I have met some

of the most unbelievable people. And we can sit down, we can talk shop, commiserate. . . . There is a core group of TYCA people who are gold. Absolute gold. And those are the ones who, for me, have done the most in terms of my own growth as a teacher and as a professional.

Seven faculty indicated that the networks they forged through professional organizations became resources they drew on throughout the year, both to tap disciplinary and professional knowledge and, in the case of the TYCA regionals, to confer about state-level policies and regional accreditation procedures.

Every instructor I spoke with believed that participating in disciplinary professional organizations had enhanced his or her teaching. Five prioritized engaging with "cutting-edge research" and "theory" at national conferences like CCCC conventions, while twelve preferred the "practical" and "hands-on" ethos of their regional TYCA—in fact, three specifically praised TYCA for always giving them something they could "use in the classroom on Monday." Seven faculty regularly attended their regional TYCA *and* CCCC or NCTE conventions, appreciating the balance of theory and practice as well as the combination of national and regional perspectives that they gained from participating in both. Nearly every instructor could recall specific conference presentations or conversations with colleagues that had contributed to their teaching in some way, including particular assignments and assignment sequences, classroom activities, readings, uses of digital media, and feedback and assessment practices, as well as broader theoretical and ethical orientations toward language and learning.

In addition to their own pedagogical development, many faculty believed that participating in professional organizations benefited their departments and institutions. Four instructors indicated that attending regional conferences gave them a chance to "bond" with departmental colleagues, and two found that engaging with the professional organizations made for richer "around-the-water-cooler-type conversations" when they returned to campus. Several faculty cited specific administrative decisions around issues such as placement, assessment, curriculum design, and professional development that had been informed by research or practice they had learned about through their involvement with professional organizations. Indeed, fourteen faculty described situations in which they were able to leverage their engagement with these organizations to assert professional authority in institutional decision making that affected their departments and programs (see Toth, Griffiths, and Thirolf, p. 595).

Finally, eight instructors believed that participating in professional organizations was important for elevating the status of two-year college English teachers more broadly and for representing their interests at the national level. Four noted that attending conferences enabled them to interact with four-year faculty "as colleagues," and viewed such communication across institution types as important for both enhancing the professional recognition to two-year college faculty and for broadening the knowledge base of the discipline of composition. As one instructor said:

> It's crucial, I think, for two-year college faculty to work with four-year college and university faculty in the discipline. We make up half of the field. . . . It just feels like it's incumbent on us to be part of this.

Such representation is particularly important in the context of current educational reform movements, which too often exclude faculty from conversations in which their local and disciplinary knowledge should be taken into account. As one instructor put it:

> Many community college instructors across the United States do feel undervalued and disconnected from college teaching as a profession. There's a lot of feeling that we aren't respected or that we aren't integral to the conversations; that we're on the periphery. . . . The conferences show that other people have that same experience, but at the same time we validate each other, and they are a chance for us to talk about how we can be involved in national conversations, how we can be involved in the profession in significant ways.

Barriers to Participation

Despite the many ways in which the faculty in this study believed they benefited from their involvement with professional organizations, nearly all of them described a range of barriers that limited their own engagement and, in many cases, prevented some of their colleagues from participating. Some of these barriers were personal. Seven, for example, described family commitments that made it difficult to travel for conferences, particularly during years when their regional TYCA conference was far from home. Eight faculty cited professional barriers. Many of their department colleagues, they said, had received little or no exposure to professional organizations during their graduate education or did not view participating in these organizations as a professional obligation, particularly if they perceived no institutional expectation that they do so.

Indeed, most of the barriers the instructors described were departmental or institutional. Nearly half of the faculty indicated that they were one of only a few instructors — and sometimes the only person in their department — who regularly attended conferences, and that the broader departmental culture assigned little value to such engagement. There was, however, great variability among the faculty participants in this regard: nine described departments where there were strong expectations, either through informal cultural norms or in hiring, promotion, and tenure criteria, that faculty be involved with professional organizations. On the other hand, sixteen indicated that their institution offered little or no financial support for conference attendance, and they often traveled at their own expense, something many of their colleagues were unwilling or unable to do. Overall, lack of resources constituted *the* major barrier for faculty in many departments.

Twenty faculty indicated that working conditions at their colleges made it hard for them and their colleagues to "get away." Their heavy teaching loads made travel difficult, particularly to multiday national conferences held in the middle of the semester. Likewise, the increasing reliance on part-time instructors at many two-year colleges meant that full-time faculty were shouldering heavy administrative burdens, further constraining their time for professional activities that are, in the words of one instructor, "extra credit." As several faculty were quick to note, it was exceedingly difficult for many of their part-time colleagues to attend conferences, even at the regional level, due to hectic teaching schedules, few financial resources, and little institutional support. Only two faculty indicated that their institutions provided any kind of conference travel funding for adjuncts, and four noted that the growing number of dual enrollment courses at area high schools was creating yet another pool of instructors who had few resources and little encouragement to participate in professional organizations.

Finally, some of the faculty participants commented on barriers that they or their colleagues perceived to be erected by the national professional organizations themselves. Six had experienced presentations at CCCC conventions to be "really theoretical," "jargon-laced," and "preoccupied with ideology"—one participant referred to presenters as "babbling theoreticians," and two commented on the number of graduate students delivering densely theoretical presentations based on little actual teaching experience. Three faculty described feeling ignored or marginalized—"like second-class citizens"—at national conferences. One said, rather diplomatically, "There is a sort of exclusion that happens a little bit, and that may not be intentionally." Another participant put it more bluntly: "TYCA's single greatest strength is we get sneered at at the Cs." While these experiences were certainly not shared by all faculty in the study, many of whom were active, long-time participants at CCCC, the perception seemed to be sufficiently widespread that it prevented some two-year college English faculty from returning to the conference, or even attending in the first place.

Getting Involved

Despite these barriers, the faculty in this study *were* involved with professional organizations, and they found this involvement personally, pedagogically, and professionally rewarding. So how did they and their colleagues overcome the barriers to entry? Ten faculty described first getting involved during graduate school, most often through the encouragement of specific faculty mentors who urged them to attend conferences and to submit presentation proposals and, in many cases, co-presented with them on panels. While many had experienced such mentorship in doctoral programs, a few received this kind of professionalization in their master's programs. As one faculty member described her experience:

> No doubt about it, I had excellent leadership from my director. . . . She gave us the full meal deal, as far as rhetoric and composition goes. She not just taught us about grading practices and composition and rhetoric theory, but she introduced us to the publications and for the first time ever, she went to the dean of the college and got some funds to take us to four Cs. Didn't just say, "Hey, let's go to St. Louis and have a good time." She sat us down, showed us the program, how to read it, what to look for, and how to meet with the book reps when you're there and to make those connections. She really instilled that in us.

This early introduction to the field made a lasting impression on the instructor, who has been an active participant in several different regional and national professional organizations for more than two decades.

The importance of this kind of mentorship extended beyond graduate school. Seven faculty attributed their involvement in professional organizations to encouragement and guidance from departmental colleagues, most often during their first few years of teaching. As one faculty put it:

> I was really lucky that I had a great mentor when I first started at my current position. She recommended that I immediately start presenting at conferences and attending conferences and doing that sort of work because I don't know that all of my colleagues are committed to getting involved in this way.

Once they became involved, faculty were no longer intimidated by the process and found the rewards of involvement well worth the time and energy. As another veteran conference-goer described:

> One of my colleagues was the program chair and got me involved [in the regional organization]. I presented, and then I presented at the CCCC in Kansas City and met a bunch of good people. . . . I was young and full of beans. I just thought that, hell, this is easy. You just write out a little thingy and send it in. You're on the program, you meet great people, you go around and talk to all these experts, and they talk to you like you're an adult and important.

For many faculty, once they had experienced this kind of engagement, they never looked back.

Fifteen faculty described stepping into a mentor role themselves, or becoming "cheerleaders" within their departments for attending conferences, participating in professional organizations, and engaging with disciplinary knowledge making. Although taking on this role could be tricky—some feared impugning the professionalism of their colleagues— such advocacy had become a career-long project for several faculty. As one instructor put it:

> I don't want to judge folks. I try to court. I try to inspire. . . . I always pro- mote the conferences and what's out there. I send people stuff constantly and say this is something you're interested in. . . . I do that constantly. It's usually well received.

In some cases, faculty took this cheerleading role beyond circulating calls for papers and sharing articles and sought to secure more depart- mental or institutional resources to support their colleagues' conference attendance. This included lobbying administrators for travel funding, as well as organizing ride-shares and other cost-saving measures so that more faculty—including adjuncts—could afford to attend regional or national conferences that were being held nearby. In a few cases, faculty also used their sway to revise position descriptions and hiring criteria, formally establishing involvement in professional organizations as an explicit expectation. At some colleges, such changes had created real shifts in departmental culture and levels of engagement over time. As one instructor described:

> I think because I was the first person trained in composition hired at my college, I always was aware that there was a world out there. I kept one part of my mind attuned to what was going on in the world, and I wanted to bring that to my faculty, my colleagues, who weren't like that. . . . We've hired a lot of comp people since then. I know we've changed the culture of the campus in that way.

Unmeasured Forms of Engagement

From my earliest interviews, it became apparent that trying to mea- sure two-year college faculty engagement with professional organiza- tions simply by counting NCTE membership and conference atten- dance was inadequate. First of all, focusing only on NCTE organizations obscures much of the range of faculty's actual involvement. The diversity of two-year college English faculty's disciplinary backgrounds, the vari- ety of courses they teach, and the range and variability of their admin- istrative duties within their institutions leads to a distinctive form of engagement with academic knowledge that I call *transdisciplinary cos- mopolitanism*: a pragmatic translation of knowledge across multiple disciplines and geographical scales that is uniquely suited to two-year college faculty professional roles (see Toth, Griffiths, and Thirolf, p. 595). In addition to NCTE and CCCC, faculty in this study indicated that they or their English department colleagues participated in professional organizations across an array of disciplines, including several closely tied to composition (e.g., Council of Writing Program Administrators, International Writing Center Association, Association of Teachers of Technical Writing), other areas of English studies (e.g., Modern Language Association, Association of Writers and Writing Programs, Teachers of English as a Second Language), and education (e.g., National Association for Developmental Education), as well as a variety of interdisciplinary organizations (e.g., Community College Humanities Association). Several also reported attending small special-interest conferences focusing on topics as diverse as information literacy, popular culture, sports literature, and folklore. Moreover, faculty participated in organizations across multiple geographical scales, attending national and international as well as regional, state, and local conferences. In sum, two-year college faculty engage with many professional organizations beyond the "standard" NCTE associations.

Furthermore, even when they could not attend conferences in person, many faculty and their colleagues engaged with professional organizations online. They reported using a range of digital technologies to stay involved, including listservs, blogs, and Facebook. These tools served as quick and informal ways to pose questions, share resources, circulate calls for proposals, and stay tuned in to regional and national professional conversations, even if it was just as a "lurker." As one participant said of the WPA listserv: "That's kind of my professional home. When people talk on that listserv, I pay attention. . . . It keeps me up on what people are talking about." Three participants noted that keeping up with these kinds of resources could be overwhelming, so they tended to check in sporadically ("I'll hop on it and then hop off"), and two admitted that they sometimes felt reluctant to post to listservs, either because they perceived those communications to be too permanent ("you know it's going to be archived and it's accessible") or because they were afraid of the response they might receive from colleagues ("I feel like whenever I say something people are gonna throw shit at me"). Whether active posters or lurkers, those two-year college English faculty engaging with professional organizations online are not necessarily dues-paying members or regular conference attendees, and their participation is difficult to quantify.

In addition to participating in various forms of digital communication, one instructor reported making creative use of online technologies to participate in conferences. As she described:

> This past year I wasn't actually able to physically attend four Cs, but I had a presentation. We were supposed to be making a presentation and actually did it virtually because it was an online presentation through Facebook. So it was an actual session that was, apparently, very well attended. We had maybe 25 or 30 people . . . [and] several people participating online via the Facebook page. In the lead-up to that session, we had

had a few weeks of just really intense conversations going on on the Face-book page.

In this case, Facebook not only made it possible for the instructor to present at a conference that she could not physically attend, but the session participants were able to extend their conversation beyond the physical *and* temporal boundaries of the conference itself. Many of these virtual two-year college participants probably did not appear on the official attendee tallies for that year's CCCC convention, but they were engaged nonetheless.

In another form of unmeasured engagement, thirteen of the twenty-four faculty described a pattern of conference attendance that I began to think of as the *delegate model*, in which one or more faculty would attend a national or regional conference on behalf of the entire depart-ment. As one instructor described it:

> I think also within our department there have been a couple of people who are sort of identified as our links to the national committees. The col-league I mentioned who is very involved in TYCA, NCTE, and CCCC, I think a lot of people have decided well, that's her role, she'll keep us in-formed. It's been, sort of, as long as we've got one person connecting us then perhaps not everybody has to.

In some cases, different faculty assumed responsibility for specific con-ferences, and then came back and shared what they learned with their colleagues, thereby maximizing the disciplinary "coverage" within de-partments constrained by limited travel funding. Another instructor described the following dynamic:

> There's a few of us that always go to Cs, there's a bunch of us that go to NADE, there's always people that go to AWP. . . . We obviously can't af-ford to have everybody go and this is — virtually none of these folks are adjuncts, 'cause adjuncts unfortunately don't get any support. What we do is, twice a year — once a semester — we have something called Institute Day where we come and present on our work, and a lot of times our work is related to things we've done at conferences or seen at conferences or workshops.

While some departments relied on delegates to share what they learned informally, in three cases the dissemination was a formal event like Institute Day that made it possible for all colleagues, including adjunct faculty, to access at least some of the disciplinary and professional knowledge being brought back from conferences. There are undoubt-edly limitations to the delegate model: many of the personal, social, and professional benefits of attending conferences that highly engaged fac-ulty describe can only be experienced in person. However, indirect en-gagement is better than no engagement at all. Because of this kind of delegation, for every two-year college instructor who appears on the attendee roster at CCCC or NCTE, there may be a dozen or more uncounted faculty back at their college who are engaging indirectly.

Indeed, whether they encountered information through conference attendance or through listservs, academic journals, or personal communication with faculty at other institutions, twenty-one faculty described formal and informal mechanisms by which they and their colleagues circulated disciplinary resources within their departments. These mechanisms included structured professional development events, discussions in department or committee meetings, regular brown bag or reading group sessions, and email or online repositories, as well as casual conversation. This kind of indirect involvement is difficult to quantify but suggests that two-year college faculty are much more engaged with disciplinary and professional knowledge than a narrow, "four-year-centric" focus on paid organizational membership and physical conference attendance reveals. In the words of one participant: "We do a lot of sharing. . . . I think you'll find that that is a very typical faculty thing. . . . I think the engagement is much deeper than it looks like on the surface." This sharing of (inter)disciplinary resources, which connects rather than isolates faculty from regional and national professional communities, is markedly different from the uncritical practitioner "sharing" that McGrath and Spear describe.

Conclusions

This study suggests several implications for two-year college English faculty. For those who are not currently involved in professional organizations, these findings provide a glimpse of what they stand to gain by participating. Likewise, these findings highlight the need to create departmental cultures that value engagement with professional organizations, and they demonstrate the importance of reaching out to early-career faculty to help bring them into the professional community. Two-year college faculty who are active participants in professional organizations should continue encouraging new instructors in their departments to attend conferences, and might provide further mentorship by inviting them to collaborate on panels, attending their presentations, and discussing how they might apply what they learn at the conference back at their home institution. More broadly, two-year faculty should continue being departmental cheerleaders for the regional TYCA, CCCC, and NCTE, as well as other relevant professional organizations. This includes reminding busy faculty about call for proposal deadlines and organizing ride- and room-shares, but also pursuing structural incentives, such as securing dedicated funding for conference travel and codifying expectations of engagement in faculty position descriptions, hiring criteria, and, where applicable, the promotion and tenure process.

Of course, securing any additional resources is a tall order in the current budget climate. Given this reality, these findings suggest several strategies that two-year college faculty might employ to engage with professional organizations despite the many constraints on their time and funding. Various forms of online engagement—listservs, Facebook pages, and the NCTE Connected Community, for example—can provide an important means of participating in professional conversations. Of course, Bateman rightly warns TYCA not to overestimate the power of technology for creating community, but as social media and other online technologies advance, we should continuously consider how they can be put to use to lower the costs of engaging with professional organizations. If nothing else, faculty and departments might think creatively about what technology could make possible before deciding that they cannot afford to participate in conferences at all.

Likewise, the delegate model offers a cost-effective means of enabling entire departments to access relevant knowledge being made across a range of disciplines and professional organizations. Consciously adopting this strategy not only encourages faculty engagement with the professional organizations most closely aligned with their academic training and professional interests but also fosters intradepartmental scholarly exchange among faculty who might otherwise be isolated in their classrooms. Additionally, faculty might continue to create structured ways of sharing disciplinary and professional resources within departments: email and online resource repositories are a start, and regular brown-bags, discussion groups, and institutional symposia can also encourage the development of departmental professional communities that are connected to disciplinary professional organizations.

This study also suggests a number of steps that the NCTE-affiliated professional organizations can take to foster two-year college faculty engagement. First, these organizations can seek to cultivate more online engagement and virtual conference attendance among two-year college faculty. Second, NCTE or CCCC could collaborate with TYCA to develop videos or other multimodal resources that share research related to pressing issues facing two-year college faculty (e.g., multilingual students, learning transfer, automated essay scoring). Such resources could be specifically designed for viewing and discussion within two-year college English departments. They would be an accessible way to share disciplinary knowledge through professional organization networks, would support the development of professional communities within departments (including adjuncts and dual enrollment faculty), and might also demonstrate the value of engaging with professional organizations to faculty who are not yet involved. Connecting research to practice in a way that takes advantage of the affordances of digital media *while being driven by TYCA-identified needs and audience considerations* might also help address the persistent impression among some two-year college faculty that CCCC has, as one instructor put it, a "blithe disregard for two-year colleges."

Likewise, the professional organizations could do more to foster exchange and mutual understanding between two- and four-year college faculty. For example, CCCC and TYCA could collaborate on a position statement regarding the specific ways in which English graduate programs, both at the master's and doctoral levels, should be informing their students about what it means to be an excellent teacher *and* engaged professional in the two-year college—nearly two decades after Nist and Raines's calls for such integration, two-year colleges still remain largely invisible in many English graduate curricula. This would be important for graduate students in rhetoric and composition *and* literature and creative writing who, whether they realize it or not, may be making their careers in two-year colleges. However, such inclusion would also provide much-needed professional development for graduate students who go on to positions at *four-year* institutions: it would give them a more accurate understanding of the landscape of postsecondary literacy instruction, help them prepare their own future students for two-year college careers, and make them better-informed colleagues to the two-year membership of NCTE.

Similarly, CCCC and TYCA could work together to establish explicit expectations regarding the responsibility that university composition programs have to serve as a resource and hub for collaboration with two-year college English faculty in their regions (see Nist and Raines; Andelora, "Teacher/Scholar," p. 579). As professionals whose job descriptions, workloads, library resources, and travel funding typically allow for greater engagement with disciplinary knowledge making, university faculty can be an important point of access for the two-year college faculty in their city or region, who in turn have a great deal of local pedagogical knowledge and classroom experience to offer four-year faculty and graduate students. Such "professional organization" across institutions could include workshops, symposia, guest speakers, and hybrid online courses on topics of particular interest to two-year college faculty, as well as collaborative research projects and other forms of scholarship that will benefit students and faculty at both institution types and could include K–12 faculty, too. In short, national professional organizations could push to make collaboration with two-year college colleagues an expected professional role of *four-year* English faculty, rather than remaining the special interest of just a handful of researchers.

Finally, this study suggests several areas for future research. First and foremost, there is a pressing need for research on the extent to which two-year college adjunct faculty are engaging with professional organizations, what this engagement looks like, and how well the professional organizations are meeting adjunct faculty needs. Second, the field needs a clearer empirical understanding of the relationship between faculty engagement with professional organizations and student learning outcomes: most faculty involved in professional organizations believe that such participation has improved their teaching, but many administrators and policymakers do not share this sense that being professionally engaged results in better "returns" for students, the institution, and taxpayers. Determining the nature and extent of these returns might, among other things, lend credence to faculty requests for conference travel funding and other institutional incentives for participating in professional organizations.

One of the faculty in this study described the annual trip to his regional TYCA as a "hero's adventure": "Departure, fulfillment, return," he said. "That's what a conference is. The character who goes out at the beginning of the story is not the same person who comes back. . . . Whatever happens, we go out and come back a new and better person." A research project is also a journey. In 2009, when I set out to learn more about two-year college faculty engagement with professional organizations, I was a shell-shocked first-semester graduate student. I missed my community college students, and I was not at all convinced that I would be able to do work within the discipline of composition that would serve the institutions I cared about most. Over the last four years, as I have moved through my doctoral program, this project has allowed me to stay connected to the students and faculty closest to my heart. It is a journey that has taken me to six regional TYCA conferences and given me the opportunity to contribute to conversations about the profession on the pages of *College Composition and Communication*. Most importantly, it has enabled me to make friends with dozens of colleagues who are, indeed, *gold*. Thanks to their mentorship, I am returning from the journey a better scholar and a better teacher, and I am also coming back with a stronger belief in the discipline of composition—albeit with plenty of ideas about how it could be improved. Fortunately, the teacher-scholars of TYCA have taught me another important lesson along the way: this field is ours for the making.

Works Cited

Andelora, Jeffrey. "Forging a National Identity: TYCA and the Two-Year College Teacher-Scholar." *Teaching English in the Two-Year College* 35.4 (2008): 350–62. Print.

———. "The Professionalization of Two-Year College English Faculty: 1950–1990." *Teaching English in the Two-Year College* 35.1 (2007): 6–19. Print.

———. "TYCA and the Struggle for a National Voice: 1991–1993." *Teaching English in the Two-Year College* 35.2 (2007): 133–48. Print.

———. "TYCA and the Struggle for a National Voice: 1994–1997." *Teaching English in the Two-Year College* 35.3 (2008): 252–65. Print.

Bateman, Eric. "Ideas for the Future of TYCA." *Teaching English in the Two-Year College* 36.3 (2009): 235–43. Print.

Bureau of Labor Statistics. "Occupational Employment Statistics, May 2012: English Language and Literature Teachers, Postsecondary." Web. 31 May 2013.

Calhoon-Dillahunt, Carolyn. "Writing Programs without Administrators: Frameworks for Successful Writing Programs in the Two-Year College." *WPA: Journal of Council of Writing Program Administrators* 35.1 (2011): 118–34. Print.

Cohen, Arthur M., and Florence B. Brawer. *The American Community College.* 5th ed. San Francisco: Jossey-Bass, 2008. Print.

Corbin, Juliet, and Anselm Strauss. *The Basics of Qualitative Research: Techniques and Procedures for Developing Grounded Theory.* Thousand Oaks: Sage, 2007. Print.

Klausman, Jeffrey. "Mapping the Terrain: The Two-Year College Writing Program Administrator." *Teaching English in the Two-Year College* 35.3 (2008): 238–51. Print.

———. "Toward a Definition of a Writing Program at a Two-Year College: You Say You Want a Revolution?" *Teaching English in the Two-Year College* 40.3 (2013): 257–73. Print.

Laster, Ann, and Beverly Fatherree. "Reminiscing about a Two-Year Regional Conference: Two Voices/One Viewpoint." *The Profession of English in the Two-Year College.* Ed. Sylvia Holladay-Hicks and Mark Reynolds. Portsmouth: Boynton/Cook, 2005. 113–24. Print.

Lovas, John C. "All Good Writing Develops at the Edge of Risk." *College Composition and Communication* 54.2 (2002): 264–88. Print.

McGrath, Dennis, and Martin B. Spear. *The Academic Crisis of the Community College.* Albany: State U of New York P, 1991. Print.

Nist, Elizabeth A., and Helon H. Raines. "Two-Year Colleges: Explaining and Claiming Our Majority." *Resituating Writing: Constructing and Administering Writing Programs.* Ed. Joseph Janangelo and Kristine Hansen. Portsmouth: Heinemann, 1995. Print.

Otte, George, and Rebecca Williams Mlynarczyk. *Basic Writing.* West Lafayette: Parlor P, 2010. Print.

Taylor, Tim N. "Writing Program Administration at the Two-Year College: Ghosts in the Machine." *WPA: Writing Program Administration* 32.3 (2009): 120–39. Print.

Tinberg, Howard B. *Border Talk: Writing and Knowing in the Two-Year College.* Urbana: NCTE, 1997.

Tinberg, Howard, and Jean-Paul Nadeau. "Contesting the Space between High School and College in the Era of Dual-Enrollment." *College Composition and Communication* 62.4 (2011): 704–25. Print.

Two-Year College English Association. "Guidelines for the Academic Preparation of English Faculty at Two-Year Colleges." NCTE. 2004. Web.

Contingent Faculty

The Problem of the Majority Contingent Faculty in the Community Colleges

Helena Worthen

In reference to the following selection, Helena Worthen writes, "Looking back on this chapter after nearly 20 years I am happy to see that I got a lot right. There are two points I would like to emphasize now. First, not only is contingency continuing to rise, but the movement of contingent faculty toward self-organization to lead the fight against it is also rising. The Coalition on Contingent Academic Labor (COCAL) holds conferences in Canada, the United States, and Mexico; the New Faculty Majority does advocacy and legislative work; traditional teacher unions (AFT, NEA, AAUP) are finally very worried about the situation; one union in particular, SEIU (Service Employees International Union) is deploying a Metro Strategy in the private sector, and sponsored an Occupy-style, anonymously inspired national Adjunct Walkout Day on February 25, 2015, designed to generate mainstream media alarm. The tone of this movement is not fearful and desperate, as it was before contingents recognized that we were the majority and the norm; instead, it is assertive, direct, and a bit rowdy. One nationally known contingent activist is on Twitter as @badjunct. Second, the trend

From *The Politics of Writing in the Two-Year College*, edited by Barry Alford and Keith Kroll. Heinemann/Boynton-Cook, 2001, pp. 42-60.

toward reshaping community colleges to serve economic development is accelerating, meaning the elimination or shrinking of adult education programs, cuts to services like writing centers, general liberal arts, and 'niche' programs like ethnic and women's studies. The tool that is being used to accomplish this, ironically, is the accreditation process; the exemplary case study is City College of San Francisco. Overall, this shift from focus on what's bad about contingency to what's bad about an industry (higher education) in which contingency is the norm is healthy and liberating. On the way to this perspective, however, contingent faculty have to shed the hope that by keeping our mouths shut and trying ever harder, we will capture the brass ring of a full-time tenured position. It's either all of us or none. The bridges being built between contingent faculty organizations like COCAL and organizations representing other low-wage contingent workers such as taxi drivers, domestic workers, and day laborers provide evidence that as workers, we have more in common with them than not."

> "The best thing about contingent faculty is that you can get rid of them whenever you want."
>
> —A president of a California community college, spring 1992; a remark made in the presence of contingent faculty

> "Little creativity occurs when faculty members are preoccupied with issues of personal security and institutional fairness."
>
> —Terry O'Banion, *The Renaissance of Innovation*

In studies of community-college issues, one or two pages out of several hundred will be typically spent deploring the overreliance of most colleges on contingent faculty (see Brint & Karabel 1989; Deegan & Tillery 1985; McGrath & Spear 1991; Richardson, Fisk, & Okun 1983). Because contingent faculty are now the substantial majority of community-college faculty (66 percent according to Mahoney & Jimenez 1992), two pages out of several hundred seems, at least to contingent faculty, like a misrepresentation of the situation. Furthermore, most descriptions of the status of faculty in the community colleges are made from the perspectives of administrators, who tend to view their work as managing an organizational structure, or from the perspectives of full-time faculty, who tend to view their work as sustaining a certain norm of academic quality and commitment on behalf of the college as a whole. From both perspectives, contingent faculty appear to be marginal, the exceptions to the norm that provide specific, narrow value. In terms of fiscal logic, they provide flexibility; in terms of curricular planning, they provide the special expertise. However, these descriptions fail to portray what the contingent majority experiences.

In this selection, I will try to write about the experience of contingent faculty from the point of view of the part-time faculty.

Impossible Choices

A contingent faculty member describes her situation at her college:

> This semester I had a very bad class. There were a lot of people in there who shouldn't have been—relatives, friends who just tagged along. I let them in because if my enrollment had fallen below twenty-five, I would have lost the class. As it was, there were just twenty-five. The result was, I gave out sixteen D's out of twenty-five students. I know this looks bad. I went to a full-timer and asked her what to do. She said, raise all the grades 5 percent. I worked the numbers every way I could and gave them all five extra points. Another full-timer said to just raise all the grades one letter. But the thing is, this was a really bad class. Many of them should have been sent to adult school instead. So I don't want to send them the wrong message. But I'm afraid the dean will look at my grades and say, "You don't belong in the community-college system. You're not in the community-college mode. You don't know your students very well. You don't adjust your teaching to your students." I'm really scared: this could be my job.

This contingent is racked by conflicting responsibilities. To prevent her class from being canceled, she must enroll at least twenty-five students. Although this is too many for the class she is teaching (remedial language arts), she is not in a position to criticize district policy. Minimum class size is set at the district level and is derived from budgetary assumptions. (Specifically, one year's state funding per full-time equivalent (FTE) times twenty-five will support one full-time teacher plus the equal amount of administrative overhead; this means that the difference between full-time and contingent salaries is the "savings" out of which district contingency and discretionary funding comes.[1])

"Not in a position" in this case should be taken literally: There is no secure footing from which this contingent faculty member can speak, no legitimate channel through which her knowledge of the minimum pedagogically sound conditions of her classroom can enter the discussion out of which comes the decision to set class size at twenty-five. There is no feedback loop from the instructor in the classroom to the district management. Although there is faculty representation on the district budget committee, contingents are never on it and information about the classroom work of contingents is not solicited in the decision-making process. So this teacher's options are to accept the students or lose the class. Losing the class means losing the income. Furthermore, she is a forty-year-old single female with no savings, a health problem, and she gets her health insurance through a district group plan (although she pays the premium). So she accepts the class of twenty-five students.

This semester, however, the high minimum class size has meant accepting some students who are unprepared or uncommitted. She worries about this; she knows what the consequences of this may be at exam time. And, sure enough, her fears are realized. At the end of the semester, she knows that if she grades honestly, her grade sheet will be more than half D's. It will look as if she either hasn't taught the students anything or has lost control of the class. When the department grade sheets are compared at the end of the semester, hers will stand out. She is right when she says that her dean will warn her she is not "in the community-college mode." The happy-face tradition of community colleges that calls tutorial centers "success centers" encourages grade sheets that either show a bell curve (indicating a competitive classroom that sorts students[2]) or all A's and B's (the egalitarian outcome). Exceptions to this stand out. Those whom she perceives as judging her include not only her dean, who hires the contingent faculty from one semester to another, but her full-time colleagues, who evaluate her and will sit on any hiring committee to which she will apply if a full-time job opens up in the future. Therefore, faced with an impossible choice, she decides to be proactive and ask their advice. At least for a few moments during the conversation she may hope to display the appropriate amount of exasperation at the conditions that have put her in this bind.

However, their advice to her essentially tells her to set aside her professional integrity. They see themselves as being helpful and supportive by advising her to adapt to coercive circumstances. They do not use the protection of their tenure to address those circumstances themselves. She (again) is not in a position to point this out to them. She is embarrassed on their behalf (embarrassed by their cowardice, as she perceives it), yet she is afraid to say what she thinks of them.

The details of this instructor's experience are an important part of what must be considered when understanding teaching in the community-college system—the "teaching colleges," as they are ironically known. No matter how much this instructor has read, how well she has grasped the arguments of David Bartholomae, Mike Rose, Min-Zhan Lu, Martin Nystrand, Andrea Lunsford, Mina Shaughnessey, or the other contemporary theorists of composition instruction, no theory, no disciplinary knowledge will help her when she faces a class half full of students who shouldn't be there, who are there because the bus doesn't leave until ten-thirty and their ride is enrolled in the class. All the theory in the world won't help her when she is told by someone whose goodwill she depends on to "raise all the grades one letter." In fact, she does read theory. This particular instructor has a Ph.D. She keeps up with the journals in her field and pays her own way to conferences. But how will professional development help her at a moment like this?

What would her knowledge of these impossible choices contribute to a discussion about initiation into the culture of the academy, polyvocalism, dialogic pedagogy, and the appropriation of discursive forms? It is at a moment like this that the concerns of this instructor's disciplinary specialty do not seem contiguous to the realities of her work.

People who are or who know contingents in the community-college system will wonder how I got this story. Stories like this do not float around as general gossip. They are told either in confidence, between people who have reason to trust each other, or else (with bitterness) by former contingents after they have left teaching. Therefore, people might think this is my story because no one would have told it to me. However, it is not my story. In fact, for about seven years I was in a position to hear many stories like that one because between 1988 and 1995 I was part of a general organizing drive to unionize California community-college contingent faculty and to negotiate job-security contract items for contingents in districts where unions were established. Working for the California Federation of Teachers, I edited a newsletter dedicated to this organizing drive. My phone number was listed in the newsletter, and, therefore, I became one of the ears for innumerable stories like this one, stories that could not be told to anyone local whom the troubled contingent knew because, without job security, to name a problem was to be a problem.

Here is another story. This is not a language-arts instructor. It is a carpentry instructor. Language arts and carpentry tend to inhabit different hemispheres of the educational globe, but note the parallels in the issues: class-size determination made at a distance, compromises made by the teacher, devaluation of educational experience, and the collusion of the tenured full-timer who wants to be helpful but does not attempt to use his or her protected status to address the problem at its root. This story also explicitly mentions the absence of a communication channel from the instructor to the administration, and the way in which the instructor's working conditions block the flow of information from the instructor to the decision-making part of the system. I offer this story to make the point that the politics of teaching anything as a contingent overwhelm the politics of a specific discipline. This is precisely because the conditions of contingent teaching silence debate about disciplinary concerns: to disagree fundamentally about how to do your job with someone who has power over your job is to risk losing your job. The only situations in which the power relations between contingent faculty and the rest of the college personnel do not matter with regard to disciplinary issues are those in which all debate has been *a priori* extinguished and there is nothing left to disagree about. It is a situation that can be achieved, of course (and is often attempted), by routinizing all aspects of teaching.

The carpentry instructor told me this story:

> This semester they just jammed me, jammed me for ADA (average daily attendance). I have thirty-five students in every class, no more than two absences on any day, and they're sticking with me, not dropping. But I can only handle twenty-five in the shop. Now I haven't had an accident in there the whole time I've been working here, but I don't have eyes in the

back of my head, and this semester, I got really worried. The students have insurance and worker's comp, but still, you don't want an accident. I went to a full-timer who teaches wood technology and asked him what I should do and he just said, "Hang in there." What I did was, I didn't let the students get their hands on power tools at all until halfway through the semester. Now if I had had job security, I would have said to the administration, "No, it's not safe, I won't take any more than twenty-five, I won't sign the add cards." And they would have just had to live with it.

This instructor has safety concerns: power tools can cut off a finger or a hand. An unsupervised student could start a fire by plugging extension cords into the wrong socket. Applying varnish in an unventilated corner could make a student pass out. Here, learning to use equipment is analogous to learning to write; the problem of instrumentality, of learning to make a tool serve one's purpose, is the same. In both cases, the instructor's hope of teaching students to use something is defeated.

The two disciplines—carpentry and composition—may seem unalike, but when they are both taught by contingents their similarities are more salient than their differences.

The Snapshot Survey

"If I had some job security . . ." became words familiar to us as our team of organizers expanded to include people at more colleges, and more and more stories like this came to our ears, stories that could only be entrusted to those of us who had earned credibility by publicly working to change the conditions that were causing the conflicts.

After four or five years of working on this effort, I began to feel inhabited by these voices. I got so I jumped when the phone rang at dinner and a voice said, "I don't think you know me, but I got your name from the union. . . ." Then I would hear a fifty-five-year-old teacher of French who was being replaced by another, younger teacher who "had better energy." I would hear a Chinese teacher of physics, who was caught explaining a concept (after class, to his mostly Chinese students) in Chinese, by a non-Chinese administrator and was being descheduled (a euphemism) because he is "racist." I would hear a young Spanish teacher who was nominated by her students as Teacher of the Year and was now being told by her dean that she had developed "a bad attitude." And there was the young man who became active in his union (at a college where contingent faculty could buy in to the health plan) and tried to organize contingents; he suddenly had no assignment. I couldn't help him; the union could not be mobilized to prove retaliation. We heard a year later that he had died of AIDS, without health insurance.

In all these stories, contingent teachers were asked or told to do something (or not to do something) that discredited or suppressed their own experience and knowledge—of their students, of their own work lives, of their disciplines. Their seniority, their bilingualism, their pride, their bravery; they each paid dearly for these.

These were difficult years for me. There were times when I could not bring myself to have a civil conversation with an administrator whom I knew from another source to have exploited the vulnerability of a contingent, or with a full-time faculty member who had failed to use his or her protected status to lessen that vulnerability.

I began to want to make these stories public. They had been told us in confidence, as part of a request for help (I have changed some details to disguise the situations I've described), so they could not be used for newsletter articles or for a study, for example, to create a cumulative, aggregate portrait. Therefore, eventually our organizing team decided to ask for, rather than just wait for, such stories. We sent out two hundred copies of a one-page survey asking people to write a few sentences, or more if they wished, about the relationship between their ability to do their jobs well and their job security. Anonymous responses were fine, but we warned people that we would use the stories they told us publicly. We asked both full- and part-time faculty and we asked at campuses where there was no job security for contingents as well as at campuses where there was a degree of job security (some kind of due process, usually). The survey was supposed to be a snapshot of how people felt at that moment in time.

We got back forty responses. One person, afraid to be identified, phoned me after mailing in his response and asked me to pull it from the stack. Another wrote, in response to our question about experiences illustrating the connection between job security and quality of work, "Not on paper, not in my handwriting!" These responses created a picture of an academic culture overcast with fear, and often confused.

Some responses seemed to be just about the banality of evil:

> I was bumped the current semester by a full-timer who had an underenrolled course. He chose my course because it was scheduled for a Tuesday and Thursday. This instructor had been getting his Fridays free for the last six years.

> One semester, my teaching schedule was changed at the last minute. I said I couldn't work that schedule and expressed anger over the situation. I was not called to teach the next semester, presumably because I didn't quietly go along with things.

> I won an election against a full-timer for a prestigious post in the honors program. He tried to have me fired; threatened me; tried to invalidate the elections; and finally cursed me, shoved me, and hit me. Thankfully, the union reprimanded him, and the administration followed suit.

I knew, from previous conversations with many people like those who answered our survey, that they loved their students and their disciplines and had a vision of good teaching. Yet when asked about their relationship to the colleges where they worked, their enthusiasm failed and they became evasive and timid. Some responses revealed contingents taking proactive measures to create a publicly safe or pleasing persona:

> I suspect that "charm" may be valued over academic accomplishments, ability to teach.

> Sometimes your teaching can be changed to conform to the powers that be.

> Anyone who says they teach exactly the same way as they would if they had full tenure is either a fool or not teaching much worth learning.

> As a contingent who wants a full-time job, I am perpetually auditioning.

> Even though I take what I believe to be the correct stance (academic, pedagogic, or political), there is always the worry that the "wrong" person will hear and disapprove. I definitely have the impression from other [contingents] that they feel the same way. One feels constantly endangered.

> As a contingent, I was threatened more than once with the possibility of losing my classes if I didn't fall into line with department policies. These included content as well as scheduling. I had to put up with a lot of unprofessional behavior.

> There is subtle pressure to post grades that look like the rest of the department (not too many D's or A's, depending on the current fad).

Others displayed a kind of quiet defiance:

> My pride will not allow me to slack even though I have no contract.

> I do a serious job in spite of being an adjunct teacher.

> I don't allow insecurity to affect me. More security, more risks one might take in terms of pedagogy, content. However, those without security might still take risks.

We asked if there were substantive issues to disagree about. Examples came from all different disciplines:

> Using material represented by the white male canon leads to different discussion than a more multicultural selection. If a dean prefers to teach

one set of values, lifestyles, goals over another, your job may be jeopardized if you fall into the latter category.

Philosophy can by nature be controversial.

I personally know people who have been let go for their choice of texts.

History is inherently political all the time.

The anti-immigrant movement bears directly on our dealings with ESL [English as a Second Language] speakers in composition class.

High standards for university transfer classes are being sacrificed to keep large classes. If an instructor holds high standards (a contingent instructor, that is), she is accused of "not being nice to students."

Some instructors dealt with the politics of their discipline by simply skirting anything controversial. We heard from a psychologist who stuck to what he considered "objective" and a chemist who avoided talking about environmental issues:

There is certainly enough to talk about that is objective in psychology, without getting into very many political issues. I am not all that much wishing to mix politics with my discipline.

Not much in chemistry. Except in environmental policy. . . . But one must feel secure to discuss one's true feelings.

Others, especially ESL and basic-skills instructors, faced the issue directly:

Teaching ESL is definitely political . . . I give my students examples of people struggling and improving their lives. I'm not just giving them skills so they can go out and earn more money and better themselves individually. It's collective betterment. Their problems are not individual, their problems are part of a group.

How can anyone teach basic skills to inner-city young people without asking why economically disadvantaged people are so often educationally disadvantaged as well?

My students are not in remedial classes because they are genetically inferior; they are there because of the world they live in, and I have to help them learn to either change it or else escape from it.

Look closely at the last clause of that statement: "learn to either change [the world] or else escape from it." It implies a certain curriculum, for which there is plenty of support in the adult-education literature (see Friere 1985; Newman 1994; Rose 1989). This may seem like a laudable, unexceptional goal for a remedial language-arts teacher, but what would become of her if she persisted in this goal after a dean decided that remedial classes should teach to a skills-focused exit test?

The logical next step for those who do their best despite not having job security is to feel contempt for faculty who have the protection of tenure but seem to be doing nothing with it. These people are an advance guard in the mounting effort to eliminate tenure:

> Job security makes some teachers fat, dumb, and happy.

> I personally feel that job security does not always nurture academic excellence: in fact, it creates inefficiency.

> Tenure permits long-term mediocrity.

> Incompetent faculty stay as long as the best of us.

Quite a few saw a connection between the job status of individual faculty and the life of the college as a whole.

> More workshops and more communication between and for faculty would occur if there were more job security.

Long-range planning on curriculum, designing and revamping programs, can only come from someone who has a full-time position. But many full-time faculty mentioned quitting teaching:

> My advice to new contingent instructors in the community-college system is to find other work. I blew it! If I had my life to do over again, I would go to work for United Airlines. I would not have invested the time, effort, and emotional capital trying to be a good teacher.

Incidentally, at about the time that we gathered these responses, I took a look at the quit rates of contingents in my own district and found that 50 percent of all contingents were gone within two years of being hired. Another organizer at another district did the same study and found the same quit rate.

These were the disturbing responses that our organizing team got when we asked contingents to summarize their experience for public consumption. With a few exceptions, they told us: I am angry, but I keep a smile on my face for my administrative manager; I try to forget about lack of job security; my discipline has deeply rooted debates, but I play it safe and don't refer to them; I don't think teachers with tenure deserve it, and I wouldn't advise anyone to go into teaching. The tone is low key and controlled (unlike the stories I would hear in phone calls, when the speaker was likely to be weeping). The overall impression these stories give me is of people who have adapted to denying to themselves a major portion of the knowledge created by their own work lives.

Unfortunately, these responses deal with instructor-administrator and instructor-student relationships only. A type of relationship we did not ask people to comment on is that between instructors, among colleagues. How much collegiality is possible when instructors are in competition with each other for the scarce resource of the approval of a manager, which leads to getting rehired? How much does the need to continually please those who have the power to hire distort the part-timers' contribution to any college infrastructure work he or she may participate in?

Conversations Minus One Voice

My own exposure to the inside stories of contingent faculty made me highly sensitive to discussions of community-college policy in which the voices of part-timers are absent. The public conversation about contingents takes place overwhelmingly among full-time faculty or among administrators, over the heads, as it were, of contingents, which means that space in the discourse gets taken up by people who do not know the whole story. As a result, we get articles like the full-page personal essay in the *Chronicle of Higher Education*, written by Eugene Arden, a vice-chancellor emeritus at the University of Michigan. Arden tells how, each semester, he tried to create an opportunity for "a collegial encounter" among contingents (a three-hour weekend breakfast or lunch in the faculty dining room). He reports that at one such encounter there was a discussion of the value of "including some classroom discussion rather than lecturing for the full period." At other sessions he brought in an expert on testing or showed a video about ethnic and gender issues. Now, these contingents were not novice teachers; in fact, Arden even mentions that "a sizeable number are travelers, who manage to piece together a low-paying full-time schedule by teaching four or five courses per semester on two or even three campuses." Yet Arden makes no mention of asking them to tell him (or each other) about their work; he assumes that they are the empty pails that he must fill. How can he imagine that they need to be told to include opportunities for discussion during a lecture? The only time we hear their voices is when they are expressing gratitude: "I was told more than once: 'This is the first time the institution has paid any attention to us.' Another adjunct asked, 'Does all of this activity mean that what we do in the classroom really matters to you?'" Arden does not tell what the next turn in that dialogue was. Maybe there was none. But if Arden had replied, "Yes, what you do in the classroom really matters," then the adjunct might have said, "Well, then, if that is the case, why don't you be quiet for a moment and listen to us tell you about it?"

Another example, an article in *Crosstalk* (January 1995, 5), a policy newsletter published by the California Higher Education Policy Center in San Jose, describes the shift of remedial English composition courses from the University of California at Davis to Sacramento City Community College, a controversial move occurring as part of a general narrowing of access to the UC system under fiscal stress. The choice to narrow access rather than broaden support for public higher education in California has been made in the context of noisy legislative debate, high-profile partisan politics, and lots of news coverage; the removal of basic English to the community colleges is a highly visible link in that process. Not incidentally (because cost-savings are the driving concern), all of the teachers of the thirty-one sections of the relocated class are contingents. Not one of them is quoted, which makes it possible for readers to get a description of the program and a judgment on the success of the program without ever hearing testimony from someone actually teaching in the program who might be able to comment on the significance of the increase in class size from fifteen to eighteen students per class (the norm at UC) to thirty per class, or how they manage to teach a composition class without paid office hours in which to hold student conferences. William Twombly, the reporter, interviewed everyone else, apparently: the coordinator of the program at the University of California at Davis, the coordinator at Sacramento City, an instructor at Davis who used to teach the course when it was run through Davis, the retired chemistry professor from Davis who set up the program, the president of Sacramento City, and a coordinator of a similar program at University of California at San Diego. There is no evidence that he interviewed someone who was teaching the course. The article does tell us that the teachers are paid about $40 an hour—$50 if they have a Ph.D. Twombly says that the program will be imitated "because the taxpayers are going to demand it." In what other field or business would such a judgment be made without even inquiring after the opinion of the people who know the most about how the program is working?

My point is not that *Crosstalk* makes a unique error, but that the absence of the perspective of the teacher from reports of teaching is so prevalent that it passes unnoted. The employment of faculty in part-time positions is treated as a policy matter, not a pedagogical matter. The silence of the majority of faculty in discussions of policy is a nonissue.

The Working Conditions of the Typical Community-College Instructor

Today the modal community-college faculty person is contingent. This makes community colleges a qualitatively different place than when the part-timers were the visiting experts or emergency temporary help.

Contingent faculty were not always the modal faculty. On August 17, 1995, in a radio broadcast about the community-college system on the NPR show *Talk of the Nation*, Arthur Cohen of the ERIC Clearinghouse said that there had been no significant change in the proportion of part-time faculty over the last thirty years. He could hardly have been more wrong. According to the Spring 1990 ERIC Information Bulletin, "Between 1973 and 1984, the number of full-time faculty increased by 22 percent, whereas the number of part-time faculty grew by 168 percent."

In 1980, Edmund Gleazer, past president of the American Association of Community Colleges (AACC), articulated the traditional academic rationale for hiring contingents to bring in "special expertise." Gleazer explained:

> A large number of faculty are active in the practice of their trade and profession as well as in their teaching. Sometimes referred to as "professor-practitioners" or adjunct professors, they work as real-estate insurance brokers, lawyers, engineers, craftsmen, and doctors and provide further means for linking up with other parts of the community's learning system. (11)

These contingents could make the college a multiplier of community culture and skills. Gleazer did not envision a faculty that was predominantly part-time. His contingent faculty were part-time because they had other full-time jobs outside teaching; that is what gave them "special expertise." Nor did he foresee that they would be used to solve budget problems or reduce the influence of tenured faculty.

Time passed. The boom years of physical expansion of colleges were over. Now the problem was to fill the buildings with students, maximize enrollment, without spending too much money, and the obvious answer was to hire contingent faculty. In 1989, the Conference on College Composition and Communication produced what is known as the Wyoming Resolution (Robertson, Crowley, & Lentricchia 1987), against the overuse of contingents. The National Education Association generated a "Report and Recommendations on Part-Time, Temporary and Non-Tenure Track Faculty Appointments." The Modern Language Association also produced a position statement. In 1992, the Association of Departments of English declared that "the conditions under which most adjunct teachers are employed define them as nonprofessionals." The American Federation of Teachers, which had produced one position statement in 1979, produced another. Faculty organizations (unions, associations, and disciplinary organizations) were across-the-board critical of the overuse of part-time faculty.

However, by this time the budgetary appeal of a low-cost faculty was enhanced by the management appeal of a "flexible" faculty. Linda Pratt in *Report on the Status of Non-Tenure Track Faculty* (1992) summarized 1991 data from National Center for Education Statistics on contingents in higher education. They noted that while the use of contingent faculty might have originated as a way to save money, it had evolved into a mechanism for creating budgetary discretion. The power to choose how to spend the saved money had become a motive for saving money in the first place:

> ... since 1970 part-time appointments as a proportion of all faculty appointments have risen from 21.9 percent to 33.9 percent in 1987 ... closer examination of the data indicates that most of the relative growth of part-time faculty occurred during the period from 1972 to 1977, a period often characterized as one of sharply reduced financial strength for both private and public institutions, and increased institutional interest in alternatives to the tenure system. If those events are important causes of the growth of part-time faculty, then the fact that the supposedly temporary situation did not improve after the economic recovery suggests a growing administrative desire for budgetary discretion. (43)

The collision of "budgetary discretion" with academic quality was becoming a central concern. In 1993, Judith Gappa and David Leslie published *The Invisible Faculty: Improving the Status of Part-Timers in Higher Education.* They argued for a respectful treatment of contingents as employees and professionals, including better professional development programs, careful evaluations, and job stability:

> We cannot think of a better investment for a college or university than its faculty. We think that relatively small investments in part-time faculty now will pay off over the next decade, when the faculty workforce will experience turbulent times. (283)

But the threefold logic for relying on contingents continues to grind inexorably forward: Part-timers bring expertise, save money, and increase management discretion, an unbeatable combination. The result is more part-timers.

In October 1994, the National Center for Education Statistics (NCES 1995) reported that there were 253,711 faculty and instructional staff as of fall 1992, of which 53.4 percent or 135 out of 518 were contingent (1–2). The NCES count, however, did not include instructors teaching in noncredit programs (where large numbers of contingents teach remedial-skills classes, ESL, and composition) or instructors in contract education programs. In addition, the NCES survey counted persons with faculty status whose assignments did not include instruction (such as some deans, researchers, administrators) and persons on sabbatical, the exclusion of whom would decrease the numbers of full-time faculty and thereby increase the percentage of faculty recorded as part-time (19). Furthermore, both the NCES and the AACC surveys were based on self-reports, leaving it to the individual institutions to define who is contingent and who is not. Both surveys probably underestimated the numbers of contingents.

As Perry Robinson (1994) points out, critiquing the previous (1988) NCES survey, "There is no national standard definition of a regular part-time faculty member," which gives institutions considerable reporting leeway (9). He lists the four states with the highest percentages of contingent community college faculty: Vermont (100 percent); Illinois (73.6 percent); Pennsylvania (73.3 percent), and Ohio (72.7 percent). California alone had 26,727 contingents and 16,012 full-timers in the fall of 1993 (California Postsecondary Education Commission 1994, 17). That means that 62.5 percent of faculty in the California community colleges were contingents in 1993. The California count is regarded as reasonably accurate because, since the major California Community College Reform Bill AB 1725, which attempted to penalize districts that hired contingents to teach over 25 percent of credit classes, it is watched closely by several competing constituencies.

The increase in low-cost, flexible contingents mirrors the increase in contingent labor throughout the economy. Robinson places part-time teaching in the context of other part-time work:

> Labor Department statistics reveal that some occupations have an even higher rate of part-time employment than higher education: food counter, fountain, and related workers, 70.9 percent; library assistants and bookmobile drivers, 63 percent; ushers and lobby attendants, 72.8 percent; child-care workers, 61.6 percent; and guards, 86.5 percent. (1994, 4)

However, he points out that:

> . . . among "professional specialty occupations" only the two categories of dancers/choreographers and musicians have a higher incidence of part-time employment than higher education faculty. And if only two-year college faculty were considered, higher education would have the highest percentage. (4, 5)

Because this book is about the politics of writing instruction, it is important to note that contingents are concentrated in programs that have seen enrollment increases in the last twenty years, such as remedial programs, ESL programs, and composition, all of which may be organized under Humanities, Language Arts, or English departments and any of which may offer the college's writing courses. Part-time faculty members float among these departments, working wherever they can get a course. Kroll (1994) surveyed public and private community colleges in the nineteen-state Council of North Central Two-Year Colleges and estimated that the proportion per institution of instructors of English who are part-time faculty is around 62 percent.

Contingents, then, have become the model faculty members. When we say that they teach under conditions in which they are likely to be fearful of losing their jobs, cannot participate fully or honestly in the institutional discourse, and lack encouragement or material support for professional development, we should remember that we're talking about the working conditions of the typical community-college instructor. Tenure is not the norm; tenure is the exception and insecurity is the norm. Writing in the *Golden Gate University Law Review*, Jeffrey Kerwin said, "The complete exposure of part-time teachers to arbitrary or repressive action has a chilling effect on their exercise of freedom of speech" (1980, 81). Because contingents are the modal community-college faculty, that sentence ought to read, "The complete exposure of *community-college* teachers to arbitrary or repressive action has a chilling effect on their exercise of freedom of speech." When this happens, all the activities that evolve in the infrastructure of an academic institution—the discussion, the reflection upon work, the collaboration, the development of new programs—become severed from their roots in the classroom, where the real knowledge of the institution accumulates.

Education policy does not yet reflect this fact. Understanding this—that the actual faculty working in the community colleges is contingent faculty working under unsatisfactory conditions—and integrating it into our assessments of the mission of higher education, into our state and local oversight and regulatory policies, and into our education school-training curriculum would require a major rethinking of the meaning of work in academia.

The NCRVE Study of Teaching in the Community Colleges

By the early 1990s I had gone back to graduate school at Berkeley, in part because I had encountered some questions about teaching and learning that I could not answer without drawing on resources that lay well beyond the walls of my classroom. I had the good luck to get a graduate research assistantship working for Dr. W. Norton Grubb on an empirical study, funded by the National Center for Research in Vocational Education, of teaching in the community colleges. The purpose of the study was to develop an aggregate empirically-based portrait of what goes on in community-college classrooms. This information is typically reported in case-study form or in terms of outcomes (number of students enrolled, retained, passed, placed, etc.). We wanted to fill the gap in the literature by actually going to see what was happening. We eventually visited thirty-two community colleges and observed 250 classrooms, interviewing instructors and administrators. This project enabled me to visit community colleges outside of California as well as to interview administrators.

Approaching community colleges through the administration as a researcher, rather than through the union as an organizer, was, as I had expected, a different experience. Upon arriving at a college I would typically be given a list of instructors to observe. My letter of introduction had asked to be allowed to observe instructors in a range of disciplines—occupational and technical, liberal arts, contingent and full-time. Usually the list would have no contingents on it. I would ask my administrator contact if it would be possible to observe a contingent faculty member. Often, it simply wasn't possible; they didn't have complete lists and didn't know how to get in touch with the contingent.

At one college in Iowa I was assured that there were no contingents. Later that day, after interviewing a full-time statistics instructor, I asked him how the college had managed to refrain from relying on contingents. "What?" he said. "Come look in the mailroom and I'll show you a whole wall of their boxes."

At another college the only person I met who could talk about contingents was the union vice-president, who had just been handed a proposal for instructor evaluations that did not include an evaluation procedure for contingents. She was angry: "They are the first contact the public has with us, and I want to know if someone's just standing out at the end of a road handing out grades," she said.

We found only one community college, Indian Hills, that did not use any part-time faculty. It expressly had a policy against "going the part-timer route." However, it was located in a rural area of Iowa, well off the freeway flyer route, and had no adjacent colleges that could have generated a critical mass of jobs for contingents. Most of the faculty at this college actually used the metaphor "one happy family" when I asked them how policy and governance decisions were made.

By comparison, other colleges used as many contingents as they could hire. Union roles varied enormously; in several states, the faculty union excluded contingents; in another, the union had negotiated contractual job security for contingent faculty and priority for full-time jobs.

Overall, my impression from visiting community colleges outside California was that, with the exception of the colleges where the union had taken up part-time issues actively, contingents were, as Gappa and Leslie (1993) noted, truly "the invisible faculty."

Looking at the Future

Two trends seem to extend into the future of community colleges: the increased use of contingents and adding industry-specific training by region. Perhaps, by noting the ways in which these trends are consistent with each other, it is possible to envision the future of community colleges.

One trend is the seemingly irresistible urge to increase the use of part-time faculty at the community college. There seems to be no brake on it except state-level legislation and unionization, which is neither easy nor a sure thing. The second trend is based on our research during the NCRVE study, which focused on occupational/technical programs. In addition to the traditional community-college missions of occupational/technical, remedial and liberal-arts, and transfer education, a fourth mission is thriving: industry-specific training for regional economic-development purposes. While some colleges had not entered this path at all, others were running a booming operation involving partnerships with industry. In these programs, the community college provides for the industry whatever kind of training the industry wants its workers to have—generic training like computer instruction, total quality management, or statistical process control, or specific training on machines, vehicles, tools, or software that only one manufacturer uses. There is no need to hire full-time faculty for these programs or to involve full-time faculty already at the college to approve or create the curriculum. Running these programs was treated as an entrepreneurial challenge: making the contact, signing the contracts, assigning the room, hiring the instructor, creating (or buying) the curriculum, and collecting the fees. In places where these programs had been set up, they were generating sufficient income for the college that they were seen as an irresistible trend.

These trends, increasing use of contingents and increasing involvement with industry-specific training programs, are not incompatible with each other; on the contrary, they are consistent with and may even amplify each other. They seem, however, to be incompatible with the traditional missions of the community college as open-access, low-cost, second-chance institutions. The result of the combination of these two trends might be to create a segment of higher education that is dedicated to the short-term needs of local industry and is run in an entrepreneurial manner by program planners using contingent instructors as they would independent contractors.

The Politics of Writing Instruction from the Point of View of Contingent Faculty

I was asked to write about the politics of writing instruction as experienced by contingents; instead, I've written about the politics of instruction in general when it is carried on by contingents. My point is that for contingents, no matter what one is teaching—writing, history, ESL, philosophy, or carpentry—the politics of the workplace overwhelm the politics of the discipline. One of our respondents said, parodying *A Streetcar Named Desire*, "I have always been dependent upon the politics of strangers."

The politics of the world our students come from embraces both the college and the classroom. The job of the community colleges (unless they become primarily instruments of economic development) is to provide educational opportunity for people who want it, but, for either academic or financial reasons, are unable to attend other institutions of higher education. The demographics of the students who are drawn to community colleges reflect this in their numbers: Of all minorities enrolled in higher education as of 1992, 47 percent were in community colleges. Fifty-eight percent of the students enrolled in fall 1992 were women; the typical woman had at least one child and was working part-time. Twenty-seven percent were minority. Eight percent were disabled; more than half of all disabled students in college were in community colleges (Phillippe 1995, 20–21). The politics of writing instruction is embedded in the politics of the community college as workplace, which is in turn embedded in the politics of being disadvantaged—minority, female, a single parent, a part-time worker, low-income, or disabled—in the United States. The politics of the world students live in penetrates to the center of this dense arrangement where it hardly matters whether one is a composition instructor or a carpentry instructor. This statement was made by a contingent carpentry instructor: "We begin with the wood, and maybe it's redwood, and we go from there to the redwood tree, and the forest, and pretty soon it's the spotted owl." The story the instructor is telling pushes back out through the dense concatenation of contexts; if he or she is very skilled, or exceptionally lucky, this instructor may be able to keep the story moving and carry the students back past all the hazards they overcame to get to the classroom, back to a world that he encourages them to weave together in a coherent master narrative.

But doing that, pushing the boundaries, entails risks, and the instructor may decide: "I say to myself, no, wait, I'm just supposed to be teaching them carpentry." And the carpenter's last line might easily have been said by a contingent composition instructor: "Sometimes I would like to give them the whole world, but I hold myself back."

Notes

1. This calculation describes the California situation, where most of the college funding comes from the state at the rate of about $3,700 per FTE per year. In other states, where the state may supply as little as 40 percent of college funding and where college districts set their tuition cost locally, a different formula holds, but the incentive to hire contingent faculty remains the same: tenured or continuing-contract faculty are a fixed cost, whereas contingent faculty are cheap and flexible.

2. In fact, contingent faculty members are more likely than full-time faculty to use a bell curve in grading students, according to the June 1995 issue of the *National Education Association Higher Education Research Center Update*, a report generated from the data of the 1993 National Study of Postsecondary Faculty by the National Center for Education Statistics. Comparing part-time and full-time faculty in terms of the way each group evaluates students' work (the possible categories were student presentations, student evaluations, multiple-choice tests, essay tests, short-answer tests, term or research papers, multiple drafts of written work, grading on a

curve, and competency-based grading), the report finds that part-time teachers tend to be more conservative than full-timers in their evaluation techniques (NEA 1995, 3). My interpretation is that contingents evaluate conservatively because they teach defensively.

Works Cited

American Federation of Teachers. April 7, 1979. *Statement on Part-Time Faculty Employment.* American Federation of Teachers Advisory Commission on Higher Education. Washington D.C.: AFT.

Arden, E. July 21, 1995. *Ending the Loneliness and Isolation of Adjunct Professors.* Point of View column in *The Chronicle of Higher Education,* A44.

Brint, S., & J. Karabel. 1989. *The Diverted Dream: Community Colleges and the Promise of Educational Opportunity in America, 1900–85.* New York: Oxford Press.

California Postsecondary Education Commission. August 1994. *Faculty Salaries in California's Community Colleges, 1993–94.* Commission Report 94–13. Sacramento: CPEC.

Deegan, W. L., & D. Tillery. 1985. *Renewing the American Community College.* San Francisco: Jossey-Bass.

ERIC Clearinghouse for Junior Colleges. Spring 1990. *Information Bulletin.* University of California, Los Angeles.

Friere, P. 1985. *The Politics of Education: Culture, Power and Liberation.* South Hadley: Bergin & Gavney.

Gappa, J. M., & D. W. Leslie. 1993. *The Invisible Faculty: Improving the Status of Part-Timers in Higher Education.* San Francisco, Calif.: Jossey-Bass.

Gleazer, E. J., Jr. 1980. *The Community College: Values, Vision, and Vitality.* Washington, D.C.: AACJC.

Kerwin, J. 1980. "The Part-Time Teacher and Tenure in California." *Golden Gate University Law Review,* 10(2): 765–803.

Kroll, K. 1994. "A Profile and Perspective of Part-Time Two-Year College English Faculty." *Teaching English in the Two-Year College.* (December): 277–87.

Mahoney, J., & E. Jimenez, eds. 1992. *Community, Technical and Junior Colleges Statistical Yearbook.* Washington, D.C.: American Association of Community Colleges.

McGrath, D., & M. Spear. 1991. *The Academic Crisis of the Community Colleges.* Albany: SUNY P.

Modern Language Association. 1982. "MLA Statement on the Use of Part-Time Faculty." *Profession* 82. MLA, 52.

National Center for Education Statistics. October 1994. *Faculty and Instructional Staff: Who Are They and What Do They Do?* Survey Report: 1993 National Study of Postsecondary Faculty. U.S. Department of Education, Office of Educational Research and Improvement. NCES 94–346.

National Center for Education Statistics. 1995. *Fall Staff in Postsecondary Institutions, 1991.* U.S. Department of Education, Office of Educational Research and Improvement. NCES (February): 95–317.

National Education Association. June 1995. *NEA Higher Education Research Center Update.* 1(1). Washington, D.C.: NEA.

Newman, M. 1994. *Defining the Enemy: Adult Education in Social Action.* Paddington, New South Wales: Stewart Victor Publishing.

Phillippe, K. A., editor. 1995. *National Profile of Community Colleges: Trends and Statistics, 1995–1996.* Washington, D.C.: Community College.

Pratt, L. R., et al. November-December 1992. Committee G on Part-Time and Non-Tenure-Track Appointments. "Report on the Status of Non-Tenure-Track Faculty." *Academe: The Bulletin of the American Association of University Professors*: 39–48.

O'Banion, T. 1981. "The Renaissance of Innovation." In *Innovation in the Community Colleges*, ed. T. O'Banion. New York: ACE/McMillan.

Richardson, R. C., E. C. Fisk, & M. A. Okun. 1983. *Literacy in the Open Access College.* San Francisco: Jossey-Bass.

Robertson, L. R., S. Crowley, & F. Lentricchia. March 1987. "Opinion: The Wyoming Conference Resolution Opposing Unfair Salaries and Working Conditions for Post-Secondary Teachers of Writing." *College English* 49(3): 274–80.

Robinson, P. June 1994. *Part-Time Faculty Issues.* Washington D.C.: American Federation of Teachers.

Rose, M. 1989. *Lives on the Boundary.* New York: Free Press.

Twombly, W. January 1995. "English 57: Cooperative Venture Unites UC and Community Colleges." *Crosstalk: A Quarterly Publication of the California Higher Education Policy Center* 3(1): 5.

Not Just a Matter of Fairness: Adjunct Faculty and Writing Programs in Two-Year Colleges

Jeffrey Klausman

Adjunct faculty working conditions create more than a sense of unfairness; they create an "energy" that works against the movement necessary to build a coherent writing program at a two-year college. In this article, Jeffrey Klausman offers a brief overview of efforts to address adjunct faculty inequities, and then reports on an original study that revealed adjunct faculty attitudes toward program development. Klausman also offers suggestions to faculty members or WPAs working toward building a coherent writing program at their college.

Several years ago, when my college first financed a writing program administrator (WPA) position—reassigned time and a budget to pay adjunct faculty stipends for program development—I met with all of our most senior adjunct faculty. "Without you," I told them, "this effort to build a better writing program won't work. Participation and buy-in among adjunct faculty is essential." I knew from experience that any

From *Teaching English in the Two-Year College*, vol. 37, no. 4, 2010, pp. 363-71.

changes to curriculum, any new assessment processes, any new professional development initiatives would be viewed with suspicion by our adjunct faculty, who have no job security and who have historically been institutionally marginalized. Yet I also knew that very little had been written about creating and sustaining writing programs (as opposed to a loosely organized collection of classes) at two-year colleges. Since the WPA position was new on my campus and very rare in two-year college English departments in general, I conducted a survey and then follow-up interviews to better understand adjunct faculty attitudes toward and expectations of WPAs in two-year college English programs.

Much of what I found corroborated what I already suspected. For example, adjunct faculty feel marginalized on their own campuses and are somewhat to very resentful at teaching so much of a program's courses while receiving so little in terms of pay and benefits. Also, adjunct faculty are often invited to join full-time faculty in program work but have very little incentive to do that. However, what surprised me was the insight that these are not merely parallel issues. I was not able to say, for example, "Yes, I know the adjunct situation is unfair, but let's get to work on the program anyway." Instead, I came to see a dynamic relation: the institutional marginalization creates a kind of energy, acts as a centrifugal force countering the centripetal efforts of building a coherent writing program. Until the institutional marginalization ends—somehow—or until we consciously address the realities, efforts to build a program out of a "collection of classes" at a two-year college will be undermined.

In what follows, I summarize the current context of adjunct faculty in two-year colleges, summarize the findings of the survey and interviews I conducted, and offer suggestions on how to work within and against this system of use and abuse.

The Context

My college is not unlike most: around two-thirds of all our classes are taught by adjunct faculty, and often the number is higher. Our adjuncts have no long-term contracts, though in our department an informal seniority system gives longer-term adjuncts—many with ten years of service or more—preference in staffing. Thanks to joint efforts at the state and local levels by our faculty union, adjunct faculty at my college, by my calculations, have a starting salary of around 93% of a full-time faculty's beginning salary (though pay increases for adjuncts fall behind that for full-time faculty); in our department, about half of our adjunct faculty receive health and retirement benefits equal to what full-time faculty receive. In contrast to the national picture, adjuncts at my college are in a relatively good situation—but we still have a ways to go.

By contrast, nationally the situation is generally worse. In 2004, 78% of two-year college faculty were non-tenure track (Bartholomae and Laurence). As bad as that sounds, Donald W. Green reports that Rio Salado College in Tempe, Arizona, "has only twenty-seven full-time faculty members but teaches 46,800 credit students and 14,000 non-credit students" (29). Perhaps at the opposite extreme, Yakima Valley Community College, in Washington State, has very few adjunct faculty, employing a majority of tenured and tenure-track faculty, probably due to the college's location, far from a major university that can offer a stream of recent graduate students and far from a major urban area (Calhoon-Dillahunt). My department has eleven full-time, tenure-track faculty (five hired within the last three years) and twenty-four to thirty adjunct faculty teaching less than 80% of a full-time load; this modest ratio is largely due to the initiative of the local union and administration to limit the exploitation of adjunct faculty. Nonetheless, a joint study by the Modern Language Association (MLA) and the Association of Departments of English (ADE) found that a "diminished and diminishing" segment of all faculty in all colleges are tenured or tenure track: in 1995, 42.2%; in 2005, 32.3%. There was a commensurate increase in full-time non-tenure-track faculty, from 16.8% in 1995 to 20.3% in 2005 (Bartholomae and Laurence; Laurence 13).

So the number of non-tenure-track faculty is growing and has been for quite some time. Against this trend is the fairly lofty ideal we sometimes hear: adjunct faculty "should be recognized and valued as professional colleagues working in collaboration with full-time faculty and administrators to achieve the teaching mission of America's community college" (Wallin 373). This sounds good. However, we are probably also aware of another more pressing reality—the financial reality: "Proponents of the business culture [of a college] view adjunct faculty in a highly bifurcated and ambiguous manner," say Richard L. Wagoner, Amy Scott Metcalfe, and Israel Olaore: "a flexible, disposable temporary work force that can be counted on for years of dedicated service" (38). These contradictory views have led to two related problems that persist today: inequality of working conditions for adjunct faculty, and "outsider" status for adjunct faculty relative to the institutional culture (Wagoner, Metcalfe, and Olaore 26).

The American Association of University Professors (AAUP) states that employment conditions for adjunct faculty means they "do their work apart from the structures through which the curriculum, department, and institution are sustained and renewed" ("Statement"). And an assessment of adjunct faculty at one university found that adjuncts experienced a "sense of isolation" from their program and felt they were "out of the [university's] information loop" (Fagan-Wilen et al. 45–46).

Further, the AAUP warns of a "shrinking Brahmin class of professorial-rank faculty [who] enjoy academic careers and compensation commensurate with advanced training, while a growing caste of 'untouchable' educational service workers [. . .] obtain only poorly remunerated semester-to-semester jobs that offer no career prospects." Mary R. Lamb, speaking of her experiences at Georgia State University, which is moving adjunct to full-time instructorship positions, does not dismiss the opportunities of these full-time positions but fears they merely create "another (underpaid, subordinated) layer" of faculty (A8).

Recently, in an effort to address these issues, unions and coalitions at the local, state, and national level have been active, though with uncertain effect (see Lynn; Jaschik; Holler). Partly in response to this uncertainty, the National Coalition for Adjunct Faculty has been formed. Leaders of the group say that they aim to be "a national voice solely for the 70 percent of faculty members who work outside the tenure track" since existing faculty unions "cater to the concerns of tenured and tenure-track professors" (June). At the same time, administrators on many college campuses have been actively working to create better working conditions and professional development opportunities (see Lydic "What"; "Integrating"; TYCA Research). Yet, as David Lydic recognizes, "doing our best" and "making great strides" does not mean that equity and fairness have necessarily been achieved ("Austin") nor that everyone is happy.

What the literature does not tell us, however, is what impact the reliance upon adjunct faculty has on the creation and development of a writing program. Those interested in writing programs know it must have an impact since so many people with whom I talk mention the need to work within the predominant climate to reach out to adjunct faculty and to create means of addressing their needs. In other words, we take it as a known that adjunct faculty issues create a challenge to the development of a writing program, but I don't believe we've asked in what ways that difficulty operates. At two-year colleges, where, if the joint MLA-ADE study is correct, 78% of English faculty are adjunct (Laurence 13), such a question would seem crucial.

Initial Surveys

It was in this context that in 2006, as my college's first WPA, I began to study the impact of adjunct faculty on program development. To form a baseline, I decided to survey adjunct faculty who said they worked in an English department that has a WPA or WPA-like person or committee. This group would give information specific to program development efforts. I set up a Survey Monkey survey and sought participants via the WPA-listserv and through colleagues who I knew had writing programs administered by a WPA or WPA-like person or committee. I asked questions about the administrative structuring of the department, the role of the WPA, the respondent's attitudes toward and expectations of the WPA, and the respondent's demographics in terms of experience, degree earned, and so on. I received 93 responses from across the country—the Southeast, the Midwest, the Southwest, California, and the Pacific Northwest (though possibly elsewhere as well). It should be noted that these respondents were self-selected—I only heard from those who made the effort to take the survey and who self-identified as working with a WPA or WPA-like person or committee. In some cases, I contacted faculty at institutions where I knew a WPA-type position was in place and asked that they solicit responses.

Some of the more interesting responses are as follows: To the question of how much input to curriculum decisions adjunct faculty should have, 52.9% said that adjunct faculty should work equally with the WPA, while 26.5% said the WPA should lead curriculum development. To the question of whether the WPA values the expertise of adjunct faculty, such as seeking input on curricular issues, only 24.2% answered "Yes, very much," while 48.5% answered "Yes, somewhat," 21.2% answered "No, not very much," and 6.1% answered "No, not at all." To the question of what would increase the respondent's sense of being more valued, the responses receiving the most affirmatives were for having expertise on curriculum more valued (63.6%), being paid more equitably (60.6%), being compensated for attending meetings (57.3%), and having flexible meeting times (51.5%). Demographically, 40% of the respondents had eleven or more years of teaching experience, and slightly over 50% had coursework or a degree beyond a master's, with 27.2% having a doctorate or being ABD.

My tentative conclusions, which I presented at the CCCC convention in 2008, are that most adjunct faculty who work with a WPA or WPA-like person or committee tend to expect the program's leadership to work with them (as equals) in developing curriculum and assessment plans, most wish to have their expertise more highly valued though they feel fairly well respected, and most cite unfair working conditions and pay as major obstacles to their contributing to program work. My final conclusion was that adjunct faculty represent tremendous experience and expertise that is probably underused.

The survey I conducted had its flaws; nonetheless, the findings on years of experience and training match numbers I have heard both from the TYCA Research Initiative Committee and the ADE-MLA joint study (Laurence; Bartholomae and Laurence). More importantly, I believe the information it offered was valuable as it fleshed out some of the concerns I had sensed among the adjunct faculty colleagues with whom I work; in particular, how being respected and having one's expertise both acknowledged and incorporated into program-building decisions were challenged by working conditions.

Follow-up Interviews

I wanted to understand the apparent disjunction in a key area of responses: that adjunct faculty feel "fairly well respected" but also feel their expertise was "undervalued." This seemed odd: How can they feel both "respected" and have their expertise not valued highly enough?

Either this displayed a disquieting low self-esteem—"Well, my expertise isn't valued very highly, but that's what I deserve"—or opposing energies at work. Given my purpose—of understanding how adjunct faculty attitudes affect writing programs—understanding this disjunction seemed crucial. In 2008–09, I followed up on this survey with targeted email interviews.

Again, through the WPA-listserv and colleagues at other institutions, I solicited adjunct faculty who work with a WPA or WPA-like person or committee to answer a few questions following upon the 2007–08 survey. In addition to demographics, I asked for responses to the key findings from the 2007–08 survey and responses to these follow-up questions:

- What is your motivation for staying current in the field, staying involved?

- How involved in the running of your writing program are you?

- Does your institution encourage or discourage you from being a "full member" of the writing program?

I received nine responses: two from adjunct faculty at a two-year college in Arizona, two from a two-year college in Illinois, and two from a branch campus of a Research I institution in Washington State, plus three from faculty at my own college, though I did not rely much upon these since none of the responses were anonymous and, of course, I knew the respondents at my own institution. The responses were in the main very detailed, and all were quite frank. For most, I asked follow-up questions and received clarifying responses.

To the question of the respondent's motivation for staying current in the field, the responses all focused upon personal interest or enrichment or sense of duty as an instructor: "I enjoy working with my peers and truly want our program to be a wonderful learning experience for our students," said one respondent. Another said, "I enjoy teaching comp-rhet; I think it's an interesting subject." And still another said, "I like to stay involved for my own professional development and enjoy the community-building conversations about writing and teaching." None of the respondents mentioned professional advancement, job security, or increased pay, suggesting to me a disconnect between their sense of selves as professionals in a field and as members of a writing program or faculty of an institution. This is borne out by the next set of responses.

To the question of how much involvement the adjunct faculty member has in the running of the writing program, the responses heavily leaned toward uninvolvement. One respondent said, "I am not allowed to become involved with my own English department's decision-making process." Another said, "These questions do not seem applicable to my position/situation." Still another replied, "Much of the [adjunct faculty] has no real loyalty or motivation to go above and beyond" to accept invitations to participate in program development. One simply replied, "None." There was an exception. One respondent reported being "lead adjunct faculty" and thus being very involved in the program, though this does not speak to the much larger majority of her adjunct faculty colleagues.

The question of whether the respondents feel the department or the college encourages or discourages them from being full members of the writing program goes to the heart, I believe, of the apparent disjunction I noted in the 2007–08 survey results—that while adjunct faculty tend to be fairly well respected, they also tend to feel undervalued. Most of the responses—much like my own thinking—seemed confused or contradictory, unable to explain this disjunction. But one response seemed to crystallize what I had been sensing and seeing:

> I believe that the department *encourages* all adjuncts to be a "full member" of the writing program; whereas the institution *discourages* adjuncts from full status. In the department, adjuncts are invited to all department meetings, serve on committees and are encouraged to interact with the dean and other faculty. . . . [However] the institution, not only by the paycheck, but also as a general attitude among top to middle administrators, have made it clear that adjuncts are pretty much "throw away" and designed for the "dirtier" jobs, as it were. Although there are now efforts to offer training to adjuncts, I don't see encouragement to do much more than teach a class and try not to organize into a union or complain too much, and thus the institution does not seem to care or even want adjuncts to take ownership of any part of the college or its programs.

I have seen this institutional disregard on my own campus. I have been a leader in our faculty union—as president twice and chief negotiator of our contract once—and so I am keenly aware of how marginalized the adjunct faculty on my campus are made to feel. But I have also been a leader in our department—as chair twice and WPA for three years—and I know that the efforts I and my full-time colleagues make to encourage adjunct faculty to be full members of the program are very real.

My error has been in assuming, naively, that my work on behalf of adjunct faculty—even going to the state capitol and knocking on the doors of state legislators to lobby for adjunct faculty pay equity—would counter the fear and suspicion adjunct faculty might have toward my role as the new WPA. That is, my error has been in assuming that the "institutional disregard" and the departmental efforts at inclusion were simply parallel phenomena.

On the contrary. The disjunction between the institutional disregard on one hand and the genuine collegiality on the other is not merely interesting or lamentable but is a very real and tangible force that actively works against the development and cohesion of a writing program.

I said at the 2009 CCCC convention in San Francisco that I noted a bi-furcation emerging from the respondents:

> Among adjunct faculty there is evident an individual and personal desire for involvement in the field both professionally and, more importantly, in-tellectually, along with a commensurate ability to do so; and yet there is also an overall dissatisfaction over being shut out from full membership in their programs, one that suggests a violation of personal identity ("pro-fessional" v. "itinerant worker"). While "we" say that adjuncts are encour-aged as professionals, the realities work against that. ("Attitudes")

The use and abuse of adjunct faculty goes beyond fairness. So long as we have powerful centrifugal realities creating an "energy" pushing adjunct faculty away from a coherent "us," our centripetal efforts to de-velop a program with shared curriculum, assessment, and professional development will be hampered.[1]

Suggestions and Reflections

Of course, we must all continue to work at the local level toward "best practices"—advocating for more tenure-track positions, pushing for eq-uity in pay and benefits, establishing systems for job security, adequate support, training, and recognition. We must also continue to push for a radical restructuring of labor practices in higher education, though that is a much more distant hope. Perhaps something more we can do is make explicit this kind of research, which sheds light on how the realities of adjunct faculty working conditions impact efforts at building a writing program. In so doing, we might short-circuit some of the blaming that might go on, disarm some of the frustration.

For me, the most important benefits of this work probably lie in the future. I look forward to exploring how the idea of professionalism in-tersects with a more or less permanent "class" of adjunct faculty; ex-ploring how personal desire and "imagined programs" (like Benedict Anderson's "imagined communities") impact program building and the perceptions and actions of a WPA in a two-year college; and how WPAs demonstrating leadership in the field of composition may affect col-leagues' sense of their own place as professionals in an evolving En-glish department and discipline.

That lies ahead. For now, I do not think I have a definitive answer to the question of how to work with adjunct faculty in building a pro-gram—certainly not one that "works" in addressing the core issues of uncertainty and marginalization. But this survey and these interviews have shed light on what I thought I knew and supposed, corroborating much and offering the one telling insight—that institutional margin-alization is a dynamic, centrifugal force working against the centrip-etal efforts to build a cohesive program. Given this, I am in a better position to address the larger "field of play" of program building in a two-year college English department.

Note

1. William Klein and Suellyn Duffey, at the University of Missouri–St. Louis, are working on a theory of WPA work based not on tasks but on the concepts of time, space, place, and energy.

Works Cited

Anderson, Benedict. *Imagined Communities: Reflections on the Origin and Spread of Nationalism*. New York: Verso, 1983.

Bartholomae, David, and David Laurence. "The Report of the ADE Ad Hoc Committee on Staffing: A Discussion." Paper presented at the annual convention of the Conference on College Composition and Communication. Hilton San Francisco, San Francisco, CA. 13 Mar. 2009.

Calhoon-Dillahunt, Carolyn. Personal interview. Annual convention of the Conference on College Composition and Communication. 13 Mar. 2009.

Fagan-Wilen, Ruth, David W. Springer, Bob Ambrosino, and Barbara W. White. "The Support of Adjunct Faculty: An Academic Imperative." *Social Work Education* 25.1 (2006): 39–51.

Green, Donald W. "Adjunct Faculty and the Continuing Quest for Quality." *New Directions for Community Colleges* 140 (2007): 29–39.

Holler, Keith. "The Proper Advocates for Adjuncts." *Chronicle of Higher Education* 52:41 (16 June 2006): B11–12. *Academic Search Premier*. EBSCOhost. Whatcom Community College, Bellingham, WA. 22 Jan. 2009.

"Integrating Adjuncts into the Community through Professional Development, Support." *Academic Leader* 21.7 (2005): 1, 6.

Jaschik, Scott. "Creating a National Voice for Adjuncts." *Inside Higher Ed*, 20 Feb. 2009. 20 Feb. 2009 <http://insidehighered.com/news/2009/02/20/adjuncts>.

June, Audrey Williams. "An Activist Adjunct Shoulders the Weight of a New Advocacy Group." *Chronicle of Higher Education* 10 Sept. 2009: n. pag. Web. 22 Jan 2010.

Klausman, Jeffrey. "Attitudes and Expectations: Adjunct Faculty and WPAs at Two-Year and Small Colleges." Paper presented at annual convention of the Conference of College Composition and Communication. Hilton San Francisco, San Francisco, CA. 14 Mar. 2009.

Lamb, Mary R. "Growing Into and Out of My NTT Lecturer Position." *Teaching English in the Two-Year College* 36.3 (2009): A5–A8.

Laurence, David. "Demography of the Faculty: A Statistical Portrait of English and Foreign Languages." *Profession* 22 (2009): 245–266.

Lydic, David. "Austin Community College: Best Practices for Adjunct Faculty Working Conditions?" *Teaching English in the Two-Year College* 36.3 (2009): A9–A11.

———. "What Teaching Conditions Promote Part-time Teaching Success? How Can Writing Programs Build Such Conditions into Their Programs?" Paper presented at the annual convention of the Conference of College Composition and Communication. Hilton San Francisco, San Francisco, CA. 14 Mar. 2009.

Lynn, Marjorie. "It's Hard Work, but Someone's Got to Do It! Unionizing in Southeast Michigan." *Teaching English in the Two-Year College* 36.3 (2009): A14–A16.

"New: The National Coalition for Adjunct Faculty." The New Faculty Majority. 8 Apr. 2009 <http://thenewfacultymajority.blogspot.com/2009/02/coming -national-coalition-for-adjunct.html>.

"Statement from the Conference on the Growing Use of Part-Time and Adjunct Faculty." American Association of University Professors. 26–28 Sept. 1997. 8 Apr. 2009 <http://www.aaup.org/aaup/issues/contingent/conferencestate ment.htm>.

TYCA Research Initiative Committee. 2005. 8 Apr. 2009 <http://www.ncte.org /tyca/research>.

Wagoner, Richard L., Amy Scott Metcalfe, and Israel Olaore. "Fiscal Reality and Academic Quality: Part-Time Faculty and the Challenge to Organizational Culture at Community Colleges." *Community College Journal of Research and Practices* 29 (2005): 25–44.

Wallin, Desna L. "Valuing Professional Colleagues: Adjunct Faculty in Community and Technical Colleges." *Community College Journal of Research and Practices* 28 (2004): 373–91.

Epilogue

At Spike's Garage

Steve Straight

At Spike's Garage near the university
I pull in for gas. It's the olden days,
and Ernie the mechanic comes out
from the bay to pump my gas.

I'm in grad school and my second year
teaching freshman English, and Ernie's
fixed my car a few times at his house
to spare me Spike's cut for parts and labor.

Ernie, a townie, about 22, bushy haired
with greasy blue coveralls, oil under
his nails, locks the pump on and says,
"So, professor, what're ya teachin'?"

It's Friday, and I remember the dazed group
I tried to teach that morning, sleepy and
hung over, leading a discussion just one more
session pulling teeth. "Hamlet,"
I tell him. "You know, Shakespeare."

He stops in mid-squeegee as blue water
streams down my window. "Hamlet!"
he spits. "Ugh. I had to read that in
high school. It was awful, so boring."

He seems to say what my students only
thought, and for a second I wonder if
I'm cut out for this, trying to teach great
works to people who hate them.

"Hamlet!" he says again, shaking
the squeegee. "He didn't even know
when to shit." Finally he pulls it across
the window, wiping the excess liquid off
the rubber with his fingers. "Macbeth,"
he says. "Now *that* was a play."

From *The Water Carrier*, reprinted edition. Curbstone, 2004, pp. 16-17.

About the Editors

Patrick Sullivan has the great honor of teaching English at Manchester Community College, in Manchester, Connecticut, where he has taught since 1987. Patrick believes deeply in the mission of the community college, and he is deeply grateful to have had the opportunity to work with so many amazing community college students. Patrick has taught a wide range of basic writing and composition classes, and he has published scholarship in a variety of journals, including *Teaching English in the Two-Year College, College English, College Composition and Communication, Academe, The Journal of Adolescent and Adult Literacy, The Journal of Developmental Education, The Community College Journal of Research and Practice, Innovative Higher Education, The Chronicle of Higher Education*, and *English Journal*.

Patrick is the coeditor, with Howard Tinberg, of *What Is "College-Level" Writing?* (NCTE, 2006) and, with Howard Tinberg and Sheridan Blau, of *What Is "College-Level" Writing? Volume 2: Assignments, Readings, and Student Writing Samples* (NCTE, 2010). He is also the author of *A New Writing Classroom: Listening, Motivation, and Habits of Mind* (Utah State University Press, 2014). Patrick is editing, with Howard and Sheridan, a new collection of essays, *Deep Reading: Teaching Reading in the Writing Classroom*, which is scheduled to be published in 2017 by NCTE. He is also at work on a book about community colleges, *Economic Inequality, Neoliberalism, and the American Community College*, which will be published by Palgrave Macmillan in 2017. Patrick is currently serving as a member of the Editorial Board of *College Composition and Communication*.

In addition to teaching and writing, Patrick enjoys running, biking, hiking, reading, and spending time with his family—his wife, Susan, and his children, Bonnie Rose and Nicholas.

Christie Toth is an assistant professor in the University of Utah's Department of Writing and Rhetoric Studies, where she teaches writing, rhetoric, and literacy studies courses at the undergraduate and graduate level. She has taught basic and first-year writing at several two-year colleges, most recently Diné College in Crownpoint, New Mexico. Her research interests include the intellectual work and professional identities of two-year college English faculty, tribal college writing instruction, community college students' post-transfer writing experiences, writing assessment, and interinstitutional collaborations in writing studies. Her work has appeared in *College Composition and Communication, Composition Studies, Journal of Basic Writing, Assessing Writing, Writing Program Administration, Higher Education: Handbook of Theory and Research, College English*, and *Teaching English in the Two-Year College*, as well as the edited collections *Class in the Composition Classroom* and *Writing Assessment as Social Justice*.

Christie also serves on the *TETYC* Editorial Board and as a four-year representative on the TYCA-West Executive Committee. She works closely with faculty colleagues at Salt Lake Community College on a variety of initiatives supporting the writing transitions of transfer students.

About the Contributors

Peter Adams retired in 2014, after thirty-six years of teaching, mostly basic writing, at the Community College of Baltimore County (CCBC). Toward the end of his teaching career, Adams, stealing ideas from the studio model, from Greg Glau's Stretch Program, and from learning communities, developed a new model for basic writing called the Accelerated Learning Program (ALP). Today CCBC offers more than a hundred sections each semester, and almost two hundred schools nationwide offer sections of ALP, and six states—Arkansas, Indiana, Michigan, Colorado, Connecticut, West Virginia, and Virginia—have initiated large-scale ALP projects. Throughout the United States, ALP is doubling the percent of basic writers who pass composition. No longer teaching, Adams devotes his time to helping other schools adapt ALP to their local conditions.

Jeff Andelora is the English Department chair at Mesa Community College in Mesa, Arizona, where he has taught since 1996. For ten years prior to that, he taught English at Mesa High School. He is associate chair of TYCA, past chair of TYCA-West, and has also served on the Executive Committee of the Council of Writing Program Administrators. His work has appeared in *Teaching English in the Two-Year College*.

John Bean grew up in a small town in Idaho where his dad owned a telephone company. Before coming to Seattle University in 1986, he taught for thirteen years in Montana at both the College of Great Falls and at Montana State University. In the early part of his career, his scholarship focused on Renaissance literature, and he published articles on Shakespeare and Spenser, but by the early 1980s his scholarly focus morphed to rhetoric/composition with a special interest in writing across the curriculum and all forms of pedagogical theory and practice connected to active learning, critical thinking, and the teaching of undergraduate research. Bean is the coauthor of several textbooks on composition and argument (with Dr. June Johnson), and the author of a widely used and cited book on writing and critical thinking entitled *Engaging Ideas: The Professor's Guide to Writing, Critical Thinking, and Active Learning in the Classroom*, which has been translated into both Dutch and Chinese. He gives faculty workshops on writing and critical thinking at institutions around the world. His most recent scholarship focuses on assessment of student learning and on teaching rhetorical use of numbers (with Seattle University colleagues from science, finance, economics, and math). Between his graduation from Stanford and when he began graduate school, he served in Vietnam as an army lieutenant. He is an avid Seattle Mariners baseball fan, and he and his wife like to bike, sea kayak, and spend time with their four grown children and their families, all of whom live in the Seattle area.

Anne Beaufort is associate professor of Interdisciplinary Arts and Sciences and coordinator of writing across the curriculum at University of Washington, Tacoma. Her PhD in education at Stanford University focused on language, literacy, and culture, and she has done ethnographic research on the ways in which adults can improve their handling of the writing process and write effectively in a range of genres both in higher education and workplace settings. Beaufort's first book, *Writing in the Real World: Making the Transition from School to Work*, received an NCTE award for best technical/professional communications book.

Mark Blaauw-Hara is professor of English and writing program coordinator at North Central Michigan College in Petoskey, Michigan. He also serves on the executive board of the Council of Writing Program Administrators and is a peer reviewer for *Teaching English in the Two-Year College*. His writing has appeared in *TETYC*, *Community College Week*, *The Writing Center Journal*, and several other journals and edited collections. Blaauw-Hara's current research focuses on threshold concepts and transfer theory, writing in occupational disciplines, and adult learning theory.

Sheridan Blau is Professor of Practice in the Teaching of English and Director of the English Education Program at Teachers College, Columbia University. He is also Professor of English and Education (*Emeritus*) at the University of California, Santa Barbara, where for 30 years he directed the South Coast Writing Project and Literature Institute for Teachers. He is a former President of the National Council of Teachers of English (1997–98), and in 2007 received NCTE's Distinguished Service Award for his professional leadership, contributions to teaching, and exemplary writing. He has published extensively in the areas of seventeenth century British literature, the teaching of composition and literature, professional development for teachers, and the ethics and politics of literacy. His book *The Literature Workshop: Teaching Texts and Their Readers* (Heinemann), was selected by the Conference on English Education as winner of the 2004 Richard Meade Award for outstanding research in English education.

Carolyn Calhoon-Dillahunt graduated with distinction from Washington State University, receiving an MA in composition in 1996. Carolyn has been teaching English at Yakima Valley Community College in Yakima, Washington, since 1999 (and taught middle school and high school language arts prior to that). She was recognized by her college with the Robert M. Leadon Award for Excellence in Teaching in 2002. Calhoon-Dillahunt is a former Two-Year College English Association (TYCA) secretary (2006–2008) and chair (2010–2013) and has served on the executive committees of TYCA, CCCC, and NCTE as well as a variety of task forces and committees for each organization. She currently serves as CCCC policy fellow and is the NCTE higher education policy analyst for Washington State. She reviews for *TETYC* and regularly presents at disciplinary conferences. She was selected as the featured speaker for the College Celebration at the NCTE Annual Convention in 2013.

Dr. Peter A. Facione is a principal with Measured Reasons, a Los Angeles–based research and consulting firm supporting excellence in strategic thinking and leadership decision making, and a managing partner of Insight Assessment, located in Silicon Valley. In academia he has served as provost of Loyola University Chicago, dean of the College of Arts and Sciences at Santa Clara University, and dean of the School of Human Development and Community Service at California State University, Fullerton. In private business, Dr. Facione was a strategic consultant with Stratus-Heery International and is a managing partner and CFO of the California Academic Press. Dr. Facione spearheaded the international study to define critical thinking, sponsored by the American Philosophical Association in 1990. His research formed the basis for numerous government policy studies about critical thinking in the workplace, including research sponsored by the U.S. Department of Education. Today, his tools for assessing reasoning are used around the world in educational, business, legal, military, and health sciences. Dr. Facione maintains an active speaking, writing, consulting, and research agenda, with well over 150 publications including essays, books, articles, case studies, and educational testing tools. These include the *California Critical Thinking Skills Test*, the *California Critical Thinking Disposition Inventory*, the *Health Sciences Reasoning Test*, the *Business Critical Thinking Skills Test*, the *Legal Studies Reasoning Profile*, the *Military & Defense Critical Thinking Inventory*, *Professional Judgment Rating Form*, and the *Holistic Critical Thinking Scoring Rubric*. Dr. Facione is the author of the popular and often quoted essay about the meaning and importance of critical thinking, "Critical Thinking: What It Is and Why It Counts." His textbook, *THINK Critically*, is published by Pearson Education, the second edition coauthored with Dr. Carol Gittens. He is the author of two books with Dr. Noreen Facione: *Thinking and Reasoning in Human Decision Making* addresses human decision making in contexts of risk and uncertainty, and *Critical Thinking and Clinical Reasoning in the Health Sciences* presents strategies for training clinical judgment.

Michelle Navarre Cleary is an associate professor and associate dean of curriculum, instruction, and assessment at DePaul University's college for adult students, the School for New Learning (SNL). Before coming to SNL to develop a writing program, she was an English department faculty member at Olive-Harvey College, one of Chicago's community colleges. Navarre Cleary has published on teaching writing with and to post-traditional students in *Teaching English in the Two-Year College* (*TETYC*); *College Composition and Communication* (*CCC*); *The Journal of Basic Writing*; *Composition Forum*; *Kairos: A Journal of Rhetoric, Technology, and Pedagogy*; *WPA: Writing Program Administration*; and *Reflections: A Journal of Writing, Service-Learning and Community Literacy*.

Dodie Forrest earned her master's degree from Oregon State University. She teaches at Yakima Valley Community College (YVCC) in Yakima, Washington, where she also directs the writing center. Recognized for her teaching and mentorship, Dodie received the inaugural Sherrie and Daryl Parker Faculty Award at YVCC (2012) and a Lisa Ede Excellence in Teaching Award from TYCA-Pacific Northwest (2007). She was a leader and presenter at the International Writing Centers Association (IWCA) Summer Institute (2007) and is an active member of the Pacific Northwest Writing Centers Association (PNWCA) as well as TYCA-PNW, having served as program chair for their joint fall conference. Currently, Forrest is in her second term as co-chair of TYCA-PNW.

Richard Fulkerson received his PhD from Ohio State University in 1970 with a concentration in Victorian fiction. He took a full-time position at East Texas State University in Commerce (now Texas A&M–Commerce). He spent his entire career there, and served many years as the director of English graduate studies and assistant to the department head. He has published articles in *The Dickensian*, *The Quarterly Journal of Speech*, *The Journal of Advanced Composition*, *Rhetoric Review*, and *College Composition and Communication*. He served one term on the executive committee of CCCC, and served as a peer reviewer for five journals. In 1996, he published *Teaching the Argument in Writing*, which became an NCTE best seller. Fulkerson's scholarly interests include historical approaches to ethnographic research in composition. He was awarded emeritus status from Texas A&M–Commerce in 2009.

Sarah Gearhart began teaching at the Community College of Baltimore County (CCBC) in 2007, the year that Peter Adams founded the Accelerated Learning Program there. Sarah taught in the program for four years, beginning in its second semester, and watched its success grow during that time, both as a teacher and as a member of the steering committee that oversaw, evaluated, and promoted the program's progress as enrollments in it began to rise both at CCBC and as it spread to other institutions across the country. She is now an assistant administrator in the ALP headquarters at CCBC, where she monitors the program's continuing national growth. Gearhart helps organize the ALP National Conference, update the list of participating schools across the country, facilitate the outreach of CCBC consultants to newly interested schools nationwide, and encourage acceleration programs that have developed in other departments at CCBC.

Kristen di Gennaro is the director of composition and an assistant professor of English at Pace University in New York City. As an applied linguist with a specialization in writing assessment and pedagogy for second language writers, she has also directed the English as a Second Language Program, the Writing-Enhanced Course Program, and placement testing for incoming students. Di Gennaro's research has been published in *Assessing Writing*, *Journal of Basic Writing*, *Language Testing*, *Teaching English in the Two-Year College*, and *Writing & Pedagogy*. She serves as a reviewer for several journals, including *Research in the Teaching of English*, *Canadian Modern Language Review*, *Assessing Writing*, and *Language Assessment Quarterly*.

Joanne Baird Giordano is the developmental reading and writing coordinator for the University of Wisconsin Colleges, a statewide, two-year institution. She teaches at the University of Wisconsin–Marathon County and for the University of Wisconsin Colleges Online. Her research interests focus on the experience of students at open access institutions, especially multilingual writers and significantly underprepared students. Her work has been published in *Teaching English in the Two-Year College*, *College Composition and Communication*, *College English*, and *Open Words: Access and English Studies*.

Brett M. Griffiths is the current director of the Macomb Reading and Writing Centers at Macomb Community College in Michigan. She completed her PhD in composition studies in the Joint Program for English and Education at the University of Michigan. Her primary research interests include writing instruction at open access institutions, first-year writing, and departmental and institutional approaches that support quality instruction and student success. She has published work on mathematics education and the effects of poverty on writing instruction at community colleges. Griffiths also publishes creative nonfiction and poetry.

Katie Hern, EdD, is an English instructor at Chabot College in Hayward, California, and has been teaching students to read, write, and think critically since 1991. She has also conducted extensive research into her department's accelerated developmental English course, an integrated reading and writing class one level below college English that is open to any student. Hern is director and cofounder of the California Acceleration Project (CAP), working with math colleague Myra Snell to support the state's 113 community colleges to transform remediation and increase student completion and equity. Hern's publications focus on the need to reform placement (*Perspectives*, 2014), design principles for teaching accelerated English and math (*LearningWorks*, 2013), and the movement to establish accelerated models of developmental education (*New Directions for Community Colleges*, Jossey-Bass, 2014 and *Teaching Developmental Reading*, 2nd edition, Bedford St. Martin's, 2014). She speaks nationally on remediation reform and integrated reading and writing.

Holly Hassel teaches writing, literature, and women's studies at the University of Wisconsin–Marathon County. She earned her doctorate in English from the University of Nebraska–Lincoln in 2002. Her work on teaching and learning in the writing, literature, and women's studies classrooms has appeared in *Teaching English in the Two-Year College*, *Feminist Teacher*, *Pedagogy*, *College English*, and *CCC*. Hassel is the coauthor of *Threshold Concepts in Gender and Women's Studies: Ways of Seeing, Thinking, and Knowing* (Routledge, 2015). She is also the current editor of *Teaching English in the Two-Year College*.

David A. Jolliffe is professor of English at the University of Arkansas at Fayetteville, where he holds the Brown Chair in English Literacy. In his forty-year career as an educator, he has published books, articles, and chapters on the history of rhetoric, writing in the disciplines, and the preparation of high school and college English teachers. Jolliffe's recent initiatives include arts-focused community literacy projects in rural Arkansas.

Susan Jones is a senior lecturer in the Graduate School of Education at the University of Exeter, England, where she is the school's director of doctoral studies. Her research areas include the developing writer, with a particular focus on integrating grammar pedagogy; and gender, especially the way this interacts with writer identity and classroom interaction. She is an active member of the Centre for Writing Research and part of a successful research team that has conducted a series of publicly funded research projects in the United Kingdom exploring contextualized grammar teaching, writing development, and composition behavior. This research has been undertaken in both primary and secondary schools and seeks to engage teachers in the research process.

Dan Keller is an associate professor of rhetoric, composition, and literacy at The Ohio State University at Newark, where he is also coordinator of the First-Year Writing Program. He teaches courses in composition, digital rhetoric, film, business writing, writing center theory, and theories of reading and writing. His work has been published in *Writing Center Journal*, *Teaching English in the Two-Year College*, and several edited collections. Keller's book *Chasing Literacy: Reading and Writing in an Age of Acceleration* was published by Utah State University Press in 2013.

Jeffrey Klausman is professor of English and writing program administrator at Whatcom Community College in Bellingham, Washington. He has served on executive committees for the Conference on College Composition and Communication, the Council of Writing Program Administrators, and the Two-Year College English Association. He served on the drafting committee for the *Framework for Success in Post-Secondary Writing* and was co-chair of TYCA's Research Committee (2013–2015), which authored a white paper on developmental education reform. He served as the review editor of *Teaching English in the Two-Year College* (*TETYC*) and serves on several editorial boards. Klausman's articles in *TETYC* have focused on writing program administration in the two-year college setting.

Galen Leonhardy teaches six or seven classes each week at a community college in Illinois. He has studied classical and contemporary rhetoric, cultural studies, assessment theory, theories of race, and composition theory, and he has published work in a variety of journals, including "The Way of Sweat" in *College Composition and Communication*; "Notes from the Trenches" in *Silent No More: Voices of Courage in American Schools*; "So This Is America" in *Becoming and Being a Teacher*; and work in *The Alternative* (a self-published journal-based ethnographic exploration of teaching). In his spare time, he reads (twice weekly) with elementary-aged kids at the local Martin Luther King, Jr. Center and gets into a fair amount of trouble for agitating autocratic administrators and by supporting the efforts of Catholic Workers and Ploughshares activists. Above all, Leonhardy's greatest joy is spending time with his two daughters, Sarah and Hallie.

Cynthia Lewiecki-Wilson, professor emerita of English at Miami University, taught on Miami's Middletown campus for over a decade, collaborating often with Jeff Sommers on issues of teaching open admissions students. After moving to the Oxford campus, she directed the Composition Program and later served as English graduate director, receiving a Miami Distinguished Educator award for mentoring and teaching graduate students. She has served on the editorial board of *CCC* and other journals, on the executive committee of CCCC, and chaired its Committee on Disability. Her research and teaching have always focused on issues of difference, especially the ways in which race, class, gender, age, and disability affect teaching and learning. Lewiecki-Wilson has published numerous articles, reviews, and book chapters and authored or coedited five books, including *Disability and the Teaching of Writing* (Bedford/St. Martin's, 2008) with Brenda Jo Brueggemann.

Helen Lines is a research fellow in the Centre for Writing Research at the University of Exeter, England, and part of the team that has been investigating the impact of contextualized grammar teaching on children's writing. She is currently involved in a longitudinal study with children aged eight to fourteen, researching the development of metalinguistic understanding and its application in writing. Lines has a particular interest in secondary teachers' and students' assessment of writing and in writing pedagogy.

Frost McLaughlin is a professor of English at Lord Fairfax Community College (LFCC) in Middletown, Virginia, where she has been teaching freshman composition and sophomore literature for twenty years. While teaching at LFCC, she earned her doctorate from George Mason University, writing her dissertation on "Live Feedback as the Primary Mode of Teacher Response to Freshman Writing," which she presented at the Conference on College Composition and Communication (CCCC). Prior to teaching at LFCC, she taught literature and composition at Florida State University, Virginia Tech, and North Shore Community College (Beverly, MA). She has served variously as writer, editor, or manager of documentation at Carnegie Mellon University's Software Engineering Institute and three software companies. With Miriam Moore, McLaughlin has presented at CCCC and TYCA-SE, and she currently serves as a guest reviewer for *Teaching English in the Two-Year College*.

Robert Miller is an associate professor of English at the Community College of Baltimore County. He has taught at City College of San Francisco, Arizona State University, and several other schools, including in Yugoslavia while on a Fulbright Fellowship. His research interests are basic writing and acceleration, and he has been involved in ALP since its inception. Miller currently focuses on professional development in basic writing. He is also a member of the Council of Basic Writing executive board.

Jody Millward is the coordinator (and cofounder) of Santa Barbara City College's (SBCC) College Achievement Program, which is designed to help students with outside responsibilities meet their English and Math requirements. She cofounded and teaches in SBCC's Multicultural English Transfer (MET) Program and the Express to Success Program. A former chair of the Two-Year College English Association, she directed the TYCA National Research Initiative's surveys on reading/writing assessment, technology, and pedagogy, community college working conditions (including adjuncts), and helped get the results of these national surveys published in *TETYC*. Millward has published in *TETYC* and in "TYCA to You," and her work has also appeared in *Cross-Language Relations in Composition*. She has also contributed to national and statewide conferences. She is a recent recipient of the William H. Meardy Faculty Award, sponsored by the Association of Community College Trustees, for excellence in teaching and contributions to the profession. She has also received TYCA's Nell Ann Pickett Service Award, the Young Rhetorician Council's (YRC) Rhetorician of the Year Award, and Pacific Coast TYCA's Nina Theiss Award for excellence in teaching and contributions to the discipline. Millward is frequent conference presenter at CCCC, YRC, and Pacific Coast TYCA.

Miriam Moore is professor of English and ESL at Lord Fairfax Community College (LFCC) in Middletown, Virginia, where she has been teaching since 2003. She discovered her passion for teaching over twenty years ago when, as a PhD student in the Linguistics Program at the University of South Carolina, she worked with ESL writers in a sheltered section of first-year composition. Before coming to Virginia, she taught first-year, developmental, and ESL composition in the English Program for Internationals at the University of South Carolina and at Raritan Valley Community College in Somerville, New Jersey. She is coauthor, with Susan Anker, of two developmental writing textbooks (*Real Reading and Writing* and *Real Skills*). In 2011–2012, she served on the team that wrote the integrated curriculum for the redesign of developmental English in the Virginia Community College System. From 2007 to 2013, she coordinated LFCC's Quality Enhancement Plan

(QEP), *Developing Critical Thinkers at LFCC*; as a result of the QEP, she collaborated with Frost McLaughlin on the rubric and symposium addressed in the article in this collection. Moore is currently developing a multilevel ESL program at LFCC.

Debra Myhill is professor of education at the University of Exeter, England. Her research interests focus principally on aspects of language and literacy teaching, particularly linguistic and metalinguistic aspects of writing, and on the composing processes involved in writing. This research is interdisciplinary, drawing on psychological, sociocultural, and linguistic perspectives on writing. Over the past fifteen years, she has led a series of research projects in these areas, in both primary and secondary schools, and has been involved in commissioned research or advisory roles for policy makers and examination boards. Myhill is director of the Centre for Research in Writing, and in 2014, her research team was awarded the Economic and Social Research Council Award for Outstanding Impact in Society. She is a fellow of the Academy of Social Sciences, joint editor of *Research Papers in Education*, and secretary/treasurer of the European Association for Research in Learning and Instruction.

Jean-Paul Nadeau is professor of English and the English and Humanities Department chair at Bristol Community College in Fall River, Massachusetts. He is coauthor of *The Community College Writer: Exceeding Expectations* (SIUP, 2010) and a first-year experience textbook, *Foundations for Learning: Claiming Your Education*, 3rd edition (Prentice Hall, 2012). He has coauthored articles in *College Composition and Communication*, *English Journal*, and the *Writing Center Journal*. Nadeau serves as a reviewer for *Teaching English in the Two-Year College*.

Nell Ann Pickett taught for many years as an instructor of English at Hinds Community College in Raymond, Mississippi (state law at that time did not permit rank or tenure at two-year colleges). Her essay in this collection is a revised version of her CCCC chair's address delivered in Phoenix in March 1997. Pickett amplifies aspects of this essay in "A Quarter Century and Beyond: My Story of Teaching Technical Communication" (Reynolds, ed., *Two-Year College English: Essays for a New Century*, 1994). The Nell Ann Pickett Service Award, NCTE's major service award for two-year college teachers, is named after her and is granted annually to an outstanding teacher whose vision and voice have had a major impact on two-year college professionalism and whose teaching exemplifies such outstanding personal qualities as creativity, sensitivity, and leadership.

Nancy Lawson Remler has taught composition and literature for the past twenty-three years at Armstrong State University in Savannah, Georgia, where she is an associate professor of English. Her research interests include first-year composition, professional writing, and teacher education. She has served on the board of the Georgia Council of Teachers of English, and she is a longtime member of National Council of Teachers of English. Currently, she serves as the director of composition for the Department of Language, Literature and Philosophy at Armstrong. She is the author of several first-year composition textbooks, including *Collages, Texting: Clear Communications for Various Contexts*, and *Word by Word*. Under her pen name, Nancy Brandon, she is the author of *Dunaway's Crossing*, a historical novel, which was a finalist for the 2013 Georgia Author of the Year Award.

Mark Reynolds retired from Jefferson Davis Community College in Brewton, Alabama, after thirty-eight years of teaching and administrative work, including chairing the Humanities Division for twenty-two years. Active professionally throughout his career, Reynolds has served on a number of committees for NCTE, CCCC, MLA, TYCA National, and TYCA-SE. He was a member of the original committee that helped create TYCA, and from 1994 to 2001, he edited *TETYC*. He edited *Two-Year College English: Essays for a New Century* (NCTE, 1994), and with Sylvia Holladay-Hicks, *The Profession of English in the Two-Year College* (Heinemann, 2005). The author of a number of articles on teaching writing and literature, he has three essays in the MLA's *Approaches to Teaching World Literature Series*. Reynolds has also won awards for teaching and service, including NCTE's Nell Ann Pickett Service Award, TYCA-SE's Doster Award, and the Alabama College System's Outstanding Faculty Award. In 2011, TYCA named its annual award for the best article in *TETYC* after him. Currently, he is an adjunct professor in Huntingdon College's Evening Studies Program, Brewton Campus, and among volunteer activities, serves as an elementary school reading coach.

Anne Roberts is a professor of English at the Community College of Baltimore County. She holds a master's degree in classical philology from the University of North

Carolina at Chapel Hill and one in English from Middlebury College, Bread Loaf School of English. She is currently completing her master's of fine arts in creative nonfiction at Goucher College. She teaches composition, literature, creative writing, grammar, Latin, and Greek.

Mike Rose is a professor in the UCLA Graduate School of Education and Information Studies. He has taught in a wide range of educational settings, from elementary school to adult literacy and job training programs. He is a member of the National Academy of Education and the recipient of a Guggenheim Fellowship, the Grawemeyer Award in Education, and awards from the Spencer Foundation, the National Council of Teachers of English, the Modern Language Association, and the American Educational Research Association. He also received the Commonwealth Club of California's Award for Literary Excellence in Nonfiction. Rose's books include *Lives on the Boundary: The Struggles and Achievements of America's Educationally Underprepared, Possible Lives: The Promise of Public Education in America, The Mind at Work: Valuing the Intelligence of the American Worker, Why School?: Reclaiming Education for All of Us,* and *Back to School: Why Everyone Deserves a Second Chance at Education.*

Richard Rothstein is a research associate of the Economic Policy Institute and senior fellow of the Chief Justice Earl Warren Institute on Law and Social Policy at the University of California (Berkeley) School of Law. He is the author of *Grading Education: Getting Accountability Right* (Teachers College Press and EPI, 2008) and *Class and Schools: Using Social, Economic and Educational Reform to Close the Black-White Achievement Gap* (Teachers College Press, 2004). Rothstein is also the author of *The Way We Were? Myths and Realities of America's Student Achievement* (1998). Other recent books include *The Charter School Dust-Up: Examining the Evidence on Enrollment and Achievement* (coauthored in 2005); and *All Else Equal: Are Public and Private Schools Different?* (coauthored in 2003).

David Russell is professor of English at Iowa State University, where he teaches in the ISUComm program (foundation composition and upper-level business writing) and in the PhD program in Rhetoric and Professional Communication. His research interests are in writing in the disciplines, international writing instruction, and recently, online multimedia case studies for computer-supported collaborative learning. His book *Writing in the Academic Disciplines: A Curricular History*, now in its second edition, examines the history of United States writing instruction since 1870. He has published many articles on writing in the disciplines (WiD) and professions, drawing mainly on cultural historical activity theory and rhetorical genre theory. He coedited *Landmark Essays on Writing Across the Curriculum*, a special issue of *Mind, Culture, and Activity* on writing research, *Writing and Learning in Cross-National Perspective: Transitions from Secondary to Higher Education*, and *Writing Selves and Societies*. He has given workshops and lectures on WiD, nationally and internationally, and now edits *Journal of Business and Technical Communication*. Russell was the first Knight Visiting Scholar in Writing at Cornell University, 1999, and Leverhulme Visiting Professor at Queen Mary University of London, 2005.

Greg Shafer is a professor of English at Mott Community College in Flint, Michigan, and former president of the Michigan Council of Teachers of English. In more than twenty-five years of teaching at the middle, high school, and college levels, he has published over sixty scholarly articles, and in 2007, his article "A Christian Fundamentalist in a Reading Response Class" was named the best article of the year by *Teaching English in the Two-Year College*. He is on the editorial boards of *Language Arts of Michigan* and *Teaching English in the Two-Year College*, and his *English Journal* article "Composition for the Twenty-first Century" (2001) has been used for years by the Baltimore County Public Schools in their training of new writing teachers. Shafer's main interests lie in multiple literacies, African American English, and post-process composition theory.

Jeff Sommers served as editor of *Teaching English in the Two-Year College* from 2006 to 2015. Currently professor of English at West Chester University, he is also professor emeritus at Miami University, where he was a member of the faculty at the Middletown two-year regional campus from 1981 to 2008, and where he served as the associate dean for his final three years. While at Miami, he was the recipient of the College of Arts and Sciences Distinguished Educator Award (1993) and the Knox Award as the outstanding faculty member at Miami University's three campuses (2005). He was West Chester University's nominee for the national Professors of the Year Award Program administered by the Carnegie Foundation for the Advancement of Teaching and Council for Advancement and Support of Education (CASE) in 2013. Sommers was also awarded a Carnegie Academy for the Scholarship of Teaching and Learning (CASTL) Fellowship (2003) and received the NCTE Two-Year College English Association (TYCA) Nell Ann Pickett Service Award (2012). Author or coauthor of four books and textbooks, he has published over forty journal articles and book chapters.

Nancy Sommers led the Harvard College Writing Program for twenty years, directing the first-year program, establishing the Harvard Writing Project, and leading a series of research studies about college writers. To honor her work at Harvard, she was awarded an endowed chair, the Sosland Chair in Writing. Sommers now teaches at the Harvard Graduate School of Education, where she leads writing workshops and mentors new writing instructors. She is the coauthor of four writing textbooks, including *A Writer's Reference* and *A Pocket Style Manual*, and the book *Responding to Student Writers*, all published by Bedford/St. Martin's. She is a blogger for *The Huffington Post* and a prize-winning essayist for her personal essays and articles about teaching writing. Over the last two decades, Sommers helped establish writing programs at universities in Asia and Europe, lectured at more than a hundred universities on all aspects of teaching writing, and created three films about the culture of college writing.

David Starkey is director of composition and director of creative writing at Santa Barbara City College (SBCC) and a long-term member of the Multicultural English Transfer (MET) faculty. In 2009–2010, he served as Santa Barbara Poet Laureate, and his poetry has appeared in seven full-length collections, as well as multiple journals, including *The American Scholar*, *The Antioch Review*, *The Georgia Review*, *The Massachusetts Review*, and *The Southern Review*. He is the editor of two books on creative writing pedagogy published by Heinemann, Boynton/Cook: *Teaching Writing Creatively* (1998) and *Writing What We Teach* (2001), and he guest-edited a special issue of *Teaching English in the Two-Year College* devoted to creative writing (Dec. 2014, 42.2). Starkey's text *Creative Writing: Four Genres in Brief* (Bedford/St. Martin's, 2012) is in its second edition.

Sandra Starkey has served as the director of Santa Barbara City College's Multicultural English Transfer (MET) Program. She has also served as director of composition. Her presentations at multiple state conferences and national CCCC's focus on how theory can translate into practice to create a culturally inclusive classroom and improve the success of marginalized students. In 2013, SBCC acknowledged her contributions to the success of underserved students with a Faculty Excellence Award. Starkey is currently a member of MET and SBCC's nationally recognized Express to Success Program, a program that offers students an accelerated path through the English sequence.

Marilyn S. Sternglass was an early advocate for open admissions institutions and developmental students, and spent many years teaching English at City College of City University of New York. Her acclaimed book *Time to Know Them: A Longitudinal Study of Writing and Learning at the College Level* received the Mina P. Shaughnessy Prize of the Modern Language Association in 1998 and the CCCC's Outstanding Book Award in March 1999. This book was among the first academic studies to explore how the writing performance of college students is "influenced by their experiences outside the college, in their homes, in their workplaces, and in their communities."

Steve Straight is professor of English and director of the poetry program at Manchester Community College, in Manchester, Connecticut. His most recent book is *The Almanac* (Curbstone/Northwestern University Press, 2012). His previous collection of poetry, *The Water Carrier* (Curbstone, 2002), was featured on the nationally syndicated radio program *The Writer's Almanac with Garrison Keillor*. For many years Straight directed the Connecticut Poetry Circuit, and for many summers he directed the Seminar Series for the Sunken Garden Poetry Festival. He has given workshops on writing and teaching throughout the eastern United States and in Ireland. In 1998, he was named a Distinguished Advocate for the Arts by the Connecticut Commission on the Arts.

Jenny Stuber is an associate professor of sociology at the University of North Florida. After growing up in Minnesota, she went on to receive a PhD in sociology from Indiana University. She also holds degrees from Northwestern University and Brown University. Motivated by her own experience as a first-generation college student, her research focuses on the cultural aspects of social class inequality. By looking at the cultural underpinnings of class inequality, her research asks questions about how people understand, enact, and use social class in their everyday lives. Her 2011 book, *Inside the College Gates: How Class and Culture Matter in Higher Education*, investigates how social class and first-generation status shape how students navigate the college environment, focusing specifically on their social interactions and extracurricular involvement. Her research has also appeared in *Sociological Forum, The Journal of Contemporary Sociology, The International Journal of Qualitative Studies in Education*, and *Teaching in Higher Education*. In 2015, she published the textbook *Exploring Inequality: A Sociological Approach* with Oxford University Press. Dr. Stuber is deeply committed to providing her students with a rigorous and personally relevant educational experience.

Kara Taczak is part of the writing faculty at the University of Denver, where she teaches first-year writing courses and advises first-year students. Her research centers on the intersection of reflection and transfer of knowledge and practices. Taczak's current research project, which was awarded a 2014–2015 CCCC Research Initiative grant, examines on four different campuses how a teaching for transfer curriculum supports students' transfer of writing knowledge to other sites of academic writing. This is the second phase of the research focused on in her coauthored book, *Writing Across Contexts*, which was awarded the 2014–2015 CCCC Research Impact Award. Taczak's publications have appeared in *Composition Forum, Teaching English in a Two-Year College*, and *Across the Disciplines*.

William H. Thelin is a professor and chair of the Department of English at the University of Akron. He received his doctorate from Indiana University of Pennsylvania in 1996 and earned tenure at the University of Cincinnati before leaving for his current position in 2001. He is the author of the textbook *Writing without Formulas*, and coeditor of the collection *Blundering for a Change: Errors and Expectations in Critical Pedagogy*. While his specialty is critical pedagogy, especially in relation to working-class students, his publications have also focused on issues such as responding to student writing, adjunct labor, and assignments for the college writing classroom. His work has appeared in *College English, College Composition and Communication*, and *Composition Studies*, among others. He has chaired or co-chaired the Working-Class Culture and Pedagogy special interest group for over ten years and is the coeditor of the journal *Open Words: Access and English Studies*. He was the subject of an interview for the collection *Listening to Our Elders: Working and Writing for Change*, as well as for the recently released documentary *Con Job: Stories of Adjunct and Contingent Labor*.

Kathryn Thirolf earned her PhD in higher education at the University of Michigan. She has published articles on community college faculty identities and coauthored a book on the organizational performance of colleges and universities. She currently works as Director of Innovation Instruction at Jackson College in Jackson, Michigan.

Howard Tinberg, a professor of English at Bristol Community College in Massachusetts, and former editor of *Teaching English in the Two-Year College*, is the author of *Border Talk: Writing and Knowing in the Two-Year College* and *Writing with Consequence: What Writing Does in the Disciplines*. He is coauthor of *The Community College Writer: Exceeding Expectations* and *Teaching, Learning and the Holocaust: An Integrative Approach*. He is coeditor of *What is "College-Level" Writing?* and *What is "College-Level" Writing? Volume 2*. In 2004, he was recognized as U.S. Community Colleges Professor of the Year by the Carnegie Foundation and the American Council on Education (ACE). From 2005 to 2006, he was a scholar in residence for the Carnegie Academy for the Scholarship of Teaching and Learning (CASTL). He is a former chair of the Conference on College Composition and Communication.

Michelle Tremmel is a senior lecturer and academic adviser in the Department of English at Iowa State University in Ames, Iowa. She teaches undergraduate writing in the ISUComm Foundation Courses program, the writing methods course in the Secondary English Education program, and a professional seminar that supports new ISUComm Foundation Courses graduate teaching assistants. She also supervises preservice English teachers and mentors teaching assistants. Before coming to Iowa State in 1998, she taught English for twenty years in a combined middle and high school in Michigan. She has published articles in *English Journal, Teaching/Writing: The Journal of Writing Teacher Education, Teaching English in the Two-Year College*, and the *Journal of Teaching Writing*, as well as a chapter in *Teachers of High School English and First-Year Composition*.

Annabel Watson is a lecturer in the Graduate School of Education at the University of Exeter, England, where she leads Secondary English initial teacher education courses and is a member of the Centre for Writing Research. Her research interests focus on high school students' writing and metalinguistic development, the use of digital technologies for writing, and teachers' beliefs and practices in the teaching of writing.

Ed White is a visiting scholar in English at the University of Arizona and professor emeritus of English at California State University, San Bernardino, where he served for many years as English department chair and coordinator of the upper-division university writing program. Statewide in California, he has been coordinator of the CSU Writing Skills Improvement Program and for over a decade was director of the English Equivalency Examination program. On the national scene, he directed the consultant-evaluator service of WPA for fifteen years, and in 1993 was elected to a second term on the executive committee of CCCC. His *Teaching and Assessing Writing* (1985) has been called "required reading" for the profession; a new edition in 1994 received an MLA Mina P. Shaughnessy Prize for outstanding research. He is author of more than one hundred articles and book chapters on literature and the teaching of writing, and has written five English composition textbooks, most recently *Inquiry* (2004) and *The Promise of America* (2006). His *Developing Successful College Writing Programs* was published in 1989, and *Assigning, Responding, Evaluating: A Writing Teacher's Guide* was published in a fifth edition by Bedford/St. Martin's in 2015. He is also coeditor of four essay collections for the MLA, SIU, and Parlor presses. His work has recently been recognized by the publication of *Writing Assessment in the 21st Century: Essays in Honor of Edward M. White* (Hampton, 2012), and by the 2011 Exemplar Award from the CCCC. White's latest book, *Very Like a Whale: The Assessment of Writing Programs*, was published by Utah State University Press in 2015.

Smokey Wilson spent many years working with academically inexperienced adult learners during her career as an instructor at Laney College, an inner-city community college in Oakland, California. She served as director of the Tutorial Center on campus, was cofounder and co-coordinator of the basic skills learning community known as Project Bridge, and was the founder and coordinator of an American Sign Language [ASL]/English bilingual/bicultural program called Deaf College Access Network (DeafCAN). Wilson retired from the English Department in 2002. She is the author of *What About Rose?* (Teachers College Press, 2007).

Helena Worthen has been writing since college, when she won a Stegner Fellowship at Stanford for a short story she published in the *Kenyon Review*. Over the next several years she became involved in union activism, traveled, and wrote two novels (*Perimeters*, published by Harcourt Brace Jovanovich, and *Damages*, published by Arbor House). She also has an MLA in landscape architecture and a PhD in education from Berkeley. She has taught at many institutions, but was especially involved in the union in the Peralta Community College District in Oakland. Her organizing efforts for part-time faculty include editing a statewide newsletter and conducting conferences. While at Berkeley, she joined a project on teaching in community colleges led by Norton Grubb. She has worked for the Philadelphia Joint Board of UNITE, the garment workers' union, and on labor education at the University of Illinois. Worthen's interest in learning theory, cultural-historical activity theory (CHAT), and collective learning inform her scholarly journal articles and her recent book, *What Did You Learn at Work Today? Forbidden Lessons of Labor Education* (Hardball Press 2014).

Acknowledgments *(continued from p. ii)*

Preface
Page viii: "How They Got Here" from *The Water Carrier* by Steve Straight. Copyright © 2002. All rights reserved. Published by Curbstone Press. Used with permission.

Chapter 1
Page 7: Excerpt from p. 101 from *Higher Education for American Democracy: A Report of the President's Commission on Higher Education. Vol. 1: Establishing the Goals, a report of the President's Commission on Higher Education* by George F. Zook. Copyright © 1947 Harper & Brothers. Reprinted by permission of HarperCollins Publishers.
Page 11: Pickett, Nell Ann. "The Two-Year College as Democracy in Action." *College Composition and Communication* 49.1 (1998): 90-98. Copyright © NCTE. Used with permission.

Chapter 2
Page 20: Rothstein, Richard. "Chapter 1: Social Class, Student Achievement, and the Black-White Achievement Gap." *Class and Schools: Using Social, Economic, and Educational Reform to Close the Black-White Achievement Gap.* Copyright © 2004 Economic Policy Institute. Used with permission.
Page 32: Stuber, Jenny. "Chapter 1: Inside the College Gates: Education as a Social and Cultural Process." *Inside the College Gates: How Class and Culture Matter in Higher Education.* Copyright © 2011 Rowman & Littlefield. Used with permission.
Page 42: Sullivan, Patrick. "Measuring 'Success' at Open Admissions Institutions: Thinking Carefully about This Complex Question." *College English* 70.6 (2008): 618-32. Copyright © NCTE. Used with permission.

Chapter 3
Page 58: Lewiecki-Wilson, Cynthia, and Jeff Sommers. "Professing at the Fault Lines: Composition at Open Admissions Institutions." *College Composition and Communication* 50.3 (1999): 438-462. Copyright © NCTE. Used with permission.
Page 82: Hassel, Holly, and Joanne Baird Giordano. "Occupy Writing Studies: Rethinking College Composition for the Needs of the Teaching Majority." *College Composition and Communication* 65:1 (2013): 117-39. Copyright © NCTE. Used with permission.

Chapter 4
Page 109: Fulkerson, Richard. "Composition at the Turn of the Twenty-First Century." *College Composition and Communication* 56.4 (2005): 654-87. Copyright © NCTE. Used with permission.
Page 139: Reynolds, Mark. "Two-Year College Teachers as Knowledge Makers." *The Profession of English in the Two-Year College.* Ed. Mark Reynolds and Sylvia Holladay-Hicks. Copyright © 2005 by Boynton/Cook Publishers, Inc. Published by Boynton/Cook Publishers, Inc., Portsmouth, NH. Reprinted by permission of the publisher. All rights reserved.

Chapter 5
Page 153: Sheridan Blau, "Performative Literacy: The Habits of Highly Literate Readers," from *Voices from the Middle*, Volume 10 Number 3, March 2003. Copyright © NCTE. Used with permission.
Page 160: Sullivan, Patrick. "'A Lifelong Aversion to Writing': What If Writing Courses Emphasized Motivation?" *Teaching English in the Two-Year College* 39.2 (2011): 118-40. Copyright © NCTE. Used with permission.

Chapter 6
Page 185: Bean, John. "Using Writing to Promote Thinking." *Engaging Ideas: The Professor's Guide to Integrating Writing, Critical Thinking, and Active Learning in the Classroom.* 2nd. ed. Copyright © 2011 Wiley. Used with permission.
Page 198: Tinberg, Howard, and Jean-Paul Nadeau. "Chapter 5: Implications for *Teaching and Research.*" *The* Community College Writer: Exceeding Expectations. Copyright © 2010 by Southern Illinois University Press. Used with permission.

Chapter 7
Page 202: Beaufort, Anne. "The Question of University Writing Instruction." *College Writing and Beyond: A New Framework for University Writing Instruction.* Copyright © 2007 Utah State University Press. Republished with permission of Utah State University Press; permission conveyed through Copyright Clearance Center, Inc.
Page 219: Hassel, Holly, and Joanne Baird Giordano. "Transfer Institutions, Transfer of Knowledge: The Development of Rhetorical Adaptability and Underprepared Writers."

Index